TEACHING SPEECH

TEACHING SPEECH

GEORGE L. LEWIS
Ohio State University

RUSSELL I. EVERETT
University of Southern Mississippi

JAMES W. GIBSON
University of Missouri

KATHRYN T. SCHOEN
Ohio State University

CHARLES E. MERRILL PUBLISHING COMPANY
A Bell & Howell Company
Columbus, Ohio

Standard Book Number: 675-09438-0

Library of Congress Catalog Card Number:
74-93121

1 2 3 4 5 6 7 8 9 10 —
73 72 71 70 69

PRINTED IN THE UNITED STATES OF AMERICA

To *Dotty, Olga, Jo,* and *Dick,*
and the students from whom we have learned

Preface

Methods should not be taught apart from the theories, concepts, and accumulated knowledge of the discipline represented. Speech, being the oldest of the schools, has collected disciplines from many areas, has presented many theories, and has developed a number of processes which lead to skilled performance.

It is not our intent to provide a book which teaches these concepts, theories, or knowledge accumulations. The authors have assumed that the students using this book will have completed courses in public address, voice science, theatre, oral interpretation, and broadcasting. Having assumed such a background, we have felt free to "force" the student to make a legitimate review of the various speech areas in the process of identifying these areas of knowledge and processes for teaching. We challenge those needing greater understanding of these disciplines to make extra study necessary to become competent. In many cases we have deliberately challenged established theory or process in order to make the student reanalyze many of the things he has taken for granted from the mythology of established practice.

We make no apology for expecting students to study in depth the wealth of literature available in each of the speech disciplines. Rhetorical, dramatic, and literary theory and content are an expected part of liberal knowledge for teachers in all fields. Students expect a teacher's background to be adequate to lead discussions and provide directions. Toward this end, supplementary readings and suggested readings have been provided throughout the book.

The projects and activities listed at the end of each chapter are based upon job description realities. Believing that theory can be learned from practice, we have attempted to provide projects and activities which would help the potential teacher understand the content, process, and theory of speech. Moreover, we have designed the various behavioral experiences so that an understanding of process will develop the independent problem-solving ability needed by teachers. Since we consider the classic speech concepts to be valid, we present them here as continuing, current processes out of which speech skills grow.

Contents

Part Two   Content

6   Resources in Speech Instruction

7   Public Speaking

8   Oral Interpretation

9   Conversation, Discussion, and Debate

10   Theatre

11   Broadcasting

12   Out-of-Class Activities

13   Professional Organizations

TEACHING SPEECH

Part One

PROFESSIONAL PREPARATION

The development of sound programs in instruction and in out-of-class activities in the field of speech begins with a consideration of the relevant goals. Consequently, the first part of this text directs your attention to the problems of selecting objectives from a sound philosophical base and building a curriculum while keeping these objectives in sight. Listening and communication theory and awareness of the impact of semantics and the mass media all contribute to a well developed curriculum.

Once the speech program is in operation, the teacher must develop a policy for evaluating student performance. Testing and grading policy must at all times remain relevant to the objectives of the program. It is appropriate, therefore, that Part One begins and ends with a consideration of the objectives of speech instruction.

1

The Objectives of Speech Education

The teaching of speech is the result of ancient pragmatism. Because citizens of Athens and Sicily were expected to act as their own lawyers and plead their own cases, Corax and his pupils (467 B.C.) gave instruction in rhetoric and persuasion. Aristotle gave clarity and meaning to speech instruction by defining the types of proof (ethos, pathos and logos) used by the rhetoricians of his time and still used today. His definition of rhetoric as "the discovery of every available means of persuasion" provides a model for the modern broadcaster. In turn, it presents the modern researcher with the problems of testing a specific "means of persuasion" against traditional and other means. By 95 A.D. speech instruction had developed to such a high art that Quintilian presented the first monograph on teaching methods, directed to teachers of oratory.[1] This document, summarized below, continues to be an excellent guide regarding the age, motivation, and attention span of the student, teaching methods, discipline, and a pragmatic approach to ethics.

---

[1]Quintilian, *The Training of the Orator (De Institutione Oratoria),* tr. Butler, 4 vol. (Cambridge: Harvard University Press, 1936); condensed version by Jed A. Cooper in *Phi Delta Kappan,* 49 (October, 1967).

1. The interest of the learner in the matter to be learned is highly important.
2. The teacher should take advantage of the pupil's early years; he is more tenacious of mind, more energetic, and highly imitative at that time. The importance of an adequate social environment cannot be overstated.
3. The pupil should take several subjects simultaneously for variety, not serially to exhaustion.
4. The teacher should be aware of his own physical fitness as conducive to his professional competence.
5. The early training in identifying the alphabet through the use of ivory letters as toys and the training of letters by following grooves cut in boards (kinesthetic method) are effective procedures in letter recognition.
6. The teacher should utilize recreational periods for play and rest and make use of games in teaching. Games are also good for character development.
7. The pupil should learn moral precepts incidentally while learning to write, rather than through the catechetical (question-answer) method.
8. Group rather than tutorial teaching should be used, thus enriching experience through sharing, providing a competitive value, and securing social learning. In group instruction the teacher must not lose sight of the individual.
9. Corporal punishment is taboo. If a child does not respond to reproof, whipping will merely harden him; also it takes time from the pedagogue's first duty to instruct; it is humiliation to a boy of spirit — he will shun society, etc.; it takes advantage of the pupil's helplessness; it creates emotional blocks to learning. The teacher should instead substitute praise, exercise tolerance, reason with the student to change his behavior, or use prizes.

The application of these principles should enable you to function as effectively as did their author, Quintilian, who practiced the art of teaching during the first century of the Christian era. Many of the items listed, and discussed at length in the original, seem significantly modern. We might turn from such classic guide lines for teacher behavior to some modern challenges in teaching speech and the pragmatic problems to be solved through communication.

HAS RHETORIC EXPANDED?

Today we find a resurgence of classical theory, canons, and concerns. Discovery of every available means of persuasion has, however, been subject to rethinking and possible reinterpretation. Modern broadcasting ethics are in conflict with the *ethical man, speaking well.* Journalists and scholars are discussing "The Rhetoric of the Streets"[2] and the role of the agitator and the activist in the area of rhetoric.[3] Truth in advertising forces consideration of the basic differences in classical concerns for communication—the differences between the ethical man and the Sophist. Pending legislation regarding the right to dissent (expanded to the right to riot, loot, and burn) attempts to establish the boundaries between legitimate dissent and infringement upon the rights of others.[4] The basic tenets of democracy as expressed in the Bill of Rights, especially freedom of speech, are forced into analysis. A part of such analysis is the concern for freedom of privacy from dissenters, rioters, and speakers. Do we have the right to dissent from dissenters?

Relevancy of Listening

From classical times to the twentieth century rhetoricians assumed that training the speaker in speaking skills is the desired goal of the teaching of speech. The speaker is often taught to analyze his audience in order to persuade. The assumption is made, however, that there is in fact a listener. Since Rankin, Nichols, and their students, we have become aware that listening is an active part of the communication process.[5, 6] The teacher of speech must understand the barriers which may hinder good listening and the process for turning on the receiver. Teaching listening has become as integral a part of teaching speech as has the teaching of speech preparation and organization. Methodology dealing with the problem of listening has been developed and tested.[7]

Rights to Speak, Listen, and Refuse to Listen

Freedom of speech and the right to refuse to listen are no longer academic problems for discussion in college classrooms only. Real

---

[2]Franklyn S. Haiman, "The Rhetoric of the Streets: Some Legal and Ethical Considerations," *The Quarterly Journal of Speech*, 53:99-114 (April, 1967).

[3]Charles W. Lomas, *The Agitator in American Society* (Englewood Cliffs, N. J.: Prentice-Hall, Inc., 1968).

[4]Abe Fortas, *Concerning Dissent and Civil Disobedience* (New York: The New American Library, Inc., Signet Books, 1968).

[5]Ralph Nichols and Leonard Stevens, *Are You Listening?* (New York: McGraw-Hill Book Company, 1957). See also Nichols, "Questions and Problems," *The Quarterly Journal of Speech*, 33:84 (February, 1947); Factors in Listening Comprehension," *Speech Monographs*, 15:154-163 (1948); "Listening Instruction in the High School," *Bulletin of the National Association of Secondary School Principals*, 36:158-174 (May, 1952).

[6]Sam Duker (ed.), "Master's Theses on Listening," *Journal of Communication*, 12:234-242 (1962); and "Doctoral Dissertations on Listening," *Journal of Communication,* 13:106-117 (1963). See also Sam Duker (ed.), *Listening: Readings* (New York: The Scarecrow Press, Inc., 1966).

[7]*Ibid.*

problems of this sort are now emerging in high school classes, inner city PTA groups, and faculty-parent working committees. Student strikes, walkouts, and boycotts are becoming interwoven with housing protests, equal job opportunities, and industrial strikes. Teacher power is placing working conditions and the right to speak and be heard on the agenda of school boards and college administration meetings. This right to be heard reflects their charges that earlier messages which were transmitted were not received. Communication models stress the importance of clarity in the encoding of the idea, efficiency in transmission, assurance of an operationally active receiver, and use of similar frames of reference by the decoder. Yet some acknowledged messages have been decoded into messages different from those transmitted.

In the classroom students are seeking recognition for their ideas. Exile or "shadow" governments sponsored by community action groups are emerging which demand equal voice in student government in well established schools in major cities. Students have filed suits to restrain school administrations and state government (including highway patrols and the National Guard) from enforcing school regulations. Some demand that civil charges be dropped for arrests derived from forcible take-over of buildings and personnel. Yet those asking that all regulatory powers be dropped have not considered the rights of other students. Here it would seem that freedom of speech, listening, and action are the prerogative of some but rights to be denied others. Is there a right to dissent from dissenters and activists? How under these conditions does the speech teacher meet the challenge of such an expanded rhetoric?

Lomas and Haiman[8] challenge the serious implications of rhetoric when it is expanded beyond *speaking and listening* into the realm of *action*. Journalists and broadcasters report demonstrations and marches into cities and neighborhood communities as part of the modern rhetoric. What is said and heard has now been expanded into what is seen. If action is a basic part of communication, the rhetorician is now using the language of the stage in which the story (message) is carried as much through action as through dialogue. If rhetoric is truly the discovery of every available means of persuasion, and freedom of speech includes the right to march into any neighborhood to express the intended message through dialogue and action, what then is the dimension of communication which includes listening and feedback? If we assume that the speaker has the right to speak, does the listener have the right to refuse to listen? If the citizen moves from the central city to the suburbs, does the speaker have the right to pursue and persuade? As a teacher of speech, will you confine your definitions of rhetoric to the verbal act or will you expand

---

[8]*Op. cit.*

it to include the very clear provocative message of the stage, the street, and the activist? One thing is certain: as teachers of speech we can no longer rest with the assumption that the speaker has a listener or that the listener receives the message intended by the transmitter. Speech teachers must remain conversant with changing terms, definitions, semantic implications, and processes.

INSTITUTIONAL PURPOSE

Institutions exist for a purpose. These purposes are spelled out in charters and legal authorizations. An institution may be subject to investigation when it participates in activities not authorized in its charter. Defining freedom of speech to arrive at a speaker rule places great pressure on definition and purpose of a school as a sponsoring institution. While restrictive definitions can infringe on freedom of speech, open definitions may allow freedom to coerce and harass. Is freedom of speech denied when a speaker can be sponsored by other groups and in other facilities than the school? A school with educational purposes may sponsor widely divergent views as a means of furthering education. Institutional objectives are of primary concern to the teacher of speech in a climate of free inquiry. Thus, supporting the basic objectives of freedom to learn, freedom to research, and freedom to express the results of that study is the fundamental goal of speech instruction. Speech teachers may find the support needed to build and protect a sound program of this type in the following statement of the Commission on Education and Human Rights of the Phi Delta Kappa.

Supplement 1.

Education and Human Rights —
A Statement of the Phi Delta Kappa
Commission on Education and Human Rights[9]

Introduction

The concept of human rights is as old as man and goes to the very core of relationships among men. It is a dynamic force rooted in basic moral and ethical values.

---

[9]Commission members include Charles R. Foster (Chairman), Glenn R. Snider, James H. Bash, Gayle B. Childs, William L. Cobb, William G. Zimmerman, Paul Clifford, John Letson, Donald W. Robinson, and Herbert W. Wey. Reproduced by permission of *Phi Delta Kappan,* 49:418-419 (April, 1968).

If human potentialities are to be realized, society must be concerned not only with theoretical and philosophical concepts of human rights, but equally with translating these concepts into realities expressed in the behavior of free men. It is imperative that human beings live together in ways which accord each person, irrespective of biological and cultural differences, full dignity, respect, and value, simply because he or she is human. This objective cannot be achieved unless each human being has the opportunity, through education, to develop his abilities and talents.

A commitment to human rights requires that no person be denied opportunity to engage in any kind of activity which is valued and rewarded by his society. While national origin, racial identity, religious preference, economic status, social class, political and economic beliefs, and other factors which differentiate human beings must be accepted as realities, none of the conditions should add to or detract from the worth of an individual as he is perceived by other human beings. Education's goals must include reducing the more mischievous differences and bolstering the concept of equal worth.

Some of the most disturbing and far-reaching problems of our society center in the area of human relationships and responsible citizenship. They will be resolved only as the capacity of individuals to deal with them is improved. This capacity is likely to be improved in a democratic society only as more people understand and become committed to the values and human rights delineated in the basic documents which constitute the legal foundation for organized government.

The purpose of this statement is to define human rights and identify the values which support them, describe the role of education in achieving basic human rights, and illustrate school policies consistent with that role.

Values

The values a people hold are beliefs giving direction and meaning to their behavior. Among the beliefs basic to realization of the rights of free men in our society are: that each individual is equal in dignity and worth to every other individual; that freedom must be granted to pursue individual goals which do not infringe upon the rights of others; that the application of reason is the best means of resolving man's problems; that institutions are established by men and should contribute to the welfare of the individual and society; that the concepts of truth and moral responsibility are crucial and fundamental.

Human Rights

The human rights most prized by our society grew out of struggles celebrated in the history of Western civilization. Man's unending search for human rights produced the tenets of Judaism and Christianity; the principles of Graeco-Roman philosophy and law; the Magna Carta; the Petition of Right; the Declaration of Independence; the Constitution of the United States; the Declaration of the Rights of Man; the Universal Declaration of Human Rights of the United Nations; and a long list of other declarations, documents, proclamations, legislative enactments, and judicial decisions, the proud product of democracy.

Among the rights these landmark statements seek to secure are life; liberty; security of person; equality of opportunity for every individual in every facet of life; freedom of speech; freedom of press; freedom of (or from) religious beliefs; the right of due process; freedom of assembly, petition, and redress of grievances; protection against unreasonable search and seizure; freedom from self-incrimination; the right to trial by a jury of peers; the right to privacy; the right to fair and equal representation in government; the right to own property and enter into contracts; the right to select leaders through the exercise of the franchise; and the right to dissent.

Education

Formal education is a powerful and effective means by which our society can realize the promise of our human rights heritage. It is important that educational programs emphasize not only the rights but the responsibilities inherent in each of them. A major challenge for education at all levels is to teach and practice these rights and responsibilities faithfully and well in every classroom.

It is impossible to teach and practice democratic values and human rights and responsibilities in a school in which the worth of the individual is not prized; consequently, every person engaged in the formal educational process, including members of governing boards, should in his behavior exemplify commitment to these human rights and responsibilities and the values which support them. It is, of course, extremely difficult to achieve the goals identified here in a school which is racially segregated, whether the segregation results from consciously adopted policy or from historical forces more difficult to reverse.

Behavior

A democratic society is attaining its goals when the thoughts, attitudes, and overt behaviors of the people exemplify the values and human rights and responsibilities we have identified.

Illustrative of behaviors which demonstrate a commitment to some basic human rights are the following examples:

1. *Freedom of speech* — All persons have the basic right to express opinions and ideas on any subject or issue. All students should have access to truth in relevant published materials and must be free to discuss controversial issues, with responsible direction, in the classroom or on the school campus.

2. *Due process of law* — A person is presumed innocent until proven guilty. Students suspected of violating school rules or regulations should be presumed innocent until guilt is established; no situation or condition, however, relieves the individual student from the necessity of exercising good judgment and responsibility.

3. *The right to privacy* — Every individual has the right to privacy of

person and action, as he develops his personality and tastes, so long as he does not infringe upon the rights of others. The school should not impose undue restrictions on patterns of dress and personal grooming on the mere assumption that they unfavorably influence the learning situation.

4. *The right of dissent* — A person should have the right to take a responsible point of view on any issue without fear of recrimination or reprisal. A student should be able to take issue with the teacher's views on a given matter without being labeled a "trouble-maker" or suffering a lowering of his grades, just as a teacher should be able to take issue with administrators, at proper times and places, without penalty.

5. *The right to equal opportunity* — No person shall be denied equal opportunity for education. Schools should not require students to take courses or educational experiences in inappropriate levels of interest, ability, and comprehension, nor should the school establish arbitrary and capricious restrictions on students as a condition for participation in programs of the school.

The values and the human rights identified in this statement apply to society as a whole. Because education is a major vehicle for the achievement of these rights, the school should make them central to its philosophy and practice.

Objectives and Policy

High level policy is the responsibility of school boards elected by, and responsible to, the democratic electorate. It is seldom delegated to the faculty or to students. These policies are most frequently based upon the primary objectives of the institution. The faculty and students often request clarification when the means of implementation of the policy seems to contradict the objectives. The speech teacher has a prime leadership responsibility to help students understand the various levels of policy-making and delegation of such processes.

A flow chart of policy within a school is shown in Fig. 1. The policy of the Board generally includes the determination to provide the personnel and facilities to educate the students. The Board may even participate in establishing certain parts of the curriculum, but this task is generally delegated to the Superintendent, whose major duties are to recommend the hiring of specific personnel and to provide facilities. The Superintendent may in turn delegate certain responsibilities and implementation policies to the Principal. Often the responsibilities for the curriculum (courses, activities, and student organization) are delegated in turn to the faculty. Selection of the curricular offerings is a step toward implementing education. In this setting the Board is in the position of approving programs and evaluating the steps of implementation. The flow chart shows that each of the personnel involved may evaluate all of the steps in the process.

Even the students participate in evaluation. However, in trying to move into policy-making which has not been delegated to them, or even to the faculty or the administration, the students reveal their confusion about the procedure for implementing policy.

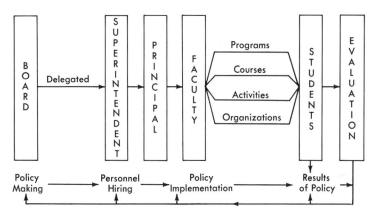

Figure 1. Policy Flow Chart

Assuming that freedom of speech is a primary objective of teaching and instruction in speech, the teacher must help the student understand the relationship of speech freedom to speech responsibility and implementation. The series of questions in the following table establishes some of the conflicting concerns in maintaining an open forum and the responsibilities of an educational institution to that forum. While the ideas expressed in the table may create more discussion than solution, they represent the type of considerations one might list regarding speakers invited onto a campus and the relation of the sponsoring group of students or faculty to such a speaker.

Speaker Invitations

1. The school should provide opportunities for students to hear many sides of controversial questions.
2. Assuming that the sponsoring group (students or faculty) is acting in good faith, the institutional sponsor need not agree with the speaker in order to approve the speaker.
   a) Is the decision of the sponsor and the student group open to review by appropriate administrative or faculty groups when information is available that the students or faculty have not acted in good faith?

b) Is there a minimum level of *academic competence* below which a speaker should not fall in order for a group to invite him to a campus? What is the basis for determining "academic competence"? As a teacher of debate, what is your position on permitting students to use proofs or points of view from obviously incompetent speakers whose opinions would not be acceptable to any group of recognized authorities in a particular field?

c) Is there a minimum level of *emotional stability* which a speaker must possess to be worthy of a university-provided platform? At what point does the university become obligated to provide teachers and speakers of a high enough degree of stability? Must the university sponsor speakers whose levels of excellence fall below that acceptable for university sponsorship?

d) Let us suppose that knowledgeable people in the field rate the speaker as academically incompetent, or that in the light of past behavior a particular community considers the speaker emotionally unstable: could the sponsoring group and adviser be questioned about their "good faith" in extending an invitation to such a speaker?

e) Do items (*b*), (*c*), and (*d*) above go beyond the legal limits of rights of invitation of the sponsoring group and the advisor?

3. Can the Board of Trustees, as charged by the State Legislature (for the total administrative responsibility of the university), delegate the authority below the level of the President of the University and divest themselves of the responsibility of final action?

Be very careful that any decisions you make on the questions above are not made on the basis of personal bias. As a teacher of speech, committed to freedom of speech, you must be able to defend your stand on such questions. The competency and reliability of the authority must be demonstrated in order to establish the speaker's undesirability. Competency generally demands some level of academic excellence in the area on which the speaker is speaking.

GENERAL SCHOOL OBJECTIVES

Religious views and the burden of several wars have heavily influenced the general objectives of the American public schools. The Old Deluder Satan Law was based upon the assumption that the individual should be able to read and interpret his own Bible. This was a major change from a position of reliance upon the priest. A desire to help western settlers solve their agricultural and vocational problems resulted in the Morrill Act which added many features to the previous Northwest land grants for public schools. Basic illiteracy in World War I identified a need for more practical education and brought about the Commission of the Reorganization of Secondary Education. The Commission modernized the objectives of education proposed by Herbert Spencer[10] and titled them *Cardinal Principles of Secondary Education.*[11] During a major economic depression these were redefined into objectives of the Educational Policies Commission.[12] Total mobilization during World War II again forced a close look at pragmatic objectives, resulting in the formulation of the *common and essential needs* of youth in a democratic society.[13] Many other professional groups have formulated similar objectives.[14] Those which follow provide the teacher with a guide to general educational objectives. *The objectives of specific programs, such as speech, must remain consistent with the overall objectives of the school. Common and Essential Needs That All Youth Have in a Democratic Society* provides the specificity needed in speech disciplines. Study the following lists closely and determine which objectives might be accomplished, or at least reinforced, through speech experience. Note particularly those which seem to terminate in skills and those which seem to have implications for behavioral change. Which objectives imply a body of knowledge, concepts, principles, or processes of inquiry? Note the relevant nature of these separate lists despite the variation in time and committee membership. Compare these individual lists with the objectives discussed in Supplement 1 above, the Phi Delta Kappa Commission's "Education and Human Rights."

*Educational Objectives**

A. *Objectives proposed by Spencer, 1911.*
  1. Activities which directly minister to self-preservation
  2. Activities which, by securing the necessities of life, indirectly minister to self-preservation

---

[10]Herbert Spencer, *Essays on Education* (New York: E.P. Dutton & Co., Inc., 1911), p. 7.

[11]Commission of the Reorganization of Secondary Education, *Cardinal Principles of Secondary Education* (Washington, D.C.: US Office of Education, Bulletin 35, 1918).

[12]Educational Policies Commission, *The Purposes of Education in American Democracy* (Washington, D.C.: National Education Association, 1938).

[13]Educational Policies Commission, *Education for All American Youth* (Washington, D.C.: National Education Association, 1944, revised 1952).

[14]For a current discussion of these and many other lists of objectives see Daniel Tanner, *Schools for Youth: Change and Challenge in Secondary Education* (New York: The Macmillan Company, 1965), pp. 1-210.

*These lists have been abstracted from sources given in earlier footnotes and vary in format in an effort to preserve the meaning of the original.

Educational Objectives (continued)

3. Activities which have as their end the rearing and disciplining of offspring
4. Activities which serve to maintain the proper social and political relations
5. Miscellaneous activities which make up the leisure part of life, devoted to the gratification of tastes and feelings

B. *The Seven Cardinal Principles of Secondary Education, 1918.*
   1. Health
   2. Command of the fundamental processes
   3. Worthy home membership
   4. Vocation
   5. Civil education
   6. Worthy use of leisure time
   7. Ethical character

C. *Objectives Stated by the Educational Policies Commision, 1938.*
   1. *The Objectives of Self-Realization.*
      The educated person
      a) has an inquiring mind,
      b) can speak the mother tongue clearly,
      c) reads the mother tongue efficiently,
      d) writes the mother tongue effectively,
      e) solves his problems of counting and calculating,
      f) is skilled in listening and observing,
      g) understands the basic facts concerning health and disease,
      h) protects his health and that of his dependents,
      i) works to improve the health of the community,
      j) is participant and spectator in many sports and other pastimes,
      k) has mental resources for the use of leisure time,
      l) appreciates beauty, and
      m) gives responsible direction to his own life.

   2. *The Objectives of Human Relationship.*
      The educated person
      a) puts human relationships first,
      b) enjoys rich, sincere, and varied social life,
      c) can work with others,
      d) appreciates the family as a social institution,
      e) conserves the family ideals,
      f) is skilled in homemaking, and
      g) maintains democratic family relationships.

Educational Objectives (continued)

3. *The Objectives of Economic Efficiency.*
   The educated producer
   a) knows the satisfaction of good workmanship,
   b) understands the requirements and opportunities for various jobs,
   c) has selected his occupation,
   d) succeeds in his chosen vocation,
   e) maintains and improves his efficiency, and
   f) appreciates the social value of his work.
   The educated consumer
   a) plans the economics of his life,
   b) develops standards for guiding his expenditures,
   c) is an informed and skillful buyer, and
   d) takes appropriate measure to safeguard his interests.
4. *The Objectives of Civic Responsibility.*
   The educated citizen
   a) is sensitive to the disparities of human circumstances,
   b) acts to correct unsatisfactory conditions,
   c) seeks to understand social structures,
   d) has defenses against propaganda,
   e) measures scientific advance in terms of its contribution to the general welfare,
   f) is a co-operating member of the world community,
   g) is economically literate,
   h) respects law,
   i) accepts his civic duties, and
   j) acts upon an unswerving loyalty to democratic ideals.

D. *Common and Essential Needs That All Youth Have in a Democratic Society, 1944.*
   1. All youth need to develop salable skills and those understandings and attitudes that make the worker an intelligent and productive participant in economic life. To this end most youth need supervised work experience as well as education in the skills and knowledge of their occupations.
   2. All youth need to develop and maintain good health and physical fitness.
   3. All youth need to understand the rights and duties of the citizen of a democratic society and to be diligent and competent in performing their obligations as members of the community and citizens of the state and the nation.
   4. All youth need to understand the significance of the family for the individual and society and the conditions conducive to successful family life.

Educational Objectives (continued)

5. All youth need to understand the methods of science, the influence of science on human life, and the main scientific facts concerning the nature of the world and of man.
6. All youth need to know how to purchase and use goods and services intelligently. They must understand both the values received by the consumer and the economic consequences of their acts.
7. All youth need opportunities to develop their capacities to appreciate beauty in literature, art, music, and nature.
8. All youth need to be able to use their leisure time well and to budget it wisely, balancing activities that yield satisfactions to the individual with those that are socially useful.
9. All youth need to develop respect for other persons, to grow in their insight into ethical values and principles, and to be able to live and work co-operatively with others.
10. All youth need to grow in their ability to think rationally, to express their thoughts clearly, and to read and listen with understanding.

Objectives and Relevancy

It is a major challenge to the speech teacher to maintain the high goals expressed in the foregoing statements and achieve the basic objectives of the school. We have stated that we are interested in behavioral goals, which are achieved by practice and repetition in school activities, the classroom, and school-sponsored organizations. The speech teacher must develop a climate of free speech with responsibility in classes, tournaments, theatre production, and school-sponsored programs. Protecting the rights of listeners is just as important as protecting the rights of those determined to speak. A further challenge arises in determining the relevance of a speech topic to the school's scheduled events and their relationship to the total purpose of the school. For example, what relevance does a discussion on the draft or Viet Nam bear to a course in chemistry or biology? While the teacher may find that such issues are relevant at some point in a speech course or a course on problems of democracy, one may question devotion of half of the course to such discussions.

Course objectives establish priorities and limits for instruction. Activities, materials, and evaluation methods help to achieve the objectives for which the institution was established. It may be proper at a given point in a course to explore and evaluate a specific national or local problem. If a course has been established with specific behavioral objectives, students have the right to expect instructional experiences which will result in a change in their skills and knowledge, leading to the expected behavioral changes. Exciting activities (productions or gab sessions) should be measured against the objectives. Speech objectives should relate to the improvement of speech skills, knowledge, and theory, leading to improved communication behavior.

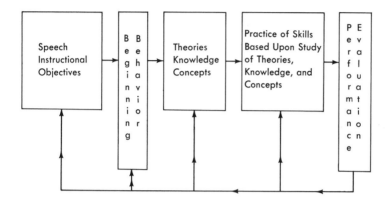

Figure 2. Learning Process: Behavioral Model with Evaluation and Feedback

Improvement of Criticism Is an Objective. Ever since Aristophanes presented his satirical commentary on Socrates' "Thinkery School" (*The Clouds*), it has been necessary to take a critical look at the purposes for which schools exist. (1) Some educators and laymen advocate that the purpose of the school is to teach *basic skills*; they asume that these skills are an end in themselves. It is assumed here that the individual will complete school and adapt his skills to meet the problems which he encounters during life. (2) Others advocate that the *school exists as an exploratory period* in which the student encounters basic life experiences. For this group *school is not a preparation for life; it is life*. It is assumed that the individual, having adjusted to the school experience, will make a satisfactory adjustment to life situations. (3) A third group of educational practitioners maintain that life is filled with problems and the basic necessity in learning is to develop processes to *solve* such problems. This group recognizes that the problems of the child's future may be similar but not identical to those found in the school. They advocate Dewey's problem solution steps as a viable process in which the student *(a) recognizes problems when encountered, (b) is able to analyze the problem in terms of relevant facts and people, (c) develops various solutions, (d) advocates the solution he feels is best,* and *(e) is able to explain and demonstrate the workability of the selected solution.* Note that the ability to comment, criticize, and support selected positions objectively and constructively is a basic tool in this approach to educational goals. Re-examine the above lists for evidence of these three approaches to objectives.

It is possible that all three groups are attempting to develop programs leading to the same goal: a thinking student capable of self-support, community leadership, and meaningful personal relationships. Such a goal reflects a need for teaching responsibility, rather than skills which may be used to exploit society. Still, the quantity and quality of current criticism indicates that the teaching mechanics and journeymen-teachers in our midst have their eyes upon skills and experiences and not upon the development of thinking, creative, responsible, problem-solving students.

Because a creative, thinking student often causes the inadequate teacher to feel uncomfortable, he is often required to read and agree with the text. This situation provides a fortress of support to cover the inadequacies of the teacher and text. In such a classroom the basic element, *freedom of speech,* is lost. The speech classroom should be mechanically and theoretically organized to guarantee this basic freedom. Multiple texts and deliberate methods of fostering dissent should be basic to the speech classroom. The speech teacher must be committed to freedom of

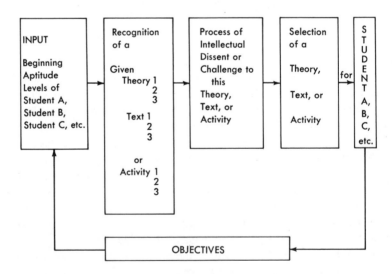

Figure 3. Learning Process: Multiple-Theory Model with Materials and Activities

thought and speech and must provide a climate for both at functional and artistic levels. This may prove a challenge to theatre directors and oral interpretation teachers who rely upon historical models of performance in blocking or line interpretation. Verbalization is not the measure of practice; practice is generally the *determinant of objectives.*

SPEECH EDUCATION AND SCHOOL OBJECTIVES

Learning involves changes in behavior that persist. Speech education concerns changes in behavior which relate to improvement of *skills in speaking, listening,* and determining the *involvement* of listeners in all types of oral communication. Speech education is concerned with these behaviors in *functional* and in *artistic* forms of oral presentation. Although speech instruction has been a part of formal instruction for more than 2500 years, it has been primarily concerned with teaching skills involved in preparing and delivering a speech or presenting a play. While early discussions of speech refer to audience study, these are mostly limited to the study of the audience by the potential speaker as a means of attracting and holding their attention. Little concern was directed to the *listening* process in the modern sense. *Audience interaction* and *feedback* studies are almost entirely a process learned from mass communication during the past half century.

Speech concerns the skills, processes, and behavior of the speaker and the listener, and the process of determining feedback. Particularly, speech instruction treats the teacher as a communicator and the class members as speaker-listeners. Modern concerns for interaction and feedback in the classroom will be fundamental to the teaching processes which follow. How can we plan instruction to improve the persistence of changed behavior in speaking situations? How can we improve understanding of the processes as well as the skills? An instructional discipline which has survived so long should have theory, content, and established procedural disciplines. Showing that these processes are relevant to the modern student is the purpose of this book.

Objectives of Speech Education

In spite of considerable effort on the part of leaders in speech education the public has, during the past two decades, continued to think of speech as a basic part of the curriculum devoted to leisure-time activities (number 6 of the Seven Cardinal Principles). While leisure-time activity may be one of its minor functions, the stress placed upon this objective has far out-weighed its more important functions and has placed a stereotype upon speech programs in the minds of administrators, teachers, laymen, and even teachers of speech. Worse yet, students in many schools have a distorted interpretation of speech. Some consider it a snap course, others a pleasant diversion, and others a depository for the rejects from the college-preparatory program. Student opinion reflects the practices used in various schools. Such attitudes can be changed by speech teachers through instruction of students, parents, fellow faculty members, and administrators. The teacher must, therefore, have clear understandings about national as well as local speech objectives.

Some of these disagreeable attitudes result from the practices of speech teachers who look for outlets for their own "arty" ambitions. We should remember that teachers are employed to educate students, and the best recommendation a teacher may gain is through accomplishing that objective. The teacher's best reward is not the contest trophy, but rather the knowledge that students have developed proficiencies and understandings which free them from the dependency of childhood and make possible better functional and artistic communication. Speech programs can achieve general school objectives while achieving the specific objectives of speech programs. When the teacher evaluates the outcomes of speech

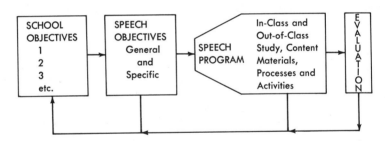

Figure 4. Outcomes Related to Instruction

instruction, he may find that the materials, methods of study, or in-class and out-of-class activities were major barriers to achieving those objectives. It is not uncommon to find that out-of-class objectives are in direct conflict with the general and specific objectives of the class. One may also discover that some school objectives may not be educational if actually pursued and may dictate faulty objectives for speech programs, such as collecting hardware (trophies).

Fundamental Processes as Objectives

If students are to communicate more effectively, they must become aware of the basic problems which act as barriers to this process. Beginning teachers with normal emotional reactions are uneasy when they enter the first classroom; they undergo "stage fright," gain understanding of the symptoms which students experience, and get practice in overcoming the causes. As a speaker-communicator, the teacher must face the *fundamentals of speech* in much the same way as the students must. These fundamentals underlie every speech course offered. As courses become more advanced the process changes to adapt to new audiences, expectations, and materials, but fundamentals remain much the same. The fundamentals in speech help to identify those processes which set speech apart from other forms of communication. They include the following:

1. Adjustment to the speaking situation
2. Phonation
3. Articulation
4. Critical use of oral symbols
5. Skills and concepts involved in listening
6. Understanding empathy, or feedback

Compare this list with that of Barnes[15] where listening is included under the first four items. Because listening is an adjustment of the audience member to the speaking of others, and because ability to listen is closely related to symbolic proficiency, it might be rated as an integral part of the first four processes. Braden[16] includes *confrontation* as a fifth process due to the immediacy of the speaker-listener "now" relationship. Speech classes must have confrontation with these concepts in order to develop behavioral skills and become proficient in speech. Cortright makes a plea for a return to fundamentals — action, voice, language, and thought — as our unique, distinctive task.[17] We should compare these concepts with those discussed by Allen, Anderson, and Hough[18] which to a great extent deal with communication theory and the impact of mass media.

If we accept certain "unique" processes as basic to oral communication, and if we are to help students master these processes, we must be proficient in knowledge, process, and demonstration ability in the use and evaluation of each process. Those who have struggled with the problems of stagefright, phonation, articulation, and symbol development will recognize the need for specialized training in these fundamental processes.

---

[15]Harry G. Barnes, *Speech Fundamentals* (New York: Prentice-Hall, Inc., 1953). See Fig. 20. Progressive Rating Scale.

[16]Waldo Braden, *Speech Methods and Resources* (New York: Harper & Row, Publishers, 1961).

[17]Rupert L. Cortright, "That Intelligence May Prevail," *The Michigan Speech Association Journal*, 2:1-5 (1967).

[18]R. R. Allen, Sharol Anderson, and Jere Hough, *Speech in American Society* (Columbus, Ohio: Charles E. Merrill Publishing Company, 1968), pp. 51-124.

Only recently, in the studies of listening and feedback, have we become aware of the dimensions of linguistic and semantic involvement which go beyond the printed symbol. We further believe that the individual skills demanded in these areas require technical training and judgment which are not provided in the preparation of teachers in other disciplines. As a final test we might make close comparisons with Kramer's objectives[19] or those discussed in The Common and Essential Needs That All Youth Have in a Democratic Society.[20]

Justifying Speech.   Because the speech teacher is often challenged to justify speech programs, he should clarify his thinking and formulate defensible objectives after study of the suggested lists above. Such objectives should include responsibility and integrity relevant to the culture of our time (whether 1969, 1976, or 1990). One might ponder the theory of *The American Challenge* as presented by J.J. Servan-Schreiber in contrast with Toynbee's discussion of the rise and fall of civilizations in selecting objectives for the future.[21] *The Teacher's Guide to High School Speech*[22] and *Speech in American Society,*[23] with its accompanying handbook for the teacher, provide some very specific guidance for thinking about objectives. A usable handbook for the student and teacher entitled "Radio and Television in the Secondary School" is also available.[24] The preface to most texts provides concise viewpoints on the author's objectives and the use of the book. Textbooks frequently indicate in appendices or prefaces the chapters useful for various types of speech courses.

Objectives, Values, and Teacher Competence

Among the "Ten Common and Essential Needs of Youth" we find an underlying need for experience leading to recognition and establishment of values. When an incompetent director directs a student play, or when the play is inadequately staged or the performance not polished, the stu-

---

[19]Magdalene Kramer, "The Role of Speech in Education: A Re-evaluation," *The Quarterly Journal of Speech,* 34:123-127 (April, 1948).

[20]Educational Policies Commission, *op. cit.*

[21]J.J. Servan-Schreiber, *The American Challenge* (New York: Atheneum Publishers, 1968); Arnold J. Toynbee, *A Study of History,* abridgment by D. C. Somerwell (New York: Oxford University Press, Inc., 1947).

[22]*The Teacher's Guide to High School Speech,* published by The Indiana State Department of Public Instruction in Cooperation with the Indiana University English Curriculum Center, Bulletin No. 503 (1966).

[23]Allen, Anderson, and Hough, *op. cit.*

[24]"Radio and Television in the Secondary School," *The Bulletin of the National Association of Secondary School Principals,* 50, No. 312 (October, 1966).

dents will conclude that *poor production is good theatre.* They may even conclude that it is honest to sell tickets to such a shoddy event. This is in the same category as teaching students that stealing is honest.

Students are frequently guided in their educational experiences by leaders who are incompetent in skill areas. In order to teach values in music, the teacher must have a discriminating skill to hear and interpret music. Flat notes never become non-flat notes by wishing. Like music, speech teaching involves technical skill in many activities where speech is used. Group discussion is more than a round-table exchange of ideas. Elimination of faulty phonation and articulation errors may be complex or easy, depending upon the nature of the problem, but misdirection can be very serious and may create more problems. Radio and theatre skills are not the province of the amateur. *Life-enriching and fulfilling experience can be gained under wise and competent guidance in speech activities. Under incompetent direction these same activities can be a detriment that the school cannot afford.*

Professional Information and Exchange of Ideas. The competent teacher of speech should be dedicated to the improvement of student adjustment to the speaking situation. He should understand stage fright and the various types of speech skills leading to the types of therapy needed. He should be critically aware of the research being performed in the areas of articulation and phonation. The professional journals (e.g., *The Quarterly Journal of Speech, The Speech Teacher,* and *The Educational Theatre Journal*), in which studies are reported and methodology is described, should be a part of his daily professional life. The teacher should act as a model in the use of language, understanding its limitations as well as its beauties.

Speech for All as an Objective

Leaders of American schools of the early forties were finally awakened to the need for education of all youth. Many books and journal articles carried this goal as part of their titles, some devoting an entire issue to the problem.[25] Thus, education (including speech) became an obvious need for all. With Sputnik the need for scientists blurred the vision of educators and the goal remained dormant. The studies of Baker, Everett, Schoen,

---

[25]Evelyn Konigsburg, "Speech Education for All," *The Speech Teacher,* 2:191-5 (September, 1953). "Speech Education for All American Youth," *The Bulletin of the National Association of Secondary School Principals,* 32, No. 151: whole issue (January, 1948).

and Harvill[26] indicate that less than ten percent of the students in high schools are able to register for speech classes.

Screening Techniques and Competition for Time.   The competition of required courses for the time of the college-preparatory student has left little time for any electives. Thus, speech instruction for potential leaders becomes somewhat remote.[27] Some speech teachers have established unfair screening systems in schools where speech registration is limited to two or three classes. Limitation of classes by the administration is an open admission that the speech teachers have failed to sell the importance of speech instruction to the administration. Screening "try-outs" imply that the teacher does not feel capable of teaching but only of coaching those students already talented. One type of screening is defensible: that of admitting to speech classes only those in obvious need of speech instruction.

Types of Programs and Courses.   Studies of inner city problems indicate a massive need for communication skills. Most of the children in the inner city areas must learn salable skills for employment in the cities. This employment includes skilled trades involving the ability to communicate with the public, with employers, and with fellow workers. The challenge of SPEECH FOR ALL is now a must. It is the firm conviction of the authors of this book that three school plays and ten debates do not comprise a program in speech. A speech program is viable when enough sections of fundamentals are offered so that all can register. This offering should be supplemented with advanced speech courses in debate, drama, radio, or combinations of these. Many teachers prefer courses with broad goals so that the interrelationships of drama, radio, and debate can be included without debating students on the course objectives and types of assignments. We can well afford to provide multi-experience in all types of speech at functional levels. Functional conversation, dealing with prod-

---

26Mary K. Baker, "An Evaluation of the Speech Program of the Secondary Schools of Ohio for the Year 1961-2" (unpublished monograph, Ohio State University, 1962); Russell I. Everett, "Speech Education: Ohio College Programs and Certification" (Doctoral dissertation, Ohio State University, 1967); Kathryn T. Schoen, "Perceptions of Speech Education in Ohio Secondary Schools" (Doctoral dissertation, Ohio State University, 1965); and Linda Harvill, "The Status of Speech Education in Accredited Mississippi Secondary Schools" (Master's thesis, University of Southern Mississippi, 1967).

27Thorrell B. Fest (ed.), "A Symposium: Fifty Years of Indecision: The Speech Curriculum for American Youth" (John W. Keltner, "Speech for All American Youth: Current Issues and Problems"; Ronald R. Allen, "The New Speech Educator: Philosophy and Standards"; William E. Buys, "Speech Curricula for All American Youth"; Robert C. Pooley, "Oral Communication in the English Curriculum"; Donald K. Smith, "Speech for Tomorrow: Concepts and Context"), *The Speech Teacher,* 15:11-33 (January, 1966).

ucts, job interviews, and ability to give and understand directions, should replace the wearisome waste of time so long devoted to social conversation. A close tie with programs in distributive education (in which on-the-job experience supplements classroom instruction) might be worked out so that the speech program can compete with the excellence found in the speech training built into the Future Farmer and Future Homemaker activities sponsored by Smith Hughes.

The major concern is not the types of speech courses offered but the variety of beginning and advanced training for students as individuals. Good bands, choruses, and orchestras are not developed in a single, one-semester fundamentals program. Quality teams are not developed by allowing students to register for football or basketball for one year only. But the purpose of speech does not permit it to depend on those processes in which only select students are found acceptable, as in choral or athletic participation. We might emulate athletic programs which are supported by well developed physical education classes for all students or music curricula in which every student is encouraged to participate in a chorus or band group. Competition for the varsity team or choir then develops meaning. A good speech program should provide sufficient classes in fundamentals for all, advanced classes for those wishing advanced classroom instruction, debate and discussion groups of sufficient number to involve one third to one half of the student body in any given year, and enough plays to provide opportunities for all. Out-of-class programs need be scheduled neither for the general public nor for interschool competition. A vigorous intra-class program is a basic means of implementing the goal of speech for all. Advanced students can act as coaches and assemblies and class meetings can provide audiences. SPEECH FOR ALL *can be a realistic objective.*

THE TEACHING PROCESS

Teaching is a process of (*a*) *selecting objectives,* (*b*) *collecting and organizing content* (knowledge and materials), (*c*) *planning experiences* (activities for teacher and student), and (*d*) *evaluation* (diagnosis and progress). It should be apparent that recipes or cook book approaches are insufficient for good instruction. The speech teacher must be competent in theory and practice, which involves a thorough knowledge of the content of the various types of speech behavior and their historical settings. You will note the *interrelationships* of rhetorical, dramatic, and literary criticism to the theories and practices of controversial discussion and production styles. You may be challenged and intrigued by the common bond of (*a*) audience analysis compared with the impact of theatre and (*b*) interpretive materials and rhetoric as a commentary or criticism on civilization. The idea of this unifying bond may cause you some concern as you watch the fragmentation of speech departments and programs into separate areas emphasizing behavioral science, fine arts, and voice science. In your own practice you will find that you cannot develop the great speaker, the informal discussant, or the theatrical performer without concern for all of these interrelated disciplines. Primarily, students expect speech teachers to be knowledgeable about all these activities which are labeled "speech" in the mind of the layman.

Due to the complexity of rehearsals, tournaments, and class meetings throughout all the periods of co-curricular activity, the teacher becomes anxious for immediate *aids* for solving specific problems. Your instructor and this text may help you find answers, but neither your instructor nor the authors of this text can find the best answer for your immediate problem in a *cook book* approach. Part of the professional task is to select the better solution after a thorough diagnosis. Your instructor and the present authors entered college teaching because they were concerned with the quality of instructional programs, contests, and festivals in schools where they taught. They developed a curiosity to know more about teaching in general and teaching speech in particular. Each wanted to experiment to find out if one type of instruction is more effective than others. Reported research of practicing teachers, found in the professional journals (*The Speech Teacher, The Quarterly Journal of Speech, The Educational Theatre Journal, Speech Monographs*, and the many regional and state journals) is extremely valuable. It is reassuring to find that other successful speech teachers have met similar problems and have suggested solutions which work for them. Inserting large capsulized reports from these journals into this text would rob you of valuable experience. Samples will be furnished to give guidance, but regular reading and reporting from the professional journals is a part of the academic training of a professional teacher. It is best to begin now.

Professional Resources and Guides

A group of speech educators formed the Speech Association of America in 1914. Since that time many articles have appeared in the professional journals listed above and in *The Bulletin of the National Association of Secondary School Principals*. Those who believe that the secondary administrator has been unfriendly to speech programs should study closely the following complete issues devoted to speech instruction.

"Role of Speech in the Secondary School," 29, No. 33 (Nov., 1945).

"Speech Education for all American Youth," 32, No. 51 (Jan., 1948).

"Dramatics in the Secondary School," 33, No. 166 (Dec., 1949).

"Speech and Hearing Problems in the Secondary School," 34, No. 173 (Nov., 1950).

"The Imperative Needs of Youth of Secondary School Age," 31, No. 145 (March, 1947).

"Public Address in the Secondary School," 36, No. 187 (May, 1952).

"A Speech Program for Secondary School," 38, No. 199 (Jan., 1954).

"Radio and Television in the Secondary School," 50, No. 312 (Oct., 1966).

The following represents but a sample of the articles from *The Speech Teacher.*

Loren D. Reid, "On First Teaching Speech," *The Speech Teacher,* 1:1-8 (January, 1952).

Karl F. Robinson, "Certification of Secondary School Teachers of Speech," *The Speech Teacher,* 1:24-28 (January, 1952).

Franklin H. Knower, "A Philosophy of Speech for the Secondary School, *The Speech Teacher,* 1:79-85 (March, 1952).

John Keltner, "Discussion Contests: Sense or Nonsense," *The Speech Teacher,* 1:95-100 (March, 1952).

Oliver W. Nelson, "Developing a Functional Speech Program for the Public Schools," *The Speech Teacher,* 1:125-127 (March, 1952).

Geraldine Granfield, "The Integration of Speech with English in the High School Curriculum," *The Speech Teacher,* 2:114-118 (March, 1953).

Hugh F. Seabury, "Objectives and Scope of the Fundamentals Course in Speech in the High School," *The Speech Teacher,* 3:117-120 March, 1954).

The Quarterly Journal of Speech, Speech Monographs, The Educational Theatre Journal, and regional speech journals show equal concern about the objectives of speech instruction, as evidenced by the writers and the space allotments within each of the journals.

The Speech Teacher and *The Educational Theatre Journal* were established in 1952 and 1949 respectively in order to share information about teaching problems. Other professional speech journals were devoting more space to research and university programs. (*Speech Monographs,* in fact, is now totally research-oriented.) Teachers of speech can find few professional resources better than the articles in these two journals in the quarter century of their existence. These journals document the modern problems of communication and the relevancy for the established theory and practice. The reference to practical considerations in these journals indicates a belief that theory can be developed from practice. Concern for on-going research reveals the forward-moving responsibility of the profession. *The Table of Contents of The Quarterly Journal of Speech, Speech Monographs, and The Speech Teacher* has been compiled and revised by Franklin H. Knower from each first volume through the current copies. This index is basic to the teacher wishing to keep abreast of the field. Articles are listed by each professional journal and cross-indexed to cover the following large areas with sub-divisions: *fundamentals of speech, public address, interpretation, radio and television, dramatics, speech and hearing disorders,* and *speech education.* Thus, the teacher may find pertinent material on theory and practice within the various speech disciplines and in speech education at all grade levels. Courses of study, selected unit plans, and discussion of projects are included.

Relation of Textbooks to Objectives

Most textbooks for secondary speech subscribe to one or more of the lists of general educational objectives. Again the teacher should study planned experiences carefully to determine if the assignments and materials can lead to accomplishment of the objectives. The practicing teacher may be permitted to change assignment suggestions to fit the selected text into behavioral concerns, but this would be to teach by organizational process. We must remember that philosophy is the outgrowth and measurement of what one does, rather than what one says he would like to do. Therefore, beginning with a problem to be solved, an individual casts about for instruments of solution. *Having recognized an instrument* (knowledge or implement), he applies it to the problem (*he uses it as a tool*). Based upon the success of these two procedures, he *develops a better understanding* of the problem and a respect for the instrument. Now we might say that he recognizes the tool at a higher level, uses it in a more sophisticated way, and understands it at a still more sophisticated level. In this sense learning becomes a cycle of *recognition, use,* and *understanding* of problem-solving instruments. Speech textbooks can be used as tools in this manner. Speech instruction might then set its objectives as providing precision tools to increase sophisticated understanding. *Tools* in this sense includes texts, subject matter, theories, processes, skills, and evaluation techniques. Through these precision skills we can aid the student in adjusting to the environment in which he finds himself. The teacher cannot furnish answers but he can help the student in developing solution processes.

Teaching Methods

This chapter has been devoted to an exploration of speech objectives as they relate to the objectives of the school and the total educational structure. Educational methods begin with *objectives*. Selection of *materials* (content or knowledge) must remain relevant to the objectives chosen. *Activities* of teacher and student can be justified only as they are oriented toward the achievement of objectives. *Evaluation* must be carried out to determine the need for selection of objectives, to measure progress toward these objectives, and finally to determine if the objectives have been achieved. The process of methodology might be illustrated as in Fig. 5.

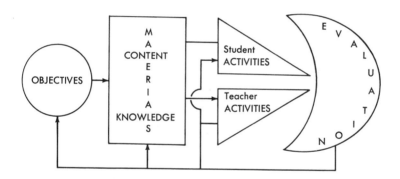

Figure 5. Teaching Methods

Care must be taken to make sure that activities do not become objectives in themselves. While content or knowledge is not an end in itself, various speech skills, concepts, and knowledge can be formed into a process for improving functional and artistic communication. Only by maintaining a program of evaluation can we determine if we are on the path to completing the desired trip.

This book is not a substitute for texts or materials in the respective speech disciplines. The potential teacher will need to make constant reference to his texts and class notes from preceding courses in communication theory, public address, speech science, theatre, oral interpretation, and broadcasting.

Planning the curriculum will be treated in Chapter 3, and Chapter 4 will cover classroom teaching and interaction. Evaluation will be discussed in Chapter 5, and the various chapters which follow in Part Two will cover content, resources, and organization of experiences in the specific speech areas. Chapter 2 will develop current concerns and trends in speech education.

Suggested Projects

1. Explain the four basic objectives of education as set up by the National Educational Policies Commission. Indicate specifically how you would attempt to achieve these goals in each of the following types of speech courses. Indicate especially the changes you would use at different grade levels.

   a) Junior high school general speech course
   b) Fundamentals of speech course at the high school level
   c) Advanced public speaking course
   d) Drama or interpretation course

2. Assume you have been appointed to a high school position to instruct students in speech. The following facts are relevant. The school has four hundred students in the ninth through twelfth grades, but only one speech course is offered. The community is agricultural in nature and expresses considerable interest in competitive sports. The first-year enrollment of the class is five boys and fifteen girls. The balance of your day is assigned to instruction in English or social studies.

   a) What specific plans will you carry out to create a demand for a second-year course by your second year? Direct these plans to the student level.
   b) What community plans will you carry out to create a demand on the part of the parents as well as the students? Be specific.
   c) What specific plans will you present to the administration to justify the change in teaching assignment and the creation of a second section or course?

3. Consider again the community described above:

   a) Give a tentative list of units or projects you would include in your first-year course. Indicate their probable order and give reasons for this order.
   b) Explain briefly your approach to teaching the fundamentals: articulation, symbolic formulation, adjustment, and phonation. What methods would you use to teach the "mechanics" you feel are

absolutely necessary? How will you interest students in studies of listening and feedback?

4. Recent studies in listening have had a considerable effect upon approaches to teaching speech. Discuss the facts and the implications of these studies as they refer to the responsibilities of speech programs in the junior and senior high schools.

5. Discuss variations in the mental, physical, social, and emotional maturity and behavior patterns of the junior and senior high school student which have a bearing upon classroom organization, planning, objectives, and activities in the speech area.

6. Discuss the reasons why a speech program in the secondary school should serve all the students. List the areas of speech instruction which should be included.

7. Describe the types of positions generally open to the speech graduate and the type of training needed to adjust the teacher to his job. Include a brief listing of personal, academic, and professional education needs.

8. Why should a study of language be included in a speech course?

References

Bettinghouse, Erwin P. *Message Preparation: The Nature of Proof.* Indianapolis, Ind.: The Bobbs-Merrill Company, Inc., 1966.

Bois, J. Samuel. *The Art of Awareness: A Textbook on General Semantics.* Dubuque, Iowa: William C. Brown Company, Publishers, 1966.

Brooks, Keith (ed.). *The Communicative Arts and Sciences of Speech.* Columbus, Ohio: Charles E. Merrill Publishing Company, 1967.

Cathcart, Robert. *Post Communication: Critical Analysis and Evaluation.* Indianapolis, Ind.: The Bobbs-Merrill Company, Inc., 1966.

Christensen, Francis. *Notes Toward a New Rhetoric.* New York: Harper & Row, Publishers, 1967.

Clevenger, Theodore, Jr. *Audience Analysis.* Indianapolis, Ind.: The Bobbs-Merrill Company, Inc., 1966.

Delbridge, Arthur and Bernard, J. R. L. *Patterns in Language.* San Francisco: Tri-Ocean Books, 1966.

Diack, Hunter. *Language for Teaching.* New York: Philosophical Library, Inc., 1967.

Duker, Sam (ed.). *Listening: Readings.* New York: The Scarecrow Press, 1966.

Fortas, Abe. *Concerning Dissent and Civil Disobedience.* New York: The New American Library, Inc., Signet Books, 1968.

Henry, Mabel W. (ed.). *Creative Experiences in Oral Language.* Champaign, Ill.: National Council of Teachers of English, 1967.

Lamers, William M. and Staudacher, Joseph M. *The Speech Arts.* Chicago: Lyons & Carnahan, 1966.

Lenneberg, Eric H. *Biological Foundations of Language.* New York: John Wiley & Sons, Inc., 1967.

Lomas, Charles W. *The Agitator in American Society.* Englewood Cliffs, New Jersey: Prentice-Hall, Inc., 1968.

Macdonald, James B. and Leeper, Robert R. (eds.). *Language and Meaning.* Washington, D. C.: Association for Supervision and Curriculum Development, 1966.

Marsh, Patrick O. *Persuasive Speaking: Theory, Models, Practice.* New York: Harper & Row, Publishers, 1967.

May, Frank B. *Teaching Language as Communication to Children.* Columbus, Ohio: Charles E. Merrill Publishing Company, 1967.

Miller, Gerald R. *Speech Communication: A Behavioral Approach.* Indianapolis, Ind.: The Bobbs-Merrill Company, 1966.

Mills, Glen E. *Message Preparation: Analysis and Structure.* Indianapolis, Ind.: The Bobbs-Merrill Company, Inc., 1966.

Nilsen, Thomas R. *Ethics of Speech Communication.* Indianapolis, Ind.: The Bobbs-Merrill Company, Inc., 1966.

O'Neil, Robert M. *Responsible Communication Under Law.* Indianapolis, Ind.: The Bobbs-Merrill Company, Inc., 1968.

Phillips, Gerald M. *Communication and the Small Groups.* Indianapolis, Ind.: The Bobbs-Merrill Company, Inc., 1966.

Thayer, Lee (ed.). *Communication Theory and Research: Proceedings of the First International Symposium.* Springfield, Illinois: Charles C. Thomas, Publisher, 1967.

Valdman, Albert (ed.). *Trends in Language Teaching.* New York: McGraw-Hill Book Company, 1966.

Wiseman, Gordon and Barker, Larry. *Speech: Interpersonal Communication.* San Francisco: Chandler Publishing Co., 1967.

Articles

Behan, David F. "A Technique for Teaching Audience Awareness and Audience Response to High School Students," *The Speech Teacher*, 12:52-54 (January, 1964).

Bemis, James L. and Phillips, Gerald M. "A Phenomenological Approach to Communication Theory," *The Speech Teacher,* 13:262-269 (November, 1964).

Brewster, Laurence W. "The Effect of a Brief Training Program in Listening Improvement," *The Speech Teacher*, 15:1-7 (January, 1966).

Bronstein, Arthur J. and Rambo, Dorothy E. "Language Analysis and the Speech Teacher — A New Frontier," *The Speech Teacher,* 11:130-135 (March, 1962).

Canfield, William H. "A Phonetic Approach to Voice and Speech Improvement," *The Speech Teacher,* 13:42-46 (January, 1964).

Carmack, Paul A. "Evolution in Parliamentary Procedure," *The Speech Teacher,* 11:26-39 (January, 1962).

Ecroyd, Donald H. "New Directions in Teaching Voice and Articulation," *The Speech Teacher,* 16:230-234 (September, 1967).

Erickson, Marceline. "Improving Speech Programs: Needs, Trends, Methods, Part I," *The Speech Teacher,* 12:26-33 (January, 1963). Individual articles as follows: Erickson, Mareline. "The Required Speech Course and the Speech Profession"; Stevens, Walter W. "The Speech Building Conference"; Hoogestraat, Wayne E. "Letters of Evaluation — An Exercise in Speech Criticism"; Watkins, Lloyd I. "Affiliating the Advanced Speech Course with a Charitable Organization"; Graham, John. "Something New in Student Legislatures."

Feany, Leo S. "Unlimited Potential to Communicate," *The Speech Teacher,* 14:63-66 (January, 1965).

Furbay, Albert L., Hedges, Carmita, and Markham, David. "A Listening Approach to Fundamentals of Speech," *The Speech Teacher,* 15:232-235 (November, 1966).

Geiger, Don. "The Humanistic Direction of Debate," *The Speech Teacher,* 14:101-106 (March, 1965).

Gibson, James W. and Kibler, Robert J. "Creative Thinking in the Speech Classroom" (a bibliography of related research), *The Speech Teacher,* 14:30-34 (January, 1965).

Gouran, Dennis S. "Attitude Change and Listener's Understandings of a Persuasive Communication," *The Speech Teacher,* 15:289-294 (November, 1966).

Griffith, Francis. "The Ideal Speech Program in the Secondary School," *The Speech Teacher,* 12:34-36 (January, 1963).

Grove, Theodore G. "Abstracted Feedback in Teaching Discussion," *The Speech Teacher,* 16:103-108 (March, 1967).

Heinberg, Paul. "Phonetics, Linguistics, and Voice Science: Where To?" *The Speech Teacher,* 16:7-13 (January, 1965).

Hildebrandt, Herbert W. and Sattler, William M. "The Use of Common Materials in the Basic College Speech Course," *The Speech Teacher,* 12:18-25 (January, 1963).

Kane, Peter E. "Role Playing for Educational Use," *The Speech Teacher,* 13:320-323 (November, 1964).

Klotsche, J. Martin. "The Importance of Communication in Today's World," *The Speech Teacher,* 11:322-326 (November, 1962).

Knower, F. H. "Interdisciplinary Research in Communication," *Ohio Speech Journal,* 1:93-98 (1962).

————. "A Model for a Communicology," *Ohio Speech Journal,* 1:181-187 (1963).

Lewis, G. L. "Do You Know Your Plays and Playwrights?" *Ohio Speech Journal* 1:42-50 (1962); 2:149-154 (1963).

————. "Secondary School Speech Textbooks: A Biblographic Analysis," *Ohio Speech Journal,* 3:3-13 (1965).

_____, and Eliopolis, J. "Problem Questions for Speaking and Discussion," 1:75-88 (1962).

Martin, Charles K. and Munger, Daniel I. "Team Teaching in a Course in Fundamentals of Speech," *The Speech Teacher,* 14:331-333 (November, 1965).

McCroskey, James C. "Toulmin and the Basic Course," *The Speech Teacher,* 14:91-100 (March, 1965).

Newman, John B. "Semantics and the Study of Speech," *The Speech Teacher,* 16:98-102 (March, 1967).

Oliver, Robert T. "One Hundred Years of Teaching Speech: An Interpretation," *The Speech Teacher,* 11:247-252 (September, 1962).

Paul, Aldrich K. "A New Concept in Sharing Speech Professors," *The Speech Teacher,* 14:63-66 (January, 1965).

Roberts, Mary M. "Improving Speech Programs: Needs, Trends, Methods, Part II," *The Speech Teacher,* 12:115-127 (March, 1963). Including articles as follows: Roberts, Mary M. "Planning a Forensic Workshop"; Kuhr, Manuel I. "Conducting a Two-Week Debate Institute"; Schmidt, Robert. "Consultant Service for a Drama Workshop"; Kline, H. Charles and Holley, Donald L. "A Contest Workshop in Television Speaking"; White, Harvey. "Some Techniques for Teaching Anatomy and Physiology"; Verderber, Rudolph F. "The One Point Debate: An Addition to the Beginning Course."

Rucker, Juanita J., Sanders, W. E., and Mitchell, Wanda B. "Resource Materials: Innovations for the High School Teacher of Speech," *The Speech Teacher,* 17:258-267 (September, 1968).

Shiraishi, Jane S. "A Fourth Type of American Speech," *The Speech Teacher,* 11:48-50 (January, 1962).

Vogelsong, Robert W. and Ettlich, Ernest E. "NDEA Institutes: A Challenge to Speech Educators," *The Speech Teacher,* 15:186-190 (September, 1968).

Walter, Otis M. "On the Teaching of Speech as a Force in Western Culture," *The Speech Teacher,* 11:1-19 (January, 1962).

Wenger, Galen L. and Schilling, Arlo L. "Speech as Preparation for High School Writing, An Experiment," *The Speech Teacher,* 14:136-137 (March, 1965).

Wheater, Stanley B. "Team Teaching in a Course in Speaking and Writing," *The Speech Teacher,* 15:242-247 (September, 1966).

Wood, Barbara Sundene. "Implications of Psycholinguistics for Elementary Speech Programs," *The Speech Teacher,* 17:183-194 (September, 1968).

Zelko, Harold P. and Knapp, Mark L. "Business and Professional Speech Communication in American Colleges and Universities: Status of Courses," *The Speech Teacher,* 15:235-241 (September, 1966).

2

Trends in Speech Education

A superficial examination of the title indexes of *The Quarterly Journal of Speech, Speech Monographs* and *The Speech Teacher* provides some insight into the vast changes and modern trends taking place in speech education. The form and substance of the entire field of speech continues to change as modern research techniques are employed in repudiating or substantiating old axioms and in formulating new principles and theories. The rapid expansion of speech content has occurred primarily as a result of the spectacular advances being made in both the behavioral and physical sciences. The scope of speech content has come to concern itself not only with message construction and delivery but also with message transmission, reception, further dissemination, and feedback.

Indeed, the changes which have taken place in content emphasis over the last two decades have given rise to the suggestion that the term "speech" itself is inadequate and should be replaced with a term which would serve as a more adequate denoter of all the areas of legitimate concern to speech educators. Further, we see emerging at the college and university level an increasing number of departments of communication. The content areas embodied in departments of communication vary. One may find all or some of the following areas included: public address, radio-television, speech education, theatre, speech and hearing science, journalism, public relations, etc.

Departmental designations are not, however, the sole barometer of changes occurring in the field of speech. The titles and contents of college and secondary speech texts reflect changing patterns in emphasis. Whereas twenty years ago many of the texts published incorporated within their titles the term *speech*, today there are an increasing number of texts employing in their titles the term *communication*. These changes reflect an evolution from the speech act conceptualized as a singular event occurring in a moment of time to the speech act viewed as only one phase in a much more complex and on-going communication process.

Many speech educators have come to realize that speech is truly an interdisciplinary study. We have borrowed heavily from sociology for our knowledge of group processes and the effects of group membership upon message reception. We find that the concepts of opinion leader, task leader, socio-emotional leader, role, norm, group sanction, status, and prestige are fruitful in the process of audience and speaker analysis, message construction, and so forth.

Speech has likewise borrowed heavily from psychology for its knowledge of personality. We are beginning to feel comfortable with the concepts of dissonance, internalization, privatization, perception, cognitive, affective, and overt behavior, congruency, inhibition, etc., as we relate them to the communication act.

Nor is speech any less indebted to the physical sciences. The concepts of feedback noise, signal, transmitter, channel, encoding, decoding, and so forth, have functioned to broaden our understanding of the oral communication process and to provide us with an appreciation of how closely the elements in the oral communication process parallel those elements existing in other forms of communication.

More recently one hears the charge, from those who find it difficult to keep pace with change, that modern speech educators have succeeded only in cluttering the field of speech with an abundance of pedagogical jargon for which there were previously quite adequate and respectable terms. Those critics seemingly fail to recognize that the concepts assimilated from other behaviorial and physical sciences have provided us with new insights and new avenues of approach to a more complete understanding of the communication process. Change has come in speech education, in many instances at the cost of dissension in the ranks.

The following sections of this chapter deal with some of the more important changes and trends which have occurred in the content and activities of speech education during the past quarter century.

CONTENT CHANGES

Language

Semantics. The works of semanticists such as Alfred Korzybski,[1] Wendel Johnson,[2] Stuart Chase,[3] C. K. Ogden and I. A. Richards,[4] and Irving J. Lee[5] have had a pronounced effect upon speech education. The writings of these men have served to redirect our attention from the "how it is said" concern of the elocutionary period to the "what is said" concern of the present day.

We know now that *meaning is within the individual*, that it is dependent upon the sum total of his experiences and that meaning is aroused within an individual and not transmitted to him. Equally important is the realization that words are representations and not the things about which we converse. These verbal representations we call symbols. Thus, the old adage "Sticks and stones may break my bones, but names will never hurt me" receives considerable reinforcement.

In a society whose very foundations are periodically rocked (often as a result of name-calling, stereotyping, and generalizing) and whose minority groups find it increasingly difficult to communicate effectively with the majority, the necessity of some formal training in semantics for speech students becomes all too apparent.

Speech texts for both the college and secondary level usually include at least one chapter on language. More often than not the chapter dealing with language is all too brief and general. The potential high school speech teacher needs to leave college with adequate training in semantics to supplement the content presented in the text. Unfortunately, few college speech departments require training in semantics for their speech education students; and the little bit that is received often comes from a single chapter in the basic speech text. The potential speech teacher who lacks training in semantics would do well to become familiar with the works cited at the beginning of this section.

Phonetics. With increased opportunities for rapid and widespread travel and the advent of the electronic mass media, Americans have be-

---

[1]*Science and Sanity: An Introduction to Non-Aristotelian Systems and General Semantics* (Lancaster, Pa.: The Science Press, 1933).

[2]*People in Quandaries* (New York: Harper & Row, Publishers, 1946).

[3]*Power of Words* (New York: Harcourt, Brace & World, Inc., 1953).

[4]*The Meaning of Meaning* (New York: Harcourt, Brace & World, Inc., 1936).

[5]*Language Habits in Human Affairs: An Introduction to General Semantics* (New York: Harper & Row, Publishers, 1941).

come increasingly exposed to a variety of regional dialects. National radio and television conform rather closely with what most linguists term the General American or Midland dialect. The Midland dialect, spoken by a majority of Americans and popularized by the electronic media, has become the dialectal pattern more often taught in speech classes.

The advantages of phonetics as a tool for teaching pronunciation have become widely recognized by speech educators during the last quarter century. Almost all texts designed for the basic speech course at the secondary and college level include a section on phonetics. The subject is often included under one or more of the following headings: language, pronunciation, voice and diction, or articulation.

The treatment of phonetics within texts varies. Some texts treat the subject extensively, presenting the whole of the International Phonetic Alphabet, while in others the treatment is so superficial that one may question the value of its inclusion. Probably no area of speech content has been more abused than the study of phonetics. Many teachers, especially at the secondary level, ignorant of the utility of phonetics, teach it or do not teach it for a number of reasons. Some have voiced the opinion that students believe the field of speech lacks real content and that requiring the students to master the phonetic alphabet impresses upon them that speech does have content.

Frequently the methodology employed in teaching phonetics is sufficient by itself to squelch all the students' enthusiasm for learning the subject. There are those teachers who have set aside three days, a week, or more for the study of phonetics. During that period of time the students drill, drill, and drill on sound and symbol. Other teachers have devised ingenious teaching techniques such as a sound bingo game which provides the student with both a challenge and an enjoyable learning experience. Phonetics, as a tool to help the student correct speech deficiencies, should be employed throughout the duration of the speech course, thus not restricting its usefulness solely to the unit in which it is introduced.

A few teachers ignore the phonetics section because they have not received training in the subject. In a study done in 1967 Everett found that only six colleges out of thirty-nine Ohio teacher training institutions required a phonetics course for the speech education major.[6] Ohio teacher training institutions are typical of those throughout the nation. While this and similar studies tend to confirm the complaint of teachers about the lack of academic training, it does not, however, excuse them from study done on their own or additional academic training. The speech education

---

[6]Russell I. Everett, "Speech Education: A Comparative Study of Ohio Colleges" (Doctoral dissertation, The Ohio State University, 1967), p. 59.

student is well advised to prepare himself to teach phonetics while still in undergraduate school!

The wise teacher views phonetics as an invaluable tool for helping students learn correct pronunciation and for correcting simple speech deficiencies. When the teacher does not intend to use phonetics as a therapeutic tool, it is probably wiser to ignore the section than to require the student to memorize a mass of symbols and sounds for which he perceives no practical application. Teachers often complain that students dread phonetics and for that reason they ignore the phonetics section or hurry over it. It might be well to remember that unless the teacher presents some realistic rationale for the study of phonetics, he should not expect his students to exhibit much enthusiasm about the unit.

Listening

The area of listening in the study of speech is enjoying wide popularity in texts and among teachers. While speech educators from classical times to the present have talked about listening in terms of the necessity of being clearly heard, modern experimental research has contributed a substantial body of knowledge to the subject of effective listening. So specialized has the subject become that educators no longer talk about just listening but more specifically about defensive listening, critical listening, listening for information, and listening for enjoyment, among other goals. Research has shown that listening skills can be taught and that most students improve their listening ability through training in listening. Further, it has been demonstrated that comprehension improves and that wide differences among students in listening ability are considerably reduced as a result of training in listening.

Speech educators justify the study of listening on the basis of its being the counterpart of speaking. Further, listening is inextricably related to the speech act in terms of its functioning as a self-correction mechanism for the speaker and as a device which makes it possible for us as listeners to more effectively adjust to our environment. With much of the content of listening closely related to thinking, the study of listening becomes significant in the modern school curriculum where heavy emphasis is being placed on turning out students skilled in critical thinking.

Almost all speech texts designed for the secondary level have at least part of a chapter devoted to listening. Many texts give chapter status to listening and a few authors have thought the subject important enough to distribute its content throughout the text, as required by its relationship to the speech act under discussion. In at least one instance the term *listening* has been incorporated into the title of a secondary school text.

In some fourteen research studies reported by Duker[7] there were no significant differences in listening skills as a result of efforts of instruction in this area. Listening is possibly more closely related to personality than to anything else. Some people have a semantic block to listening to particular types of people; this block may be based on the speaker's appearance, race, or complexion, or even on a prejudgment about the potential value of the speaker. Such findings challenge us to continue research in the area of listening.

Though listening is receiving considerably more attention in basic texts, college training beyond the level presented in the basic speech texts has not yet infiltrated the undergraduate program of most college speech departments. Invariably, the potential speech teacher interested in this area will need to embark upon a self-taught program in listening.

It is not surprising that added emphasis is being given to the teaching of listening, but rather that attention to the area has so long been delayed. The relationship between speech, listening, and critical thinking should have made listening a major concern of speech educators long ago.

Radio

The incorporation of radio speech into the secondary curriculum began in the early 1930's. Elmer B. Eklo, writing in the June, 1934, issue of *The Quarterly Journal of Speech*, observed:

> While radio speech in its entirety is a little explored field, it is very much undeveloped and untried in high schools. The better equipped universities and colleges now include in their departments radio speech, but it seems that its application to high school equipment, conditions, and students has been somewhat overlooked. It should be of interest to progressive high school speech instructors to see the possibility and practicability of radio speech in their own schools to broaden and supplement the work that is now being done.

Today radio is found in the secondary school in a variety of forms. In some schools radio is taught as a unit in the basic speech course, while in other schools one or more separate courses in radio may be offered. In those schools where only one unit on radio is taught, the concern is primarily with producing the various types of radio programs. More often the emphasis is upon newscasts, short dramatic skits, and interviews. Where separate courses in radio are offered, radio programming and broadcasting are emphasized. Most teachers of speech perceive the unit

---

[7]Sam Duker (ed.), *Listening: Readings* (New York: The Scarecrow Press, 1966).

or course in radio as a medium for the improvement of speech skills and the understanding of communication theory. There are those few, however, who stress the technological aspects of radio and appear dedicated to turning out students skilled in the various aspects of radio technology.

The equipment needed to teach radio on a closed circuit system is minimal. Teachers have employed such devices as public address systems and tape recorders. In the larger schools one may find a control board, turntables, and microphones readily available. Many teachers are able to utilize the facilities of a local radio station. Frequently programs written and produced in the high school are aired over the local radio station.

Remedial Speech in the Classroom

Except for recognition of dialectal differences, most of us pay relatively little attention to the speech of those about us. However, our attention is drawn to the speech of others when we detect sounds (or the absence of them) which do not fall within our set of sound expectations. When our perception is thus diverted from the ideas expressed by a speaker to the vocal process he employs in expressing those ideas, we conclude that the speaker has a speech defect. Charles Van Riper refers to speech as defective "when it deviates so far from the speech of other people that it calls attention to itself, interferes with communication, or causes its possessor to be maladjusted."[8]

The speech defects which the teacher is more likely to encounter in the classroom are functional articulatory disorders, stuttering, and voice disorders.[9] Functional articulatory disorders are those which have no organic basis and are characterized by sound substitution, omission, distortion, and addition. Stuttering, while it may appear in a variety of forms, is typically characterized by prolongation and repetition of speech sounds and syllables. Voice disorders are of three general types: intensity, pitch, and quality. Disorders of intensity are related to the degree of loudness. Pitch disorders are commonly classified as monotone, or too-high or too-low pitch. Disorders of vocal quality as identified by Van Riper are hyper-nasal (commonly referred to as "nasal twang"), denasal, strident or harsh, falsetto, breathy or husky, and hoarse.[10]

Identifying the Speech Defective Student. Speech teachers in attempting to determine what constitutes a speech defect must keep in mind

---

[8]Charles Van Riper, *Speech Correction: Principles and Methods* (4th ed.; Englewood Cliffs, N. J.: Prentice-Hall, Inc., 1963), p. 16.

[9]*Ibid.*, p. 36.

[10]*Ibid.*, p. 30

the distinction between defective speech and what is generally called substandard speech. Any of the speech practices reviewed earlier as articulatory errors may not in fact represent a speech disorder but rather the use of substandard speech. Differentiating which of the two it is will require some investigation into the linguistic background of the student. Generally if he is a native of the school community his speech habits will be reflected in the speech patterns of the other students. If he is not a native and his speech differs from that of the other students, the teacher should attempt to ascertain his linguistic background. His speech may reflect the linguistic environment of his childhood and not necessarily a disorder due to some deficiency. In terms of functional articulatory disorders, the treatment remains the same regardless of the underlying cause of the problem. The student, however, should be told whether his problem stems from exposure to substandard speech or originates from within himself.

A number of oral reading tests have been devised for use in detecting articulatory disorders. Some of these tests have also been employed as exercises for the improvement of pronunciation. Van Riper presents a passage which the teacher may find useful in testing the student's ability to produce acceptable speech sounds. The passage includes all of the speech sounds found in American speech.

My Grandfather

> You wished to know all about my grandfather. Well, he is nearly
> ninety-three years old; he dresses himself in an ancient black frock
> coat, usually minus several buttons; yet he still thinks as swiftly as
> ever. A long, flowing beard clings to his chin, giving those who
> observe him a pronounced feeling of the utmost respect. When he
> speaks, his voice is just a bit cracked and quivers a trifle. Twice
> each day he plays skillfully and with zest upon our small organ.
> Except in the winter when the ooze or snow or ice prevents, he
> slowly takes a short walk in the open air each day. We have often
> urged him to walk more and smoke less, but he always answers,
> "Banana oil!" Grandfather likes to be modern in his language.[11]

The speech teacher may wish to devise his own screening test. Tests are usually of the word, sentence, or paragraph type. The important point to keep in mind is that all sounds, as well as all possible blends of

---

[11]Charles Van Riper, *Speech Correction: Principles and Methods,* Fourth Edition © 1963. By permission of Prentice-Hall, Inc., Englewood Cliffs, New Jersey.

consonant sounds, are included. The teacher should also attempt to vary the position of the sounds, i.e., to place each sound in initial, medial, and final positions in words. For example, in testing for the production of the [k] one should provide for the [k] to appear in the initial position *(camp)*, in the medial position *(encourage)*, and in the final position in words *(lock)*. With some imaginative effort the teacher should encounter relatively little difficulty in composing a set of words, sentences, or a short paragraph which encompasses all of the American speech sounds.

Following is a series of sentences, each of which is designed to test the production of a selected consonant sound.

1. [p]   Penny peppered the potato soup.
2. [b]   Bob, always ambitious to foment trouble, called his buddies into a secret confab.
3. [m]   Murmuring and mumbling to himself, the strange old man managed to climb the stairs.
4. [n]   The sands silently filled the cavern and no longer can man walk through the narrow tunnels.
5. [ŋ]   England, no longer willing to linger, instinctively rose to defend the free world.
6. [t]   Tim thought that the sun rotated around the moon.
7. [d]   Donna played with the tender dandelions in the meadow.
8. [θ]   Three days passed before his thirsty, dry mouth knew the thrill of cold water.
9. [ð]   Though he could barely breathe and all in lather from exhaustion, he pursued the heathen down the path.
10. [f]   Half of the framework was found to be defective.
11. [v]   The bereaved relatives stood bravely in the vanguard of mourners assembled in the grove.
12. [k]   The cold, clear creek smacked against its banks and cascaded over the falls to the rocks below.
13. [g]   Getty, his finger still gripping the trigger, grimaced as the bullet hit the log instead of the target.
14. [s]   You simply press the crimson button and the electricity activates the alarm.
15. [z]   As a cold breeze arose, he zipped his jacket and the drizzle began to fall.
16. [ʃ]   Surely fashion is one question in the minds of socially conscious women.
17. [ʒ]   The garage mechanic fixed the motor at his leisure but the job was done with great precision.
18. [tʃ] The child chuckled as the pitcher clutched the ball and began his ritualistic pitch.

19. [dʒ] The judge thought the jewel thief was incorrigible and suggested he never be paroled.
20. [hw] Which wheel whines when the car runs?
21. [w] The weasel snapped the walnut but quickly discovered it was not what he had expected.
22. [j] The ewe in her usual manner yielded the patch of clover to the huge ram.
23. [r] It was a reasonably thrilling movie but reading the book was more enjoyable.
24. [l] Laura sulked under the elm tree, resolving never to spill the milk again.
25. [h] The hatchet had a heavy head.

Thus far we have concerned ourselves with identifying articulatory disorders. The other two major speech disorders of stuttering and voice are in general easily discernible. The teacher may also discover these deficiencies in the process of administering the articulation screening test or in requesting a short impromptu speech.

Understanding the Speech Defective Student.   Most of us find it difficult not to express in some fashion our feelings of revulsion or sympathy for those individuals who are obviously handicapped. Others of us tend to ignore the handicap completely. The handicapped person generally seeks neither of these two responses. The person handicapped with a speech disorder seeks acceptance rather than pity, and understanding rather than total indifference. While not all speech handicapped students are aware of their disorder, most of those with a severe speech disorder are usually painfully aware that their speech deviates from the normal pattern. The teacher should condition himself to talk with the student about the disorder in an objective manner with as little emotion as possible. The teacher's attitude should be one of understanding and desire to help.

Many students who have an articulatory disorder are totally unaware of their problem. The teacher should demonstrate some sensitivity when creating in the student an awareness of the problem. The reaction of students to learning that they have a speech defect may be expected to vary. In most cases, however, the individual will express his appreciation for having the problem brought to his attention.

Assisting the Speech Defective Student.   Creating within the student an awareness of his problem is the first essential step in any planned program for assisting the speech handicapped individual. Second, he must be persuaded that he has a speech problem which requires a remedial program. Third, he must be motivated to want to participate in a planned remedial program. In some instances it may be difficult to persuade the student to curtail his extracurricular activities for the purpose of receiving remedial assistance. The teacher in attempting to motivate the student to participate in a remedial program ought to know the prognosis for the particular case. The student ought not to be motivated on the basis of total rehabilitation when total rehabilitation is not a reality. Further, he should not be told that the problem is a simple one when it may require months or years of continual attention.

Except for cases of simple articulatory disorders which are of a functional origin, most speech teachers are professionally unequipped to make decisions about the cause of a speech disorder or the necessary remedial procedure. Such cases, without exception, ought to be referred to the professional speech therapist.[12] The speech teacher should consult with the speech therapist, however, about the possibility of assisting the remedial program of the student in the speech classroom. The consequences of an inaccurate diagnosis and treatment can be tragic. Brong cites the following:

> An uninformed teacher of speech, noting the hoarseness of one of his pupils, searched for exercises to correct the condition. Realizing that the girl's voice was weak, he chose drills designed to strengthen the voice. Under his direction she read poems demanding excessive loudness to large imaginary audiences. A year later the girl died of cancer of the larynx. Whether the inappropriate procedures contributed to the malady will never be known. This much is certain: if the teacher had recognized the danger potential of a chronically hoarse voice and had sent the girl to a laryngologist for examination, he might have been instrumental in saving her life.[13]

To this point we have not discussed the hearing handicapped student. Any student who appears to have a hearing impairment should be referred to an audiologist or a speech and hearing therapist. Further, the teacher should seat the student in the classroom in a location providing maximum opportunity for hearing and for using visual cues.

If there is not a speech and hearing program in his school system the teacher may wish to refer the case to an institution which has such a program. Often these services can be obtained through rehabilitation centers and university or hospital clinics, through other school systems which have such a program, or through professionally certified private

---

[12]Immediate referral is often vital, as in the case of chronic hoarseness, which may be symptomatic of cancer of the larynx.

[13]C. Cordelia Brong, "Helping Speech and Hearing Defective Students," *Speech Methods and Resources*, ed. Waldo W. Braden (New York: Harper & Row, Publishers, 1961), p. 461.

speech therapists. Obviously such referrals must be made with the knowledge of the student's parents. Funds for assisting remedial work are sometimes available through local, state, and federal agencies.

Evaluating the Speech or Hearing Defective Student. At some point in his teaching career almost every teacher is faced with the problem of evaluating the performance of the speech or hearing handicapped student. No hard and fast rules can be made, but the teacher of speech particularly may find the following suggestions helpful.

1. Design his assignments so that they fall within his range of capabilities and yet meet the general requirements of the course. The student should not be discriminated against when some aspect of his disorder prevents his adequately fulfilling an assignment required of all students.
2. Expectations of improvement must take into consideration the student's limitations and the opportunities for improvement provided within the course.
3. Do not fail to challenge the student. Expect him to engage in all speech activities which are within the realm of his abilities.

Discussion

Discussion is becoming increasingly popular as a unit in the secondary school speech course. While various forms of discussion are taught, emphasis appears to be upon problem-solving discussion. Some teachers prefer to have the discussion unit come very early in the course, often supplanting the introductory speech as an ice-breaker. It is felt that the student is more at ease performing in a group situation than he would be giving an individual speech performance. Some educators argue that most of the public speaking done by individuals today is in small group problem-solving situations. Therefore, they contend that the emphasis in the basic speech course ought to be on group performance. The argument appears to have some merit.

Objections have been raised among teachers as to the length of research time needed by students to become adequately informed on discussion subjects. They see the time factor as a limitation on the number of discussion experiences possible for each student and as a barrier against the use of discussion early in the speech course. It might be noted that while discussion subjects should be worthwhile, the perceptive teacher will be able to draw from the experiences and interests of his students for meaningful discussion topics.

Many of the techniques employed in discussion have been borrowed from business and industrial management procedures. Particularly popular have been the Phillips 66 buzz session technique and the brainstorming technique. The forms of discussion more often taught are the symposium, round table, case conference, and panel.

Psychiatry and sociology alike have also contributed certain techniques especially useful in problem-solving situations. Role-playing, as in sociodrama, often provides the student with insights which he would not otherwise have obtained. In addition, the use of discussion in the basic speech course provides the student with an understanding of group norms, functions, and goals and prepares him to function more effectively within small groups and organizational settings. Finally, when the discussion evaluation is conscientiously executed, the student discovers his strengths and weaknesses in relation to other group members.

Debate

Debate has been a popular high school activity for a number of years, and more recently its subject content has appeared in the basic secondary speech texts. A discussion of debate as an extracurricular activity appears later in this chapter. Our concern at this point is the teaching of a unit of debate in the basic speech course, a practice which has met with varying degrees of success.

The primary complaint of teachers seems to be that students lack both the time and facilities to do adequate research on the debate topic. Some instructors have attempted to remedy these two problems by providing the research materials for the students and, in some instances, by providing speech class time for research and case construction. Neither of these two practices seems desirable. Providing the research material deprives the student of valuable research experience, and consuming class time for debate preparation seriously curtails the number of total speaking opportunities available to each student enrolled in the course. In the process of selecting debate topics the teacher should be sure that adequate research material is available. Often the selection of a local controversy as a debate topic will provide the student with a topic about which he already has considerable knowledge. Further, the choice of a topic of local concern gives the student the opportunity to employ the interview as a research technique. The selection of a local issue as a debate topic also tends to insure that the student will find some information about the topic in the local newspaper.

The use of published debate handbooks as research material on the national high school debate topic appears to negate many of the principles of effective speech teaching. First, it alleviates the need for the student to do research. Second, it provides for the student many if not all of the issues involved in the topic thus restricting his creativity in defining the issues.

The time allotted to a debate unit varies, but generally most teachers devote from four to six weeks to the subject. It should be noted that while the debate format is highly structured, it provides the student with the experience of having his ideas challenged. Further, it affords him an opportunity for a kind of give-and-take interaction more closely paralleling the experiences he will encounter in his daily communication.

There is an apparent increase in the number of debate courses being offered at the secondary level, an encouraging trend for the growth of the speech curriculum in our high schools. This increase is especially noticeable in the larger metropolitan schools. No doubt every debate course being offered in high school represents a considerable effort on the part of the teacher who instituted the course, because it is not easy to convince administrators of the need for an additional speech course. The potential teacher should be aware of two possible pitfalls when seeking to have a debate course added to the curriculum. First, never jeopardize your professional credibility to sell the course to school administrators. In short, do not promise a showcase full of trophies as the inevitable result of a debate course. Second, never use the debate course for the sole benefit of the high school debate team. All students enrolled in the course should receive equal attention and opportunities to actively participate. Probably no practice will squelch enthusiasm and enrollment more quickly than the showing of favoritism in the speech classroom.

Drama

The teaching of drama at the secondary level occurs in basically two forms. In those schools in which a basic drama course is not offered, a unit in drama is often included in the basic speech course. Where a drama course is offered, the units more frequently taught are acting, history of the theatre, stagecraft and production, and dramatic literature.[14]

The addition of a basic drama course to the secondary school curriculum appears to be an increasing practice. This increase in drama courses probably reflects an increasing popular interest in drama generated by television dramatic productions as well as by the increasing popularity of children's theatre, creative dramatics, and state-wide dramatic contests. Unfortunately, the content emphasized in the basic drama course is all too often determined by the particular interests of the teacher. This tendency may be due to a number of factors, but often

---

[14]Kathryn T. Schoen, "Perceptions of Speech Education in Ohio Secondary Schools" (Doctoral dissertation, The Ohio State University, 1965), pp. 64-65.

it reflects the narrow scope of dramatic training received by the teacher in his undergraduate career. Some colleges require only one drama course for the speech education student while others have a speech education program composed almost exclusively of drama courses. Neither extreme is desirable for the needs of the speech teacher.

A special subcommittee of the American Educational Theatre Association Committee on Secondary Schools published in 1950 "A Suggested Outline for a Course of Study in Dramatic Arts in the Secondary School." The scope of the dramatic arts as presented in the outline was in keeping with the philosophy of the committee that

> The audiences of tomorrow are in the high schools today; therefore one of the major responsibilities of the dramatic arts course in the secondary schools should be to train discriminating audiences who will demand a high standard of dramatic entertainment. The student's ability to discriminate, and to evaluate the dramatic performances with which he is in constant contact, is surely one of his fundamental needs. . . .[15]

In 1963 a special committee of the Secondary School Theatre Conference presented an outline for a course of study at the secondary level. This outline also stressed the importance of theatre appreciation as opposed to the mastering of highly specialized dramatic skills.[16] Nevertheless, many teachers today, perhaps in an effort to compensate for their own thwarted ambitions, dedicate themselves to turning out highly skilled actors, designers, and technicians.

In those speech courses which include a single unit on drama, the teacher should select for emphasis that content and those activities which will tend to reinforce the principles of effective communication taught throughout the course.

Television

Television in the secondary speech curriculum is a relatively new development and may be considered as still in the experimental stage. Many teachers now include a unit on television in the basic speech course. For the most part the content of the unit and the approaches to teaching the subject represent no drastic departure from the content and methodology of the unit taught in radio. The objectives in teaching

---

[15]American Educational Theatre Association," A Suggested Outline for a Course of Study in Dramatic Arts in the Secondary School," *American Educational Theatre Journal*, 2:15-31 (March, 1950).

[16]Secondary School Theatre Conference of the American Educational Theatre Association, Inc., *Course of Study in Theatre Arts at the Secondary School Level* (Washington, D. C.: American Educational Theatre Association, Inc., 1963, revised 1968).

a unit on television ought to be correlated with the principles of effective communication taught throughout the course. In addition, the student should gain a general understanding and an appreciation of the broadcast medium.

At this point we can only speculate as to the effects of the portable video-tape recorder on the teaching of speech in the secondary school classroom. With the slowly decreasing cost of the portable video-tape recorder, we may expect to see a rise in the number of secondary schools employing this device in the teaching of speech. The device offers the opportunity for more realistic self-evaluation. Previously, students under the stress of speaking were often unaware of their speaking mannerisms and experienced considerable difficulty in remembering them when they were pointed out by the teacher or by student critics. The portable video-tape recorder offers the speech student the possibility of instantaneous self-correction. He can for the first time see himself as he speaks. Further, it provides a visual as well as an aural record of his performance which he may review at a later time. The teacher's comments about bodily actions should certainly become more meaningful as the student is able to see how he appears to others. Generally, less classroom time may be needed for teacher and student oral critiques.

Teachers employing the portable video-tape recorder will find that there are some problems posed in the use of the device. First, replaying the tapes in class would consume an inordinate amount of time. Therefore, a room adequate for replay will need to be secured. The operation of the video-tape recorder has been so simplified that students should encounter little or no difficulty in operating the mechanism. Second, while the ordinary classroom is adequate for this type of video-taping, one should not expect an acoustically accurate reproduction of the live performance. There will be some acoustical distortion in most cases but the distortion will more often prove to be minimal. Third, the video-tape recorder will require adjustment on occasion, but the cost factor involved in that operation is nominal. Finally, the teacher should expect some initial inhibition among students to appearing before the camera. Inhibition, when it occurs, should dissipate through continued use of the device and should constitute no more of a problem than the often experienced mike-fright encountered in the teaching of radio.

SPEECH ACTIVITIES

Probably no other area of speech education has done so much to promote the inception and growth of secondary speech programs as have the various speech activities. Paradoxically, when secondary speech programs are discontinued or fail to materialize, the finger of guilt can often be pointed at speech activities. Perhaps we should clarify by saying that the success or failure is not within the activity itself but more fundamentally within the manner in which the activity is conducted by the teacher. There can be no doubt that speech activities appeal to high school students. It is not difficult to generate interest in such activities as debate, drama, interpretative reading, or oratory. As enrollment in the activities increases, the teacher strengthens his position in requests for expansion of the total speech program. Wide interest and participation in the drama club may dispose administrators to add to the speech program a basic course in theatre. More often than not speech courses have entered the secondary curriculum as a result of the popularity and success of speech activities. In some schools, however, the speech program has never progressed beyond the activities level. There may be a number of causes for such stagnation, only a few of which will be discussed here.

A few teachers suffer from what might be termed "trophy-itis." These teachers measure their success in terms of the number of trophies they are able to bring back to their school from the tournaments. Those suffering from "trophy-itis" can be readily identified. Teachers struck with this malady usually restrict membership in an activity to the talented few. Their primary goal is not learning but winning. They are the teachers who promise the administrator "a case full of trophies" in return for subsidizing their favorite activity. The teacher with "trophy-itis" experiences feelings of extreme elation or depression in relation to the extent of his trophy winnings. Further, a poor year in terms of trophies won may spell doom for the activity the following year. The wise teacher will base his request for the subsidization of speech activities on the rationale that it will provide a learning experience, not for a select few, but for all those who are interested.

The stagnation of speech programs may also occur as a result of an excessive preoccupation with one activity. The speech teacher with an intense interest in drama may find himself involved in so many dramatic productions that he lacks the time to generate interest in debate or other speech activities.

More often, stagnation occurs as a result of the limited interests of the speech teacher. Many speech teachers enter the field of speech education as a result of successful experiences in some high school speech activity. While in college they arrange their academic programs to suit their special interest and neglect training in other speech activities. Thus, many teachers arrive on the high school scene ill-equipped to direct activities or to teach in all areas of speech education. Where these situations have occurred, the blame must be shared by both the teachers and the college speech departments from which they graduated. Perceptive college speech educators distribute their required courses over the entire spectrum of speech areas in an effort to help assure some level of competency in all phases.

Debate

Debate, as an extracurricular activity, enjoys increasing popularity in the secondary schools. Tournaments for high school debaters are increasing in frequency and in size. In most states a state debate tournament is held under the auspices of the state department of education. In addition to the state-sponsored debate tournament, many colleges and universities conduct high school debate tournaments as well as debate workshops. College speech educators perceive the college-sponsored high school debate tournament as an excellent medium for the recruitment of future speech students.

Where state departments of education sponsor state debate tournaments, participation in the state tournament is dependent upon winning records in the district and regional meets. The high school debate coach should not feel that failure to place in the district or regional meets signals the end of debate activity for the year. In addition to an ever-increasing number of tournaments sponsored by colleges and universities, many teachers have found it a profitable experience to arrange debate meets with other high schools in their district or region. Before arranging any outside conference debates, it is always wise to consult conference rules regarding such practices. In some states, participating in other than conference-scheduled debates may lead to ineligibility to participate in the conference debates. While conference rules vary, for the most part the states often permit debates between schools which will not meet in conference. For example, debate meets may be arranged between Class A and Class B high schools without jeopardizing the conference standing of either.

The outline of a forensic tournament, based on an educational format, is presented below and should be compared with the more typical format furnished in Chapter 12, which is used in many state meets and in National Forensic League contests. Contest situations dictate a need for knowledge of this more typical style of contest, but the format of the tournament given here can be used for a variety of invitational meets as a means of motivating mass debating and providing opportunities for many students to participate. Any four schools within transportation range could participate with six teams each. In fact, several such tournaments might be in session at the same time within a single metropolitan district. This format was used within a single region to select the regional representatives for the state tournament. All the schools involved were developing from twelve to thirty teams each and from these teams the individual schools selected the six teams for the regional meet from records of previous tournaments. Rounds of debate were adjusted for time in order to utilize regular classroom audiences. This procedure in itself was highly educational and resulted in many more active debaters the following year.

The format for the tournament was designed to provide the best educational laboratory possible. Policy meetings were held four months prior to the tournament and were attended by the forensic coaches of each school accompanied by the school principal or an administrator. The host school presented the suggestion that all debates be held in front of student audiences (English, social studies, speech, and even mathematics classes). The administrators were the first to applaud this innovation as an excellent learning experience for debaters and audience. Debating time was accordingly shortened in order to adapt the debate rounds to class schedules. These points of policy were adopted:

a) Each team would debate both sides of the question, change sides after each round, be matched against a different school each round, and have a different judge each round.

b) Each school would bring six teams. Half of the teams for each school would begin as affirmative teams and the other half would begin as negative teams, changing sides each round thereafter. The coach for each school would draw a block of numbers (1-6, 7-12, 13-18, 19-24) and assign numbers to his teams without consultation with other coaches. The first three numbers in each block would be affirmative teams; the last three, negative.

c) All teams would debate five rounds. State participants would be selected from those teams with no defeats. If the number of teams with no losses exceeded the quota for the state contest, or if the number was not sufficient to meet the state quota, then a play-off match of those teams involved would follow until the required number was selected.

During the tournament itself speech students were assigned to each team to guide competing teams to the next classroom. By the third round the members of the student audiences were beginning to get involved as critics of content, speaker efficiency, and use of proof. Many were pointing out faulty reasoning and distorted statistics. Obviously, this criticism was not made during a debate but in the classroom at the conclusion of the debate.

The tournament outline follows.

Supplement 2.

Region III Forensic Tournament

Brigham Young University Secondary Laboratory School welcomes the participating schools of Region III of the Utah High School Activities Association to its campus and extends to them the heartiest wishes for a successful and profitable experience. All events and rules will be run for the convenience of the tournament as follows:

SCHEDULE OF EVENTS

Friday, March 23

8:15 a.m.   Registration of debate teams by coaches in Room 110E. General meeting of all debaters in Room 115E.

8:50 a.m.   First Round of Debate as indicated in the room assignments.

9:55 a.m.   Second Round of Debate as indicated in the room assignments.

11:00 a.m.   Third Round of Debate as indicated in the room assignments.

12:00-1:00   Lunch. Contestants will find milk and pop on sale in the archway. They should bring their own lunches! B.Y. High has no student lunch program.

12:45   Fourth Round will be posted. Please do not attempt to find out what the team standings are. No notice will be posted until the time indicated.

1:10   Fourth Round of Debate in the rooms as indicated.

2:20   Fifth Round in the rooms as indicated.

3:00   Meeting of all debaters and coaches in 115E to award the certificates to the eight teams which have been selected to represent the Region at State. (Note: If more than five rounds are needed, there will be a brief meeting of the coaches at this time and the final round will be scheduled. Awards will be held up until the finish of the final round.)

Saturday, March 24

8:15   Oratory begins. Rooms will be posted.
Drawing of topics for First Round of Extemporaneous Speaking 280E.

8:50   Beginning of continuous session of Legislative Forum 115E.
Beginning of Second Round of Oratory Rooms 210A and 220A (260A 9:55).

8:50	Beginning of Extemporaneous Speaking First Round 290E.
9:55	Continuation of Oratory, Extemporaneous Speaking, and Legislative Forum. Sixth Round (if necessary).
1:00	Awards.

GENERAL

1. Each school may enter the following:
   Debate, 6 teams
   Oratory, 6 students
   Extemporaneous Speaking, 6 students
   Legislative Forum, 6 students
2. The following will be chosen to represent the Region at State:
   Debate, 8 teams
   Oratory, 6 students
   Extemporaneous Speaking, 6 students
   Legislative Forum, 10 students
3. As a reminder on the choice of teams and representatives of the Region to the State Meet, the instructions from the State Forensic Committee are included below. Special note should be made of Item No. 2. Item No. 1 has been ruled to eliminate the topics no longer a part of the final debate resolution.
4. The time limit is to be 8 minutes for the constructive speech and 4 minutes for the rebuttal.
5. The time limit for extemporaneous speaking is 4 to 6 minutes (not less than four). Notes are not to be used.
6. The Student Legislature will consist of both a Senate and a House. The ten regional winners are to draw lots for 3 Senators and 7 Representatives to participate in the Student Legislature.
7. The time limit for oratory is to be 7 to 10 minutes (not less than seven). No notes are to be used. The oration must be original, with not more than ten per cent quoted material. Each student shall select a topic for oratory that he feels is important and timely.

JUDGING AND JUDGING SHEETS

Judging sheets will be available to all judges in room 110E and should be picked up prior to leaving for the assigned room. At the request of the coaches the following rules should be observed by the judges:

1. Judgment should be made according to what the judge feels is the best presentation of the problem involved. All participants have the responsibility of proving to the judge that their point of view is the most desirable solution to the problem on which they are speaking.
2. Judges are requested not to "coach" teams or speakers. The meet is closely timed in order to furnish audiences for the speakers and there will be no time for critique sessions.

REGION III DEBATE MEET

	Round 1				Round 2				Round 3				Round 4				Round 5		
Affirm.	vs.	Neg.	Room	Affirm.	vs.	Neg.	Room	Affirm.	vs.	Neg.	Room	Affirm.	vs.	Neg.	Room	Affirm.	vs.	Neg.	Room
1	vs.	10	150A	23	vs.	1	150A	1	vs.	17	150A	11	vs.	1	150A	1	vs.	16	140A
2	vs.	16	140A	12	vs.	2	140A	2	vs.	24	140A	18	vs.	2	140A	2	vs.	22	110A
3	vs.	22	210A	11	vs.	3	110A	3	vs.	18	110A	23	vs.	3	120A	3	vs.	10	120A
7	vs.	4	260A	24	vs.	7	210A	7	vs.	16	250A	5	vs.	7	210A	7	vs.	17	260A
8	vs.	17	250A	5	vs.	8	260A	8	vs.	22	260A	16	vs.	8	260A	8	vs.	23	360A
9	vs.	23	360A	18	vs.	9	250A	9	vs.	6	210A	24	vs.	9	115E	9	vs.	4	115E
13	vs.	5	395E	22	vs.	13	170E	13	vs.	12	120A	4	vs.	13	170E	13	vs.	24	170E
14	vs.	11	170E	6	vs.	14	180E	14	vs.	23	290E	10	vs.	14	280E	14	vs.	5	180E
15	vs.	24	180E	4	vs.	15	280E	15	vs.	10	380E	22	vs.	15	290E	15	vs.	12	280E
19	vs.	6	280E	17	vs.	19	290E	19	vs.	11	395E	12	vs.	19	380E	19	vs.	18	285E
20	vs.	12	290E	16	vs.	20	380E	20	vs.	5	140E	6	vs.	20	395E	20	vs.	11	290E
21	vs.	18	380E	10	vs.	21	115E	21	vs.	4	285E	17	vs.	21	110A	21	vs.	6	395E

3. Teams are to be known by numbers only and *should not* identify themselves either by school or name.
4. Ballots should be returned without consultation with other judges or listeners.
5. Judges of Extemporaneous Speaking and Oratory should number their contestants from 1 through 10 in order of excellence. Six winners and two alternates must be selected for the State panel.
6. Any student or team more than 10 minutes late will default.

AWARDS: All contestants winning placement in the State meet will receive Superior awards. Those lasting until the final rounds, but eliminated from the State Meet will receive Excellent awards. Alternates will receive Excellent ratings.

OFFICIALS IN CHARGE OF MEET

Chairman of Region III Speech Activities	M_____	S_____
General chairman of local meet	W_____	M_____
Committee on local arrangements		
Registration and room assignments	W_____	M_____
Arrangements and Legislative Forum	D_____	M_____
General advisor on meet	G_____	L_____
Chairman of Extemporaneous Speaking	R_____	H_____
Chairman of Legislative Forum	F_____	N_____
Chairman of Oratory	N_____	W_____
Debate Judges and pairing	C_____	R_____
Awards and certificates	R_____	S_____

Drama

Dramatic activity in the form of class plays has been and continues to be an important segment of the high school speech program. In addition to the traditional class plays, speech teachers are also producing children's plays. The rising interest in children's theatre promises a much needed rejuvenation of interest in dramatic activity at the high school level. Given adequate publicity, the high school children's theatre play will not want for an audience. Parents in most localities, realizing the limited opportunities to expose their children to acceptable dramatic experiences, support the children's theatre productions. It should be noted here that in speaking of children's theatre we are not referring to child actors but rather to plays for children.

The speech teacher may find the children's plays a profitable venture, supplying him with funds for the acquisition of long-needed theatre equipment. Further, it will be found that, as members of past audiences become students, there will be growing interest and participation in the dramatic program.

Participation in dramatic productions, as in any other speech activity, should be open to all interested students and not confined to those enrolled in speech or drama courses. Moreover, the perceptive teacher will avoid the emergence of a star system in which a favored few are consistently cast in the leading roles. The star system is likely to stifle student interest in participating actively as well as in being members of the audience.

Creative dramatics is another facet of dramatic activity which enjoys increasing popularity in the public schools. While creative dramatics appears more appealing to children of the elementary grades, it has been used successfully with teenage students and has proven to be a highly successful technique in problem-solving situations at the secondary level. Creative dramatics has been successfully employed to help student actors gain a better understanding of the characters they are portraying in student productions. Frequently creative dramatics reveals hidden talents in the shy and retiring student.

Platform Activities

Whether sponsored by the state department of education or by colleges and universities, platform activities have traditionally included such events as declamation, extemporaneous speaking, impromptu speaking, oral interpretation, and original oratory.

Declamation is typically described as the delivery of a non-original speech. That is, it is a speech composed and delivered at some former time by someone other than the present speaker. If one can judge interest in an event by the number of students who volunteer to participate in it, then interest in declamation seems to be on the wane. Indeed, so hard pressed are speech teachers for participants in the event that they often resort to conscripting students who exhibit above average talent in speaking skills.

Humorous and dramatic declamation are still often classified as part of oral interpretation in many states. In other states the controversy continues over the arbitrary boundaries which would separate oral interpretation, impersonation, drama, and Readers' Theatre one from another. The fact that the purists find many reasons for ignoring their own rules reveals the basic error of creating such boundaries in the first place. To effective teachers there is a close kinship among all these forms of storytelling; for instance, Readers' Theatre is an offspring of the discipline of oral interpretation. The division among these forms, then, is one of degree and emphasis. Television has given a rebirth to the humorous storyteller, whose memorized material is written for the special characters which he has developed. Many students are highly motivated to attempt to match such storytellers as Bill Cosby, Bob Hope, Henry Gibson, or Flip Wilson.

Extemporaneous speaking as a competitive platform activity appears to be gaining wide popularity. The event requires the speech student to apply all of the principles of effective speaking including adaptation of his topic to his specific audience. Unlike declamation, the abilities of the speaker are reflected through more than the delivery. Further, this form of delivery has about it a spontaneity and vitalness not evident in declamatory speaking.

Impromptu speaking represents another form of delivery often encountered in competitive platform activities. The inclusion of impromptu speaking in platform speaking events also appears to be on the increase. Impromptu speaking, like extemporaneous speaking, requires the speech student to be familiar with all of the principles of effective speaking. Unlike the extemporaneous speech, the content of the impromptu speech often lacks depth. This is understandable since the speaker receives his topic just before he is to speak. This form of delivery does, however, reflect the speaker's ability to organize his ideas. Unfortunately, many students engaged in impromptu speaking are prone to make light of the event and the speeches very often take on the characteristics of speeches intended to entertain.

Original oratory often appears on the schedule of events for platform speaking. There is little dispute about the definition of original oratory. Most speech teachers agree that it is the work of the student speaker. However, there is considerable controversy about the method of delivery. It is wise to check with the program director as to the form of delivery desired for this event. In some instances the teacher will find the speech is to be delivered from memory; in other instances it is to be read from manuscript. The values of this event with its concomitant forms of delivery are questionable. Generally, the memorized speech appears rhythmical, sometimes bombastic. The manuscript speech limits good bodily action and thwarts effective speaker-audience relationships.

Oral interpretation continues to have widespread popularity among competitive platform events. If one is to judge on the basis of participation, the event appears more popular among female than male students. In some respects public interpretative reading is an anachronism. Few audiences, generally speaking, assemble for an evening of interpretative reading.

The mass media, especially television, have presented from time to time an interpretative reading program. Viewer ratings for interpretative reading programs have on the whole been disappointingly low. Interpretative reading reached the zenith of its popularity during the late elocutionary period in America. It has tenaciously remained in the college speech curriculum primarily as a result of the nostalgic zeal with which many of its adherents remember its heyday. Interpretative reading has valiantly fought to preserve a special niche in the speech curriculum. Its adherents have been so powerful that in some states it is a specific requirement for certification to teach speech. It appears to this writer that the value of interpretative reading lies not in its being a form of public performance but in its usefulness as a technique through which the serious student of public speaking can improve his vocal and bodily expression.

PROFESSIONAL ORGANIZATIONS

The past quarter century has seen a dramatic rise in the number of professional speech organizations in America. These organizations provide the speech teacher with a forum for the exchange of ideas, keeping him abreast of developments in the area of speech education. Forty-five of the fifty states have a state speech association. In addition to the state speech associations, there are five regional associations which publish a journal that the speech teacher will find helpful as a source of new ideas and developments in speech education. Most of the state associations and all of the regional associations hold annual conventions. In addition to the state and regional associations, there is the national Speech Association of America which holds two conventions each year and publishes three journals. Of specific interest to the teacher of speech is *The Speech Teacher,* a quarterly journal published by the Speech Association of America.

A few of the larger cities have recently organized city speech associations. These local associations address themselves to the problems involved in building the secondary speech curriculum and planning competitive inter-school speech activities. With the variety of speech organizations available, the secondary school teacher has ample opportunity for association with other members of his profession. The speech teacher will find that association membership not only provides him with new and stimulating ideas but also with an awareness of developments in his field, which contribute to his professional development.

COMMUNICATION PATTERNS

The verbal communication patterns of our society today raise serious doubts concerning the value of continued emphasis upon public speaking in the secondary school curriculum. The primary goal in teaching public speaking is to teach the student to communicate his ideas more effectively. While there can be no quarrel with that goal, we need to find out under what circumstances the student will express his ideas. That is to say, is the training given the speech student consistent with the kinds of experiences he will encounter as a citizen in a democratic society? Further, how extensive are the opportunities for a high school graduate to engage in platform public speaking and with what frequency does the average high school graduate engage in such an activity? Obviously, high school graduates rarely face the need to engage in platform public speaking. Their oral communication experiences appear generally restricted to conversation and small group interaction. Significantly, only a relatively few citizens engage in the type of public speaking emphasized in today's secondary school. Why then this misplaced emphasis?

Platform public speaking emerged in the curriculum of the secondary school in an age when a high school education was readily available only to a minority of our citizens. The high school curriculum of that era was primarily college-preparation oriented. The opportunities for service in public life were far more extensive for the high school graduate of that day than they are for today's high school graduates. Thus, it was felt that America's future leaders ought to be trained in the art of platform public speaking. Concomitant with that philosophy was the widely held belief in the omnipotent power of the spoken word. Parents supported public speaking courses in the naive belief that oratorical excellence assured success in almost any endeavor. Speech educators, struck with a new-found popularity, seemed loathe to disspell the notion. Moreover, there were many men who had gained their fortunes through oratorical excellence. A parade of such men constantly marched before the American public during the period of the Chautauqua movement.

Despite the fact that the citizens of this nation are highly group-oriented and that almost all of their verbal communication acts take place in that context, we still persist in presenting the principles of effective communication primarily through the format of the formal public speech. In short, we are providing our students with content and skills in a highly specialized and seldom used mode of communication. We are in the position of paying homage to a form of verbal communication rarely employed by a vast majority of our citizenry while almost totally ignoring those communication forms in which most of us take part on a daily basis.

There are those who would justify the emphasis on public speaking on the basis that there exists a set of common principles underlying all communication activity. While this is true, it is likewise true that each of the communication activities has its own peculiar set of principles and skills not necessarily shared by other communication activities. Those who propose that public speaking is the medium through which the principles of effective communication should be taught attempt to justify their position by citing the principle of transfer. They contend that the student will transfer the skills and knowledge which he has mastered in public speaking to other speaking situations. Most of our college and secondary basic speech texts adhere to this theory and begin by applying the principles of effective communication to public speaking and then to discussion, debate, oral interpretation, and so on. Unfortunately, many of the skills of public speaking are inappropriate to the kind of verbal communication activities in which most of us engage. Further, if we are to teach verbal communication theory and skills, then let us put the emphasis upon the more frequent verbal communication activities.

There have been recent attempts in secondary speech texts to break away from the traditional formal public speaking approach to forms of communication more in keeping with the communication patterns of modern society. A few authors of secondary speech texts, recognizing weaknesses in the traditional approach to preparing students to effectively participate in current communication practices, have included in their texts sections on informal and formal speaking. The informal speaking sections treat such subjects as conversation, telephone speech, and interviewing. The sections on formal speaking present the various types of formal public speaking including the informative, persuasive, and entertaining speech as well as debate and formal public discussion. Typically, the section on informal speaking comes first. Thus, the student is provided the opportunity of progressing from the study of communication practices well known to him to those in which he has had relatively little personal experience.

In terms of learning this approach has much to recommend it. First, the student perceives the immediate practicality of the subject with which he is concerned. He is able to relate the content and skills of the subject to his daily communication needs. Second, he is provided with a basis upon which to build a more thorough understanding of the more complex style of formal public speaking.

References

Brong, Cordelia C. "Helping Speech and Hearing Defective Students," *Speech Methods and Resources,* ed. Waldo W. Braden. New York: Harper & Row, Publishers, 1961.

Chase, Stuart. *Power of Words.* New York: Harcourt, Brace & World, 1953.

Hayakawa, S. I. *Language in Thought and Action.* New York: Harcourt, Brace & World, 1954.

Johnson, Wendell. *People in Quandaries.* New York: Harper & Row, Publishers, 1946.

Knower, Franklin H. "Communicology, An Overview: Philosophy, Objectives, Content," *The Communicative Arts and Sciences of Speech*, ed. Keith Brooks. Columbus, Ohio: Charles E. Merrill Publishing Company, 1967.

Korzybski, Alfred. *Science and Sanity: An Introduction to Non-Aristotelian Systems and General Semantics.* Lancaster, Pa.: The Science Press, 1933.

Lee, Irving J. *Language Habits in Human Affairs: An Introduction to General Semantics.* New York: Harper & Row, Publishers, 1941.

Ogden, C. K. and Richards, I. A. *The Meaning of Meaning.* New York: Harcourt, Brace & World, 1936.

Secondary School Theatre Conference of the American Educational Theatre Association, Inc. *Course of Study in Theatre Arts at the Secondary School Level.* American Educational Theatre Association, Inc., 1963.

Van Riper, Charles. *Speech Correction, Principles and Methods.* 4th ed.; Englewood Cliffs, N. J.: Prentice-Hall, Inc., 1963.

Articles

American Educational Theatre Association. "A Suggested Outline for a Course of Study in Dramatic Arts in the Secondary School," *American Educational Theatre Journal*, 12:15-31 (March, 1950).

Eklo, Elmer B. "Radio Speech in High School," *The Quarterly Journal of Speech*, 20:414-418 (June, 1934).

Unpublished Materials

Everett, Russell I. "Speech Education: A Comparative Study of Ohio Colleges." Doctoral dissertation, The Ohio State University, 1967.

Schoen, Kathryn T. "Perceptions of Speech Education in Ohio Secondary Schools." Doctoral dissertation, The Ohio State University, 1965.

Trends in Speech Education

"New Directions in Speech Education," series of articles by authors as listed, ed. Waldo Braden. *The Speech Teacher*, 17:50-70 (January, 1968).

 Henning, James H. "An Exemplary Speech Arts Program for Secondary Schools," pp. 68-70.

 Hopkins, Thomas A. "Pennsylvania's Speech Consultant System," pp.64-67.

 Matlon, Ronald J. "Model Speeches in the Basic Speech Course," pp. 50-57.

Street, Marion L. "Speech Improvement Program in Philadelphia," pp. 58-63.

"Instructional Uses of Videotape: A Symposium," *The Speech Teacher*, 17: 104-122 (March, 1968).

Becker, Samuel L. "Videotape in Teaching Discussion," pp. 104-106.

Gibson, James W. "Using Videotape in Training of Teachers," pp. 107-109.

Hirschfeld, Adeline G. "Videotape Recordings for Self-Analysis in the Speech Classroom," pp. 116-118.

Nelson, Harold E. "Videotaping the Speech Course," pp. 101-103.

Ochs, Donovan J. "Videotape in Teaching Advanced Public Speaking," pp. 110-111.

Pennybacker, John H. "Evaluating Videotape Recorders," pp. 119-122.

Reynolds, R.V.E. "Videotape in Teaching Speech in a Small College," pp. 113-114.

"Honors Courses: A Symposium," *The Speech Teacher*, 17:193-206 (September, 1968).

Gilbert, Jack G. "Honors for the Best," pp. 193-195.

Heisey, D. Ray. "An Honors Course in Argumentation," pp. 202-204.

Hill, Donald. "Honors in Theatre," pp. 199-201.

Kenner, Freda. "An Honors Course in High School," pp. 205-206.

Peterson, Owen. "Teaching the Honors Course in Fundamentals of Speech," pp. 196-198.

"The Effect of Audience Feedback on the Beginning Public Speaker," *The Speech Teacher* 16:56-60 (January, 1967) and 17:229-234 (September, 1968).

Amato, Philip and Ostermeier, Terry H. "The Effect of Audience Feedback on the Beginning Public Speaker," 16:56-60.

Combs, Walter, and Miller, Gerald. "A Counter-View," 17:229-231.

Ostermeier, Terry H. and Amato, Philip. "A Rejoinder," 17:232-234.

"Symposium on Using Speech Models," *The Speech Teacher*, 16:11-27 (January, 1967).

Baird, A. Craig. "Speech Models and Liberal Education," pp. 11-15.

Bosmajian, Haig A. "Using Readings in Speech in the Introductory Course, pp. 21-23.

Gehring, Mary L. "The Inductive Approach to Speech Models," pp. 16-18.

Kerr, Harry P. "Using *Opinion* and *Evidence*: The Case Method," pp. 19-20.

White, Eugene E. "Supplementing Theory and Practice," pp. 24-27.

"Symposium: Evaluation in the Public Speaking Course," ed. J. Donald Ragsdale. *The Speech Teacher*, 16:150-164 (March, 1967).

Baker, Eldon E. "Aligning Speech Evaluation and Behavioral Objectives," pp. 158-160.

DeVito, Joseph A. "Learning Theory and Grading," pp. 155-157.

Hance, Kenneth G. "Improving the Instructor as a Critic," pp. 150-154.

Ragsdale, J. Donald. "Post Hoc and Synchronic Criticism," pp. 161-164.

"Instructional Uses of Recorders: A Symposium," *The Speech Teacher,* 16:209-224 (September, 1967).

Dallinger, Carl A. "Purposes and Uses of Recorders," pp. 209-211.

Dickson, Phoebe L. "Using the Tape Recorder in the Elementary School," pp. 221-224.

Kenner, Freda. "Using the Recorder in Teaching Speech in High School," pp. 217-218.

Niles, Doris. "Recorder Projects for High School Classes," pp. 219-220.

North, Stafford. "Increasing Teaching Resources through Tapes," pp. 212-214.

Scheib, M. E. "Extending the Perimeter of the Classroom," pp. 215-216.

"Symposium on Using Common Materials," *The Speech Teacher,* 16:259-283 (November, 1967).

Brandes, Paul D. "The Common Materials Approach to the Teaching of Speech," pp. 265-269.

Graham, John. "Speech as a Subject for Common Materials," pp. 274-276.

Hildebrandt, Herbert W. "A Rationale for Non-Fragmented Topics," pp. 259-264.

Hopkins, Jon. "The Syntoptican and Ideas for Speeches," pp. 277-278.

McNally, J. R. "Lecture-Panel Method," pp. 271-273.

Tedford, Thomas L. "Teaching Freedom of Speech through the Use of Common Materials," pp. 269-270.

White, Hollis L. "The Commons Materials Approach: A Negative View," p. 279.

"A Symposium: Fifty Years of Indecision," *The Speech Teacher,* 15:11-33 (January, 1966).

Allen, Ronald R., "The New Speech Educator; Philosophy and Standards," pp. 19-20.

Buys, William E., "Speech Curricula for All American Youth," pp. 20-25.

Fest, Thorrel B., "The Speech Curriculum for American Youth: An Introduction." pp. 11-12.

Keltner, John W., "Speech for All American Youth: Current Issues and Problems," pp. 13-17.

Pooley, Robert C., "Oral Communication in the English Curriculum," pp. 26-29.

Smith, Donald K., "Speech for Tomorrow: Concepts and Context," pp. 30-33.

"A Symposium: Learning in the Speech Classroom," *The Speech Teacher,* 15:99-125 (March, 1966).

Clevenger, Theodore, Jr. "Some Factors Involved in Classroom Procedures for the Acquisition of Verbal Concepts," pp. 113-118.

Edwards, Allen J. "Response Generalization and Language Behavior; Review and Prospect," pp. 102-107.

Harms, L. S. "Two-Person Learning Programs for Speech," pp. 119-125.

Kibler, Robert J. "An Introduction," pp. 99-101.

Knower, Franklin H. "The College Student Image of Speech Communication and Speech Instruction," pp. 108-112.

"Opening Assignments: A Symposium," *The Speech Teacher*, 18:18-25 (January, 1969).

Hootman, Richard, and Ochs, Donovan J. "Audience Analysis: An Exordium for the Basic Course," pp. 23-25.

King, Thomas R. "An Inductive Opening Exercise," pp. 21-22.

McNally, James R. "Hermeogenes in the Modern Classroom," pp. 18-20.

3

Curriculum

Human intelligence is too rare and precious a thing to squander on a haphazard program of instruction.[1]

All of the experiences provided by the school which are intended to influence the behavior of pupils may be described as the school curriculum. This broad definition also applies to the speech curriculum. Since most of our education depends upon oral communication, the speech curriculum is viewed as extending beyond the immediate confines of the classroom. Societal sources which affect the total school curriculum affect the development of the speech curriculum. These *societal sources,* identified by Taba[2] as the learner, the learning process, the cultural demands, and the content of the disciplines, are the factors which influenced the formulation of the broad educational objectives outlined in Chapter 1. Using the basic framework of what might be described as traditional curriculum thought, the speech teacher is confronted with

---

[1]Philip H. Phenix, *Philosophy of Education* (New York: Holt, Rinehart & Winston, Inc., 1958), p. 59.

[2]Hilda Taba, *Curriculum Development: Theory and Practice* (New York: Harcourt, Brace & World, 1962), p. 10.

(1) formulating specific speech objectives, (2) selecting content and learning experiences, (3) organizing content and learning experiences, and then (4) evaluating them with respect to objectives and student behavior. This is no easy task, for human behavior is multidimensional; thus, objectives, experiences, and evaluational procedures must also be multidimensional.

SPEECH OBJECTIVES

The specific speech objectives selected should be related to the general objectives of educational programs and school policies, which describe areas of life needs and behavioral goals. Such objectives as those proposed by the Educational Policies Commission (self-realization, human relationships, economic efficiency, civic responsibility) define the broad purposes of education.[3] These broad objectives furnish an overview of educational goals, but they are not specific enough to identify which speech content and activities to select or how to organize them. As the speech teacher determines what kind of behavior the student should acquire as the result of a particular program or unit, he seeks to select and organize content and activities which will lead to this behavioral outcome. Good teaching objectives are student, not teacher, oriented, thereby providing for an evaluation of the student. Speech objectives should realistically and specifically describe desired student behavior and course content, should be broad enough to include all the types of outcomes for which the speech program is responsible, and should allow for developmental sequence and continual growth. The modern speech teacher will be more concerned with classifying types of behavior rather than content, since content does not describe all the processes by which knowledge is acquired and utilized. The emphasis on the need for acquiring life-long systems for learning requires the speech teacher to examine both content and process.

Various educators have considered *cognitive, affective,* and *psychomotor learning* as useful in describing human behavioral characteristics. The cognitive domain involves levels of knowledge and related intellectual skills and abilities. The affective domain includes objectives expressed as values, attitudes, interests, emotional sets or biases and appreciations. The manipulative or motor-skill area fills out the psychomotor domain.[4]

---

[3]Educational Policies Commission, *The Purposes of Education in American Democracy* (Washington, D.C.: National Education Association, 1938).

[4]Benjamin S. Bloom (ed.), *Taxonomy of Educational Objectives* (New York: David McKay Company, Inc., 1956), p. 7.

Diagnosis

To help determine which objectives to emphasize, and to keep the speech curriculum timely and appropriate to student needs, diagnosis of learners, materials, and methods must be a continuous part of the speech program. Such an analysis reveals cultural and social backgrounds, motivational patterns, concepts of program, peers, teacher, and self, interpersonal relations, present and potential achievement levels, weaknesses and strengths, and realistic standards and learning approaches. Diagnostic information about the nature of learners and the factors which affect learning provides direction for creating optimal learning conditions. Stephen Corey's action research[5] is essentially a method of diagnosing practical curriculum problems by involving those teachers affected by the problems.

The Learner and Learning

To effectively obtain and interpret this diagnostic information, the speech teacher should be proficient in analyzing individual needs, interests, and abilities. Students enroll in speech programs for many reasons but not always because of an intense interest in speech. When the interest factor is pronounced, the teacher may not feel as great a need for obtaining various information. Yet what a student *wants* may not necessarily be what he *needs*. In an attempt to arrive at sound educational decisions the teacher may employ several formal and informal diagnostic devices such as achievement tests, predictive tests, and sociometric tests, special assignments and exercises, observation, and personal and group discussion. Various approaches help the teacher to analyze quality and level of the student's feelings, judgments, knowledge, sensitivities, skills, work habits, understandings, and creativity. From such diagnoses emerge indications and suggestions for program emphasis.

The more informal diagnostic devices are subjective; therefore, judgments from them are dependable only if the conclusions drawn from data from several sources are consistent. Without a design or specific criteria, diagnoses will lack focus and it will be difficult to determine the important from the unimportant. For example, if student sensitivity to problems of human relations is important, the teacher will analyze the discussion differently than when his chief concern is to distinguish the student's immature reactions from the mature reactions. Rather than look at an isolated aspect of behavior, such as the IQ, one should look for rational constellations of factors to discover meaning in the data.

---

[5]Stephen M. Corey, *Action Research to Improve School Practices* (New York: Teachers College Press, 1953).

Educational evaluators may furnish assistance to insure that the devices are dependable and that interpretations are as objective as possible.

Several ideas about the learner and how he learns have influenced curriculum development. The concept of *development* assumes that all growth and development (physical, social, emotional, and mental) follows a sequence, proceeds from less mature to more mature, and is organismic and cyclical. This concept provides a basis for planning curricula. The concepts of *maturation* and *motivation* require a curriculum which permits selectivity and a range of study possibilities. In a system which groups students in grades and falsely assumes uniform behavior, it is easy to view as slow any individual whose variations in the developmental cycle deviate from the so-called normal. Yet a speech teacher knows that the maturation level of a fourteen-year-old boy may be quite at variance with the maturation level of a fourteen-year-old girl and learning experiences need to recognize these differences. Enforcing static norms of achievement and progress is inconsistent with the idea of development. Through diagnoses and knowledge of the patterns of development, the speech teacher should be able to more accurately predict future achievement and plan a better program.

The concept of *developmental tasks*[6] represents an effort to provide for an individual's needs and still help him to meet society's expectations. If a teacher is to make educational use of this concept, he will not only be aware of the development of the biological organism but will meet the student's needs as an individual and a member of society. The junior high school student's motivation for developing oral communication skills might be to help him relate more comfortably to his peer group. As this same student reaches the senior high level, his motivation for improving speech skills might be his desire to more effectively persuade others to accept his ideas.

What is included in curriculum materials and how it is taught is often based on the concept of what *intelligence* is and how it functions. Intelligence appears to be affected by native potential, motivation, and environmental stimulation.[7] This seems to indicate that with proper stimulation and a wish for learning, speech experiences such as debate, usually reserved for the more intellectual or advanced students, might be effectively handled by the less intelligent student.

The problem of *transfer* has been an educational concern for some time. Whatever is taught produces some transfer. It is hoped that

---

[6]E.H. Erikson, "Growth and Crises of the Healthy Personality," *Personality in Nature, Society, and Culture*, eds. C. Kluckhohn, H.A. Murray, and D.M. Schneider (rev. ed.; New York: Alfred A. Knopf, Inc., 1955), Ch. 12.

[7]J.B. Miner, *Intelligence in the United States* (New York: Springer Publishing Co., Inc., 1957).

whatever is learned in school may somehow be used in later life in positive transfer. The idea of transfer is currently supported by the newer theories of learning which stress the cognitive nature of learning. They assume that all learning is a meaningful organization of experience and response. Kohler demonstrated learning by "insight" when he showed that apes grasped a relationship between the objects around them and their goals. Hilgard demonstrated the importance of understanding in problem-solving situations for transfer of learning to take place. Bruner indicated that transfer of learning appeared to be aided by an understanding of the structure of the subject matter. These and other ideas about transfer suggest that transfer depends on whether the curriculum materials and learning experiences stimulate the discovery of basic principles, provide practice in applying principles, and develop an expectation that whatever is being learned will be used later in some way. This means that speech teachers must create reality experiences in understanding concepts and in applying these concepts practically. By devising meaningful educational experiences which permit a student to discover fundamental principles for himself rather than contriving artificial drills and assignments, the processes of transfer are enhanced.

Since speech is social behavior occurring in a social setting and influenced by it, the concept of *social* or *cultural learning* becomes important. Different meanings may be attached to words, symbols, or events represented in the curriculum. The particular culture of a person determines what these meanings are. Often the meanings learned in a subculture do not coincide with meanings assigned to them in school, and the resulting confusion interferes with learning. Approved ways of showing anger in a certain cultural environment might be considered unacceptable behavior in a school environment. Training in new habits would then become necessary before an effective speech program could be implemented. The teacher should recognize cultural conflicts, misunderstandings, and their effect on the ability to learn; then he should seek ways to resolve these conflicts. Looking at life through dramatic literature, by creatively dramatizing situations or by role-playing, is an approach which the classroom teacher can employ to diminish cultural distance.

Selecting and Organizing Learning Experiences

Diagnostic data provide the clues which the insightful and imaginative teacher will find helpful in selecting and organizing learning experiences. Effective learning is achieved when both *content* and *processes* are fruitful and significant.[8] Educators interested in the curriculum, such as Schwab, Parker, and Rubin, reflect in their works the importance of

---

[8]Taba, *op. cit.*, p. 265.

process and application in enquiry.[9] Thus the speech teacher must have an understanding of the content and the processes (the what and the how with which students learn). Some speech objectives are served by content, while others are best implemented by organization and learning experiences. Students can learn the content of the historical development of rhetoric, but an exposure to the content of such a course is not a sufficient guarantee that their rhetorical skills will be commensurate with this knowledge. An awareness of the need for a constant interaction of content and learning experience will add meaning and balance to the curriculum. Factors in selecting content are scope and depth, accuracy and significance, consistency with life facts, appropriateness and adaptability to the learners, and provision for various types of behaviors. Provisions for heightening student interest help to minimize discipline problems which might result from a dull speech program.

In designing a speech program, one must look at many factors which will influence the extent and depth of course offerings as well as co-curricular activities. Scope and depth of speech content are often determined by the teacher's knowledge, interests, and skills, the available facilities, speech sources, time, budget, class size, and scheduling, the types of students, and the attitudes of the school and the community with reference to the status of the speech program. The wise teacher will attempt to achieve some kind of functional balance in establishing dimensions for a proposed speech program. A study of various texts and professionally prepared guides will help identify what content belongs in a fundamentals course and what content belongs in a more advanced speech course.

Accuracy and significance depend upon how well the curriculum content reflects contemporary knowledge as well as how fundamental the knowledge is. Decisions of this nature are not easy to make, especially if the teacher is not trained to teach speech or not sufficiently acquainted with the frontiers of knowledge in speech. The speech profession assists in this matter through professional meetings, journal articles, and publications in which "basic" content is identified by recognized authorities.

State courses of study may be obtained by contacting the various state departments of public instruction usually located in the state capitals. Some state speech associations, such as the Michigan Speech Association at the University of Michigan in Ann Arbor, offer speech curriculum guides for a nominal fee. The Secondary School Interest Group of the

---

[9]Joseph J. Schwab, "The Concept of Structure in the Subject Fields" (paper delivered to the Council on Cooperation in Teacher Education of the American Council on Education, Washington, D.C., 1961); J. Cecil Parker and Louis J. Rubin, *Process as Content: Curriculum Design and the Application of Knowledge* (Chicago: Rand McNally & Co., 1966).

Speech Association of America prepared "Fundamentals of Speech: A Basic Course for High Schools," which was published in *The Speech Teacher,* March, 1959. A special subcommittee for the Committee on Secondary Schools of the American Educational Theatre Association compiled "A Suggested Outline for a Course of Study in Dramatic Arts in the Secondary School," *American Educational Theatre Journal,* March, 1950. This was followed later by *Course of Study in Theatre Arts at the Secondary School Level,* 1963 (revised 1968). The National Thespian Society published *The High School Drama Course* by Willard J. Frederick, 1955. In some issues of the *Bulletin of the National Association of Secondary School Principals,* November 1945, January 1948, December 1949, November 1950, May 1952, January 1954, and October 1966, monthly issues have been devoted to the high school speech curriculum. *The Quarterly Journal of Speech* and *The English Journal* feature articles which focus on defining, preparing, and improving speech programs.

Speech-English sectional meetings of teacher organizations, regional and national speech groups, and workshops and seminars offer assistance to speech personnel. Textbook writers influence our secondary speech programs, especially when teachers use a course of study as outlined by units or chapters in a text. The teacher of speech needs to be knowledgeable enough to be discriminating in the use of these materials.

If the speech curriculum is to be useful, it must provide a useful orientation to the world around us. Since change is an aspect of our contemporary life, the speech program should include sufficient experiences and materials to develop an understanding of the phenomenon of change, its attendant problems, and reasonable techniques for coping with an unpredictable future. Society requires a variety of communication processes with increasing emphasis upon group decision-making under a variety of circumstances. A study unit on understanding individuals and groups — how they function, interact, and make decisions — can be integrated with studies of group participation and leadership skills in school situations for more effective human relationships.

The teacher must take an approach to learning which connects what the student already knows with what is yet to be learned. This does not necessarily mean "bringing the subject matter down to a level the student has already experienced. It could mean extending the student's experience so he experiences the subject matter."[10] The teacher needs to be aware of student deficiencies and needs. Meaningful content and

---

[10]Eugene T. Gendlin, "The Discovery of Felt Meaning," *Language and Meaning* (Washington, D.C.: Association for Supervision and Curriculum Development, NEA, 1966), pp. 60-61.

experiences increase student understanding and motivation. To be able to adapt or translate such learning to appropriate student levels requires teacher flexibility and perception.

Since different behavior requires different types of learning experiences, the speech teacher must select educational experiences which will allow students to practice appropriate behavior. It is possible to engage in the learning of content in such a way that there are opportunities for learning several processes or functions at one time (e.g., analyzing a problem, making a judgment as to the best possible solution, organizing ideas, and practicing speech skills).

Organization of learning experiences within the speech program requires establishing scope, sequence, continuity, and integration. These decisions of determining what time to introduce certain learning experiences are too important to be decided at the moment of actual teaching. Therefore, much careful planning must be involved in this aspect of the curriculum. Some speech programs build from the basic to the advanced; some are based on prerequisite learnings (e.g., Readers' Theatre based on oral interpretation principles). There are speech programs which concentrate on parts of the whole (e.g., staging and make-up of production), but probably the most popular organization is the topical arrangement of courses and units. A basic public speaking course might consist of the following units: principles of effective speaking, speech composition, speech delivery, types of speeches, audience analysis, and controversy. An advanced public speaking course could incorporate the elementary principles but might strive for in-depth coverage in areas such as reasoning and language. It might also introduce abstracts, informal and technical reports as types of speeches; these more technical speeches would fit better into an advanced course. A unit on audience analysis could introduce a body of research on the psychology of the audience. Most programs will provide steps or levels for a progressively more demanding performance. Hopefully, the student will see relationships among experiences and will be able to integrate learning. Focusing on several major concepts and offering a variety of learning techniques will not only provide for the needs of heterogeneous groups but will make it possible for students to translate subject matter into educational process.

Evaluating Learning Experiences

Evaluation, defined in its broad sense, is an integral part of the speech curriculum, beginning with the objectives which concern the processes involved and ending with an assessment of the degree to which students attained these objectives. The way of evaluating what is learned dictates the way in which learning takes place. Students will concentrate on that learning in which they are to be examined, regardless of what the teacher says. *Consistency between evaluation and objectives* is important. To maintain this consistency, the teacher must constantly examine what he is planning, doing, and evaluating to see if these efforts relate to what he originally said he intended to do. Unless one makes continual reference to course goals, it is understandable that one might during the year lose sight of desired outcomes. When this occurs, evaluative criteria bear no resemblance to the objectives. Evaluation may include mastery of content, reactions of students to the content, or mastery of skills. The contribution evaluation makes to the teacher's improvement of the instructional process by examining student response should not be dismissed lightly. To design valid instruments or procedures is a challenging task. The teacher's mastery of a body of knowledge becomes important in constructing effective instruments and identifying basic concepts. Methods of evaluation need to be varied to allow for individual student differences as well as differences in the expected behavior. Written tests, records of various types, observations of behavior and performance, and products or projects (e.g., models, displays) may furnish assessment information. If data are to be useful for improved learning situations, interpretation must be related to curriculum purposes. One must also provide criteria by which student achievement is appraised. What level will be excellent, good, fair? Which level requires greater discrimination? Which project demands more skill, and in what way? Types of evaluation, instruments, techniques, and interpretation of data are discussed in greater detail in Chapter 5.

THE METHODOLOGY FOR PLANNING
A COURSE OF STUDY IN SPEECH

Step I. Diagnose Needs

This involves a general analysis of the problems, conditions, and difficulties pertaining to the speech program. The following factors demand consideration:

A. Students
   1. Age, grade assignment
   2. Education, speech training
   3. Interests

    4. Characteristics and abilities: intellectual, physical, emotional, social, cultural

B. Teacher
  1. Personal characteristics, abilities, interests
  2. Training and preparation
  3. Teacher responsibilities
    a) General
    b) Classroom
    c) Co-curricular

C. Resources
  1. Physical facilities (availability)
    a) Classrooms (size, type)
    b) Equipment
    c) Library
    d) Auditorium and lab work space
  2. Teaching aids
    a) Tests and resource materials
    b) AV (audiovisual) media
  3. Budget
  4. Scheduling opportunities
    a) Availability of speech for all grades
    b) Number of periods per week
    c) Class size
    d) Elective subject vs. required subject
    e) Opportunities for program continuity and expansion

D. Status of speech program
  1. Attitude of administrator
  2. Attitude of students
  3. Attitude of faculty
  4. Attitude of community

In examining these factors, one needs to know about the developmental level of the students, how much exposure to speech activities they have had, and what their speech potential might be in relation to scheduling and school facilities. If speech becomes merely a substitute for the slow learners — consisting of meager course offerings, few resources, and scheduled at inopportune times in poor speech facilities — it is difficult to build an effective program. Professional journals and speech texts emphasize the need to deal with these factors effectively. While it is true that speech facilities and equipment may not determine the speech program, they can influence it.[11]

---

[11]Karl F. Robinson, *Teaching Speech in the Secondary School* (New York: Longmans, Green and Co., 1954), p. 5; Andrew Thomas Weaver, Gladys Louise Borchers, and Donald Kliese Smith, *The Teaching of Speech* (Englewood Cliffs, N.J.: Prentice-Hall, Inc., 1952), pp. 78-82; Waldo W. Braden (ed.), *Speech Methods and Resources* (New York: Harper & Row, Publishers, 1961), pp. 5-10.

Much of the responsibility for excellent speech programs depends on the administration's *attitude*. When those in a position to influence speech programs are convinced of the central role speech plays in communication, they can provide for a better speech curriculum.[12] Attitudes concerning the status of speech in a local school situation usually reflect the type of program in operation.[13] It is paramount that speech teachers understand the purpose of a speech program and try to communicate this purpose to others.

One of the key individuals in the total picture, of course, is the *speech teacher*. Unfortunately, some teachers of speech have not had adequate speech training, do not feel comfortable in conducting a program, are often burdened with heavy classroom and co-curricular responsibilities, and therefore do not always have the energy, desire, or knowledge to build effective programs.[14] Education in oral communication should not be regarded as a part of the English curriculum. Unfortunately, "too many still assume that skill in oral communication is a by-product of instruction in reading and writing."[15] There is also the teacher-administrator group which may not view the local speech program in a favorable light, which would indicate that speech is not adequately covered in the language arts program.[16] While it is desirable that one is at least adequately prepared for the instructional obligations he will incur, it occasionally becomes necessary to engage in self-instruction to fulfill a responsibility.

Each speech teacher needs to become familiar with the *basic body of knowledge* associated with the fields of speech for which he is responsible. The Speech Association of America Subcommittee on Curricula and Certification presented "Principles and Standards for the Certification of Teachers of Speech in Secondary Schools" in the November, 1963 issue of *The Speech Teacher* (p. 336) and hoped these standards and principles would serve as a basis for guidance in the certification of secondary teachers of speech. More recently an Ad Hoc Committee of the Speech Association of America stated that "all teachers charged with the task of developing pupils' competence in oral communication need preparation in the following:

1. Knowledge of how the child develops through processes, language, and speech.

---

[12]Mark Chesler, Richard Schmuck, and Ronald Lippitt, "The Principal's Role in Facilitating Innovation," *Theory into Practice*, 2:269-277 (December, 1963).

[13]Kathryn T. Schoen, "Perceptions of Speech Education in Ohio Secondary Schools" (Doctoral dissertation, The Ohio State University, 1965), p. 118.

[14]*Ibid*, p. 116.

[15]Mary Kinane, "Promoting Speech Education," *The Speech Teacher*, 15:313 (November, 1966).

[16]Schoen, *op. cit.*, p. 102.

2. Knowledge of the basic linguistic and phonetic structures of American English.
3. Knowledge of the forms of oral communication: conversation, creative dramatics, choral speaking, discussion and debate, improvisation, interviewing, oral interpretation, oral reporting, public speaking, story telling, and dramatic production.
4. Personal proficiency in oral and written communication.
5. Skill in motivating and guiding pupils to develop correct and effective habits of oral communication.
6. Training in the skills and special methods of teaching oral communication and in evaluating the results obtained."[17]

This training may be acquired through formal university course offerings, reading, exposure to various speech experiences, and professional involvement with colleagues. The speech teacher should be acquainted with numerous sources: people, resource materials including books, audiovisual aids, and related speech activities (drama, debate, etc.). As the teacher increases his own background of understanding and experience, he can more capably and flexibly develop effective speech programs. He should be more sensitive in evaluating and responding to individual students by offering varied approaches to the learning task.

Most secondary speech teachers do not have time to engage in individualized speech therapy or else do not have sufficient training in corrective speech to feel qualified to cope with *speech disorders*. However, since over seven million people in the United States are handicapped by serious speech deviations,[18] the speech teacher should have some basic understanding of speech improvement. The classroom teacher should have a working knowledge of the speech mechanism, be able to recognize defective speech, and know when students should be referred to a speech pathologist. Once a diagnosis has been made of the disorder, the speech teacher can often help in the rehabilitation.

Many speech problems are due to faulty learning. The speech teacher may correct such functional disorders by making the student aware of his faulty pronunciation so that he will learn to produce correct speech sounds. If the teacher sets a poor example, he reinforces speech problems. Sometimes students cannot hear differences in sounds either because of faulty hearing or poor listening ability. Assistance in these areas permits the student to identify and correct his articulation, rhythm, rate, and

---

[17]Ad Hoc Committee of the Speech Association of America, "Speech Education in the Public Schools," *The Speech Teacher*, 16:82 (January, 1967).

[18]Sheila Morrison Goff, "Speech Pathology," *The Communicative Arts and Sciences of Speech*, ed. Keith Brooks (Columbus, Ohio: Charles E. Merrill Publishing Company, 1967), p. 229.

phonation defects. Hearing tests, exercises, and group drills may be scheduled as part of a unit on voice improvement to teach discrimination among sounds. Continuation of these corrective measures for those who need further work may have to be arranged on an individual basis. If no speech therapist is available, the classroom speech teacher may have to assume this responsibility. Sometimes school therapists will supply suggestions for improving poor speech habits but still require the classroom speech teacher to assist in implementation. Neurological, organic, and emotional causes of speech defects should be referred to those qualified to cope with these problems.

Step II. Determine the Philosophy of Speech Education

After considering the factors which affect the speech program, one should determine his philosophy of speech education in terms consistent with generally accepted educational and speech objectives within a framework of practical reality. This requires a consideration of national and local goals since one must function in relation to both. The ability to revise and adapt to local needs is essential if an effective program is to result. This attitude determines ultimate values and helps to clarify what is desirable in a total speech program. What one should reasonably hope to accomplish is reflected in a combination of Steps I and II.

Step III. State Specific Course Objectives

One should state specific course objectives for those courses which he expects to develop. Objectives and course titles should accurately reflect purposes and experiences. While some objectives may be stated as teacher goals, the discussion here centers on student objectives and desired behavioral outcomes. Some objectives refer to information which the student must acquire, such as "identifying lighting areas of the stage" or "knowing standards of criticism for broadcasting." Objectives concerned with *understanding* include "perceiving the structure of a speech" and "comprehending differences between propositions of fact and propositions of policy." These last imply intellectual power to form reasoned judgments. Some goals relate to *skill* areas and are described by such phrases as "analyzing a speech which one hears," "selecting and wording a question for discussion," or "cultivating proper breathing."

To write statements of *attitudinal objectives,* one might use phrases such as "developing a belief in the value of discussing controversial issues." Attitudinal objectives, like those relating to appreciation and interests, are easier to write than to achieve. To help students acquire an "appreciation of individual differences" or "an interest in dramatic literature" may prove to be a commendable but difficult goal.

Here are two guides which might prove beneficial in formulating objectives: (1) good objectives are consistent with one's philosophy of education, with psychologies of learning, and with available resources; and (2) good objectives should consider student behavior, content, and standard of performance and should be capable of being evaluated. One test of a good objective is how well it communicates your intent to a student or colleague.

Step IV. Select the Content and Learning Experiences

Once the objectives have been carefully defined, their fulfillment depends upon the skill with which the teacher can select and organize the educational experiences. This means choosing content related to the scope of the program as well as using appropriate teaching procedures. "Program" is a broad concept which includes not only classroom content and procedures but also co-curricular speech. Co-curricular activities become the laboratory experiences for the classroom in an integrated curriculum.

The scope of a course in *basic speech* includes the fundamental concepts (articulation, phonation, language, thought, adjustment to the speech situation), debate, discussion, public speaking, parliamentary procedure, bodily action, critical listening and thinking and critical appraisal of controversy, oral interpretation (indivdual and group), radio and television, semantics, phonetics, drama, and organization and research. Source materials, course of study, lecture notes, and study sheets may be consulted to establish content.

The scope of a course in *basic drama* might include units on the history of theatre, acting, stagecraft and production, creative dramatics, children's theatre, dramatic literature, the Readers' Theatre, the theatre as commentary, and playwriting. Again, the depth of content for the various units or the breadth of experiences selected will depend upon many factors. One of the most critical factors is the teacher's knowledge of the field. Gilbert Highet states, "First and most necessary of all, he must know the subject."[19] If the speech teacher knows his subject, he will be aware of resources for the field.

Selection is followed by refinement and applicability to the existing situation. If speech can only be scheduled two periods a week or for only one semester, the amount of content will be adjusted accordingly

---

[19]Gilbert Highet, *The Art of Teaching* (New York: Random House, Inc., 1959), p. 12.

in scope and depth. If there are no school radio and television facilities, learning experiences within the school in these content areas will probably be minimal.

Step V. Organize the Learning Experiences

Content should be organized into some type of meaningful presentation or *sequence*. Identification of major concepts within a field is one type of course framework. A popular arrangement is *units*. For many years the separate-subject approach was the accepted curriculum organization. In an attempt to organize the curriculum to be psychologically consistent with learning theories, unit teaching developed. A unit is described as "any combination of subject-matter content and outcomes, and thought processes, combined in learning experiences suited to the maturity and needs of the learners, which clearly serves the needs of those learners; which is a whole with internal consistency determined by immediate and ultimate goals."[20] The unit of work involves a theme or central problem or study. This becomes the organizing principle for the learning experiences. Unfortunately, unit teaching has often been misunderstood. Traditional daily textbook assignment of lessons is not the integrated process and content of the true unit. Occasionally textbook writers change chapter headings for units, but this does nothing to alter the traditional organization. The textbook should serve as instructional source material which is combined with many other aids. If the unit drags on with no climax in understanding, its purpose — a recognition of the importance of learning episodes — is defeated.[21]

The *resource unit* is a summary of an area of study for the teacher. This is a broad framework which will include an outline of the basic content to be contained in the unit, a list of authoritative sources to consult for content, reference materials, available films and audiovisual aids, and suggestions of possible activities, projects, or experiences which might relate to the development of the unit. This summary furnishes the teacher with a broad base from which to work as he produces a unit "custom-made" for a particular group. The plan which the teacher uses with a specific group of students is the *teaching unit*. This is the unit which he takes into the classroom and which he uses in planning and executing the course in cooperation with his students.

Speech teachers can plan resource units in public speaking, debate, drama, or other areas with only general information about a group of

---

[20]William H. Burton, Ronald B. Kimball, and Richard L. Wing, *Education for Effective Thinking* (New York: Appleton-Century-Crofts, 1960), p. 314.

[21]Jerome Bruner, *The Process of Education* (New York: Random House, Inc., 1963), p. 49.

students. However, as soon as the group becomes identifiable as individuals, he must tailor the resource unit with students' assistance to provide for their individual variations and environmental factors. Each unit will have its own specific objectives and sequence, continuity with the total speech program, and evaluation procedure. Units may be as short or as long as need and interest dictate. Some may be terminal within the class period (although this would be unusual); others may last three days or three weeks. These units are then organized into daily lesson plans which also follow the general pattern of objectives, selecting and organizing learning experiences, and evaluation. It is this step which describes the methods which the teacher uses to create a climate for learning. Facilities, equipment, and activities are scheduled to integrate content and process. These are means, not ends, to establish desired behavior.

A *unit on discussion* might be planned with daily lesson plans on the purpose of discussion, types of discussion, selecting and wording discussion topics, leader participation, member participation, and opportunities to practice discussion. Appropriate procedures for implementation should be clearly defined. Some of these might be scheduled as co-curricular activities to furnish increased opportunity and variety for student participation. A sample *daily lesson plan* on the purpose of discussion might be as follows:

Daily lesson plan: *Purpose of Discussion*
Unit: *Discussion*
Objectives of the day:
  The student should be able to
    1. describe possible ways in which discussion is used in our society,
    2. identify situations in which discussion appears to be effective and why, and
    3. suggest a definition of discussion which includes purpose.
Ideas to be presented:
    1. recognition of a common problem,
    2. some problems best solved by groups of people,
    3. problem-solving steps (reasoned discourse),
    4. importance of cooperation,
    5. leadership–participant roles,
    6. limitations of group discussion, and
    7. speech skills involved.
Materials needed:
  Board and chalk.
Procedures:
  Informal discussion of an accurate definition of *discussion* by examining ways in which discussion is used, why and when it appears to

be successful, and how people interact. List student reactions on the board and frame the purpose of defining *discussion* from their cooperative efforts to solve the problem.

Evaluation:

Did students fulfill objectives?

What types of behavior, understandings, and skills are needed by this group of students for more effective discussion?

Suggested materials for further reading:

List several sources available in the local school library, speech rooms, or community which would include material on group discussion, e.g., R. Victor Harnack and Thorrel Fest, *Group Discussion, Theory and Technique* (New York: Appleton-Century-Crofts, 1964); Paul Brandes and William Smith, *Building Better Speech* (New York: Noble & Noble, Publishers, Inc., 1966), Chapter 10; Barry Collins and Harold Guetzkow, *A Social Psychology of Group Processes for Decision-Making* (New York: John Wiley & Sons, Inc., 1964).

Assignment for students:

1. Identify common types of group discussion.
2. Select a realistic problem area which could be used for a group discussion topic.
3. Observe a group discussion situation (television or otherwise) and note characteristics of participants.

Further lesson planning in group discussion should not only involve a more detailed study of the concepts of this form of oral communication but also introduce the student to activities as an observer-participant so that he may develop the necessary skills for effective discussion. If this were expanded to a semester course of study, each of these content areas could be approached as separate units.

A *unit on debate* might include the purposes of debate, debate propositions, the nature of the proposition, research, organization, proof, refutation, rebuttal, the brief, debate speech composition and delivery, controversy, types of debate, and judging debate. Such content, when supplemented by activities, could be expanded to a semester's work or shortened to a six-weeks' unit which would be more of a survey-orientation approach. For instance "Library Research" might be scheduled as a *daily lesson plan* using the following format:

Daily lesson plan: *Library Research*

Unit: *Debate*

Objectives of the day:

The student should be able to

1. identify the location of library resource materials (books, pamphlets, vertical file information, and pictures),

    2. select and use reference materials, and

    3. develop skill in recording references.

(Note: If the library serves as a resource center for all audiovisual materials and aids, these should also be included.)

Ideas to be presented:

    1. services of school library for debate research (kinds of information and professional assistance available),

    2. location of important reference materials,

    3. how to use the materials, and

    4. importance and preparation of reference cards.

Materials needed:

Cards (4 x 6 in.) for recording reference sources, and the poster indicating information on note-taking for reference cards.

Procedures:

    1. Reconfirm arrangements with school librarian.

    2. Class assembles in library.

    3. Librarian explains location, types, and use of available debate resource materials.

    4. Note-taking procedures; use AV aid in lieu of board.

    5. Pass out cards so students can practice locating and recording data.

Evaluation:

    1. Oral questioning for comprehension.

    2. Practice in library research process.

Assignment:

Prepare reference cards utilizing library materials relating to the current topic which the class is preparing to debate. (This may be the national topic of the high school speech leagues or several topics selected by the students.)

Sometimes the speech teacher will choose to house resource materials in the speech classroom, but this may present a problem in making certain that these materials are available at all times. By using the library rather than the speech classroom as the resource center, students have access to materials and assistance at all times. Better control and utilization of materials can also be maintained. The speech teacher should know what materials are housed in the library and when these materials are available to speech students. The school librarian is often one of the most helpful sources within the library.

A *unit in oral interpretation* might be built around a study of American twentieth-century poetry. The development of the unit should include an introduction to the type of speech activity described as oral interpretation and should be justified in terms of its contribution to the educational program. Specific areas might be developed in the following categories: (1) criteria for selecting literature, (2) introductions, (3) vocal responsiveness, (4) physical responsiveness, and (5) general effectiveness. As these specific areas are discussed and developed, sub-elements are emphasized. Lesson plans for the area of vocal responsiveness would focus on elements of the voice such as audibility, intelligibility, rate, volume, pitch, quality, phrasing, and appropriateness to the literature. Literary selections would be chosen from American twentieth-century poetry. Student experiences in this connection involve listening to recordings, working for self-improvement in vocal responsiveness, analyzing the literature for appropriate vocal cues, reading selections to the class, and evaluating individual presentations. Although the student improves skills through analyzing, the process of analysis must enhance, not diminish, the general effectiveness and enjoyment of the literature. Selections of the poetry prepared in the unit of study may then be read to groups outside the regular speech class as a way of enlarging student experiences and sharing fine literature. The amount of time required to properly develop an oral interpretation unit on American twentieth-century poetry depends upon several factors: the number of times the class meets per week, the length of the class session, the availability of literary materials, and the number of students per class. Each student should have several opportunities to read individually for evaluation and criticism in order to improve his skills and should be able to participate in listening to and evaluating other students.

Other units which might be planned are units in choral reading, Readers' Theatre, storytelling, prose or poetry relating to certain periods of time, and specific authors or themes.

If a study of drama must be included in the basic speech course, the teacher can only arrange a unit which permits an *overview of drama*. In schools where the speech programs include basic as well as advanced drama each aspect may be expanded and additional student experiences provided. The general structure of suggested topics for basic drama (mentioned earlier in the chapter) could be used as separate units; some might serve as semester courses of study. It is questionable how meaningful any of these topics might be if a speech teacher would attempt to offer information in lecture sessions without providing experiences for student involvement. A unit on the history of the classical theatre could be quite dull if approached only through a reading of the recorded facts. However, history learned through researching and building models of early theatres, creating masks, designing costumes, reading plays, acting, discussing the socioeconomic, political, and religious effects of the times, studying the playwrights, listening to records, viewing films, attending plays, and other kinds of student involvement heightens interest and provides meaningful lessons. Unfortunately, because of time limitations, some speech courses follow such a format. It would seem wiser for a teacher hampered by scheduling difficulties to select one or two topics and with carefully planned learning experiences achieve effective results rather than to strive for too much and endanger the entire program.

An interesting approach suggested in a publication of the American Education Theatre Association is a course guide which seeks to involve the student in a series of discovery opportunities.[22] The approach is not based on "units" in the ordinary sense. Behavioral evidences of desired student awareness and response are suggested in the guide to aid the teacher in evaluating student achievement. This guide is a revision of the 1963 *Course of Study in Theatre Arts at the Secondary School Level* published by the American Educational Theatre Association. Section headings are labeled "Discovering an Approach to Theatre," "Discovering the Process of Acting," "Exploring a Drama Through Improvisation," "Placing Theatre in Perspective," and "Organizing the Play for Production." Several supplements recommend new approaches to student involvement.

How much development and detail should be devoted to a topic will depend upon the factors mentioned in Step I. If the teacher is widely acquainted with resource materials and is imaginative in selecting sound learning experiences, the environment for learning will be greatly enriched. The wise teacher recognizes the need to select and organize experiences which will not only gain attention but retain attention. The teacher seeks priority for his activities in competing with all the influences operating in a student's life. Involvement and visualization help keep his attention on learning experiences in school.

Even the most carefully planned units or lessons must often be revised during the actual learning situation because of the nature of the learner and other variables which the teacher can never control or predict. *Flexibility* is essential if learning is to be meaningful in a world of change.

During the course of a lesson there are natural motivations which initiate "teachable moments." The sensitive teacher will take advantage of these opportunities by recognizing these interests and needs and providing satisfaction for the student. Such moments may or may not be a planned part of the lesson. The lesson plan is necessary to guard against haphazard experiences which provide no purposeful direction. However, this procedure does not mean that the teacher and students become "slaves" to the plan. The teacher may estimate what learning

---

[22]Secondary School Theatre Conference of the American Educational Theatre Association, Inc., *A Course Guide in Theatre Arts at the Secondary School Level* (Washington, D. C.: American Educational Theatre Association, Inc., 1968), p. i.

experiences might be organized within the framework of a daily class session, but the framework does not guarantee that this daily class plan is the most desirable or will be accomplished. Organization in terms of *concepts* allows one to adjust to natural motivations and unexpected demands without the frustrations encountered by the teacher who thinks the student learns because the content is covered. The teacher is continually exercising professional judgments in deciding what projected experiences may reasonably be discarded and what experiences need to be expanded for meaningful learning.

School activities (e.g., athletics, music) involving student participation may influence the amount of energy or time which may reasonably be expected in speech participation. Even the time of day that classes are scheduled affects student reaction. Evaluations, such as written tests, may have to be re-scheduled if results are to be valid. A teacher may be testing a student's energy level or endurance rather than his comprehension of basic speech content if he forces the student into competitive situations.

This matter of *timing* becomes important in organizing learning experiences to be compatible with seasonal interests. For instance, a storytelling unit might be more readily acceptable at Hallowe'en or Christmas. There is not only a body of literature to serve as resource material, but these can be grouped in levels of difficulty. To heighten interest, elementary pupils, lay groups, or other secondary students might furnish appreciative audience situations. Encouraging creativity in student planning develops the student's potential and promotes the total speech program. Some students may choose to combine several communication skills by writing original stories and presenting them. Involvement in projects which give personal satisfaction to the student in being able to communicate effectively increases his desire to improve speech skills. Student evaluation of such projects develops his ability to discriminate in levels of speech performance, audience analysis, and speech understandings which need to be reinforced. Goals must be clear and meaningful to the student if he is expected to know how to evaluate.

If a teacher were to use a prepared course of study rather than initiate his own, he would still have to make adjustments. The suggested *unit on preparation and delivery of talks* submitted by a special committee of the Secondary School Interest Group of the Speech Association of America might furnish the base from which to work.

Preparation and Delivery of Talks

Time: Three weeks

I. *Introduction:* In our highly organized society, it is reasonable to expect that numerous occasions will arise in most lifetimes when addressing an audience becomes a civic or social obligation which may not be avoided and should be welcomed. Every high school pupil has a right to be trained to meet these opportunities in such a way that his chances for advancement are enhanced.

II. *Objectives:*
   A. General

      To equip the pupil with a specific technique for assembling, organizing, and presenting material so that both he and his audience may enjoy his performance.

   B. Specific
   1. To eliminate fear of a speech situation.
   2. To convince the pupil that there is a definite technique for speech-making developed over a period of several thousand years.
   3. To convince the pupil that, no matter how short or casual a speech may seem, real preparation is required.
   4. To convince the pupil that to produce and manage ideas requires a disciplined mind.
   5. To teach the pupil that written and spoken English are very different and that a speech must convey the sincerity, honesty, and enthusiasm of the speaker to his audience with spontaneity.
   6. To develop a system of sentence-outlining which will enable the pupil to organize material quickly, logically, and effectively.

III. *Approach:* Stress is placed upon the usefulness of the skills to be developed and the number and type of occasions for which the skills will be needed. The students may be encouraged to tell times in their lives when they have been or may be called upon to speak.

IV. *Organization and Content:*
   A. Value of public speaking
   1. Influence upon the audience
   2. Influence upon the speaker
      a) Personality development
      b) Opportunities for leadership
      c) Opportunities for advancement
      d) Opportunities for service
   B. Preparations for speaking
   1. Selecting a subject
      a) Appropriateness to audience
      b) Adaptability to time limit
   2. Determination of purpose
      a) To entertain or interest
      b) To explain or inform

      c) To convince or stimulate
      d) To persuade or arouse to action
   3. Research for material
      a) Possible reliable sources
      b) Note-taking on cards
      c) Filing
   4. Divisions of outline
      a) Introduction
      b) Body
      c) Conclusion
   5. Sentence-outlining
   6. Rehearsal of delivery
  C. Types of public speaking
   1. Impromptu speech situations
   2. Extempore speeches
      a) Anecdotes
      b) Explanations using visual aids
      c) Informative talks
      d) Talks which convince or stimulate
      e) Persuasive or selling talks
      f) Speeches for special occasions
   3. Memorized speeches (not advisable for high school pupils)

V. *Pupil Experiences and Activities:*
  A. Preparation and submission of a sentence outline at least two days before each assignment is due.
  B. Assignments
   1. A speech of explanation with visual aids to be used as a first assignment (because the natural movement needed for demonstrating tends to overcome fear and give the pupil a feeling of security as he discusses his hobby).
   2. A speech to entertain, using a personal experience such as a most embarrassing moment.
   3. A speech to convince or stimulate, requiring reliable proof or support material.
   4. A speech to persuade followed by a heckling period during which the pupil must support his points under pressure. (Two separate grades are given for this assignment.)
   5. Speeches for special occasions, using a different kind of speech for each pupil.
   6. Impromptu speeches for which the pupil draws a subject and tests his ability to organize material on the spur of the moment.
   7. A final examination speech assigned well in advance and requiring a great deal of research, note cards properly filed, a noun topic outline, a sentence outline, and a biography.

VI. *Evaluation and Testing:*
   A. Selection by each pupil of another member of the class to act as his official commentator and supply him with written comments about each performance.
   B. Careful grading of outlines and notebook by the teacher.
   C. The final examination speech.
   D. The record sheet kept by the teacher for each pupil so that improvement and problems still existing are evident at a glance.[23]

The suggested time allotment for this unit is three weeks. This may or may not prove to be feasible. Objectives, which are teacher-oriented, should be revised to be student-oriented so behavior can be evaluated. The conceptual approach requires each teacher to adapt the suggested content and process to his individual group. The development of this unit might even be expanded by presenting various approaches to outlining, the responsibility of the listener, and critical thinking. If critical thinking becomes a part of the unit, there must be stated objectives for critical thinking, content and learning experiences, and evaluation.

Beginning public speaking courses at the university level have for some time utilized the *"common materials"* approach. This "problem method" or "controlled method" depends on the ability of the teacher to direct students to assigned readings.[24] Such an approach may help the teacher to do a more adequate job of criticizing content and may elevate the level of information presented by the student. Some of the weaknesses which exist would be in trying to decide on a theme which would have sufficient interest for all students, and in obtaining an adequate supply of resource material. Involvement in current issues helps the student to find relevancy in studying speech and to appreciate the concept of an "expanded rhetoric."

Another prepared course of study is the topic outline by Lewis for *radio-television* stated here in brief form. The complete course outline including recommended, selected resources and student activities is found in the *National Association of Secondary School Principals Bulletin,* 50, No. 312, October, 1966. See also Chapter 11 of this book, entitled "Broadcasting."

   I. Objectives
  II. Content
      A. Broadcasting equipment, studio, personnel

---

[23]Speech Association of America, "Fundamentals of Speech: A Basic Course for High Schools," *The Speech Teacher,* 8:103-104 (March, 1959).

[24]Waldo Braden (ed.), "Symposium on Using Common Materials," *The Speech Teacher,* 16:259 (November, 1967).

  B. Announcers and "talent"
  C. Program analysis and classification
  D. Sound and music effects in broadcasting
  E. Analysis and writing of various program types
  F. Development of broadcasting in America
  G. Appreciative, informational, and critical listening
  H. List of audience size measurement services
 III. Inductive learning activities
 IV. Equipment
  A. Ideal Equipment
  B. Operators
  C. Textbooks
  D. Radio scripts
 V. Selected resources for teacher and student

Secondary speech teachers should carefully examine their goals and objectives before choosing any approach. Undue emphasis upon the elements of voice and bodily activity at the expense of sound content presents a distorted picture of the accepted principles of communication. The focus should be on setting an environment which will help the student become a more effective communicator by synthesizing all that he has learned about enhancing the speaker-listener relationship.

Step VI. Evaluate

As indicated in an earlier paragraph, evaluation consists of determining objectives, diagnosing, selecting and organizing learning experiences, appraising progress, and determining changes. This process requires decisions on what to evaluate as well as how to evaluate. Continual assessment of the total program reveals student growth and needs, compatibility of program operations with program goals, and weaknesses to be avoided or overcome in future planning. Practical considerations of economic efficiency for both teacher and students are a part of this appraisal, and better organization and more selective learning experiences can improve not only the quality but also the quantity of speech education. Certainly many of the materials and approaches used in teaching need to be reviewed.

It has been suggested that a revolution is needed in the speech field to attain a greater relevance to pressing social problems. Those who are involved in this interdisciplinary field of study, described by Dr. Franklin Knower of The Ohio State University as "social achievement in symbolic behavior," must keep in touch with social changes. Persons who have been interested in language acquisition and modification for children have become interested in the culturally deprived, where language emerges as a learning disorder. In an effort to cope with the language problems of the disadvantaged, recent interdisciplinary dialogue has focused on ways to resolve these problems.[25] The speech teacher who is working in an economically disadvantaged area may be involved in problems of social dialect which need to be understood before it is possible to motivate students to participate in any kind of a successful speech experience. Research on bilingualism and dialect takes the view that disadvantaged children speak in a language different (rather than deficient) from that of the middle-class school. Those researchers who advocate that dialect is a different language system suggest that when disadvantaged students are forced to function with a middle-class dialect, all kinds of communication and emotional barriers result. They propose that "standard English" should be taught as a second language. The speech repertoire is an important aspect of language development since it is acquired through imitation.[26] Reading acquisition is based upon the imitative speech repertoire; thus, a failure in one aspect of the formal education process often precipitates a failure in another aspect. Teachers of speech need to be informed as to how they can contribute to resolving these problems.

For the beginning speech teacher, especially for one with little formal speech education, it may be more desirable to obtain existing patterns — courses of study — prepared by professional groups. These patterns should only serve as temporary measures and should be tailored to fit elements of the particular situation. If the speech program is already established, one can, at least for the initial year, maintain the status quo. As the need for *improvement* becomes apparent, the speech teacher must recognize that the task of initiating change is twofold: changing ideas and changing human dynamics. Thus, the successful teacher needs training in human engineering as well as professional skills. (Curriculum *improvement* and *change* are used interchangeably here although technically curriculum change might be viewed as changing ideas, goals, means and people. Curriculum improvement can be interpreted as an extension of the existing conception of the curriculum and its organization.) The speech teacher must be involved in cooperative efforts with school personnel, students, administrators, and lay groups to establish rapport and understanding of the speech program. Progress may be slow since attitudes and values do not change quickly. Some administrators have only a vague idea of speech goals; thus programs may falter

---

[25]"Summary Transcript: Interdisciplinary Meetings on the Language Problems of the Disadvantaged," New York City, January 26, 1968, convened by Speech Association of America.

[26]Arthur W. Staats, *Learning, Language and Cognition* (New York: Holt, Rinehart & Winston, Inc., 1968), p. 398.

because the teacher fails to adequately communicate purposes. In order to influence administrators, the teacher must have well-formulated objectives supported by recognized leaders in the field, a knowledge of content and process, and a means of determining success. He needs to be convinced that "no aspect of the curriculum is more important to the school of a democracy than the teaching of speech."[27]

All *curriculum improvement* should not be expected to originate with administration or professional groups. The speech teacher must study the practical problems encountered in daily instruction. Sometimes an experimental testing of some aspect of curriculum revision or materials within his own speech program provides a *pilot unit* to be tested in

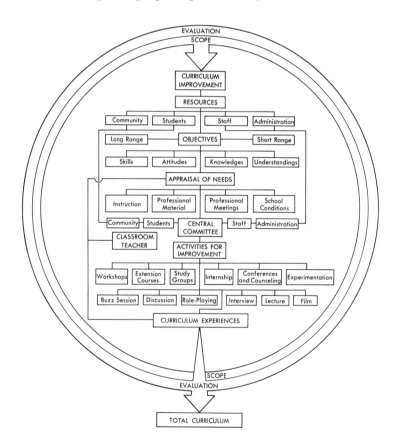

Figure 6. Flow Chart for Curriculum Improvement

---

[27]Ruth E. French, "The Potential of Speech in the English Program," *An English Teacher's Reader* (New York: Odyssey Press, 1962), p. 206. (Reprinted from *English Journal*, November, 1960).

other classrooms under different conditions. From this experimentation may evolve a model which other speech teachers will find desirable. Further refinement may be obtained as this design is shared with those who are qualified to evaluate such change. This way of viewing curriculum responsibility requires the speech teacher to function in a creative and dynamic role. Hopefully, this procedure of curriculum-making on the local level will be reflected in national speech programs.

The flow chart for curriculum improvement in Fig. 6 suggests that the classroom speech teacher can reconsider and replan learning-teaching units as a first step in curriculum improvement. The teacher who wishes to initiate curriculum improvement must do so through a systematic program design. The flow chart indicates that any change must relate to the total school program and be evaluated not only on its own merits, but also on its relationship to the entire structure. The scope of the proposed improvement depends upon appraisal of needs, school-community resources, and perceptions. The nature of curriculum change is a type of social change, changing people. The suggested improvement should be expressed in objectives and prescribed activities. Some of these activities will be planned to induce those involved to accept the change and to prepare for its installation. Other activities will be curriculum experiences essential for implementation.

Suggested Projects

1. Using the Speech Association of America's "Fundamentals of Speech: A Basic Course for High Schools," divide one of the suggested units into daily lesson plans. State objectives in behavioral terms (what you expect of the student), list the activities and materials you expect to provide, the learning environment which will make these objectives possible, and state how you expect to evaluate student behavior to determine if the objectives have been achieved. It is also important for students to understand how they are to be evaluated.

2. Create a public speaking resource unit which focuses on selected current issues. Establish outcomes in terms of understandings, skills, and attitudes. Suggest a variety of learning activities and resources giving some consideration of local field trips. Request a classmate to evaluate this unit and make recommendations.

3. State what you believe is one of the important concepts in the speech curriculum. Identify some specific behaviors which you feel students should develop if this concept is to be realized. How might you evaluate this?

4. Read and abstract professional speech journals on the national and state levels for articles which relate to curriculum development. Abstract only those which are meaningful.

5. Develop a file of various courses of study in basic speech. Identify concepts and units. What appears to be considered as "basic"? Do you agree? Suggest the concepts, units, and order of appearance you believe should be included in a basic speech course with supporting statements for your decisions.

6. Present an innovative approach to teaching in any of the speech areas. Justify this approach and state how one might evaluate its effectiveness.

7. List several specific steps which you feel might be appropriate in initiating curriculum change.

8. Make a list of educational objectives consistent with the broad purposes of education. State specific speech content and activities which you feel might realistically contribute to these outcomes.

9. Identify several of the most critical current problems of the adolescent in American society and their implications for the secondary speech curriculum. Name specific activities one might plan which relate directly to these problems.

10. List several major ideas in modern learning theory and plan classroom procedures which are consistent with these ideas.

References

Bloom, Benjamin S. (ed.). *Taxonomy of Educational Objectives.* New York: David McKay Company, Inc., 1956.

Braden, Waldo (ed.). *Speech Methods and Resources.* New York: Harper & Row, Publishers, 1961.

Bruner, Jerome. *The Process of Education.* New York: Random House, Inc., 1963.

Burton, William H., Kimball, Ronald B., and Wing, Richard L. *Education for Effective Thinking.* New York: Appleton-Century-Crofts, 1960.

Corey, Stephen M. *Action Research to Improve School Practices.* New York: Teachers College Press, 1953.

Educational Policies Commission. *The Purposes of Education in American Democracy.* Washington, D.C.: National Education Association, 1938.

Erikson, E. H. "Growth and Crises of the Health Personality," *Personality in Nature, Society, and Culture,* eds. C. Kluckhohn, H. A. Murray, and D. M. Schneider. Rev. ed. New York: Alfred A. Knopf, Inc., 1955.

French, Ruth E. "The Potential of Speech in the English Program," *An English Teacher's Reader.* New York: Odyssey Press, 1962, p. 206. (Reprinted from *English Journal,* 49:556-562, November, 1960.)

Gendlin, Eugene T. "The Discovery of Felt Meaning," *Language and Meaning.* Washington, D.C.: Association for Supervision and Curriculum Development, NEA, 1966.

Goff, Sheila Morrison. "Speech Pathology," *The Communicative Arts and Sciences of Speech,* ed. Keith Brooks. Columbus, Ohio: Charles E. Merrill Publishing Company, 1967.

Highet, Gilbert. *The Art of Teaching.* New York: Random House, Inc., 1959.

Miner, J. B. *Intelligence in the United States.* New York: Springer Publishing Co., Inc., 1957.

Parker, J. Cecil and Rubin, Louis J. *Process as Content: Curriculum Design and the Application of Knowledge.* Chicago: Rand McNally & Co., 1966.

Phenix, Philip. *Philosophy of Education.* New York: Holt, Rinehart & Winston, Inc., 1958.

Robinson, Karl F. *Teaching Speech in the Secondary School.* New York: Longmans, Green and Co., 1954.

Secondary School Theatre Conference of the American Educational Theatre Association, Inc. *A Course Guide in Theatre Arts at the Secondary School Level.* Washington, D. C.: American Educational Theatre Association, Inc., 1968.

Staats, Arthur W. *Learning, Language and Cognition.* New York: Holt, Rinehart & Winston, Inc., 1968.

Taba, Hilda. *Curriculum Development: Theory and Practice.* New York: Harcourt, Brace & World, 1962.

Weaver, Andrew Thomas, Borchers, Gladys Louise, and Smith, Donald Kliese. *The Teaching of Speech.* Englewood Cliffs, N. J.: Prentice-Hall, Inc., 1952.

Articles

Ad Hoc Committee of the Speech Association of America. "Speech Education in the Public Schools," *The Speech Teacher,* 16:82 (January, 1967).

Braden, Waldo (ed.). "Symposium on Using Common Materials," *The Speech Teacher,* 16:259 (November, 1967).

Buys, William E., Carlson, Charles V., Compton, Hite, and Frank, Allen D. "Speech Communication in the High School Curriculum," *The Speech Teacher,* 17:297-317 (November, 1968).

Chesler, Mark, Schmuck, Richard, and Lippitt, Ronald. "The Principal's Role in Facilitating Innovation," *Theory Into Practice,* 2:269-277 (December, 1963).

Kinane, Mary. "Promoting Speech Education," *The Speech Teacher,* 15:313 (November, 1966).

Lewis, George. "Radio and Television in the Secondary School," *The Bulletin of the National Association of Secondary School Principals*, 50, No. 312: 67-70 (October, 1966).

Speech Association of America. "Fundamentals of Speech: A Basic Course for High Schools," *The Speech Teacher*, 8:103-4 (March, 1959).

Unpublished Materials

Schoen, Kathryn T. "Perceptions of Speech Education in Ohio Secondary Schools." Doctoral dissertation, The Ohio State University, 1965.

Schwab, Joseph J. "The Concept of Structure in the Subject Fields." Paper delivered to the Council on Cooperation in Teacher Education of the American Council on Education, Washington, D.C., 1961.

"Summary Transcript: Interdisciplinary Meetings on the Language Problems of the Disadvantaged." Convened by Speech Association of America, New York City, January 26, 1968.

4

Preparation and Classroom Management

PREPARATION AND CERTIFICATION

Teacher preparation and certification are determined by several forces: (*a*) standards of teacher preparation institutions (public and private colleges and universities), (*b*) certification codes of various State Boards of Education, (*c*) recommendations of professional organizations at national, state, and regional levels (Speech Association of America, American Educational Theatre Association, Central Speech Association, etc.), and (*d*) job description analysis (from records of associations of superintendents and principals).

Most reputable teacher preparation institutions exceed the minimal standards set by state certification offices because states codes are designed to provide a "floor" below which the most limited college should not prepare teachers. The minimal standards recommended by the professional organizations (SAA and AETA) more nearly match the standards of the better teacher preparation institutions. Both provide a constant constructive pressure to assure that the more limited institutions will improve their programs.

State certification boards often delegate responsibility and grant "provisional teacher certification," valid for a set number of years, upon the recommendation of the degree-granting institutions. Providing qualified teachers is, therefore, a joint responsibility covering (*a*) *preparation* of qualified personnel, (*b*) *recommendation* by college administration and supervisory officers, (*c*) *definition* of the professional job by the hiring institution, and finally (*d*) *assignment* of the qualified personnel in a manner which makes satisfactory job completion possible. The quality of teaching is diminished when the prospective teacher has not been adequately prepared, is not adaptable to the realistic job description, or when the job assignment has been extended into unrealistic dimensions. The latter exists when teachers are assigned outside their areas of certification.

Certification standards prescribe the nature of the content to be mastered,[1] the skills to be learned,[2] and the attitudes to be instilled[3] in an acceptable preparation program for speech teachers. Kerikas described many of these facets in a multi-state study of speech education.[4] Marceline Erickson reported the results of a study on undergraduate course preparation for prospective speech teachers,[5] analyzed in terms of the minimum standards recommended by the Certification Committee of the Secondary School Interest Group of the Speech Association of America.[6] Data for her study was taken from the catalogues of 339 four-year colleges and universities of thirteen central states. She found that 105 of the institutions (about 31 per cent) required a course in the processes of speech, 118 (about 35 per cent) required a course in theatre, 58 (17 per cent) required a course in speech correction, 147 (43 per cent) required a course in public address, and 126 (37 per cent) required a course in speech methods. The figures may be misleading due to the fact that they are based upon the 339 institutions surveyed rather than the 264 institutions indicating a major or minor program.

---

[1]Karl F. Robinson, "Training the Secondary-School Teacher of Speech," *The Quarterly Journal of Speech*, 30:225-227 (April, 1944).

[2]Frederick W. Haberman, "Toward the Ideal Teacher of Speech," *The Speech Teacher*, 10:4 (January, 1961).

[3]SAA Subcommittee on Curricula and Certification, "Principles and Standards for Certification of Teachers of Speech in Secondary Schools," *The Speech Teacher*, 12:336-337 (November, 1963).

[4]E. J. Kerikas, "Current Status of Speech Education in the Public Secondary Schools of the Intermountain States" (Doctoral dissertation, Northwestern University, 1962).

[5]Marceline Erickson, "Undergraduate Course Preparation in Colleges and Universities of the Central States for Prospective Teachers of Speech in Secondary Schools," *The Speech Teacher,* 12:308-316 (November, 1963).

[6]A recent study, Linda Harvill, "The Status of Speech Education in Accredited Mississippi Secondary Schools, 1966-67" (Master's thesis, University of Southern Mississippi, 1967), indicates a close correlation of certification standards and job load descriptions of Mississippi and Louisiana to those of Ohio and Michigan.

Trauernicht, in 1949, employed the questionnaire technique to determine which courses given in a prescribed list were more frequently required of prospective high school speech teachers. The study encompassed 116 training institutions for speech teachers over a 41-state area as well as 44 of the state departments of public instruction.[7] The replies are presented below in tabular form. The Trauernicht study does not account for courses and areas of content such as television, history of theatre, communication theory, etc. One is reminded that speech content and the concerns of speech professionals have changed since 1949, particularly in relation to broadcast media.

Number and Percentage of the 86 Speech-Training Institutions Requiring the Various Courses for All High School Speech Teachers with the Average Number of Semester Hours of Each Course[8]

Course	Number of Institutions Requiring	Percentage Requiring	Average Number of Semester Hours
Fundamentals of Speech*	67	77.90	3.19
Oral Interpretation	49	56.96	3.24
Methods of Teaching Speech	42	48.83	2.60
Public Speaking	42	48.83	3.21
Practice Teaching in Speech	37	43.02	4.26
Speech Pathology and Correction	36	41.86	2.90
Play Production and Direction	36	41.86	3.41
Acting	23	26.74	2.88
Radio	23	26.74	2.90
Debate	23	26.74	2.59
Stagecraft	18	20.93	3.02
Observation of Teaching of Speech	17	19.76	2.86
Discussion	17	19.76	2.89
Phonetics	16	18.60	2.62
Voice Science	16	18.60	2.83
Basic Communications†	10	11.62	5.38
Speech for the Classroom Teacher	10	11.62	3.03
Psychology of Speech	9	10.40	3.00

*Embracing training in such skills as adjustment, communicativeness, bodily action, voice, diction, original speaking, reading aloud, listening, and the use of the microphone.
†Reading, writing, speaking, and listening.

---

[7]Maxine M. Trauernicht, "The Training of High School Teachers of Speech," *The Speech Teacher*, 1:29-36 (January, 1952).
[8]*Ibid*, p. 30.

Concerns of Professional Associations and Leaders

The apparent unsystematic and variable nature of education in speech has been noted at the national, regional, state, and local levels by speech educators and by others dedicated to providing quality education for the youth of America. The primary concern of these educators has been with the quality of speech education at the secondary level. In focusing national attention on the problem, the Speech Association of America declared:

> The disorganized and erratic nature of education in speech has been a matter of deep concern to the Speech Association of America since its founding. The Association has sought to provide through its publications both theoretical guidance and practical curriculum materials for sound programs in speech education.[9]

A committee of the Central States Speech Association, in conducting a poll of state superintendents of public instruction, found there was a general feeling that

> Speech is inconsistent in its requirements from teacher to teacher and from school system to school system. It refuses to be *nailed down. It is improving the techniques and the mechanics of communication, or memorizing and reciting lines, or developing the arts of conversation,* or many other things, dependent on the teacher's preference and range of interests.[10]

The last of the above statements — "dependent on the teacher's preferences and range of interests" — is probably the most disconcerting to speech educators. Lewis, writing in *The Central States Speech Journal,* noted that

> Many teachers of speech, graduated from all types of speech and/or education departments, are not good representatives for speech. Many are seeking outlets for isolated speech interests. To them, debate, the school play, or the contest is an end rather than a means to improve the communication of students.[11]

---

[9]Speech Association of America Interest Group: Speech in the Secondary Schools, *Newsletter* (September, 1963), p. 2.

[10]G. Bradford Barber, "Questions to be Considered by Panel Members for the Central States Speech Association Program" (report of a 1963-64 survey to be discussed at CSSA Convention, St. Louis, Missouri, April, 1964).

[11]George L. Lewis, "Speech Teacher Certification: Communication and Self Reception," *The Central States Speech Journal,* 11:84 (Winter, 1960).

At the state level, the first comprehensive survey of speech education in Ohio was conducted some seventeen years ago by Franklin H. Knower. The Knower study revealed an urgent need, as have subsequent studies, for not only more state certified teachers of speech but also better trained teachers of speech. Ohio high school principals in replying to the Knower questionnaire indicated that speech teachers were inadequately prepared and their recommendation was to "broaden teacher education in speech."[12] While Baker found that there were more certified teachers of speech in Ohio secondary schools than at the time of the Knower study,[13] Schoen reported that a great many teachers of speech lacked the minimal semester hours for certification to teach speech but taught by virtue of administrative appointment.[14] Knower found in his 1950 study that only about one-third of the speech teachers responding to his questionnaire had any academic preparation for teaching speech.[15] In 1965 Schoen reported that approximately 44 per cent of the speech teachers lacked Ohio speech certification.[16] A study conducted by McManus and Petrie for the 1965-66 academic year confirmed that well over one-third of the speech teachers in Ohio lacked the eighteen semester hours in speech required for a provisional teaching certificate in speech,[17] although both the Knower and the McManus-Petrie studies indicated that almost all of the speech teachers in Ohio secondary schools have their bachelor's degree from an Ohio college or university and are certified to teach.

In addition to the recommendations of the Certification Committee of SAA's Secondary School Interest Group, the literature is replete with suggestions for improvement of speech education programs.[18] Karl Robinson recommended at least a major of 30 or 40 semester hours in speech content, student teaching experience, course work in related fields (English or social studies) as minor areas, and general education courses.

---

[12]Franklin H. Knower, *Speech Education in Ohio* (Columbus, Ohio: Department of Speech, The Ohio State University, 1950), p. 39.

[13]Mary K. Baker, "An Evaluation of the Speech Program of the Secondary Schools of Ohio for the Year 1961-62" (paper submitted for a seminar, The Ohio State University, 1962), p. 13.

[14]Kathryn T. Schoen, "Perceptions of Speech Education in Ohio Secondary Schools" (Doctoral dissertation, The Ohio State University, 1965), p. 95.

[15]Knower, *op. cit.*, p. 77.

[16]Schoen, *op. cit.*, p. 93.

[17]Thomas R. McManus and Charles R. Petrie, "Speech Education in Ohio High Schools, 1965-66," *The Ohio Speech Journal* (1967), 9-14.

[18]Fred Alexander and Gordon Thomas, "The High School Speech Teacher in Michigan," *Speech Teacher*, 9:189-190 (September, 1960). Knower, *loc. cit.* Charles L. Balcer and Hugh F. Seabury, *Teaching Speech in Today's Secondary Schools* (New York: Holt, Rinehart & Winston, Inc., 1965), p. 50.

Specific courses in voice and phonetics, debate and discussion, interpretation, radio and dramatics were included.[19] Balcer recommended courses in the fundamentals of speech, oral interpretation, discussion and debate, dramatics, stagecraft, speech science and pathology, and parliamentary procedure. Balcer, a former high school principal, noted that

> Often one of the principal's biggest problems arises from the inability of a speech teacher to handle satisfactorily extra-class activities. Speech teachers should make every effort to participate, while in college, in speaking activities: debate, discussion, interpretative reading, drama, radio and television so that when they become members of a high school staff and of a community they will have available a practical knowledge of speaking situations.[20]

Haberman puts considerable emphasis upon the mastery of speech theory rather than upon the development of speech skills.

> The speech teacher needs to know the fundamental physiological processes involved in human communication, including the sounds of the language, how they are formed, and how received, . . . the psychological processes, including conceptions of meaning, attention, social control, and satisfaction of wants, . . . the linguistic processes including rhetoric, . . . poetics, . . . logic, . . . the aesthetic processes including the form of speeches, of drama, and the like, . . . the functional processes involved in the media which carry human communication, including the platform, radio, and television. He needs to understand the history of human communication, including the history of theory and the history of practioneers, . . . to possess some measure of above-average competence in a basic speech form: acting, reading, debating, public speaking.[21]

Continuing Recommendations of Professional Organizations

In 1960 the Secondary School Interest Group of the Speech Association of America recommended to the legislative assembly of the SAA a resolution setting forth certain minimal requirements for certification of teachers of speech in secondary schools. "A Resolution Adopted by the

---

[19]Karl F. Robinson and E. J. Kerikas, *Teaching Speech* (New York: David McKay Company, Inc., 1963), pp. 49-51. Robinson, "Training the Secondary-School Teacher of Speech," *loc. cit.*

[20]Charles L. Balcer, "The High School Principal and the Teacher of Speech," *The Speech Teacher,* 4:184 (September, 1955).

[21]Haberman, *loc. cit.*

Legislative Assembly of the Speech Association of America," dated December 28, 1960, sets forth the following requirements:

Section I. *General Requirement.* For permanent certification in speech, the teacher should offer at least twenty-four semester hours in speech, taken at an accredited college or university, and distributed as specified in Section II. For provisional, temporary, or "second field" certification, the teacher should offer at least eighteen semester hours in speech, taken at an accredited college or university, and distributed as specified in Section II.

Section II. *Subject Area Preparation.* To insure breadth of preparation, each certified teacher of speech should have completed at least one course in each of these divisions:

(A) *Speech Sciences and Processes,* such as phonetics, physiology of the voice mechanism, basic speech development, voice, articulation, et cetera; (B) *Theatre and Oral Interpretation,* such as oral interpretation, acting, directing, technical theatre, play production, radio, television, et cetera; (C) *Speech Correction,* such as speech correction, speech pathology, clinical practices in speech correction, et cetera; (D) *Public Address,* such as public speaking, discussion, argumentation, debate, radio, television, et cetera.

Section III. *Professional Preparation.* In addition to the preparation specified above, the teacher certified in speech should offer at least one course in methods of teaching speech in the secondary school, together with appropriate student teaching.[22]

The resolution as adopted is basically consistent with the recommendations for certification made by the Secondary Interest Group of the Speech Association of America in the years 1951 and 1959. In 1963 the Subcommittee on Curricula and Certification of the Speech Association of America gave the following statement of principles and standards as a guide in meeting the certification of teachers of speech for the secondary schools:

Principles and Standards for the Certification of
Teachers of Speech in Secondary Schools[23]

School administrators, colleges, accrediting agencies, and state departments of public instruction look to professional associations for direction regarding

---

[22]SAA Subcommittee on Curricula and Certification, *op cit.,* p. 336.

[23]This statement was prepared by a special subcommittee of the Committee on Curricula and Certification. It was accepted as an official document of SAA by action of the Administrative Council in Denver, Colorado, August 19, 1963.

principles and standards for certification of teachers in various subject matter fields. The following statement is offered as a basis for guidance in the certification of teachers of speech in secondary schools.

1. *The competent teacher of speech should have an understanding of the nature of speech.*

   a. The teacher of speech knows that speech, with its counterpart listening, constitutes the primary means whereby man most commonly comes to an understanding of himself and his universe. It is the basic means through which he formulates thought and the major process through which our society operates and maintains itself. It is central to the functioning of religious, political, social and economic life.

   b. The teacher of speech sees speech as complex behavior which involves thought, attitudes, use of language, sound, and action. He views it as a social process, an interaction among people whose purpose is to effect commonality of understanding.

   c. The teacher of speech recognizes that through speech the individual is helped to integrate knowledge. He knows that in a democratic society it is vital that intelligent individuals also be made articulate in order that intelligence may prevail.

   d. The teacher of speech knows that speech is learned behavior. He is aware that upon its proper learning depends much of the individual's self-realization and his development as a thinking, mature, responsible person. He realizes that to improve speaking is to contribute importantly to an individual's mental and emotional health and well-being.

   e. The teacher of speech appreciates that to be most effective such learning is best achieved through organized instruction under competent teachers.

2. *The competent teacher of speech in secondary schools must be prepared to execute effectively any or all of the following duties:*

   a. Teaching classes in speech fundamentals, discussion and debate, public speaking, oral reading of literature, dramatic production and/or speech before microphone or camera.

   b. Directing and/or coordinating co-curricular or extracurricular activities in debate, discussion, speech contests and festivals, theatre and radio and television production.

   c. Planning and preparing or assisting others in the preparation of programs for assemblies, community ceremonies and special occasions.

   d. Preparing courses of study, making textbook selections, procuring audio-visual and other teaching materials, and planning extracurricular programs.

e. Serving as consultant in matters of speech to the entire faculty and to the community.

3. *The competent teacher of speech in secondary schools must demonstrate:*

   a. Personal proficiency in oral and written communication.

   b. Functional knowledge of the basic forms and uses of speech as listed in 2a and 2b.

   c. Ability in stimulating and guiding the speech development of students.

To meet these qualifications for certification, the prospective teacher shall be expected to complete in an accredited college or university not fewer than eighteen semester hours (or their equivalent) in courses in speech appropriately distributed, and related to the duties listed in Section II above. In addition, he shall be expected to complete at least one course in Methods of Teaching Speech in Secondary Schools together with appropriate successful experiences in directed or supervised teaching.

It is assumed, of course, that the prospective teacher of speech will have selected courses in at least three of the academic areas of humanities, social studies, biological sciences and physical sciences.

The Speech Association of America recommends that school administrators assign only certified teachers of speech to classroom instruction in speech and to the direction of speech activities.

The position of SAA regarding the minimal requirements for speech teacher certification appears to have changed little despite the fact that membership of the committee has changed several times over the intervening years. This leads us to the conclusion that among speech educators actively participating at a national level, there is a considerable amount of agreement on the nature of the training which should be required of potential high school teachers of speech.

A special subcommittee for the American Educational Theatre Association Committee on Secondary Schools published in 1950 a suggested outline for a course of study in dramatic arts in the secondary school. The scope of content presented in the outline was in keeping with the philosophy of the committee that

> The audiences of tomorrow are in the high schools today; therefore one of the major responsibilities of the dramatic arts course in the secondary schools should be to train discriminating audiences who will demand a high standard of dramatic entertainment. The student's ability to discriminate, and to evaluate the dramatic performances with which he is in constant contact, is surely one of his

fundamental needs. In addition, of course, the student should develop individual skills that will enrich his life and help him develop
a more interesting personality.[24]

The suggested units of study in the outline included exploring the
field (a survey), the actor, the play, the director, the technician, history
of the theatre, and optional units in television, motion pictures, and
radio.[25]

In 1963 a special committee of the Secondary School Theatre Conference presented another outline for a course of study in drama at the
secondary level. Section headings of this outline are "Creating an
Attitude," "Exploring a Drama through Improvisation," "Widening Per-
spectives," and "Organizing the Play for Production."[26] The content to
be covered and the suggested activities of this outline are not unlike
those of the earlier AETA publication, but the emphasis on involvement
seems to have shifted from the instructor to the student. Further, a wider
range of activities designed to heighten creativity and appreciation of
the student for theatre and somewhat fewer activities for theatre skills
development are included.

It is obvious that leaders in the field and the representatives of professional speech and theatre organizations expect the teacher to be
informed in content, skilled in demonstration, and efficient in developing
the skills, concepts, and understanding of students in all speech experiences. The speech teacher is a teacher of students and has a body of
knowledge and processes to teach to them.

Certification and Reciprocity

Many practicing teachers and teachers in preparation ask enough
questions to warrant a discussion of certification and its types and
terms. The best text is a current certification code. The one which follows
(in Supplement 3) is typical of those in a majority of the states. Terms
may vary from state to state and requirements may change, but clarification of this code in contrast with or comparison to the state code of the
resident student will eliminate misunderstanding. Deletions have been

---

[24]American Educational Theatre Association, "A Suggested Outline for a Course
of Study in Dramatic Arts in the Secondary School," *American Educational Theatre
Journal,* 2:15-31 (March, 1950).

[25]*Ibid.*

[26]Secondary School Theatre Conference on the American Educational Theatre
Association, Inc., *Course of Study in Theatre Arts at the Secondary School Level,*
American Educational Theatre Association, Inc., 1963.

made of various certification areas to save space and focus upon the general and specific problems of speech certification.

With leadership at state and national levels, certification requirements have improved throughout most states during the past two decades. Establishment of minimum standards has increased *"reciprocal" certification* in many states. This is an aid to those responding to the residential mobility in our country. This reciprocity has come about because graduates of reputable college programs in one state meet the requirements of another without excessive "bending of the rules" in interpreting scope or quality of individual courses and professional experience. The edited excerpts directly from the appropriate sections of Ohio law governing teacher certification follow in Supplement 3.

Supplement 3.

Sections of Ohio Law Governing Teacher Certification

1. Necessity for Certification

Section 3319.30. "No person shall receive any compensation for the performance of duties as teacher in any school supported wholly or in part by the State or by federal funds who has not obtained a certificate of qualification for the position as provided for by section 3319.22 of the Revised Code and which certificate shall further certify to the good moral character of the holder thereof. Any teacher so qualified may, at the discretion of the employing board of education, receive compensation for days on which he is excused by such board for the purpose of attending professional meetings, and the board may provide and pay the salary of a substitute teacher for such days."

2. Grades and Types of Certificates

Section 3319.22. "Teachers" certificates of Statewide validity shall be issued pursuant to sections 3319.22 to 3319.31, inclusive, of the Revised Code, or in accordance with standards, rules, and regulations authorized by law. The grades of certificates shall be designated as "temporary certificates," "provisional certificates," "professional certificates," and "permanent certificates." Each of such grades of certificates may be issued in each or any of the following types:

A. Kindergarten-primary, valid for teaching in kindergarten, first, second, and third grades;

B. Elementary, valid for teaching in grades one to eight, inclusive;

C. High school, valid for teaching the subjects named in such certificate in grades seven to twelve, inclusive;

D. Special, valid for teaching any subject named in such certificate in all grades of the elementary and high schools, or in such other special fields as are included in public school curricula;

E. Elementary principal, valid for teaching or supervision in the elementary schools;

F. High school principal, valid for teaching the subjects named in such certificate or for supervision in junior or senior high schools;

G. Supervisor, valid for supervising and teaching subjects named in such certificate in elementary, special, or high school fields;

H. Superintendent, valid for teaching the subjects named in such certificate, for supervising in elementary and high schools, or for administrative duties in a school system;

I. Vocational, valid for teaching and supervising vocational agriculture, vocational distributive education, vocational home economics, or vocational trades and industries as named in such certificate;

J. Assistant superintendent, valid for supervising in elementary and high schools, or for administrative duties in the school system;

K. Pupil-personnel workers, valid for the conduct of all home-school-community relations incident to the adjustment of pupils to the facilities available for their education.

L. Executive head, valid for teaching the subjects named in such certificates and for supervision and administration in a local school district.

M. Educational administrative specialists, valid for those special areas of educational administration in a school system, other than superintendent, assistant superintendent, executive head, supervisor, or principal, as are specified and defined in such certificate.

3. Standards for Teacher Education and Certification

Section 3319.23. "The State Board of Education shall establish standards and courses of study for the preparation of teachers, shall provide for the inspection of institutions desiring to prepare teachers, shall approve such institutions as maintain satisfactory training procedure, and shall properly certificate the graduates of such approved courses and institutions.

The standards and courses of study for the preparation of teachers together with the standards, rules, and regulations set for each grade and type of certificate and for the renewal and conversion thereof shall be adopted and published by the Board in accordance with Chapter 119., of the Revised Code and no change therein shall be effective for at least one year from the first day of January next succeeding the publication of the said change."

4. Provisional Certificates

Section 3319.24. "Provisional certificates valid for four years shall be issued by the State Board of Education to those who have completed the respective courses prescribed therefor by the Board in an institution approved by it for the type of preparation required; provided that the requirements shall not be lower than graduation from a two-year course for types (A) and (B) as set forth in section 3319.22 of the Revised Code and graduation from a four-year course for all other types, except vocational trades and industries for which the training shall be as prescribed by the State Board and approved by the Board. The Board may renew for like period and for like type and validity any provisional certificate upon satisfactory evidence of the applicant's professional standing, and, if experienced, teaching success."

5. *Professional Certificates*

Section 3319.25. "The State Board of Education may convert any provisional certificate or renewal thereof into a professional certificate of like type valid for eight years, provided the applicant has met the standards of preparation, experience, and teaching success set by the Board for the conversion applied for."

6. *Permanent Certificates*

Section 3319.26. "The State Board of Education may convert any professional certificate or renewal thereof into a permanent certificate of like type provided the applicant has met the standards of preparation, experience, and teaching success set by the said Board for the conversion applied for. All permanent certificates shall be countersigned by the Superintendent of Public Instruction."

7. *Renewal of Certificates*

Section 3319.27. "The State Board of Education may renew for like period and validity, any provisional certificate issued prior to September 5, 1935 upon satisfactory evidence of the applicant's professional standing, and, if experienced, teaching success.

The Board also shall establish standards in accordance with which it may convert provisional and life certificates issued prior to September 5, 1935 into certificates of the various types provided for in section 3319.22 of the Revised Code. All such certificates issued prior to September 5, 1935 shall, without such conversion, retain their validity for the kinds of positions for which they were valid when issued."

8. *Temporary Certificates*

Section 3319.28. "The State Board of Education may establish standards, rules and regulations below those set for provisional certificates by which it may grant temporary certificates valid for one year of the types provided for by section 3319.22 of the Revised Code and by which it may renew the same for like periods. It may receive applications for such temporary certificates only upon the request of the superintendent of a city, county, or exempted village school district, a superintendent of diocesan schools, or the administrative head of any non-tax supported schools, and upon evidence of a scarcity of suitable teachers otherwise certified. Such certificate shall be valid for teaching only in the school or schools in the administrative jurisdiction of the official signing the request."

9. Revocation of Certificates

A. Section 3319.31. "If at any time the holder of a certificate is found intemperate, immoral, incompetent, negligent, or guilty of other conduct unbecoming to his position, the State Board of Education shall revoke the certificate. Such evidence must be presented in writing, of which the accused shall be notified, and no certificate shall be revoked without a personal hearing in accordance with sections 119.01 to 119.13, inclusive, of the Revised Code."

B. Section 3329.10. "Superintendent, supervisor, principal, or teacher not to act as sales agent for textbooks or supplies.

A superintendent, supervisor, principal, or teacher employed by any board of education shall not act as sales agent, either directly or indirectly, for any person, firm, or corporation whose school textbooks are filed with the Superintendent of Public Instruction, or for school apparatus or equipment of any kind for use in the public schools. A violation of this section shall work a forfeiture of their certificates to teach in the public schools.

A teacher employed by a board of education may not act as sales agent for any person, firm or corporation whose school text books have been filed with the Superintendent of Public Instruction, but it is not unlawful for such teacher to act, during his spare time, as sales agent for publisher of an encyclopedia or other general reference work in the sale to private individuals of such work, if such publisher has not filed with the Superintendent of Public Instruction any school text books which he proposes to furnish for the use of schools." 1949 OAG 4251.

10. Fees For Certificates

Section 3319.29. "Each application for any grade or type of certificate, renewal or duplicate thereof shall be accompanied by the fee of two dollars. Upon the acceptance of such applications the fees shall be paid into the State Treasury to the credit of the general fund."

11. Failure to File Certificate or Reports

Section 3319.36. "No clerk of a board of education shall draw a check for the payment of a teacher for services until the teacher files with him such reports as are required by the State Board of Education, by the school district board of education, and the superintendent of schools, and a written statement from the county, city, or exempted village superintendent of schools that the teacher has filed with him a legal teacher's certificate, or true copy thereof, to teach the subjects or grade taught, with the dates of its validity. The State Board of Education shall prescribe the record and administration for such filing of certificates in county school district.

Upon notice to the clerk of a board of education given by the State Board of Education or any superintendent of schools having jurisdiction that reports required of a teacher have not been made, the clerk shall withhold the salary of the teacher until the required reports are completed and furnished."

12. Suspension of Certificate.

Section 3319.15. "No teacher shall terminate his contract after the tenth day of July of any school year, or during the school year, prior to the termination of the annual session, without the consent of the board of education; and such teacher may terminate his contract at any other time by giving five days' written notice to the employing board. Upon complaint by the employing board to the State Board of Education and after investigation by it, the certificate of a teacher terminating his contract in any other manner than provided in this section may be suspended for not more than one year."

13. Qualifications of Superintendent

Section 3319.01 provides in part, "No person shall be appointed to the office of superintendent who is not possessed of a certificate of the superintendent type, as defined in section 3319.22 of the Revised Code, unless such person had been employed as a county, city, or exempted village superintendent prior to August 1, 1939."

14. Teachers in Non-Tax Supported Schools

Section 3301.071. "In the case of non-tax supported schools, standards for teacher certification prescribed under section 3301.071 of the Revised Code shall provide for certification without further educational requirements of any administrator, supervisor or teacher who has attended and received a bachelor's degree from a college or university accredited by a national or regional association in the United States, or who, at the discretion of the State Board of Education, has an equivalent degree from a foreign college or university of comparable standing."

Definitions

1. Additional Training: Credit earned by an applicant after the granting of the initial certificate.

For the renewal of certain certificates, or for the conversion of certain certificates into certificates of another grade, additional training is prescribed.

To be acceptable for these purposes additional training credit must meet the following criteria:

A. It shall have been completed since the granting of the certificate to be renewed or converted.

B. It shall be part of a planned program pertinent to the applicant's field of teaching.

C. It shall be applicable to an undergraduate or graduate degree in the institution offering the course.

D. It shall be earned in an approved institution.

2. Approved Institution: One which has been approved for the preparation of teachers by the State Board of Education.

3. Certificate: A license issued by the State indicating the grades or subjects in which the holder has satisfied the minimum requirements prerequisite to employment in the schools of Ohio.

4. Certificated Employee: A person employed in any one of the twelve categories enumerated in Section 3319.22 of the Revised Code, and who holds a certificate valid for service in that category.

5. Continuing Contract: An employment agreement according to which teachers hold their positions continuously without the necessity of periodic applications, election, and contracts. Commonly referred to as tenure. (Eligibility for, requires possession of a professional, permanent, or life certificate.)

6. Elementary School: Section 3301.16 R. C., defines an elementary school as "one in which instruction and training are given in accordance with sections 3301.07 and 3313.60 of the Revised Code and which offers such other subjects as may be approved by the State Board of Education. An elementary school may also include a preparatory kindergarten year. In districts wherein a junior high school is maintained, the elementary schools in that district may be considered to include only the work of the first six school years inclusive."

7. High School: Section 3301.16 R. C. defines a high school as "one of higher grade than an elementary school, in which instruction and training are given in accordance with sections 3301.07 and 3313.60 of the Revised Code and which also offers other subjects of study more advanced than those taught in the elementary schools and such other subjects as may be approved by the State Board of Education."

8. Junior High School: The lower part of a divided secondary school comprising usually grades 7, 8, and 9.

9. Executive Head: The administrative head of a school unit in a county school system.

10. Majors and Minors: Areas of concentration in programs of teacher education. (Majors and minors are no longer designated as such on certificates. The strength of preparation in semester hours of credit in each teaching field is designated.)

11. Pertinent Electives: Those related subjects which make a contribution that functions intimately and frequently in the life and work of the teacher.

12. Principal: The administrative head of an elementary or high school whose administrative and supervisory duties require more time than his teaching load.

13. Professional Courses: Those which deal primarily with developing an understanding of the learner, the learning process and the role of the school in society.

14. Quarter Hour: Equivalent to two-thirds of a semester hour.

15. Semester Hour: The unit, point, or credit granted for the satisfactory completion of a course requiring one one-hour classroom period a week for a semester. Since a semester is usually 18 weeks in length, a semester hour is equivalent to 18 clock hours.

16. Special Subjects: Those subject matter areas which are frequently taught in grades one to twelve, inclusive, and for which a higher degree of specialization is required than for teaching of the same subjects at a given grade level.

17. Substitute Teacher: A properly certificated teacher employed for service only in the absence of the regularly employed teacher.

18. Successful or Satisfactory Experience: A requirement for the renewal or conversion of a certificate. Such experience must be in, or related to, the field in which certification is sought and must be rated as satisfactory by administrators, supervisors, and associates in the school in which the applicant has been most recently employed.

19. Superintendent: The administrative head of a city, county, or exempted village school system.

20. Supervisor: Any school officer charged with the responsibility of working with teachers in the overseeing and improvement of instruction and instructional methods, or of working with pupils who are assigned to classes regularly taught by other teachers.

General Information

1. *How To Apply for Certificate*

A. Provisional

The Ohio law provides that provisional certificates be issued "to those who have completed the respective courses prescribed therefor by the State Board of Education in an institution approved by it for the type of preparation required."

Application forms for this grade of certificate are processed by the proper authorities of the institution in which the applicant has completed preparation for teaching.

B. Professional

Certificates in this grade are issued only to teachers who have had successful teaching experience in Ohio under the provisional certificate. Only those who are employed in the schools of Ohio at the time of application, and who have completed the requirements prescribed elsewhere in this bulletin are considered for this certificate. Application forms may be obtained from any school superintendent.

C. Permanent

The permanent certificate, valid for life, is issued only to those employed in the schools of Ohio, under a professional certificate at the time of application, and who have completed the requirements prescribed elsewhere in this bulletin. Application forms may be obtained from any school superintendent.

D. Temporary

The temporary certificate is one of sub-standard grade and is issued only when a suitable teacher holding one of the standard grade certificates cannot be found.

Application for this certificate is made by the proper employing school official.

2. *Regulations are Minimums:*

The regulations prescribed by the State Board of Education are minimums and, except where specifically stated, should not be construed as either optimum or maximum. They are designed to provide adequate professional preparation, a breadth of general education, and adequate basic preparation in teaching fields.

3. *Out-of-State Credentials:*

Applicants for certification in Ohio whose preparation for teaching has been completed in an institution in another state may be certificated in Ohio providing:

A. The pattern of training is substantially equivalent to the Ohio requirements.

B. The applicant holds a valid certificate, of the type applied for, from the state in which the training was completed.

C. The institution in which the training was completed is currently approved for teacher education by its own state department of education.

"A"
Teaching Certificates

I. PROVISIONAL CERTIFICATES

A. Elementary

. . .

B. Kindergarten-Primary

. . .

C. High School

The provisional high school certificate will be issued to the holder of a baccalaureate degree, conferred by an institution approved for the preparation of high school teachers, provided the pattern of training leading to the degree conforms to the following requirements:

The minimum professional preparation outlined in (1) below, and a minimum of 100 semester hours of credit, including the required general education course requirement; health and physical education, and the required courses in teaching fields in which certification is requested. The certificate issued will be limited to the teaching of those subjects listed in (3. a to x) below in which the applicant has completed the minimum requirements.

1. Professional Education.

The student shall complete the minimum preparation in professional education courses as indicated in each of the four areas below. Additional credit shall be completed in one or more of these areas to bring the total to 17 semester hours.

    a. Human Growth and Development .... 2 sem. hrs.
      (Prerequisite—General Psychology)
    b. The School in Relation to Society .... 2 sem. hrs.
    c. The Secondary Curriculum and Instructional Materials and Methods in the Major Teaching Areas 4 sem. hrs.
    d. Student Teaching and Related Laboratory Experience in Secondary Education .... 6 sem. hrs.

2. General Education ....30 sem. hrs.
    a. Science and/or Mathematics .... 6 sem. hrs.
    b. Social Studies .... 6 sem. hrs.
    c. Literature and/or Language .... 6 sem. hrs.
    d. Fine and/or Applied Arts
    e. Religion and/or Philosophy
      Credit in either or both (d) and (e) .... 6 sem. hrs.
    f. Excess credit in any or all areas above .... 6 sem. hrs.

Note:

(1) Required service courses in health education or physical education may not be included in the above 30 semester hours.

(2) The course requirements in any area above may be satisfied by either basic or integrated courses.

(3) Types of courses acceptable in group (d) include art, crafts, music, industrial arts, home economics, radio and dramatics.

(4) Types of courses acceptable in group (e) include logic, ethics, philosophy, religion, Bible.

(5) The student electing to satisfy the requirement in (c) with foreign language shall submit a minimum of six semester hours of credit in one language, unless he has two units of high school credit in the language elected.

(6) The Department of Education encourages institutions to exceed the above minimum requirements wherever possible, in the belief that approximately 45 semester hours of credit, in any pattern of teacher education should be devoted to the area of general education.

3. Teaching Fields
    (Grades 7-12 inclusive)
    a. Art ....24 sem. hrs.
    b. Biological Science ....15 sem. hrs.
    c. Bookkeeping .... 9 sem. hrs.
              . . .
    t. Science (comprehensive major) ....45 sem. hrs.
    u. Social Studies (comprehensive major) ....45 sem. hrs.
    v. Speech ....18 sem. hrs.
      (1) Speech fundamentals ....2-4 sem. hrs.
      (2) Electives well distributed over four of the five areas listed below ....14-16 sem. hrs.
      Interpretive reading
      Speech correction and voice science

                              Theatre: dramatic production, history
                                 and criticism
                              Public Address: debate, discussion
                                 and rhetorical theory
                              Radio and Television: history,
                                 programming administration and
                                 performance

                                        . . .

Any of the above subjects appearing on a certificate issued by the State of
Ohio is valid for teaching that subject or any subject listed as a required course
in that area, in grades 7 to 12, inclusive.

The above list is not all-inclusive, for example, subjects such as Economics,
Sociology, Geography, Physics, etc. will, upon the recommendation of the
institution, be added to a certificate providing the applicant has completed 15
semester hours of appropriate credit.

Teaching areas are not designated as majors or minors. The certificate will,
however, indicate in semester hours the strength of preparation.

To facilitate placement, the applicant is advised to prepare for certification
in at least two of the above areas, including one of the comprehensive majors.
Those who do not include one of the comprehensive majors should elect a
logical combination of three teaching fields.

D. Dual Certification

Pattern of training leading to the baccalaureate degree in education and to
the provisional elementary and secondary or special certificates:

	Sem. Hrs.
1. Professional Requirements	34

The student shall complete a minimum of 34 semester
hours in professional courses distributed among the
following areas:

a. Understanding The Learner	6-9

Principles of Learning, Child Growth and Development, Educational Psychology

b. Teaching and The Learning Processes	12-15

General and Special Methods, including reading,
language, arts, and arithmetic evaluation, classroom
organization and control, instructional materials

c. Purposes of Education in American Democracy	3-6

Educational Aims; the School Curriculum

d. Student Teaching	8-12

Actual classroom teaching, under supervision, preferably in large blocks of time per day

2. General Requirements	60

The Student shall complete not less than 60 semester
hours of credit distributed among the following areas:

    a. Language Arts 12-18
English Composition, Literature, including 3 sem. hrs. of Children's Literature, Speech. Demonstrated competency in correct use of English

    b. Social Studies 18-24
World Civilizations, Government, Geography, Socio-economic Problems, United States History. A basic course in American Government or United States History must be included

    c. Science 8-12
Science in Everyday Living (Biological and Physical)

    d. Health and Physical Education 3-6
Personal and Community Health, Physical Development, Play and Games

    e. Music, Art and Crafts 6-9
Music Appreciation and Expression and Music Literature for Children. Art (Appreciation and Expression), Crafts

    f. Arithmetic 3-6
Functional Arithmetic. Demonstrated competency in elementary school arithmetic

3. Electives
Elective credits shall be limited to service courses in physical education and the courses required for the fields of teaching at the secondary level in which certification is requested.

E. Special Certificates

  1. Professional Education
(Same as C. 1 . . . except that student teaching and related laboratory experience shall be at both the elementary and secondary level)

  2. General Education
(Same as C. 2 . . .)

  3. Minimum Requirements in Areas of Specialization

    h. Speech ....40 sem. hrs.
Courses shall be distributed over each of the following areas, with at least one course in each area:
(1) Speech fundamentals
(2) Interpretive reading
(3) Speech correction and voice science
(4) Theatre; dramatic production, history, and criticism
(5) Public address: debate, discussion, and rhetorical theory

(6) Radio and television: history, programing, administration, and performance

Note: The above subjects may also be added to the provisional high school certificate.

II. PROFESSIONAL CERTIFICATES

C. High School

Any provisional high school certificate may be converted into an eight-year professional high school certificate upon evidence of:

1. Twenty-four months of successful teaching experience under the provisional certificate to be converted, and

2. The satisfactory completion of 18 semester hours of additional training credit. Such credit shall represent a purposeful pattern of teacher education and shall be taken in an institution approved for the training of teachers.

III. PERMANENT CERTIFICATES

C. High School

Any eight-year professional high school certificate may be converted into a permanent high school certificate upon evidence of:

1. Forty months of successful experience under the eight-year certificate to be converted, and

2. The completion of an appropriate master's degree or the equivalent. (By equivalent is meant 30 semester hours of graduate credit representing a purposeful pattern of teacher education.)

College Programs Leading to Preparation and Certification

Professional personnel representing teachers' schools are often critical of assigning teachers to speech classes without adequate preparation in speech. Teachers often complain about inadequate preparation for the realistic job description from required college classes. Everett[27] found that more than half the speech teachers in Ohio were graduates of small, private, or parochial colleges. His concern was to find out if these graduates were selected because of better preparation, or because they were more *available*. A review of the studies by Baker, Schoen, and McManus and Petrie[28] revealed many qualified and unqualified teachers in the field. The number of uncertified teachers causes us real concern when Baker reminds us that many teachers, certified to teach speech, are teaching in other subject areas. Some state institutions seemed to be shortchanging their graduates. Noting that *certificates are granted* to graduates *upon the recommendation of the institution of teacher preparation*, we wondered about the responsibility level of institutions and superintendents where uncertified teachers were assigned to teach speech

---

[27]Russell I. Everett, "Speech Education: Ohio College Programs and Certification" (Doctoral dissertation, The Ohio State University, 1967).

[28]*Op. cit.*

and where "certified" teachers lacked background in the areas specified by the law governing certification. A statement of the problems and the findings follows and should be compared to the standards of teacher preparation in other states.[29]

Job Description Responsibilities

Schoen performed a study of 305 Ohio high school speech teachers and found that basic speech was the most prevalent course offered in about 80 per cent of the schools. Next in frequency was basic drama, taught in approximately 20 per cent of the high schools.[30] The units most often incorporated into the basic speech course were, in order of popularity, speech fundamentals (95 per cent of the classes), public speaking (93 per cent), bodily action (85 per cent), oral interpretation (81), critical listening (78), debate-discussion (73), organization (68), parliamentary procedure (59), and drama (56). Those units most often included in the basic drama course were acting (in 88 per cent of the classes), history of the theatre (in 76 per cent), stagecraft and production (71), and dramatic literature (63). These findings are comparable to those of Knower in his 1948-49 study of speech education in Ohio schools.[31]

In terms of speech teacher activities, Schoen found that 92 per cent of the speech teachers were involved in activities other than classroom instruction and that the typical teacher was expected to present one or two plays per year. About one-third of the speech teachers were responsible for forensic or debate activities. The average number of hours spent weekly with speech-oriented activities was about seven.[32] The 92 per cent of speech teachers engaged in speech activities represents a 30 per cent increase over the percentage involved in speech activities as reported by the earlier Knower study.[33]

The academic responsibilities and activities of Ohio secondary school speech teachers appears to be comparable to those of high school teachers in other states. Alexander and Thomas in a 1960 study of the high school speech teacher in Michigan reported that 78 per cent of the speech teachers surveyed taught a course in public speaking and 23 per cent a course in dramatics. The researchers reported that the average teacher is responsible for two extracurricular speech activities in addition to his regular teaching load. Fifty-six per cent of the teachers are required to

---

[29]Harvil, *op. cit.*, a comprehensive diagnosis and comparison of Mississippi and Louisiana to Ohio and Michigan standards.
[30]Schoen, *op. cit.*, pp. 62-3.
[31]Knower, *op. cit.*, p. 33.
[32]Schoen, p. 57.
[33]Knower, p. 40.

engage in some form of student dramatic activity, 60 per cent are involved in forensic activities and 36 per cent in debate activities.[34]

From the foregoing studies we may conclude that the average secondary school speech teacher will teach courses in the fundamentals of speech, or public speaking or drama, and in over 60 per cent of the teaching positions he will be responsible for some form of dramatic activity.

College Speech Education Programs

Everett's study indicated that 39 colleges and universities in Ohio offered a program in speech education, leading to certification at the secondary level. Of the 33 offering a major in speech education, 31 (93.93 per cent) listed course requirements beyond a teaching methods

Speech Education Major Required Courses*

Total No. of Institutions Requiring	No. of Private Institutions Requiring	No. of State Institutions Requiring
Speech Methods (25)	Speech Methods (21)	Speech Methods (4)
Fundamentals of Speech (24)	Fundamentals of Speech (21)	Oral Interpretation (4)
Oral Interpretation (22)	Oral Interpretation (18)	Debate (4)
Debate (18)	Debate (14)	Discussion (4)
Public Address (15)	Public Address (12)	Fundamentals of Speech (3)
Theatre History (14)	Theatre History (11)	Public Address (3)
Play Production (14)	Play Production (11)	Theatre History (3)
Voice and Diction (12)		Play Production (3)
		Play Direction (3)
		Voice and Diction (3)
		Speech Production (3)
		Speech Disorders (3)
		Radio-TV Programming (3)
		Phonetics (2)
Mean Required Courses 7.93	6.96	14.50

*This table is based on a sampling from 32 private institutions and 7 state institutions.

---

[34]Fred Alexander and Thomas Gordon, "The High School Speech Teacher in Michigan," *The Speech Teacher,* 1:189-191 (September, 1960).

course. Seventy per cent of those offering a minor listed course requirements beyond a methods course. The table below shows the distribution of required courses on the basis of course frequency. They are further classified according to mean distribution by private or state institutions.

The next two tables summarize the extent (in percentages) to which the courses required for the majors and minors of each college meet

SAA and AETA Recommendations and State Requirements for Speech Education Major Programs

Insti-tution	SAA Areas	AETA Areas	Secondary Speech Course Areas	Secondary Drama Course Areas	Meets Certification Requirements	Rank
1	100.00	75.00	71.42	60.00	yes	3
2	80.00	25.00	57.14	20.00		
4	100.00	50.00	71.42	60.00	yes	10
5	80.00	75.00	71.42	80.00	yes	3
6	100.00	75.00	85.71	60.00	yes	1
7	100.00	50.00	71.42	40.00	yes	7
8	60.00	25.00	42.85	20.00		
11	100.00	50.00	71.42	60.00	yes	6
13	40.00	75.00	42.85	60.00		
14	80.00	00.00	71.42	00.00		
15	100.00	25.00	71.42	20.00	yes	11
16	100.00	25.00	57.14	60.00	yes	9
17	100.00	25.00	57.14	00.00	yes	13
18	100.00	50.00	57.14	40.00	yes	8
21	40.00	00.00	28.57	00.00		
22	80.00	25.00	42.85	20.00		
23	80.00	25.00	42.85	20.00		
24	80.00	100.00	28.57	100.00		
26	80.00	100.00	42.85	80.00		
27	80.00	00.00	42.85	00.00		
28	60.00	00.00	42.85	00.00		
29	80.00	00.00	28.57	00.00		
31	100.00	75.00	71.42	60.00	yes	3
32	60.00	25.00	28.57	20.00		
33	80.00	75.00	71.42	60.00	yes	5
34	60.00	25.00	28.57	20.00		
35	60.00	75.00	57.14	60.00		
36	60.00	50.00	42.85	40.00	yes	12
37	100.00	25.00	71.42	20.00		
38	40.00	50.00	28.57	40.00		
39	80.00	25.00	28.57	20.00		

(1) the recommendations of professional organizations (AETA and SAA), (2) the job description responsibilities of secondary school teachers, and (3) certification requirements of the state. Only thirteen colleges (of the 39) appeared to satisfy state certification requirements and yet all recommend that the state issue certificates to their graduates upon college authorization. It would appear that the colleges are as guilty of inadequate preparation as the superintendents are of improper assignment of uncertified teachers. Other states may need to make analysis of the extent to which their colleges meet the state standards, which are low enough as it is.

*SAA and AETA Recommendations and State Requirements
for Speech Education Minor Programs*

Insti-tution	SAA Areas	AETA Areas	Secondary Speech Course Areas	Secondary Drama Course Areas	Meets Certification Requirements	Rank
1	100.00	75.00	57.14	60.00	yes	2
3	80.00	25.00	42.85	20.00		
4	80.00	25.00	42.85	20.00		
5	80.00	50.00	71.42	40.00	yes	3
6	80.00	75.00	85.71	60.00	yes	1
8	60.00	00.00	28.57	20.00		
11	40.00	00.00	14.28	00.00		
12	80.00	50.00	42.85	40.00	yes	5
15	100.00	25.00	71.42	20.00	yes	4
17	80.00	25.00	42.85	20.00	yes	8
19	60.00	25.00	57.14	20.00		
20	40.00	25.00	42.85	20.00		
21	40.00	00.00	14.28	00.00		
25	80.00	25.00	57.14	20.00	yes	7
26	80.00	100.00	57.13	80.00		
27	40.00	00.00	14.28	00.00		
28	60.00	00.00	42.85	00.00		
30	20.00	75.00	14.28	60.00		
31	60.00	00.00	42.85	00.00		
32	80.00	25.00	85.71	20.00	yes	6
34	60.00	25.00	28.57	20.00		
36	60.00	25.00	57.14	20.00	yes	9

Pressures for Specialization

Periodically we find pressure from students and faculty to "strengthen" teacher preparation by requiring greater concentration in a single area of speech (in theatre, debate, etc.). Erickson's Midwest poll of institutions of teacher preparation indicated that the majority of those responsible for future teachers felt such preparation was neither in the best interest of the prospective teacher nor of the profession. Job description studies furnish ample evidence that few specialized positions exist. Moreover, these misguided specialists in their pursuit of excellence frequently exploit students. Too often the students needing the most help are screened out of projects (plays and debates), while those with talent already evident are exploited to enhance the reputation of the teacher. Most speech positions are less than full time, resulting in the speech teacher's teaching in a second field, most frequently English. It is difficult to imagine a teacher of speech who is well prepared in his own field but who does not have considerable academic knowledge in literature. Since communication is more than 70 per cent oral, one might assume that the speech teacher then has the prime responsibility for teaching appropriate English usage. With such a need for broad knowledge and preparation in a related field, the speech teacher should be conversant with the areas immediately adjacent to the field of speech.

We have noted the concern of the professional speech and theatre committees for adequate preparation. As recently as October, 1967 the Theatre and Drama Interest Group of SAA in joint action with the Teacher Training Project of AETA submitted the following resolution to its national convention:

Be it resolved that the Theatre and Drama Group of the Speech Association of America supports the general position taken by the Teacher Training Project of the American Educational Theatre Association in its attempt to gain minimum standards in the certification of teachers of speech in the specific areas in which they are to teach or direct extracurricular activities.

Further be it resolved that the group approves of the following statement of guidelines for certification of teachers of speech in the secondary schools recommended by the AETA Teacher Training Project.

I. A teacher should be certified in the field of speech before being assigned to classroom instruction in speech and to the direction of speech activities.

II. Speech is generally understood to include the classroom study of public speaking, oral interpretation, dramatics, debate and discussion, and radio and television, as well as the extracurricular directing of these events.

III. Since the field of "speech" is broad and includes several discrete subject areas, a teacher should not be assigned to teach courses or direct activities in which he is not specifically qualified.

IV. A teacher assigned to teach classes in drama, theatre, dramatic production, theatre arts, etc. should present educational qualifications of at least 15 semester hours in theatre courses, including courses in theatre history, acting, directing, and technical courses.

V. The extracurricular production of plays is an integral part of theatre training, and in many schools provides the students with their only experience with the theatre arts. Therefore, the direction of plays should be assigned only to a teacher who is qualified to teach theatre arts classes.[35]

While the above list would focus upon strengthening the preparation of teachers of drama, it seems equally important to strengthen preparation for the rest of the speech field. It seems that constant surveillance of college programs leading to certification is just as important as scrutiny of teacher assignment by school administrators. Students preparing to teach should be critical of programs leading to certification and ask that they be job-oriented.

Recommendations Regarding Certification

Certification requirements at national, regional, and state levels should be revised to suggest (*a*) that the minimal semester hour average for certification to teach at the secondary level be set at no less than thirty semester hours, (*b*) that specific course content rather than broad areas of study be designated in keeping with what the organization feels will provide the highest level of competency to teach the areas of concern at the secondary level, (*c*) that the areas of study included in the AETA *Course of Study in Theatre Arts at the Secondary Level* be used as a guide in determining what specific drama content is necessary to establish a background adequate to the teaching of these areas and the production of plays, (*d*) that frequent checks should be made by the state certification office to ascertain whether college graduates recommended for certification have fulfilled the requirements for state provisional certification to teach speech at the secondary level, and (*e*) that speech

---

[35]Submitted to the resolutions committee December, 1967 and printed in the *Newsletter* October, 1967.

education students should be required to have formal training in discussion and debate.

Having identified the areas of preparation and the need for academic background, we turn now to the problem of helping students master those skills, processes, and concepts intended to improve their ability to communicate. This takes us from the problem of acquiring knowledge to the classroom and the process of teaching.

CLASSROOM MOTIVATION AND MANAGEMENT

Classroom management is a key to successful teaching. Much of the successful management is a direct result of good communication and organization. One of the first concepts to be established is that the teacher is a communicator and is responsible for planning the instructional activities and the arrangement of the room. Many unsuccessful teaching periods can be avoided through clarification of objectives, clearly stated goals, and an understanding of the types of behavior acceptable. Speech teachers, trained in communication, should be highly efficient in the use of these methods leading to teaching excellence. If properly prepared in audience analysis, they should be proficient at anticipating student behavior and thus should plan instruction with the student audience as the center of the lesson plan.

Eliminating barriers to communication should be one of the first considerations of the teacher. Seating arrangements can hinder instruction and hold back student projects. As the leader, the teacher should establish the right to maintain a climate for instruction and learning. All decisions regarding classroom climate should be made in terms of educational objectives. The teacher then becomes a moderator rather than a dictator, acting in terms of the welfare of other students when dealing with misbehavior. One of the marks of the professional teacher is the constant analysis of the "workability" of the teaching laboratory. Experimentation can be an excellent tool for making new arrangements of personnel and furniture to improve a project. It may quietly eliminate barriers to instruction at the same time.

MOTIVATION

Motivation is also a key to successful teaching. Research in motivation has been the focus of many scholars in speech for the past forty years. It is unfortunate that this focus has been on the motivation of audiences without the awareness that a classroom of students is an audience. Let us apply a landmark contribution to speech, Alan H. Monroe's "Motivated

Sequence,[36] to the process of teaching. Monroe stresses the sequential order of (*a*) gaining attention, (*b*) establishing a need, (*c*) providing satisfaction, (*d*) providing visualization, and (*e*) requesting action. Utilize this sequence in the teacher's planning guide below. Such a sequence might be used in making an assignment.

A Teacher's Planning Guide

I. In selecting the experiences of learning to be used within the classroom the teacher must determine those activities he will use as a teacher to

A. Gain and retain *attention*.
   In order to accomplish this goal the teacher must recognize the student goals, interests, and wishes which are in competition for class attention: time of day, previous activities, classes, inactivity or over-activity, reason for being in class, etc.

B. Establish a *need* based upon the needs of the student for the learning. Long range goals are not as effective as immediate reinforcement needs.

C. Provide *satisfaction* for the necessary student investment.

D. Provide visualization of the skill, concept, or behavior in terms that the student can understand.

E. Provide for learning experience in terms of *student action*.

II. Listed below are a number of teaching techniques which can be creative and effective if they are applied with regard to student ability and age, and if the time involvement is sufficient to be effective but not so long that it becomes a device for avoiding other learning. Small children have an attention span of five to ten minutes. Pupils in the lower grades of elementary schools have an attention span of ten to twenty minutes. By junior high students still must have a change of activity in a class lasting 40 minutes. This change provides a balance between physical and mental activity.

Questioning
Using the chalkboard
Pictures
Speech activities
  panels
  debates
  reports
  courts
  dramatizations
    creative dramatics
    productions
  story-telling
  demonstrations
  speeches
  knowledge contests
  socio-drama
  role-playing

Open textbook lessons
Globes and maps
  commercial
  student-created or teacher-created
Committee planning and projects
  films, film strips, slides
  tape recordings, phonographs
  diagrams, charts, dioramas
  flannel boards, bulletin boards
  field trips
  magazines
    pictures and stories
  newspapers
    test for authenticity
  photography
    distortion and selection

---

[36]Alan H. Monroe, *Principles and Types of Speech* (Glenview, Ill.: Scott, Foresman and Company, 1955), Chap. 16.

Supervision

Supervisors assume that the certified teacher is prepared in terms of the subject matter and then focus upon the instructional presentations and the learning taking place. They are particularly concerned about student involvement and thinking, teacher flexibility and adaptability under student questioning, and the ability of the teacher to turn problems back to the student for clarification and solution. If excellent questions are left undeveloped or sidetracked, student concern may develop. Routine details directly related to attendance, teaching load, and records are noticed only when accompanied by limited instructional efficiency.

The evaluation form which follows is the outgrowth of a lesson plan and a series of anecdotal comments regarding the efficiency (or lack of efficiency) of student teachers over an extended period. It may be used by a visiting supervisor as well as a practicing teacher. Self-evaluation is one of the best forms of improvement. Awareness of highly effective techniques as well as inefficient procedures may be speeded up by comparing teacher rating given by the teacher himself with that of the supervisor. The supervisor acts as a video-tape or visiting camera, functioning much the same way as the speech teacher functions with student speakers.

Objectives. In the upper left-hand corner of the form we find a number of objectives to be checked off. The objective for the day might be (*a*) acquiring new knowledge, (*b*) developing an interest great enough to begin study of a unit, or (*c*) drill (application) of knowledge already acquired. More specific objectives might be checked for the entire class, or for certain students. Secondary goals might be checked, such as habitual behavior (projection, enunciation, placement, or inflection). Objectives chosen for the day, or for an entire unit, should be precise and clear to the teacher. A supervisor, with no knowledge of the subject, should be able to identify the objectives by watching the activities and listening to the teacher-student discussions. If such objectives are not clear to a trained observer, it would be obvious that the *reason for activity* is not clear to most of the students.

Materials and Activities. Still working on the left side of the form, the visiting supervisor should be able to discover the *objectives* (the conceptual elements selected for development) the *materials* selected and their relevance to the objectives, and the *activities* for the students and teacher which result in the teaching methods. Activities should also have direct relevance to the objectives to be gained. Utilization of teaching devices (charts, films, make-up materials, forms of outlining, or even demonstrations of various types of discussion) should be relevant to conceptual or behavioral goals. By the end of any given lesson (or series of lessons) the supervisor, teacher, and student should be able to

Objectives of the day:

Knowledge

Interests

Attitudes

Use of knowledge (drill)

Use of knowledge (new application)

Organization of knowledge

Developing sources (library)

Unit ideas taught

Assignment given

Assignment checked or called for

Teacher's evaluation of the day's achievements (List good and bad points on the back of the form.)

Habits:

Appreciations	Drill
Ideals	Projection
Creative expression	Enunciation
Skill	Voice placement
Adjustment to audience	Characterization
Listening	Inflection
Critical thinking	Vitality & variety

Materials used   Method of instruction
                        (list devices)

Method of evaluation

_____ Test _____ Rating sheets

_____ Questions _____ Other

Classroom study period

From _____ to _____

Student teacher _____

Hour _____ Date _____

Class started quickly, enthusiastically?
no 1 2 3 4 5 6 7 8 9 10 yes

Expected assignment clear to students?
no 1 2 3 4 5 6 7 8 9 10 yes

Assignment conducive to achievement of aims?
no 1 2 3 4 5 6 7 8 9 10 yes

Examples adapted to students' daily interests?
no 1 2 3 4 5 6 7 8 9 10 yes

Teacher's voice alive, varied, interesting?
no 1 2 3 4 5 6 7 8 9 10 yes

All students involved in classroom project?
no 1 2 3 4 5 6 7 8 9 10 yes

Did materials contribute logically to aims?
no 1 2 3 4 5 6 7 8 9 10 yes

Were methods varied to maintain interests?
no 1 2 3 4 5 6 7 8 9 10 yes

Adequate help for individuals in need?
no 1 2 3 4 5 6 7 8 9 10 yes

Evidence of adequate teacher background?
no 1 2 3 4 5 6 7 8 9 10 yes

Evidence of skill in diagnosis of problems?
no 1 2 3 4 5 6 7 8 9 10 yes

Skill in demonstration to aid students?
no 1 2 3 4 5 6 7 8 9 10 yes

Were problems turned back to student thinking?
no 1 2 3 4 5 6 7 8 9 10 yes

Skill in thought-provoking questions.
no 1 2 3 4 5 6 7 8 9 10 yes

Handling of stage fright skillful, tactful?
no 1 2 3 4 5 6 7 8 9 10 yes

Culmination clear and orderly?
no 1 2 3 4 5 6 7 8 9 10 yes

verbalize the ideas gained, the skills developed, and the appreciations established. A lesson may be confined to one idea or skill or may develop several ideas or skills. Much concomitant learning may be developed at the same time.

Assignments. Giving and calling for assignments is often the greatest strength or weakness of many teachers. First, assignments should not be given which are beyond the capability of the student. *Is the material available in the room, library, home, or community?* Many classrooms do not have classroom library facilities. Teachers should not make a school or community library assignment without first checking on the specific availability of the specific material in quantity. It is impossible for sixty students to use one copy of dramatic literature, or one debate handbook within three or even four days. The reading time, organization time, and available study time of each student must be considered.

Open hours of the library are also crucial. When libraries close an hour after school, or scheduled after-school rehearsals (for speech, music, athletics, etc.) fill the available library time, the teacher may have guaranteed failure on an assigned library project by failing to acknowledge *legitimate competition.* The solution in such a case is to acquire the quantity of needed material and provide classroom study time. Again we measure the assignment against the objective. If acquisition of materials relevant to the objective is important, the assignment should provide realistic means for a successful solution. Too often we find the librarian harassed because of a limited supply of books needed by several classes. It may be that students in various classes might be programmed to the materials on different weeks. Few libraries are designed to handle a class of thirty students at a time without warning. School and public libraries generally have limited desk help and limited space around shelving or check-out areas. Often library-oriented assignments are most successful when a review of library facilities and techniques is made and students are programmed into the library a few at a time, by a prior appointment with library personnel. Where quantity is needed, the teacher may well arrange to have such materials deposited well ahead of the assignment.

An assignment should specify what is expected and when it is due. The process for culminating the assignment is a worthy activity for clarification. *The teacher might well ask students to repeat the assignment and the process by which they will carry out the presentation* (individually and collectively). Experienced teachers are not dismayed when this procedure must be repeated several times, orally and in writing. Speech teachers may learn something about the process of communication in this effort. The problem cannot be blamed upon the listening students until the teacher can be sure they have received the message as it was intended to be transmitted. Making the assignment relevant to the established objectives of the course may also improve motivation and better guarantee completion of assignments.

Classroom Procedures

On the right side of the form is a linear rating scale which can be used independently of the lesson form. Some of the items are clustered and represent the various dimensions of a successful class. Assignments and materials have been discussed above, but some of these combine into clusters of three or four relationships which make the difference between a highly successful class and a guaranteed failure.

Getting the class started immediately (with the bell) avoids the loss of the entire class period, problems arising from inefficient roll calls, re-arrangement of the laboratory, or delay while answering the questions of students clustered around the desk. One soon learns that roll call takes four or five times longer if students are asked to explain the absence of their classmates. Let him explain it when he arrives. Empty seats can be marked while class is in session. Get the students working and then expedite rolls and money changing. Teachers teach students to waste time and students soon find they can plan on time-consuming sessions.

Involvement.   Involve all students when questions begin. Questions raised by a few are problems of many. By establishing planned question periods the teacher can eliminate unnecessary repetition. Further, students not involved will mentally check out and will be much more difficult to bring into the class activity later. When *problems are turned back to all the students* for thinking and their solutions are expected, when a teacher is skilled in involving students with thought-provoking questions, students become excited about learning. Speech teachers should know the value of establishing the empathy of active listening and should be familiar with the many processes of establishing it. It is not the sole responsibility of the student to "engage the action." When students remain out of the action it is the responsibility of the "professional" in the room to establish communication. Students may often share in analysis and criticism periods. They easily identify artificial criticism periods in which they are led into evaluation and then their opinions are discarded for teacher summaries. Students are very capable of finding the relevancy of materials, assignments, and ideas to their own interests and needs.

A professional teacher must be capable of self-evaluation. The back of the form is used to describe those parts of the teaching day which were successful (or unsuccessful) and why. Materials and processes may then be redesigned to avoid repetitions of methods which resulted in low motivation, lack of preparation, or lack of necessary quantities of materials. For several days a teacher may know that something is not working but may be unable to identify the cause. After three or four days of verbal photographs the causes become apparent. It is equally important to identify the techniques and materials which proved successful and plan to repeat them.

COMMUNICATION AND INTERACTION ANALYSIS

Teaching is an act of communication concerned with the total effectiveness of teacher-to-student and student-to-student communication. This point is so obvious that it seems incredible that speech teachers do not apply communication theory and empathy to the daily act of communication in the classroom. We turn to recent studies in other disciplines to find models for our own field.[37] These studies range from quantitative classification techniques to process and qualitative models. Flanders' *Categories for Interaction Analysis* is widely used and is discussed in relationship to many other models for improving learning. The purpose of interaction analysis is to gain a visual process chart, or quantitative photograph, of the type of talking going on and who is doing it. The type or quality of the talk is also desired. We may find that the teacher talks for thirty minutes during a forty-five minute period and that the other fifteen minutes are taken up by two students. The teacher may believe that many students were involved and may not be aware that she talked for more than a few moments. A quantitative photo focuses upon the need to involve students. Students with good questions might have provided much of the teacher's talk. They might even be critically involved in providing the questions.

Frymier's types of structure[38] illustrate many obvious teacher-student relationships and furnish interesting flow charts to focus upon the problem. These flow charts have been reproduced below as they apply to speech situations. We might recognize ourselves and our past teachers where such patterns were used, not always in productive ways. Selecting a proper structure implies that the type of project dictates structure.

---

[37]John P. DeCecco, *The Psychology of Learning and Instruction* (Englewood Cliffs, N.J.: Prentice-Hall, Inc., 1968), Chapter 1.

[38]Jack R. Frymier, *The Nature of Educational Method* (Columbus, Ohio: Charles E. Merrill Publishing Company, 1965), Chap. 6, pp. 156-192.

Single and Multi-Source Communication Patterns Illustrated

Figs. 7 and 8 are self-explanatory. The teacher may dominate all communication or may cause students to talk with each other and with the teacher. Single-source implies the teacher as a dispenser of informa-

Figure 7. Single-Source Communication Pattern

Figure 8. Multi-Source Communication Pattern

tion and the students as receivers. In this system there is even a lack of questioning in order to clarify the information given. With multi-source the assumption is made that all members of the class, including the teacher, may make valuable contributions.

Most of us have seen the *manipulative structure* (Fig. 9) used in play rehearsals where the director has pre-blocked all action and has made precise decisions on line interpretation. We often overlook the fact that his classes reveal the same attitude toward student thought and ability. A self-appointed god is seldom wrong. His methods may be so subtle that the subjects of his benevolent despotism believe he is teaching them to think and create.

Figure 9. Manipulative Structure

Directive structure (Fig. 10) is similar to the manipulative structure but is more open. The director talks and gives direction, and the class members are not led to believe they are making decisions. Goals are clearly set and the students expect to reach them. If guidance is needed they may question and will be told the routes to select. The teacher using this method may offer a selection of routes or solutions from which they may choose. Speech students may be told to use an inductive approach on the next round of speeches. This procedure can be much more valuable than allowing complete freedom.

In *persuasive structure* (Fig. 11) the "teacher moves from an unearned authority toward one of earned authority" by becoming one of the group. This new position is based upon respect for the teacher's knowledge, leadership, or talent. It may be better for teachers unable to attain or maintain leadership through this earned respect to keep some aesthetic

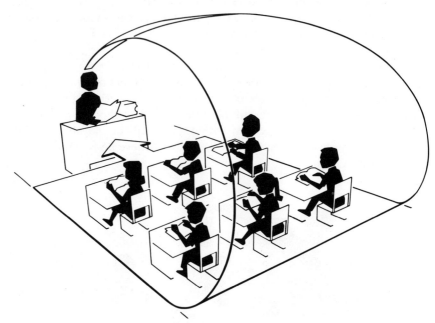

Figure 10. Directive Structure

Figure 11. Persuasive Structure

distance. Primarily this type of teacher convinces students that they have worthy ideas and are capable of thinking out solutions. Such a teacher is creative in that he *assumes multiple solutions to complex problems* and "helps" students select appropriate solutions involving time, place, and personnel. Such a teacher helps the student arrive at the appropriate outline for his speech, be it problem solution (inductive or deductive), chronological, or logical sentence. He does not manipulate a solution.

The *discussive structure* (Fig. 12) involves the pooling of ideas from the total group. It is the most difficult to achieve because all members of a group may not be willing to communicate openly. Many remain silent or echo the opinions of others. Out of class they may voice opinions to be carried back by more vocal members. Discussive structure differs from recitation in that the teacher gives consideration to ideas expressed rather than repeating them for reinforcement. Frymier identifies two types of discussion: *exploratory* and *decisive*. The first is based upon understanding by considering points of view while the latter is decision-

Figure 12. Discussive Structure

making with a purpose to convince. The speech teacher may choose to review various purposes of group discussion and particularly the problem solution types in evaluating this classification. Education books often refer to "buzz" sessions as discussion. For the purpose of gaining group rapport or helping one to *belong,* it may be called discussion but more often is merely congenial conversation over a chosen problem. The *exploratory discussion structure* as a teaching device would concentrate upon the first three stages of problem-solution discussion. The *decisive discussion structure* would begin with the selection of the "best solution" and would prove its workable desirability. In either case the chart shows the teacher acting as a traffic control agent to involve all students in the process. If the teacher abdicates this role the *advocates* take over and may practice mass *manipulation* or *directive* structures.

Supportive structure (Fig. 13) is identified by the teacher's role as a guide and a questioner, helping students map their own intellectual trips. Care must be taken to keep from asking questions which become *manipulative* or *directive.* This is the role of the director of creative dramatics in contrast to the "super-marionette" director of formal theatre. Some directors of formal theatre can effectively use this technique to blend the creative talent of the total production team and actors into a work of art. In this role the teacher is the developer of the talents of

Figure 13. Supportive Structure

others. In the manipulative or directive structure he is the artist using actors, lights, and scenery as materials to be arranged into artistic patterns.

The *non-directive structure* (Fig. 14) "truly lets students do as they please." This method does not furnish the mature assistance of the *supportive structure* and in Frymier's opinion has no place in an educational institution. The authors of this book soundly support this opinion. Any group wishing a new experience at a reasonable investment of time or energy should hire a guide who is acquainted with the type of terrain to be travelled. He may offer choices or explain the dangers and allow a consensus, but he has failed as a teacher-guide if he merely goes along to gather up the rubbish and the bodies as they fall.

Figure 14. Non-Directive Structure

Graded Interaction

Interaction charts can do more than classify. They may be used to plan constructive teaching. Because the Flanders system demands a measurement of stipulated time intervals it is not practical in speech classes where speeches may be several minutes in length or in situations

Teacher-Student Interaction Analysis[39]

1. Make a seating chart of the class showing the special arrangement. (See sample.)
2. The legend may vary according to the needs of the particular teaching discipline (language, social science, literature, etc.). (See sample.)
3. Record each question and response between student and teacher. Note the quantity for each student.
4. A question with no response may be cancelled (/). This system allows (*a*) a record of volume response, (*b*) a graded response to fit student ability, (*c*) an analysis for future challenge, and (*d*) possible problems for motivation and discipline. It may be confined to any period of active interaction.

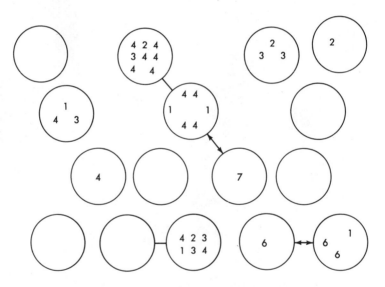

Figure 15. Teacher-Student Interaction Analysis

Legend:
1. Affirm or negate (yes or no response).
2. Describe.
3. Repeat content (of previous response).
4. Analysis.
5. Read aloud.
6. Negative response to student interaction.
7. Positive response to student interaction.

[39]Designed by George L. Lewis, 1968.

of extended quiet study. Interaction deals with actual interrelationships of student-to-student and student-to-teacher. All students are not equally verbal, so the need to grade response becomes important. The following student-teacher interaction analysis was developed for use in foreign language classes where students of wide aptitude were classed together. The flexibility of its use and the grading of responses are two of its main values. The recorder first prepares a seating chart. Any arrangement of student seating is permissible. Arrows may be used to show the direction of a comment from one student to another or from the teacher to a student. Like the Flanders chart each number is given a value based upon the type of response expected. For the moment let us use the following legend for each type of response.

1. Affirmation or negation (yes or no).
2. Read content from printed page.
3. Repeat content in your own words.
4. Describe the action or process which the script, or copy, requires.
5. What does this mean (analysis)?
6. Negative reaction (objects to participation).

As questions are directed to various class members, a number classifying the expected response is placed in the circle representing the student called. A diagonal line might be used to indicate no response. After a class period we may find that four students have fielded most of the questions and one third of the others were never called upon. This is quantitative and valuable, but the greatest value is found in analysis of types of response. Student *A* may not be able to handle a question demanding analysis or description, while Student *B* is wasting time dealing with a question requiring a yes or a no. By deliberate process Student *A* may be promoted from yes-no questions to reading content from the book. Later he may be able to repeat it in his own words. With patience and good instruction he may be able to develop abilities to analyze. In many classes we have students who cannot rise to questions demanding analysis but who may still profit from instruction at graded levels within their reach. The chart below is an actual reproduction of a twenty-minute interaction with the teacher using the *discussive structure* to talk about a piece of literature.

Effective Questioning

A teacher's efficiency frequently depends upon the skilled use of questions. The teacher also tries to involve students in asking questions as well as giving answers. Eventually he may become the class moderator, with students searching for answers by asking their own questions. Questions are of these several types:

1. situation questions
2. general questions
3. thought questions
4. summary questions
5. follow-up questions
6. questions to encourage observation
7. questions about sources of information

A few sample questions from each of the above types, taken from classroom situations, are listed below. The topic under discussion is either inherent in the question or else is furnished in parentheses.

1. Situation questions

Suppose you owned and operated a radio station and needed a new advertising salesman. Why would you (or would you not) choose Willy Loman? How about a long-haired hippy with a beard?

Assume you are Thespis. Describe the theatre you must work in and the problems you must solve to be heard.

Place yourself in the time of Ibsen. (1) Would you leave your husband for the same reasons Nora did? Why? What were her reasons? (2) How would you react as the wife of Alving, if he were alive today? (3) In escaping from reality we often find ourselves in "boygs," attached to unpleasant situations and people. Describe some of the "boygs" and "pigs" which result from present-day escape. (*Peer Gynt*)

Scientific knowledge taught in the school and used in the speech assignments of students is undermining religious teachings in your family. How will you react in relation to your younger brothers and sisters? In terms of your own beliefs? These teachings may defeat you at the polls in the next election because you depend upon "fundamentalist voters." How would you relate to these teachers? (*Inherit the Wind*)

Assume you are the head administrator of a large high school or college. You believe in free speech, but protest groups hold meetings at the same time and in facilities previously scheduled by others. How would you provide for various groups to meet and speak freely without interruption?

2. General questions

How, and to what degree, has drama influenced twentieth century religion?

How has Reuben's lack of affection affected his home life and his family? (*Dark at the Top of the Stairs*)

What are some of the important unifying themes in *Hamlet*?

How does *The Crucible* reflect the deep religious culture of the Puritans? What was man's relationship to the Church and to God under this group?

In what way has high school debating influenced the social and economic life of modern American citizens?

3. Thought questions

Did justice triumph in *The Visit* or *Winterset*? Why? Why not?

Why do you think Ionesco wrote the scene in *The Bald Soprano* in which Mr. and Mrs. Martin can't remember where they've met?

What is the meaning of the many references to "moon" in *Our Town*?

In what ways can a man protest a law he feels is unjust? Must he be willing to risk arrest and imprisonment? What is the impact upon those whose rights are lost by having the law broken?

Students frequently denounce the elected student council as being non-representative. In what ways are the non-elected leaders of small groups representative?

4. Summary questions

"It is better to have loved and lost than never to have loved at all."—Alfred Lord Tennyson.

We have studied several poets during the past few weeks. Which of them would have agreed with this statement?

We have read several selections where lovers have overcome many types of barriers. Name some of them and illustrate the types. How do such barriers enrich the story and develop characters? Do barriers help us?

"The most dangerous foe to truth and freedom in our midst is the compact majority. Yes, it's the confounded, compact, liberal majority."

How can this comment from *Enemy of the People* describe the conditions in America today?

How does the following promise of Mrs. Antrobus (*Skin of Our Teeth*) reflect the theme of the play? "We can suffer whatever's necessary; only give us back that promise."

5. Follow-up questions

John has said that one characteristic of a box set is three walls showing the interior. What other characteristics does a box set have?

That is an excellent point. How does it compare with the comment Sara made a moment ago?

You have commented upon the power and viciousness of the professor's wife in *Who Is Afraid of Virginia Woolf?* How does she compare with Mrs. Alving (*Ghosts*) or Hedda Gabler in the play of that name? Why was Mrs. Alving unusual for a nineteenth-century woman?

That is a very important point in the discussion. What other contentions do we have that can be used to support this issue?

6. Questions to encourage observation

The affirmative have stated that pollution is caused by drainage from cesspools and inadequate sewage systems. What types of pollution do you see in streams near your community which are caused by drainage from parking lots? From industrial waste?

How do Hamlet's costumes and their color affect his character? How do they contrast him with the scenery and the other actors?

How many levels and rooms are included in the set for *Death of a Salesman*? How are the levels used to help indicate the small crowded attic in *The Diary of Anne Frank*?

How many sets are needed in *Our Town*? What elements are used to establish a "set"? How were scene changes carried out?

In what ways are the audience members involved directly in *Inherit the Wind*?

7. Questions about sources of information

What sources can you use to help you make drawings for a flat? Where can we purchase new spot lights for the beam position? Where can we borrow the props we need?

What is the most reliable source of information regarding recent legislation on the topic? How can we find out if the source is reliable?

Statements representing the American Medical Association's point of view regarding medical legislation will generally have what bias?

Compare Mayor Daley's statements about Chicago security with those of the news media. How do you determine the authenticity of each report? In what ways does the camera act as a censor? What happened before the camera was turned on and focused? What action was left out? Were there any quiet, hard-working efforts at the convention? Where do we find evidence of it?

Some General Advice on Questioning

1) Avoid yes-no questions. This type of question contributes considerable talk with a minimum of reaction from the student. He may guess at the answer. This is a true-false type of evaluation instrument.

2) Avoid asking two questions at a time. The student may attempt to answer the second before the first, or even attempt to answer both at the same time.

3) General questions should be precise. They should avoid the "what do you think?" phrase since any response to this question is acceptable.

4) Care must be taken to avoid clues in the question.

5) Student questions may best be turned to other students for reaction. The teacher should not become the source of all knowledge. Don't be afraid to admit you don't know the answer.

6) Answer irrelevant questions quickly and then return to the topic, or postpone the question until a time when it is relevant, or arrange to deal with the question after class. If the question is "hot" and worthwhile you might depart from the lesson, but arrange specifically to return to the lesson. You may need to capsulize in order to regain needed time.

7) During inquiry periods be willing to wait for answers. During drill the rapid fire technique helps to "package" the review material.

8) Relate question examples to personal interests and experiences.

9) Repeat questions in several forms and in graded difficulty to make inclusion of slower students possible. Don't waste the time of superior students with simple or descriptive processes. On the other hand, don't expect slow students to react well to questions demanding analysis.

Use Speech Principles to Teach

Logically, the speech-trained individual should use speech concepts in teaching. Let us consider a few of these concepts. *Start where the students are* and prepare them for what is to come. Substitute the word *audience* for the word *student* and the point should be clear. We insult an audience if we assume they know nothing and begin at primary levels. We may also begin at levels far beyond their sophistication and they will never gain an understanding. This applies equally to public address and to teaching. We may also frighten an audience or class of students by indicating the difficulty of some process or tool. Let us show them how much they already know and then teach the new concepts to be added.

Phonetics is an excellent example. College students enter the speech class terrified at the complexity of phonetics. If we begin with the consonants and utilize the motor kinesthetic method of placing the articulators in the position for the first consonant in the alphabet, they soon note that by lessening the tension the sound has two dimensions. These can be labeled *voiced* and *unvoiced*. Soon, within one class period, the students have helped to identify all but eight of the consonants in English and have classified them into voiced and unvoiced lists. They have also noted that some sounds have voiced and unvoiced pairing while others do not. With only eight new symbols to learn for other consonant sounds the burden is lessened and the students are already able to make rough transcriptions. Writing a few jokes on the board in phonetic transcription helps to drill the symbols already known.

Almost all the steps in writing a speech or preparing a play for production can be drawn from students and placed on the blackboard in a random "scattergram." Learning can then be developed as the processes are arranged in order and further refined. When students are shown how much they already know, when the learning lists and ordered processes seem to be their own, they are much more easily motivated and retain the information much longer.

TEACHING AND GROUP PROCESSES

Teaching processes improve with the realization that teaching-learning is a group process and that group dynamic theories apply to classroom management. The research in speech related to communication within groups is designed mostly for adults in industry and community programs. Much information related to school situations is also available. The following has been extrapolated from a pamphlet on teaching applications of research on group processes.[40]

What Research Says About Group Process

1. Group processes are the changes in the social unit (a number of individuals who interact or are interdependent
    a) in the *cognitive domain* (including addition in knowledge and development of intellectual skills),

---

[40]Louis M. Smith, "Group Processes in Elementary and Secondary Schools," *What Research Says to the Teacher*, No. 19 (Washington, D.C.: Dept. of Classroom Teachers, American Education Research Association of the National Education Association, 1959).

b) in the *psychomotor domain* (reading, writing, and laboratory skills), and

c) in the *affective domain* (attitude changes, beliefs, and mental health).

2. The classroom is affected by the larger social system and subgroups beyond the class. These alignments cannot be ignored. Individuals cannot leave groups and join others as readily as may be desired. The child cannot readily leave the classroom group but may realign within it with some limitations.

3. The sociometric test is a device for identification of group alignments and attitudes toward many things. Choices may be ranked. Some teachers may perceive these attitudes better than others, without use of tools.

a) Sociometric tests may be used to help in seating, grouping, and changing motivation.

b) Sociometric testing may be used to identify student acceptance or rejection by groups, and also individual isolation by personal anticipation or interpretation of group attitudes.

c) Sociometric tests operate in stages:

(1) charting of response in a series of ranking choices, and

(2) charting of individuals by placement in a "group" or in isolation. Lack of empathic response can be shown.

4. A student participates in contagion, conformity, and deviation as a part of subgroup processes where members of the subgroup make deliberate and direct attempts to influence him. The members soon increase or terminate interaction and comment upon response by rejection or tightening the group feeling following the challenge. Students with strong needs for friendliness are affected most by small group pressure.

5. The teacher in the classroom is the leader of the group in *initiating structure* and in *consideration*. Initiating structure refers to the clarity of his feeling for the group, his willingness to try new ideas, criticism of the work, the emphasis on deadlines and routine (fairness, consideration). It works best when the teacher is directive, takes action, initiates without destroying human relations, makes membership in the group pleasant, maintains equality among members, is willing to make "justifiable changes," and protects the personal welfare of the members. Ability to routinize without worship of routine is crucial. Students learn best when the teacher initiates, has direction, does not waste time, but is capable of consideration. Initiation or consideration used separately result in ineffective classrooms.

The results of research on group process, activity, or experience curriculum indicate no basic differences in effectiveness from "traditional processes."

Application of Group Process Theory to Classroom Practice

I. The teacher needs to understand and recognize the various existing groups and may utilize sociometric devices to determine membership and degree of volume acceptance of various members to each other.

II. The teacher has, and should exercise, the prerogative to change groupings within the class in order to expedite learning.

    A. Student choices are not always most conducive to learning.

    B. Changes in grouping may be made frequently for the purposes of

        1. experimentation,

        2. maintaining attention, and

        3. improving motivation and creativity. Established groupings tend toward group conformity in thinking and problem solution.

        4. Group changes listed above may include seating, team membership, or any other desirable arrangement.

    C. Seating in a classroom should be flexible and should provide open aisles to allow movement of the teacher and students without disturbing other seated students. Chairs closely arranged encourage notes and talking which may be irrelevant to the classroom business. Classroom interaction can more readily be directed into interaction of student-to-student and student-to-teacher-to-student if the teacher establishes the total room as a base for questions, challenges, and responses. It is possible to identify and detour possible diversions in a constructive way if the teacher is at work among the students or even at the back of the room. A movement to a position behind the desk can then establish a "directive, authoritative position." Such flexible seating as a working basis then is more conducive to individual projects, assistance in specific instructional needs, and in discipline.

III. By identifying individual groups and analyzing possible causes of the groups, the teacher may vary groupings and even plan projects to create new groupings in order to achieve (*a*) the goals of the school, (*b*) the objectives of the specific course, (*c*) the development of leadership within the student groups, (*d*) the protection of "creative" isolation, and (*e*) assistance for projects needing such individual effort.

IV. The principles of group dynamics show that:

    A. The so-called buzz session is not group discussion but is a tool to establish a sense of belonging, allowing everyone the right to be heard, or to develop "status equality."

    B. Group discussion is a precise tool for action analysis or problem solution. It is designed as a scientific approach to group problem-solving as in policy-making, learning, or resolving value conflicts. As a tool in the classroom or community, it is time consuming, often necessitating long recesses for committee research and analysis of information. It follows the famous Dewey format for problem solution:

1. awareness of a problem,
2. definition and analysis of the problem (including research and the history of its causes and the attempts at solution).
3. suggested solutions (Note the plural; single solutions generally short-circuit and result in a power failure with bigger problems.),
4. selection of the best solution through comparative simulation or debate, and
5. testing the solution for workability.

V. The responsibilities of the leader-participant in the classroom use of questions and moderation include these points:

   A. The teacher is the constant group leader and moderator. He is not desk-bound and may delegate leadership for a designated period. It is always necessary to retain the ability to recall the delegation and to maintain a climate for the thinking and involvement of the students.

   B. The development of a climate for "discussion-learning" depends on

     1. transferring responsibility for thinking to the students,

     2. developing a thinking leadership attitude in all the students,

     3. developing mechanisms for involving all the students in questions and discussion, grading expected responses according to abilities of the students,

     4. developing rapid drill periods as well as thought provoking delayed solution problems needing research and analysis,

     5. identifying minority domination, over-development of single arguments, and lagging discussion,

     6. utilizing the constructive, limited complement for partial or potential answers in contrast to a negative response to wrong answers which limits the discussion and breaks the climate of exploration and discussion, and

     7. emphasizing that all studies of creativity recognize the existence of multi-solutions to most complex problems, and that the best solutions come from realignment of old solutions and materials into new forms (e.g., today's extensive use of plastics).

Research then tells the teacher that interaction structures are best when the teacher maintains a directive structure, or at least a directive-discussive structure. It is amusing to hear student teachers speak of using lecture methods when they mean teacher-led discussive structures. Often, however, they are more nearly manipulative structures.

The Sociometric Test

The sociometric test is a means of planning instruction in terms of student need. Simple mechanical procedures of arranging chairs may eliminate potential discipline problems and focus upon intended learning experiences. Much teaching methodology might be extrapolated from the chapter on discussion in this book and applied to the teaching situation. In order to find what the student attitude is, one might fashion any number of sociometric devices. The following volume acceptance type, shown in Fig. 16, can be used to determine existing groupings, antagonisms, hobbies, etc. It can then establish activities to realign teams or casts into groups of mutual or conflicting interests. Isolates may be

---

Instructions for Sociometric Chart

I. Within the circles in the following chart place the people in the room with whom you are acquainted. Place those you know best in the circle next to center, those you know only by sight in the outside circles.

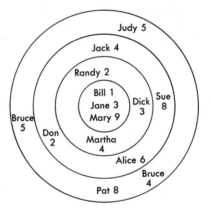

Figure 16. Volume Acceptance Sociometric Chart

II. Place behind each name listed a number as given in the list below, indicating your attitude *at present* toward that individual.
   1. Like the individual very much.
   2. Like the individual as a close companion.
   3. Like the individual as a member of the crowd.
   4. Individual is OK but attitude toward him cool.
   5. Never noticed the individual.
   6. Slightly irritating to me.
   7. Envious of the individual.
   8. To me the individual seems snobbish or conceited.
   9. Dislike the individual very much.

identified and worked into active student teams. Care should be taken to avoid placing isolates together. Potential leaders can be identified through analysis charts of student selection, such as those focal figures in Fig. 17. A teacher may also identify antagonisms but care must be taken for student critiques of speakers or performers.

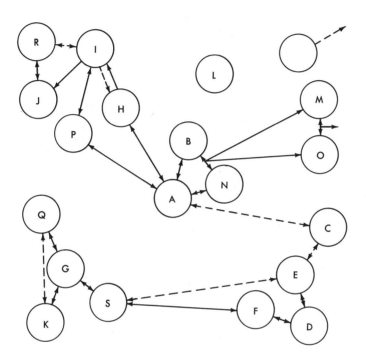

Figure 17. Sociometric Grouping Analysis

Legend: Lines can be solid or broken and can also be shown in colors to reflect various attitudes toward other people, concepts, practices, and activities. In the above chart you might interpret the solid line as positive (friendly) and the broken line as negative (unfriendly) in the direction of the arrow.

TEACHING COMPETENCY

The balance of this book is to be devoted to the problems of selecting materials, planning the methods, and evaluating the results of teaching. Personnel offices are highly interested in the professional ability of a teacher in these specific skills. We might say that few teachers are removed from office or denied renewal of contract for lack of knowledge. The issues which force the action of administrators are those which deal with a lack of efficiency in teaching.

Interviews attempt to evaluate the prospective teacher's ability to *(a) organize wholesome learning experiences, (b) motivate student interest, (c) provide for individual differences, (d) use life situations, (e) use creativity in the approach to teaching, (f) stimulate critical thinking, (g) use resources and teaching aids, and (h) evaluate student progress.* This is a profound list which justifies closer scrutiny. Each item could be treated as an individual chapter but each deserves brief comment as it pertains to the qualities of the teacher.

Speech teachers often organize activities on the assumption that busy students learn something. They may learn that to act busy keeps them from getting heavier assignments. Actually no activity should be planned or continued unless it has well justified goals and can test out under evaluation. These goals must be educationally sound.

Speech teachers are challenged to demonstrate the prime test of the good speaker when they are asked to motivate students through the interests of the students themselves. Since all means of persuasion are methods of motivation for an audience, the teacher of speech should be well trained to analyze interests, age group affiliations, and all other "springs of action" by which students can see value in instructional projects. If the teacher cannot find any means of persuasion, she should reevaluate the goals. If the goals are still worth obtaining, she should reexamine the methods or projected activities for attaining the goals. Such analysis leads to the study of *individuals* which make up the group as well as the group impact. Very often the teacher, like the good speaker, finds the concrete analogy of every day life a valuable aid to persuasion. *Good speaking takes the audience from where they are to that point where you wish them to go. Good teaching constantly connects what is to be learned with the known and applies theory to life situations.*

Creative teaching is an art, based upon sound social engineering. If we have screened out the incompetent, the balance of teachers capable of maintaining school classes might be described in three levels of proficiency: The first group maintains class order, covers the content and expected activities, and needs a reasonable and predictable amount of supervisory help. With supervisory help they would be slightly more efficient but not exceedingly so. These we classify as *teaching mechanics* (rough carpenters). While these teachers might do the heavy work, they should not be left to work alone or to design new buildings. The joints never quite fit tightly, but the structure seems solid. Let us classify the second group as *journeymen*. Here the teacher can be his own boss, has considerable judgment, knows when to ask for advice, and is capable of using all the advice he gets. He works well alone, or with a crew, and can be used as a foreman or supervisor of students. One of his attributes is that he will follow a plan, once drawn, without making impulsive changes. He does everything well and adequately. Seldom, however, does he do new things on his own initiative. He is blessed and cursed with the desire for security in position and expectations.

The third classification we designate as the *master craftsman*. He has a discriminating ear and eye. He looks for causes of problems others have not yet detected. He sees opportunities to develop students and himself, through the improvement of personal skill and new methods of instruction. He is seldom worried about security because he is too busy teaching. You should not jump to the conclusion that he is a poor organizer. He blueprints his plans to save waste motion and to test his techniques. He is able to relate results on tests to parallel processes and to draw conclusions and generalize from sound investigation. His curiosity leads to probing questions which perplex students but leave them eager to search for answers; thus he develops in them an ability to do critical thinking. Often he may appear over-busy or even uninformed so that quick students will be trapped into voluntary contribution of service and leadership. He and his students develop new resources and aids to learning through available materials. Although he knows the value of time and the importance of a balanced diet, he may aid the student in evaluation of student time and energy output on any project. Thus the price of the ticket is weighed against the value of the trip. This is the creative teacher. This is the master craftsman. His greatest reward is the relief from tensions felt by his fellow colleagues who itemize their work load and worry about the extra time they are putting in. This teacher sees the development of students, the maturity of men and women in the making. This is the "master builder" of youth.

Interviews and Employment

The master teachers can justify interviewing the prospective employer as well as being interviewed by him. Such a teacher will be interested in the potential flexibility of the program and the support given to innovative efforts. Teaching in a fixed or rigid system where enrollment is limited, where new courses cannot be developed, or where nationally recognized programs cannot be offered can make a teaching mechanic from a potential "craftsman." Conversely, a teaching mechanic or journeyman may successfully teach in such a system and fail if creativity and innovative programs are expected. In an interview the interaction is not one-way.

Most employment contracts are finalized following an interview with the hiring officer of a school board (the superintendent of personnel). The interview follows a study of the academic record and recommendations which have been filled out by advisors, teachers, supervisors of student teaching, and previous employers. The applicant is generally invited to submit rating forms or anecdotal forms to these individuals, who in turn mail them to the teacher placement agency "in confidence." Most teacher preparation institutions maintain such an office at no cost to the student or the hiring district. You will find this office much more satisfactory than contracting through a commercial agency, which charges a percentage of your contract for placement services and often deals in difficult placement positions. Professional organizations (SAA and AETA) also have excellent placement offices. Personnel officers travel from coast to coast to obtain the best personnel to fit their needs. Therefore, you may be interviewed for positions in California, Washington, New York, or any other state while in residence at any institution.

Presentation of your person as well as your papers is important to this interview. The hiring officer looks at the transcript of credits, the rating forms and the letters of recommendation and conducts his interview in terms of the strengths and weaknesses evident. He will be interested in (*a*) the amount and level of experience (teaching, production responsibilities, participation in college speech activities, leadership in campus organizations, or work with student groups off campus), (*b*) student teaching, and (*c*) your reaction to such experience. *The applicant should also interview* in terms of the job description, the opportunity to expand the program and the facilities available.

Professional Ratings. A reproduction of a composite rating sheet used by many school boards is given in *Rating Form A*. Many superintendents use only selected sections of such a rating device (personal traits, class management, and teaching methods), assuming that they can view the scholarship from the transcript. Others wish to get a reaction concerning scholarship related to the ability to teach from supervisors and colleagues of the applicant. We frequently find that students with extremely high grades cannot "communicate" knowledge or process to students. They sometimes lack any understanding of students willing to do adequate work in one field while saving time and energy to achieve excellence in another. Frequently a student ranking in the upper half but not in the upper ten percent of a graduating class is a very effective teacher. In spite of or because of this ranking, he has learned patience, the need for review, and the ability to explain processes to a student with great limitations. Teachers with limitations of knowledge, process, or self-discipline (shown in the scholarship ratings) seldom become good teachers. They fail to understand good questions from students and often miss excellent contributions of students as they follow the text page by page. Rating sheets used to evaluate and rank potential teachers focus upon behavioral evaluation: How will the teacher respond to the total school effort? Can he work effectively with limited supervision? Will he ask for and accept advice and assistance without fear of losing status? Can he accept negative administrative reaction to proposed plans or professional performance without bitterness or sulking? Self-rating is a way of seeing oneself on the job.

Rate yourself using Rating Form A as a superintendent or supervising principal might fill it out when a teacher applies for a second position.

Specific and general scholarship do not exist separately, but one reflects the other. Outside the specific areas of speech the teacher is concerned with a need for general knowledge of the world at work — current scientific theory, historical perspective, correct and fluent use of English, and the ability to correlate all this knowledge with the specific interests of the students.

During the past several years the debate questions which have fascinated curious high school students have included foreign tariffs, labor and management relations, socialized medicine, comparative educational systems, weapons control, and guaranteed annual wages. During the past years students in favorable television areas have had the opportunity to see plays of the classic Greek period and several Shakespearian productions, all presented in various styles by a variety of production groups. Student questions following such productions place a knowledge demand upon the teacher. He who knows the historical periods, and the implications of cross-indexing ideas can help students compare the tragic philosophies of the Greeks with the tragic interpretations of Tennessee Williams and Arthur Miller. Such comparison will soon find eager students waiting to be instructed. The teacher who merely looks blank when eager students ask intelligent questions can hardly hope to recruit students or sell speech. Teaching success is often measured by the intellectual curiosity and enthusiasm of the teacher.

Scholarship for the teacher of speech must be concerned with specific knowledge within the field of speech and general knowledge of areas outside but related to speech. Following a period in education in which the generalist has been deified, it appears that we are turning to the problem of how to develop the generalist. It is difficult to believe that one becomes a good general scholar by a little bit of training in many things. A quick analysis of the great teachers we have known will remind us that those

Rating Form A

Personality traits:	P	F	G	VG	O		Responsive to suggestions:	P	F	G	VG	O
Dependability							Sense of humor					
Judgment							Voice: quality & articulation					
Industry							Personal appearance					
Health							Genuine interest in students					
Promptness							Ethical qualities					
Poise							Constructive independent					
Initiative							work					

Analytical statement:

Scholarship (mastery and use of content, and historical and cultural background):

Speech:	P	F	G	VG	O		General:	P	F	G	VG	O
Fundamentals							General educational back-					
Public speaking							ground					
Dramatic lit.							Knowledge of current events					
Stagecraft							Correct and fluent English					
Radio							Correlation with student					
							interest in other courses					

Analytical statement:

Class management:	P	F	G	VG	O			P	F	G	VG	O
Emotional climate							Motivated control					
Routine details							Adaptability					

Teaching methods:	P	F	G	VG	O	
Org. wholesome learning experiences						Analytical statement:
Motivation of student interest						
Provision for individual differences						
Awareness and use of life situations						
Creativity						
Stimulation of critical thinking						
Use of resources and aids						
Evaluation of student progress						

Professional attitude:	P	F	G	VG	O	
Support of fellow teachers						Analytical statement:
Attitude toward teaching profession						

Summary statement and comments:

Legend: P=poor, F=fair, G=good,
VG=very good, O=outstanding.

Signature

with great general knowledge were well specialized in two or more areas. Finding that the answers to their problems could only be found outside the specialty, they broadened their training and the application of the knowledge they had already acquired. Students with a small amount of knowledge in many areas are seldom well enough trained to be aware of the problems, let alone have the tools to search for the answers. Speech is the content area of the speech teacher. In order to recognize problems

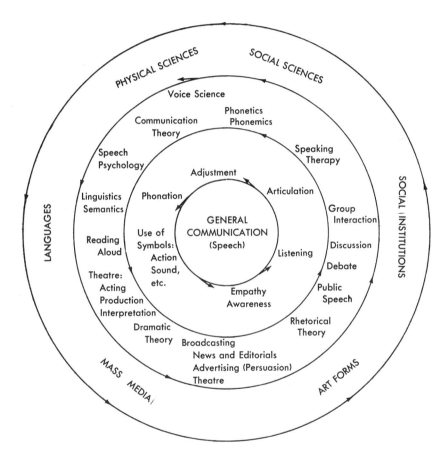

Figure 18. The Communication Wheel

Adjacent wheels indicate the variable nature of relationships from the simple desire to communicate to the physical and psychological processes of making sound, dealing with symbol systems, and selecting the necessary content from academic disciplines. The wheel at any level may vary to select the appropriate relationship for the type of speech form or format (discussion, dramatization, speech).

in this area he must be adequate in (1) the fundamental processes of speech, (2) public speaking and debate, (3) dramatic literature and oral interpretation, (4) stagecraft, (5) radio and television, (6) speech correction, (7) linguistics, and (8) communication theory.

The Communication Wheel.   Fig. 18 is based upon a chart originally prepared by Knower, indicating one design for the necessary training of the speech teacher. The chart furnishes a picture of the relatedness of the training received in speech with many other areas. You will note the core of areas at the center which might be designated as general speech. Beyond this are the areas of specialization many students wish to pursue within the typical speech department (theatre, public address, speech science, interpretation, or broadcast programming). While any of the specific areas of speech can apparently train students to perform in other areas without specific courses, such courses are highly valuable. One might seriously question if the actor, speaker, announcer, or interpreter can function without a working knowledge of voice production and phonetics. True, the speech scientist needs more knowledge from the medical science areas than do the other areas of the speech field. But actors and interpreters need training in the defective problems if for no other reason than to understand how not to misuse the vocal instrument.

The adjacent areas arranged in the chart are not necessarily those most pertinent to the speech area involved. While theatre and interpretation utilize materials from English literature, they also must work with philosophical, historical, sociological, and economic disciplines. The speech teacher will find training from such areas a constant aid in teaching and coaching out-of-class speech activities.

Personal Traits

Personal traits requested are numerous and interrelated. *Dependability* and *promptness* on the job can be rated by the college advisor based only upon the student's attention to these items in his attendance at classes, rehearsals, and other appointments. Secondary school students are like radio listeners. If the teacher is not there when the bell rings, and if attention is not gained in the early seconds, the dials begin to spin. Often the unsuccessful class can be traced to a lack of attention, lost in the beginning minutes.

Students will seldom be more industrious than the teacher, so employers wish some indication of the *initiative* and *industry* of the person they are considering. It may be fallacious reasoning to assume that attention and devotion to employment will be similar to the attention and devotion to study in the major and minor subjects, but we can generally expect that the student is reflecting his personal habits while in college. Employers may be wrong, but they assume that loyalty to the job is equal or more important than loyalty to family, community, or social organizations. They are eager to find if the student can make balanced *judgments* in terms of industry and initiative related to professional assignments and involvement in off-the-job interests. A balance of professional student obligations, dating, sleep, part-time work, rehearsals, and *attention to health* is one measurement of future balance of work, family, and community responsibility. It is possibly a measurement of a crucial personal quality desired in teachers.

Mature Judgment. Students during adolescence and early college are faced with many problems. Many decisions are made hastily with and without sufficient basis on fact or experience. Often the student turns to the teacher for guidance. When this happens, the teacher is no better than his judgment. Often the best action in terms of student good is to help him think through his problem and then let him solve it himself. In a few rare cases, the maturity of the teacher, his knowledge of policy and implications, will demand that he make the decision related to the student problem. In either case the teacher is making value judgments, an ability important to school administrators in search of staff. They wish to know if the teacher can differentiate between the important and the unimportant. Can the teacher isolate basic underlying issues and causes of problems without getting lost in the surface emotionalism related to his own student situation? Can the teacher identify personal interpretations as compared with those of the student?

Teachers of speech, like other coaches, are placed in positions where their qualities of judgment are sorely tried. It is not uncommon to find student loyalty developing around a "good coach" to the extent that students turn to that source in search of opportunities, privileges, and support.

Because the students are willing to devote time and energy, without pay, to projects which "interest the coach" and to projects which seem to him excellent educational opportunities for students, it is easy to lose perspective when the program or the students come into conflict with other members of the faculty. When, in the judgment of any teacher, the student is right and the colleague is unfair or wrong, the teacher is professionally obligated to defend the student. He must learn to do this without jeopardizing his professional relationship with colleagues, with students, or with other teachers. It is not an easy art to walk professional tightropes. More pertinently, it is important to critically evaluate the situation and determine whether (as a coach) you are identifying with the students and their problems, or studying all the ramifications of the problem. Students are quick to search for champions of causes (questionable and appropriate). All such projects are not defensible. There are differences between student desires and solutions which are to their advantage. Many problems are complex and have an impact upon other student groups. Let us look at one incident of on-the-job education reported by letter from a neophyte teacher:

Dear Professor:

Early in my third year as teacher-advisor, the Thespian Troupe invited me to join them in a toboggan ride and moonlight ski trip following rehearsal. It was Thursday evening and the rehearsal had been excellent. Moonlight promised an excellent evening of excitement on skis, without risk. Rehearsal finished at seven thirty and the outing culminated after two hours — early enough that the students returned home by ten p.m. without any complaint from parents.

The next morning was shattered by unexpected tension and the best dressing-down I have ever received in my professional capacity as a teacher. Several teachers were now on the "hot seat" because students under one teacher's sponsorship could have mid-week parties while the rest of the student body could not. Several basic questions were asked: To what extent, as a sponsor of the Thespian organization, did I feel justified in violating basic school policy? Since when did a rehearsal extend itself into a party as a means of circumventing policy? Were the students or sponsor interested in remaining active in the school? Would it be necessary to cancel productions and rehearsals as a means of preventing further occurrences?

To beginning teachers or college groups fighting for freedom without responsibility, this may sound like expanding a simple problem far beyond its importance. Actually, this school had spent more than three years dealing with unscheduled, unsponsored and highly questionable events which interfered with the efficiency of instruction and the primary purpose of the school. The error had not been intentional. I was guilty of allowing students to plan, what to me was a few minutes of earned relaxation, without analyzing the total picture in light of school problems or policy. The students may have gone on the same outing without me, with a parent. I gave official approval by my presence.

Apologies were accepted by administration and fellow staff members. My responsibility and oversight were discussed with my students and thus directly with the malcontents wishing similar privileges, but it was some time before other groups accepted the limitations which continued as established policy. Our evening of fun reappeared to haunt me many times in dealing with student control in various classes during the balance of the school year.

A neophyte.

Teachers are well advised to join faculty groups rather than student groups.

Health. The maintenance of health on the part of the teacher is an important factor in the professional life. Speech teachers find themselves in late rehearsals and long hours in planning. They find it necessary to curtail certain activities with students preceding an opening of a production. In many ways they treat themselves with open disregard to their teaching responsibilities or the success of their work. Susceptibility to respiratory infection can spread disease from the teacher throughout a cast. Poor discipline in early stages of illness may cause a teacher to be absent from the job for long periods of time. Teachers and administrators know that the substitute teacher is challenged to teach by students and that the regular teacher often returns to find that the class has been kept, but that instruction is behind rather than ahead of the point attained when absence began. Thus your health is important to the success of your teaching. You may have identifiable limitations. If so, you must learn to live with those limitations if you intend to remain active in the profession. The first obligation is to the students and includes responsibilities to protect them as well as direct their learning opportunities.

Poise. Speech teachers expect to aid students to adjust to the speaking situation. The *teaching situation is an adjustment* for many teachers. More than any teacher in the school the teacher of speech should rate high in poise, should be relatively free from negative reactions to praise or blame, and should be a glowing example as a speaker in many types of situations (formal and informal). The speech teacher should demonstrate the enthusiasm of the master storyteller and be able to demonstrate acting techniques in classroom and public and should be able to move into situations requiring extreme adjustment without losing status in his own eyes. Only by such poise can he hope to develop such qualities in his students. Like stagefright for students, he would know that steps in the direction of poise are a recognition and acceptance of his own abilities as they actually are. This recognition includes the ability to judge the responsibilities he accepted against the ability to produce, and an ability not to misevaluate the importance of a single event or challenge. He would also know that preparation is the best guarantee of poise (adjustment) in a given situation.

Initiative. Tradition may determine some of the duties which take many of the hours expected of the speech teacher. Even in these traditions the teacher is expected to be a self-starter. More importantly, however, the speech teacher must continue to develop ways of keeping the students interested in speech activities and to make opportunities for shy and isolate students to join in the projects. If a fundamental process is to help students adjust to speaking situations, then the teacher must provide the situations. These should not be confined to the artificiality of the classroom. Many opportunities can be provided to take the speaker, reader, or actor into the community where speech performs its natural function. The speech teacher who lacks *initiative* will find the demand for speech classes diminishing each year. Many schools find no demand for speech where a program was once active and the quality good. The frequent complaint is that the administration was unfriendly to speech. In most cases the fault may be laid directly at the feet of a teacher whose interests turned away from the school with the final bell, or whose initiative was so lacking that the means of persuasion did not include the numerous ways of getting more students involved through functional application of the instructional program. Without a high level of *initiative* few speech teachers will build or maintain a good program.

Responsiveness. Professional people don't know all the answers. In most professions the individual practitioners join with other colleagues to exchange ideas in order to continue their professional growth. The teacher of speech finds many problems which may be new to the beginner but may have been met many times by other teachers. The nature of in-class and out-of-class activities may create new problems which reach beyond the scope of the speech program. One of the duties of the administrator is to coordinate the programs in various areas of the school. The speech teacher who is still open to suggestions and *responsive to advice* will find fewer crises in his relations with other teachers and students. This is not, however, an invitation to spend most of one's time attempting to find out where the school is going. Leadership does not mean running madly in an attempt to keep up with the crowd or the administration. There are many honest differences of opinion and the teacher with leadership abilities will find new ideas at variance with the established traditions and the desires of others. The efficient teacher must always be capable of reevaluating goals as well as methods of reaching these people. He must further be capable of seeing the goals and opinions of others in the light of their professional views and must be responsive to suggestions where compromise is the intelligent action.

Humor. Most teachers remember the instructor who made learning fun. The essence of good comedy is the power to drive home a point with a laugh or at least a chuckle. The teacher who can see the humor in life and can translate the content to be learned into interesting daily analogies will find classes interesting for many years to come. In a sense, the teacher who takes herself and her subject so seriously that there is little time for humor will find that the total learning is diminishing and the desire to report for work each day is motivated by the paycheck rather than by a love of work well done. There are many humorous opportunities in every daily class. All of them cannot be used or little might be accomplished, but enough must be used to give comic relief. Care must be taken that the humor puts the point across rather than acting as a camouflage.

Vocal Efficiency. Vocal efficiency is important to any teacher. For the teacher of speech it is a professional necessity. Students should not be subjected to nasal, muffled, raspy or guttural vocal qualities. Articulation and enunciation standards should include the proper sounds clearly understood. This certainly does not include the over-precise speech so often found among the "effete artistes" who have done so much harm in the fields of speech, art, and music. The ability to curse without sounding precocious is just as important as the ability to make rounded or pear-shaped tones when the occasions call for such technique. The speech teacher should have such control of the vocal instrument as to be able to demonstrate rather widely the various uses to be made of the vocal mechanism. Band teachers in the secondary schools should be highly proficient on at least one instrument, but they must be able to demonstrate and teach students to play the many instruments included in the band. The teacher of speech is expected to develop vocal proficiency among the students whether their voices are immature, high, or low. He should know enough voice science to be aware of the type of instrument with which the student is working, but first and foremost he should be vocally proficient himself and able to set a worthy example for students.

Appropriate Dress. One of the paradoxes of teaching is that the teacher is expected to dress wisely and neatly, like the banker, but on the wages of a semiskilled workman. This is reconcilable for most because the conservative nature of the job helps make the chosen clothing last longer if cared for wisely. The teacher should dress with functional neatness balanced by a studied attempt not to appear a fashion model. The latter part of the problem soon disappears when the college student finds himself furnishing his own clothing rather than expecting parents to do so.

The speech teacher is often challenged to provide more functional methods of dress to avoid the destruction of valuable clothing during stagecraft emergency construction periods. Few of us can boast that we have always worn a shop coat or remembered to change into painter's clothing until after a valuable suit was ruined.

Research in speech is replete with evidence that clothing, posture, appearance, and attitude have a direct effect upon audience reception. Clothing or appearance can act as a barrier to communication. Parents react negatively to teachers who lead or reinforce extreme fashions. Extreme fashion in the school room frequently results in cancelled contracts and tensions with colleagues. *Appearance* brings many little problems to the teacher.

Interest in Students. This is a widely misinterpreted quality on teacher rating sheets. Sympathy is not necessarily synonymous with understanding of motives or respect for needed discipline and skills. Often the teacher gains the respect of the student when the teacher insists on standards and thus develops a sense of responsibility and values. Students, like adults, make many bad judgments and often procrastinate. Because of his youth the student may make even more mistakes, but with less serious effects. A medical doctor once stated "the medical practitioner is done when he begins to suffer the symptoms of his patients. You cannot save them all and the sympathizer saves even fewer." Understanding is essential to the teacher of speech. He must understand that the student will willingly devote unbalanced proportions of time and energy to those things he likes, including speech. A true interest in the student is to help him find balance, values, responsibilities, and satisfaction in knowing he is maturing in these respects. The teacher should exhibit kindness, understanding, patience, and perseverence. The courage to insist on standards in the best interests of the student is also important.

Ethics. In a status-ridden society the matter of ethics is of utmost importance. Good teachers do not verbally dismantle others in the presence of students. Students are eager and quick to find a friendly ear to discuss their sufferings due to the behavior of other teachers. The teacher who is complimented by such voluntary confiding may feel that the students are right. Teachers are not all wise, nor do they agree on all matters of policy or value. Still the student who will willingly assist in tearing one teacher apart will share the same activity with another using the first willing listener as the object of dissection. Teachers may discuss problems among themselves during their meetings, but cheap gossip is not ethical. It is immature and otherwise detrimental to the school, the students, and to the individual who participates in it. The faculty lounge is often the den of iniquities where sick teachers air their grievances about their colleagues. *Professional problems, not personalities should be discussed. If a personality is involved, focus on the problem.*

Constructive Independent Work. Like industry, initiative, and good judgment, constructive independent work is a desirable quality for the teacher of speech. The teacher who has this personal trait seldom picks a play two weeks before it is to go into production. Neither is such a teacher saddled with a play picked by members of a committee. If a committee is to make final selection, the teacher with this trait will already have presented several plays within the abilities of the students and director, one capable of being staged within the limitations of the school. An advantage-disadvantage case for each play is likewise presented. Thus the committee soon becomes aware that they are dealing with a professionally competent teacher and interference is minimized. In the balance of the teacher's day the constructively independent teacher is so busy with projects of value that the office protects such a valuable teacher from important "busy work" that can be done by teachers without out-of-class loads. The teacher who works independently on constructive projects for the welfare of students soon finds full-time teaching loads in the area of her interest because the enthusiasm is contagious with students and administration. With such enthusiasm the time and the budget soon follow.

Scholarship. In an age of specialization we are tempted to delve into interest areas until we lack the ability to converse intelligently in our own fields. A public school is typical if it employs one full (or part-) time speech teacher. In the eyes of the community of students and parents anything dealing with speech should be a part of the province of this teacher. Unlike the college professor, who may be able to fence off a corner of the field, the public school speech teacher must teach speech fundamentals, debate, various types of public speaking, oral interpretation, and theatre.

Certification in many states requires a variety of course backgrounds for the teacher of speech. General speech, or fundamentals, is considered basic in most of the certifying areas. In a few states the teacher may then specialize in public speaking or in theatre, but most states require credit hours in four or five of the basic areas of speech to guarantee competence to teach classes and to direct the out-of-class activities in radio, oral interpretation, theatre, and debate. In addition, enough speech correction is required to help the teacher decide whether the student should be sent to a therapist or given classroom therapy.

Even if the school is large enough to provide one teacher in theatre, another in public speaking, and a third in radio or therapy, these teachers are, in the eyes of the students, "speech teachers" and should furnish some common ground of communication. Fragmentation (specialization) is an easy cover for the incompetent.

Content Preparation. The teacher of speech seldom asks the student to speak about "speech," the content of the course for which he is registered. In most cases the public speaking topics deal with current events, science, or other student interests. Plays are selected which deal with problems of family or community. Thus the teacher of speech must know theory, content, and process in his own field and also be well enough educated to judge with competency the speech content and the performance of the student. *It is not enough to judge his delivery or confine evaluation to the presentation of elements confined to speech skill.* In fact it is almost impossible to speak of speech skill without dealing with the skill of handling content. The speech act is a composite of the idea, its organization, and its presentation. The speech teacher must include educational proficiency leading to efficient judgment in all these. Thus we are concerned with adequate general education and also specific knowledge in the area of speech.

The word "adequate" used above demands some explanation. Obviously, even in speech, one cannot be a specialist in all of these areas. Still the speech teacher is called upon to teach courses labeled "fundamentals" and must often teach fundamental processes of speech in the most advanced courses and out-of-class projects. The advanced public speaker often utilizes acting techniques in reading and public debate. The speech teacher is expected to be qualified to work within this boundary. More importantly, he must know when he has reached his own limits and refer questions to a specialist. Otherwise, in his ignorance, he may delegate authority to a student who knows less than the teacher but who does not hesitate to tear a control console apart in the radio room, thus costing the school much money. Even this type of damage is preferable to the damage which might be done through the misuse of psychodrama and T-group technique in treating cases needing intensive psychotherapy.

What are speech fundamentals? Barnes classifies them as those processes which deal with *phonation, articulation, adjustment to the speaking situation,* and *symbolic formulation of language* into vocal use. Obviously the teacher then needs to have a thorough knowledge of voice science, phonetics as a tool of diagnosis, training in personality and its manifestations, and some ability to hear and to interpret what is heard. A reasonable score on the Seashore test of musical aptitude might be considered a minimum tool.

Having established adequate scholarship and skill necessary for diagnosis and the finger exercises necessary for beginning speakers, the teacher must then furnish evidence that he is competent in the skill leading to polished performance in public speaking. Much of his teaching career will be spent helping students (*a*) choose acceptable topics, (*b*) gather material, (*c*) analyze audiences, (*d*) determine purpose, (*e*) limit the topic, (*f*) clarify the theme, (*g*) outline, and (*h*) write the speech. Very soon he will wonder when he will find time to (*i*) teach speech delivery. Later he will find that delivery is partially accomplished when all the ground work of preparation is completed.

As the teacher turns from public speaking to interpretative projects of acting and reading literature from the printed page, he will again find students needing help in (*a*) finding suitable material, (*b*) analyzing it in terms of attention steps, build steps, climax steps, colorful words, and other features before going on to (*c*) helping them with projection, intensity, placement, resonance, and patterns of inflection. These things can be taught through inquiry and analysis. With more limited students, they must be demonstrated. Thus the teacher's scholarship must be judged by what is known and what can be demonstrated. It is a rare and wonderful teacher who can help students go beyond the teacher's own ability. Somehow, he must have the knowledge and the ability to use a variety of technical processes to reach individual students.

Students working in college theatrical projects see many specialists solving complex problems with light, paint, design, accoustics, and construction. In the small college and in most secondary schools there is no staff of specialists. Each crew (costume, light, props, construction, painting, and box office) is headed and taught by the teacher — the SPEECH TEACHER! The play will be no better than the ability of that teacher to instruct the crews. There is too much to be done for him to do the work himself, even if stagecraft is his selected hobby. Students are eager to do such work. They work efficiently if taught properly and if the work delegated is within the reach of the students' capacity. Therefore scholarship in this area means that the teacher of speech must know the subject and have some functional knowledge of what limitations must be placed upon students working at any part of the theatre problem.

Broadcasting furnishes considerable challenge and motivation for the teacher of speech. Microphones are valuable devices of motivation. Many students love to work consoles or plan various types of programs. Knowledge in this field must include the ability to distinguish busy work with gadgets from profitable learning experiences. Some of the best learning comes from listening, if one knows what he is listening for. Teachers of speech should know enough about the broadcasting industries to answer many of the students' questions about how program ratings are obtained by audience studies and how special effects are obtained in sound and light to make productions effective. It is equally important to know about the control of broadcasting by the FCC and its relation to the advertising agencies which represent sponsoring industries. Knowledge of broadcasting should be parallel to the same services in newspaper news and advertising, to theatres in terms of entertainment and programming, and to the related interests of the students in the media available in most homes in the nation.

Suggested Projects

1. Self-evaluation is a major step in professional growth. The professional must learn to see himself accurately and be objective about the perceptions others have of him.

   a) If you are still a student, rate yourself on personal traits and have another adult member of the family or a roommate rate you. Then compare the rating and discuss major differences. Use rating forms A and C. (Form A appears on p. 156.)

   b) If you are a student teacher or practicing teacher, rate yourself on the total form and have a supervisor rate you on preparing yourself for promotion or salary increase. Use forms B and C.

   c) Using form A, make a composite rating and compare it with your academic transcript regarding grades in general education and in specific speech areas: public address, oral interpretation, fundamentals, stagecraft, and radio. How do you explain the differences? Have your courses had an accumulative effect towards justifying a higher rating than the score on individual courses? Did you deposit your notes in a safety box, sell your books, and now find yourself wanting? Is the urgency for employment causing you to review?

   d) Have a cooperating teacher or supervisor rate you using form B. Rate yourself and compare results.

Rating Form B

Class started quickly, enthusiastically?
    no 1 2 3 4 5 6 7 8 9 10 yes

Expected assignment clear to students?
    no 1 2 3 4 5 6 7 8 9 10 yes

Assignment conducive to achievement of aims?
    no 1 2 3 4 5 6 7 8 9 10 yes

Examples adapted to students' daily interests?
    no 1 2 3 4 5 6 7 8 9 10 yes

Teacher's voice alive, varied, interesting?
    no 1 2 3 4 5 6 7 8 9 10 yes

All students involved in classroom project?
    no 1 2 3 4 5 6 7 8 9 10 yes

Did materials contribute logically to aims?
    no 1 2 3 4 5 6 7 8 9 10 yes

Were methods varied to maintain interests?
    no 1 2 3 4 5 6 7 8 9 10 yes

Adequate help for individuals in need?
    no 1 2 3 4 5 6 7 8 9 10 yes

Evidence of adequate teacher background?
    no 1 2 3 4 5 6 7 8 9 10 yes

Evidence of skill in diagnosis of problems?
    no 1 2 3 4 5 6 7 8 9 10 yes

Skill in demonstration to aid students?
    no 1 2 3 4 5 6 7 8 9 10 yes

Were problems turned back to student thinking?
    no 1 2 3 4 5 6 7 8 9 10 yes

Skill in thought-provoking questions?
    no 1 2 3 4 5 6 7 8 9 10 yes

Handling of stagefright skillful, tactful?
    no 1 2 3 4 5 6 7 8 9 10 yes

Culmination clear and orderly?
    no 1 2 3 4 5 6 7 8 9 10 yes

Rating Form C

Desired Outcomes

Development of a greater and greater degree of mastery of subject matter content and of educational principles and implications involved.

P F G VG O   Can you select, organize, and use teaching materials effectively?

P F G VG O   Do you know enough of the subject matter of related teaching fields to relate it to teaching speech?

P F G VG O   Do you know the visual and auditory aids which will be valuable in teaching speech?

P F G VG O   Are you well acquainted with texts and reference materials in the field of speech?

Development of a measure of skill in certain fundamental methods, procedures, and techniques of teaching.

P F G VG O   Can you administer classroom routines effectively (roll, ventilation, room conditions)?

P F G VG O   Can you use specific methods of instruction effectively (individual group discussion, contract plan, laboratory situations, directed study)?

P F G VG O   Can you construct and use wisely tests and examinations (different kinds for different purposes?)

P F G VG O   Can you effectively use detailed techniques such as questioning, drill, assignments, illustrative materials, visual and auditory aids?

P F G VG O   Can you recognize and control situations which may lead to disciplinary problems?

Development of desirable personal characteristics and desirable relationships with others.

P F G VG O   Can you establish and maintain satisfactory relationships with your supervising teachers?

P F G VG O   Can you recognize and make an effort to eliminate any undesirable characteristics or habits you may possess?

P F G VG O   Is there indication of increased and justified confidence in your abilities in a teaching situation?

Development of desirable professional interests, attitudes, and ideals.

P F G VG O   Has there been more reading of professional literature on your part?

P F G VG O   Have you gained in knowledge of professional opportunities and organizations?

P F G VG O   Have you a better understanding and appreciation of higher teaching standards and professional ethics?

Legend: P = poor, F = fair, G = good, VG = very good, O = outstanding.

Rating Form D

Below are listed several areas which are included in Speech and Drama disciplines. Each person differs in his competencies in each of these areas. So that we may assist you during your student teaching experience and in the future, please rate yourself on each of these categories using the following criteria.

1. I could teach it tomorrow without research preparation.
2. I could teach it a week from now — a little research would be necessary.
3. I could teach it six weeks from now — a fair amount of research would be necessary.
4. I could teach it a quarter from now — a considerable amount of research would be necessary.
5. Without some additional professional instruction in this area, I could probably not teach the subject adequately.

Public speaking	1	2	3	4	5
Debate	1	2	3	4	5
Discussion (all types)	1	2	3	4	5
Oral interpretation	1	2	3	4	5
Drama (history)	1	2	3	4	5
Drama (technical: stagecraft, lighting and scenery)	1	2	3	4	5
Drama (costumes and makeup)	1	2	3	4	5
Drama (acting)	1	2	3	4	5
Parliamentary procedure	1	2	3	4	5
Radio-TV	1	2	3	4	5
Voice and diction	1	2	3	4	5
Phonetics	1	2	3	4	5

Using the same five criteria given previously, assess your ability to engage in directing one of the following high school activities.

Debate team	1	2	3	4	5
Producing and directing	1	2	3	4	5
Radio-TV club	1	2	3	4	5
Oratory club	1	2	3	4	5
Oral readers club	1	2	3	4	5
Parliamentarian for the P.T.A.	1	2	3	4	5

2. The Use of Student Evaluations. The present concern for the improvement of teaching has focused upon methods of rating oneself, supervisory rating, and student rating. With the increased early exposure to knowledge and learning experiences, students are becoming far more sophisticated in perceiving their learning environment. A number of studies have suggested that students can perceive and describe with validity the learning taking place in the classes they attend.

If a teacher improves with experience, he may improve much more rapidly if he can visualize the classroom through the student's frame of reference. It is important that the students describe and evaluate the environment they are in, rather than assume they have authority to hire, fire, or promote the teacher. Such responsibility may distort the validity of the evaluation. To insure validity, it is also important that students be allowed to remain anonymous, if they so desire. This eliminates fear of identification and retribution. The student's perception of himself as a good, poor, or average student is an additional variable. If a student rates himself as a poor student in terms of ability but feels he is learning effectively, or if a student sees himself as a student who learns easily but rates a teacher low in making ideas clear, each has made a valuable comment upon the class concerned. Some teachers are very effective with students of high ability but fail to identify the problems of the students of average and below-average ability. Some teachers fail to drill enough; others drill so much that students feel it is a waste of time. Grouping, drill groups, acceleration of instruction, or other techniques might be redesigned by use of student evaluations.

The following rating forms for student evaluation were designed by Brian P. Holleran and are used with his permission. Research based upon their use as an instrument should be available by early 1970.

Rating Form E, Part 1

DIRECTIONS:

Student opinion on a teacher and his course is important and valuable in determining what has been taught and learned. Therefore, will you give your opinion on each of the statements presented below using the key provided. Place the number of the phrase which most closely expresses your opinion in the space preceding the statement you are considering.

To be most objective, try to consider each statement separately. None of us are perfect or complete failures, so every statement may not be given the same value.

Feel free to give additional comments on any statement. Use the space at the bottom of this form or the reverse side and write the number of the statement and then your comments.

You need not put your name on this form but please indicate your age, sex, and the type of class this is, such as, Speech I, English III, Chemistry, Drama I, etc. Your frank and honest opinion is wanted, so give each statement serious thought.

Age_____   Sex_____   Class_____

KEY: 1. Never really achieved
      2. Still needs a lot of improvement
      3. Still needs some improvement
      4. Did an average job
      5. Did better than some teachers I have had
      6. Did better than most teachers I have had
      7. Did as well as the best teacher I ever had

1. _____ The voice used in teaching and discussing ideas was lively and pleasant to hear.
2. _____ A friendly classroom atmosphere was developed.
3. _____ A pleasing personality was evident.
4. _____ Anything that happened in class was noticed and dealt with effectively.
5. _____ An atmosphere was established where many important ideas were learned.

6. _____ Student ideas were appreciated and used when possible.
7. _____ The work assigned to students was reasonable and necessary for them to get the most out of this course.
8. _____ Testing and grading were fair and did not favor anyone or anything to an extreme.
9. _____ Everyone participated in class discussions because they were lively, enlightening and interesting.
10. _____ Homework and in-class assignments were made quite clear.
11. _____ A lot seemed to be known about the topics taught.
12. _____ A sense of humor was evident and enlivened discussions and lectures.
13. _____ Very few discipline problems occurred and a minimum of control was necessary to keep the class running smoothly.
14. _____ Rather than just giving busy work, the homework assignments were made challenging and interesting.
15. _____ Learning of the subject matter was not rushed and it was explored in depth.
16. _____ Everyone looked forward to coming to this class.
17. _____ The words used to discuss ideas were easily understood by everyone.
18. _____ Personal appearance and dress were appropriate and neat.
19. _____ Certain gestures drew attention and thus became distracting.
20. _____ Additional individual help was pleasantly given on any idea or problem that was not immediately understood.
21. _____ Student questions and answers were understood and effectively fitted into the class discussions.
22. _____ No trite phrases, such as OK or all right, were unnecessarily repeated.
23. _____ Questions were always asked in words understandable to all the students.
24. _____ The subject matter was made meaningful and related to current ideas and events.
25. _____ This subject has been made exciting and interesting.
26. _____ Considering everything, the teacher did a satisfactory job of teaching this class.

Not only are your opinions about this class important but also what you have learned is important. Therefore please list at least three things that you have learned well.

1.

2.

3.

There might have been some things that you have not learned so very well, so list any that now comes to your mind.

1.

2.

3.

ADDITIONAL COMMENTS:

Rating Form E, Part 2

Following are eleven statements on which we are asking you to give your opinion. For each statement being considered, choose *one* of the descriptive adjectives which most closely describes your opinion of that ability. In order to clarify and denote the meanings of the adjectives, specific descriptive statements are presented for the levels of excellence. Once you have checked *one* of the adjectives, please underline the phrase or phrases under the adjective grouping which most influenced your choice of the descriptive adjective. Your teacher will never know how you, as an individual, answered the statements presented below. We only ask that you give your age and sex in the spaces provided.

Age _____   Sex _____

	OUTSTANDING	EXCELLENT	GOOD	AVERAGE	FAIR	WEAK	UNSATISFACTORY
1. How was your teacher able to stimulate pupils to learn?	☐ Secures willing participation cooperative class climate; strong evidence of pupil initiative in planning activities.		☐ Some evidence of pupils using what they have learned; generally secures participation; pupils generally cooperative; pupils doing required assignments.			☐ Pupils uncooperative; pupils indifferent; secures limited participation.	
2. How well was your teacher able to communicate subject matter to pupils?	☐ Exceptional ability to apply knowledge to given situation or question; consistently seeking new ways to teach subject; exceptionally broad background.		☐ Able to enrich pupil experiences; applies knowledge but at times talks over heads of pupils; informed in several related fields; usually able to apply knowledge to fit situation or question.			☐ Lacks ability to apply knowledge to pupil question or situation; inadequate background; lack of depth in subject matter; narrowly specialized.	

	OUTSTANDING	EXCELLENT	GOOD	AVERAGE	FAIR	WEAK	UNSATISFACTORY
3. Was your teacher mentally alert in dealing with pupils?	☐	☐ Consistently alert; creative in replying to pupils; exceptionally quick to understand; communicates from pupil's frame of reference.	☐ Grasps pupils ideas; uses good judgment; usually able to answer pupil's questions; uses suitable vocabulary.	☐	☐	☐ Easily confused; shows poor judgment; is not spontaneous in replying to pupils; somewhat inarticulate; disorganized; overuses trite expressions.	☐
4. How well did your teacher develop discipline?	☐	☐ High degree of self-discipline; pupils enjoy attending class; considered fair in administration of discipline.	☐ Established a well-structured discipline; pupils responding with good work and satisfactory attitudes.	☐	☐	☐ Unfair in administration of discipline; insensitive to pupils' attitudes; distant; unsympathetic.	☐
5. Did your teacher provide for recognition of individual needs?	☐	☐ Sensitive to pupil differences; seeks causes and skillful in discovering solutions; encourages pupils to satisfy own needs.	☐ Somewhat aware of differences; frequently knows how to satisfy needs; sometimes motivates pupil initiative.	☐	☐	☐ Seldom recognizes needs; unaware of responsibility for providing for individual needs.	☐
6. How was student morale?	☐ Morale very high.		☐ Morale good.			☐ Morale very low.	☐
7. How well did your teacher execute his plans?	☐	☐ Lead students to adequate understanding; unusual effectiveness in adapting in-	☐ Fairly well-executed; some understanding of what was being achieved; instruction	☐	☐	☐ Plods through plans; little comprehension of what is being achieved; pupils	☐

	OUTSTANDING	EXCELLENT	GOOD	AVERAGE	FAIR	WEAK	UNSATISFACTORY
	struction to pupils; development of plans interesting and creative.			usually adapted to pupils needs and interests.			often confused; misses opportunities which arise.
	□	□	□	□	□	□	□
8. Was your teacher emotionally poised?		Radiates warmth and sincere concern for pupils; consistently acts with good judgment.		Usually well-controlled; responsive to class mood; recognizes tense situation but not able to relieve it.		Unduly uncertain in difficult situations; poor self-control; fails to feel tension in classroom.	
	□	□	□	□	□	□	□
9. How well did your teacher react to constructive criticism?		Invites criticism; makes discriminating use of it; responds creatively to criticism; exerts effort to improve.		Accepts criticism well; does not seek criticism; sometimes gets confused in effecting suggestions.		Finds it difficult to accept criticism impersonally; defensive; fails to realize need for improvement.	
	□	□	□	□	□	□	□
10. How do you rate your teacher on general effectiveness?	□	□	□	□	□	□	□
11. How would you rank yourself as a participating member of this class?	□	□	□	□	□	□	□

If you have any specific comments you would like to make, please feel free to do so on the back of this form. To insure anonymity, print or use a backhand slope.

References

American Council on Education. *Accredited Institutions of Higher Learning.* Washington, D.C.: American Council on Education, February, 1966.

Balcer, Charles L., and Seabury, Hugh F. *Teaching Speech in Today's Secondary Schools.* New York: Holt, Rinehart & Winston, Inc., 1965.

Ferguson, George A. *Statistical Analysis in Psychology and Education.* New York: McGraw-Hill Book Company, 1959.

Friederich, Willard J. *The High School Drama Course.* Cincinnati, Ohio: The National Thespian Society, 1955.

Knower, Franklin H. *Speech Education in Ohio.* Columbus, Ohio: Department of Speech, The Ohio State University, 1950.

Robinson, Karl F., and Kerikas, E.J. *Teaching Speech.* New York: David McKay Company, Inc., 1963.

Secondary School Theatre Conference of the American Educational Theatre Association, Inc. *Course of Study in Theatre Arts at the Secondary School Level.* American Educational Theatre Association, Inc., 1963.

State of Ohio Department of Education. *Educational Directory.* Columbus, Ohio: State Department of Education, 1965.

————. *Laws and Regulations Governing the Certification of Teachers, Administrators and Supervisors and School Employees in Pupil Personnel Service.* Columbus, Ohio: State Department of Education, 1963.

Articles

Alexander, Fred, and Gordon, Thomas. "The High School Speech Teacher in Michigan," *Speech Teacher*, 1:189-191 (September, 1960).

American Educational Theatre Association. "A Suggested Outline for a Course of Study in Dramatic Arts in the Secondary School," *American Educational Theatre Journal*, 12:15-31 (March, 1950). Revised 1963 and 1968.

Balcer, Charles L. "The High School Principal and the Teacher of Speech," *Speech Teacher*, 4:184 (September, 1955).

Erickson, Marceline. "Undergraduate Course Preparation in Colleges and Universities of the Central States for Prospective Teachers of Speech in Secondary Schools," *Speech Teacher*, 1:29-36 (January, 1952).

Haberman, Frederick W. "Toward the Ideal Teacher of Speech," *Speech Teacher*, 10:4 (January, 1961).

Lewis, George L. "Secondary School Speech Textbooks," *Ohio Speech Journal*, 3:16-18 (1965).

————. "Speech Teacher Certification: Communication and Self Reception," *Central States Speech Journal*, 11:84-87 (Winter, 1960).

Petrie, Charles R. and McManus, Thomas R. "Status of Speech in Ohio Secondary Schools," *The Speech Teacher*, 17:19-26 (January, 1968).

Robinson, Karl F. "Recent Trends in Certification of High School Speech Teachers and the Report of the S.A.A. Committee to the North Central Association," *The Speech Teacher*, 8:114-119 (March, 1959).

_____. "Training the Secondary-School Teacher of Speech," *The Quarterly Journal of Speech*, 30:225-227 (April, 1944).

Speech Association of America Interest Group: Speech in the Secondary Schools. *Newsletter* (September, 1963), p. 2.

Speech Association of America Subcommittee on Curricula and Certification. "Principles and Standards for the Certification of Teachers of Speech in Secondary Schools," *The Speech Teacher*, 12:336-337 (November, 1963).

"The Status of Speech in Secondary Schools: A Symposium," *The Speech Teacher*, 18:39-53 (January, 1969).

Fausti, Remo P. and Vogelsang, Robert W. "In High Schools of the State of Washington," pp. 50-53.

Ogilvie, Mardel. "In High Schools of New York State," pp. 39-44.

Ratliffe, Sharon A. and Herman, Deldee M. "In High Schools of Michigan," pp. 45-49.

Trauernicht, Maxine M. "The Training of High School Teachers of Speech," *The Speech Teacher*, 1:29-36 (January, 1952).

Unpublished Materials

Baker, Mary K. "An Evaluation of the Speech Program of the Secondary Schools of Ohio for the Year 1961-62." Paper submitted for a seminar, The Ohio State University, 1962.

Barber, Bradford G. "Questions to be Considered by Panel Members for the Central States Speech Association Program." Report of a 1963-64 survey to be discussed at the CSSA Convention, St. Louis, Missouri, April, 1964.

Everett, Russell I. "Speech Education: Ohio College Programs and Certification." Doctoral dissertation, Ohio State University, 1967.

Harvill, Linda. "The Status of Speech Education in Accredited Mississippi Secondary Schools, 1966-67." Master's thesis, University of Southern Mississippi, 1967.

Schoen, Kathryn T. "Perceptions of Speech Education in Ohio Secondary Schools," Doctoral dissertation, Ohio State University, 1965.

5

Evaluation

The overall purpose of evaluation is to determine whether instruction is needed or has taken place. The process of evaluation includes the design and use of appropriate instruments by which this might be determined. The present chapter will deal with the specific purposes of evaluation, the development of *objective* and *subjective* instruments used in the process, the strengths and weaknesses of various instruments in use, and the system of grading by using test results.

PURPOSES OF EVALUATION

The purpose of evaluation dictates the type of instrument to be selected and the interpretation of the results. In an instructional setting the first purpose of evaluation is to *diagnose the need for instruction.* Various techniques might be used to find the present status of the student as an individual, or as part of a group. One might wish to determine the student's knowledge of content, or his proficiency in skill to implement the content. He may know the facts but not understand them clearly. Thus *diagnosis* gives the teacher a basis for (*a*) selecting goals, materials, and activities, (*b*) reviewing partially understood concepts, or (*c*) launching into new areas of knowledge, skills, or understandings.

The second purpose of evaluation is to *measure progress*. This is also referred to as achievement testing. After a period of instruction it is desirable to determine the amount of learning achievement in facts, skills, or concepts that the student now understands or practices. This method uses instruments similar to those used to diagnose.

On a delayed time basis we might wish to find out how much material is retained after an extended period with or without specific drill on established skills or concepts. The use of diagnostic and progressive instruments on a pre-test and post-test basis measures the relative effectiveness of one method of instruction against another. Thus, we refer to *experimental instruction* as a third purpose in evaluation.

As instructional tools the various evaluation devices might be used to *enhance drill* by *increasing repetition* in learning, or by *increasing the intensity of involvement* during the learning process. Unfortunately, students are so conditioned to the use of evaluation scores as grading devices that they use tests as a means of *focus* on the expectations of the teacher. A teacher may unwittingly fail to meet her objectives by focusing attention on a narrow range of content or skill because students will prepare for the test rather than the objectives of the course.

Combined use of diagnostic and progressive instruments may help a teacher eliminate activities which reinforce bad habits, contribute little to new understandings, or confuse students in the process of instruction. Techniques proving effective may be expanded and improved. Carefully designed instruments may help to identify those students speaking from intuition rather than knowledge, or those able to "parrot" processes by imitating the teacher or other students without the ability to interpret for themselves. In either case the teacher should be professionally informed in order to select new goals, materials, and activities.

Principles of Evaluation

1. All attempts to ascertain the extent to which pupils have advanced toward their educational goals constitute the technique of appraisal.
2. The functions to be served by all techniques of appraisal are
    a) to supply evidence of the presence or absence of desired learning products, and
    b) to supply evidence of the degree of progress toward desired outcomes of learning.

3. The complete instructional program consists of
   a) the curriculum,
   b) the techniques and procedures of teaching, and
   c) the techniques of appraisal.
4. Appraisal is an integral part of the complete instructional program; properly conceived and adequately developed it must
   a) provide the pupils with the means to evaluate their own activities,
   b) provide the teacher with a basis both for planning the activities of the pupils and for continuous evaluation of the results, and
   c) provide a basis for constant revision of the curriculum.
5. The techniques of appraisal derive from and are determined by the purposes to be served by the appraisal.
6. Appraisal implies a recognition of these sources of pupil growth:
   a) direct outcomes of instruction,
   b) indirect outcomes of instruction,
   c) outcomes of co-curricular activities, and
   d) other sources.
7. The outcomes of teaching-learning activities may be classified into these types:
   a) increased or required knowledge,
   b) new or improved habits or skills, and
   c) new or improved attitudes and appreciations.
8. Instruments and techniques of appraisal which attempt to measure the direct outcomes of instruction must take into consideration all the factors which condition learning, especially
   a) the pupil,
   b) the curriculum, and
   c) the technique of instruction.
9. The emphasis given to appraisal directly affects the content of the curriculum. The published statement of the curriculum may not reveal this, but the administration of it will be greatly influenced both by the purpose which the teacher recognizes in appraisal and by the form of the tests used. The choice of content and the teaching procedures are likely to be modified to fit the expected tests. Such modification is especially likely when commercial tests are used. One of the most common criticisms of the state scholarship tests is that teachers reduce teaching to coaching for the tests.
10. The type of test to be used on any given occasion is determined by the purpose to be served. No single test will adequately measure the desired outcomes from any significant unit of instruction.
11. Available commercial tests have conspicuous limitations when compared with the broad program of appraisal outlined above.

a) They are based on the assumption that the curriculum is uniform in all schools. Two aspects of supposed uniformity are to be noted:

(1) that the content taught is the same in all schools, and
(2) that the time of teaching (i.e., grade level) is the same in all schools.

School practices vary greatly in regard to both of the foregoing.

b) Available commercial tests measure only a few of the outcomes of instruction in a given field. Many worthwhile outcomes cannot be measured by paper and pencil tests.

c) Most commercial tests are based on the work of a semester or more in a particular field and are therefore of limited service to a teacher who organizes his work into units requiring two, three, or four weeks for completion and who wishes to test the learning of each unit.

12. Commercial tests when properly used are especially helpful in the following ways:

a) They provide a means of objective comparison between the achievements and abilities of different groups of children (i.e., they function as a survey).

b) In many cases they have diagnostic values.

c) Many of them are superior to any teacher-made test because they incorporate skill and technical knowledge which is not at the command of the average teacher.

13. As much as possible the evidence of pupil growth must be gathered from the behavior exhibited by the child when he is living in a life-like situation.

The Process of Evaluation. The process of evaluation begins with the selection of goals and includes the creation and refinement of the instruments and the interpretation of the results. Assuming that the objectives of instruction have been chosen and that the materials have been selected and utilized in activities, we must see if the outcomes are those planned in the objectives. To determine this the teacher follows a process of evaluation, such as the following six-step procedure. (1) An item of knowledge or mode of behavior is selected as worth knowing or doing. (2) The concept is constructed with a key into a test item or statement on a rating sheet. (3) The concept is assembled with related items in an objective test or into a general rating sheet. A key or instruction for the evaluator is made for the total test. (4) The test is administered and scored. (5) An item analysis is made to determine the number of students doing well or poorly in the use of the instrument. Items missed frequently and those not missed are classified as to ambiguity, vagueness, clues, etc. and thrown out or reworded for the next use of that test item. (6) Policy decisions are made about the use of the test results. A flow chart on this process would appear as in Fig. 19.

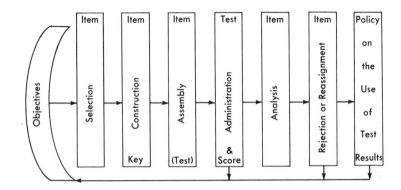

Figure 19. Evaluation Flow Chart

Diagnostic and Progressive Instruments

Samples of *diagnostic* and *progressive* rating forms are given in the following pages. The first, shown in Fig. 20, is a diagnostic form designed by Harry G. Barnes and is so constructed that the student, beginning with easy assignments, alternates through a variety of speaking activities. By the time he has completed eight performance projects, the teacher has been able to rate him on (*a*) the fundamental processes of speech, and (*b*) his performance ability in speaking and reading aloud. Remedial needs can be noted in phonation and articulation. The teacher and the student can then systematically plan activities to eliminate problems and strengthen talents.

The second rating sheet, designed by George L. Lewis, includes many of the same necessary items from speech fundamentals but also provides a system of rating for many processes, concepts, and skills which should be basic objectives of the speech course. It is shown in Fig. 21. Following Lomas's guidance on stage fright,[1] this form was designed to place attention on subject matter rather than on the speaker. Note that such course objectives as using the library intelligently, making appropriate outlines, analyzing the audience, and using demonstration materials are among the early concerns. Moving from processes common to all speaking, the teacher may then concentrate upon a number of basic objectives

---

[1]Charles W. Lomas, "Stage Fright" *The Quarterly Journal of Speech*, 30:479-485 (December, 1944).

Assign one rating to each item as required. Mark other items and make comments as appropriate
RATING SCALE: 1, Very Poor; 2, Poor; 3, Adequate; 4, Good; 5, Very Good.

FUNDAMENTAL PROCESSES OF SPEECH, Assignment I
(Encircle appropriate descriptive terms.)

1 2 3 4 5

ADJUSTMENT TO THE SPEAKING SITUATION: Ill at ease, unnatural, tense, inhibited, nervous, excited, frightened, hesitant, uncertain, chaotic, bodily mannerisms; unable to speak coherently, fluently, emphatically.

FORMULATION OF THOUGHT: *Successive thoughts:* unrelated, interrupted, inconsistent; *Statements:* ambiguous, obscure, inexact, incomplete, frequent grammatical errors; *Vocabulary:* limited, inaccurate, colloquial, dull, inexpressive; *Pronunciation:* noticeably incorrect, inaccurate.

ARTICULATION: Organic abnormality; jerky, uneven utterance, stuttering; incorrect formation of some speech sounds; inaccurate formation of speech sounds; inactivity of the articulators, rapid rate of utterance; foreign accent.

PHONATION: Organic abnormality; *Pitch:* too high, upward slide, pitch pattern; *Intensity:* too weak, too loud; *Duration:* tones held for too short a time; too long a time; *Quality:* improper balance or control of resonance, unpleasant, peculiar; voice lacks flexibility.

Date _____ Observer _____

PHONATION, Assignments III and IV

	Comments	Severe	Faulty
ORGANIC			
QUALITY			
Muffled			
Metallic			
Nasal			
Denasal			
Harsh			
Hoarse—Husky			
Breathy			
Infantile			
PITCH High ☐ Low ☐ Medium ☐ Rising inflection ☐ Pitch pattern ☐			
DURATION Staccato ☐ Too fast ☐ Too slow ☐			
INTENSITY Weak ☐ Too loud ☐			
FLEXIBILITY Poor ☐ Satisfactory ☐ Good ☐			

ARTICULATION, Assignments V and VI

			Severe Faulty
ORGANIC	Teeth ☐ Lips ☐ Tongue ☐	Palates ☐ Facial Muscles ☐	
RHYTHM	Jerky ☐	Stuttering ☐	
FOREIGN ACCENT	Nationality:		
ORAL INACCURACY	Rapid rate ☐	Oral inactivity ☐	

INCORRECT SPEECH SOUNDS

	Severe Faulty		Severe Faulty
1. s ☐ z ☐		10. æ ☐	
2. ʍ ☐ w ☐		11. aɪ ☐	
3. θ ☐ ð ☐		12. aʊ ☐	
4. ʃ ☐ ʒ ☐		13. ɔɪ ☐	
5. tʃ ☐ dʒ ☐		14. ɜ,ɝ ☐	
6. t ☐ d ☐			
7. m ☐ n ☐ ŋ ☐			
8. l ☐		Others	
9. r ☐			

184

Figure 20. A Diagnostic Rating Form

Rating (Encircle one.)
1 2 3 4 5

Date ___ Observer

Rating (Encircle one.)
1 2 3 4 5

Date ___ Observer

SPEECH MAKING, Assignment VII

SUBJECT ___

1 2 3 4 5

Choice of Subject
Choice of Thought
Choice of Material
Organization of Material
Use of Language
Projection to the Audience
Control of Bodily Activity
Rhythm
Pronunciation
Voice Control
Audience Response

Total Score ___

Score
Above 38 — Above Average
28-38 — Average
Below 23 — Below Average

Date ___ Observer

READING ALOUD, Assignment VIII

SELECTION ___ AUTHOR ___

1 2 3 4 5

Choice of Material
Arrangement of Material
Projection of Thought
Projection of Emotion
Control of Bodily Activity
Rhythm
Pronunciation
Voice Control
Audience Response

Total Score ___

Score
Above 31 — Above Average
23-31 — Average
Below 23 — Below Average

Date ___ Observer

*"Speech Fundamentals Inventory, Teacher's Record Blank" for use with Harry G. Barnes and Loretta W. Smith, *Speech Fundamentals* (Englewood Cliffs, N. J.: Prentice-Hall, Inc., 1953).

PROGRESSIVE RATING SCALE

Place appropriate number from the linear scale in box at right.

General speech skills and background

Did the student make intelligent use of library?
no 1 2 3 4 5 6 7 8 9 10 yes

Did the student complete clear outlines?
no 1 2 3 4 5 6 7 8 9 10 yes

Was there a realistic analysis of audience?
no 1 2 3 4 5 6 7 8 9 10 yes

Were demonstration materials shown to advantage?
no 1 2 3 4 5 6 7 8 9 10 yes

Did the speaker indicate a vital interest in subject?
no 1 2 3 4 5 6 7 8 9 10 yes

Speaker's rating sheet

Did the speaker evidence poise, control, and good posture?
no 1 2 3 4 5 6 7 8 9 10 yes

Was your attention and interest turned to the subject?
no 1 2 3 4 5 6 7 8 9 10 yes

Did the speaker present interesting materials, facts?
no 1 2 3 4 5 6 7 8 9 10 yes

Were illustrations based upon fundamental wants of people?
no 1 2 3 4 5 6 7 8 9 10 yes

Was there a good speaker-audience relationship?
no 1 2 3 4 5 6 7 8 9 10 yes

Was the thesis emphasized enough to be well understood?
no 1 2 3 4 5 6 7 8 9 10 yes

Did the speaker accomplish his purpose?
no 1 2 3 4 5 6 7 8 9 10 yes

Was the voice projected, resonant, pleasant?
no 1 2 3 4 5 6 7 8 9 10 yes

ASSIGNMENTS

1	2	3	4	5	6	7	8	9	10

INCORRECT SPEECH SOUNDS

Check basic problems for this student.

	Severe	Minor	Improved	Correct
Adjustment				
Phonation				
Pitch				
Quality				
Muffled				
Harsh				
Nasal				
Rate				
Fast				
Slow				
Pattern				
Breathy				
Organic				
Articulation				
Rhythm				
Foreign				
Sounds				
θ—ð				
tʃ—dʒ				
s—z				
ʃ—ʒ				
t—d				
æ				
Others				

Oral reading, dramatics of storytelling

Did the speaker establish the desired atmosphere early?
no 1 2 3 4 5 6 7 8 9 10 yes

Did the speaker evidence an understanding of material?
no 1 2 3 4 5 6 7 8 9 10 yes

Was phrasing, rhythm, and pausing an aid to thinking?
no 1 2 3 4 5 6 7 8 9 10 yes

Was the voice pleasing but strong and projected?
no 1 2 3 4 5 6 7 8 9 10 yes

Did the reader establish an empathic response?
no 1 2 3 4 5 6 7 8 9 10 yes

Was the tempo in harmony with the desired effect?
no 1 2 3 4 5 6 7 8 9 10 yes

Were the transitions of pantomime smooth and intelligent?
no 1 2 3 4 5 6 7 8 9 10 yes

Was the character consistently portrayed?
no 1 2 3 4 5 6 7 8 9 10 yes

Debate and discussion

Did the introduction include a plan of development?
no 1 2 3 4 5 6 7 8 9 10 yes

Was there a steady, logical development of the case?
no 1 2 3 4 5 6 7 8 9 10 yes

Did the argument show support of points with evidence?
no 1 2 3 4 5 6 7 8 9 10 yes

Did the argument evidence adequate study and knowledge?
no 1 2 3 4 5 6 7 8 9 10 yes

Was the argument challenging to the thinking of opponents?
no 1 2 3 4 5 6 7 8 9 10 yes

Did the speaker answer the challenge of opponents?
no 1 2 3 4 5 6 7 8 9 10 yes

Did the member participate intelligently, easily?
no 1 2 3 4 5 6 7 8 9 10 yes

Were the ideas of the argument easily understood?
no 1 2 3 4 5 6 7 8 9 10 yes

1	2	3	4	5	6	7	8	9	10

1	2	3	4	5	6	7	8	9	10

Name

Class   Section

Comments:

Figure 21. A Progressive Rating Form

187

in public speaking, oral reading, drama, or debate. The form also carries out an overriding philosophy, that audience analysis, organization ability, logical thinking, accomplished purpose, and delivery are common to all types of speaking. Space is provided for noting remedial problems to be isolated and corrected. This form provides for ten ratings in each major area, or forty speaking projects. Copies of this or the Barnes rating sheet may be placed in the hands of student and teacher.

Evaluation and Relationship to Objectives. Extreme care must be taken in construction of evaluation instruments that the *objectives of the course are reflected in the instruments used.* Most lists of objectives for education include "the development of critical thinking." Students learn that "parroting expected answers" often results in higher grades. Thus, this objective becomes the regurgitation of expected answers, which replaces critical thinking. Developing creativity soon disappears as a course objective when students are told specifically how to inflect lines, block action, or interpret a part. In this way artistic excellence, as measured by "teacher creativity," supersedes the creative development of the student. The best that the student can get is "re-creation" with teacher applause.

An instrument may measure the frequency of activity but may fail to measure the *quality* or *quantity* of learning. It may focus upon acquisition of facts or concepts. Whether dealing with the *diagnostic, progressive,* or *instructional* purposes of evaluation, the teacher must develop proficiency in constructing and using many instruments of evaluation and must keep them in harmony with the course objectives.

Can Speech Proficiency or Knowledge be Measured? The challenges for instructional space and personnel compel a constant examination of the criteria used in measuring speech knowledge and performance. It is relatively easy to identify the speaker who is unable to support tone and placement adequately to be understood throughout the room. It is also possible to identify the individual who can be heard but not understood. Many skills, including selection, organization, interpretation, and delivery of information can be quantified. The major challenge is to defend the various *qualitative* measurements used in speech instruction. Teachers should be familiar with the many studies available in order to be proficient in developing new instruments based upon new research.

CONSTRUCTING MEASURING INSTRUMENTS

Measuring instruments must be designed so that the terms used in them are precisely defined. The basic terms which must be understood are *validity, reliability, usability, scope, speed, power, item analysis, objectivity, and subjectivity.* Judgments made without the precise use of these terms can only end in faulty conclusions.

Validity

Validity is gained if the instrument measures that which it was designed to measure. This involves use of the appropriate instrument in the proper place. An instrument designed to measure organizational ability is inappropriate to measure vocal quality; therefore, it would be invalid for this purpose. If the language used to ask a question is complicated, it may measure reading ability but not word knowledge. A student may recognize a type of outline or certain stage lighting instruments without knowing how to use either. A valid instrument can be designed to determine (*a*) recognition of a tool, fact, or process, or (*b*) ability to use the tool, fact, or process. It is also possible to design a measuring instrument to determine (*c*) the ability to generalize from association and recognition. The misuse of an instrument invalidates the information drawn. A student may be able to "think" without the skills of punctuation and spelling.

Reliability

Reliability refers to the consistency of a measurement with validity. Questions may have face validity and experience one or more apparently successful administrations. Under continued administration the test may reveal that reading ability, prerequisite training, or clues aided a class with high reading ability, awareness of sources, or previous acquaintance with the teacher's approach to testing. A breakdown in reliability may identify a lack of instruction in one group which occurred in other groups.

Usability

Usability refers to the ease with which the student can take the test and the teacher can administer and evaluate results. The *design,* or layout of the questions, and the *instructions* determine to a large extent the ability of the teacher and student to use the instrument. On one occasion a student teacher was asked to administer a term test in a public school. The test was written in longhand on legal size "ditto." Instructions were lacking and it was difficult to follow any part of the test to its culmination. Written in two columns, part of column one was continued in column two. The highest score on 100 points was 38. After redesign the same test, given by surprise, netted a low score of 73. The content remained the same, but instructions were included and the layout of the material changed so that the test could be followed. This criterion refers to *usability*. A test loses *validity* if the lack of instructions or layout makes the instrument a challenge to follow hidden paths or "read the mind" of the instructor.

The ability to apply a key is an element of usability. The teacher should be able to apply a key and correct the test without having to read every question in order to determine the correctness of the answers. With objective type tests the item to be selected, or the blank to be filled, should be arranged so that the student places his answer in the right hand margin or on a separate answer sheet. This enables the teacher to apply a mechanical key beside the answers or over the answers. Thus if the correct answer fails to show through the cutout, or beside the key, an incorrect response can be marked.

Instructions are important. The teacher may spend much time during a test giving oral instructions regarding the test in general or test items in particular because adequate instructions are not given on the test itself. Instructions should include the use of answer sheets and what is expected in each type or section of the test. Whenever the style of the test items change, there is an opportunity for confusion, since the validity of a test suffers if the student is rated on his knowledge of content on the one hand but is challenged in adaptability and intuition regarding expectations due to inadequate instructions. Time taken to figure out expectations may make the difference of several points on the total examination score. Even in essay type examinations the *instructions should place a boundary around the problem* so that the response can be checked by the teacher without rereading the question in order to determine the correctness of the answer. Students with greater adaptability may thus gain points. When this happens, the measurement has been in terms of adaptability rather than content, and the test is invalid for the purpose for which it was constructed.

Usability should be considered in terms of cost. Rating sheets are an item of cost to the speech teacher and school. How often should they be used? When should they be used? If students are asked to rate each other, should all students be so involved with each speaker? How big, in terms of paper size, should a rating sheet be? These questions deal with many issues other than cost, but let us look at the construction of a small rating scale below which can be duplicated with four or six copies on a sheet of paper 8½ x 11 inches. If each student in a speech class of twenty members rates each student, four hundred copies will be used for each round of speeches. The cost of the paper plus the secretarial time of the teacher and the office raises a serious question on the cost values of all students rating all students. Some variations may be equally valuable. *Five raters may be selected at the completion of a speech,* thus keeping the class involved as listeners.

Rating Sheet

Debate
Did the introduction include a plan of development?
    no 1 2 3 4 5 6 7 yes   _____
Was there a steady, logical development of the case?
    no 1 2 3 4 5 6 7 yes   _____
Did the argument show support of points with evidence?
    no 1 2 3 4 5 6 7 yes   _____
Did the argument evidence adequate study and knowledge?
    no 1 2 3 4 5 6 7 yes   _____
Was the argument challenging to the thinking of opponents?
    no 1 2 3 4 5 6 7 yes   _____
Did the speaker answer the challenge of opponents?
    no 1 2 3 4 5 6 7 yes   _____
Did the member participate intelligently, easily?
    no 1 2 3 4 5 6 7 yes   _____
Were the ideas of the argument easily understood?
    no 1 2 3 4 5 6 7 yes   _____

Scope

Scope refers to the inclusion of all the areas of knowledge covered in a period of instruction. If the teacher designs a test based predominantly on one or two areas (oral interpretation and acting) and excludes other areas, the students interested in the excluded areas (production, lighting, debate) are automatically penalized in the evaluation process. Care must be taken, particularly in semester and final examinations, that the *scope* of the test recognizes areas of interest in the total instructional experience of the course.

Speed and Power

Speed refers to a challenge to those who know and can respond upon signal, while *power* refers to preparing the instrument in increasing stages of challenge so that solutions may be reached at levels of *fact, content, association, analysis, performance,* or *ability to generalize* from any of these. Again, many students may know the content but may not be able to solve problems with these tools. Others may be able to classify or associate things belonging together without the ability to generalize or see new relationships. Thus, students may have considerable speed without power or may have both speed and power. Some of our best students have power without speed. They may represent the methodical but deep-thinking scholars.

Item Analysis

Item analysis is the basic process for determining *validity*. After a test has been administered, each item is analyzed in regard to the number of times missed. If most students miss a given item, the teacher should first check the key to determine if a wrong answer is on the key. If the key is correct the teacher must then make an *analysis of the wording* to find any *ambiguity, vagueness,* or *misleading cues.* It may be that *design* or *lack of instructions* has caused the difficulty. Clues do not help the poor student for whom they are frequently planted. They help only the brilliant student, who is able to spot the clue and take advantage of it by distributing the score even wider.

Objectivity and Subjectivity

After selecting the content or speech processes to be evaluated, the teacher must select *objective* or *subjective* instruments. An *objective* instrument is one in which the teacher or evaluator makes no judgment during the time of correction, using only the key. Keys are constructed at the time the instrument is designed. Tabulation and marking of the test could be done by someone with a key but without training in the content. An *objective* item should be selected so that an answer can be selected from two or more choices. Other answers have been eliminated from the alternate choices and thus the individual correcting the test is not influenced by the language or personality of the speaker or by the test situation. Objective types of instruments include (*a*) true-false, (*b*) matching, (*c*) multiple choice, (*d*) completion, and (*e*) arrangement.

Subjective instruments demand critical judgment when correcting them. Factors influencing the rater's judgment include the completeness of the content, the ability to see relationships, linguistic proficiency, the legibility of the writing, and most importantly the rater's ability to hear and discriminate sound and thought. *Rating sheets and anecdotal records frequently used in evaluating speech performance are no more valid than the ability of the person doing the rating.* The essay examination is a subjective form and is the most difficult to design validly.

Central Tendency and Halo Effect

The *validity* and *reliability* of subjective instruments such as rating sheets and anecdotal records are most frequently reduced by *central tendency* and *halo effect*. *Central tendency* refers to the behavior of raters who seek a middle ground rating rather than commit themselves to a rating of failure or excellence. In constructing rating sheets the teacher might follow the research guidance that a scale of fewer than three lacks effectiveness and more than seven points on a linear scale is equally uneffective. One will note that due to central tendency a ten point linear scale was used on the progressive rating sheet in Fig. 21. Refusal of raters to use a *1, 2, 9,* or *10* left a six-point scale in the center. Central tendency can be avoided or reduced by *forced ranking* of speakers.

The *halo effect* occurs constantly in the use of subjective forms and comes in polished and tarnished forms. *Halo effect* refers to ratings affected by (*a*) the past experience of the rater with the performer, (*b*) the appearance of the performer's clothing or hair style, (*c*) phonation and articulation, (*d*) organization, (*e*) grammar and spelling, or even (*f*) experiences of the rater prior to the performance. If the speaker is aware of rater bias, he may gain a polished halo. *The halo may be polished or tarnished* by overcompensation or negative reaction to a bad breakfast, a family fight, or stalled traffic as the rater reported for work. The halo effect can be reduced by using well structured rating scales which infuse as much objectivity into the rating process as possible.

The teacher must be able to identify the objective and the subjective qualities in any evaluation instrument. Even the selection of items for a test is subjective. Classifying phonetic errors in a diagnostic test is a subjective act but becomes more objective as the rater increases his skill in seeing as well as hearing the placement of the sound. Subjective judgments deal with opinions, comparisons, contrasts, and performance. They are valid insofar as they are used to measure that for which they were designed, and insofar as the rater possesses the necessary skill for interpretation and maintains a stability from performance to performance. Apathy resulting from a long series of speeches can negate the validity in the use of rating sheets. Change of rater, order of speaker, or style of speech may change the rating.

Breakdown in Validity and Reliability

From the above discussion we note that validity and reliability are reduced, and may completely break down, due to

a) lack of instructions (inability to read the mind of the instructor),
b) scope out of balance,
c) wrong instrument or misuse of instrument,
d) vagueness of wording,
e) ambiguity,
f) design (too many items, poor arrangement, lack of space),
g) clues, and
h) ability or bias of evaluator.

CONSTRUCTING OBJECTIVE INSTRUMENTS

Types of Objective Tests

Objective testing includes *true-false, multiple choice, matching,* and *completion* type test items. Each has certain strengths and limitations. The total effectiveness of the testing is determined by the skill and care taken in the construction and use of each item. Frequent use of objective instruments is due to the simplicity of administration and the ease and speed in scoring. This does not imply that they are easy to construct, but once constructed each student can be given an individual copy of the test, with or without a special answer sheet.

If the teacher chooses to use an answer sheet, *alternate* or *equivalent* forms may be used within one class, or from class to class. The originals of the test may be retained for files and thus the teacher is saved considerable labor in future construction. Systems of *alternate forms* may provide for a series of tests within one classroom group across a period of time, or the teacher may select from several forms the items to be used in a final examination. Considering the amount of time and skill necessary to refine a good test item, the teacher should find ways to discuss the results of testing without distributing the tests throughout the school. Because the test can be administered with a minimum of writing, the symbol, word, or letter can be recorded on an answer sheet as easily as on the original copy.

Care should be taken to design the answer sheet so that scoring is rapid, but more important, so that the student is not confused in recording his answer choice. The student will be less likely to be confused when the answer sheet corresponds to the margin of the original sheet, than when the design of the answer sheet has no relation to the layout of the original copy. See the spacing for answers on the matching tests which follow. An answer sheet should match this printed spacing. When a student misses one blank in recording his answer, he may then follow through with the right answers in the wrong spaces of the answer sheet for the balance of the examination. We then have a measurement of his ability to follow a schematic pattern rather than his knowledge of the subject being tested. If the intent is to test his ability to follow directions and trace a pattern, a different instrument should have been chosen. In attempting to translate the test results, the teacher may detect a misuse of the answer sheet instructions, but he is then involved in a matter of subjective translation and is no longer dealing with the "objective" test.

Alternate and Equivalent Forms

Alternate forms of a test utilize the same items, worded in the same way from form to form but presented in a different order. Such an arrangement guarantees the same degrees of difficulty and the same content or process measurement. Its basic use is to make it difficult for students to take a test during an early class period and invalidate the test for all other classes through conversations. By use of the alternate form the student may talk about the content but cannot place any type of key or "pony" in the hands of a classmate. Alternate forms can be constructed with limited effort by the following process: (1) Select the items and arrange them for form A typed on cards along with the key. (2) Type out the examination following the order of the cards, but omitting the key. (3) Shuffle the cards and type out form B. (4) Reshuffle and type out as many other forms as desired. Keys can be made up at the time of the typing for each form. The form selected for any given class can be varied to discourage cribbing. The students need not know whether this is an alternate, or equivalent form.

Equivalent forms employ the same content with the same degree of difficulty in each item, but individual questions must be rewritten so that the tests are not just alternate forms. This is a difficult test to design since the student's language proficiency must not have a bearing on the test results. The simplest test of validity of an equivalent form is to word the content of each item in two or more questions. After the test has been administered the upper fourth of the class using form A of the test item is compared with the upper fourth taking forms B, C, or D. If the number of correct and missed responses correlates for this upper fourth and for a similar lower fourth of classes taking various forms, then each item may be said to be equivalent.

The Completion Test

The completion test includes a statement which is incomplete until a word, a date, or a short phrase is added. To reduce time in administering the test, the blanks should be at or near the end of the statement and the blank to be filled should be at the margin on the right side of the paper. This allows the student to read into the final position without having to cut back to the beginning of the statement to fill in the blank. This takes only a few seconds, but in a test of one hundred items the addition of five seconds per item adds considerably to the time spent working on the test and reduces the time spent analyzing information. Good test construction attempts to streamline the mechanical features so that attention can be focused upon the concept or skill to be measured. Any mechanical feature which reduces concept involvement reduces the accuracy of examination.

One of the more difficult features of the completion test is to provide an item with only one answer. Care must be taken that verbs, adjectives, and adverbs are not used to complete the test item. The problem of synonyms provides more than one answer. Selecting and refining an item to the point where there is no other acceptable answer may make the answer so obvious that it lacks value as a test item. The main advantage to the completion test item is that it requires *recall*, which is not a feature of tests where *recognition* is the only challenge. Completion is not a good test to measure reasoning, but this instrument may be used to develop test items for multiple choice testing. The correct answers may be used as right choices while the wrong answers may be used as incorrect choices. A similar application could be made of the material for true-false items.

Several other features of the completion test must be carefully watched. Cues or hints to the answer in the item must not be given. These cues are often partial quotations in which the length of the line or the breaking of the line indicates the number of words. These cues aid the better student, who does not need such help, and enlarge the point spread in the final results. Information given within a test item should not point obviously to the answer. Above all, items should not be included in the test which furnish the answers to other items. Again it is the rapid reader, the highly proficient student, who is given the advantage by such techniques. Better methods of finding the most proficient student should be used. Knowledge of the subject is more important than speed in reading when we are dealing with a "subject" item examination. If we wish to examine reading skills, we should use an instrument designed for that purpose. A few examples of good and poor items follow. Poor items, as classified by fellow students, are marked with asterisks (*).

*1) A voice with too much nasal resonance is_____.
*2) A voice that shows a lack of nasal resonance is_____.

*3) A vocal tone which includes noises as in exhalation is_____.
*4) When all the details can be combined into a related whole, a thought has_____.
*5) When a thought is free from error in grammatical structure, the thought is_____.
 6) Highness or lowness of vocal tones is called_____.
 7) The length of time a tone is held is called_____.
*8) The overall individuality of a voice is its_____.
 9) The loudness of a tone is the_____.
10) The production of tones is_____.
11) In speaking, the modification of tones of the voice to form the speech sounds is called_____.
12) The initial sound in the word *then* is indicated by the symbol _____.
13) The initial sound in the word *thin* is indicated by the symbol _____.
14) The initial sound in the word *judge* is indicated by the symbol_____.
15) The symbol for the final sound in *garage* is_____.
16) The symbol for the initial sound in *yet* is_____.
17) The symbol for the final sound in *sing* is_____.
18) The symbol for the initial sound in *shed* is_____.
19) The symbol for the beginning sound in *cheap* is_____.
20) The symbol for the beginning sound in *what* is_____.
21) The voiced counterpart of [p] is_____.
22) The voiceless counterpart of [d] is_____.
23) The voiced counterpart of [k] is_____.
24) The voiceless counterpart of [z] is_____.
25) The voiced counterpart of [f] is_____.

The Matching Test

This type of test deals with more than one item at a time and builds around a central group of items. Two related lists of words, phrases, pictures, or other symbols are presented. The student is expected to select from one list the item which most closely relates to a specific item in the second list. The two lists should cover only one topic and be closely enough related to make the selection a challenge: (*a*) Plays and authors might be used. (*b*) If one wished to challenge a more mature group, the items might include a sequence of lines from a play to be matched with a second list of play titles. (*c*) Types of outlining might be included in one list with examples in a second list. (*d*) Pictures including staging equipment or vocal mechanisms might be matched against identifying terminology.

The two columns should not employ an equal number of items, since the student would find the test a process of elimination. If less than five items in one list are used, process of elimination also makes the test relatively easy. If more than twelve or fifteen items are used in either list, the student will spend more time hunting than discriminating on the selections to be made.

Four errors are built into the sample test given: (1) the number of items in each column is equal, (2) too many items are included in each column, (3) part of each column is continued on a second page, and (4) items 20 and *t* were omitted due to crowding at the bottom margin. (See *A Sample Matching Test* below.)

By keeping the lists between six and twelve items and by having more items in one list than in the other, the teacher forces the student to discriminate closely between the items to be chosen. The student must choose items with skill and necessarily leave some items blank. Use of such a list could determine the readiness of a group to intelligently use the library for study purposes. Sections from the *Reader's Guide,* the card catalogue, or reference books would determine whether a trip to the library would be *wasted in hunting,* or *spent in using the facilities available.* Many library excursions are little more than an "outing" in which the students eagerly vote their way out of class. The same applies to field trips. Matching tests may be used to determine the amount of

---

A Sample Matching Test

1. Thespis	a. Throws a strong light
2. Iszonous	b. Handing pipe
3. Proscenium	c. Used for blocking
4. Baton	d. Unit of scenery
5. Ratchet	e. Device to cut glare
6. "In one"	f. Stage opening
7. Aristophanes	g. Used for locking ropes on a fly system
8. Ground row	h. Used for flying
9. Deux Ex Machina	i. Additive color
10. Fresnel	j. Electronic lighting
11. Lamp	k. Producer
12. Barometer	l. First actor
13. Floor plan	m. Playwright
14. Ellipsoidal	n. Died in 1950
15. Barn door	o. Amount paid to put on play
16. Counterweight system	p. Source of light
17. 3 fold	q. Mechanical screwdriver
18. Pin rail	r. Greek device to elevate actor
19. G. Bernard Shaw	s. Soft, diffused light

21. No	u. Report of business done
22. L.C.	v. Japanese theatre
23. Red, blue, green	w. Combination of all colors
24. White	x. Chinese theatre
25. David Belasco	y. Left center
26. Royalty	z. A floor piece to simulate distant mountains or foliage

recognition on what was seen and talked about or what material is to be used after the trip has been completed.

The matching test takes more time for the student to read and reread in making his choice and allows him some opportunity for guessing despite great care in construction, but it is a good tool for measuring recognition, classification, or association of specific parts of ideas and the relation of things to terminology. Because learning often moves from recognition to use and then to understanding, this test is an aid in developing understanding between the steps of instruction.

Assume for the moment that the teacher wishes to develop a light crew capable of selecting the proper instruments for a given play. The students have seen various lighting instruments in storage facilities and many have been aware of their use in actual production. The teacher may have taken time to teach the uses to be made of each instrument. A test might be designed like this one:

Instructions: Match the instruments listed in column 1 with specific use or description of its function in column 2. Place the appropriate letter from column 1 in the blank following the number in column 2.

a. lekolight (elipsoidal reflector)	1. a three-circuit light unit used to light scenery rather than actors	1_____
b. plano-convex (baby spot)	2. a spotlight whose light distribution is greater at the center of the spot than at the outside edges	2_____
c. fresnel	3. a highly efficient spotlight with shutters used to frame an object without spilling light on the scenery around the object	3_____
d. ollivete		
e. par-38	4. an inexpensive lamp designed for multi-use which has a high heat ratio to the amount of candlepower; often used in window decoration	4_____
f. striplight		

If the majority of the students can answer these items, the teacher hardly needs to accompany a student to the storage area to select two fresnel spotlights and one section of strip lights to set up a scene in a classroom or assembly. Pictures could have been used in the second column for an *alternate form* test. One might note that tests need not be long to be effective. The above item might begin a class as a means of introducing the problem and determining the need for instruction. If the concepts are known, instruction may be changed or omitted.

Terms Related to Interpretation — A Matching Test

Match the concepts in column 1 with the terms in column 2. Some of the terms in column 1 may be used more than once. Some of the blanks at the right may be left blank if no answer from column 1 is correct.

a. pause and phrasing	1. dialect	1._____
b. number of words in a period of time	2. rate	2._____
	3. tempo	3._____
c. feeling along with	4. monologue	4._____
d. high pitch	5. dialogue	5._____
e. local characteristics of speech	6. empathy	6._____
f. one person speaking	7. fright	7._____
g. rising and falling pitch	8. vocal variety	8._____
	9. inflection	9._____

Basic Principles — A Matching Test

Match the concepts in column 1 with the terms in column 2. Place the answers in the blanks at right.

a. most persuasive form of public speaking	1. impersonation	1._____
	2. acting	2._____
b. presentation of cases on a controversial subject	3. oratory	3._____
	4. mood	4._____
c. original, interpretive	5. discussion	5._____
d. between acting and oral reading	6. debate	6._____
e. exploration of a topic to clarify thinking	7. kinds of speaking	7._____
f. becoming a character	8. speaking situations	8._____
g. convincing an audience of a specific point of view	9. expression	9._____
h. informal, formal		

The True-False Test

The label of this test (true-false, alternative-response, right-wrong, or correct-incorrect) does not change the style or the use to be made of the instrument. Each item is listed as a positive or negative statement and the student must indicate in an appropriate place (on an answer sheet or on the original) his reaction to the item. He is asked to indicate if he agrees or does not agree with the statement.

The symbol to be used in making the choice varies with the teacher. Because a written *T* may be confused with a hurriedly written *F*, some teachers prefer other symbols. So long as the symbol eliminates confusion there is little place for argument over relative values. If, however, students are using one set of symbols in one class and a contradictory set in a second class, the test may be invalidated by the confusion between the two teachers' systems. Some teachers prefer the use of plus (+) and minus (—) but others prefer to eliminate discussion following a test when a minus can easily be changed. Thus they may use the letter (*T*) and the letter (*O*). A check on the practices of other teachers may aid the teacher in making the necessary choice. Consistency in later practice should eliminate confusion among the students and focus their attention on the content or process to be measured rather than on the mechanics of the testing procedure.

A good true-false item should require the student to approach a decision concerning knowledge in a new way. Good items are not taken directly from text books where the student is merely asked to recognize that which he has seen before. Forced choice items such as matching or multiple choice are better for that purpose. Mental photographic skill is hardly a measurement of knowledge or the application of knowledge. The statement must be very clear, definite, and free from opinion.

If the wording of the statement leaves room for debate, or if more than one answer is possible, the item should be reworked or omitted. Short sentences are better than long ones in this type of test item. Students who are more test-wise are aware that verbiage involves more and more qualifying features. The greater the number of qualifications the greater is the chance of negation of the concept. Many students will therefore mark long items as negative (false) on the assumption that qualifications cause the entire item to be negative. Students also learn a semantic principle in objective testing. Items with *absolutes* of positive or negative nature are generally false. The use of "allness" ("always" or "never") is a cue to use the negative response on the true-false test.

Whether in a complete unit of true-false items or in a mixed set of various types of items, the basic rule is not to include items in one section which furnish answers to items elsewhere in the test. Again the teacher is reminded that the student needing the least help is given the most assistance in this type of item selection. The brilliant student easily detects slight clues, but the slow reader working hard on one item at a time seldom has the time or the awareness to detect that this item was included in the multiple-choice or matching section of the examination.

The true-false test has certain disadvantages in its use which teachers seldom recognize. As with all tests we are concerned with *validity* and *reliability*. Will the instrument test that for which it is designed and do so consistently? The true-false test lacks reliability if it lacks a sufficient number of items or if the scope of material to be covered (information or abilities) gives an inadequate sampling. The teacher may be led into traps since constructing items for one section of the material may be easier than for another. He must be careful to outline the material to be covered, make sure the total weight of the items is evenly distributed throughout the test, and present enough items in each section to gain reliability.

In order to gain reliability on the true-false test, fifty to one hundred items must be included. These may be distributed across short tests given each day or may be included in one large test. The individual scores may lack reliability, but the total scores take in the factors of scope and quantity to regain the overall picture. Students can be expected to process two to four items per minute, and therefore a large number of items can be used as a total test or as a review test on a daily basis.

This type of a test is of little diagnostic value because the teacher is not aware of the reasons why students are uninformed. He is merely aware of what is known from the total of what was asked. Many teachers find it difficult to stimulate class discussion of the test using this instrument. Once the students have their scores they may wish to debate about some of the questions but seldom wish to develop a discussion of understandings. Its greatest value is to test for specific knowledge. It is a difficult test to construct but is extremely fast to correct when the keys are designed to fit the margin of the test or the answer sheet. The construction of other forms of this test (alternate and equivalent) is one advantage of this instrument. Suggestions for these other forms were explained earlier. To make this test most efficient the teacher must eliminate opinion questions, keep the items simple, and avoid clues and specific determinants.

The Arrangement Test

The arrangement test is little used but is one of the better tests for determining the ability of students to order items according to importance or relationship. Numerous items can be listed and the student is expected to arrange them in chronological, logical, or cause-to-effect order, or in order of importance in outline form. Experienced teachers recognize the ability to outline as one of the continuing challenges of teaching. Students complain that they have had outlining before, but their themes and speeches continue to indicate a lack of understanding of the process of outlining and even the various types of outlining available to develop a particular idea. Drama teachers may use this instrument in preparing materials for drama to determine the understanding of order in scenery construction. Speech teachers may use it to measure the problems which cause poor speech construction, or emphasize the order needed to prepare for debate, radio programming, or play production.

Multiple-Choice Tests

Like the matching test, the multiple-choice test has two basic parts. The first part is an introduction to a concept or a question; the second part presents several possible answers from which the student selects the one he believes is the best choice to complete the statement.

The multiple-choice item is often referred to as a "forced choice" instrument because the student is forced to select one of several possible items. All items must be so well constructed as to be a challenge to the thought and judgment of the student. Thus each of the alternate choices must possess elements which make its choice desirable. If the item includes less than five alternate choices, the student may successfully guess the right answer through the process of elimination. Inclusion of choices which are obviously wrong merely diverts attention and contributes nothing to the reliability or validity of the item. It is better to have four good alternate choices than to have a fifth which is nonsense in relation to the concept. All alternate choices need not be completely false — they may be true but simply not relevant to the introduction. Further, if the choices exceed five or six, the student spends too much time in elimination and hunting. Care must be taken in constructing the correct and incorrect choices if the student is to be forced to make a discriminating selection. Be sure to vary the location of the "correct" item in the alternate choices. Simplicity in the introduction and the conclusion, relatedness in all alternate choices, possible and likely situations, positive rather than negative statements, and noncontradiction between the introduction of the statement and the conclusion are all necessary.

Although the student will spend considerable time taking the test, the teacher can correct the test in a relatively short time. The teacher can also detect from his item analysis the types of misconceptions which the students hold and can take steps toward remedial teaching. A single concept or generalization may provide one good multiple-choice item and several true-false items for alternate forms, but be sure not to include them in the same form since they may act as cues for items in other parts of the test.

The multiple-choice test is highly valuable for measuring judgment as well as the depth of reasoning in the use of knowledge. A student who is prone to talk around a subject on an essay might be forced to discriminate in this type of test. Like the matching test it can be used to identify the correct part of a diagram, instrument, or type of reading matter. Thus it is helpful in outlining, speech construction, stagecraft, and other instructional processes.

---

*Questions on Speaking—A Multiple-Choice Test**

Select the best answer to complete the thought.
1. The expression of the thoughts, moods, emotions,   1._____
   and feelings of another by a speaker is called
   (*a*) public speaking, (*b*) interpretation, (*c*) discussion, (*d*) conversation, (*e*) none of these.
2. The process of interpretation is (*a*) simple,   2._____
   (*b*) easy, (*c*) hard, (*d*) complex, (*e*) none of these.
3. The basic unit of interpretation is (*a*) the sentence,   3._____
   (*b*) phrasing, (*c*) pause, (*d*) grammar, (*e*) none of
   these.
4. Mood in oral interpretation refers to (*a*) how the   4._____
   author feels about some phase of life, (*b*) the state
   of mind of the reader, (*c*) the feelings of the major
   character, (*d*) the scene, (*e*) none of these.
5. The most frequently used means of emphasis in   5._____
   presenting thought is (*a*) pause, (*b*) force, (*c*) inflection, (*d*) pitch, (*e*) none of these.
6. Changes in the quality of your voice probably indi-   6._____
   cate changes in your (*a*) eye contact, (*b*) pitch,
   (*c*) interest, (*d*) mood, (*e*) none of these.
7. For the purposes of diagnosis, training, and retrain-   7._____
   ing, the speech act may be divided into (*a*) types
   of phonation, (*b*) types of articulation, (*c*) types
   of formulation of thought, (*d*) fundamental processes, (*e*) none of these.

---

*An answer sheet could be made to match the spacing of the numbered column on the right. The second column might have spaces for answers 11 through 22, and the third column questions 23 through 40. Thus five columns on each side of an 8½ x 11 page might become the answer sheet for 100 questions.

8. Adequate formulation of thought is evidenced by 8._____
(*a*) ideas that are well expressed, (*b*) repetition of ideas, (*c*) unconnected ideas, (*d*) poor grammar, (*e*) none of these.

9. Thoughts that are expressed orally should always 9._____
have a (*a*) punch line, (*b*) moral, (*c*) purpose, (*d*) direction, (*e*) none of these.

10. The production, modification, and variation of the 10._____
tones of a speaker's voice as he speaks is known as (*a*) the process of phonation, (*b*) the process of articulation, (*c*) the process of oration, (*d*) the process of interpretation, (*e*) none of these.

CONSTRUCTING SUBJECTIVE INSTRUMENTS

Types of Subjective Instruments

The speech teacher utilizes many *subjective* forms of evaluation in teaching. A considerable amount of information needed to clarify the reasons his students are motivated or fail to learn can be isolated for study. *Personality inventories* may help in clearing up the picture but do not furnish the complete pattern of behavior. A single speech needs many *rating instruments* to measure all the aspects which lead to a successful performance. Still the teacher must use such information as he has to make judgments, diagnose the problems, and relate them to the success or lack of success in the speech performance. In a sense the speech teacher is little better than his ability to make worthwhile subjective evaluation and improve instruction to meet the needs of the student. The good teacher combines all the "objective" judgments possible to ramify his "educated guesses" in the subjective evaluation he is forced to make.

Rater Competence

The teacher is involved in two basic types of evaluation of a subjective nature. The first involves diagnosis to determine the status of the student. With this procedure he hopes to determine the student's potential and limitations as well as isolate specific problems to be studied and corrected. The subjective evaluations made often call for specific skills. Seeing and hearing are used in many observational tests where anecdotal records or rating sheets are used. *If the teacher is limited in his ability to view or listen with discrimination the evaluations will lack validity and reli-*

ability. For example, one student teacher was finding fault with a student in an interpretive exercise for lacking variety in his speech patterns. In order to better understand the problem the two of them went to the laboratory for a hearing test. Audiometric and Seashore tests for musical talent were given to the student and the teacher. The experience proved very interesting since the tests showed that the teacher had almost no aptitude in pitch discrimination and virtually no melody discrimination. Using some worn-out, mechanical cliches, he had rebuked the student but was unable to hear the actual variation which the student used. Since the speech teacher uses so many applications of tonal sound quality, where musical aptitude is necessary to teach interpretive techniques properly, it seems almost a necessity that his pitch discrimination be acute. He should also have precision in the other basic features of the musical elements of speech — rhythm, duration, melody, and volume.

In a discussion of what a speech test[2] is, the following qualities were listed as requirements for anyone expecting to evaluate by observational means. The observer must have (1) efficient sensory capacities, (2) the capacity for alertness and concentration, (3) the ability to make fine distinctions, (4) the ability to make observations quickly, (5) the ability to interpret, (6) the knowledge of what to look for, and (7) freedom from prejudice. When one realizes that the spoken word is fleeting and that the observer is bombarded with new symbols of sound and rhythm each new minute, then one can understand that the observer is considerably challenged. Intuition is hardly a good instrument for use in such a situation and thus the teacher must strive to improve instruments to aid in observational measurement. The teacher should turn to a form of analysis that is more systematic. The observer improves his ability when he begins to look for something definite. The validity of the rating improves when the specific item to be observed is related to actual performance.

Considerable discussion is generated when one begins to select or build a rating scale for use in classroom or contest speaking. In actual situations of speaking to the public the impact on the audience is the only valid measurement. Some parts of this impact can never be measured. Many people are affected by a given performance but do not reduce their reaction to a measurable quantity. In some instances a very simple rating sheet is useful, whereas in more complex cases a more complicated instrument is needed.

In selecting judges for a debate the more experienced often refuse to use multi-factor scales on the grounds that paying attention to so

---

[2]Franklin H. Knower, "What is a Speech Test?" *The Quarterly Journal of Speech*, 30:485-493 (1944).

many items on the rating scale diverts attention from the speaker and thus reduces the judge's ability to listen to the basic thing to be measured — the speech. If the rater is experienced, he may choose to look for *content, organization,* and *delivery* in the polished speech. In the classroom, however, each of these may need to be subdivided for purposes of analysis. Delivery may comprise many things related to the production and formulation of sound; it may include poise and manner in speaker-audience relationships; it may deal with variation of pace, tempo, speech patterns, and rhythm. Organization and content may be equally complex, but can all these items be approached at one time?

Lomas discusses criticism as it relates to stagefright and warns that the criticism must be graded to the degree that the speaker is prepared to accept it constructively.[3] Little has been accomplished to help the speaker if the degree of criticism destroys his ability to contend with the speaking situation at a future time. Lomas also implies that in graded criticism a few items at a time focus the attention on those things done well and those things one can work on for immediate challenge and improvement. As in any skill the student must isolate and do the finger exercises in speech. An accumulation of skilled finger exercises leads to a composite of polished performance. *The difference between the skilled speech teacher and the general classroom teacher should be the ability of the one to recognize the specific problems of the student and understand the amount, degree, and quality which he may profitably attack at one time.*

Diagnostic Ratings

Early rating sheets may deal with diagnosis for teacher and student use. These, like the Barnes charts, may concentrate upon three or four items. Adjustment to the speaking situation may be a broad concept but adequate for the first speech. The teacher may even keep his attention on one process while the student may be focusing upon another. The teacher may be looking for phonation and articulation problems while the student is working on the improvement of a speech of demonstration or information. The teacher may not necessarily get a true picture of the student's speech habits while he is concentrating on the same problem. His habit is that which will become evident when he concentrates on his message.

Later charts may deal with more specific aspects of speech organization, audience analysis, choice of language, or any specific goal the teacher has been developing. Sample rating sheets may be found in

---

[3]Lomas, *op. cit.*

large number in the many books prepared for high school use — those rating sheets developed for methods courses and those developed for adjudicating contest speaking. A complicated form, like the progressive rating sheet of Fig. 21, may be used only with certain items as the focal concern on any one day. This plan may be desirable in that the student is able to see the total expectation of the speaking act and then pick the "finger exercises" for a given lesson or performance.

Several of the available rating sheets utilize the numerical rating system as used by Barnes. Here a number of specific items are listed and the student is scored from 1 through 5 according to the judgment of the evaluator. The instructions indicate whether the 1 or the 5 is the highest rating. The biggest problem in using such a scale is that a rating of 3 varies with the emotional attitude of the rater, the time of day, the student preceding the speaker, and so forth.

Some teachers use a linear scale in an attempt to approach specificity. Such a scale is implicit in the chart which follows. The purpose of this particular linear scale is to focus attention on the speech and not on the speaker. For early speech assignments this plan is desirable in aiding the student to diminish stagefright. Note the attention to preparation through use of the resources, attention to an outline, analysis of the audience, and use of any illustrative materials. The speaker's interest in the subject is the most direct focus upon the individual but does not point attention to his fear or self-consciousness.

General Speech Skills

Did the student make intelligent use of resources?
    no 1 2 3 4 5 6 7 8 9 10 yes
Did the student complete clear outlines?
    no 1 2 3 4 5 6 7 8 9 10 yes
Was there a realistic analysis of the audience?
    no 1 2 3 4 5 6 7 8 9 10 yes
Were demonstration materials shown to advantage?
    no 1 2 3 4 5 6 7 8 9 10 yes
Did the speaker indicate a vital interest in the subject?
    no 1 2 3 4 5 6 7 8 9 10 yes

Rating the Speaker and the Speech

After several speaking experiences in which the attention has been placed upon the performance, the speaker may be ready to begin looking more critically at himself. The varied success of previous speaking experiences may have readied him for more critical appraisal of the speech act as measured against audience reaction. The rating scale may even include specific instructional aids. The questions raised by the scale may give specific guidance in preparing for the speech.

For the moment let us look at a rating scale for instructional use. The first item immediately focuses attention upon the poise and control of the speaker and the relevancy of this to posture. Again the importance of turning the attention of the audience to the speech rather than the speaker is emphasized in item two. The importance of materials and types of evidence is reflected by the relation of items three and four. Only as the evidence is related to the fundamental wants of people can it prove effective, thus these items should be close together. Inclusion of such items suggests the content of instruction to prepare students for this speaking experience. The speaker-audience relationship is included, possibly reduntantly. Thesis, purpose, and audibility follow. Note that being heard was not referred to through volume but through the basic elements of placement, resonance, and quality.

Speaker's Rating Sheet

Did the speaker evidence poise, control, and good posture?
   no   1   2   3   4   5   6   7   8   9   10   yes
Was your attention and interest turned to the subject?
   no   1   2   3   4   5   6   7   8   9   10   yes
Did the speaker present interesting materials and facts?
   no   1   2   3   4   5   6   7   8   9   10   yes
Were illustrations based upon the fundamental wants of people?
   no   1   2   3   4   5   6   7   8   9   10   yes
Was there a good speaker-audience relationship?
   no   1   2   3   4   5   6   7   8   9   10   yes
Was the thesis emphasized enough to be well understood?
   no   1   2   3   4   5   6   7   8   9   10   yes
Did the speaker accomplish his purpose?
   no   1   2   3   4   5   6   7   8   9   10   yes
Was the voice projected, resonant, pleasant?
   no   1   2   3   4   5   6   7   8   9   10   yes

Any one item might be selected as the goal for the day from all the items on a rating sheet. A specific speech following concentrated instructions on audience analysis may be confined to those items dealing specifically with audience factors.

The task of the teacher in a particular activity is reflected in the items included in the rating sheet. Debate items focus attention on order, logical development, support of the argument with evidence, thorough knowledge of the subject, challenge *to* the opposing points of view as well as meeting the challenge *of* the opposition. If these are important to the speaker in a discussion or debate they should likewise be a vital part of the instruction and should also be reflected in the instrument for evaluating classroom performance. The student soon adapts to the types of stimulation which gain satisfaction for him. It behooves the teacher, therefore, to make sure that important concepts are used as a means of judgment. Since the ability to think and to make mature value judgments is more important than the ability to adjust to policy, the student should frequently be judged on the basis of value and thought application.

STANDARDIZED TESTS

The school often participates in the administration of certain standardized tests. These are highly structured, often machine-scored if desired, and have been administered in many geographic areas to various groups of students of similar ages until the results can be said to have established a *standard,* or *norm.* Thus a new school may take such a test and determine the degree of relationship of the total *school to the norm,* or of each *student to the norm.* In this way the school may evaluate its own instruction and its way of meeting the problems of instruction. Such tests are available in various subjects which influence speech, but few are available to measure factors which are directly pertinent to the speaking act. Among the types useful to the speech teacher are those dealing with verbal aptitude, intelligence quotient, social studies, reasoning, and even personality inventories. Great skill of judgment is needed to interpret and use the results of some of these tests. Unfortunately, few teachers are qualified to interpret the data properly. Even fewer classroom teachers have enough training or skill to deal with the therapy involving personality deviation and other factors important to the speech-personality relationships. Those knowing least, too often, have the most courage in launching therapeutic programs.

GRADING POLICY

Some Relationships of Testing, Grading, and Evaluation. Considerable time is spent in the public schools giving *tests.* In-service teacher programs devote time to discussing *evaluation, testing, and grading procedures.* These concepts have many similarities and in some cases are treated as though they were synonymous. Too often the only purpose of test administration in the classroom is to determine grades. In some cases the grades have been predetermined — by inherent ability, study facilities, or other factors outside the course. In many cases the test is little more than a motivational whip to guarantee the reading of text material or the completion of certain drill activities. The teacher must analyze any test and determine the purpose for which it is given.

Evaluation seems to be the biggest concept of the three elements being considered. It includes all *objective* and *subjective* means to determine status, progress, or policy.

Grading is a problem of *policy* and is established when the student receives a rank, position, or grouping assignment relative to others in his class or school, to national norms, or to his previous position. The judgment of the teacher is improved by using valid instruments.

Teachers sometimes describe grading as a great evil which acts as a barrier to motivation, while at the same time they continue to threaten students with grades as a form of motivation. Administratively, schools are required to make some type of ranking of the various class groups and individuals. Many schools have attempted to replace the traditional forms of grading with conferences, letters to the parents, or new symbols. Ultimately someone asks for a recommendation for a student and he is placed in the top fourth, above or below the median, in relation to his classmates. Parents and students find new grading systems difficult to interpret after being conditioned to a five-step scale of marks. They are further confused when three different children bring home report cards using three different systems of grading. Thus the pressures continue to retain the old techniques or use dual systems. Behavioral rating may be ignored if rankings on subject skills are high.

Establishing Grading Policy. Grading will continue. The teacher must determine how the grade is to be established. Should it be established according to *knowledge of the content* of the course? If so, how is one to determine whether you have a true measurement of what is known? Should it be established on the *basis of effort* or the *amount of growth* during a given period of instruction? How shall the teacher determine these quantities or qualities? If the grade is to reflect a *prediction of success* in other experiences in a competitive society, to what extent will *knowledge, effort, and ability to grow* be reflected in the grade? If the student is overrated on his knowledge and proficiency by behavioral traits (effort and growth factors), will he later suffer in competition due to a poor sense of values which have been established by the use of *effort* and *growth* in grading? Such questions lead one to fear the effects of grades and avoid the responsibilities of grading. In some cases tests are used as criteria to defend the grade when the student or parent challenges the report card. Thus, *testing may become a part of the defense mechanism of the teacher.* The important point at this time is to *determine the goals of instruction and relate all grading to those goals.* Grading policy can remain educationally sound when related to sound objectives. In some cases policy is set by administrative edict without reference to any instructional objectives. School policy may determine cut-off points and the ratio of final examination scores to project scores.

Grading is Necessary and Profitable. The student and the parent expect a report on the progress and status of the student. Like the employee in a factory or on the farm, the student likes to have some indication as to whether he is to be retained, promoted, or fired. Many are aware of a degree of satisfaction between the student and the teacher. This awareness increases with the communicative ability and sensitivity of both. The student attitude depends upon the instruments used and the frequency of evaluation. The instruments should assist in helping the student become aware of how others feel about his speech effort.

Grading is a Process of Communication. Grading, in spite of all its weaknesses, is a constant part of learning procedure. Grading may be faulty and may be based upon misevaluations, but the student will also suffer these experiences in the world of work. Often his knowledge of status may increase his motivation and rank. The basic rating is necessary to improve communications between the school, the student, and the home. If the parent speaks Italian and the grades are issued in Arabic, little communication takes place. In fact suspicions may be aroused resulting in a breakdown in communications. The inability, or unwillingness, to interpret new grading symbols (such as satisfactory, unsatisfactory) has forced some school districts back to the five letter grade systems which "parents can interpret."

The cutting line between satisfactory and unsatisfactory is relative and is affected by many things. Is ten percent error satisfactory in arithmetic, or measurement of chemical compounds? If so, who will take care of the unbalanced bank accounts, sales slips, or tax reports? Can we accept 10% error in mixing medicines? Who is to determine the right or wrong of policy questions related to economics or social problems?

The use of class ranking often determines whether the student will be admitted to college, receive a scholarship, obtain a job, or complete school. Such ranking is not always based upon potential or intelligence. The application of knowledge, the attitude which leads to completed work, the patience to rework and drill until proficiency is reached, and attendance and punctuality oftentimes are reflected in the quantity and quality of the student's learning. Human nature often leads one to do the expected. Grading policy is an indication to the student of satisfactory expectations with those classmates who receive grades at variance from his own.

There has been a great deal of criticism about the competitive elements of the school. Some have even assumed that, if the school would abandon all competition, the next generation would be free from such evils. Selection of a mate and possessions is as primitive in a sophisticated society as among savages. The elimination of competition may lead to racial suicide. The job of the school is to teach values so that the student more wisely selects the things for which he expends great energy in competition. G. Stanley Hall has said, regarding the instincts of youth and their implication for education, that

> "Youth loves combat, and this may be developed into debate; it loves distinction and to exert influence, and this suggests oratory; it loves to assume roles and to widen sympathy by representing at this circumstating stage, with its keen sense of character, manifold types of human life; and has a passion for the theatre and this suggests the drama, which always has this supreme moral quality that the good is victorious."

Grading Curves and Use of Test Results

Grading curves are instruments used in grading practices. If the sampling is sufficiently large, students tested will distribute themselves in roughly a bell-shaped curve, as shown in Fig. 22. A distribution of top scores will correspond to an equal distribution of low scores (the number of A grades equals the E grades). The center of the curve will indicate the largest distribution of scores (C), while the number of scores distributed between the center and the high scores will be matched

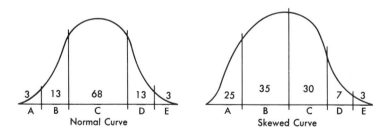

Figure 22. Normal and Skewed Grading Curves

by equal numbers between the center and the low scores (B equals D). Various studies place this distribution over a variable range depending upon its use. Although it is a theoretical curve, it is often used as though it were fact.

Teachers using this curve may distribute the grade cut-off points arbitrarily at 3% A, 13% B, 68% C, 13% D, and 3% F, or at 7% A, 14% B, 58% C, 14% D, and 7% F. If the sampling within their classrooms were sufficiently large to gain a valid measurement, they would find the total scores falling approximately into such a distribution. Some studies indicate a need for not less than one thousand samples to establish any validity in use of the curve. Even this number may be insufficient if the sample is skewed rather than random. Skewing occurs when a sample includes a selected group with or without training in a field. Thus a course with prerequisites has a skewed sample.

Misuse of this curve theory takes many variations. One teacher with thirty-three college-preparatory students in biology administered the same test to them and to a group of non-college-preparatory students. Two curves were established. A score of 79 in the "college-prep" group was marked a failure but given an A in the non-college group. Neither sample was large enough to justify the use of the curve. The norm had been arbitrarily established by the teacher — rather than by a distribution of grades. Needless to say, one should question this grading policy. Should both groups have been taught the same course in the same way? If there were variations in the course presentation, then the weighting as well as the selection of items called for variation.

Attitudes toward testing and rating scales often diminish the effectiveness of teaching. Student attitudes may invalidate an instrument. The student is often frightened by test situations. The student who is test-wise is not blocked by the knowledge that he is being rated or graded. The student with "test-phobia" may overreact to the outcome of the test. Some teachers believe that frequent tests acclimate the student to the testing situation. Frequent tests also serve to furnish many test results and thus diminish (in the student mind) the importance of any one test score. Surely a teacher should question the policy that one-third or one-half of the final grade will be based upon a single final examination. Research does not support the theory that any one test, or any one performance, is a true measurement of what has been learned or what can be applied.

Grading is directly associated with the philosophy of the teacher and the policy of the school. National objectives for education subscribe to the statement that "education is for all American youth" and even go so far as to proclaim loudly that "speech (art, music, mathematics,

English, history) is needed by all students." These are the verbalizations. Teaching and grading practice indicate that *"only the talented* can hope to pass this course." Only the talented in a particular content or subject area can hope to do passing work? The critical question for any teacher to determine is answered in his philosophy of education. More specifically, what is the purpose of the secondary school? What is the contribution of this particular course to the secondary school? Care must be taken that required courses not be used as screening devices for advanced classes.

How much specific instruction is needed? Many educational specialists maintain that the secondary school is the time for exploration. The student should have brief introductions into the aspects of any field of study. They discourage depth probing on the basis that such depth is too time consuming and thus limits the exploration. The frequent question asked by generalists is: How much do students need to know? By this they imply that there is a breaking point at less depth than many subject-centered teachers feel is an adequate level of accomplishment.

Other educational leaders support the view that the best way to explore is to give depth study into fewer experiences. By carefully selecting a few representative experiences the student should gain usable skills for exploration, thus leading him to choose or eliminate more wisely. The student should develop a sense of values and establish tools by which he can become capable of knowing. It is preferable that he talk less and talk more accurately. Both points of view champion programs which would require students to enroll in courses in many areas, but *the grading practices are not always in agreement with the verbalization of the philosophy. One might raise the question as to whether the practice or the verbalization is the philosophy.*

The Challenge of Honest Grading. For dedicated teachers the problem of giving failing grades to those students who evidence little aptitude, proficiency, or adaptability to the learning situation in a given area results in frustration and heartache. To those less dedicated this group of students offers the easy way to establish some type of curve predetermined by the teacher or school policy. Regardless of the need for grade distribution and policy it seems reasonable to expect a system of evaluation to encompass the matter of helping the student realize that there are some areas in which he is not, nor will become, highly efficient. We do not expect the shetland pony to pull the load of an elephant, nor do we expect the elephant to race the thoroughbred. We do not expect equal performance of the draft horse and the racing breed in either of the other's developed specialty. Thus, we must help students to find those areas in which they are most proficient, to widen their areas of proficiency insofar as the broadening concept is profitable to them. It seems imperative, however, that they learn that in all activities there may be some who can demonstrate proficiency better than they. The school, it seems, is charged with teaching the child to evaluate his own abilities and to work out his problems and challenges. The school cannot do this if it fails to help him face reality in evaluating himself. Many students underrate their abilities and this is equally as serious (in the limitations they place upon themselves) as it would be to consistently overrate themselves. The teacher must help the student in honest self-evaluation. Speech teachers should be particularly concerned with this type of student.

Because grading policy is so controversial, a number of individuals and departments of schools have attempted to rationalize the existing policy with specific criteria. Charles R. Gruner redesigned the items used at Penn State in order to gain *grading objectives based more on behavioral criteria*. A total of 328 usable returns (52.3%) were analyzed, giving some guide as to the grading policy practiced by teachers in the profession. His statement follows in Supplement 4.

Supplement 4.

Behavioral Objectives Expected by Teachers of Speech as Criteria for the Grading of Classroom Speeches*

Charles R. Gruner

Baker[4] has pointed out the lack, except for incidental remarks,[5] of published material on speech behavioral objectives, and Kibler[6] has stressed the importance to the speech student and teacher of clear behavioral objectives. Since the rating or "grading" of speeches seems to vary greatly among raters,[7]

---

*Reproduced by permission of the author. The study also appears in *The Speech Teacher*, 17:207-209 (September, 1968). See also Henrietta Cortright, Doris Niles, and Dorothy Weinrich, "Criteria to Evaluate Speech I in the Senior High School," *The Speech Teacher*, 17:217-224 (September, 1968).

[4]Eldon E. Baker, "Aligning Speech Evaluation and Behavioral Objectives," *The Speech Teacher*, 16:158-160 (March, 1967).

[5]Theodore Clevenger, Jr., "Some Factors Involved in Classroom Procedures for the Acquisition of Verbal Concepts," *The Speech Teacher*, 15:113-118 (March, 1956).

[6]Robert J. Kibler, "Developing Behavioral Objectives for Undergraduate Speech Instruction," Paper presented at the 1963 SAA convention, Denver.

[7]For instance, see Wayne N. Thompson, "An Experimental Study of the Accuracy of Typical Speech Rating Techniques," *Speech Monographs*, 11:65-79 (1944).

the present study was undertaken to see what agreement, if any, exists among speech teachers on what behaviors are expected of student speeches in order to obtain different grades.

Procedures. The "behavioral objectives" used were basically those standards for speech grading used at Penn State and published by Oliver.[8] They were re-written to conform more closely (although not completely) to the concept of "behavioral objectives" as defined by Mager[9] and by Kibler.[10] In the spring of 1967 the objectives were randomly ordered, mimeographed, and mailed, with a cover letter, to the 651 Undergraduate Speech Instruction Interest Group members listed in the 1966-67 *SAA Directory*. Each USI member was to check whether he required the objective's achievement for a C, B, or A speech. It was assumed that any objective required for a C speech would be required of a B and an A speech; that one required for a B would also be required for an A; and that an objective not required at all would be left unchecked. Respondents were encouraged to write on the back of the page their own objectives not on the list.

Results. Of the 651 questionnaires sent out, 23 were returned as "undeliverable," resulting in a net total of 628 sent out. By June 9, 1967, 336 had been returned; 8 were not filled out and were thus not usable, resulting in a total net return of 328, or 52.3% of the net total sent out. This was considered a sufficient sample for the purposes of this study, so a follow-up letter was not mailed.

The following chart lists the objectives in the questionnaire in the order they appeared in the questionnaire and the total number and percentage of respondents checking that objective as required for each grade. For any one objective the percentages may not total 100%, since some respondents did not consider it an objective necessary for any grade.

Behavioral Objective:		REQUIRED FOR:		
		"C"	"B"	"A"
1. The speech style was distinguished by elements of vividness, such an analogies or comparisons, metaphor, specific instances, humor, concreteness, etc.	#:	19	177	125
	%:	5.8	54.0	38.1
2. The speech had a clear purpose in terms of auditor response sought, supported by main heads easy to identify.[11]	#:	227	87	9
	%:	62.9	26.5	2.7
3. The speaker demonstrated reasonable directness and communicativeness in delivery.	#:	287	36	3
	%:	87.5	11.0	0.9

[8]Robert T. Oliver, "The Eternal (and Infernal) Problem of Grades," *The Speech Teacher*, 9:8-11 (January, 1960).

[9]Robert F. Mager, *Preparing Instructional Objectives* (San Francisco: Fearon Publishers, Inc., 1962), p. 12.

[10]Kibler, *op. cit.*

[11]One respondent indicated objective required for a "D."

REQUIRED FOR:

		"C"	"B"	"A"
4. The speaker did not detract from his message through gross errors of grammar, pronunciation, or articulation.	#: %:	278 84.8	37 11.3	7 2.1
5. The speaker made a genuinely individual contribution to the thinking of his audience.	#: %:	17 5.2	126 38.4	170 51.8
6. The speech was intellectually sound in developing a topic of real worth, using adequate and dependable evidence.	#: %:	73 22.3	221 67.4	33 10.1
7. The speech conformed reasonably to the assigned time limit.[12]	#: %:	294 89.6	17 5.2	6 1.8
8. The speaker made understandable an unusually difficult concept or process; OR he won *some* agreement from an audience initially inclined to disagree with him; OR he won *some* tendency to act from an audience initially inclined not to so act.	#: %:	16 4.9	136 41.5	161 49.1
9. The speaker achieved a variety and flexibility of mood and manner suited to the multiple differentiation of thinking and feeling demanded by the subject matter and by the speaker-audience relations.	#: %:	19 5.8	130 39.6	159 48.5
10. The speech was of the type assigned (to inform, to convince, to actuate, etc.).[12]	#: %:	313 95.4	8 2.4	5 1.5
11. The speaker moved the audience progressively from initial uncertainty (of knowledge, belief, or tendency to act) toward the acceptance of the speaker's purpose, by orderly processes, toward a final resolution of the uncertainty in a conclusion that evolved naturally from the materials used by the speaker.	#: %:	18 5.5	138 42.1	158 48.2
12. The speech was better than most classroom speeches in *stimulative quality*, that is, in challenging the audience to think, or in arousing depth or response.	#: %:	5 1.5	230 70.1	88 26.8
13. The speaker established rapport of a high order with apt style and direct, extemporaneous delivery, achieving a genuinely communicative *circular response*.	#: %:	10 3.0	96 29.3	212 64.6
14. The speech was presented on the date for which it was assigned.[13]	#: %:	286 87.2	14 4.3	5 1.5

---

[12]Two respondents indicated objective required for a "D."
[13]Five respondents indicated objective required for a "D."

Hand-written statements that could be considered "grading objectives" or criteria came back on 67 returns, but no clear *pattern* was discernible in them. Several of these were considered included in the questionnaire check-list. For instance, 3 mentioned a vivid *style*; 2 required a speech to be "understandable" to get a C; 5 mentioned some facet of *organization*; 7 mentioned meeting the assignment's *requirements*; 7 mentioned good *evidence* and/or *research*, while 5 mentioned good *reasoning*; 4 wanted good vocal quality and 8 specified good *visible* (bodily, facial) *delivery*; 5 mentioned *poise* or lack of *stage fright*; 9 mentioned *suitability* of speech *topic* for audience and/or speaker; 2 mentioned *personal credibility*, and 10 required "creativity" or *originality* for higher grades; 1 mentioned ability to "get information across"; and 6 mentioned "accomplishing the speech purpose" as necessary for a higher grade.

Several other criteria were mentioned, but again with no definite pattern: 1 mentioned "audience reaction and contribution"; 2 mentioned "use of notes"; 2 demanded that students "work to potential"; 1 required an "A" speech to be "entertaining"; 2 admitted to "therapeutic grading," awarding a higher grade as *encouragement*; 4 said they graded on a few skills at first, and on more skills as the semester progressed; 2 counted outline quality as part of a speech grade; 1 mentioned "smooth" transitions, 5 wanted "interesting introductions," and 3 required "memorable" conclusions for an A. Six respondents sent rating scales which they use; 5 sent copies of the Oliver standards, which they said they used; and two replied that they did *not grade speeches*, one even reporting that he graded students on criteria quite apart from their speaking.

Returns making evaluative comments on the survey numbered from 40 to 50, depending upon what one accepts as "evaluation." Comments ranged from "study appears to me to be quite worthwhile," to "answering your questions [*sic*] (is) a pointless task." Negative comments outnumbered positive about 3 to 1. One attacked the objective checklist with the observation that he had "taught public address since 1955" and had "never heard of a 'circular response'." Thirty-two respondents mentioned the justifiable criticism that many of the objectives were obtainable *by degrees* instead of simply on an either/or basis.

A couple of responses, at least, deserve special mention. One gentleman aptly generalized his standards as: "C — do well everything expected of you; B — show that you learned something from me; A — I learn something from you." Another reported a delightfully honest "grade-from-the-guts" subjectivity: "Seems OK — C; Seems better than most — B; Gad, he's doing a good job! — A."

Conclusion. A Chi-square analysis of the results on page 2 would be pretty meaningless; but a judicious study of the data indicates some considerable agreement among speech teachers on what achievements set the C speech apart from the B and A. The C objectives pretty well specify minimum "*mechanical*" objective requirements whereas the A and B objectives tend to infer actual communicative *impact* upon the *audience.* Perhaps this is the major molar difference speech teachers should recognize between the C and better speeches, especially since the point is bolstered by other evidence. Gruner, *et al.*[14] found that an "average" classroom speaker was not *persuasive* whereas a "good" speaker was, and that speeches graded by a panel of teachers as C or lower were not effective whereas speeches so graded as B or better *were,* in terms of attitude change. The A speech is not well differentiated from the B speech by this study, but at least partly because "true" behavioral objectives were not used; a great many concepts not universally defined were contained therein. But it is hoped that speech teachers find the data in this study helpful in grading.

Grading is Related to Motivation. In the faculty lounge and in un-guarded moments we hear teachers wish they could be freed from the responsibility of some student or students. But students do not drop dead merely because some teacher wishes it. If the teacher is untactful enough to make such a wish openly, in plain or guarded terminology, the student does not become a lesser problem, but in most cases stands up just as high, twice as healthy, and with a great deal more organized opposition to his well-wishing teacher. The problem, if a student is less than desired, seems to be one of getting him into an attitude to improve his situation. By doing so the teacher in most cases makes the job much easier on himself. Open opposition to a slow or obstinate student is profitable only when opposition is the best therapy. Detours may not necessarily be the best action either. Even when the student must be failed in a course, there is seldom a need to have open warfare. The mutual understanding that the student did not apply himself and thus did not learn the necessary concepts important to the course is possible without establishing an enmity between student and teacher. Students are aware enough of working situations that the teacher can establish a parallel in that reporting for work does not establish the claim for pay if no work is done. We have not yet developed student unions protecting the pupil's right to loaf and get portal-to-portal pay with fringe benefits on report cards or transcripts.

Suggested Projects

1. Teachers must frequently obtain "feedback" on the retention of facts, concepts, and process understanding to determine the effectiveness of their

---

[14]Charles R. Gruner, Marsha W. Gruner, and Donald O. Olson, "Is Classroom Evaluation Related to Actual Effectiveness of Classroom Speeches?" *Southern Speech Journal,* in press.

teaching. This feedback is measured by objective type instruments. Design a comprehensive test for use as a semester or final examination. Utilize true-false, matching, multiple-choice and completion types of items. Utilize approximately 100 items in each test.

a) Make three copies of each test (two may be carbons) and a key.

b) Make one test in the area of voice science and fundamentals.

c) Make one test to cover areas of oral interpretation and theatre.

d) Make one test to cover areas of public address, discussion, and debate.

e) Make one test to cover areas of parliamentary procedure, semantics, communication processes of transmission — feedback and linguistics.

f) Make one test to cover broadcasting as it applies to communication, public address, discussion, persuasion (advertising), and oral reading, etc.

All items should be validated on appropriate texts available for teaching the class level for which the test is designed (junior high, senior high, or college). Items may be further validated against the content of college texts.

2. Utilizing the tests designed above, administer this test to three classmates using answer sheets designed for the test. Each test should be scored and hypothetical grades assigned as though these tests had been administered to a regular class with the three participants representing score distributions of 30 or 60 students. Grades should not be determined until item analysis has been completed.

3. Each person taking the test should "simulate" the role of a substitute teacher or a supervisor with knowledge of the field. After taking the test, utilize the rating sheet which follows. Instructions and criteria are listed on the rating sheet.

An Evaluation Form for Student-Authored Tests

Name of Author

Name of Evaluator

Instructions:

a) Take the test, marking all items as instructed by the author.

b) Circle the number on the answer sheet for any item you consider "poor" (vague, ambiguous, too obvious, opinion, etc.).

Evaluation:

Instructions: Instructions were furnished where needed and were understandable.

no   1   2   3   4   5   6   7   8   9   10   yes

Scope: This test covers a representative list of items from the total unit or course (fundamentals, preparation and delivery of speeches, discussion, etc., *or* interpretation, acting, scenery construction, lighting, and history of theatre).

no 1 2 3 4 5 6 7 8 9 10 yes

Design: This test is designed to be clear, easily read, neat, usable for the student taking the test and the person correcting the test.

no 1 2 3 4 5 6 7 8 9 10 yes

Quality: In general the test is made up of items which are *valid* and *reliable*. In terms of *power* it includes items which will challenge the best students. In terms of *speech* it will challenge what is known.

no 1 2 3 4 5 6 7 8 9 10 yes

Validity and reliability: The items included are true and can be verified by competent authorities; they are free from opinion.

no 1 2 3 4 5 6 7 8 9 10 yes

Arrangement of items: Items dealing with identification and association are not intermixed with items asking for a value judgment.

no 1 2 3 4 5 6 7 8 9 10 yes

Comparison: In terms of the test created by the evaluator this test is better than, or less well done.

better   about the same   less well done
_____

_____Number of items completed with the correct answers.

_____The approximate grade if the student tested had been a high school student.

On a separate sheet write any response you feel should be added concerning this test as a instrument of instruction and diagnosis.

4. Analyze the comments and make an item analysis on the returned tests and turn in the test package to the instructor (three tests, key, evaluation sheets, and your own comments).

5. The next class period should be devoted to the discussion of the test items and total test improvement, including the analysis of items and the reasons for confusion, multiple answers which were unexpected, comments on design improvement, and general concepts gained from the project.

6. Teachers of speech utilize many subjective forms of evaluation. Survey texts for high school and college and make a comparison of those found with those presented in the present chapter. Evaluate each in terms of usability and economy in terms of instructional efficiency.

7. Write a paper based upon your reading from the selected bibliography. Confine your paper to grading, evaluation as a teaching process, or to test item construction and validation.

The Speech Teacher as Critic and Analyst

8. Into every speech teacher's life comes the student with an anguished look and plaintive cry, "Help, I must give a speech at a community event!" A few questions establish the facts: he has not taken any speech courses, he

has not received instruction for this type of preparation in other class programs, and he is not aware of the process or sources for preparing a speech. The teacher might respond by asking him to register for speech next semester. This, however, is not the help he needs now, nor is he likely to register. This is not a "dry run" simulation of a speech event. Here is an opportunity and challenge. Can the teacher instruct a student with a real speech? So a capsule course in public address is produced during a hurried conference after school or during a free period. Following this session the student is asked to prepare his speech (for a specific occasion, to a known audience, with appropriate language to fill the designated allotment of time). The purpose of the speech is determined and the student is asked to provide a copy for advice and criticism prior to delivering the speech. The outline and the speech may have to be reworked in order to save the student's and teacher's time before a lengthy oral rehearsal. In short, the teacher is a critic-analyst of student speeches.

Every opportunity for *real* speaking occasions should be encouraged in preference to *simulated* experiences in the classroom. The purpose here is to provide the potential teacher with models for speech analysis. Several speech models have been selected to provide variety in construction and strategy. First, make a thorough study of the speech analysis in Supplement 5, "Vital Speeches As a Teaching Device," by Lionel Crocker. An outline of Crocker's *Principles of Speech Composition* and their application to Robert M. Hutchins' "Where Do We Go from Here in Education" is furnished. Second, make an equally detailed analysis of (*a*) "Editor's Choice—You Couldn't Do Woise," by Bergen Evans and (*b*) "General Patton's Prayer." These speeches are Supplements 6 and 7, respectively. Or select two current speeches from those in the press or current magazines and make the appropriate analysis. Note the unique circumstances which must be known to the critical analyst. Furthermore, you are committed to *freedom of speech* and therefore should identify, classify, and evaluate the format of the speech, the types of proof used, the levels of language (analogies, metaphors, similes), and the types of reasoning, humor, and use of repetitions. You may help the speaker arrive at his chosen thesis, but do not criticize his right to speak on a given subject.

Supplement 5.

Vital Speeches As a Teaching Device

Lionel Crocker*

Foreword

The study of public speaking should be geared to the present, like journalism. We speak to solve pressing problems of the present. The use of such

*Dr. Crocker is Emeritus Director of the Department of Speech at Denison University, Granville, Ohio. He is former national secretary of Tau Kappa Alpha and author of *Public Speaking for College Students*, *Argumentation and Debate*, and *Oral Reading*. Reprinted by permission of the author.

publications as *Time* and *Newsweek* in classes in public speaking give the student the panorama of passing events. In addition to this study of current events, the student of public speaking should have *Vital Speeches* which contains the thought on current affairs by distinguished leaders in the national scene. The student will learn much about the problems of education by studying this speech by Robert M. Hutchins. Before the advent of *Vital Speeches*, classes in public speaking had to depend upon volumes of speeches like *Modern Eloquence* which contain speeches on issues long dead.

In addition to knowing the thought of such important men, the student can gain public speaking power by trying to digest their thoughts and by saying them in his own language from the platform. *Vital Speeches* used with a text on public speaking makes an almost unbeatable combination for the study of speech composition. And as a by-product, students in other fields, like economics and government, find helpful materials to aid them in their study.

To the Student

Robert M. Hutchins is a good example of a man in business and professional life who is expected to know how to speak. His position in our national life gives him an opportunity to influence greatly through speech our thinking on themes of interest to us all. He has learned many lessons in the gathering, arrangement and expression of his ideas. Can we learn from his experience? It is with the hope that younger men and women, who are destined to occupy positions of importance and who will have the opportunity to speak out, will profit by some of the rhetorical devices employed by Mr. Hutchins that this study is offered. For example, where does Mr. Hutchins get his materials? Does he use logical, personal and emotional proof? Does he use inductive and deductive reasoning? Does he use the enthymeme? Does he call upon opinion to support his position? Does he use interesting illustrations to arouse the interest of his audience? How does he secure humor? How does he apply his materials to a specific audience? How does the speaker get into his theme? How does he close? What employment does he make of transitions? How does the speaker arrange his materials? What sort of language does the speaker use? It is with the hope of answering some of these questions that this study is presented. The study is not exhaustive but merely suggestive. You and your teachers will undoubtedly find many other rhetorical devices employed by this powerful speaker.

Principles of Speech Composition to Apply to Vital Speeches

A. INTRODUCTION
  1. *Purposes:* To secure goodwill, to secure attention, to prepare audience, to suggest speech purposes. (Quintilian)
  2. *Material:* May emphasize speaker, theme, audience, occasion.
  3. *Faults:* False assumption, excuses and apologies, ill-advised funny stories, false leads. (O'Neil & Weaver)

B. DISCUSSION

4. *Steps in composition:* Getting the idea, thinking over the idea, immediate preparation, delivery of the idea.

5. *Selection of subject:* Fit the speaker, the audience, the occasion.

6. *Kinds of materials:* Facts, reasons, opinions, examples.

7. *Uses of illustrations:* Clearness, proof, memory, imagination, rests the audience, provides for various hearers, presents argument differently, tact, educates audience to use illustrations, ornaments the address, introduces narrative element, introduces humor. (Beecher)

8. *Factors of interest:* Animate, antagonistic, concrete, unusual, similar, vital, uncertain. (Phillips)

9. *Impelling motives:* Self-preservation, property, power, reputation, taste, sentiment, affection. (Phillips)

10. *General ends:* To inform, actuate, entertain, impress, convince.

11. *Outlines:* Topical, simple list, causal relation, time order.

12. *Patterns of speech structure:* Extended analogy, string of beads, partition of a text, repetition of a pattern, problem-solution, motivated sequence, exclusion, deduction, induction, negation and affirmation.

13. *Reference to experience:* Principle: the more the speaker brings his ideas within the vivid experience of the audience the more likely will he be to attain his end, and obversely. (Phillips)

14. *Factors governing reference to experience:* Originally intense, experienced frequently, frequently recollected, recent.

15. *Imagination:* Helps with construction, helps speaker to invent or discover, produces images, realizes the invisible, stimulates the imagination of the audience.

16. *Humor:* Disappointment theory, derision theory. Exaggeration, understatement, parody, satire, grotesquery, ridicule, irreverence, sarcasm.

17. *Figures of speech:* Synecdoche, metonomy, simile, metaphor, personification, apostrophe.

18. *Rhetorical principles:* Coherence, unity, emphasis.

19. *Language:* Choice of words, phrases, slogans, repetition, rhythm, imagery.

20. *Principles of style:* Clearness, energy, ease.

21. *Types of reasoning:* Inductive, deductive, causal relation.

22. *Definition:* Negation, example, application, etymology, context, authority, function.

22. *Development of theme:* Definition, particulars and details, comparison and contrast, illustration, presenting reasons, applying a principle, cause and effect.

24. *Three kinds of proof:* Logical, emotional and personal.

25. *Ways of getting material:* Observation, corresponding, talking, reading, thinking.

26. *Analysis of audience:* What does the audience know about you? about your subject? What influence do occasions have on audience? Young? homogenous? sex? status? affiliations?

27. *Patterns of persuasion:* Competition, cooperation, immediacy, delay, precedent, ideals, conformity, adventure, status quo, exclusive.
28. *Suggestion:* Confidence in speaker, elementary impulses, convention, prejudices.
29. *Deliberation:* Important matters, unusual talking points, new ideas, complicated ideas.
30. *Sentences:* Short, long, antithetical, interrogatory, declarative, simple, complex.

C. CONCLUSION

31. *Types:* Summary, recapitulation, application.
32. *Warnings:* Brevity, simplicity, unity, energy.

"Where Do We Go from Here in Education"

American University Has Developed Power to Destroy; Ill Equipped to Save the World

Robert M. Hutchins*

1. Mr. Chairman, Mr. Lovett, gentlemen: I appreciate Mr. Lovett's remarks very much indeed. From one point of view I do deplore them. I deplore them because of the emphasis on the word "new." I must say that I feel very far from "new." Now that Nicholas Murray Butler is out of the way, I am the senior executive in the American Association of Universities, closely pushed by that young man at Ann Arbor, Mr. Ruthven, who had the misfortune to be elected president of the University of Michigan four months after the University of Chicago had the misfortune to elect me.

See how the speaker pegs his opening remarks on the remarks of the chairman. Pay attention to the courtesy of the opening sentences and how one sentence leads into the ad lib introductory remarks. Names are interesting. Here you have Butler, Ruthven and Lovett. The speaker secures humor by self depreciation. He does not take himself too seriously. The speaker seizes upon a point of common interests — the universities.

2. From the gray eminence which I occupy, I survey American education with a detachment, a disinterestedness, and, I may add, a pessimism which nobody, except possibly Mr. Ruthven, in the state of Michigan can approach.

Note the style, — "gray eminence." Again depreciation. Might he have said "doubtful eminence?" Note the use of the climax, a sort

---

*Dr. Hutchins is former chancellor of the University of Chicago. He is now president of the Center for the Study of Democratic Institutions and editor-in-chief of *Great Books of the Western World*. This speech was delivered before the Economic Club of Detroit, May 12, 1947. The comments on the principles of speech, following each paragraph of Dr. Hutchins' talk, are by Dr. Crocker.

of anticlimax. Here is the climax made of three parts. This is a favorite device of the speaker. See paragraphs 68 and 71.

3. I have worked long, and occasionally hard, and have seen very little done. My one solid accomplishment I owe to Michigan, — it procured a team which defeated mine 85 to 0. Because of this, I was able to abolish football in Chicago.

The speaker gets a laugh but leaves a sting behind. This result epitomizes what the speaker has been trying to do. Note the specific reference 85 to 0. Not by a "big score." Do not escape the thrust of the word "procure."

4. For this and many other favors, I shall never cease to be grateful to you.

The speaker summarizes his ad lib introductory remarks and prepares for launching into his prepared speech which he undoubtedly read.

5. Now, in the twenty-five years, and more, that I have been in American education, I have noticed that it has certain permanent and abiding problems. They are caused by various paradoxes or contradictions in our educational system, and in our attitude toward it. It is about these problems, paradoxes, and contradictions, that I wish briefly to speak.

The speaker gives proof of his right to speak: "Twenty-five years."
The speaker is giving the results of his observation. This is to be a problem-solution speech. The speaker tells the audience what he is going to do in the speech. The speaker introduces the key word paradox. *If there be those who do not understand this word, the speaker tells them what it means,* contradictions. *See paragraphs 23, 47 and 66. The speaker has four paradoxes.*

6. The first paradox appears in our national behavior in the support of education. It is often said that American education is the American substitute for a national religion, but many countries have been able to reconcile support of an official religious establishment with disregard of its principles, and American support of education often appears to be of this kind. The devotion seems to be the symbol, rather than to the activity, and is rather rhetorical than real.

Note the number of times the word education — the thing the speaker is talking about — is mentioned. I counted 76 times. Pick up the speech at any point and you'll find the speaker is talking about education. Note the thoughtful analogy. Note the rhythm of the speaker:

> *The devotion seems to be to the symbol*
> *rather than to the activity*
> *and is rather rhetorical*
> *than real.*

The repetition of the s *and* r *sounds is pleasing to the ear.*

7. Popular education is a splendid subject for a Fourth of July address; yet, 350,000 teachers have been driven from the profession by the pitiful salaries now offered.

Note the scorn of the speaker. He is graphic all the time. Fourth of July orations are pompous and empty. One of the four types of material is facts. He does not say "a lot of teachers," but 350,000. And note the verb "driven." See how the speaker musters supporting data to maintain his first contention, his first paradox.

8. In some parts of this country, a teacher may count herself fortunate if she receives $500 a year, and we can be certain, I think, that if there is another depression the experiences of the last one will be repeated. The expenditures on the schools will be the first cut and the last restored.

The speaker is hard hitting. He uses facts and historical examples to prove his point. Would anyone in the audience doubt his supporting material. Is he not telling them what they already know?

9. I have come to Detroit directly from the plane that brought me home from a month in England. There is a country in which there is a shortage of all goods; a country whose empire, if not dissolving, is at least changing its shape; a country which has neither manpower, building materials, books, nor paper.

The personal authority, the prestige, of the speaker is used as proof. Here is a man who knows what he is talking about. To support his contention he employs contrast and comparison: *What they are doing in England. Note the sentence made up of three parts. To drive home his point he paints a dark picture of England. Note repetition of "a country." This gives style to public speaking.*

10. What is it doing?

In the preparation of his manuscript the speaker uses many one sentence paragraphs. See paragraphs 20, 26, 32, 52. This technique helps in the effective reading of a manuscript.

11. It is putting into effect the provisions of the Education Act of 1944, the main result of which is an extension of the period of compulsory education from 14 to 15 years of age. I do not say that this is a wise decision, or that a mere increase in the school-leaving age produces necessarily sound educational results. I do say that this action which, under the circumstances, is so courageous as to be almost reckless, shows that the British really mean what we say about education.

Note the personal style of the speaker, the "I," "you," "we." Again note how exact the speaker is. There is an echo of his first paradox here: "the British really mean what we say about education." The speaker keeps his audience on the mental track.

12. They mean that education is important; it is more important than food, tobacco, or even beer; more important than capital equipment, military equipment or houses. They mean that man does not live by bread alone, and that an intelligent nation is more likely to succeed economically and militarily than one which has great material resources but does not know what to do with them.

Note the use here of the three elements of the sentence. Note also the use of the climaxes of three, — "food, tobacco, or even beer," "capital equipment, military equipment, or houses." The speaker likes to repeat his sentence forms. "They mean . . . . They mean . . . ."

13. It is true that our own country is now committed, in the GI Bill of Rights, to the greatest educational expenditure in the history of the race. The appropriations for educational purposes under the GI Bill of Rights will run between ten and fourteen billion dollars. This legislation originated, not in the desire to educate veterans, but in the forebodings of the economist that there would be six to eight million unemployed within six months after the war.

The speaker anticipates the objections raised by his audience. He knows what they are thinking. He introduces refutation into his speech. The speaker develops his themes by means of illustrations. In debating parlance he turns the tables. He proves his point by material which opponents of his contention might use to prove their contention. The audience cannot but agree.

14. The genesis of the National Youth Administration during the depression was the same. It did not result from the conviction that young people must be educated even if the stock market falls, but from a desire to keep young people off the labor market.

The speaker does not hesitate to speak unpalatable truths. He uses an historical example to substantiate his point.

15. I applaud the expenditure and the consequences of the National Youth Administration, and the GI Bill of Rights, although I must say it will be a little unfortunate if the young men now studying under the GI Bill of Rights come to the end of their grants and the end of their studies in a period of unemployment.

The speaker challenges attention by his forthrightness. He does not let his audience enjoy the pleasantness of the thought of educating so many millions. He makes the audience face unpleasant possibilities. Such speaking may disturb an audience but it holds attention.

16. I am concerned here, not with what such measures accomplish, but with what they reveal of the American attitude toward education. They do not require any revision of my thesis that the American people, whatever their professions, do not take education very seriously. And, in the past there has been no particular reason why they should.

The speaker comes back to his first contention. He ties up his illustrations with his theme. This paragraph is in the nature of an internal summary. The speaker wants to carry his audience with him. He does not want them to miss the point. The speaker is excusing the American people for their attitude and is getting ready to introduce another turn in his thinking. If in the past there was no urgency to take education seriously, there is today.

17. This country was impregnable to enemies from without, and apparently indestructible. It could not be destroyed even by the hysterical waste

and mass stupidity of the people and its government. Foreign policy, for example, could be the blundering ground of nice old southern lawyers, and education could be regarded as a means of keeping children off the street; the schools kept young people out of worse places until we were willing to have them go to work.

> *The irony, the sarcasm, the wit of the speaker reaches a high point in this paragraph. There is no pandering to the audience here. Our sins are hurled at us: "mass stupidity of the people and its govern-ment." What did the speaker say about being "detached?" Pay attention to the choice of adjectives in this paragraph: hysterical, mass, blundering, nice, old, southern, worse.*

18. Now, when the Russians have the atomic bomb — which I am happy to say was not solely the product of the University of Chicago — and the Russians certainly will have it within five years; Langmuir's prediction is about a year and a half — when the Russians have the atomic bomb, the position of the United States automatically undergoes a dramatic change. The position of the United States, then is very little beyond that of Czecho-Slovakia before the war, — one false step in foreign policy can mean the end, not only of our institutions, but also of civilization. In a war in which both sides have atomic bombs, the cities of both sides will be destroyed.

> *Note the transition word* Now. *The speaker could put much mean-ing into this by inflection. The importance of the atomic bomb is un-derscored by his disclaiming full responsibility for its manufacture. Opinion is one of the four types of material. Note the use of the literal analogy: the United States is compared to Czecho-Slovakia.*

19. And, we cannot place our hope on those agreements for the control of atomic energy, which are just around the corner in the sense in which Mr. Hoover remarked, in 1932, that prosperity was just around the corner. These agreements are absolutely imperative; but they will simply guarantee, if they are effective, that the next war will end with atomic bombs instead of begin-ning with them. And, if these agreements are ineffective, they will simply increase the element of surprise which the atomic bomb has added to the arsenal of the aggressor. And, if it becomes possible, as it theoretically is, to manufacture atomic bombs out of helium and hydrogen, all plans for control based on the control of uranium must fail.

> *Pay attention to the transition words of the speaker. See paragraphs 5, 23, 49. Here* and *is used. See how the speaker refers to the experience of his audience. Anyone who lived through the depres-sion would remember Hoover's prediction with a wry smile. Note the series of conditional enthymemes. The speaker shakes his audi-ence out of any apathy they may feel regarding the atomic bomb by a terrible prediction.*

20. We have now reached the point where we cannot have war and civili-zation, too!

> *Here we have the disjunctive enthymeme, — it is a case of either or.*

21. Last week in Paris, I met with a staff of the United States Scientific and Cultural organizations. There is a group operating, by the way, on an

annual budget which is about 25 per cent of the amount which the United States Government spent every year during the war at the University of Chicago alone for the production of new weapons. And, this group is dedicated to the proposition that, since war begins in the minds of men, and since education is supposed to have some effect on the human mind, the way to prevent war is to do something about education.

> *The audience cannot escape the thought that it is sitting on the front seat. They are listening to a man who is in the know. A speaker reveals himself to an audience in the course of his speech. Again the rhetorical device of contrast and comparison is employed. The speaker permits the audience to draw its own conclusion, i.e. that more money is spent on weapons than on the prevention of war. See how the speaker returns to his theme, how this paragraph bears out the point that Americans do not believe in education.*

22. I put it to you that this proposition is sound; that education, as the British have decided, is the most urgent business before us, and that we must show, by our actions rather than by our speeches, that we regard it in this light.

> *Here is the concluding paragraph on the first paradox. The speaker uses the echo of his remark in paragraph 11 about the British. Such cross references help knit the speech together. Read over this first section (¶ 6 to ¶ 23) and see that every word, phrase, sentence, contributes to the total effect that Americans do not take education very seriously. The speaker devotes 17 paragraphs to point 1, 26 paragraphs to point 2, 18 paragraphs to point 3, and 8 paragraphs to point four. The speaker has a psychological development of his theme. He is governed by the ability of his audience to listen. He terminates quickly.*

23. Now, while we are about it, we might attack another paradox in American education, which is that a system, nominally democratic, operates in an oligarchial way. An oligarchy, I need not remind you, was a form of government based on wealth.

> *The speaker gets away from the mechanical "the second paradox." But in order that the audience may know where he is in the development of his points he does in paragraph 47 refer to the "third paradox." He does not say "fourth paradox" but says in paragraph 66, "The final paradox. . . ."**
>
> *The speaker retains his key word, — paradox. The speaker does not let the word oligarchial pass without definition. He knows the truth of the remark, "Never underestimate the intelligence of the audience but do not overestimate their information."*

---

*The organization of the material under the first paradox looks something like this:
I. The first paradox appears in our national behavior in the support of education, for
A. The devotion seems to be the symbol, for
  1. Teachers (350,000) have been driven from the profession.
  2. The expenditures on the schools will be the first cut in a depression and the last restored.

24. American education is founded on the belief that democracy is served if its schools, colleges, and universities charge low fees, or none; and if, at the same time, there is no discrimination among students in terms of their intellectual ability.

> *The speaker takes this paragraph and the next to set up his assumptions which he will tear apart. Most of us unthinkingly accept these beliefs. The speaker shows his reasoning power in analyzing the falsity of these assumptions.*

25. We have democratic education, then, if we do not charge for it, and if we make clear that every citizen is entitled, as a matter of right, to as much free education as every other citizen.

> *This paragraph restates what paragraph 24 set forth. The speaker uses the conditional syllogism:*
> *If we do not charge for education, we have democratic education.*
> *We do not charge for education,*
> *Therefore, we have democratic education.*
> *(If we affirm the antecedent, we must affirm the consequent.)*

26. This assumption is false in all its parts.

> *But the speaker examines the truth of the assumption, and declares it false. Here is the debater who states what his opponents say and then denies it.*

27. Actually, the important cost of education is not fees. It is the cost of the pupil's subsistence if he lives away from home, and the loss of his earning power. In this country, however, scholarships given by private foundations rarely cover more than fees.

> *We have development by definition. The speaker tells what education is not and then proceeds to tell what it is. The speaker shows he has thought through his theme by including earning power. The speaker draws upon his own experience.*

B. England is putting into effect the provision of the Education Act of 1944, for
 1. The British really mean what we say about education.
 2. An intelligent nation is more likely to succeed.
C. Our expenditures for education are for ulterior puposes, for
 1. The G.I. legislation originated in the forebodings of the economist.
 2. The genesis of the NYA during the depression was the same.
D. In the past there was no particular reason why Americans should take education seriously, for
 1. This country was impregnable to enemies from without and apparently indestructible.
 2. Now, however, when the Russians have the atomic bomb one false step in foreign policy can mean the end, not only of our institutions, but also of civilization.
E. The United States Scientific and Cultural organizations are operating on an annual budget which is about 25 per cent of the amount which the United States Government spent every year during the war at the University of Chicago alone for the production of new weapons.
 (The teacher may wish to require the student to outline other portions of the address).

28. The educational institutions, managed by local and state governments, feel they have performed their full duty if they charge low fees, or none. The books of the University of Chicago will show an expenditure on student aid of more than $600,000 a year, but the figure is meaningless, for almost every cent of this money is paid back to the University in the form of fees by the students who receive it.

> *Development by example. The audience is instructed. Informing is a way of holding attention. The speaker uses facts. The speaker uses tax supported institutions and private institutions to support his paradox.*

29. Universal education in America has therefore, meant that all those who could afford to continue in school have been able to, and those who have not had the money, have not.

> *The speaker draws his conclusion which reinforces his second contention that American education operates in an oligarchial way, i.e. education depends upon the pocketbook and not on brains.*

30. Hence the paradox, that in a country which provides free education for all, the length of a young person's education varies directly with his capacity to pay; and since, at these age levels, at least, and probably at all age levels, there is no relation between intellectual ability and capacity to pay, the educational system has been overwhelmed with students who are not qualified for the work they are supposed to be doing, and whose presence inevitably dilutes and trivializes the whole program.

> *The speaker emphasizes by repetition his paradox and shows what results flow from that paradox. Note the effect of the verb* trivializes. *The speaker quarrels with modern education because it deals in trifles. So there is much thought behind this word. The verb* overwhelmed *is masterful. Swift said, "Style is proper words in proper places."*

31. Every study that has been made in this country shows that there are more good high school graduates out of college than in. The reason is that the ones who go to college are the ones who have the money to go, and it would be undemocratic to say they were not bright enough to go. And, those who are bright enough to go, cannot go unless they have the money to go, because we have no adequate system of financial aid to those who are bright, but impoverished.

> *The speaker generalizes from statistical studies. See how the speaker hammers his point. Note the concern of the speaker with what is democratic as opposed to oligarchial. The speaker is not afraid to end his sentence with a preposition. Why is* impoverished *better than* poor?

32. Here I think it is safe to say that we fall behind every country in the Western world.

> *The speaker emphasizes his point by placing it in a separate paragraph. The excellent device of contrast and comparison is used. The speaker appeals to the desire to be the equal of others or better.*

33. Until the National Youth Administration and the GI Bill of Rights, nothing was ever done by anybody to recognize the cost of living as an element in the cost of education.

> *The speaker weaves in a previous reference. The speaker develops his thesis by examples.*

34. Before the war, we used to boast that a student could go to the University of Illinois for $75 a year. He could. That is, he could, if in addition, he could command not less than $750 a year to live on, and if his family could do without his earnings.

> *The speaker uses his home state as an example. He knows most about it. Note the use of facts. He does not deal in generalities. Note the everyday English of the speaker. He does not say "subsistence" but "to live on." And he repeats, "if his family could do without his earnings."*

35. By contrast, every European country has long since made provision that those who show themselves qualified through a rigorous system of competition to receive aid in their education shall receive aid which enables them to live as well as to study.

> *This evidence bolsters his contention in ¶ 32. The previous two paragraphs show that in the U.S.A. we do fall behind. Note the use of generalization. Would the audience accept this without further proof? Would it have been better if he had cited an example of "every European country?"*

36. As a self-supporting student, who tried to live first and study afterwards, I can testify that the combination is possible only because the American university demands so little study.

> *The speaker knows what is going through the minds of his audience, and he spikes it. He uses himself as an example of one who "worked" his way through college. But is it clear whether the speaker means college or university? He went to Oberlin and Yale.*

37. If we had in this country real intellectual competition in our universities, it would at once become apparent that it is not possible for a boy to work eight hours a day in a factory, as I did, and get an education at the same time. Under those circumstances it must be clear that I did not get an education; I simply graduated from college, which is quite a different thing.

> *Further personal proof is given. Such proof coming from such a speaker carries great weight. The speaker elaborates on the problem. He scores a favorite American delusion that it is possible and desirable for a boy to work his way through college.*

38. What we need is an adequate system of financial aid for those who deserve it, a national system of competitive scholarships, — scholarships which are large enough to enable the student to study as well as live.

> *Here is the solution to this part of the address. This will take care of the bright students who can benefit from a university education.*

39. We also need a system by which those students, who are not qualified for university work, may be effectually excluded from the university. The basic task of education for citizenship should be performed outside the universities. The universities should be devoted to advanced study, professional training, research, and the education of leaders. Therefore, the university must be limited, if it proposes to succeed in any of these tasks, to those who have demonstrated their qualifications for advanced study, professional training, research, or leadership.

> *But what will happen to those who fail the competitive examinations? This and the following paragraphs take up the solution for those who can not benefit from a university education. Note the structure of the speech. The speaker has thought through the problem. You have in this paragraph the speaker's conception of a university: a four fold program. Note that he repeats the four functions. Is "leadership" a vague term?*

40. The notion that any American, merely because he is one, has the privilege of proceeding to the highest university degree must be abandoned. A six-year elementary school, a three or four year high school, a three or four year college, locally organized, would give us a system which would take care of the fundamentals of education, and would relieve the university of the necessity of doing so. Students graduating from this system would come to the end of it between the ages of 18 and 20, and only those who had demonstrated their qualifications to go on should be permitted to do so, — at least at the cost of the taxpayer.

> *The speaker again is very definite as to this solution. This is the product of much deliberation, much conference with educational leaders. The speaker is as clear as crystal.*

41. In order to induce the others not to go on, I should be perfectly prepared to have them receive the Bachelor's degree at the age of 18 to 20.

> *The speaker introduces some sarcasm directed toward the Bachelor's degree.*

42. I have, in fact, a good deal of sympathy for the proposal of Barrett Wendell of Harvard, that every American citizen should receive the Bachelor's degree at birth.

> *Further depreciation of the A.B. degree is contained in this reference to Barrett Wendell. It undoubtedly raised a laugh.*

43. With a six-year elementary school, a three or four year high school, and a three or four year college, from which only carefully selected graduates should be permitted to proceed to the university, we might have a truly democratic system of education, democratic in the purest Jeffersonian sense.

> *The speaker reiterates his contention and supports it by appealing to the founding fathers. The speaker attempts to link up his concept with a concept which his audience may already have accepted.*

44. Jefferson's proposals for the University of Virginia contemplated a rigorous selection of students, the like of which has never been seen in this hemisphere.

The speaker elaborates for the sake of those who did not know of
Jefferson's plan. The speaker never leaves his audience in the dark.
He takes time to explain.

45. There is nothing undemocratic about saying that those who are to receive education at public expense should show they are qualified for it. On the contrary, it is most undemocratic to say that anybody can go as far as he likes in education, when what it actually means [is that] he can actually have all the education he can pay for.

Fearful that his audience might think his plan undemocratic the
speaker uses refutation. Here is another paragraph by way of sum-
mary. He says in effect, "What I am proposing is democratic; what
we have now is undemocratic."

46. The creation of local colleges as the culmination of the six-four-four, or six-three-three system of education would give us a chance to develop institutions devoted to liberal education, free from the domination of the university, and would give us a chance to develop universities free from the domination of collegiate interests.

Here is the plan:
1. six-four-four college for all.
2. liberal arts for those who can afford it.
3. universities for those who pass competitive examinations sup-
   ported by taxation.
The speaker shows the advantages of this system. It is no wonder
that Dr. Hutchins is listened to with respect for he has thought
through the problems confronting our college and university set-up
and has arrived at a solution satisfactory to himself.

47. We should then have an intelligently organized educational system, democratically operated, and equipped to play its part in the New World that is struggling to be born; but, when all this is done, we shall be left confronting a third paradox, namely, the paradox presented by what the people expect of educations.

This paragraph is in the nature of a peroration for the second para-
dox. The third paradox is introduced.

48. Our country, in which the rapidity of technical change is more dramatically presented than anywhere else in the world, has an educational program which largely ignores the rapidity and inevitability of such change.

In this third section of the address the speaker inveighs against voca-
tional training, social climbing and financial success. This paragraph
dwells upon the paradox of a static educational program in a
rapidly changing world.

49. Now, vocational training assumes that the machinery on which the boy is trained will be in use when he goes to work. Actually, the machines

and the methods are likely to be so different that his training will be a positive handicap to him.

The speaker amplifies what he means by technical change. The speaker blasts a common assumption. The speaker is getting ready to bring forward his theory of the Great Books which set forth everlasting principles.

50. As our experience in war time shows, the place to train hands for industry is in industry. The aircraft companies produced better mechanics in a few weeks than the schools could produce in years. And, it must be obvious that education on a democratic basis cannot supply social standing, as Gilbert and Sullivan pointed out, when "Everybody is somebody and nobody is anybody."

An example from army experience is used to prove the point against vocational training. The futility of expecting social position from education is emphasized by quoting Gilbert and Sullivan. Every speaker tries to get the audience to remember in one way or another, what he says. Here the speaker associates his idea with what is already accepted.

51. Moreover, these who seek education for financial success are doomed to disappointment. Direct training for the purpose of producing financial success, like a course in how to make money, is obviously a fraud, and the number of occupations, I regret to tell you, in which what are known as college conditions are more of a help than a hindrance is certainly limited. Yet, the belief that education can in some way contribute to vocational and social success, has done more than most things to disrupt American education.

A skilled speaker uses transition words that carry the audience along with him. Note the cumulative effect of the word moreover. *Here is another of the false expectations. Education can not and should not be expected to yield vocational training, social success or financial power. Evidently the speaker's concept of education and the prevailing concept of education are in conflict.*

52. What education can do, and about all it can do, is to produce a trained mind.

The audience is no doubt asking. "What can education do?" And the speaker hastens to answer the paramount question.

53. Now, getting a trained mind is hard work. As Aristotle remarked, "Learning is accompanied by pain." Those who are seeking something which education cannot supply are not likely to be enthusiastic about the pain which what it can supply must cause; and, since our false sense of democracy requires us to admit them to education anyway, then something must be done with them when they get into it, and it must, of course, be something which is not painful. Therefore, it must be something which interests them.

The speaker reinforces his contention that getting a trained mind is hard work by a quotation from Aristotle. Here is a hint of a knowledge of the Great Books. A little further on there is to be

another reference to one of the great Greeks. Note the logic of
these next few paragraphs. The quarrel that the speaker has with
our false sense of democracy appears again.

54. The vocationalism of our schools results, in part, from the difficulty
of interesting many boys and girls in what are known as academic subjects,
and the whole apparatus of football, fraternities, and fun, is a means by
which education is made palatable to those who have no business to be in it.

The logical result of trying to interest students is vocational educa-
tion. Note the alliteration, football, fraternities and fun. The speaker
does not mince words.

55. The fact is that the best practical education is the most theoretical
one. This is, probably, the first time in human history in which change on
every front is so rapid that what one generation has learned of practical
affairs, in politics, business, and technology, is of little use to the next, just
as to what the father has learned of the facts of life is almost useless to his
son. It is principles — everlastingly principles — which are of practical value
today; not data, not methods, not facts, not helpful hints, but principles are
what the rising generation requires if it is to find its way through the mazes
of tomorrow. No man among us can tell what tomorrow will be like; all
we know with certainty is that it will be different from today.

The speaker seems to utter a paradox of his own. Here is a good
example of the epigram. Notice the repetition of the word rapid.
See how the speaker uses the familiar "the father has learned of
the facts of life is almost useless to his son." There is always a
sense of speaking to the audience. Note how the speaker defines
his concept of principles by negations, — four of them. There is
style in the phrase "mazes of tomorrow." The rhythm of the
concluding sentence of this paragraph is worth noting.

56. We can also see that it is principles which the adults of May 12, 1947,
must understand if they are to be ready for May 13. The notion that education is something concerned with preparation for a vocational and social
success, that it is composed of helpful hints to housewives and bonds salesmen, has permeated the education of adults in the United States.

In this particular section the key word is principles. *Principles*
are set in opposition to "helpful hints to housewives and bonds
salesmen." The speaker keeps to his attack on vocational and social
success. The final part of this paragraph leads into an attack on
adult education as it is now conceived, this in turn gives the speaker
an opportunity to dwell upon adult education as it should be.

57. Adult education, in general, is aimed at making third rate bookkeepers
into second rate bookkeepers by giving them classes at night, and in the
general population, this process has not aroused much enthusiasm because
we have thought of education as something for children, anyway; we have
thought of it as something like the measles — having had education once,
one need not — in fact, one cannot — have it again.

Instead of saying that adult education today is concerned with vocational interests the speaker is vivid by stating that it is "aimed at making third rate bookkeepers into second rate bookkeepers." Dr. Hutchins' speeches would make good hunting grounds for the student of public speaking in learning how to be vivid. The speaker gets a laugh by means of ridicule. The simile "like the measles" is masterful, and note how he scores a point by driving the analogy home.

58. Apart from mathematics, metaphysics, logic, astronomy, and similar theoretical studies, it is clear that comprehension comes only with experience. A learned Greek remarked that young men should not listen to lectures on moral philosophy, and he was right. Moral philosophy, history, political economics, and literature, can convey their full meaning only in maturity.

The speaker gets a new twist to his theme. He is now talking about comprehension. *This paragraph is the result of much thought. An echo of the Great Books theme is contained here, "a learned Greek."*

59. Take Macbeth, for example. When I taught Macbeth to boys in preparatory school, it was a blood and thunder story — a very good blood and thunder story, one well worth reading, but a blood and thunder story still. Macbeth can mean what it meant to Shakespeare only when the reader has had sufficient experience, vicarious or otherwise, of marriage and ambition to understand the issues and their implications.

The speaker is talking to adults. He wants to get them interested in furthering their education. He is preparing them for their part in his program. The speaker has a mission. The speaker is now adapting his subject to his audience.

To make his point even more clear the speaker draws upon a classic example. He uses an example known to his audience, drawn from his own experience. One learns much of the speaker by reading his speech. He worked his way through college. He taught in a preparatory school.

60. It happens that the kind of things we need most to understand today are those which only adults can fully grasp. A boy may be a brilliant mathematician, or a musician — and I have known several astronomers who contributed to the international journals at the age of 13 — but, I never knew a child of that age who had much that was useful to say about the ends of human life, the purpose of organized society, and the means of reconciling freedom and order. But, it is subjects like these about which we are most confused, and about which we must obtain some clarification if our civilization is to survive.

The opening sentence of this paragraph makes the audience sit up and pay attention. The speaker still feels that his audience may not take him at his word so he illustrates once more. Note the use of the magic three: "ends of human life, the purpose of organized society, and the means of reconciling freedom and order." These are

*the problems that only adults can understand. The speaker takes up
the climax of his speech and that is the survival of civilization.*

61. The survival of civilization, if the Russians are to have the atomic
bomb in five years, depends on those who are adults today. We cannot wait
for the rising generation to rise. Even if we succeeded in giving them a perfect education, it would be too late.

*The speaker drives home the point that it is up to the adults. The
urgency of the time element is in the clause, "if the Russians are to
have the atomic bomb in five years."*

62. Therefore, it is imperative that we enter into a program of mass adult
education such as we have never contemplated before. The beginnings of this
program are already under way. They can be seen here in Detroit, in the
efforts which your library and universities are making to force the consideration of fundamental issues through the study of the Great Books of the
Western World. At the rate at which this program is now expanding, I expect
to see fifteen million people in it within five years.

*The speaker wants his audience to do something about this prob-
lem. The speaker is definite. He refers to Detroit. The vision of the
speaker comes out in this paragraph. It is bold and holds attention.
The speaker answers the question, which every audience asks,
"What has that got to do with us?"*

63. I do not suffer from the illusion that, if fifteen million Americans are
studying the Great Books of the Western World within five years, we shall
avert the next war. Education alone cannot avert war; it may increase the
chances of averting it. Nor do I deny that, if by reading the Great Books, or
otherwise, the hearts of the Americans are changed, and the hearts of the
Russians remain unchanged, we shall merely have the satisfaction of being
blown up with changed hearts rather than unchanged ones. I do not expect
the American audience to have enough faith in the immortality of the soul
to regard this as more dubious consolation. But, if we do not avert war by
this kind of education, we can at least provide ourselves, in the time that is
left to us, with some suitable alternative to liquor, the movies and — if I may
say so in Detroit — running around the country in second-hand cars, and
catching glimpses of the countryside between the billboards.

*Again the speaker is conscious of the objections of his listeners. He
meets two possible objections. He no doubt gets a laugh from his
witty, "I do not expect the American audience to have enough faith
in the immortality of the soul to regard this as more dubious consolation." And he follows this with a sentence that is an anticlimax.
Note the vividness of the picture, "suitable alternatives to liquor,
the movies and — if I may say so in Detroit — running around the
country in second-hand cars, and catching glimpses of the countryside between the billboards."
For a further explanation of the Great Books idea see the education
page of* The New York Times *for Sunday, August 24, 1947.*

64. At the age of 48 I can testify that all forms of recreation eventually lose their charm. I mean all!!! Partly as a result of the universal recognition of the great truth that eventually all forms of recreation lose their charm — partly in recognition of this great truth, the Great Books discussion classes have now begun to sweep the country from New York to Seattle.

Again the speaker offers personal proof. The speaker implies more than he says. He lets the audience fill in what he means by all. *The speaker seeks to justify the study of the* Great Books.
This is one reason for the study of the Great Books.

65. Another explanation of their success is that the people are beginning to realize the shortcomings of their own education. They see now that the books they never read in school or college, the issues they never discussed, the ideas they never heard of, are the books, discussion and issues that are directly relevant here and now. It may be that this generation of parents will see to it that the shortcomings of their children are overcome so that the American of the future may not have to get all his education after he becomes an adult.

In thinking through the question of the Great Books the speaker comes back to his thesis that American education is faulty. Here is an echo of the thesis that American education is concerned with vocations rather than principles.
Here is another reason for the study of Great Books, not only by adults but by oncoming generations.

66. The final paradox of American education which I wish to mention will become apparent when you look at what the world requires, and what American education has to offer.

The conclusion of the treatment of the third paradox leads directly into the fourth paradox. Can you think of any other paradoxes of American education?

67. American education excels in every technological activity, every applied sphere, and it excels as well, in pure science. The British, French, or German physician or engineer who had a chance to study in the United States would be a fool to decline the opportunity; but, he should be educated first and not count on the possibility of getting an education afterward. In every technological, applied, scientific field, the United States is, without question, preeminent today.

Rhetorically you have the sentence built on the magic three, "every technological activity, every applied sphere, and it excels as well, in pure science." To make his point the speaker takes up the foreign student in American universities. He shows that such a student would not get an education, in the sense that he is using the term, in the U.S.A.

68. We know, therefore, one thing with certainty about the American university — it can produce weapons of war. Any time that you would like to have weapons of war produced, the American universities will undertake to supply them, and they will be bigger, better, and more deadly than ever.

The speaker is frightening in his insistence that the American uni-
versity can produce weapons of war, "bigger, better, and more
deadly than ever."

69. On the other hand, another great segment of the American university, the modern medical school, has done almost as much to lengthen life as the schools of engineering and physics have done to shorten it.

The speaker knows that through the minds of his audience there
has been running an objection. He takes it up.

70. In short, wherever the material conditions of existence are in question, the American university can deliver the goods. If you want better bombs, better poison gases, better medicine, better crops, better automobiles, you will find the American university able — and usually willing — to help you.

But the advances are in material things. The speaker takes four
paragraphs to develop the idea that American education can pro-
duce the goods.

71. Where the American university cannot help you is where you need help most. Because of the paradoxes I have listed, because of our indifference to the real purposes of education, and because our pre-occupation with the trivial, frivolous, and immediately impractical, the American university is gradually losing its power to save the world. It has developed the power to destroy it; it is ill equipped to save it.

This paragraph is the pay-off. This is where the speaker releases his
dynamite. Look back at paragraph 2. Note that the speaker said, "I
may add, a pessimism which nobody, except possibly Mr. Ruthven,
in the state of Michigan can approach." Here is indeed pessimism.
Note how the speaker piles up his becauses. The paragraph is
enough to make the audience cry out. Here is the word trivial
again. The speaker believes that American education is trivial. Note
the three again: "the trivial, frivolous, and immediately impracti-
cal?" Note the balanced sentence that concludes the paragraph.

72. What is honored in a country will be cultivated there. A means of cultivating it is the educational system. The American educational system mirrors the chaos of the modern World. While science and technology, which deal only with goods in the material order, are flourishing as never before, liberal education, philosophy and theology, through which we might learn to guide our lives, are undergoing a slow but inevitable decay.

Another epigram opens this paragraph. It is a truism. Note the
logic of this paragraph. Each sentence grows out of the preceding
one. The verb mirrors *is suggestive. The rhythm of the final sen-*
tence of this paragraph is beautiful. This sentence truly has the oral
style.

73. It is not enough to say, then, "Let us have lots of education," or even "Let us have lots of expensive education." We must have universal education — let it cost what it may — of the right kind, and that is the kind through which we may hope to raise ourselves by our bootstraps into a different spir-

itual world; that is the kind which places a sound character and a trained intelligence above all other aims, and which gives the citizen a scale of values by which he can learn to live. Only by such a scale of values, rationally established and firmly held, can a democratic individual hope to be more than a transitory phenomenon lost in the confusion of a darkening world.

Note how the speaker dramatizes the various solutions. He introduces conversation into the speech. The speaker tells the audience what he wants "a sound character and a trained intelligence." What a masterful phrase "a transitory phenomenon lost in the confusion of a darkening world." The speaker emphasizes the "spiritual world" as opposite to the "material world" of American education.

74. In a democratic country there is a sense in which there is never anything wrong with education. A democratic country gets the kind of education it wants. I have no doubt that, if the people of the United States understand the urgency of education today, and understand the kind of education they must have, they can get it. I hope they will make the effort to get it before it is too late.

The speaker is a philosopher. Note the directness of the sentence, "A democratic country gets the kind of education it wants." There is hope in the third sentence. The prophet takes his seat after pointing the way. Would it have helped if the speaker had said, "I hope we will make the effort to get it before it is too late." Yet, the speaker warned that he viewed the scene with detachment. This is an application type conclusion. The speaker wants action.

Supplement 6.

Editor's Choice — You Couldn't Do Woise
Bergen Evans*

I am greatly honored at being asked to address so august and influential a body as the Managing Editors of The Associated Press and I would be embarrassed at the flippant aggressiveness of the title of my talk were it not that

---

*Dr. Bergen Evans is Professor of English at Northwestern University and a noted authority on American and British usage. This speech, on the subject of language, was delivered at the annual convention of the Managing Editors Association of the Associated Press. Like the speech by Robert M. Hutchins (Supplement 5) this is an after-dinner speech — the audience intended the speaker to be the main course. Dr. Evans establishes his right to speak (ethical proof) and gives us an excellent lesson in language growth and the purpose of dictionaries. You will develop an extra dimension in language knowledge while making a rhetorical analysis. Note specifically the divisions of the speech, the transitions, and the various uses of factual, ethical, and logical proof. We can find no better source to establish the priority of oral language over the written form.

first, it was selected from among more dignified titles by one of your own officers, and second, the press itself exploits sensationalism and stirs up aggressiveness so consistently and recklessly that it can't complain if a little of it bounces back, but most of all because the absurdity of the title makes it plain, I hope, that I do not regard myself as a Delphic oracle or intend to do any thundering out of Zion.

I want to lay down a few postulates or axioms just to save time. First, speech is the most important thing life has produced. The brilliance of speech, the amazingness of it is something that those of us who use it don't bother to stop to think about. There are no organs of speech. Man invented speech. It is purely parasitic upon organs that have other physiologic functions. Second, speech is spoken. This is so basic, so fundamental to any discussion of speech that, although it seems almost idiotic to state it, it has to be stated over and over again. The ordinary person will talk more in one good, gabby, excited day when he has some real dirt to dish out and meets enough people to listen, or he is angry about something, than he will write in his entire lifetime. Now this doesn't apply to people who, like ourselves, make a living of writing, but we'll do pretty well.

Man's speech is a living thing; hence, it is constantly changing. Speech is organic and hence, in relation to speech, the word *correct*, which one so often hears, and so often asks about, is utterly meaningless. If you found a mouse, and took it to a mousologist of some kind, and you said to him, "Is this a correct mouse?" he would think you were balmy or something. He would say, "It is a mouse of this species, it seems to be a mouse of this age, it's a mouse of this sex, it's a mouse of this weight, it seems to have had a hard winter." He could go on talking about it all day, but he can't tell you that it's a correct mouse or an incorrect mouse.

The third postulate is that grammar is simply a description of any language. This is not obvious immediately in your own language where status is so much involved and one's ego is at stake, but all you have to do is to translate it to another language to see this at once. Suppose you and I decide for some reason that we want to write an Eskimo grammar. All we can do is go where Eskimos are and write down what they say. If somebody is with us who takes correctness very seriously and he says to you, "Yeh, yeh, yeh, but is this correct Eskimo?" the answer is "I don't know." He says, "Well, look, this is the way they talk here in Baffin Bay but over in Greenland I heard different sounds." All you can say is "This is Baffin Bay Eskimo — that's Greenland Eskimo," and in your grammar, if somebody is willing to finance a hundred-volume grammar on Eskimo, then you will make these distinctions.

The fourth postulate is that use and custom alone — and here I know many people disagree — determine what each generation and each locality finds acceptable. If in the South they say *clean* and in the North they say *clear* — you went *clean through town* and so on — you cannot say one is wrong and one is right. Forty million people have a right to speak their own language, whether it be southern French, Romanian, or anything else. And incidentally, everybody used to say *clean*. Many of the things that people find wrong are old forms. They never recognize the really new as wrong at all. They are so much a part of it that they don't really realize the language has been actually changed.

The last postulate I want to state is that there are many forms of English. And no one of them can be unconditionally claimed to be good English to the total exclusion of the others. What passes for rules of grammar — this phrase we often hear — is usually simply half a dozen shibboleths that assert status. That is, they simply are part of the great game of oneupmanship. Somebody learns half a dozen forms — when he hears any deviation from them, he likes to pull rank and usually it terrifies people.

Now there is no way you can scare a man quicker than by using such horrendous words as *pluperfect, future indicative, clausitory subjunctive, nonrestrictive clause, mood, passibles,* and the like. The minute you hit a man with something like this, he crumbles. He heard stuff like this in high school and he wasn't listening, and in the innocence of his heart, he assumes that other people were listening. And it doesn't enter his mind that for the most part they were meaningless and the teacher herself hadn't the faintest idea what they meant, and that not listening to them was a highly salutary exercise.

The ordinary man is annoyed and he says, "Come on, you guys, cut it out." He has employed two colloqualisms, a verb in the imperative, the third person singular pronoun and he's made an idiomatic application of an adverb. Well, he'd be startled to be told all this, because all of these horrendous words merely describe what this man is doing.

Speech is incredibly subtle. You just don't know how clever you are to be able to speak. Speech is infinitely more subtle than writing. Writing is a poor, numb, stumbling, inadequate, approximate thing compared to speech, and always must be. The only one way you could hope to equate speech and writing would be if you could orchestrate it. So much of our meaning in speech is conveyed by emphasis, pause, rising or falling voice, and so on and so on. "He gave her *dog* biscuits." "He gave her dog *biscuits.*" I've exaggerated a bit there. In ordinary speech you wouldn't even make that sharp an emphasis to make two wholly different meanings. "The car stopped with a jerk at the wheel." The very slightest emphasis conveys totally different meaning.

This year I teach a course at Northwestern in Literature and in the course we read from the Bible and I had been lecturing about the Beatitudes. In reading an examination paper of an otherwise intelligent boy, I found a reference to the "B attitudes." Now this boy must have thought, "What are the A attitudes?" That is, he must have gone on, you know, on a totally different thing. The slightest shift of emphasis could reduce meaning to nonsense.

Now people get very excited about problems of grammar. They're not really problems of grammar at all; they are actually very excited about the challenging of their own status somewhere or they're determined to pull rank, and I just want to go into one or two of these statements with you.

Here is a nervous explosion from the *Christian Science Monitor* quite recently entitled "Cheap and Childish." It's objecting to the use of what they call incorrect English and attacking some wicked place called Madison Avenue. The *Monitor* is blowing up because the language is being corrupted. Says the *Monitor*: "To read or to listen, in advertisements in particular, one would get the impression that the American people is a race of semi-illiterates that neither speaks correct English nor is interested . . . The ineffable monstrosity of Madison Avenue is the substitution of *like* for *as*; we are now told that a certain type of bread is baked just like Mother baked it." Then the editorial concludes by saying: "It is a fact, long noted by Europeans and a fact which has done nothing to increase their opinion of American cultural standards, that the United States is one of the few countries in the world in which public indignation is not stirred by offenses to the language. In most European countries quick and strong resentment is shown whenever the priceless heritage of the national speech is abused." You couldn't get more balderdash in fewer words.

Let me for a moment go into this business of *like* as a conjunction, since not only the *Monitor*, but many other papers, including the *New York Times* made an issue of this. Most half-educated people, or three-quarters-educated, well, I'll be generous, 9/10-educated people, will tell you with very great assurance, that *like* cannot be used as a conjunction when introducing a clause and they look you right in the eye when they say this. And most people, not being quite sure what a conjunction is, usually wilt at this point.

But let me show you how complex the problem really is by giving you four examples of the use of *like* as a conjunction in sentences each one of which has a status different from the other. "He takes to it like a duck to water." Here the clause verb *does* has been suppressed. Now sentences of this kind are not only acceptable but preferable. If anyone said, "He takes to it as a duck to water," you'd move your seat over a few inches away from him. This is a little lofty for my taste at least.

Now take what we are told is the most monstrous debauch of the English language ever known. "Winstons taste good like a cigarette should." Madison Avenue, that wicked place, couldn't believe its luck when they got so much mileage out of that. Here where the clause verb is actually expressed, *like* and *as* have long been competing forms.

When this advertisement was stirring up all this furor that it caused, my sister and I were completing our book on the American language and we amused ourselves by questioning and cross-questioning people who got excited about things like this. I met one of my colleagues one day who said, "By God, I'll never smoke another Winston." "Why?" "They're corrupting the language." Then I said to him, "What's wrong with it, what's wrong with 'Winstons taste good like a cigarette should'?" And the answer almost invariably was the same "What's wrong with it? My God, what's wrong with it?" "Yep, what's wrong with it?" "What do you mean, what's wrong with it?" "What's wrong with it?" Then they start to splutter. Finally they may be trapped into saying *like* should not be used as a conjunction. We found many people, when you press them, thought in some way something was wrong with *good*.

Now, what are the facts? *Like* is found in sentences of this kind as far back as 1579. For 300 years some people have used *like* and some have used *as* and steadily and consistently, and within this century in a very rapidly ascending curve, *like* has dominated. About the middle of the 19th century, not until then, somebody decided that the use of *as* in these constructions marked you as a very superior person. This person and his or her followers, whom I call the *ases*, have been very militant on this point, and they have done you in any time they could.

However, for the moment, *like* is certainly in the ascendency. The use of *as* in constructions like "He takes to it as a duck to water" puts you in the minority. You may say you are the correct minority, but if you are enough of a minority, you cannot go on even claiming to be correct. I would say at the moment that the *ases* have lost the battle and that the *likeables* have won.

Now take another use of *like* as a conjunction. "Life is hard for a girl like I." This is from Anita Loos' *Gentlemen Prefer Blondes*. The use of the nominative *I*, implying the suppressed *am* makes this *like* a conjunction. Had it been *me*, it would have been a preposition. Now this sentence differs from "He takes to it like a duck to water" only in the fact that *like* is here followed by a pronoun instead of a noun. Yet nonetheless this construction is substandard. That is, the use of this construction would mark you as an uneducated person. You could not hold a job requiring a normal education if you used this construction. Why? Because usage says accept one, not the other.

Then take a fourth. "You act like you are a combination of Socrates and Napoleon." Is this right or wrong? You try it on people and they are puzzled. They don't know — they are uneasy. What it is, actually, is a regional matter. You will hear this in the South. This is acceptable in the South — it is not acceptable in the North and East.

All I meant with these *likes* is to demonstrate that the use of *like* as a conjunction is a very involved matter. If you just arbitrarily say you can't use it as a conjunction, you're not representing the English language as it is spoken and has been spoken for centuries. You cannot say "Well, everybody was wrong for 400 years and I'm right." Well, you can say it, but you don't earn vast respect by saying that.

When I did, with Mr. John Mason Brown, a TV show called *The Last Word*, which ran on the Columbia network for three years, by giving away a Britannica among other bait, we got an enormous amount of mail — we got 2,000 letters a day. We got over a million and a half letters, and I read over 50,000 to 60,000 letters myself.

One of the things that emerged was how passionately the North disapproves of the South's speech, and how supremely indifferent to the North the South is. I don't believe we got a single letter from the South saying "Why do these ignorant damnyankees talk this way?" I think the feeling is they are scum anyway and what does it matter — why do you expect people like that to talk English? But the North is very much on the defensive. We got more angry letters because people said "It's real hot today" instead of saying *very*. *Real* simply means "very." *Very* simply means "real." "Thou art the very

God," the Bible says. Yet nonetheless, people assumed in the North the one thing was absolutely criminal and you better call out the militia again.

Now people who talk about rules of grammar, unless they are grammarians, are talking for the most part pretentious nonsense. You cannot understand the rules of English. English is so enormous a language. So amazingly complex. You can't understand it by rules. Fortunately, you have to understand it before you can even go to the kindergarten. You couldn't be admitted to kindergarten if you were not already fairly conversant with the English language; and the great place for learning English in the school system is the schoolyard. This teaches you a great deal more than you get in school. One sneer in the schoolyard will do more to correct the deviation from the norm of that group than any amount of parental thundering.

My children both said *tooken*, and I never correct anybody's speech unless he pays me, and they didn't pay, and we let them go, and they don't say *tooken* now. They are grown up; they are both in college. Somewhere along the line somebody snickered, or some one of their contemporaries in the schoolyard said "yea, yea, yea, tooken, tooken, tooken." That'll do it — that'll do it far better than talking about regular past forms, the present, or gerundive, believe me.

When we were on the air in *The Last Word*, a schoolteacher wrote from Atlanta. She was obviously on the verge of a complete nervous breakdown and needed a sedative very badly. She wrote: "Can you give me some simple rules for teaching my students to use the word *the* properly?" Well, obviously, she had reached the point that all teachers and parents reach, the feeling of getting nowhere. You pick out some trifle like, "You will pick up your clothes tonight," or "You will close the garage door." Concentrate on this one or you are always licked — you never get anywhere. She decided apparently she couldn't teach them anything, but she could pick one simple word and some way they would learn to use that.

Well, I wrote her a letter — I felt rather sorry for her — and pointed out that in Jespersen's *Modern English Grammar*, which is a great English grammar, seven thick volumes in small print and double columns, 75 closely printed, double column pages are devoted to the word *the*, and at the end of this, Jespersen throws in the towel. He says that he knows this treatment is superficial and inadequate, but he has to move on. Three score and ten years is all a man has.

The idiomatic uses of T-H-E — we pronounce it three different ways, depending whether or not it is followed by a stressed vowel or whether it is followed by a comma — the idiomatic uses of T-H-E are beyond bewildering. We go *to college, to the university*; we go *to church*, but *the hospital*. The British don't. They go *to hospital*. We go *to town*, but *to the city*. Americans look *out of the window*; British look *out of window*. We may be found *at home, at the house*; we catch *typhoid*, but *the smallpox*; we catch *a cold*, but *the flu*; we have *diphtheria*, but *the measles*. And this goes on and on and on.

Now, suppose this woman decided, nonetheless, she was going to carry on. Let's assume she becomes deeply paranoid and is determined to teach *the*.

Let's suppose she gets a year off with pay in order to understand Jespersen, to codify, to make up rules, and subdivisions, and exceptions, and all the other stuff. With fire in her eye and with Jespersen in her hand, she meets the class the next year and she means this. This is the first grade. She puts the rules down and by God, they shall memorize them. What would she do? She would utterly frustrate the education of those children. Boys would stutter and stammer all the rest of their lives, all of them would be ill at the sight of a book, none of them would ever learn to read. I'm serious about this. She would produce a class of complete and absolute illiterates, with nervous breakdowns.

What's the alternative? The alternative is very simple. Never in my life have I heard a native-born speaker misuse the word *the*. Leave them alone, since they learn it anyway, enormously complicated as it is. No American says "I'm going to hospital." And no Englishman says "I'm going to the hospital." And no American says, "I caught the cold." He says *a cold*, if he is a native-born speaker. Since he does all this, amazing as it is, since his ear taught him all this and he will do it anyway and I've never known anyone who didn't, just let him alone. Don't try to teach the use of *the* by rules.

Now writing cannot equal speech. It cannot be the exact reproduction of speech. The language is changing so rapidly. We pick up so many new words. You know the much attacked *Webster's Third New International* had to add 100,000 words to the list they had in 1934. It seems incredible to think that in 1934 people simply didn't have, therefore had no words for, the atom bomb, baby-sitters, coffee breaks, electronic computers, astronauts, nylons, parking meters, antibiotics, and so on and so on. New experiences are bringing floods of new words. And what's more, they are changing old words.

Many of the letters that we got on the show asked us, "Can this word mean that?" Almost anytime anyone asks you that question, the answer is yes. Otherwise, he wouldn't have asked you the question. Nobody asks, "Can *hippopotamus* mean 'pumpkin pie'?" Nobody's ever heard it used that way. You don't ask this question until you have heard the word used and by the time you have heard the word used, and your ear notices it enough so that you don't think it is an idiotic aberration of some kind, then that probably means that, incredible as it may seem, that has become the meaning of that word.

The most common meaning, for instance, of *silo*, that one reads in the papers now is the concrete pit in the ground from which a missile is being launched. The other word, my idea of silo, a thing sticking out of the ground in which you put food for cattle, is still known, is still used, but the word is completely changed. And this is the meaning, which by the way, I see all of the time in the *New York Times*.

The *New York Times* wrote a very silly editorial on the appearance of the Third Webster, in which they stated that they were not going to use it — they were going to stick to the good old Second Webster. If they were, they would be out of business right now. You can't publish a newspaper in '63 or '61 with the language of 1934. Poor Webster, they had very poor public relations, but in their bleating, Webster pointed out that the largest single source they had drawn from was the *New York Times*. Obviously, the editors don't read their own paper.

Incidentally, I happened to be in the hospital at the time this came out, just convalescing. I had a little time on my hands, and I took that issue, the issue of the *Times* in which they made this bold and lunatic announcement and there were over 170 usages in that issue which were countenanced by the Third Webster which they said they wouldn't use, and were not countenanced by the Second, which they said they would use, and in the very editorial there were two of them.

People often hurl at me the word *permissive*. They say, "You are permissive." What do you mean "permissive"? There are 300 million who speak this language. What am I to do? Club them all on the head? What have I got to do with it? I permit Niagara Falls to go over, too. I don't know what to do about it. I permit the Grand Canyon to remain just where it is. To talk about people being permissive of what 300 million people do every day — back of this is an incredibly arrogant assumption that we who have to do with observing and using speech in some way control it. We don't. The masses control speech. And all we do, ultimately, is follow on.

Now some people believe that words have only one meaning. Of course words have, as we all know, many meanings. And only the context will show you, but the context will show you very clearly. The verb *run* is listed in the *Oxford English Dictionary*, which is now 100 years out of date, as having 265 clearly distinguishable verbal meanings. Now we don't have all those meanings in our vocabulary, but I expect any educated person has maybe 30 meanings of the word *run* in his vocabulary. Well, how do you know which one you mean? You never falter. It's like using *the*. You know. The context almost always tells you.

For instance, what does the word *locks* mean? Well, it means one thing to a locksmith, it means another thing to a delicatessen, it means another thing in a missile base. Anybody who says in a missile base "put some lox in the missile" and finds he's stuffing salmon into it — this isn't likely to happen. Nor is a locksmith likely to shove liquid oxygen through the keyhole.

The words in context almost always define their own meaning. People get unnecessarily agitated about these things. They also get agitated about the use of words. People who believe that words have only one meaning also seem to think they have only one function and they will get very angry and they will say, "You can't use that as a verb, it's a noun." Verbs and nouns are just words which describe what the word is doing at the time you are using it. They don't come first, that is, a verb doesn't mark a species like a dinosaur as against a rabbit.

I have some stuff here from the *Washington Post*, which has gotten very agitated about the English language and isn't always justified in its agitation. The *Washington Post* was very upset about the Third Webster. And, after the usual discharge of rage in such phrases as "abdication of authority," "barbarism," they then accused the dictionary of pretentious and obscure verbosity and illustrated the accusation by referring to the Third Webster's definition of so simple an object as a door.

The editor seemed to think that a door is a door, and that any damn fool ought to know that it is a door, and why do you have to take 94 words to tell someone what a door is? The point is that doors have changed like anything since 1934. We have more strange closing contraptions today. Are they doors or aren't they?

This word has come into the courts. I have a little article here from the *Boston Globe* in which a gentleman too eager to leave a modernistic post office walked through a glass partition to his own damage and then sued the United States government on the grounds that he thought it was a door. And this had to come into court and the judge had to decide not only what is a door, but what is a reasonable man in a reasonable hurry, leaving a reasonable post office, reasonably likely to think is a door? And the judge's decision was that there was no ground for suit here, that, damn it all, you ought to look at least for a handle, a knob, or something, before you start walking out of modern buildings.

But in 1963 the problem of defining a door is a much more difficult thing than it was in 1934. Take these accordion sort of things that slide shut in apartments. Your apartment rent is based on the number of rooms; the landlord may look you right in the eye and tell you that that thing marks a room, because it's a door. You may go to court — and people have gone to court on this, and the courts have ruled it's a door all right. So the dictionary has to take cognizance of this.

Now a more serious charge against the *Post*. I am in a way sorry to single out any paper, because a great many did this, but one has to deal with specific instances. The *Post*, having got its blood pressure up on the matter of usage, ran another editorial. It got very agitated, because it had come across the word *trimester*. Some college was going to go on a trimester system and the editor, huffing and puffing about this, said: "Beginning next fall, state universities will operate on three equal terms each year instead of the present semester system. Incidentally, they are calling the plan a 'trimester system' which implies a miraculous improvement indeed, for *semester* derives from the Latin word *semestris* meaning 'half-yearly'. And trimester, by analogy, must mean 'three halves'. That will be crowding it, even for Florida."

Unfortunately, that isn't what *semester* means at all. Now there is no reason to expect the editor to know Latin, but before he states what Latin means, he ought to look it up. *Semester* is based on *sex mensis*, "six months, a six months period." *Semester* has been in the language very long. *Trimester* has been in the language over a hundred years. All *trimester* means is a "three month period." This is no great crime, except that the indignation is simply unjustified and it is uninformed. And if a man is going to write editorials, scorning the dictionary, and invents facts to his fancy, then he shouldn't get too excited about the incorrect use of words.

Now many words pass in the language simply as errors. We have many established errors. Once an error is fixed by usage, it will stay and you have to use it. For instance, if a child said *gooder, knowed, me am* or *girlses,* he would agitate his parents deeply. Most children do something like this and most parents are agitated. Nonetheless, we all use words like that every day because we don't know that they are corruptions. *Lesser* and *nearer* and even the word *more* are historically exactly the same as *gooder*.

The historical word, which didn't change until Shakespeare's time, is *moe*. When Macbeth says "Send out moe horses, skirr the country round," he is not talking Dixie talk — this is the old English word. The *r* was then added by somebody who didn't perceive that *moe* was an irregular comparative. *Me am* would seem unthinkable to anybody, yet we all say *you are,* which is exactly the same, exactly the use of the accusative for the nominative and fairly recent. *Girlses* sounds awful, but we all say *children,* which is even more awful: *children* is a triplication of a plural.

Let me call your attention to some real changes that are taking place in the language that don't bother these people at all because they simply go on using them. There has been a great increase in empty verbs, that is, where people used to say, "Let's drink, Let's swim," they are now inclined to say "Let's have a drink, Let's take a drink, Let's have a swim, Let's take a swim." Where our fathers said "It snowed heavily," we're likely to say "There was a heavy snow." Our fathers "decided," we "reach a decision." Why we put these extra verbs in, I don't know. I have only some theories and won't bother you with them, but this again is a marked change in the language.

There is a great increase in the use of the passive, which probably reflects a civilized or degenerate — the two things are often the same — awareness of the fact that we are being acted on. The barbarian is never aware of this; he is acted on, but he is too aggressive to know it. The barbarian lives in the active present indicative. "I eat," "I steal," "I rob," "I rape," and eventually he drops dead. But the civilized man knows that the forces are working on him. The Greeks had a very elaborate passive, Romans didn't have much of a passive, our language has very little passive.

There is an increased use of the subjunctive in modern American English for some reason. The true subjunctive has now retreated almost entirely. Among illiterate Negroes you will hear the proper use of the subjunctive. "Be he there, see him I will." This would sound very strange, but I heard our laundress the other day, who comes right out of the Delta, say she was going back to see her grandpappy, "Be he still living." This is good, good, fine old historical English.

The new subjunctive you hear in such phrases as "I wouldn't know." In the quiz shows, if someone says "Who was George Washington?" instead of saying "The first president," you'll say "That would be the first president." There seems to be a feeling here that the subjunctive gives a touch of gentility in some way or protects you in some way. I don't know exactly why it's used.

Well now, most people don't know anything about grammar and there's no earthly reason why they should. You don't have to know any more about grammar to speak effectively than you have to know about physics to drive a car. The one is the theory of the other, but you don't have to know the theory. The people who get agitated usually fall back on logic, and there they are on completely false grounds because language isn't logical.

Language knows no logic except itself. You cannot apply mathematics to language. Classical Latin is logical, but classical Latin is a mandarin language; nobody ever spoke it. Spoken Latin was quite different from what Cicero and Virgil wrote. If language were logical, for instance, *unloose* ought to mean "tie up," but it doesn't. If language were logical, an outlaw ought to be the opposite of an inlaw. But it isn't.

One of the commonest charges people make who get logical about languages, for instance, is that you cannot use the plural with *none*. You say, "Well, none of them are coming" and they seem to think you should say "None of them is coming." They base this on the triumphant grounds that none doesn't include one. Well, if it doesn't include one, then you can't use the singular either if you want to be logical. I don't know what to do at that point.

Nonetheless, the simple fact is that people use the plural increasingly. Most people would say "None of them are coming," rather than say "None of them is." When our *Dictionary of Contemporary American Usage* was published, the *Chicago Tribune* did us the honor of ten separate attacks. The thing seemed to agitate them very deeply, and they picked on this. We had said that contemporary usage countenances plural with *none* more often than the singular. This doesn't mean that either one is wrong. They said absolutely no, and I wrote them a letter, pointing out Shakespeare used *none* with the plural, though I didn't expect that to bother them much, but I thought I had a real topper — I pointed out that God uses *none* with the plural in the very first commandment as in Deuteronomy 5:7 — but I guess my authority was regarded at the *Tribune* as secondary and they weren't impressed.

We've all heard the business of double negatives — we're all taught in school that you mustn't use two negatives. That's all right if you want to say to a class, "If you use two negatives in a certain way, you will mark yourself as a part of a certain level of education and particularness." "But I was told two negatives make a positive." A more absurd statement in relation to language was never made. Two negatives may make a positive in algebra, but they don't in any Teutonic language. In every Teutonic language, the duplication of the negative simply heightens the negation. When Chaucer says of his Knight that he "hadn't never yet said nothing nasty to no man in all his life," you would be feebleminded to say "well, did he or didn't he"? Chaucer has knocked himself and the language out trying to tell you this man never said anything nasty to people. You ought to know that by that time.

Furthermore, if you want to be logical, if you want to say logic does not countenance a double negative and you say two negatives make a positive, then three negatives make a negative again. So that if it is wrong to say "It doesn't make no difference," then it must be all right to say "It don't never make no difference." This is not true.

No, it isn't all right to say either of these simply because neither is accepted by educated people in either America or England today, though they were in the past. Not because of logic, but simply because custom doesn't countenance them, either one.

Usage is capricious and illogical, but it is tyrannical. Many times the charge has been brought: "Well, then you are saying anything goes." Oh, no, anything does not go at all. There is no activity of human life in which less goes. In speech you are not permitted to deviate one iota from the customs of your group without being severely punished. Consider what was made of Al Smith's pronunciation of what other people call *radio* and he called *raddio*. Maybe his constituents called it *raddio*. I don't know. Actually, *radio* is an artificial word made up of Latin. *Raddio* is nearer what we know of Latin than *radio*. Nonetheless, when I was a boy and the campaign was going on, I heard nothing about his career as governor of New York — all I heard was *raddio*. This man said *raddio*, just as today you hear another man say *Cuber* over and over. If you have any doubt that society will punish you for a deviation, go into a cheap restaurant in Chicago and ask for *tomahto* soup. You will feel public disapproval very quickly. If you can afford the Pump Room, they will furnish you with *tomahto* soup; don't try it in Joe's Beanery. It won't go.

All *idiom* means is something we do in this language which doesn't make any sense, but we do it all the same. And the very people who get so upset about English idioms, because they don't conform to some preconceived theory, are proud of their use of idioms in another language. We say *a couple of dollars,* but we say *a dozen eggs.* Our great grandfathers said *a dozen of eggs* and I suspect in backward rural parts today you would hear *a dozen of eggs.* We say that we *adore* God, but would be shocked if some one would say that he is *adorable.* But centuries ago, this was said quite seriously in very solemn words. We say *later on.* This sounds all right to us. The English say *early on* and *earlier on* and this baffles us.

Suppose for instance, you want to be an innovator in language and you just decided that you would say *squoze?* Why *squeezed? Squoze* sounds better. We say *freeze, froze,* and so on — why not say *squoze?* What would happen if you decided on just that one little thing? You are going to change the language. You come down to the office and say "Well, I squoze some oranges for breakfast this morning." The general look would be, "Very funny very early in the morning," and nobody would be vastly amused and they would say, "He thinks he's a card." But suppose you keep up. Day after day you're going to be a "squoze" man. You keep at it. People would begin to say, "Look, this guy has a screw loose. He says *squoze.* What's the matter with him?" And they would be right. That would cost you advancement. I'd be willing to swear that in any organization if you stuck to *squoze,* they wouldn't promote you, and they'd be right. "This guy, there is something wrong with this guy" and there is something wrong with everyone who would deliberately deviate that way.

We have deviations, but usually they are not deliberate. Men have been driven out of public life for deviating one syllable. In our speech, for instance, one of the signs of what we regard as supreme illiteracy is making stops of certain *th* sounds. That is, instead of saying *th-*, saying *dese, dem, dose.* This is supposed to mark you as a person absolutely outside the pale. Yet these sounds don't bother us if we all agree. They don't bother us in the least if we all say *bedlam* instead of *Bethlehem,* which is the proper word. We all say *murder* instead of *murther,* as it used to be. We say *burden* instead of *burthen,* as it used to be, and so on.

Certainly Mr. Kennedy, who is a highly educated man and speaks very effectively, has come in for plenty of criticism for that Boston pronunciation of the last vowel of *Cuba.* I don't know whether he does it deliberately or whether it was necessary in the early parts of his career that he might identify himself with East Boston. I don't know. It comes natural to him. Why shouldn't he speak his own language?

I speak Ohio east overlaid with English where I got my early and later education plus considerable personal idiosyncrasy as a result of adenoids, I guess. At any rate, that's the way you speak. No man ought — I would mistrust a man who changed his speech much more than I would mistrust one who went right ahead.

Truman is a wonderful speaker. Truman's voice is purely American, purely — it's western Missouri.

Well, in conclusion, what are we supposed to do about all this? Are you just to drift? Are you to permit anybody to write the way he wants to? Well, you can't do much about it. You are not going to hire illiterates. You are not likely to hire them as teachers or editorial writers or reporters, though they might make very good ones. That is, there might be a freshness in their speech.

What you have to do is admit that there is a very wide range in this great language we speak. There are many local ways of speaking. There are different ways of speaking at different levels. Everybody has several languages. You couldn't possibly speak at home as you would speak in public. We have highly formal ways of speaking on highly formal occasions, and then we have relaxed ways of speaking with our friends and then you have ways of usually grunting within the family. This conveys your feeling and you shift without any trouble from one level to another.

When you're dealing with the public as with a class or as in a newspaper or an editorial, naturally you conform to whatever the usage of that group is and I mean naturally. And I don't mean naturally in the sense that you make an effort to do it. It doesn't occur to you to do anything else.

Rules, good rules, are those which state as best they can what cultivated, sensitive people who want passionately to express their meaning now say. Bad rules are those which state what such people used to do. Very bad rules are those which state what somebody thinks they ought to do, but don't. And anyway, all rules are simply a means to an end and the end is being understood, expressing ourselves exactly and competely and expressing our emotions as well as our thoughts.

I read, as you probably do also, "Winners and Sinners," put out by Mr. Bernstein of the *New York Times*. I find it very fascinating, and it is high on my list of preferred reading. I often disagree with Mr. Bernstein on questions of grammar, but I don't disagree with him for one moment — indeed I am usually wracked with admiration for the subtlety of his perceptions — that this word in this context is loaded, that you colored this statement by putting this word in there. That is very fine editing indeed. That helps make the *Times* the very great paper it is. What you want to do is express the exact meaning. If you want to color it, fine, but you've got to know that you are coloring. The only sin is not to know this is a loaded word, not to know this word conveys something else to the average reader because you have to know what the average reader means by these words.

All writing is a form of communication and all communication is a form of translation from one man's observation and experience into another's and when you are translating, the important one is the language into which you are translating. You have to know it, of course — reporters do. The advantage of newspaper writing, the reason it is often fascinating reading, is that it has to be written with great haste. You have to meet a deadline. The thing happens, you want to beat another man with the account of it. This compels you to write in contemporary — as close to contemporary as you can, because you haven't time to think of how Shakespeare would have done it, very fortunately. Shakespeare never took time off to think how anyone else would have done it, he just did it his way.

The difficulty seems to be, the reason you get these editorials of the kind I quoted, is that only superannuated reporters become editors. You are far advanced, apparently, into the veil of arteriosclerosis by the time you become an editor. And as you are aware of the change in the language, all you see in it is corruption whereas it isn't corrupt at all, it's very live.

Language isn't made in classrooms, language isn't made in dictionaries, language isn't made in grammar books, language isn't made in editorials. Language is made by the three hundred million people of the English language who are living, who are angry, who are excited, who are greedy, who are passionate about something, and out of this enormous vocabulary that time and fate has given us, put these wonderful words together. I don't believe I've ever heard a remark in a faculty meeting that has suddenly excited me with glory and wonder, at the brilliance, the humor, the aptness of it. You don't hear that sort of thing in faculty meetings, but you do hear it on the street. Suddenly you hear a phrase, you hear something in a bus or somewhere and your heart will leap up and dance with the daffodils.

I remember at a football game once a referee who was introduced as the head of the YMCA league or something. He made a number of decisions which angered one side very much, and when he finally blew the whistle and the whole thing was over, I remember a guy behind me just yelling at the top of his voice:

"Goodbye for good, you Sunday School son of a bitch."

That was good language for that man's purposes at that moment, I thought.

Supplement 7.

General Patton's Prayer*

Sir, this is Patton talking. The last fourteen days have been straight hell. Rain, snow, more rain, more snow — and I'm beginning to wonder what's going on in Your headquarters. Whose side are You on, anyway?

For three years my chaplains have been explaining this as a religious war. This, they tell me, is the Crusades all over again, except that we're riding tanks instead of chargers. They insist we are here to annihilate the German Army and the godless Hitler so that religious freedom may return to Europe.

Up until now I have gone along with them, for You have given us Your unreserved cooperation. Clear skies and a calm sea in Africa made the landings highly successful and helped us to eliminate Rommel. Sicily was comparatively easy, and You supplied excellent weather for our armored dash across France, the greatest military victory that You have thus far allowed me. You have often given me excellent guidance in difficult command decisions and You have led German units into traps that made their elimination fairly simple.

But now, You've changed horses in midstream. You seem to have given von Rundstedt every break in the book, and frankly, he's been beating hell out of us. My army is neither trained nor equipped for winter warfare. And, as You know, this weather is more suitable for Eskimos than for southern cavalrymen.

But now, Sir, I can't help but feel that I have offended You in some way. That suddenly You have lost all sympathy with our cause. That You are throwing in with von Rundstedt and his paper-hanging god. You know without me telling You that our situation is desperate. Sure, I can tell my staff that everything is going according to plan, but there's no use telling You that my 101st Airborne is holding out against tremendous odds in Bastogne, and that this continual storm is making it impossible to supply them even from the air. I've sent Hugh Gaffney, one of my ablest generals, with his 4th Armored Division, north toward that all-important road center to relieve the encircled garrison, and he's finding Your weather much more difficult than he is the Krauts.

I don't like to complain unreasonably, but my soldiers from the Meuse to Echternach are suffering the tortures of the damned. Today I visited several hospitals, all full of frostbite cases, and the wounded are dying in the fields because they cannot be brought back for medical care.

But this isn't the worst of the situation. Lack of visibility, continued rains have completely grounded my air force. My technique of battle calls for close-in fighter-bomber support, and if my planes can't fly, how can I use them as aerial artillery? Not only is this a deplorable situation, but, worse

---

*This is General George S. Patton's famous prayer, delivered just before Christmas during the Battle of the Bulge. It was originally published in *The American Legion Magazine* and is reprinted here by permission.

yet, my reconnaissance planes haven't been in the air for fourteen days, and I haven't the faintest idea of what's going on behind the German lines.

Dammit, Sir, I can't fight a shadow. Without Your cooperation from a weather standpoint, I am deprived of an accurate disposition of the German armies, and how in hell can I be intelligent in my attack? All this probably sounds unreasonable to You, but I have lost all patience with Your chaplains who insist that this is a typical Ardennes winter, and that I must have faith.

Faith and patience be damned! You have just got to make up Your mind whose side You're on. You must come to my assistance, so that I may dispatch the entire German Army as a birthday present to Your Prince of Peace.

Sir, I have never been an unreasonable man. I am not going to ask You for the impossible. I do not even insist upon a miracle, for all I request is four days of clear weather.

Give me four clear days so that my planes can fly: so that my fighter-bombers can bomb and strafe, so that my reconnaissance may pick out targets for my magnificent artillery. Give me four days of sunshine to dry this blasted mud: so that my tanks may roll, so that ammunition and rations may be taken to my hungry, ill-equipped infantry. I need these four days to send von Rundstedt and his godless army to their Valhalla. I am sick of this unnecessary butchery of American youth, and in exchange for four days of fighting weather, I will deliver You enough Krauts to keep Your bookkeepers months behind in their work.

Amen.

References

Ambrester, Roy, Conklin, Forrest, Allbritten, Robert, and Beaty, Ray, "An Experimental Study of the Relative Effectiveness of Direct and Indirect Compliments in Persuasive Speeches," *The Ohio Speech Journal,* 4:63-65 (1966).

Baker, Eldon E. "Aligning Speech Evaluation and Behavioral Objectives," *The Speech Teacher,* 16:158-160 (March, 1967).

Becker, Samuel L., and Cronkite, Gary L. "Reliability as a Function of Utilized Scale Steps," *The Speech Teacher,* 14:291-293 (November, 1965).

Bos, William H. "Grades in Speech," *The Speech Teacher,* 15:86-88 (January, 1966).

Bostrom, Robert N. "Dogmatism, Rigidity, and Rating Behavior," *The Speech Teacher,* 13:283-287 (November, 1964).

Borchers, Gladys L. "A Symposium on Evaluation, Criticism and Grading," *The Speech Teacher,* 9:1-22 (January, 1960).

Bowers, John Waite. "Training Speech Raters with Films," *The Speech Teacher,* 13:228-231 (September, 1964).

Callaghan, Calvin. "Testing the Ability to Organize Ideas," *The Speech Teacher*, 13:225-227 (September, 1964).

Clevenger, Theodore, Jr., Clark, Margaret Leitner, and Lazier, Gilbert N. "Stability of Factor Structure in Smith's Semantic Differential for Theatre Concepts," *The Quarterly Journal of Speech*, 53:241-47 (October, 1967).

Crocker, Lionel, "Guide Lines for Objectivity in Grading in Speech Courses," *The Ohio Speech Journal*, 4:11-16 (1966).

Crocker, Lionel, "The Comprehensive Examination in Speech at Denison University," *The Speech Teacher*, 7:127-129 (March, 1958).

Crowell, Laura. "Rating Scales as Diagnostic Instruments in Discussion," *The Speech Teacher*, 2:26-32 (January, 1953).

DeVito, Joseph A. "Learning Theory and Grading," *The Speech Teacher*, 16:155-157 (March, 1967).

Douglas, Jack. "The Measurement of Speech in the Classroom," *The Speech Teacher*, 7:309-319 (November, 1958).

Dow, Clyde W. "Testing Listening Comprehension of High School Seniors and College Freshmen," *The Speech Teacher*, 4:239-246 (November, 1955).

Ellis, Dean S. "A University Speech Placement Test for Entering Freshmen," *The Speech Teacher*, 15:158-164 (March, 1966).

Faules, Don. "Quantitative Analysis of Peer-Group Evaluation," *The Ohio Speech Journal*, 4:60-62 (1966).

Hance, Kenneth G. "Improving the Instructor as a Critic," *The Speech Teacher*, 16:150-154 (March, 1967).

Harris, Chester W. "Some Issues in Evaluation," *The Speech Teacher*, 12:191-199 (September, 1963).

Holtzman, Paul D. "Speech Criticism and Evaluation as Communication," *The Speech Teacher*, 9:8-11 (January, 1960).

Kelly, J. C. "The Classroom Communication Test in a Voice and Articulation Course," *The Speech Teacher*, 4:89-97 (March, 1955).

Kelly, Win D. "Objectivity in the Grading and Evaluation of Speeches," *The Speech Teacher*, 14:50-53 (January, 1965).

Knower, Franklin H. "The Analysis and Validation of Tests and Test Items in Speech," *The Speech Teacher*, 10:228-231 (September, 1961).

————. "The Graduate Record Examinations Advanced Speech Test," *The Speech Teacher*, 3:199-201 (September, 1954).

————. "What is a Speech Test?" *The Quarterly Journal of Speech*, 30:485-493 (December, 1944).

Laase, Leroy. "The Measurement of Instruction in Speech," *The Speech Teacher*, 7:47-53 (January, 1958).

Lewis, George L., and Schoen, Kathryn T. "The High School Drama Course, A Project in Test Item Analysis," *The Ohio Speech Journal*, 2:161-180 (1963).

Linkugel, Wilmer A. "Student Evaluation of Assignments in a Course in Fundamentals of Speech," *The Speech Teacher*, 7:154-156 (March, 1958).

Miller, Gerald R. "Agreement and the Grounds for It: Persistent Problems in Speech Rating," *The Speech Teacher*, 13:257-261 (September, 1964).

Monroe, Alan H. "Testing Speech Performance," *The Bulletin of the National Association of Secondary School Principals*, 29:159-163 (1945).

Montgomery, K. E. "How to Criticise Student Speeches," *The Speech Teacher* 6:200-204 (September, 1957).

Myers, Gary C. "The Examination and the Learner," *The Educational Review*, 54:274-284 (October, 1917).

Oliver, Robert T. "The Eternal (and Infernal) Problem of Grades," *The Speech Teacher*, 9:8-11 (January, 1960).

Osgood, Charles, Tannenbaum, Percy, and Suci, George. *The Measurement of Meaning*. Urbana, Illinois: University of Illinois Press, 1957.

Pfister, Emil R., and Schilling, Arlo L. "A Procedure for On-the-Spot Oral Evaluation of Performance by Students in Speech Contests," *The Speech Teacher*, 14:132-135 (March, 1965).

Ragsdale, J. Donald (ed.). "Symposium: Evaluation in the Public Speaking Course," *The Speech Teacher*, 16:150-164 (March, 1967).

Rees, Norma S. "Measuring and Training Pitch Discrimination Ability in Voice Improvement," *The Speech Teacher*, 11:44-47 (January, 1962).

Robinson, Karl F. "Teaching Listening Through Evaluation and Criticism" *The Speech Teacher*, 2:178-180 (September, 1953).

Sawyer, Thomas M. "A Grading System for Speech Classes," *The Speech Teacher*, 9:12-15 (January, 1960).

Seiger, Marvin L. "The Speech Teacher: Listener and Critic," *The Speech Teacher*, 5:259-261 (November, 1956).

Sikkink, Donald E. "A Numerical Grading System for the Required Basic Speech Course," *The Speech Teacher*, 13:293-295 (November, 1964).

Smith, Raymond G. "A Semantic Differential for Theatre Concepts," *Speech Monographs*, 28:1-8 (March, 1961).

Stevens, Walter W., and Hildebrandt, Herbert W. "Blue Book Criticisms at Michigan," *The Speech Teacher*, 9:20-22 (January, 1960).

Thompson, Wayne. "Is There a Yardstick for Measuring Speaking Skill?" *The Quarterly Journal of Speech*, 29:87-91 (1943).

Tiemens, Robert K. "Validation of Informative Speech Ratings by Retention Tests," *The Speech Teacher*, 14:211-215 (September, 1965).

Utterback, William E. "Evaluation of Performance in the Discussion Course at Ohio State University," *The Speech Teacher*, 7:209-215 (September, 1958).

Weaver, Carl. "The Construction of an Objective Examination in the Fundamentals Course," *The Speech Teacher*, 10:112-117 (March, 1961).

White, Eugene E. "A Rationale for Grades," *The Speech Teacher*, 16:247-252 (November, 1967).

Wiksell, Wesley. "New Methods of Evaluating Instruction and Student Achievement in a Speech Class," *The Speech Teacher*, 9:16-19 (January, 1960).

Part Two

CONTENT

Teachers of speech are often challenged to justify speech as a discipline of learning. The second part of this text presents the several precise disciplines of speech, each of which contains enough content to form a complete course. Each has a rich historical literature: rhetoric, the oldest of the schools of speech; interpretation, the art of the storyteller and its modern variations in film, radio, and television; and drama, still the best medium for critical comment. On the domestic and international level, problems evolve into oral confrontations demanding skill in large and small group communication. And broadcasting permits the individual citizen to view each of these speech disciplines every day; the media thus carries its impact beyond the recorded message.

While each of these fields could be studied as separate and self-contained, each profits from new ideas and techniques borrowed from the others. The common bond which they all share — that of a live audience *reacting to a* message *— demands that we continue to develop ways of using the speech disciplines in efficient, functional, and artistic forms.*

6

Resources in Speech Instruction

Resources in speech instruction should be selected to improve learning. Through the wise choice of people and materials, direct experiences can contribute to student behavior which will closely resemble the behavior sought in the instructional process. What or how much is learned in "non-media" situations as compared with that in certain media situations is still a matter for much research.[1] The recent rapid expansion of audiovisual materials available to the schools has aroused concern for better utilization, administration, and evaluation of these materials. Speech resources have not been as available as materials prepared for other fields, such as science, yet the relationships of these resources to the total program must receive the same scrutiny.

RESOURCE UNIT DEVELOPMENT

Since 1930 various groups have made attempts to develop resource units in different fields. This was an outgrowth of the emphasis on

---

[1]Jack V. Edling, "Educational Objectives and Educational Media," *Review of Educational Research,* 38, No. 2:189 (April, 1968).

democracy in the classroom which sought to create situations in which students and teacher worked democratically. In contrast to the textbook-assignment-recitation procedure, this approach involved a systematic and comprehensive survey, analysis, and organization of possible resources with suggestions for use and evaluation. These resource units are usually developed cooperatively with students or other teachers as they engage in preplanning a learning unit in the classroom. (Chapter 3 discusses these units more fully.) Such resource guides or reservoirs of ideas and materials permit the teacher to select those best suited to his group and daily situation. Flexibility rather than rigidity and creativity rather than comformity become the guiding philosophy. For the teacher whose guiding philosophy has been to cling to the traditional ready-made plans for teaching by faithfully following a prescribed course of study utilizing a single source, this poses a serious problem. In an attempt to move from very traditional to more modern teaching methods, there is often a tendency to formulate resource guides with suggestions which may become rigid requirements. In such cases, the labels have changed, but the purpose has not. When the controlling factor becomes ground-to-be-covered rather than presentation of a variety of purposeful educational experiences to meet individual needs, the focus is on accommodating the teacher rather than the student.

To view a textbook, a course of study, or any other instructional aids as sources to be adapted to particular situations requires that the speech teacher discover and use a wide variety of resources. Because this procedure requires more time for planning, some teachers with already burdensome instructional loads feel it is necessary to accept an established pattern or outline. If the pattern, such as a single text, reflects quality speech instruction and if the teacher is fairly creative and sensitive in adapting this prescribed outline to individual students, effective teaching may result. However, the tendency appears to be for teachers to become too reliant upon someone else's suggestions. For the teacher of speech who has insufficient training in speech, using an established outline may be a better course of action, but the sooner a teacher becomes acquainted with the variety of available speech materials the more knowledgeable and comfortable he may become. He is then better qualified to recommend resources for speech instruction.

A word of caution to those who seek to employ newer approaches for improved instruction. To initiate organizational innovations may solve organizational problems, but to teach differently than one taught before requires a greater amount of work than simple organizational restructuring.

Selecting Resource Materials

There are several basic considerations which should govern the selection of instructional material. One of these is the rationale or *purpose* in their selection. Different objectives usually demand different experiences for the student. Some may be simple and direct, some contrived and dramatic, while others may be complex and abstract. Directly related to purpose is the appropriate and intelligent *use* of the selected resources. This requires adaptation to the learner and the learning situation if their use is to be effective. The *availability* of these tools of learning is also a concern in the acquisition of suitable instructional materials. One must have access to these resources to foster learning activities and be assured that provisions are made for budgetary concerns.

Types of Resource Materials

Innovations in electronic learning devices have taken place so rapidly that many teachers are overwhelmed by all the materials and equipment available today. As soon as one begins to feel proficient with certain types of media, newer models replace the familiar but obsolete ones. It has become increasingly apparent that with a profusion of types of resources, no classroom teacher can serve as an expert in the intelligent use of all of them. Specialists are required to help faculty and students develop their competencies or to offer services as technicians. In local schools where such a service center is unavailable, classroom teachers must develop competency in utilizing those resources which are available and seem to have the most potential in the particular learning experience.

People, textbooks, charts, dioramas, diagrams, graphs, maps, specimens, models, globes, photographs, mock-ups, three-dimensional displays, overhead transparencies, tradebooks, pamphlets, forms, references, tests, films, filmstrips, slides, closed-circuit TV, audio- and video-tapes, language laboratories, disc recordings, programmed texts, radio, computer programs, multi-media communication systems, and various reproduction, projection, listening, and response devices are some of the types of resources available for educational purposes. It is essential for teachers to understand the educational implications of the newer media and provide for humanizing rather than dehumanizing their educational use.

We may conveniently group various resources as follows: (1) community resources, (2) printed materials, and (3) audiovisual aids.

Community Resources

Community resources may be classified as people, institutions, objects, and natural resources. Although *people* have been used as educational resources for many years, it is doubtful that secondary teachers have utilized them to augment and improve the instructional program the way elementary teachers have. There are many different types of communicators in a community who could strengthen secondary speech and drama curricula.

The speech teacher is a resource person as is each student who brings some kind of personal experience and background to the class. In some instances these individuals become authorities and are capable of making outstanding educational contributions. Personal experience in various performance skills increases the potential resource background. Community people such as attorneys, actors, labor leaders, ministers, and others who successfully employ speech skills can serve to encourage students to participate in speech experiences. Persons involved in communication efforts during election campaigns might be useful resource people. Individual students may participate as audience members or conduct interviews with candidates and report results to their classes if the candidates and the total speech groups cannot be involved in a mutual situation. Parents can become more powerful educative agents as they discuss local, state, and national concerns with children. Through the use of telelecture techniques, verbal presentations transcend physical boundaries which once restricted learning.

Just as materials must be evaluated to determine their educational worth, so people must be evaluated for the contribution they can make to the educational objective. If these evaluations are not made carefully, the use of such people may prove to be unwise.

Institutions, like people, may become resources for a speech program. Students need to study the role of speech in the life of basic institutions in order to lead better lives in society. Freedom of speech, respecting rights of others, and responsible debate are but a few of the speech concerns with which institutions are involved. Field trips to study how speech is used in various institutional settings, such as a court room, may increase understanding.

Objects, while related to people and institutions, often serve as a focal point in an educational experience. A study of Greek theatre history could be enhanced by viewing in the local museum Greek costumes, masks, and art objects which tell in a visual manner the history of early drama.

Natural resources, although they are community resources, would appear to be more beneficial in a study of our way of life or features of our geographic environment than as a related speech experience. However, students need an understanding of physical environment to appreciate the aesthetic and artistic. Sensory appeals are important for creative dramatics.

Printed Materials

Textbooks are a potent source of curriculum content and in an environment of limited printed materials often play the major role in determining the content of speech programs. In schools where there is an abundance of books, textbooks and printed materials are often used as guides or references. The teacher sometimes condemns these materials because of improper use — when a single text becomes the sole basis for an educational speech program. When it becomes an aid, not the sole source, its role can be a very positive one. To teach without a textbook can be hazardous. The program may lack substance and direction. Lack of organization could lead to frustration and prove to be time-consuming. To teach with a good textbook, especially if it is used with supplementary material, will provide a common basis for discussion. The less experienced speech teacher may feel the need to rely on a textbook for guidance.

Regardless of whether the teacher uses one textbook or many, he needs to establish some criteria to help him evaluate the quality of the textbooks he examines in order to exercise sound educational judgments. Factors to be considered in choosing a textbook are (1) the professional competency of the author and publisher, (2) the author's educational philosophy, (3) the scope and emphasis of the content, (4) the accuracy and appropriateness of its content, (5) the format of the book (size, color, prints, paper, organization, etc.), (6) the literary qualities and readability of the materials, (7) how well the book relates to course objectives, and (8) the supplementary materials which accompany it, such as bibliographies, teaching aids, etc. It is also helpful to consult book review sources in making decisions concerning textbooks.

The library is often the center for housing printed materials within the school or community. It serves as a research center for information and pleasure. Reference materials, periodicals, and books of many categories supplement textbook materials in enlarging the scope of the speech program. This learning resource for areas such as debate, public speaking, oral interpretation, and drama, when used wisely, will enrich a purposeful speech program.

Also included in this research center, the library, are various *non-standardized materials* which are highly desirable. Some may be included in the picture file and the vertical file, which is a depository of various articles, clippings, and pamphlets supplying current information on a variety of subjects. Free or inexpensive materials are published by private and industrial concerns. One should recognize the possibility of propaganda inherent in these materials and use them accordingly, Frequently these sources serve as evidence for a debate. Such materials are similar to those supplied through the state high school speech leagues to member schools.

Speech teachers should not overlook the value of *personal collections* of printed materials acquired during their undergraduate speech programs. A personal library of professional speech journals and books in all skill areas of speech, including forensics, interpretation, general speech, theatre, speech correction, and broadcasting-television, should prove helpful. Any graded materials or handouts for drill, motivation, and remedial use in these skill areas are resource materials. Catalogues from theatrical supply houses, drama publishing companies, and other commercial agencies may prove useful in selecting and producing a play or purchasing equipment for speech programs. Collections of general culture such as short stories, dramas, histories, periodic literature, and subscriptions to current magazines of general interest which reflect current events provide excellent sources for stories, topics, theatrical settings, costuming, characterization, discussion, and other needs of a speech program.

Audiovisual Aids

Audiovisual materials, materials that do not depend primarily upon reading to convey their meanings,[2] have been used for years as instructional aids. Formerly the emphasis was on graphic materials such as charts, globes, diagrams, pictures, etc. With the advent of electronic technology and the multi-media approach, a profusion of learning devices has invaded our classrooms bringing with it excitement, confusion, distress, disappointment, research experimentation, production, and revised curricula.

In the area of *mass media* the views of Marshall McLuhan have been unusually influential. His contention that the "medium is the message" has been widely quoted and analyzed. The medium *per se* is important in that different media place different restrictions on the kinds of messages they can communicate. However, there is at best only a

---

[2]Edgar Dale, *Audio-Visual Methods in Teaching* (rev. ed.; New York: Holt, Rinehart & Winston, Inc., 1964), p. 3.

low-order correlation between message and medium in an instructional context.[3] Most *media research* during the past fifty years has been media comparison. If attention could be focused on learning variables — why the person does or does not meet progress criteria — then insight might be gained as to how instructional media might provide for individual needs. It would be advisable for the secondary speech teacher to review some of the research literature on educational media and technology to be aware of the "state of the art" and its implications for the speech curriculum. The teacher might refer to the April, 1968 issue of the *Review of Educational Research* entitled "Instructional Materials: Educational Media and Technology," published by the American Educational Research Association, and *Teacher Education and the New Media* by Herbert Schueter, Gerald Lesser, and Allen Dobbins, published by the American Association of Colleges for Teacher Education, 1967. The role of mass communications in contemporary society and its impact on cummunication process is discussed extensively in *Speech in American Society*.[4]

Extensive and varied resources have created a need for an *instructional materials center*. This center, sometimes organized as a branch of the school library, requires specialized personnel to purchase, service, and aid the classroom teacher in the selection and utilization of the newer media. If the center houses all printed materials, teaching aids, and media used in the school environment, it is often called the learning resource center or laboratory. As teachers struggle to understand the techniques and educational implications, there is sometimes a tendency to become involved in the gadgetry and to forget relevance, readiness, and the learner's uniqueness. None of these inventions should take the place of the special relationship between the teacher and student. Yet many of these enhance the learning process by involving the student in direct purposeful sensory participation. The more concrete experience minimizes confusion in trying to establish a uniform mental image among the group and eliminates unnecessary questions resulting from abstract verbalization.

Once the speech teacher has established behavioral objectives, he will attempt to select materials and methods relevant to his desired outcomes. He may examine existing audiovisual materials, prepare his own, or plan for student endeavors. Students may plan, direct, and implement radio programs, films, television shows, or other communication efforts

---

[3]Paul Saettler, "Design and Selection Factors," *Review of Educational Research,* 38, No. 2:122 (April, 1968).

[4]R. R. Allen, Sharol Anderson, and Jere Hough, *Speech in American Society* (Columbus, Ohio: Charles E. Merrill Publishing Co., 1968), Chapter 15.

employing audio or visual media. These efforts may serve as *controlled educational experiences* for the participating students or may result in preparing instructional aids for other student groups. Speech experiences which involve action for the student are more *direct speech experiences* and are usually more meaningful. There may be actual speech situations like giving speeches, telling stories, debating, discussing, or employing parliamentary procedure in a non-contrived meeting. These are typical of curricular and co-curricular activities.

Often it becomes necessary to contrive speech experiences in order to furnish opportunities for large numbers of students to participate or because it is impossible to supply the "real" situation. *Simulated experiences* are fairly concrete and include public speaking and dramatized and oral interpretation activities. The "pretend" radio and television programs with all the attending props are substitutes for the genuine experience but may be meaningful educational opportunities for the students.

Within the past few years, *video-tape* has been used in many university and college speech departments for teaching speech fundamentals, discussion, advanced public speaking, and teacher education programs. In most cases the results have been encouraging. As the equipment becomes more accessible, it is reasonable to assume that more secondary school speech programs will adopt the video-tape as a teaching aid. It allows the student to view the replay of his own speaking behavior either immediately or at a later time. Non-verbal messages as well as verbal messages are recorded and more easily evaluated. Critiques of speech behavior are often more meaningful when accompanied by the playback. Student self-analysis often increases the student's motivation for improving his speech skills. The portability of the equipment makes it possible to use it within the regular classroom setting. It should be remembered that effectiveness of this or any other teaching aid in the secondary speech program depends upon its intelligent use.

Models and mock-ups are used to represent the real thing. They are important for understanding speech science and anatomy and the technical aspects of theatre, where it is often impossible to view objects and processes any other way. In dramatized experiences the student may share participation and observation. He may create a dramatic situation or may reconstruct one. These may be in the form of pantomime, role-playing, sociodrama, plays, puppetry, pageants, or creative dramatics. Such activities not only teach basic speech skills but also help the student to understand himself and to be more understanding of others.

Experiences which are more abstract because they involve more observing and less doing may be demonstrations or activities involving only listening or seeing. Exhibits, charts, graphs, chalkboards, maps, flannel boards, bulletin boards, tackboards, picture displays, television, films, slides, recordings, and radio can provide auditory and visual aspects of speech performance. Listening laboratories have been utilized effectively in various speech areas. Recent studies on speech instruction through programmed textbooks have demonstrated success.[5] Computer-assisted instruction is also receiving attention as a device to enhance the learning process, but the potential utilization of this medium is largely unexplored.

When verbal symbols without the aid of any other form of representation are used to convey meaning, the experience becomes quite abstract and meaningless unless the listener can supply meaning for the symbol. Carefully selected and properly used media will more effectively communicate the intent of the message, but the teacher must still control technology by asking, "What instructional problems do I want it to solve?

If the speech teacher is not familiar with the school's audiovisual services, he can inquire as to what is available and the policies for obtaining technical assistance, *hardware* (equipment), and *software* (films, slides, etc.). Suppliers of audio-visual media often furnish assistance by providing displays for educational meetings, school demonstrations, and workshops. Universities and colleges also conduct seminars and workshops devoted to instructional aids and audiovisual media.

The limitations and advantages of various devices as well as suggestions for evaluating their effectiveness are listed in numerous publications pertaining to such aids. General rules applicable to all media are:

1. Are the media relevant to the objectives?
2. Is this the best media to accomplish the learning process?
3. Is this audiovisual material of acceptable quality?
4. Can it be utilized in an appropriate manner?
5. How will its use be evaluated?

The Relation of Various Audiovisual Materials to the Speech Program

Verbal Symbols. Either in spoken or written language verbal symbols are a part of many audiovisual presentations. They may be used as a part of the preparation process or in the actual communication

---

[5]Philip P. Amato, "Programed Instruction in Teaching Parliamentary Procedure," *The Speech Teacher,* 17, No. 2:145-149 (March, 1968).

experience. This common mode of expression uses designations or symbols, such as words, which bear no physical resemblance to the objects or ideas which they represent (e.g., the label "dog" is not the animal itself).

Visual Symbols. A combination of pictures and written words contribute much to the instructional activities of the speech program. Simplicity of the visual materials adds clarity and comprehension. These abstract representations help to communicate ideas and facts, stimulate interest, and entertain. Sometimes these materials are arranged in meaningful displays for exhibits, focusing on a theme which is meant to inform, entertain, or persuade the observer. Debate schedules, rehearsal calls, notices, clippings, and models of stage sets are examples of application of visual symbols to speech areas. Many of the technical aspects of theatre and speech science employ such visual aids. Audio-visual materials of this type might be chalkboards, drawings and sketches, diagrams, charts, cartoons and comics, graphs, globes, maps, felt boards, posters, bulletin board displays, models, and mock-ups which show only specific parts of the process.

Still Pictures and Equipment. Still pictures and slides can contribute much to the visual elements of bodily movement and expression, and aspects of dramatic production such as theatre history, lighting, costuming, and make-up.

Still Pictures Non-Projected (for individual use)

Photograph: picture obtained through the process which produces an image on a sensitized surface by the action of light.
Illustration: reproduction of an image through drawing, not photography (e.g., lithograph, etching, color print).
Stereograph: two three-dimensional pictures of the same subject, each viewed separately but simultaneously by the right and left eye through a specially designed device.

Still Pictures Projected (for group use)

Photograph, illustration, and *stereograph* (see preceding definitions).
Slide: transparent picture or image, either black and white or in color, individually mounted on cardboard or between pieces of glass; standard size, 2 x 2 in. or 3¼ x 4 in.
Filmstrip: strip of 35-mm film on which is placed a related sequence of transparent pictures or images.
Microfilm: printed matter reproduced on 35-mm, 8-mm, or 16-mm film.

Equipment

Opaque projector: projector which throws any non-transparent picture (e.g., sketches, maps) on a screen by means of very intense reflected light.

Overhead transparency projector: equipment which projects a transparency on a screen located behind instructor, who faces the students. The instructor may write, draw, or color on plastic material using an overlay technique.

Stereoprojector: device which projects a pair of stereographic transparencies on a screen. The viewer must wear specially designed glasses to receive a clear three-dimensional image.

Slide projector and filmstrip projector: this type of projector is designed to handle a slide carriage and filmstrip fitting interchangeably for 2 in. x 2 in. slide and filmstrip or to accommodate a 3¼ in. x 4 in. slide.

Microprojector: this equipment (an attachment on a microscope) projects microscopic slides so that the entire group can view a specimen simultaneously.

Tachistoscope: a diaphragm-type shutter attached to an overhead slide projector which can control the exposure periods of material thrown on a screen from one second to one-hundredth of a second.

Radio and Recordings. These auditory devices provide speech experiences which may be heard as they occur or may be recorded for later listening. Although the visual dimension is lacking, there is much emotional impact in a stirring radio debate, speech interview, dramatic production, or recorded interpretative reading. Records of good speech models may be repeated and analyzed. Radio experiences help to identify speech weaknesses ranging from ability to read a manuscript properly to vocal elements. Recordings may be made on magnetized tape, wire, or discs which vary in size and speed. Instruments like record players or tape recorders, which are capable of accurate sound reproduction, help the student audit his speech problems and improve. Records furnish background music and sound effects and serve as an instructional device to teach a dialect.

Closely related to effective use of any auditory device is the development of listening skill. Commercial organizations have prepared recordings to assist individuals to become more sensitive and critical in this aspect of communication. Secondary speech teachers by the wise use of radio and recordings can create opportunities for students to become more discriminating and eager listeners.

Educational FM radio broadcasting, sponsored by local school systems for the purpose of transmitting community educational programs with complete freedom in programming and scheduling, often involves speech teachers and students who assist in producing the broadcasts. FM radio, transmitted a fairly short distance by frequency modulation, has grown in popularity since it usually gives high quality reception. Most commercial radio broadcasts, which are transmitted considerable distances by amplitude modulation, are AM radio.

Motion Pictures and Equipment. With the advent of color and animation in the motion picture industry, it has become almost imperative that color, an illusion of motion, and a coordinated sound track be incorporated into educational films if one is to compete for the student's attention. Sound motion picture films are beneficial to the secondary speech program in presenting visible processes. These may relate to speech and hearing mechanisms, dramatic productions, techniques of public speaking and discussion, fundamentals of voice production, bodily movement, illustrations of interpretative reading, and all aspects of speech instruction which lend themselves to the visual mode of presentation.

The series of still pictures taken in rapid succession, developed, and projected again upon a screen, by means of a mechanical device to give the viewer an illusion of motion, may seek to entertain, inform, or persuade. Eight-millimeter, super 8, and 16-mm sound motion pictures are often used in conjunction with textbooks on the basis of relevancy, grade level, and subject matter to complement, clarify, and enrich unit concepts.

Television. The media which converts a scene into an electronic image which is sent through space, picked up on an antenna, and translated into a duplicate scene on the surface of a picture tube has had great impact on our society today. It is estimated that by the time a student graduates from high school, he has spent more time watching television than he has spent in the classroom.[6] Some educational television is presented over commercial channels as a public service, and in addition, programs with an educational focus are telecast by the non-profit stations. Programs relating to speech activities, such as dramatic productions, public-speaking situations, and special conferences or reports, can contribute to sound educational experiences. Sometimes students participate in these telecasts. Closed-circuit television, which has become a popular method for instructing large groups, usually functions within a large public school system or university to link classrooms with a central place from which the program is telecast. In this situation the students may learn to plan, program, direct, produce, and

---

[6]Allen, Anderson, and Hough, *op. cit.,* p. 484.

operate equipment necessary to create a television program. Students have an opportunity to become acquainted with the limitations and demands of the media and adapt to it for optimum use.

Video-tape. An electronic recording on magnetic tape can be replayed following the recording to provide an opportunity to immediately evaluate the speech experience, or it can be reviewed later.

Kinescope. A sound motion picture record preserves the original program as it is telecast so that it may be replayed at different times. Experiences with this kind of media help the student understand selection of material, preparation of visual aids for telecasting, limitations of movement, color and make-up, focus of attenton, and various problems relating to effective use of television in the learning situation.

Programmed Instruction and Computer-Assisted Instruction. The potential of computer technology to simulate events should be considered in future programs. Much work needs to be done to establish usable patterns for the teacher. Factors relating to learner dependence on or independence of the system, teacher roles and responsibilities, cost and management, attitudes, and educational objectives and media also need to be studied.

It must be remembered that "the value of any technology in education depends upon our ability to direct its capabilities with purpose."[7]

CURRENT EVENTS AS RESOURCES

Speech instructors have long sensed the need for students to know what is going on in the world about them and have programmed activities into broadcasts and magazines which deal with current news. National speech contests have also recognized the value of this resource in the selection of the topics for extemporaneous speaking from the weekly news magazines, such as *Newsweek, Time,* and *U. S. News and World Report.* One of the most valuable resources during the past several years was a list of questions compiled by Crocker and Meyers and based upon the format of the news magazines. Although this was designed for discussion questions, it proved equally valuable for public speaking, debate, and creative drama. Students who claimed they could find no subject for a speech were referred to copies of this list posted in the room. Often a cross reference from sports and highway safety provided at least a dozen questions to be researched and discussed. Students often

---

[7]John R. Ginther, "Let's Challenge Technology," *Educational Leadership,* 25, No. 8:716 (May, 1968).

took a more provocative stance than that suggested by the question. Acknowledging the value of the original list, we recommend a standard assignment to update the list each year. Many of the items used in the original list are still current, i.e. *Does McCarthyism still exist? Have we developed a McCarthyism of the left as well as the right?* A major advantage was the question which caused the student to recognize the conflict and speak about a problem rather than report uninteresting facts about a topic. These questions demand research.

The list of questions which follows resulted from the efforts of one class in speech methods. Many of the questions are posed in the same irrational way they were heard on the street, in classes, or over broadcast media. Such a list should be maintained at a current level.

Selective Questions for Public Discussion

Government and Politics

1. Why don't more people vote? How do US voting records compare with other countries? How many people vote in the national elections? Are half of our citizens just not interested? Is representative democracy outdated?

2. Is the government of Great Britain better than that of the US? Would Britain's type of government work in this country? Is the British system more responsible to the will of the people? Is the parliamentary system as efficient as the US system?

3. Should the US recognize the Communist government in Vietnam and China? Would better world understanding evolve from this? Are the oriental peoples better off now than they were? What would be the consequences of letting them into the UN?

4. How effective/destructive is the "new left"? What is its purpose? Has it achieved this? Has it gone too far? Is it helping or hurting America? Does it compare to Hitler's Putsch?

5. How can we best combat Communism in the US? Should we try to combat it? Is it a threat? In what way? Would legislation achieve desired ends? Education? Propaganda?

6. Are pre-election polls honest or representative? Do they have an unfair influence on voters? On candidates? How are the polls taken? Why can polls sometimes show extremely opposite results? Should polls be allowed?

7. Does the government have the right to control or license the sale and ownership of guns and ammunition? Are there any alternate answers to the problems? Do we really need gun laws?

8. Does an independent candidate for the presidency stand a chance? Who has done it in the past/present? What would be the consequences if an independent won? Should there be just a two-party system? Faults? Advantages? Should parties hold open conventions? Are the conventions really fair ways

to choose candidates? How about a direct primary system for presidential candidates?

9. How effective is the electoral college today? Is it fair to an independent candidate? What happens to the independent candidate if Congress has to choose a president because no majority exists in the electoral college?

10. Should eighteen-year-olds be allowed to vote? Are they qualified? If they can be in the service, should they be allowed to vote?

11. What should be the role of television in political news coverage? Should coverage be controlled by the Government? Does TV coverage actually influence the news?

12. To whom should the US give foreign aid? How much should it give? Why? To whom shouldn't we give? Why? Does foreign aid help us? Is it a waste?

13. In what respects is the Soviet Union concerned with the revisionist activities in the eastern European countries? How can Soviet diplomacy save and renew the once tightly integrated Soviet and eastern European politics? What is Moscow's policy toward liberalism and reform? How are the liberals reacting?

14. Should candidates for public office appear only on TV and radio? Would this be safer? Is it fair to the people? To the candidates? Should this only include presidential candidates?

15. Has the Supreme Court handcuffed politics? What have been the harmful results of their recent decisions? Do they adequately protect individual rights? In what directions should future courts move?

16. How can the US best respond to the force of nationalism in the rest of the world? What is the role of foreign aid? Military assistance? Military intervention? Power politics? Subversion?

17. What is the best solution to riots? Provide money for relief? Massive public works? Tougher police?

18. Is there any hope for small businesses? Is our economy a monopoly? Is it up to our government to help the small business? Who else might help? What does the owner of a small business have to say about this? Does he want government aid?

Economics

1. What is the current amount of food surplus in the United States? What is done with the food stuffs taken and stored by the government? Is this food being used? Is it simply stored away to rot? How does this relate to population growth?

2. What happened to the poverty program? How do programs like Head Start and Job Corps help America? Should business be allowed tax cuts for supporting model cities and urban redevelopment?

3. Should the US continue to trade with Communist-bloc countries? Should we allow free or restricted trade? Would it be better to trade within our own "bloc"?

4. What is the problem of inflation in the US? Is inflation desirable? Is the high standard of living going to cause an ever-increasing inflation until finally we hit a depression? What are the causes of inflation? What can help solve the problem of inflation?

5. Do the states need financial assistance? Do they have adequate sources of revenue for future needs? Should the Federal Government assist them? How? Block grants? Matching funds?

6. Should the US enact a guaranted income for all citizens? Would a negative income tax, enacted for the benefit of the poverty-stricken be a trend toward the classless society? Would it leave an incentive for the poverty-stricken to seek employment and earn money? Is it fair to ask the working man to support the capable non-working man? Are there jobs for the capable non-working man?

7. What is the national debt? Is there ever a chance of paying it off? Should we pay it off? If so, how? Does the debt remain stable, increase or decrease? Why? What effect does it have on the national budget?

8. England was recently in a financial crisis. Explain what caused this devaluation of the pound and how they managed to save their economy. Did the US have anything to do with stabilizing England's economy? If so, what did they do? Why? Why not?

9. Should non-profit organizations, such as churches, be taxed? Should church-owned companies be taxed? Churches themselves? Should churches be subject to gambling control (bingo)?

10. What can be done to improve economic conditions in South Vietnam? What are the chief problems? Will education and trained specialists help in this country? Should programs be started during the conflict or after the fighting has ended?

11. Should farmers receive government compensation for their crops? If so, how much? Do the majority of the farmers like to receive government support? Do government regulations go with this aid? If so, to what degree? Is this making the country more socialized? Should farmers be paid by the government for destroying a crop as well as for growing one? How does this compare with government support of steel, airlines, railroads, and labor?

12. Should the countries of the world consider adopting a free trade policy? Would such a policy ruin our economy? What would be the advantages? Would American manufacturers ever consent to such a program? Would it build up backward areas of the world?

13. Are present American laws effective against the formation of monopolies? Do a few people or companies control the majority of the weath of this country? What laws are in effect now? How much do they control big business? Could/should they be improved?

War and Peace

1. Will the war in Vietnam ever end? Is this a stalemate war? What is the price of victory? Is victory possible? Should America just withdraw its troops?

What Communistic countries are aiding the North Vietnamese? Are we keeping South Asia free from Communism?

2. Should we be in Vietnam? Why are we there? Should we withdraw? If we do, how will we look in the eyes of the world? How do we look now? What could have been done to avoid the Pueblo crisis? Should the ship have been sunk rather than captured? Should the men and the US have confessed to this alleged crime?

3. Should present draft laws be abolished or amended? Should we create a volunteer army? Would this be feasible? Should a lottery replace the draft?

4. What is international law? Can we instigate it and benefit from it? Why are some people afraid of international law? What are the criteria that would have to be met to use it effectively?

5. How effective is the UN? What were its purposes? How well is it following them? What are some of its main problems? Will effectiveness come through experience? What is it accomplishing?

6. A united Europe? Is this kind of a program feasible? How could it be done? What would be the handicaps? Would it solve any of Europe's problems? How much stronger would Europe become under this sort of plan? Militarily? Economically? Socially?

7. Why do people fight wars? Do they fight because they have to (compulsion)? Do they fight for their homeland? Rights? Freedom? Do they have a desire to conquer the world? Do they fight because they don't understand the other fellow?

8. Is peace through world government probable? Is peace that desirable? Could some type of world government settle our problems? Could all countries agree as to what kind it should be? What would be the intermediary steps?

9. Why continuous war in South America? Are the people too hot-tempered? Do they like to have an unstable government? What have been the reasons for it? Have the countries prospered in spite of it? Are the present governments more stable?

Crime and Safety

1. Should there be an age limit for driving? Is everyone unfit to drive once they pass a certain chronological age? Should tests be required at frequent intervals after one passes a certain age?

2. Does violence on television induce aggressive acts in all viewers? What type of viewers are most affected? Is there a direct connection? Is there any true value to be gained from watching violence on TV?

3. Should gambling be legalized? Could state-controlled lotteries supplement income tax? Will legalized gambling produce an increase or a decrease in such organizations as the Mafia and other such groups?

4. Can anything be done to prevent drivers from mixing gasoline and alcohol? Can anything be done to keep intoxicated drivers off the highway?

5. Should minors be tried in the same court as an adult for a serious crime? Should a minor be sentenced to prison for a serious crime?

6. Is there any justification to the charge of "police brutality"? Are police really being brutal, or are they only doing what they have to do to protect the citizens? What events brought the term "police brutality" to the attention of the public?

7. Is America really a violent society? How do other countries see the US? Has there been an increase in violence in this or other countries in the past years?

8. Capital punishment has been evaluated in several states. Should capital punishment be done away with? Is it really a crime deterrent? Do people have the right to kill others?

9. How equal are American citizens? Do you have as many rights as the person sitting next to you? How equal are you before the law? In your own community? In school? Can you reach the top economic bracket through hard work?

10. What causes riots in our urban areas? Poverty? Inadequate housing? Racism? Lack of respect for law and order? Are stronger measures by law enforcement bodies needed? What can be done to prevent riots in our cities?

11. Is there a drug problem in the US? What types of illegal drugs are passing through our borders? Can this be stopped? How? What is presently being done?

12. Why is crime on the rise? Do we have adequate police protection? What can be done to reduce crime? Can the private citizen help? How can this be done?

13. Has law enforcement been too lax with civil disobedience? What tactics have been used by the police force? What further measures should be taken? Has the police department been overly brutal? If so, why? Is civil disobedience sometimes justifiable?

14. Does the government really have a legitimate right to force certain safety controls on auto makers? Have these controls been effective? How can we get people to use them more?

15. What is the present state of our penal institutions? Are they adequate? Is there a personnel problem? What funds support them? Should more money be spent on such institutions? What are the programs for rehabilitation?

16. Life or death on our highways? What are the causes of auto accidents? Do new cars have too much speed? Do we have enough traffic officers? How can the accident rate be cut? Should licenses be more difficult to obtain?

17. Has the threat of an atomic war destroyed our feeling of national security? How safe would we be? What provisions have been made in our community? Are they adequate? Do we know what to do in case of an attack? Do we feel more insecure now?

18. Can graft be kept out of the Federal Government? What causes graft? Not enough honest officials? Too low a salary? Can the public more effectively check on officials? Does there have to be a change of administration every few years?

Science and Health

1. Should we adopt a program of compulsory health insurance? What would be gained by this? Would it hurt more than help? What does the AMA think of this? Might it be a waste of money? Could the possible benefits be incorporated into some other plan?

2. Do scientific principles deny the existence of God? What are some of these principles? Is it the principles themselves or the interpretation of them that matters? What percentage of scientists have disregarded the concept of God?

3. Has sex education lowered our moral standards? Does this knowledge affect moral standards? Would sex education be the cause? Do doctors and nurses have lower standards than anyone else?

4. Is the American personality neurotic? What have recent personality tests shown? Are these reliable? Does the American way of life upset mental balance? Can you prove it?

5. How good is psychology? What does it cure? Does it teach you to get along with other people? What are some advantages made in the field? How promising is it?

6. What can be done to improve mental hospitals? In what condition are mental hospitals today? Should the Federal and state governments increase the number? What better facilities would help? Are scientific techniques better?

7. What is the incidence of venereal disease in our present society? Is it increasing or decreasing? Why? What might be done about it?

8. Is it necessary for us to participate in the space program? Are our funds being used wisely? Could we use them more beneficially in other areas?

9. Are heart transplants morally wrong? Who thinks they are/are not? Under what conditions could they be considered moral for all? Should animal hearts be used?

10. What are the most recent findings regarding the relationship between smoking and cancer? Smoking and heart disease? When the news first was announced in 1964, what was the reaction? What was the reaction in the 1968 announcement? Has the sale of cigarettes declined?

11. What can be done about the dope/hallucinogen problem? Are hallucinogens really "dangerous" drugs? Where can they be obtained? What is being done to prevent their illegal sale? Can dope addiction ever be overcome?

12. What is the abortion revolution in the US? What is the cause of it? Are abortions ever justifiable? Are state laws becoming more liberal? Who is the deciding party? Should abortion laws be nationwide instead of statewide?

13. Why suicide? What causes it? Our way of life? What can be done to reduce it? What is the chief method used? Why? Can forms of better education reduce the rate?

14. How can the world feed its hungry people? Do we have enough land to grow food? What about synthetic foods? Sea foods? Will the entire world eventually starve?

15. What can be done about the current population explosion? Has the pill been effective? Compare the US with countries with the pill. Do governments have the right to enforce birth control for the sake of the whole population? What effect could such control have?

16. Smoking has been proven to be linked to cancer. What responsibility has the cigarette industry and society to youth concerning smoking? What are some new links to the causes of cancer under research?

17. What is being done in the areas of air and water pollution? What are the dangers involved? What proposals have been made to solve the problem? Have any communities instituted them?

18. Americans lead a fast pace of living. Compare US mortality rates to those of other countries. Do we have more leisure time to relax than others? Do we know how to relax? If not, why?

19. Is alcoholism a health problem in America? How can we combat it? How does alcoholism compare with dope rates, etc.? How can US alcoholism compare with other nations?

20. Is the average person of today happier because of scientific improvements? What scientific advancements have changed living conditions? What has accompanied these improvements? Does the pace balance the benefit received? Does happiness come through an increased life span? What effect does compulsory retirement have on this?

Education

1. Is there more to college than books? Is social life important? If so, how much? Does it improve character? Is learning to live with other people also a factor? Do extracurricular activites count?

2. Does college prepare one for the business world? Should it? Should it give one an overall education? Does it prepare one for life? Could it be improved?

3. Does high school prepare one for college? Is there sufficient preparation in high school for college? Is it different in certain parts of the country? Should it prepare one for the business world? The home? Should it offer more mechanical or practical training?

4. Is academic freedom advisable in schools? Do teachers have the right of freedom of speech in the classroom? Should they have it in high school as well as in college? Should students have the right to read any type of literature they please? Could it be prevented, even if they didn't?

5. What standards should be emphasized in the schools to lay the foundation for better citizenship? What are the benefits of honor codes? Would they work in public schools as in colleges? Would less emphasis on competition help? Could/should instructors treat students like equals instead of inmates?

6. Should the countries of the world further the practice of exchanging students? What are the advantages of this practice? Would it help world friendship if all countries adopted this? How could this be done? How much more expense would it involve?

7. Should a course on family hygiene be compulsory for all high school students? Would such a course be helpful to them in later life? Is it necessary? What would be some drawbacks? Might there be objections from civic groups?

8. Should TV and radio stations sponsor more educational programs? What is the quality of most TV and radio programs now? Would educational programs increase the present audience? Would the present audience like such a change? What programs are educational now? Should these be increased or be replaced?

9. Why are teachers no longer afraid to strike? Why are teachers walking out of their classrooms? What groups are leading these walkouts? For what purposes?

10. How does the role of the vocational school change the role of education? Is it good? Are they helping young people to really be equipped to enter the business world? How many vocational schools are there in this state?

11. How has the television media affected education? Are TV courses as effective as classroom lecture courses? How expensive is it to equip schools and maintain TV courses?

12. What effect has the new draft law had on higher education? How widespread is the dissent on US campuses? Is this added pressure on the college student harmful? Are graduate students the "vanishing Americans"? Will other countries now gain educational ground on the US? Why are some professional schools exempt?

13. Should everyone go to college? Do you have to further your formal education in order to be a success? What are other ways of furthering education besides at the university? How important is education in the business world?

14. How many liberties should high school students have? Is it as important to follow as it is to lead? Are some rules and regulations a handicap to learning, rather than an aid? Are we teaching democracy in books only?

15. Does the school have the right to "loco parentis"? Should it have? Where does the parent's authority end and the school's begin? Should school authorities be able to punish students? To paddle them?

16. Do PTA groups serve a purpose? Are they a good means of parent-teacher communication? Do they put undue pressure on the teacher? How could the PTA be improved?

17. Could teaching and grading methods be improved? What is wrong with our present grading system? Would a plus/minus system be acceptable? Is there too much homework and not enough teaching? How can this be solved?

18. Do schools have a right to demand what type of clothing a student should wear? What style haircut? Should students be allowed to dress according to style? What are some reasons for allowing these styles in the schools? Why have they not been allowed?

Religion and Philosophy

1. Does organized religion have a place on the college (university) campus? Does it have a stabilizing effect? Is this good? Should it be organized? If organized, is it a form of pressure? What is the use of religious groups on campus?

2. Does higher education lead to atheism and agnosticism? Why so many radicals and confused people just out of college? What courses promote this? Why do they have this effect? Would more unbiased facts on a precollege level help?

3. Does philosophy have a purpose? In what professions does philosophy help? What is its aim? What has it accomplished? Is it any better than it used to be? Can it help toward solving world problems?

4. Could there ever be a world religion? Is there enough similarity in the major religions for a synthesis? Would people be willing to make their old religions more general? Would anything desirable evolve from this?

5. Would/could going to church improve our morals? Would a better atmosphere help? How good is the average minister? Could it do more harm than good? Can you make a person believe something he doesn't want to?

6. Why has man always had religion? What is this need? Why has it persisted? Has man benefited from it? How? Will there always be some religion?

7. How much do the great religions have in common? Could they ever be combined? At what cost? What effect would this have upon the world? Would harmony result?

8. Do scientific principles deny the existence of God? What are some of these principles? Is it the principles themselves or the interpretations of them that matter? What percentage of scientists have disregarded the concept of God?

9. Is God dead? Why? Why not? What brought this issue into the public eye? Why is it such a hard issue to discuss? What are the conflicting issues? Will the answers ever be known? What can you do to assure yourself of the correct answer?

10. Is the new ecumenical movement modernizing the Catholic Church? Bringing it closer to other religions? To what extent?

11. Are present Catholic marriage laws in the public interest? Are they merely protecting religion or imposing unfair rules? What might be the results of the Pope's recent decree prohibiting birth control?

12. Should religion be part of the school curriculum? Is this really unconstitutional? Is religion an important part of our culture? Of our heritage?

13. Is religion declining in the United States? In the world? Why? Why do people turn away from the church today? Can the church offer a solution to our world's problems?

14. Is the church fulfilling its obligation to mankind? Has the church become at least in part corrupt? Does it really practice what it preaches? How effective could the church be in participating in social reform? Does the average minister fulfill his role of shepherd? Should he?

The Arts

Music

1. Why does popular music in the US have a more general appeal than classical? Is classical music on its way out? How do you account for this trend? What has contributed to it? Radio? Jukebox? Movies? Is classical music considered highbrow?

2. From what did psychedelic music and sound develop? What makes this form of entertainment enjoyable (or not) for you?

Ballet

3. What has happened to ballet in the past fifty years? Why is the form being changed? Why the trend toward "impressionism"? Will modern dance eventually supersede all?

4. What has happened to modern dance in the last decade? Has it replaced ballet as the dance of the "arts"? What are their differences? Which one do you prefer and why?

5. Consider Balanchines' statement that ballet is women and that men are only present to support the women. Do you agree?

Opera and Theater

6. Should opera and theater be brought within easy reach of the average American? Is it now? If not, why? How could it be done? Would it be advantageous to do so? Is there a tendency to do so now?

7. Should American theater (and other forms of the arts) be subsidized by the federal government? Does this work in Russia or any European countries?

Drama

8. Is TV replacing the movies and the theater? If so, why? What is Hollywood doing to combat this? Are the programs on TV better than the average stage play or movies? Why?

9. Are there any new innovations in the movies today? What happened to 3-D and why? Are the movie houses of today any different than ten years ago? If so, how?

10. What impressions are foreign films making on the American people? The American movie industry? How popular are they in the US? Have they caused a change in the quality of American films? Why are American companies making more films abroad?

11. Entertainment, both movies and live theater, is an expensive pastime. Why is this so? How could expenses be cut down to enable more people to enjoy more than TV?

Art

12. Is "modernism" in drawing, painting, and sculpturing degrading art? Does this type of art have quality line and harmony? How does it measure

up to the "old masterpieces"? What are some of the criticisms of it? Do you like it?

13. How can paintings of soup cans, busses, etc., be justified as "art"? How do these fit into the trend of modern society?

Architecture

14. Is "functionalism" abolishing beauty in modern architecture? What is the purpose of modern architecture? Is this watching of the scenery always beneficial? Advantageous? Disadvantageous? In housing projects is one form overworked?

15. Are construction costs ruining the aesthetics of architecture? That is, can anyone afford *not* to be practical?

Literature

16. What kind of literature do the American people read? What quality is it? Is there too much "cheap" literature in circulation? How much reading does the average American do? How biased is it?

17. What about the paperback book? What are its advantages? Disadvantages? Does it give more people an opportunity to read? Is it desirable literature? From whose viewpoint? What about good books that are reprinted in these editions?

18. Who are some current authors and their works? Why are they popular? What determines a book's popularity? Who makes up the best seller listing?

Extracurricular Activities and Sports

1. Is there too much emphasis on sports in our universities? How much is there? Do sports help the university? Financially, or otherwise? Do they detract from the academic part of school life? Are many sports scholarships given?

2. How important are extracurricular activities in the schools? Should every person be compelled to take part in at least one? What are their purposes? How effective are they? What types are the most important?

3. How can civic-sponsored activities reduce the rate of juvenile delinquency? What causes juvenile delinquency? Would civic-sponsored activities reduce these causes? What types of activities can be sponsored? What group ages would these cover?

4. Does too much rivalry in sports lead to unethical acts? What does the past show? Is this true in professional and nonprofessional sports? What kind of rivalry is good and what kind is bad? What is an unethical act?

5. Should students be allowed to participate in extracurricular activities if a certain grade average is not maintained? How many students neglect their academic work because of too many other activities? Would denying them access to these activities cause them to work harder in school? Might it have some other effect? How much do extra activities mean to the average students?

6. Should dramatics and speech in the public schools be considered extra-curricular? Co-curricular? What status are they now? Could the activities be extracurricular, whereas the classes would not? What are some objections to having dramatics and speech on a regular basis? How should they compare with other high school subjects?

7. Is the profit-sharing aspect stressed too much in extracurricular activities? Is this true of some activities and not of others? If so, could this cause overcompetition in these activities? Is this good for the morals of the participants? Why the profit-making stress?

8. Would more international sports contests increase friendship among nations? What are the results of such contests as the Olympics on international feeling? Could there easily be more contests (money, transportation, etc.)? What are international ideas about sports contests? What sports would be best?

9. Is competition in high school sports helpful to the average student? Do only special students get to participate in extracurricular activities? Why doesn't everyone belong to some activity or club?

10. Is baseball a dying sport? Why? Just how popular is baseball today? Compare with the era of Babe Ruth. Compare with the popularity of other modern day sports?

11. What is the most popular American spectator sport today? Why? Do the majority of Americans share an interest in it? Do the majority of Americans show interest in at least one sport?

12. What will we do with our increased leisure time as automation takes away much of the work we have to do? Do we know how to use leisure time? Do we use it well? Will this leisure benefit our society or harm it?

13. What about high school fraternities and sororities? Advantages and disadvantages? Do they take away potential school participants in extracurricular activities? Are they too selective? Do they help out in the community in constructive and creative ways?

Family and Society

1. Should the US adopt a system of compulsory service for all citizens? Could the US effectively employ all citizens at some time in their life? What would be the harm to the economy? Would it help to make all citizens equal? What types of service could be used?

2. Is marriage and divorce too easy in our society? Does a high percentage of marriages end in the divorce court? How does this country compare to others? What are the reasons for this failure? What can be done to better prepare youth for marriage?

3. Are situation ethics good foundations for morality? Why? Is this form popular in the United States? Should morality be absolute?

4. Can you trust anyone over 30? What is the generation gap? Are youth restless with the adult world? Why? Are youth becoming escapist? Why? Has this been the expense of the fast pace of society, of adult moral laxity and societal permissiveness?

5. How honest are Americans today? What is the trend of honesty in all aspects of societal living? Is the honest man jeered today?

6. Trace the civil rights movement since WW II. Are the Negroes farther ahead today? What organizations aided them with their cause? Why do Negroes rebel? The exponents of CORE differ in their philosophy from members of SNCC and the NAACP. What are the differences and why? What will happen to the movement now that Martin Luther King is dead?

7. Are people getting married too young? What happens in many of these marriages? What are the causes for youthful marriages? If pregnancy is the cause, should the couple have to get married?

8. What is the incidence of venereal disease in our present society? Is it increasing or decreasing? Why? What might be done about it?

9. Is the woman's place in the home? How many women are in the business world? Are they happy? Are they making too much competition? Can a woman have a career and be a good homemaker too? Should women be allowed in certain professions? Should women earn equal pay and have equal opportunities for advancement? Can women do an equally good job?

10. Are American moral standards declining? What are our moral standards? Are things actually worse than they used to be? Explain. If yes, what are the reasons for this? Can we do anything to make them better?

11. Is family life what it used to be? Is the family, as a whole, as much of a unit as it was? Why the changes? Are these good or bad? Do parents have the same status now?

12. How serious is juvenile delinquency? What causes it? What is being done to alleviate the problem? Is the problem widespread or sectionalized?

13. Is "sex" emphasized too much in America? Is there a trend? What has caused it? How does it compare with other countries?

14. What are the reasons for racial prejudice? Are most of them groundless? How did they begin? Does there have to be prejudice? What can be done to lessen the problem?

Picture File as a Resource

Teachers find an expanded picture file an excellent resource for current events problems. The index which follows was formed from the picture file of one city library. Individual teachers may build a classroom file by having students bring in old magazines and mounting pictures of events, characters, objects, and situations from the pictorial news, or even from advertising. The index included here was made from such a clip-and-mount set of pictures and was used by teachers from the surrounding schools for room decoration and for motivation on writing or art assignments.

Many students hide behind "lack of preparation" as a camouflage for stage fright. If the teacher begins with an assumption that no one can be unprepared in a speech class, he might hand the student a file of pictures and ask him after a short preparation to give an analysis or creative response from the pictures included. In this way he avoids reinforcement of the stage fright and may provide many interesting speeches. Student involvement in creating such a file may make it more relevant to the age group in the class. Once started, the file may be added to each year. A similar resource might be built around selections of music.

Subject Index for a Picture File

Africa
  Congo
  East Africa
  Egypt
  Ethiopia
  North Africa
  North Africa, Tunis
  Sahara Desert
  South Africa
  West Africa
Agriculture
Alaska *see also*
  Polar Regions, North Pole
  Polar Regions, South Pole
Alfalfa *see* Hay
Animals (alphabetical)
Arabia
Arbor Day
Armenia
Armistice Day
Armor
Army and Navy
Assyria
Astronomy
Australia
Austria
Automobiles
Aviation
Babylonia
Bacteria
Bays
Belgium
Bible *see* Religion

Birds (alphabetical)
Book Week
Boy Scouts
Bridges — Natural
Bridges and Bridge Building
British Isles
  England
  Ireland
  Scotland
  Wales
  History
Bulgaria
Burma
Canada
Canals *see also* Panama
Castles
Cathedrals and Churches
Cattle
Caves
Central America *see also* Panama
China (the country)
China *see* Pottery
Christmas
Circus
Civics
Clean Up and Paint Up Week
Cliff Dwellings *see also*
  National Parks — Mesa Verde
Clothing, Care of
Cocoa
Coffee
Communication
Community Chest

Italy
  History
  Rome
Japan
Jugoslavia
Jute
Knots and Splices
Korea
Labrador
Lakes
Landslides
Lapland
Latvia
Leather
Libraries
Lifesaving
Light
Lighthouses
Lightning *see* Weather
Lumbering *see also* Lumbering,
  Trees
Machinery
Malay Peninsula
Maps
Marionettes *see* Puppets and
  Marionettes
Masks
Mayas
Meat
Medicine
Memorial day
Mesopotamia
Mexico
  History
Middle Ages *see also* Armor,
  Crusades, British Isles:
  England, History
Mines and Mining
  Aluminum *see* Bauxite
  Bauxite
  Coal
  Copper
  Diamonds
  Gold
  Graphite

Iron
Lead
Manganese
Mica
Molybdenum
Nitrate
Phosphate
Platinum
Radium
Silver
Sulphur
Tin
Tungsten
Vanadium
Zinc
Mollusks
Monaco
Monasteries
Money and Banking
Mother's Day
Mountains
Museums
Music
  Dancing
  Instrument
  Musicians
  Operas
Mythology
National Forests
National Monuments
National Parks (alphabetical)
Natural Bridges *see* Bridges Natural
Navy *see* Army and Navy
Negroes *see also* U.S., Georgia,
  Slavery, Music: Musicians
Netherlands
Newfoundland *see* Labrador
New Year's Day
New Zealand
Norway
Nuts (alphabetical)
Nylon
Oats *see also* Grain
Occupations
Ocean

Vietnam and the Philippines
Valleys and craters of the Moon
Astronauts
Apollo moon shots
Volcanoes
Washington, State of
Industries
Stepping stone to Alaska
Inside passage
Washington, D. C.
Congress
House of Representatives
Senate

Judicial system
Presidential inaugurations
Shakespeare Library (Folger)
Smithsonian Institute
White House
Washington Monument
Potomac conservation
Yukon-Alaska Territory
Canada
Yangtze Basin
River
Warlords still rule

Suggested Projects

1. Examine carefully five current secondary speech textbooks. Evaluate them on the basis of the criteria for textbooks listed in this chapter. Rank the books in the preferred order of choice and write a justification for the rating.

2. Select, preview, and evaluate several audiovisual aids which would be appropriate in teaching some aspect of speech. State how you would include these in a lesson plan.

3. Build a resource file of instructional materials suitable for a specific speech unit. Secure a variety of aids with some bulletin board displays, written materials, and other audiovisuals.

4. Prepare a speech demonstrating the use of some kind of audiovisual equipment. Evaluate yourself and request your classmates to offer critiques.

5. Select several recordings. Describe how you would use these to develop listening skills. State criteria and how you would evaluate them.

6. Prepare a bibliography of free and inexpensvie materials suitable for the speech teacher. Consult the librarian for possible sources.

References

Allen, R.R., Anderson, Sharol, and Hough, Jere. *Speech in American Society.* Columbus, Ohio: Charles E. Merrill Publishing Co., 1968.

Amato, Philip P. "Programed Instruction in Teaching Parliamentary Procedure," *The Speech Teacher*, 17:145-149 (March, 1968).

Dale, Edgar. *Audio-Visual Methods in Teaching*. Rev. ed.; New York: Holt, Rinehart & Winston, 1964.

Edling, Jack V. "Educational Objectives and Educational Media," *Review of Educational Research*, 38, No. 2:177-194 (April, 1968).

Ginther, John R. "Let's Challenge Technology," *Educational Leadership*, 25, No. 8:706-721 (May, 1968).

Saettler, Paul. "Design and Selection Factors," *Review of Educational Research*, 38, No. 2:115-128 (April, 1968).

Wiman, Raymond V., and Meierhenry, Wesley C. *Educational Media: Theory into Practice*. Columbus, Ohio: Charles E. Merrill Publishing Co., 1969.

Selected Speech Resources

General References

National Education Association. *Catalog of Publications and Audiovisual Materials*. Washington, D.C.: National Education Association, June, 1968.

Dale, Edgar. *Audio-Visual Methods in Teaching*. Rev. ed.; New York: Holt, Rinehart and Winston, 1964.

Wittich, Walter A., and Schuller, Charles F. *Audio-Visual Materials: Their Nature and Use*. 4th ed.; New York: Harper & Row, Publishers, 1967.

Textbooks for the Secondary School

Adams, Harlen M. and Pollock, Thomas C. *Speak Up*. New York: The Macmillan Company, 1964.

Allen, R.R., Anderson, Sharol, and Hough, Jere. *Speech in American Society*. Columbus, Ohio: Charles E. Merrill Publishing Co., 1968.

Balcer, Charles L. and Seabury, Hugh F. *Teaching Speech in Today's Secondary School*. New York: Holt, Rinehart & Winston, Inc., 1965.

Brandes, Paul D. and Smith, William S. *Building Better Speech*. New York: Noble and Noble Publishers, Inc., 1964.

Elson, E. Floyd, *et al*. *The Art of Speaking*, 2nd ed.; Boston: Ginn and Company, 1966.

Hedde, Wilhelmina G., Brigance, William N., and Powell, Victor M. *The New American Speech*. Philadelphia: J.B. Lippincott Co., 1963.

Hibbs, Paul, Fessenden, Seth A., Larson, P. Mesville, and Wagner, Joseph A. *Speech for Today*. New York: Webster Division, McGraw-Hill Book Company, 1965.

Robinson, Karl F. and Lee, Charlotte. *Speech in Action*. Chicago: Scott, Foresman and Company, 1965.

General Textbooks

Textbooks in Print, New York: R.R. Bowker Co.

Records and Recordings

Caedmon Records, 277 Fifth Avenue, New York, New York. (Send for catalog of literary selections.)

Filmstrips

McGraw-Hill Book Company, 330 West 42nd St., New York, New York 10036.

Society for Visual Education, Inc., 1345 West Diversey Parkway, Chicago, Illinois 60614.

Films

NET Film Service, Audio-Visual Center, Indiana University, Bloomington, Indiana 47401.

Coronet Films, 65 East South Water Street, Chicago, Illinois 60601.

Encyclopedia Britannica Films, Inc., 1150 Wilmette Avenue, Wilmette, Illinois.

Plays and Programs

Plays, Inc., 8 Arlington Street, Boston, Massachusetts 02116.

Dramatists Play Service, Inc., 14 East 38th Street, New York, New York 10016.

Professional Speech Journals

The Quarterly Journal of Speech
Speech Monographs
The Speech Teacher
    Speech Association of America
    Statler Hilton Hotel
    New York, New York 10001
Various regional and state speech journals

Sources for Audiovisual Aids

Braden, Waldo W., ed. *Speech Methods and Resources.* New York: Harper & Row, Publishers, 1961, pp. 504-514.

Robinson, Karl F. and E. J. Kerikas. *Teaching Speech, Methods and Materials.* New York: David McKay Company, Inc., 1963, pp. 511-526.

Other Sources

Education Index. New York: H. W. Wilson Company.

Educational Media Index. New York: McGraw-Hill Book Company.
Educational Screen and Audiovisual Guide. 434 S. Wabash St., Chicago, Illinois 60605.
A Guide to Learning Resources in the Human Communication Process. Athens, Ohio: Resource Center for Speech in the Secondary Schools, School of Communication, Ohio University, 1967 bibliography.
Pepe, Thomas J. *Free and Inexpensive Educational Aids*, 3rd rev. ed., New York: Dover Publications, Inc., 1966.
Vertical File Service. New York: H. W. Wilson Company.

State departments of curriculum and instruction
State high school speech leagues

Instructional Materials Centers

Educational Research Council of Greater Cleveland, 1967 bibliography.

7

Public Speaking

This chapter assumes that the reader is familiar with the various areas of speech content. Our primary concern at this point is to present some of the more perplexing problems which face the speech teacher in teaching either a unit or a course in public speaking. While a sample unit outline for public speaking is provided in this chapter, it is included only as a guide and should not be considered as either representative or comprehensive in relation to the content areas which may comprise either a unit or course in public speaking. The order, depth, and manner in which the teacher presents the content will of course depend upon his approach to the teaching of public speaking in relation to the various other areas of speech content which may be taught in the speech course, basic or advanced.

Beginning teachers admit they have three major problems in teaching public speaking. First among these is the problem of selecting an approach to the teaching of public speaking. Second, there is the problem of stage fright and how to cope with it. The third major problem concerns the diagnostic and evaluative procedures to assess the students' speech needs, progress, and comprehension of the material presented. This chapter will attempt to discuss each of these three problems.

Before discussing the problem of which approach to public speaking should be taken, perhaps we should ask the even more fundamental question of what is public speaking. *Public speaking,* as it is used in this chapter, refers to the process employed by a speaker in communicating his ideas to an audience in an attempt to manipulate one or more of their three behavioral systems. Thus the speaker whose primary goal is to present information concerns himself with the cognitive (intellectual) behavioral system of his listener. The speaker whose primary goal is to entertain addresses himself to the affective (emotional) behavioral system of his receiver, while the speaker whose primary goal is to persuade directs his attention to the overt (psychomotor) behavioral system as well as to the affective and cognitive systems. Obviously, one cannot easily affect one of the behavioral systems without affecting the other two. Our attention is given here to that behavioral system which is instrumental to the attainment of the speaker's goals (with the recognition that all three behavioral systems will be affected to some extent).

Another question which emerges regarding the teaching of public speaking is at what point in the basic speech course should it be taught. First, let us put public speaking in the formal sense (i.e., as a speaker before a relatively unknown audience) into its proper perspective. The vast majority of our citizens rarely engage in formal public speaking. More often than not their communicative behavior involves conversation and discussion both informal and formal. Furthermore, their communications are directed to well known, not to relatively unknown, audiences. For those who would take issue with the formalized concept of public speaking presented here, we need only review those sections of speech texts which present subject matter pertaining to public speaking. In most of the texts a relatively unknown audience is presupposed and the suggestions given the student for adapting himself and his topic to his audience would, if heeded, prove ludicrous in a known audience situation. Further, it is with this formalized concept of public speaking that the beginning student of speech enters the classroom. There is little wonder then that the student often approaches the course with fear and trepidation. He envisions himself before a sea of unknown faces evaluating his every word, gesture, and movement. He sees himself alone, separated physically and psychologically from the group to whom he speaks. He has in effect lost all sense of group identification and security. These are some of the preconceived images of the public speaker which the beginning student brings with him to the classroom. It should be apparent that these images of the public speaker are not only a result of cultural conditioning but also of constant reinforcement from the many basic speech texts which pursue public speaking from a formal orientation.

However, the issue here is not with the formal concept of public speaking but with the concept that it constitutes a major role in the daily communication behavior of our high school graduates. It would seem that an activity so rarely engaged in by most citizens ought not to represent the major area of emphasis in the basic speech course. Much of the stage fright teachers witness in the classroom may to a substantial degree be due to having the student engage in an unnatural and highly specialized communicative act. The formal public speech is unnatural in that it is not a part of the communication behavior frequently engaged in by most citizens. It is highly specialized in that it requires not only a thorough understanding of speech context but also because it is engaged in as a function of a particular role in which most of us seldom find ourself cast.

Thus it is that the teaching of formal public speaking probably ought to fall somewhere near the end of the basic course. The formal speeches to inform, entertain, stimulate, convince, and persuade (as they are variously designated) are representative of formal public speaking.

Initially the speech teacher ought to attempt to involve the student in small group activities thus permitting him the security of the group. Such activities may involve two-way purposeful conversation formal and informal, the interview, and group discussion, as well as choral and dramatic reading when the teacher feels they are applicable.

Many well-meaning teachers begin their speech courses with what is commonly called an introductory speech. In this assignment the student is expected to stand before the group (thus isolating himself from it) and talk about himself. The assignment therefore tends to substantiate the preconceived ideas of the student about speech-making. Most often the rationale given for such a speech is that the student is engaged in talking about the subject which he knows best, namely himself. While that may be true, relatively few of us feel comfortable talking about ourselves before a group. A second reason often given for the introductory speech is that it tends to familiarize the students with one another as well as to provide the teacher with information about each of the students. Many teachers have found that the objectives of the introductory speech can be achieved just as easily through having one student introduce another, thus diminishing the necessity of acutely focusing attention on oneself.

APPROACHES TO TEACHING PUBLIC SPEAKING

The four most often employed approaches to the teaching of public speaking are (1) the principles approach, (2) the activities approach, (3) the theory or subject matter approach, and (4) any combination of the foregoing.

The Principles Approach

This approach to the teaching of public speaking involves the construction of a series of assignments such that each develops one or more speech principles. The principles or fundamentals commonly include: (1) language, (2) voice (enunciation, articulation, and pronunciation as well as pitch, rate, force, and quality), (3) thought (ideas, organization of ideas, development, and support of ideas), (4) action (gestures, facial expression, bodily movement), (5) adjustment to the speaking situation, and (6) listening.

With this approach the student is given the opportunity to apply each one of the principles in at least one specific situation. For example, if the concern of the teacher is with teaching the development and support of ideas, the following assignment might be given.

> Prepare a three-minute speech in which you present only one main idea, developing it by four or more of the following methods:
> 1. Instances or examples
> 2. Statistics
> 3. Analogies
> 4. Authority
> 5. Anecdote
> 6. Cause and effect relationship
> 7. Definition
> 8. Quotations

Representative of the principles approach is the following unit plan for a six weeks unit in the fundamentals of speech. Note that the teacher attempted to plan each student activity so that it demonstrated the speech principle currently under study in the class.

Fundamentals of Speech: A Course Outline

I. First Day — Adjustment
    A. Objectives
        1. To help student become a poised speaker
        2. To rid student of self-consciousness and excess tension
        3. To cultivate positive speaking attitudes
    B. Materials
        A self-rating poll for student to take
    C. Content — Cultivating Positive Attitudes
        1. Student's attitude toward the study of speech
           a) Interchange between speaker and listener

   b) Develop conversational rapport
   c) Acquire knowledge
   d) Acquire skills
  2. Students attitude toward himself as a speaker
   a) Take an objective look
   b) Minimize self-consciousness
 D. Activities — Time 45 minutes
  1. Teacher — lecture — Time 20 minutes
  2. Student rating poll — Time 25 minutes
II. Second Day — Adjustment
 A. Objectives
  1. To help student become a poised speaker
  2. To rid student of self-consciousness and excess
   tension
  3. To cultivate positive speaking attitudes
 B. Materials
 None
 C. Content — Cultivating Positive Attitudes
  1. Student's attitude toward audience
   a) Adopt positive attitude
   b) Seek response of individuals
  2. Student's attitude toward criticism
   a) Constructive
   b) Destructive
  3. Explanation of types of criticism used when
   students evaluate others
 D. Activities — Time 45 minutes
  1. Teacher — lecture — Time 25 minutes
  2. Student discussion — Time 20 minutes
III. Third Day — Stage Fright
 A. Objectives
  1. To help student become a poised speaker
  2. To rid student of self-consciousness
 B. Materials
 None
 C. Content
  1. Causes of stage fright
   a) Little confidence caused by being poorly
   prepared
   b) Negative attitudes
  2. Effects of stage fright on speech
   a) Nervous use of gestures
   b) Loss of thought in speech
  3. How to overcome stage fright
   a) Pick a familiar topic

      b) Be prepared
      c) Correct posture
      d) Know audience

  D. Activities — Time 45 minutes
    1. Teacher — lecture — time 20 minutes
    2. Student — Have student introduce himself and tell something about himself for one minute. If class is larger than twenty students, cut lecture short.

  E. Assignment — start reading on voice mechanism in textbook.

IV. Fourth Day — Voice and Diction

  A. Objectives
    To produce a voice that is more expressive of the student

  B. Materials
    1. Text — *Fundamentals of Speech: A Basic Course for High Schools*
    2. Chart of voice mechanism — mimeographed
    3. Recording—*American Speech Sounds and Rhythm*

  C. Content
    1. Speech as an "overlaid" function
    2. Brief summary of the vocal systems
      a) The directing
      b) The phonating
      c) The breathing
      d) The resonating
      e) The articulating

  D. Activities — Time 45 minutes
    1. Teacher — Time 25 minutes
      a) Lecture — 15 minutes
      b) Explanation of handout — 10 minutes
    2. Student — Listen to recordings — Time 20 minutes

V. Fifth Day — The Breathing System

  A. Objectives
    1. To produce a voice that is more expressive of the student
    2. To stress the importance of breathing correctly in speaking

  B. Materials
    1. Text
    2. Chart handout sheet

  C. Content
    1. The mechanism
      a) Skeleton of trunk
      b) Rib cage

       c) The lungs

       d) Intercostal muscles

       e) Windpipe

       f) Bronchial tubes

       g) Diaphragm

    2. The functions

       a) Supplying blood stream with oxygen and removing carbon dioxide

       b) Providing motive power for speech

  D. Activities — Time 45 minutes

    1. Teacher lecture — Time 25 minutes

    2. Student question-answer period—Time 20 minutes

VI. Sixth Day — The Process — How to Breathe

  A. Objectives

    To show student proper breath control for speaking

  B. Materials

    Reading and poems

  C. Content

    1. Inhalation

       a) Muscles lift ribs upward and outward from lungs

       b) Diaphragm contracts and moves downward

       c) Enlargement of chest cavity — air rushes down trachea, through bronchial tubes and into lungs

    2. Exhalation — opposite process

  D. Activities — Time 45 minutes

    1. Teacher lecture — Time 15 minutes

    2. Student — reading of verses — Time 30 minutes

  E. Assignment — read in text on other vocal systems

VII. Seventh Day — The Directing System

  A. Objective

    To show importance of this system and its equipment in the total process

  B. Materials

    1. Text

    2. Handout sheet

  C. Content

    1. The mechanism

       a) Nervous system

       b) Sense organs

    2. The functions

       a) Regulates behavior of internal organs

       b) Sense organs receive stimuli which evokes speech responses

    3. Process

D. Activities — Time 45 minutes
    1. Teacher lecture — Time 25 minutes
    2. Student — class discussion — Time 20 minutes

VIII. Eighth Day — The Phonating System
  A. Objectives
    1. To show the importance of this system and its mechanism in the total process
    2. Review of other systems
  B. Materials
    1. Text
    2. Handout chart
  C. Content
    1. Mechanism
      a) Larynx
      b) Glottis
      c) Vocal folds
      d) Epiglottis
    2. Function
      The production of sounds
    3. Process
  D. Activities — Time 45 minutes
    1. Teacher lecture — Time 25 minutes
    2. Student review — Time 20 minutes

IX. Ninth Day — The Resonating System
  A. Objective
    To explain importance of system and mechanism to whole voice process
  B. Materials
    1. Text
    2. Handout
    3. Films
      a) High Speed Motion Pictures of the Human Vocal Fold — 20 minutes
      b) Using Your Voice — 11 minutes
  C. Content
    1. The mechanism
      a) Throat or larynx
      b) Mouth
      c) Nasal passage
    2. Function
      Amplifies tone produced by your vocal folds
    3. Process
  D. Activities — Time 45 minutes
    1. Teacher lecture — Time 15 minutes
    2. Student — films — Time 30 minutes

E. Assignment — read about the articulating system

X. Tenth Day — The Articulating System

  A. Objective

    To explain importance of system and mechanism to whole voice process

  B. Materials

    1. Diagnostic test for articulation. Read onto tape the passage "My Grandfather." Play back for analysis by class

    2. Handout chart

  C. Content

    1. Mechanism

      a) Tongue

      b) Lower jaw

      c) Lips

      d) Palate

        1) Soft palate

        2) Hard palate

      e) Teeth

    2. Function

    Formation of connected speech sounds

  D. Activities — Time 45 minutes

    1. Teacher lecture — Time 20 minutes

    2. Class analysis of poem — Time 25 minutes

  E. Assignment — Have class listen to some of the great speeches by such men as Winston Churchill and Franklin D. Roosevelt. During the thirteenth day of lessons, students will indicate how they used the "elements of voice." Have students turn in written indications also. (They will have to read in text first.)

XI. Eleventh Day — Articulating System, continued

  A. Objectives

    1. To explain importance of this system to whole voice process

    2. To show difference between articulation and pronunciation

  B. Materials

    1. Chart

    2. Film — *Articulation and Pronunciation*

  C. Content

    1. Articulating process. The use of the first articulatory structures in forming sounds

    2. Pronunciation as it differs from articulation

      a) Articulation — Process of forming the sounds characteristic of connected speech

           b. Pronunciation — The way you intend to sound
             a word
    D. Activities — Time 45 minutes
        1. Teacher lecture — Time 15 minutes
        2. Student — film — Time 30 minutes
XII. Twelfth Day — The Elements of Voice
    A. Objectives
        1. Explain use of elements to convey differences in
           meaning and reveal your feelings
        2. Meaning of elements
    B. Materials
        1. Text
        2. Experiments in vocal expression (included in
           materials)
    C. Content
        1. Pitch
           a) Meaning
           b) Importance to speech
        2. Quality
           a) Meaning
           b) Importance to speech
        3. Force
           a) Meaning
           b) Importance to speech
        4. Tempo or Timing
           a) Meaning
           b) Importance to speech
    D. Activities — Time 45 minutes
        1. Teacher lecture — Time 20 minutes
        2. Student — experiments in vocal expression — Time
           25 minutes
XIII. Thirteenth Day — How to Use the Elements
    A. Objective
        To explain importance of elements of voice for
        emphasis, etc.
    B. Materials
        None
    C. Content
        1. You convey difference in meaning
           a) When you emphasize a word in a statement
           b) When you indicate finality or suspension
           c) When you ask questions
           d) When you divide a sentence into phrases
        2. You reveal your feelings
    D. Activities — Time 45 minutes
        1. Teacher lecture — Time 20 minutes

2. Student — analysis of elements used in famous speeches — Time 25 minutes

XIV. Fourteenth Day — Improving Your Voice

A. Objective

To learn to apply the elements of voice in order to improve the voice

B. Materials

Text

C. Content

1. Improving pitch
   a) Find your optimum pitch
   b) Regulate tensions
   c) Cultivate flexibility
2. Improving quality
   a) Speak in correct pitch range
   b) Avoid undesirable nasality
   c) Try to keep "open throat"
3. Improving force
   a) Adjust loudness to occasion
   b) Follow safeguards against fear
   c) Seek balance in emphasis
   d) Use amplifying equipment properly
4. Improving tempo
   a) Give audience time to absorb ideas
   b) Space pauses intelligently
   c) Recognize the power of silence

D. Activities — Time 45 minutes

1. Teacher lecture — Time 25 minutes
2. Student — question-answer period — Time 20 minutes

XV. Fifteenth Day — Lesson on Listening and Observing

A. Objectives

1. To teach student listening and observation
2. To help student analyze speech for voice elements

B. Materials

Questions students answer in their written listening report

C. Content

1. Use instructor or lecturer in another class as speaking model
2. Have students take notes and prepare a written listening report
3. Discuss

D. Activities — Time 45 minutes

1. Lecturer or instructor — Time 20 minutes
2. Written assignment — Time 15 minutes

3. Discussion — Time 10 minutes
E. Assignment — Have class bring pronouncing dictionaries and make a list of twenty most mispronounced
words.
XVI. Sixteenth Day
A. Objectives
1. To help student analyze and improve poor articulation
2. To help student in correct pronunciation
B. Materials
Pronouncing dictionaries
C. Content
1. Improve articulation
a) Analyze causes of poor articulation
b) Avoid extremes of carefulness and carelessness
c) Train your ear to be discriminating
2. Improving pronounciation
a) Listen to persons with approved standards of
speech
b) Consult pronouncing dictionaries
XVII. Seventeenth Day — Bodily Action
A. Objectives
1. To teach student that the body is the bridge between him and the eye of his observer
2. To teach the student the use of natural gestures
B. Material
Communicating Effectively: Bodily Action
C. Content — Gestures
1. Meaning of gesture—all meaningful visible activity
2. The origins of gesture
3. The nature of gesture
4. Types of gesture
a) Instinctive
b) Descriptive
c) Conventional
d) Overt and covert
D. Activities — Time 45 minutes
1. Lecture — Time 25 minutes
2. Film — Time 20 minutes
E. Assignment — Have students write a brief report on
observations of gestures, facial expressions, and bodily
actions of fellow students in ordinary conversational
situations. To be turned in on twentieth day.
XVIII. Eighteenth Day — Bodily Action
A. Objectives
1. To teach student that the body is the bridge between him and the eye of his observer

2. To teach the student the use of natural gestures
B. Materials
None
C. Content — More about Gestures
1. Gesture naturally
   a) Understand purpose
   b) Feel meaning of words
   c) Assume position that contributes to purpose
   d) Maintain eye contact with audience
2. Gesture appropriately
   a) Exaggerate gestures in practice
   b) Use platform aids as help, not as hindrance
   c) Adapt gestures to audience and occasion
D. Activities — Time 45 minutes
1. Teacher lecture and illustration of points — Time 25-30 minutes
2. Student — question-answer period — Time 15 minutes

XIX. Nineteenth Day — Bodily Action
A. Objectives
1. To explain the cause and effects of physical responses in speaking
2. To learn how to avoid some common faults in physical responses
B. Material
Exercise in facial expression (included)
C. Content
1. Cause and effect in physical response
   a) The learner
   b) The jingler
   c) The caged tiger
   d) The drummer
   e) The firing-squad victim
2. Common faults in physical response
3. Improving physical responses
D. Activities — Time 45 minutes
1. Teacher lecture — Time 20-25 minutes
2. Student's exercise on facial expression — Time 20-25 minutes

XX. Twentieth Day — Bodily Action
A. Objectives
1. Show importance of posture to speech act
2. Show importance of eye contact to speech act
B. Materials
None
C. Content — Posture and Eye Contact
1. Posture

    a) Part posture plays in speaking

    b) Part posture plays in breathing

   2. Eye contact — Why important

  D. Activities — Time 45 minutes

   1. Discussion of reports due — Time 25 minutes

   2. Teacher lecture — Time 20 minutes

  E. Assignment — Pantomimes for next lesson

XXI. Twenty-first Day

  A. Objectives

   To have student display what was taught about the use of gestures

  B. Materials

   None

  C. Content — Pantomimes — examples

   1. Playing a sport

   2. Brushing teeth

   3. Putting in contacts

   4. Rolling hair, etc.

  D. Activities — Time 45 minutes (Time divided among students according to number.)

  E. Assignment—Have students bring dictionaries to class

XXII. Twenty-second Day — Semantics

  A. Objectives

   1. To learn to use words responsibly

   2. To learn to use words correctly according to meanings

   3. To learn the meaning of words

   4. To learn how to achieve clarity in words

  B. Materials

   1. Text

   2. Dictionaries

  C. Content — Semantics

   1. The meaning of words

    a) Words are symbols

    b) Concrete words

    c) Connotations and denotations

    d) Descriptive language

    e) Directive language

   2. Do's and don'ts of word choice

    a) Avoid "loaded" words

    b) Avoid abusive labels

    c) Beware of equivocation

   3. Achieving clarity in words

    a) Use accurate words

    b) Use specific words

            c) Avoid counter words
            d) Avoid unfamiliar or too technical language
            e) Avoid jargon

    D. Activities — Time 45 minutes
       1. Teacher lecture — 25 minutes
       2. Student — Have students look up meanings and pronunciations of certain words—Time 20 minutes (Words)
            a) Diction
            b) Vowels
            c) Consonants
            d) Discreet
            e) Dialect
            f) Diacritical
            g) Pronunciation
            h) Polysyllabic
            i) Phonetic

XXIII. Twenty-third Day — Semantics
    A. Objectives
       1. To teach the structure and make-up of a good definition
       2. To teach that words have different meanings for different people
    B. Material
       Dictionary
    C. Content — Logical Definition
       1. Placement of word within class
       2. Distinguish words for class
       3. Requirements of definition
            a) It should cover all cases or instances of word, idea, or thing being defined.
            b) The definition of the word or idea being defined should be amplified in language that is familiar and clear to the audience.
            c) The definition should be as brief as is consistent with accuracy.
       4. The different meanings of a word
    D. Activities — Time 45 minutes
       1. Teacher lecture — 20 minutes
       2. Student — Say a word such as house, tree, or car and have students draw a picture of each. Show these to class. Time 25 minutes

XXIV. Twenty-fourth Day — Phonetics
    A. Objectives
       1. To clear up the confusion between the sounds of

the English language and the symbols we use to represent them

2. To aid in the correct production of sounds

B. Materials

1. Text

2. Charts of phonetic symbols and manner and place of production (included)

3. Record of John S. Kenyon's speech sounds

C. Content — Consonant: Place of Articulation

1. Labial sounds — lips block up or change the course of outgoing breath stream

2. Labio-dental — lower lip comes in contact with upper teeth

3. Lingua-dental — tip of tongue comes in contact with upper teeth

4. Post-dental—obstruction of outgoing breath caused by tip of tongue coming in contact with area behind upper front teeth

5. Alveolar — tongue tip placed against alveolar ridge

6. Palatal — point of articulation is central palate

7. Velar — back of tongue makes contact with soft palate

8. Glottal — friction in the variable opening between vocal folds, or glottis

D. Activities — Time 45 minutes

1. Teacher lecture — Time 20 minutes

2. Student — Write symbols as teacher makes sounds

XXV. Twenty-fifth Day — Manner of Production

A. Objectives

1. To explain how consonants are produced

2. To aid in the correct production of sounds

B. Material

Charts

C. Content

1. Plosive sounds — explosion of air from lips or by tongue touching post-dental area

2. Fricative sounds — breath forced through opening

3. Nasal sounds — soft palate drops, opening nasal passage

4. Glide sounds — tongue, lips, or both completely change position

5. Lateral — sound placement of tip of tongue against dental or alveolar ridge, allowing air to escape at sides

      6. Affricates — composed consonant sounds formed by combining a stop sound with a fricative

  D. Activities — Time 45 minutes

    Teacher lecture — Time 45 minutes using charts

XXVI. Twenty-sixth Day — Phonetics: Consonant sounds

  A. Objective

    To learn correct pronunciation of consonant sounds

  B. Materials

    None

  C. Content

    1. Plosives (six)

      a) Put — voiceless bilabial plosive

      b) Bat — voiced bilabial plosive

      c) Tap — voiceless alveolar plosive

      d) Dip — voiced alveolar plosive

      e) Kite — voiceless velar plosive

      f) Got — voiced velar plosive

    2. Nasals (three)

      a) Map — voiced bilabial nasal

      b) Nap — voiced alveolar nasal

      c) Sing — voiced velar nasal

    3. Fricative (nine)

      a) Far — voiceless labio-dental fricative

      b) Veer — voiced labio-dental fricative

      c) Sit — voiceless post-dental fricative

      d) Gaze — voiced post-dental fricative

      e) Ship — voiceless palato-alveolar fricative

      f) Azure — voiced palato-alveolar fricative

      g) Thesis — voiceless dental fricative

      h) That — voiced dental fricative

      i) Hat — voiceless glottal fricative

  D. Activities — Time 45 minutes

    Students orally produce the sounds as given, paying attention to the position of the articulators

XXVII. Twenty-seventh Day — Consonant Sounds

  A. Objectives

    1. To learn correct pronunciation of consonant sounds

    2. To learn manner and place of production

  B. Materials

    Phonetic Bingo Cards

  C. Content

    1. Glides

      a) Rip — voiced palatal glide

      b) Yet — voiced, palatal glide

        c) *Wish* — voiced, bilabial velar glide
        d) *What* — voiceless, bilabial glide
    2. Lateral
        Lap — voiced, aveolar lateral
    3. Affricates
        a) *Pitch* — voiceless, post-dental affricate
        b) *Ridge* — voiced, post-dental affricate
    4. Sometimes syllabic
        a) [m]
        b) [n]
        c) [l]
  D. Activities — Time 45 minutes
    1. Teacher lecture — Time 20 minutes
    2. Student — Sound Bingo — Time 25 minutes

XXVIII. Twenty-eighth Day — Vocal Sounds
  A. Objectives
    1. To learn correct pronunciation of vowel sounds
    2. To learn place of production
  B. Materials
    Word drills on consonants
  C. Content
    1. Front vowels
        a) *Beet* — high front
        b) *Bit* — high front
        c) *Bait* — mid front
        d) *Bet* — mid front
        e) *Bat* — low front
    2. Back
        a) *Blot* — low back
        b) *Off* — low back
        c) *Bought* — mid back
        d) *Boat* — mid back
        e) *Book* — high back
        f) *Boot* — high back
    3. Middle
        a) *But* — mid back (stressed)
        b) *About* — mid central (unstressed)
        c) *Bird* — mid central (stressed)
  D. Activities — Time 45 minutes
    1. Teacher lecture — Time 20 minutes
    2. Drills on consonant sounds — Time 25 minutes

XXIX. Twenty-ninth Day — Diphthongs
  A. Objectives
    1. To aid in correct pronunciation of diphthongs
    2. To review vowel sounds

B. Materials
Word drill on vowel sounds (included)
C. Content — Diphthongs
   1. *Bow*
   2. *Bite*
   3. *Boy*
   4. *You*
D. Activities — Time 45 minutes
   1. Teacher lecture — Time 10 minutes
   2. Student's production of diphthongs—Time 10 minutes
   3. Word drill on vowels — Time 25 minutes

XXX. Thirtieth Day — Objective Test
Objective—An objective evaluation of knowledge learned by student during unit

The Activities Approach

Underlying the activities approach is the rationale that "we learn by doing." Therefore, the teacher plans a series of activities through which the student may demonstrate his skill in and understanding of the principles involved in the particular activity. The emphasis in this method is upon the pragmatic application of rhetorical principles. Rather than isolate principles, as is commonly done in the principles approach, they are perceived collectively as comprising the sum total of the speech situation. Thus with the activities approach we would expect to find some of the following assignments:

1. Speech to inform
2. Speech to demonstrate
3. Speech to stimulate
4. Speech to persuade
5. Speech to entertain
6. Speech to convince
7. Speech for special occasions.

The Theory or Subject-Matter Approach

Probably the least used method of teaching speech at the secondary level is the theory approach. Student assignments consist of identifying rhetorical principles through (1) a study of speech models and (2) listening assignments in which the student is directed to analyze a speech he has heard. This approach emphasizes the development of the student's analytical and critical powers.

Generally, students taught with this method feel a lack of development of their own personal speaking skills. There also appears to be a question of personal involvement in the assignments given. The student may fail to relate what he knows to his own communication problems.

Following are typical assignments which serve to illustrate this particular approach:

1. Listen to a political campaign speaker and deliver a three-minute oral report on the techniques employed by the speaker to adapt his speech to his immediate audience.
2. Listen to a speaker and submit a written critique on the relationship of his bodily activity to his speaking effectiveness.
3. Interview a local speaker and prepare a five-minute oral report on his techniques of speech preparation. Evaluate his techniques in terms of the principles of speech preparation taught in this course.

The Eclectic Approach

Most teachers of speech at the secondary level adopt an approach which combines the best features of the principles, activities, and theory approaches. A successful combination of the three should provide the student with a knowledge of speech principles, an adequate set of speech skills for effectively communicating his ideas, and the ability to function as a critic-analyst in the speech situation.

The following outline for a six weeks unit in public speaking typifies the eclectic approach to the teaching of public speaking.

Public Speaking, A Course Outline

Time: Six weeks

Text*: Sarett, Foster, McBurney. *Speech.* Boston: Houghton Mifflin Company, 1956.

Supplementary texts: Hedde and Brigance. *American Speech.* Philadelphia: J. B. Lippincott Company, 4th ed., 1955.

Weaver, Borchers, Smith. *Speaking and Listening.* Englewood Cliffs, New Jersey: Prentice-Hall, Inc., 1956.

---

*The student will note that the example texts given are editions of some vintage. The wide adoption of these books speaks for their quality. Since many such texts will be revised and published by the time the current student is in teaching, the texts cited are given as examples only. They were deliberately selected to force the student to study and make lesson plans from up-to-date sources.

I. Basic Assumptions

This unit is begun with the assumption that the student has been exposed to a previous unit dealing with the basic skills of communication, i.e., articulation, enunciation, projection, listening, delivery, etc. Further, it is assumed that the teacher has provided the student with a proper motivation for the study of speech.

II. Objectives

A. General

1. To have the student discover and correct his weaknesses in communicating
2. To have the student employ effective communication skills
3. To provide the student with tools enabling him to better cope with his environment
4. To create in the student constructive attitudes concerning public speaking and its importance in a democratic society

B. Specific

1. To instruct the student in effective interviewing techniques
2. To help the student efficiently and effectively employ the telephone as a tool for the reception and dissemination of information
3. To have the student recognize the desirability of preparation for both formal and informal speaking situations
4. To provide the student with techniques for speech preparation and delivery
5. To have the student acquire skill in evaluating ideas

III. Approach

Emphasis is placed upon student discovery and recognition of the principles and skills to be learned through the mediums of teacher-directed classroom discussion of speech models, films, text and supplementary reading, and of student speaking activities.

IV. Content

A. Informal Speaking

1. The Telephone Conversation: answering procedures
planning remarks
articulation and projection
listening

    a) Materials for students

        1) Text: *Speech*, p. 250-253

        2) Supplementary readings:
           American Speech, pp. 26-28
           Speaking and Listening, pp. 330-341

    b) Student activities

       1) Have several students demonstrate before the class the way in which they think a good telephone conversation should be conducted. After each demonstration, observing students will critique the activity.

       2) Discuss how telephone conversation differs from face-to-face conversation.

    c) Teacher activities

    Supervision of student activities and summation of principles learned.

  2. The Interview: purpose
                preparation
                atmosphere

    a) Materials for students

       1) Text: *Speech*, pp. 253-254

       2) Supplementary readings:
         American Speech, pp. 30-37
         Speaking and Listening, pp. 175-179

    b) Student activities

       1) Have students interview each other for a hypothetical job.

       2) Discuss ways in which the interview was effective or ineffective.

    c) Teacher activities

    Supervision of student activities and summation of principles learned.

B. Public Speaking

  1. Selecting the topic: appropriate to the speaker
                     appropriate to the audience
                     appropriate to the occasion
                     appropriate to the time limit

    a) Materials for students

       1) Text: *Speech*, pp. 151-157

       2) Supplementary readings:
         American Speech, pp. 165-173

    b) Student activities

       1) Prepare a list of five speech topics the student may use in a class speech.

       2) Have the student orally defend the selection of the topic on the basis of the requirements set forth in the text.

       3) Class discussion of the four requirements of a good topic.

    c) Teacher activities

    Supervision of student activities and summation of principles learned. Evaluation of student performance using rating scales attached.

2. Determining the purpose: speech to entertain
                                    speech to inform
                                    speech to stimulate
                                    speech to persuade or activate

    a) Materials for students

      1) Text: *Speech*, pp. 157-164

      2) Supplementary readings: *American Speech*, pp. 173-180

    b) Student activities

      1) Discussion of the kinds of daily communications which are designed to entertain, inform, stimulate, and persuade us: songs, weather reports, advertisements.

      2) Discussion of the purpose of "The Gettysburg Address," Patrick Henry's "Give Me Liberty or Give Me Death" speech, daily weather reports, daily traffic reports, the "State of the Union" message.

      3) Have students suggest topics appropriate to the four purposes and discuss their applicability.

    c) Teacher activities

    Supervision of student discussion and summation of the factors which determine each purpose.

3. Gathering speech materials: experiences
                                    printed sources
                                    interviews
                                    visual aids
                                    note-taking

    a) Materials for students

      1) Text: *Speech*, pp. 165-169

      2) Supplementary readings: *American Speech*, pp. 167-168

      3) List of printed sources for research

    b) Student activities

      1) Select a speech topic for a five-minute informative speech to the class. Make a preliminary bibliography of speech materials you can employ from printed sources including indexes, standard reference works, current magazines, and visual aids.

    2) Class discussion of purpose and proper handling of visual aids.

    3) Class discussion of purpose and procedure involved in note-taking.

    4) Have student give a two-minute informative speech using a visual aid.

  c) Teacher activities

  Supervision of student activities and summation of principles learned. Evaluation of student performance.

4. Outlining the speech

  The Introduction: establishing rapport
                  revealing the subject
                  relating the subject to the audience
                  revealing the main ideas

  The Body: patterns of outlining: logical
                                       topical
                                       chronological
                                       problem-solving

          stating the main ideas
          stating subordinate ideas

  The Conclusion: simple summary
                abstract of the speech
                action appeal
                prophecy
                question
                humor

  a) Materials for students

    1) Text: *Speech,* pp. 173-180

    2) Supplementary readings: *American Speech,* pp. 183-195

      Speaking and Listening, pp. 138-140

    3) Handout of MacArthur speech

  b) Student activities

    1) Viewing and discussing of a film on speech preparation.

    (*Speech Preparation.* 16 minutes, C-B Educational Films, 690 Market Street, San Francisco 4, California.)

    (*Planning Your Talk.* 13 minutes. Young America Films, Inc., 18 East 41st Street, New York 17, New York.)

    (*Speak Up.* 13 minutes, Alturas Films, Box 1211, Santa Barbara, California.)

(*Making Sense with Outlines.* 11 minutes. Coronet Films, Coronet Building, Chicago 1, Illinois.)

2) Discussion of what should be accomplished in the introduction.

3) Evaluation through discussion of the introduction of MacArthur's "Address to Congress" speech.

4) Evaluation through discussion of the introduction of "Impatience and Generosity," by Margaret Chase Smith.

5) Have the students write a one-minute introduction for the five-minute informative speech for which they have prepared references.

6) Using the board, have the class select a topic for an informative speech developing the main ideas in a topical, chronological, and logical order.

7) Using the board, have the class select a topic for a persuasive speech developing the main ideas in a problem-solving sequence.

8) Class discussion of the purpose and types of conclusions.

9) Presentation of a five-minute informative speech.

c) Teacher activities

Supervision of student activities and summation of principles learned. Evaluation of student speeches.

5. Patterns of Reasoning: inductive and deductive (syllogistic)
causal
analogy

a) Materials for students

1) Text: *Speech,* pp. 209-232

2) Supplementary readings: *American Speech,* pp. 254-258

3) Model of speech using the inductive order by J. T. Nason.

4) Model of speech using deductive order by George W. Cabaniss.

b) Student activities

1) Discussion of the model speeches.

2) Discussion of advertisements frequently heard and their use of causality and analogy.

3) Presentation of a three-minute speech employing either the inductive or the deductive method.

c) Teacher activities

Supervision of student activities, evaluation of speaking performance, summation of principles learned.

6. Amplifying and developing ideas: definitions
   - repetitions
   - emphasis
   - examples
   - analogies
   - quotations
   - statistics
   - visual aids
   - facts
   - opinions

   a) Materials for students
   1) Text: *Speech* pp. 191-201
   2) Refer to the speeches of Nason and Cabaniss.
   b) Student activities
   1) Deliver a two-minute speech in which you employ as many of the techniques of amplification as you can to get across a single idea.
   2) Analyze through discussion the speeches of Nason and Cabaniss. What kinds of amplification did they use?
   3) Deliver a five-minute speech to persuade.
   c) Teacher activities
   Lead the class in a discussion of the methods of amplification based on the text assignment. Evaluate student speaking performance.

SPEECH PERFORMANCE EVALUATION

Evaluating the student's comprehension of speech content and the student's speech performance is another problem which constantly plagues the conscientious teacher. The extent of the student's knowledge of speech content can be rather accurately determined through the use of objective measuring instruments.[1] Unfortunately, the evaluation of the speech performance remains subjective. The degree of teacher subjectivity in determining the student's performance grade may be controlled, however, through the use of a common set of criteria for evaluating all students involved in a particular speaking assignment. It has been the concern of those involved in the construction of rating scales to perfect an instrument which would both reduce the intuitive rating tendency

---

[1]For a detailed discussion of objective measuring instruments, see Chapter 5, "Evaluation."

and provide an analytical and systematic rating scale or check list. Knower suggests that such a scale not be too long, that terms be precise, and that the discrimination units not exceed five to seven degrees.[2]

In some instances pragmatic tests (those designed to test the effects of the speech on the listener) have been employed. Such tests are concerned with comprehension, retention, and change in the attitude or behavior of the listener. However, for classroom use, such devices have been found to be too cumbersome in relation to the time involved in administering the test and scoring it.

Early rating scales in speech consisted primarily of outlines for classroom criticism, but the selection of specific criteria with which the student is judged was arbitrary. One of the reasons teachers hesitate to adopt many rating scales is the desire for a device which not only assists evaluation but also teaches.

Philosophies on how a speech should be evaluated abound. A preponderance of the writers who have devised rating scales recommend that the evaluation be made of the entire act, which is, of course, different from the summation of its parts. Most rating scales and check lists in use today conform to this philosophy. The Knower General Speech Performance Scale, which has been rather widely adopted in college speech classes typifies the speech content and skills upon which the student is to be evaluated. Based upon the evidence that raters recognize and agree on negative qualities more readily than on positive qualities, the scale is composed entirely of negative statements. Recognizing the possibility of creating a negative or defeatist attitude in the student Knower recommends that the rater should comment on strong points in the section provided. This particular scale, when used without written explanatory comments of the weaknesses checked, may not be a meaningful learning device for the student.

The teacher faces the three-fold problem of learning, evaluation, and time. Ideally he wishes an instrument which will serve as both a learning and evaluative device and will require relatively little time to complete. Some teachers have oral critique periods immediately after each speech. Certainly such a practice conforms to sound learning theory in that it provides immediate reinforcement, but it can, if not rigidly controlled, consume an inordinate amount of time.

While most of the rating scales appearing in the literature provide a systematic set of criteria for evaluating the student, their categories are too general to serve as a learning device for the student. The student

---

[2]Franklin H. Knower, "What is a Speech Test?" *Quarterly Journal of Speech,* 30:485 (December, 1944).

needs to know not only in what general areas he is weak but more precisely the exact nature of his weaknesses and, if necessary, specific recommendations on what could have been done to strengthen the areas of weakness. If the teacher accepts this premise, then it appears that he will find it necessary to employ either the oral critique method or detailed written comments or both. Most teachers resort to both, and in the oral critique period they give meaning to the rating marks and sometimes vague comments they have made on the critique sheet.

Another procedure which is sometimes employed by speech teachers is to hold a general oral critique period at the end of each class performance

---

Speech Performance Scale*

Name_____Date_____Instructor_____
Project_____Time_____
Subject_____

Criteria	Rating 1-9†	Comments
1. *General effectiveness:*		
2. *Speech attitudes and adjustments:* Indifferent ____ Loses thought ____ Fidgety ____ Evasive ____ Tense ____ Inappropriate ____		
3. *Voice:* Weak ____ Loud ____ Fast ____ Slow ____ Poor pitch ____ Poor quality ____ Monotonous ____ Poor rhythm ____ Excess vocalization ____		
4. *Articulation:* Substitutions ____ Foreign dialect ____ Additions ____ Regional dialect ____ Slighting ____ Mispronunciation ____		
5. *Physical activity:* Indirect ____ Unresponsive ____ Random ____ Inappropriate ____		
6. *Language:* Ambiguous ____ Wordy ____ Inaccurate ____ Needs force ____ Needs vividness ____ Needs variety ____		
7. *Ideas:* Poor purpose ____ Not clear ____ Poor central idea ____ Dull ____ Weak support ____ Needs originality ____ Undeveloped ____ Insignificant ____ Inaccurate ____		

8. *Organization:*	
Introduction _____	Sequence _____
Division _____	Conclusion _____
Transitions _____	
Total	

*A. Craig Baird and Franklin H. Knower, *General Speech* (New York: McGraw-Hill Book Company, 1963), p. 24.

†Rate the speaker in each square by using a scale of 1 to 9 for each of the numbered items. Use 1, 2, or 3 to indicate various degrees of deficiency in the use of the process; use 4, 5, or 6 if he is slightly below average to slightly above average in the process; and use 7, 8, or 9 to indicate relative degrees of skill in his use of the process. Add ratings to get total score.

period. During this specific time speeches given during the class period are evaluated as a whole. The rationale given by some for such a practice is that it avoids spotlighting individual students. Another dangerous and unfounded assumption underlying this practice is that the student will relate the comments made to his own specific speech performance. Such a practice is not recommended, for the comments about all speeches given must of necessity be general in nature and, secondly, there is no assurance that the student will relate the appropriate general comments to his own specific case.

STAGE FRIGHT IN THE SPEECH CLASSROOM

No logical discussion of stage fright should take place without first considering the situation in which stage fright takes place. We are not wholly convinced that what many teachers of speech diagnose as stage fright is not more simply a case of teacher fright. This is teacher fright in the sense that the teacher has established within the classroom an atmosphere so fraught with tension that a Demosthenes would be hard put to feel comfortable in the situation. Such teachers need to closely examine their own personalities in an effort to determine why they feel such an atmosphere is necessary or even desirable. We might find that the atmosphere has been established for any number of reasons but ultimately that the teacher has found it necessary as a defense mechanism. He may wish to camouflage his own feelings of insecurity about (1) his ability to maintain a friendly but orderly classroom atmosphere, (2) his knowledge of the subject matter which he is designated to teach, (3) his ability to arouse and maintain student interest in the subject matter, or (4) any number of other supposed or imagined deficiencies.

Further contributing to the classroom atmosphere is the specific role the teacher chooses to emphasize. In the course of a single day the teacher will find himself playing many roles. Among these are the critic, the evaluator, the information-giver, the friend, the counselor, the encourager, and so forth. The perception of the teacher as primarily a critic-evaluator probably contributes substantially to a tense atmosphere within the classroom situation. The teacher who perceives himself primarily as an evaluator will generally attempt to motivate students by reminding them of his role as evaluator. He makes frequent references to his function of determining grades for each particular assignment. The teacher who must rely on the threat of grades as the primary motivation for the completion of required assignments lacks initiative. As you reflect on the effective teachers you have had in the past, you will doubtless remember that you perceived them primarily in roles other than that of the evaluator. For many of us the primary roles of our most effective teachers were those of encourager and information-giver.

The student knows without being constantly reminded that he is being graded, and there appears to be little need of heightening that awareness and thus contributing to a situation which already has several built-in tension producing factors. It is these built-in factors (personality deficiencies, physical deficiences, or the illusion of being deficient in either or both) which appear to form the basis of stage fright. For example, many students with an adequate vocabulary admit fears of being unable to express their ideas with language appropriate to the situation.

There are divergent opinions about what approach the teacher should take in handling the problem of stage fright. Some conclude that the subject is better handled by avoiding all reference to it. Others believe that a full and frank discussion of the problem is warranted. The following are several views on how the problem of stage fright should be approached through discussion in the classroom:

1. Give the students an account of the possible causes of stage fright and explain the psychological and physiological symptoms which they may experience.
2. Have a class discussion in which students are encouraged to talk about their fears in speaking.
3. Have each student, through a process of introspection, study the causes of his fears in speaking.
4. Minimize the uniqueness of stage fright by admitting that the problem is universal and the symptoms are normal occurrences.
5. Avoid reference to it if at all possible.

Most of the more recent texts designed for the secondary speech course provide sufficient content for the teacher and the student to accomplish any or all of the first four approaches reviewed. Few teachers find it possible to totally avoid the subject. Obviously the problem does not dissipate through ignoring it. As one former student put it, "I'm relieved to know I'm normal. I secretly thought I was some kind of freak."

Other suggestions which have been made in addition to a discussion of the problem of reducing stage fright include developing favorable student attitudes toward speaking, reducing tension before speaking (usually involving some form of physical exertion), reducing tension during speaking through the use of good bodily posture, movement and gestures and the use of visual aids, instilling confidence in oneself before the speech by being thoroughly familiar with the content to be presented (having orally practiced it), and finally, giving the student as many speaking opportunities as possible.

References

Baird, A. Craig, and Knower, Franklin H. *General Speech.* New York: McGraw-Hill Book Company, 1963.

Articles

Fotheringham, Wallace C. "Measuring Speech Effectiveness," *Speech Monographs,* 23:31-37 (March, 1956).

Knower, Franklin H. "What is a Speech Test?" *The Quarterly Journal of Speech,* 30:485-493 (December, 1944).

Oliver, Robert T. "The Eternal (and Infernal) Problem of Grades," *The Speech Teacher,* 9:8-11 (January, 1960).

Sawyer, Thomas J. "A Grading System for Speech Classes," *The Speech Teacher,* 9:12-15 (January, 1960).

Wiksell, Wesley. "New Methods of Evaluating Instruction and Student Achievement in a Speech Class," *The Speech Teacher,* 9:16-19 (January, 1960).

8

Oral Interpretation

Oral interpretation, or oral reading, is the oldest of the speech arts.[1] Storytelling and oral recitation predate recorded history and have continued to the present day. However, the emergence of oral interpretation as a field of study was delayed until the nineteenth century because of the confusion with oratory and rhetoric.[2]

HISTORICAL BACKGROUND

In ancient *Greece*, poets, historians, minstrels, and rhapsodes recited verses handed down from generation to generation or delivered original works at festivals and other events. These people were highly respected for their historical knowledge, their speaking ability, and the content of their recitations. Reading and recitation were also used by philosophers

---

[1]Keith Brooks, Eugene Bahn, and L. Lamont Okey, *The Communicative Act of Oral Interpretation* (Boston: Allyn and Bacon, Inc., 1967), p. 3.

[2]Charlotte I. Lee, *Oral Interpretation* (3rd ed.; Boston: Houghton Mifflin Company, 1965), p. 449.

to refine lectures as critical comments from students forced revisions in their works.[3]

The *Romans* adopted much of the Greek civilization, and the custom of reciting became popular. Public recitations ranged from gifted readings to performances which could scarcely be called mediocre. Even the emperors delighted in giving recitals. The importance of this art was reflected in the educational system where pupils read and recited. Both Quintilian and Cicero offered instructions for good oral reading.[4]

Since most of the scholars were associated with the church during *the Middle Ages,* much oral reading focused upon religious literature. While Biblical selections were read in monasteries, stories of romance and adventure were recited by minstrels in the castles. With the decline of the minstrels storytelling was provided by the people.

In England during the *sixteenth and seventeenth centuries,* Bible reading was emphasized in the church, school, and home. Oral reading received attention as an art, and readers were encouraged to convey meaning with voice and body. Those who were not skilled readers enjoyed listening to those who were.

By the *eighteenth century,* England was attempting to improve the poor delivery of the clergy in both speaking and reading. Reason was to be the keynote and nature's laws were to prevail.[5] This led to the rise of a group of writer-speakers known as the *English Elocutionists* who believed that since nature gave to the emotions certain gestures and tones, these gestures and tones should be reproduced as naturally as possible in reading literature. Two of the outstanding English Elocutionists were *Thomas Sheridan* and *John Walker.* While both men claimed to take their cues from nature, each attempted to establish specific rules and markings which led to a mechanical approach. However, Sheridan's name was linked to the *natural school* and Walker's name was associated with the *mechanical school.* Many of the elocutionists of the day embraced both schools as well as an imitative approach, but followers of these men emphasized the differences. Much attention was given to the reading of prose and poetry, the role of gesture, emotion, and reading style. These English Elocutionists through their publications exerted a strong influence on oral reading in Colonial America.

By the *nineteenth century,* speech training in America was under the aegis of colleges and private schools. Two of the best known were

---

[3]Brooks, Bahn, and Okey, *op. cit.,* p. 5.
[4]*Ibid.,* p. 7.
[5]Eugene Bahn, "Epochs in the History of Oral Interpretation," *The Communicative Arts and Sciences of Speech,* ed. Keith Brooks (Columbus, Ohio: Charles E. Merrill Publishing Company, 1967), p. 288.

Boston's Curry School of Expression and the Emerson College of Oratory. During this period many eighteenth century trends continued. Memorization vs. reading, speaking vs. reading, and poetry vs. prose reading were still discussed. Important influences during this period were *James Rush,* an American medical man, and *Francois Delsarte,* a Frenchman. Dr. Rush's contributions to the field of speech included his studies of the mechanism of the human voice, his scientific approach to vocal technique, and speech terminology. He developed elaborate charts and markings for time, quality, force, pitch, and abruptness and thus supported the mechanical method. Delsarte, who did not visit America but whose teachings were promulgated by his student, the actor ever, this system with its elaborate charts and diagrams became extremely mechanical.

Near the end of the nineteenth century, *Samuel Silas Curry* presented his theory "Think the thought" which was a welcome change from the artificiality of the mechanical method to those followers of the natural school. Unfortunately, this theory became misunderstood by some teachers of speech who interpreted it to mean that comprehension of the thought would automatically guarantee appropriate delivery without a need to develop skills in the use of voice and body. The term "elocution" was displaced by the term "expression" as the earlier exaggerated and exhibitionistic style became less favored. Gradually "oral reading" and "interpretative reading" became accepted terms.

A few of the colleges and universities offered some courses in speech, but most of these were to train students in certain specialized fields such as the ministry or law. The majority of those who wished to be "readers" enrolled in the private elocution schools or studios and were taught by previous pupils of some teacher of expression. These schools varied in quality and purpose. Those who were fortunate enough to study with people like Charles Wesley Emerson, S. S. Curry, Leland Powers, and Arthur Edward Philips learned the methodology and philosophy which later became compatible with the educational standards of oral interpretation adopted by the colleges and universities.

At the outset of the *twentieth century,* men like Thomas C. Trueblood and Robert I. Fulton supported the speech arts in higher education and gained academic respectability for faculty in oral interpretation. Attention was turned from the mechanical techniques in the use of voice and body to an appreciation and analysis of the literature. The formal study of interpretation as a part of the field of speech gained status with the founding in 1814 of the National Association of Academic Teachers of Public Speaking which later became the Speech Association of America. The modern concept of oral interpretation is "eclectic" in that it borrows

from both the "natural" and "mechanical" schools.[6] Delivery is not a
display per se, but the voice and body are used to effectively communicate
the meaning and thought. Oral interpretation as a form of communication
emphasizes the role of the listener as well as that of the speaker.

Oral reading in the twentieth century has ranged in popularity from
the early Chautauqua programs held at Chautauqua, New York (which
also sent readers throughout the country) to presentations on records,
radio, and television.

Charles Laughton helped to increase interest in oral reading through
his programs of literary selections, many of which were from the Bible.
Laughton was one who was instrumental in using groups for oral reading
and helped to establish the popularity of the Readers' Theatre which is
based on oral interpretation principles. Through the 1950's and early
1960's this group activity remained primarily in professional and university circles. It gradually gained acceptance with secondary speech
teachers and now exists as another speech art form in an increasing
number of institutions. In some state high school speech league contests
students have their choice of participating in the medium of Readers'
Theatre or the one-act play.

DEFINITION OF ORAL INTERPRETATION

"The communicative act of oral interpretation is the process of stimulating a listener response which is favorable to the intent of the literature
in terms of the reader's judgments, as communicated from the manuscript
through vocal and physical suggestion."[7] This definition describes the
three elements inherent in the act of oral interpretation — the literature
the reader, and the listener. Each is dependent upon the other if the
communication process is to be effective. With the literature as the
source, the reader analyzes the selection as to its intent by availing
himself of all sources such as biographies of or interviews with the
author, literary reviews, a study of the cultural setting, or other related
information which would help to reveal an understanding of the literature. The interpreter examines the literature for suggestions of vocal
and physical cues; then uses his voice and body in such a way as to
suggest what is consistent with the literature. The potential of the literary
experience must be fulfilled in the listener's imagination. Unlike the

---

[6]Lee, *op. cit.,* p. 455.
[7]Keith Brooks, "The Communicative Act of Oral Interpretation," The *Communicative Arts and Sciences of Speech,* ed. Keith Brooks (Columbus, Ohio: Charles
E. Merrill Publishing Company, 1967), p. 298.

actor, who strives to re-create before the eyes of the audience the literal fulfillment of the literary experience, the interpreter employs the art of suggestion to stimulate and assist the listener to re-create and fulfill the literary experience in his mind. Thus the listener is involved in a dynamic process in which stimulus-response patterns are constantly being exchanged. Each individual participating in this act will respond to the various cues in relationship to his background and associations. This allows for greater imagination and creativity in response to the literature.

The oral reader attempts to develop skill in the use of the voice and body so as to convey more artistic and accurate cues. Awkward or inaccurate vocal and physical suggestions confuse the listener and prevent him from responding favorably to the intent of the literature. Since the reader's purpose is to enhance and communicate the literature more effectively, he controls the voice and body to respond unobtrusively to the literature's demands.

By using a manuscript, the reader or interpreter establishes the printed page as the source or as symbolic of the source. With his skills he re-creates the literary experience for the audience. He maintains his own identity and does not become the source in the same way that an actor becomes the source — a character in a play. Although the material remains before him, the reader must have such a firm mental grasp that he is able to concentrate on communicating with the audience rather than on reading.

Closely related to successful interaction in this process is the ability of the reader to maintain emotional control — to remain an observer. While the reader must *empathize* or *feel* into the literary experience in order to convey proper cues to the listener, he must not become so emotionally involved that he loses control in response to the literary selections. If he fails to maintain an *artistic detachment* or *aesthetic distance,* he attracts attention to himself and the listener is no longer able to focus on the literary experience. There must be enough empathy or emotional involvement on the part of the reader to help the listener experience the literature, but also enough aesthetic distance or intellectual awareness to allow the potential of the literary experience to be fulfilled.

Interpretation, Impersonation, and Acting

Students often confuse *interpretation, impersonation, and acting*. All three are closely related and sometimes difficult to separate as the performer moves in and out or employs a blending of these arts. However, the interpreter usually recognizes his audience in a more direct manner than do the other two. He may suggest characteristics through vocal and physical cues but makes no attempt to lose his own identity: "The impersonator is more indirect and involves a more complete characterization."[8] He tries to imitate a character, to make the audience believe he is someone other than himself. He goes beyond suggesting vocal and physical cues to become more literal. He employs greater freedom of movement, facial expression, and vocal display. The actor usually attempts to lose his identity by becoming involved in a complete identification with the character. Audience contact in acting is generally indirect. By employing all kinds of theatrical devices such as make-up, costuming, properties, lighting, and stage settings, his identification becomes complete. Brooks identifies some of these differences as differences in function, attitude, focus, identity, and environment.[9]

The reader must understand that these definitions are merely guidelines. Occasionally one finds a play which appears to violate these boundaries. The stage manager in *Our Town* establishes direct audience contact as he addresses them. Certain modern dramatic forms involve the actor in a direct audience relationship. However, the more conventional practices follow the guidelines suggested here in helping the interpreter understand his relation to these arts and where the emphasis should be. At all times he must be concerned about stimulating a listener response that in the reader's judgment is favorable to the intent of the literature. A skilled interpreter may employ liberties with techniques in order to enhance communication. These same exaggerations on the part of an unskilled reader would detract from the literature and lead to ineffective communication. The speech teacher will probably cause less confusion in the minds of students by placing some limitations on oral interpretation in the initial exposure to it. However, once the basic principles are understood, as evidenced by the students' behavior, there should be some opportunity for experimentation without distortion of the literary intent.

Charlotte Lee describes the writer of the literary selection as the creative artist; the interpreter, as the one who assumes the responsibility of re-creating the total entity.[10] This means that the interpreter must break down the literary selection in order to study its parts, but after this analysis must constantly reassemble the material to communicate the total effect of the literary work of art.

---

[8]Charles H. Woolbert and Severina E. Nelson, *The Art of Interpretative Speech* (rev. ed.; New York: F.S. Crofts & Co., 1940), p. 6.

[9]Brooks, *The Communicative Arts and Sciences of Speech, op. cit.,* p. 306.

[10]Lee, *op. cit.,* p. 3.

Oral interpretation in the secondary school encompasses activities such as oral reading of poetry, prose, dramatic literature, storytelling, verse or choral speaking, Readers' Theatre, and chamber theatre. Since the trend among today's outstanding teachers of oral interpretation is to refer to a manuscript, either literally or symbolically, the declamation (humorous, serious, and dramatic), memorized monologues, and play recitals have waned in popularity. More emphasis is placed on stories which are read rather than told because of the necessary or symbolic function of the manuscript. However, storytelling, especially for the purpose of stimulating creative dramatics, has a significant contribution to make in the speech curriculum.

While good oral reading is desirable for communicating many kinds of information, such as news reports, the interpretative reader focuses on literature for pleasure. Traditionally the arts of language have been described as *rhetoric* and *poetic*. Although these forms are not mutually exclusive of one other, the interpreter and actor are more concerned with the art of the poetic which involves material (feelings and ideas) organized to give pleasure to the reader or listeners.[11] The public speaker is more concerned with the art of rhetoric which involves ideas and feelings organized to influence practical action. In public speaking, one may express his own ideas and feelings in his own words; in interpretation, the reader is expressing the ideas and feelings of someone else (the author) and has an obligation to remain true to the intent of the literature.

VALUES OF ORAL INTERPRETATION

The values of oral interpretation are many. Robinson and Kerikas identify seven.

1. It furnishes a vital approach to the study of all types of literature which come alive when read orally.
2. "It allows students to build values acquired through discovering the finest ideas and emotional sensitivity in literature."
3. It is an expressional or therapeutic experience which, when done effectively, gives one a real sense of achievement.
4. "It develops a basic artistic skill that is desirable for itself as a part of speech education."

---

[11]Wilma H. Grimes and Alethea Smith Mattingly, *Interpretation: Writer-Reader-Audience* (Belmont, Calif.: Wadsworth Publishing Company, Inc., 1961), p. 14.

5. It provides a foundation for and acts as a supplement to other kinds of speech training.
6. It motivates and provides the vehicle for improvement in vocal and physical expression.
7. It furnishes excellent opportunities for participation in various interpretative activities both in and out of class and helps to develop cooperative attitudes with group experiences.[12]

Beloof states that a full comprehension of a literary work of art can come only through the participation of our bodies — that the rational process itself is a kind of emotional set which is learned through a certain control of the body. He further validates the study of oral interpretation by declaring that oral interpretation forces the reader and his audience to a realization of their reactions to the work of art. Without this experience, they might not have been aware of these disagreements in interpretation.[13] Veilleux sees oral interpretation as important not only for some of these same reasons but also because such aims "recognize the vital importance of an individual's reaction to literature, and, in a sense, his reaction to the real world around him."[14]

Through vicarious experience the student gains an understanding of other people, an appreciation of aesthetic qualities, and pleasure in literature.

THE LITERATURE, THE READER, THE LISTENER

The interpreter has a wealth of *literature* from which he may choose. He may select poetry, prose, or drama. Lyric, narrative, didactic, and humorous poetry furnish many kinds of selections. Sometimes poetry is classified by topic or theme such as American, twentieth-century, or nature. Prose may be chosen from diaries, essays, short stories, biographies, novels, and other kinds of prose writing. Drama may range from selected scenes to the full-length play. Collections, paperback editions of the selected works of one author, and anthologies are helpful sources. When wide selections are available in a few volumes, hours of searching are lessened. Selecting the proper material requires as much time, if not more so, than preparing the selections for reading.

---

[12]Karl F. Robinson and E.J. Kerikas, *Teaching Speech, Methods and Materials* (New York: David McKay Company, Inc., 1963), p. 440.

[13]Robert Beloof, *The Performing Voice in Literature* (Boston: Little, Brown and Company, 1966), p. 9.

[14]Jere Veilleux, *Oral Interpretation: The Re-creation of Literature* (New York: Harper & Row, Publishers, 1967), p. 2.

Some students have estimated that as much as two hours have been spent selecting material for every minute of reading. This part of the process, however, is usually an enjoyable one for students and allows them to become acquainted with a wide range of material. Sharing sources of potential oral interpretation materials should be a part of the course.

In choosing a selection, the interpreter must be concerned with its literary merit, appropriateness for the audience, and appropriateness for him. Lee has suggested extrinsic and intrinsic factors to consider when evaluating a tentative piece of literature.[15] These extrinsic factors, *universality*, *individuality*, and *suggestion* reveal the literature's relationship to life. *Universality* means that the expressed idea touches on a cultural experience that is common to all people. Thus "love" becomes potentially interesting and meaningful as it evokes a familiar emotional response. Of course, one must recognize that in attitude responses may vary. *Individuality* is the author's ability to approach a universal subject with a creative or fresh approach. Love has been the topic of many literary selections, but when an author through his choice of words or organization or imagery makes it a unique experience, he treats it with individuality. One must have had this experience in some relationship to be in a position to make a comparison. *Suggestion* in writing allows the reader to enrich the subject matter from his own background of experience. This does not mean that the author fails to clarify ideas. It means, rather, that the author permits the reader to participate imaginatively in the literary experience by not telling him everything. For the beginning student, this may be the easiest factor to recognize.

With these guidelines for evaluating the literary selection, the reader should be reasonably assured of audience interest and response. Each of the three may not be equally present in the material but should be identifiable. The intrinsic factors are balance and proportion, unity and harmony, variety and contrast, and rhythm. These are elements which exist within the bounds of the work itself. An appreciation of them does not depend upon one's personal experience, as does the appreciation of extrinsic qualities which are related to human experience. These intrinsic elements give lyrical quality to the literature, lend interest, and blend elements of style into a unifying total effect with clarity and smoothness. Some literature lends itself better to oral reading than other literature. This may be because of content, style of writing, or skill required of the reader.

---

[15]Lee, *op. cit.*, pp. 8, 22.

The *reader* has an obligation to select material which not only interests him but is suitable for him. Since the reader's vocal and physical cues stimulate the listener to respond, they should evoke a listener response favorable to the intent of the literature. If the reader does not have rapport with the literary intent, it becomes difficult to project appropriate cues. Some literary selections are more appropriate for male readers than female, and vice versa. If one does not have vocal or physical qualities which are capable of stimulating the listener to respond properly to the imagery, attention is directed to the reader rather than the literature. What was intended as a serious reading may then become humorous to the listener. When the reader is interested in the literature, it is easier for him to empathize — to become more involved — and to project better cues to the listener. Since the reader responds in terms of his own background of experiences and associations, he will understand some life experiences better than others. If he cannot empathize because he has not encountered the described situation, or anything even remotely associated with it, his reaction may confuse and disturb the listener.

The reader also assumes the responsibility for selecting literature appropriate for the audience. As in any speech situation, the needs of the audience and the occasion must be considered. The same audience dimensions, such as age, sex, education, attitudes, interests, etc., which apply to other communication activities must be examined before the reader can pass judgment on the appropriateness of the literature. Effective communication involves audience analysis.

The *listener* has some responsibilities too. He needs to be a good listener, meaning that he has an obligation to establish an environment for interaction and make an effort to engage actively in the communication process. Since the reader responds to listener stimulus as well as to literature stimulus, the three elements are involved in effective communication. As the listener's literary background becomes more sophisticated in responding to imagery and as his listening skills increase, the quality of his interaction in this communicative act improves.

Preparation of the Literature

After the literature has been selected on the basis of its appropriateness for (1) oral reading, (2) the reader, (3) the occasion, (4) the listener, and (5) its literary worth, the interpreter is ready to engage in *analysis* procedures. As he studies the literature he seeks answers to the questions "Who is speaking?" and "To whom is he speaking?" When the reader discovers the writer's role or viewpoint, he will then have a clue as to how he should adjust his oral style to the written style. It is important to identify the purpose and theme. Titles may reveal themes. Themes may also be an expression of an author's attitudes and are sometimes discovered in the style of writing. A study of both Dickinson's and Poe's works reveal their respective attitudes to an oft-repeated theme — death. To study an author's life is a way of discovering the motivation for his writing. The location, time, and characters along with various details and imagery are used to evoke atmosphere, moods, and emotions. An understanding of the historical period and cultural environment in which a story takes place helps the reader to project more accurately the appropriate cues. The choice of subject, organization, use of language, punctuation, or lack of it (e.g., E. E. Cummings) may all contain clues to help the reader arrive at some judgments concerning the intent of the literature. Unusual words, figures of speech (e.g., allusion, simile, metaphor, analogy, personification, apostrophe, synecdoche, metonymy), repetition, symbolism, emphasis and climax, use of imagery, and numerous other elements aid the reader in finding and expressing the meaning of the printed page.

Through *denotation,* the author is able to express meaning with precision, but the reader must go beyond exact words to the author's indirect appeal (meaning beyond meaning). Through *connotation* or suggested meaning the author forces the reader to gain new insight into experience. The teacher increases the student's ability for implications of poetry as he acquaints him with figures of speech and imagery.

Research is often necessary to render accurate literary judgments. In the poem "When the Hounds of Spring are on Winter's Traces," Swinburne makes frequent references to classical Greek culture. The "mother of months" is Artemus or Diana, virgin goddess of the moon and hunting; the "Maenad" are female worshippers of Pan and Bacchus. The entire selection is a hymn or invocation to a great spirit and suggests the largeness of the Greek chorus. If students fail to analyze the literature, they diminish considerably the possibility of effectively communicating the meaning. Library materials and literary resources must be made available not only to aid the student in selecting the literature but also to help him engage in proper literary analysis. The speech teacher needs to assist the student in how to approach this process and to suggest a reasonable sequence to follow.

If the author's intent is to stress rhythm or sound, as is often the case in Vachel Lindsay's works, the student will learn this as he reads Lindsay's poetry, biographies, or critical reviews of his works. Thus he will better understand the need for exaggerating the rhythm in a selection such as "The Congo."

Just as words give clues to meaning, so they also indicate how that meaning might best be expressed vocally and physically. As the language stimulates the senses to respond, the voice and body feel compelled to react accordingly. As the student becomes involved in the *imagery*, he will respond with a greater sense of freedom. *Imagery* amplifies an idea, intensifies an emotion, and contributes to the total work. The words serve as stimuli to help the reader recall past experiences and recapture impressions. Sometimes the appeal in imagery may be visual; sometimes auditory. It could also include other varieties or combinations of images with sensory appeal. The following passages are examples of words being used to evoke such a response.

"Love, with little hands
Comes and touches you." (tactile)

"The cold within him froze his old features, nipped his pointed nose, shrivelled his cheek, stiffened his gait, made his eyes red, his thin lips blue, and spoke out shrewdly in his grating voice." (visual, auditory, and kinesthetic[16])

"The good smell of old clothes." (olfactory)

"Furious, single horsemen gallop.
Hark! A shout — a crash — a groan." (auditory)

As students are asked to identify the different kinds of imagery, they develop more awareness of how the author uses it. The reader, as he empathizes with the literature, should select vocal and physical responses which give the listener cues consistent with the literary experience.

In some selections it is impossible to determine the literary intent. This is where the reader must make some judgments concerning the literature and how it is to be interpreted. The decision might be based on some related experience. It then becomes the responsibility of the reader to justify his interpretation of the intent of the literature by attempting to evoke a listener response favorable to his judgment.

Students may neglect to prepare the literature carefully in their eagerness to "perform." However, several thorough critiques should be effective in revealing weaknesses in this phase of the process. Students may also have a tendency to select too many pieces of literature for the allotted preparation time. It is part of the instructional process to acquaint them with the desirability of quality preparation. To help students acquire a sense of performance — a desire to share the litera-ture — and to maintain control of what appears to be an easy and natural presentation often requires hours of concentrated work.

Some literary selections, especially novels, are too long to use without *cutting*. There may also be other factors which would make them inappropriate. It is permissible to eliminate, adapt, or condense without

---

[16]Kinesthetic imagery refers to muscle tension and relaxation.

destroying the effect. The teacher should direct students to make cuttings which will not distort the meaning of the book. Students should never be permitted to deface books. Introductions can help the audience to understand the portion selected for oral reading. Sufficient numbers of copies, access to duplication services, readability, and folders for easy use of materials are a part of good course organization.

Presentation of Material

Once the student feels he has discovered the intent of the literature, he practices orally his *vocal and physical responses* to the literature which he believes will elicit a favorable response from the audience. Training in the use of body and voice learned in a basic speech course relates to this phase of the process. The more skillful the interpreter is in utilizing gesture, posture, movement, facial expression, and muscle tone (degree of body tension to suggest an emotional state), then the more capable he is of enhancing the literature. He must constantly remember that it is a suggestive physical cue for which he strives. The actor may literally strike out in a physical response; the interpreter tenses the muscles and merely suggests such an action. This controlled restraint is often difficult for beginning oral interpretation students who find it easier to literally fulfill the action rather than suggest it to the listener and let him fulfill the experience. The reader does not engage in lateral action on stage as fully as an actor, nor does he employ all the theatrical devices of drama. The skill with which he is able to suggest a literary experience, primarily through auditory appeal, requires artistry. Once the student has learned these arts, he often finds oral reading challenging and exciting.

Similar restraints apply to the use of vocal elements. Voice production and word production exercises are important to help the interpreter gain vocal facility. Subtleties in pitch, quality, rate, volume, and pronunciation lend much vocal variety. Basic speech books which contain breathing exercises and voice and articulation drills furnish supplementary opportunities to improve range and intelligibility of speech. The use of a tape recorder may help to sensitize students to meaningful sounds. Phrasing (reading words together which belong together according to meaning) usually requires additional attention, especially for poetry, since students often read line by line rather than by the idea. Of course, all responses must be dictated by the literature. No student should be permitted to engage in these techniques for any other reason. To do so is to return to the exaggerated and artificial displays of the elocutionist.

If the student has not had a basic speech course in which he has had an opportunity to develop physical and vocal skills, supplemental work will be needed to help him in the skillful presentation of the literature.

It is not difficult for oral interpretation students to recognize the contribution of a basic speech course and a basic drama course in developing techniques and skills to enhance oral reading. Likewise oral interpretation skills complement those skills emphasized in other speech arts. The speech teacher who has worked in various speech forms should recognize these relationships and help students develop a similar awareness for meaningful learning.

To prepare the audience for the literature, the student should establish the proper setting so that listener will understand the meaning more readily. This is the purpose of the *introduction*. It should not duplicate what is to be read but should capture attention and focus on the selection. Sometimes the reader wishes to establish a mood rather than an intellectual understanding. In the introduction the student has direct audience contact and establishes rapport with a conversational mode of speaking. A slight pause should follow the introduction before the oral reading commences. The more subjective the literature, the more indirect the audience-reader contact. Looking into the realm of the audience does not demand direct eye contact, especially in a selection where the reader appears to be expressing personal thoughts within himself.

Beginning students of interpretation should work initially with only one or two characters in the story. To handle the placement and *focus* in the realm of the audience with more than two characters demands greater skill in suggesting physical and vocal differences and in maintaining consistency of focus. It is also difficult for students to engage in rapid conversation between or among characters while still suggesting characterization and attempting to read effectively from a manuscript. It may be necessary to memorize this portion of the literature or at least be familiar enough not to worry about losing one's place while referring to the manuscript.

It is easy for the listener to identify the well motivated reader — the one who desires to communicate the literature. Such a person assists the listener to respond and to find pleasure in doing so. As in all communications, those characteristics which we describe as personality are an inherent part of the reader in this process.

Evaluation

If the listener responds to the literature in the way in which the reader intended, then the oral reading is successful. Success is also determined by the apparent ease and naturalness with which the interpreter presents his material. When the audience is painfully aware of the struggle involved in the oral and literary analysis, the focus is not on the literary experience.

Speech teachers should be concerned about the total effect or *general effectiveness* of the communicative act of oral interpretation. Criteria relating to the total effect include the worth of the literature, the desire of the reader to communicate, the relation of the reader's personality to the selected literature, and the ease with which the reader handles the manuscript. Also included in the total effect are the relationships of the vocal and physical cues to the literature. These may be separated into specific elements to aid students in identifying and improving the readings. *Vocal responsiveness* should be examined for motivation, intensity, pause, tempo, volume, phrasing, pitch, and meaningful and intelligible sounds. The teacher and students should also listen for mispronounced words when evaluating readings. *Physical responsiveness* should be examined for motivation and totality of the response. Other criteria are appropriate focus (in the audience realm) and maintaining suggestion, not literally fulfilling the response. The *introduction*, which establishes the setting for the literary selection, should be evaluated for stimulating content and a delivery of a more direct conversational mode than is used for the actual reading.

A checklist which would expedite the evaluation process but also allow for additional comments permits the teacher or students to move quite rapidly from one reading to another. It is suggested that if students use such a checklist that they not be required to evaluate several consecutive readings. It is also recommended that comments and criticism of students be averaged to avoid a distorted response from students. A suggested interpretation checklist for classroom use follows.

Classroom Interpretation Checklist[17]

Name_____ Assignment_____

INTRODUCTION:

Effective delivery	_____	Content stimulating	_____
Ineffective delivery	_____	Content not stimulating	_____
Effectiveness inconsistent	_____	Content uneven	_____

---

[17]Developed in the Communication Division, Department of Speech, Keith Brooks, Chairman, The Ohio State University.

VOCAL RESPONSIVENESS:

Meaningful sounds	___	Intelligibility good	___
Sounds not meaningful	___	Intelligibility not good	___
Meaningfulness inconsistent	___	Intelligibility inconsistent	___
Volume appropriate	___	Pitch appropriate	___
Volume inappropriate	___	Pitch inappropriate	___
Appropriateness inconsistent	___	Appropriateness inconsistent	___
Tempo appropriate	___	Phrasing appropriate	___
Tempo inappropriate	___	Phrasing inappropriate	___
Appropriateness inconsistent	___	Appropriateness inconsistent	___
Intensity appropriate	___	Well motivated	___
Intensity inappropriate	___	Not well motivated	___
Appropriateness inconsistent	___	Motivation inconsistent	___

Mispronounced words:_____

PHYSICAL RESPONSIVENESS:

Totality of responsiveness	___	Realm of suggestion maintained	___
Lack of totality	___	Responsiveness too literal	___
Inconsistent	___	Responsiveness inconsistent	___
Responsiveness motivated	___	Appropriate focus	___
Responsiveness not motivated	___	Inappropriate focus	___
Motivation inconsistent	___	Appropriately sustained	___

GENERAL EFFECTIVENESS:

Reader's personality helpful	___	Desire to communicate obvious	___
Personality not helpful	___	Desire not obvious	___
Sufficient manuscript familiarity	___	Material worthy	___
Insufficient familiarity	___	Material challenging	___
		Not challenging	___

*ADDITIONAL COMMENTS:*_____

_____

_____

_____

                          Grade_____

Evaluation may involve objective or essay tests asking students to offer constructive oral comments, or requiring them to furnish written responses to the literature. Such questions as the following might be asked:

1) What do you think the literature meant?
2) Could you hear and understand the reader?
3) Where, if anywhere, did you feel the vocal or physical cues were inconsistent with the literature?
4) Was the realm of suggestion maintained?
5) Was the introduction effective?
6) Were you motivated to respond to the literature?
7) Any additional comments?

Self-evaluation procedures are helpful. Once students realize that critiques are valuable for improved readings, they will view evaluation as an integral part of the total process.

It must be remembered that since the listener is an element in the communicative act of oral interpretation, all evaluation must not focus only on the reader. Any suggestions for increasing and developing better listening skills and sensitivity to imagery belong to this process.

ORGANIZING THE COURSE

It has been the general practice in teaching speech at the secondary level to include a unit on oral interpretation in the basic speech course. Seldom does oral interpretation exist as a separate course of study at the high school level. Sometimes oral interpretation is included in an English course. Since most instruction in this area must be organized in a unit usually ranging from two to six weeks and occasionally may be expanded to one semester, all of the content which rightfully belongs to oral interpretation cannot possibly be included in such a limited experience. The better informed the teacher, the greater will be his ability to see the total field and to select from that field the content he feels will be the most meaningful. Each student should understand the process of literature selection, analysis, preparation, presentation, and evaluation.

One way of getting students involved immediately is by asking each student to share orally some prose or poetry which he especially likes. Interest is further stimulated by reading to the students. If the teacher is not a skilled reader, one can invite guest readers or utilize commercial recordings. Criticism and theory should become a part of the reading activities. When problems which relate to vocal elements are noted, the teacher may wish to suggest some drills to sensitize students to these particular problems. Recording students' initial readings and then comparing them with readings made later in the unit helps students to evaluate their own progress. Self-evaluation is an important part of the oral interpretation unit.

Class programs are often based on various themes or works of one author. When students are motivated by a desire to share the literature, they may wish to extend the reading experience to a situation outside the classroom. This acquaints them with different audiences and contributes to their ability to engage in evaluation and further growth.

A possible organizational structure for a unit on oral interpretation is as follows:

1) Principles of oral interpretation
2) Interpretation of poetry
3) Interpretation of prose
4) Interpretation of drama
5) Group interpretation

Elements of narration, which would be discussed in interpretation of dramatic literature, could be used to introduce storytelling. If creative dramatics is included in the school's program, one might choose to offer experiences in storytelling as a part of the creative improvisations.

If one decides to use the organizational structure of immediately involving students with the sharing of literature, the principles of oral interpretation will evolve instructionally as a part of the process of sharing and evaluating. Students who are encouraged to share literature will be encouraged to read more widely.

Group Interpretation

Most classroom experiences in oral interpretation involve solo readers. However group readings have become more popular at the secondary level, largely because of the increased emphasis and interest at the university and college level in Readers' Theatre. *Choric interpretation* or choral speaking, which has been in existence since the early Greek chorus, can be a moving experience when group readers react in a unified manner. However, this orchestration is sometimes quite difficult. Choric groups are usually divided into "light" and "dark" voices. Male voices are generally the "dark" voices. Groups may be further divided if necessary. The basic principles of oral interpretation apply to choral reading. For initial experiences, it may help to select literature which utilizes many opportunities for solo work with designated lines, or refrains employing group response. Since many nursery rhymes use this approach, the teacher might include these as drill to acquaint students with choral effect and then move into other types of literature, such as Biblical psalms. The teacher, or director of the choir, serves as a coordinator. Once a group has had some practice in working together, vocal blending and unified meaning contribute to an expressive literary experience.

Readers' Theatre, or interpreters' theatre, has been variously defined but generally refers to group reading of literature involving delineated characters, with or without a narrator, in such a way as to establish the focus in the audience realm. The principles of oral interpretation apply to keep the action in the imagination of the audience and not onstage with the readers. Group reading of expository prose, which involves no readers assuming character parts, would not be considered Readers' Theatre according to this definition. All group reading is not necessarily a specialized form. Readers' Theatre strives primarily for auditory effects rather than visual, dialogue rather than action. Some lighting or suggestive costuming or props may be used but these should not shift attention away from the literature. Staging for Readers' Theatre is primarily psychological rather than literal and emphasizes the relationships of the characters to each other. The number of readers may vary according to the demands of the literature and the stage area.

Students have a tendency to confuse Readers' Theatre and drama. The difference primarily is one of emphasis and proportion.[18] The interpreter, with a manuscript and few theatrical devices, succeeds best on the whole when he places his scene offstage; the actor, without a manuscript and with fuller use of theatrical devices, usually succeeds best when he places his scene onstage.[19] Students who are just starting to use this convention should restrict themselves to the principles of oral interpretation. Once they are working rather well with this medium, more flexibility may be permitted. In fact, as students become more

---

[18]Wallace A. Bacon, *The Art of Interpretation* (New York: Holt, Rinehart & Winston, 1966), p. 317.
[19]*Ibid.*

skillful and confident, experimental techniques which enhance the literary experience may be encouraged. The literature itself should determine what is appropriate. For example, a play which is dependent upon stage business or make-up may prove unsuitable. In some cases, the play may be adapted by using descriptive passages to accomplish through auditory appeal what the author originally planned as visual. It is better to use another medium than to distort the intent of the literature.

Chamber Theatre has been described as a method of staging prose fiction, retaining the text of the story but locating the scenes of the story onstage.[20] The narrator may summarize or describe, and then scenes may be dramatized. It is not a fully staged play, but the narrative form moves from direct discourse to stage performance. Chamber Theatre attempts to retain through the narrator the past tense of fiction while simply staging present tense scenes (drama) in the past tense. Thus it becomes necessary to continue asking some of the questions mentioned earlier in this chapter about whose story it is, and so forth, if one is to maintain perspective within prose fiction. Since most stories are too long for a reasonable performance time, adaptations must usually be made. Stories with pronounced psychological interest or conflict between the narrator and characters appear better suited for Chamber Theatre.

Contests and Festivals

Secondary forensic contests still contain some declamation events, but emphasis on oral interpretation activities usually occurs in the festivals. Within recent years there has been an increase in secondary prose and poetry reading and Readers' Theatre. Much of the interest has been created by the colleges and universities which have sponsored such events or have promoted these activities through professional channels. Teachers feel the educational values of festivals are justified by the critiques offered by professionals and the opportunities to observe other presentations. The major emphasis is on improving quality. In an attempt to focus on educational aspects, such elements as competition, awards, and rank are minimized. Sometimes group oral interpretation activities are scheduled as dramatic events.

In selecting literary material for such events, teachers and students are using fewer professionally prepared readings. Students are encouraged to read widely in contemporary literature to become acquainted with material suitable for these special occasions. Students, under the teacher's supervision, often make appropriate cuttings. Each year more stimulating

---

[20]*Ibid.*, p. 319.

and challenging selections are being presented in the secondary festivals. The Interpretation Interest Group of the Speech Association of America can supply some guidelines for use of material in oral reading contests.

Since there are some specific rules to be observed in a contest or festival, the speech teacher should inquire of the sponsor as to their expectations. State speech leagues also furnish information governing presentations. Chapter 12 discusses more fully these out-of-class activities.

ORAL INTERPRETATION RESOURCES

Numerous sources for suitable oral interpretation materials are available to the secondary teacher of speech. These may exist in the form of general popular magazine stories and articles or in the form of specific materials prepared for the oral interpreter. Indexes are useful in locating selections. Some of these are the *Short Story Index, Granger's Index to Poetry and Recitations, Index to Plays,* and the *Speech Index.* Anthologies, paperbacks, collections of prose, poetry, and plays supply important sources. Bibliographies prepared by a special group such as a committee of the Interpretation Interest Group of the Speech Association of America may be obtained upon request. Other bibliographies (e.g. Readers' Theatre bibliographies) are excellent sources. Oral interpretation textbooks, especially those prepared for college teaching, contain many suggestions and selections. Professional speech journals and English journals should not be overlooked. Many recordings prepared by professional readers are also available.

The problem today is not one of how and where to obtain sufficient material, but rather of what material to select and how to prepare that material for presentation. Students indicate they are sometimes frustrated by the abundance of literature and often require more assistance in this phase. Once they select what they believe is appropriate, they usually become more independent in applying the analysis procedures. The teacher acts as a critical advisor in the synthesis phase as the student works for the total effect and requests professional reactions.

Currently oral interpretation activities are popular with teachers of speech and English. A review of professional programs indicates a strong interest in this area. By affiliating with a professional group interested in developing oral interpretation, the secondary speech teacher will have access to services and materials which he as an individual could not provide. These opportunities should be investigated by the teacher who is attempting to develop a sound educational program in speech.

Suggested Projects

1. Abstract ten articles which would be helpful to high school students of oral interpretation.

2. List ten resources for oral interpretation which you would recommend that the school librarian purchase. These may be books, records, films, or other materials. State the unique contributions each resource makes to the speech program.

3. Prepare a twenty-minute program based on the works of one author. List materials consulted in researching his life and works. Request classmates to react by using the evaluation checklist given in this chapter.

4. Prepare a twenty-minute group program based on a theme. In addition to the evaluation checklist in this chapter, direct specific attention to the relationship of the physical arrangement of the group to the theme and the continuity of the program. Request oral self-evaluation from the group.

5. Compile a list of suitable selections for the following categories of a high school interpretation festival:
>   poetry reading
>   prose reading
>   drama reading

6. Select three suitable stories for each of the following age groups:
>   primary (grades K-3)
>   upper elementary (grades 4-6)
>   junior high
>   high school

Consult with the school librarian to determine their appropriateness.

7. Prepare a cutting for a thirty-minute Readers' Theatre program using a narrator. Briefly describe suggestive staging, lighting, props, or costuming. Request class evaluation.

8. Attend an oral interpretation event (Readers' Theatre, festival, poetry or prose program, choral speaking, etc.). Prepare a written critique based on literary worth, audience analysis, preparation, and presentation.

9. Prepare a resource file of selections for drill exercises on articulation, phrasing, inflection, rate, breathing, dynamics, and use of imagery.

10. Using a twentieth-century poem, list steps in the process of literary and vocal analysis, preparation, presentation, and evaluation.

11. Prepare a two-week oral interpretation unit with lesson plans and resource materials. Include behavioral objectives and explain how the unit is to be evaluated.

12. Select and arrange a piece of literature for choral speaking. Make copies and experiment by using your classmates as the speaking chorus. Evaluate.

References

Bacon, Wallace A. *The Art of Interpretation*. New York: Holt, Rinehart & Winston, 1966.

Bahn, Eugene. "Epochs in the History of Oral Interpretation," *The Communicative Arts and Sciences of Speech,* ed. Keith Brooks. Columbus, Ohio: Charles E. Merrill Publishing Company, 1967.

Beloof, Robert. *The Performing Voice in Literature*. Boston: Little, Brown and Company, 1966.

Brooks, Keith, Bahn, Eugene, and Okey, L. Lamont. *The Communicative Act of Oral Interpretation*. Boston: Allyn and Bacon, Inc., 1967.

Brooks, Keith. "The Communicative Act of Oral Interpretation," *The Communicative Arts and Sciences of Speech,* ed. Keith Brooks. Columbus, Ohio: Charles E. Merrill Publishing Company, 1967.

Grimes, Wilma H. and Mattingly, Alethea Smith. *Interpretation: Writer – Reader – Audience*. Belmont, California: Wadsworth Publishing Company, Inc., 1961.

Lee, Charlotte I. *Oral Interpretation*. 3rd ed.; Boston: Houghton Mifflin Company, 1965.

Robinson, Karl F. and Kerikas, E. J. *Teaching Speech, Methods and Materials*. New York: David McKay Company, Inc., 1963.

Veilleux, Jere. *Oral Interpretation: The Re-creation of Literature*. New York: Harper & Row, Publishers, 1967.

Woolbert, Charles H. and Nelson, Severina E. *The Art of Interpretative Speech*. Rev. ed.; New York: F. S. Crofts & Co., 1940.

9

Conversation, Discussion, and Debate

CONVERSATION

One of the curses of the speech profession is the misconception that the study of speech and speech-making is analogous to studying how to walk or swim — most of us can do it anyway, and since we can do it, we can do it well. We are derided when certain practices are mentioned, practices such as teaching how to talk on the telephone and how to get a date.

The population at large has a somewhat unfavorable image of professionals in speech education because many of our colleagues have taught telephone and personal conversation as a kind of "social nicety," like flower arrangement or social etiquette. Our concern with conversation is of a different character. We do not propose to establish a set of rules for conversation. What we shall do is to enumerate the basic principles of interpersonal communication and suggest that most if not all of them are appropriate in developing effective personal relations in conversational situations with our fellow man. The effective individual (or conversationalist, or communicator) is one who adapts to and thus is sensitive to people and things about him.

We shall view conversation as *interpersonal behavior,* operating according to certain principles, with a body of knowledge about this operation. The kind of conversation we shall discuss is founded in behavioral research. It involves speaker awareness and adaptation of his listeners and is the most difficult and yet the most intimate form of interaction with other humans. Interpersonal communication occurs in a variety of forms and circumstances. These situations can be viewed as points on a continuum of formality ranging from highly informal conversation on one end through discussion and to debate at the formal end of the scale.

Principles of Communication Applicable to Conversation

(1) Individual attention is highly selective and comparatively brief.[1] We choose to attend to those stimuli about us which are attractive to us, and we shift from stimulus to stimulus as our attention for those simuli varies. Because of the brevity of attention, we should make our verbal contributions as short as possible. No one wants to listen to someone who is long-winded. Brevity, if for no other reason than it is novel, will help to keep the person with whom you are communicating tuned in to you.

(2) People grasp and are more interested in examples than they are in abstractions. Examples come alive, anchoring us to real life experiences. Lengthy abstractions or complex thoughts which do not make frequent reference to concrete matters are difficult to follow. To be sure that others are listening and are interested in what you have to say, distribute illustrations liberally.

(3) Determine your listeners' interest. There is no greater insurance against failure in communication than a thorough job of audience analysis. You cannot adapt if you do not understand. Whether by question, inference, or information provided by others, decide what resources your listener(s) have—knowledge, attitudes, interest, attention—and then adjust your remarks to those variables.

(4) Speaking is an ego-building behavior so let the other fellow have the floor. Don't build just your own ego. There is nothing more tiring than a one-sided conversation in which a speaker outlines all his interests and experiences for his silent partner. The other person is silent likely because he cannot get a word in edgewise. Give someone else a chance to express himself, and he will then be more willing to listen to you.

---

[1]Jon Eisenson, J. Jeffrey Auer, and John R. Irwin, *The Psychology of Communication* (New York: Appleton-Century-Crofts, 1963), p. 238.

(5) Organized ideas are easier to follow than disorganized ones.[2] A person who is totally disorganized in his thinking is generally regarded as having certain mental deficiencies. A common but not institutionally curable mental shortcoming of many of us is some disorganization of thinking. We may jump from one phase of a subject to another; our pattern of thinking or development may not be at all clear or sensible to others. If we systematically organize (and nearly any system is better than none at all) what we want to say, it will mean more, will more likely stimulate a response from another, and will be a positive contribution.

(6) Listen to what is said. That's a very easy piece of advice to accept but one that most of us have great difficulty putting into practice. Studies of listening behavior have demonstrated that most of us are inefficient listeners, capable of recalling only 25 per cent of what we hear a few moments after we hear it.[3] One of the reasons for this failure of listening is that we are thinking ahead or going off on tangents as a result of some word or phrase uttered by the speaker. The speaker hits on a pet prejudice we hold and immediately we begin to think about our conception of that idea instead of listening to what the speaker is saying. By this time he has made his point and we, if we want to discover what he has said, must ask him to repeat it. Most of the time this would be an embarrassing act so we merely nod and act as if we heard and understood everything.

DISCUSSION

Moving from the highly informal and casual context of conversation at one end of our continuum to formal, structured problem-solving at the other, we come next to discussion. A more adequate understanding and appreciation of discussion is gained if we first define the term. Discussion can be distinguished from casual social conversation, ". . . which is undirected and seldom sticks long to one topic."[4] It is unlike other forms of public speech in which one person speaks in a rather formal context, while others listen. In discussion there are no speeches delivered, no rebuttals presented, no hard stands taken. In short, *discussion is a group effort to solve problems and arrive at decisions through an oral inter-*

---

[2]*Ibid.*, pp. 248-249.
[3]Ralph Nichols, "Do We Know How to Listen? Practical Helps in a Modern Age," *The Speech Teacher,* 10:120 (March, 1961).
[4]William E. Utterback, *Group Thinking and Conference Leadership* (New York: Holt, Rinehart & Winston, 1957), p. 7.

change of ideas. Discussion stresses a spirit of inquisitiveness and not advocacy. Discussion is often regarded as a preliminary to debate because through discussion and group interaction we attempt to explore the merits of the various available positions before we commit ourselves to the advocacy of one.

Discussion as Social Interaction

There are two useful ways of looking at discussion: (1) as social interaction and (2) as problem-solving behavior. These categories are not mutually exclusive, but they reflect the primary emphasis given to the dynamics of group behavior.

In teaching discussion as social interaction we ought to place the emphasis on learning to understand one another. This "understanding" is not merely an acknowledgment that the other person exists; it is an attempt to appreciate the influences, forces, and motivations which lead an individual to say a particular thing or to behave in a particular way. This is an exceedingly difficult task, but it is possible to achieve if we ask certain key questions about the person being analyzed. Why is he associated with this group? Is he interested in the question being discussed? Does he have a vested interest in supporting a given position? This is only the beginning of a long list of very basic questions that must be answered to determine the reasons for individual behavior.

Through this study of motivations and influences, we can develop more "trust" for the other person and understand what he is likely to say or feel in a discussion situation. When we understand, we do not disagree frequently; much of discussion disagreement arises because persons are suspicious or ignorant of the feelings or motives of others. The development of "trust" through knowledge of others may result in the following dimensions of behavior:

1) accepting the influence of others,
2) accepting the motives of others,
3) accepting deviant behavior of others,
4) nonconformity to group opinion,
5) increased communication with others,
6) increased communication of one's personal opinions, and
7) increased liking for others.[5]

---

[5]Kim Giffin, "Interpersonal Trust in Small Group Communication," *Quarterly Journal of Speech,* 52:234 (October, 1967).

Trust thus becomes a two-way street. We learn to accept the reactions of others because we have a basic understanding of the motives for their behavior. At the same time we are more willing to reveal our true feelings and reactions because we realize that the others are, at least, aware of our probable response to the idea under discussion. Trust then becomes the removal of uncertainty, and the discussion participants develop more of an interest in the process and an appreciation and liking for it.

Small Group Behavior. Group behavior is essentially a composite of the individual behaviors. Certain actions are more likely in group situations than they would be alone, but no action which would be alien to the individual when alone is likely to be carried out when in a group. Perhaps the key to social interaction in the small group is the matter of conformity. Individual identification is lost in the process of behaving in ways which are positively reinforced by the group:

> Thus it is that group opinion often influences belief and behavior more than does expert opinion, and that a tendency to conform is common enough to be called a characteristic of groups.[6]

Students, even in small groups, are creatures of conformity and can be expected to behave in a way that will be accepted and rewarded by their peers.

Discussion as Problem-Solving Behavior

The more traditional approach to group activity has been that of discussion as exploration oriented toward problem solution. Discussion is an instrument for cooperative investigation and the evaluation of thought. The emphasis is placed on the end product instead of upon the ways persons behave as they work toward the product. Since the emphasis is upon outcomes, the method for arriving at decisions is more prescriptive; the steps are more exacting and more clearly defined than when discussion is considered as social interaction. Utterback refers to the matter of "the discipline of thinking together."[7] He is talking about the formally constituted discussion group with an appointed leader, a prepared agenda following the steps of reflective thinking, and a membership aware of their individual functions as effective discussants. The approach to the "discussion process" is far removed from what Hare describes as:

---

[6]Eisenson, *op. cit.,* p. 256.
[7]Utterback, *op. cit.,* p. 9.

The description of the behavior of an individual from the interactional point of view . . . how he acts toward others (output) . . . how others respond to him (input).[8]

Modern investigators of discussion are coming to a concept of discussion which utilizes the best of both forms — a problem-solving procedure which places primary emphasis on the behavior of the individual as he engages in exploratory, interpersonal activity.

At the high school level, since most students are unfamiliar with the process of reflective thought and its values and adaptations, the most usable format for instruction and participation in discussion probably is the problem-solution approach. Emphasis is upon the definition and the consensus of the group process. Leadership is clearly defined. A discussion leader usually is appointed and his responsibilities are explicitly stated, as are the behaviors of the discussants. The advantages of the social interaction approach can be integrated with the problem-solution method, but since emphasis must be placed on one of the two methods, the problem-solution attack will provide the advantage of structure as well as a clear understanding of the responsibilities of each participant.

A FORMAT FOR DISCUSSION

Types of Discussion Questions

It would be impossible to identify all of the kinds of questions which lend themselves to consideration through discussion. Utterback's categories are useful in "pigeonholing" questions as types that are useful for discussion. These are (1) problems of group action, and (2) problems of public policy.[9]

Problems of Group Action. A group action question is one that is immediate and usually local; it is the type of problem that relates only to the community or group in which it is discussed. For example, a discussion of such questions as "How can we raise money for the new band uniforms?" or "How can we increase student support for the track team?" fit into this category. When questions of this type are chosen for discussion, a solution is imperative; there is no choice about the existence of a problem. The objective is action by the group on a matter

---

[8]A. Paul Hare, *Handbook of Small Group Research* (New York: The Free Press, 1962), p. 13.
[9]Utterback, *op. cit.*, pp. 18-19.

which calls for the formulation of a policy. Classroom discussions of this character would probably involve some kind of activity by the members of the discussion group on the recommended action.

In most school systems and communities there is no dearth of problems. So many of the discussion questions used in classrooms and in extracurricular participation are group action in type. Students also find it relatively easy to become involved in questions of this type. The problem is near at hand and they have become familiar with it; now they are asked to assist in formulating an answer to the question. Group action questions are useful to initiate discussion activity.

Problems of Public Policy. Matters which relate to the state, national, or international community are problems of public policy. The question usually is one of substantial public concern and is a matter which has received considerable coverage in the media. Among discussion questions which are public policy are: "What action should we take to curb inflation?" or "How can our relations with Red China be improved?" or "How can we reduce the number of deaths from traffic accidents?" Each of these has implications outside the immediate community, and the questions are of significant interest to society at large.

These questions should also be timely and controversial. For instance, there are several suggestions available about how we could improve our relations with Red China. It might be appropriate for us to drop our opposition to UN membership for Communist China. Perhaps we should recognize two Chinese governments: one in exile and one on the mainland. We might discontinue our overt assistance to the government of Nationalist China on Formosa. Each of these possible solutions is, to say the least, controversial. But these questions are the heart of discussion and they stimulate student involvement. They are not as immediately involving as are the questions of group action, but they are questions that *should* matter to students.

Characteristics of Good Discussion Questions

All discussion questions should be: (1) *Immediate.* They should be matters of the moment. The questions should concern issues which are in dispute at the time of the discussion. Although the question of income tax is a perennial issue, the discussion of "Should we adopt a graduated income tax in the US?" is clearly out of date. Students could understandably not become excited about the prospect of discussing a topic which might have been current twenty-five years ago but is no longer current.

(2) *Controversial.* The sample topic of graduated income tax was at one time a highly controversial matter, but it no longer is. Social security was a "socialistic" activity when it was initiated, but it has now come to be part of our way of life. In view of the recent spate of assassinations of public figures, the question of "Should presidential candidates be permitted to campaign freely in this country?" has become a highly controversial question. Likewise, "What kind of firearms control is needed in this nation?" is a matter of substantial public dispute. Controversial questions encourage student participation and insure the success of the discussion process.

(3) *Worthwhile.* The matter should justify giving time to it during class. Occasionally, some questions which fall into the category of group action may not be worthwhile in the mind of the teacher. Usually though they are of substantial significance from the point of view of personal appearance or responsibility. In this category we could place questions related to the length of student's hair, skirt length, or loud mufflers on automobiles.

(4) *Cultivate involvement.* If the preceding guidelines are followed, then students will become involved because of the demanding nature of the question. They will see the question as worthwhile and immediate to them, and on these bases they will become involved. If the question does not encourage involvement, then the discussion process is of negligible value.

Wording of Good Discussion Questions. Discussion questions are substantially different from, for example, debate propositions. Since discussion is a method of inquiry and not advocacy, the discussion topic must reflect this spirit of investigation.

(1) *Objective and unbiased.* The discussion question should be phrased as an interrogative permitting a variety of answers. For example, the discussion question, "How should the President of the US be elected?" is open to several answers. The outcome of this discussion might be "through a direct vote of the people," "through the Electoral College only," "by a vote of the representatives and senators in each state," or any one of a variety of other approaches.

The question should not bias the outcome of the discussion and should not "beg the question" by assuming that something is proved which has not been proved. For example, the following discussion question fits in this category. "How should the spendthrift policies of the present administration be reduced?" The consideration of a question of this type will bias the outcome of the discussion.

(2) *Brief and clearly stated.* The less cumbersome and involved the discussion question is, the greater the probability that fruitful discussion

will result. The question used earlier is illustrative. "How should the President of the US be elected?" is clear and brief, but one who did not understand the process of wording a discussion question might phrase a topic of this type in one of the following manners: "Should the President of the US be elected by a proportional electoral system in which electoral votes are allocated on the basis of the percentage of the popular vote, or should he be elected by a direct vote of the people?" "In Presidential elections, how should the outcome be decided?" Both of these wordings are certainly less than clear, and in the case of the first question the wording is very cumbersome.

(3) *Timely.* Discussion questions should be matters of significance to the participants in relation to contemporary society. Students find it difficult to become excited about a topic which is not relevant to them, so whether the question is one of public policy or group action, it should be phrased in terms of the *here and now.*

Getting Organized for Discussion

After we have arrived at a tentative phrasing of the question and before the actual discussion begins, certain procedures must be specified. These procedures include (1) the preparation of the agenda, (2) the preparation of the participants, (3) the cultivation of proper attitudes, and (4) discussion thinking.

Preparing an Agenda. An *agenda* is an outline of the course of action or investigation. Preparing an agenda for a discussion requires that we "map" the direction of our discussion. This map will identify major "boundaries" or steps in the discussion and will enable us to follow the "route signs" or directions that will take us to our destination. Utterback outlines the agenda steps as:

1) Statement and definition of the problem.
2) Examination of the facts out of which the problem arises.
3) Consideration of the criteria to be used in evaluating solutions.
4) Examination and appraisal of solutions.
5) Consideration of the steps to be taken in carrying out the solution adopted.[10]

To be able to state and define the problem for discussion, we must first analyze the problem. Students must be encouraged to discover what the situation really is—the background and implications of the problem. This statement and definition of the problem involves deciding what to

---

[10]*Ibid.,* p. 34.

exclude from the discussion and what to include. Student research will reveal, in the background of the question, what matters are truly relevant to the inquiry — what the facts are.

Let us use, for illustrative purposes, the discussion question phrased earlier: "How should the President of the US be elected?" We first want to determine what the nature of the present situation is in respect to the election of the President. What strengths and weaknesses exist? The President may be elected by a minority of the people. In fact, in the election of 1888, President Harrison was elected with only 47.8 per cent of the popular vote. His major opponent, Grover Cleveland, received 48.6 per cent of the popular vote, but Cleveland was defeated in the electoral college by a count of 233 to 168. It is also interesting to note, when cataloguing weaknesses, that one vote in a large state like New York, may actually count less than one vote in a state such as Wyoming. We might consider, in our research on the present system, the facts presented above to be weaknesses of our electoral system.

In examining the strengths of the system we might point to the fact that this is the system felt most desirable by our founding fathers, and that the will of the people has been thwarted on only a few occasions in all the years during which this system has been used.

The research into the background of the question will reveal some of the causes of the problem. Using the sample discussion, if we do have a problem with our use of the electoral college, what are the causes of this difficulty? Did the founders of the country feel that our destiny should be determined by a group of gifted leaders acting upon the advice of the people? Was the system designed to operate at a time when our nation was much smaller and our governmental process much less complex than at present? This kind of question-asking and research-directed behavior will assist us in arriving at an answer to the query about the causes of the problem.

Likewise, investigation of the causes will lead us to the issues in the question. We will be able to pinpoint the areas of major disagreement and controversy. Is the question one of the use of the electoral college, or is there general agreement that the system should be modified in some way to insure that the direct popular vote is reflected in the final electoral count?

At this point in agenda preparation and problem exploration, we should be able to state the problem with reasonable precision and define the critical terms in the problem. We are able to do this because we have systematically surveyed the problem, examined the history and implications in the question, and arrived at some agreement upon the basic issues in the discussion question. We can now state the general nature of the problem and agree upon our grounds for disagreement or exploration. With the facts now at our disposal, and before we move on to an evaluation of the possible solutions to our problem, we must decide what standards or criteria should be followed in examining the solutions. Some of our standard criteria are: (1) Is it workable? (2) Is it desirable? (3) Is it economically feasible? (4) Is it philosophically acceptable? Each criterion must be evaluated on the basis of its application to the discussion question. It often may be necessary to formulate new or additional criteria according to the question being discussed.

Our next step is: what are the possible solutions? There will be, of course, many suggestions that have been offered before. This is not meant to be a derogation of the use of familiar solutions, but discussion and inquisitive processes should encourage students to develop new and imaginative solutions. It is difficult, if not impossible, to describe the components of imaginative thinking. Without exploring the area of imaginative thinking and creative behavior we might recommend the following kind of activity as a partial basis for novel solution formulation.

> How does a group go about discovering new and better ways of solving a problem? To begin with, intelligent solutions are partly a product of adequate fact-finding. As group members study and isolate the conditions that underlie the problem, they inevitably will be led to thinking about some of the hypotheses or correctives that may be needed . . .
>
> . . . One of the great barriers to the optimum use of human intelligence lies in our intense desire to cling to traditional theories and familiar practices. To draft new hypotheses requires, perhaps most of all, courage.[11]

With the possible solutions before the discussion group, the evaluation of these answers in terms of the criteria for evaluation is next. The standard criteria suggested earlier are used to assess the acceptability of each of the possible solutions: "How effective will this solution be in correcting the difficulty?" and "What new problems might be created through the adoption of a solution of this type?" Each solution should be examined closely on all counts before additional solutions are evaluated; rarely will any solution be acceptable on all counts. Instead, the solution which appears to offer the least number of shortcomings and seems to deal effectively with the problem as described is usually accepted.

---

[11]Dean C. Barnlund and Franklyn S. Haiman, *The Dynamics of Discussion* (Boston: Houghton Mifflin Company, 1960), pp. 88-89.

Often the students will wish to consider the implementation phase. Essentially implementation involves the steps to be followed in putting the most desirable solution into operation. How easily the solution can be put into operation is the key question. If the solution appears desirable but would require the re-making of much of society, clearly it is not feasible to adopt it. It is appropriate that the matter of ease of utilization be a standard criterion when assessing the merits of each of the proposed solutions to discussion questions.

Individual Preparation. Discussion can only be fruitful when the participating students prepare for it. Students should examine both the background and the present state of the problem before they participate in discussion activities. But as important as individual study of the question under examination is the matter of individual *behavior* preparation for discussion participation. Below, we examine the *phenomenological* approach to discussion, its implications for the group and the individual, as well as the behavior characteristics of participants considered successful and desirable members of a group.

Phenomenology in Discussion

Phenomenology, when applied to discussion, means an attempt "to understand behavior from the behaver's point of view."[12] Teachers who encourage this type of discussion attempt to develop on the part of their students strong feelings and beliefs about the subjects discussed but, at the same time, a willingness to reexamine their beliefs and convictions.[13] Obviously this approach encourages freedom of interchange and interchange that sometimes becomes heated. But if we feel that profitable discussion assumes free and honest participation by all its members and that such discussion results in the modification of most points of view, then we are phenomenologists. Perhaps you prefer to describe this concept of discussion in terms of individual behavior like "flexible," "not opinionated," "honest," or "willing to compromise." Regardless of the name attached to the attitude or behavior, these behaviors encourage more responsible and effective discussion.

Discussant Characteristics. As we noted earlier, the group is, in a sense, the sum of the traits of individual members. The behavior and attitude of the members of the group obviously has a significant impact upon the outcome of group processes. It would be useful at this point to

---

[12]Remo P. Fausti and Arno H. Luker, "A Phenomenological Approach to Discussion," *The Speech Teacher,* 14:20 (January, 1965).
[13]*Ibid.,* p. 21.

identify some of the personality characteristics of effective and ineffective group members.

1. It is possible to isolate relationships between the behaviors of individual group members and the characteristics or "syntality" traits of small groups.
2. Individuals who are chosen by co-workers as good leaders or as persons with whom others like to work "facilitate" group functioning, while individuals who "depress" group functioning are not generally chosen by other members of the group.
3. Individual behavior patterns which include cooperativeness, efficiency, and insight — Factor I behavior — tend to "facilitate" or be positively related to effective group function as measured by ratings of group morale, cooperativeness, productivity, cohesiveness, motivation, and interest in job competition.
4. Individual behavior patterns which include aggressiveness, self-confidence, initiative, interest in individual solutions, and authoritarianism — Factor II behavior — tend to be somewhat negatively related to ratings of group cohesiveness and friendliness.
5. Sociable behavior — Factor III — tends to reduce group motivation and competition but to increase group talkativeness, friendliness, and interest in social interaction.
6. Personality traits involving maturity, adaptability, and acceptance of others tend to be positively related to smooth and effective group functioning.
7. Personality traits involving suspiciousness, eccentricity, and coolness toward others tend to be negatively related to smooth group functioning.[14]

These behaviors identified by Haythorn — cooperativeness, efficiency, insight, maturity, adaptability, and acceptance of others — appear to be those positively related to effective group functioning.

Helpful Habits in Discussion

Besides the personal traits already discussed, there are several habits of speech and thought which serve to further the discussion process. These habits apply to our conversation-discussion-debate continuum, and particularly to the first two activities in this continuum.

---

[14]William Haythorn, "The Influence of Individual Members on the Characteristics of Small Groups," *Journal of Abnormal and Social Psychology*, 48:283 (1953).

(1) *Speak out.* Discussion can only be as profitable as the participation by its members. When we have students who are exceedingly shy and self-conscious and, as a result, do not express their feelings or ideas on the topic, there is really no discussion. No matter how much effort is made, none of us is able to fathom the mind of another; our main basis for understanding is the communication coming from that person. Openness, friendliness, and interest are all based upon the assumption that the discussants will speak their minds freely and openly. Students must make their ideas known and their disagreements clear.

(2) *Stay on the subject.* Although the progress of a discussion sometimes seems to be in a direction contrary to the interests of some of the participants, the contributions should be at least indirectly appropriate to the phase being discussed. We tend to "hitchhike" on the ideas of others; a thought expressed by one student may trigger an irrelevant idea in the mind of another participant. It is often difficult to stay on one phase of the subject until a thorough analysis has been completed; in fact, it may sometimes be more interesting to abandon one phase and move to more alluring aspects. But if there is to be any continuity to the discussion, each student must discipline himself to stay on the subject. Before making comments, students should be sure that what they want to say is being considered at that point on the agenda. Keeping the agenda in front of each participant is one way of reducing the amount of irrelevant material.

(3) *Keep your comments brief.* All of us have seen how a good thought can be ruined by excessive talking. Whenever we have the floor and the attention of others, we're reluctant to give it up. This is precisely the kind of behavior we are so prone to criticize in others but loathe to admit in ourselves. Unless there are questions when an idea is introduced, the idea is probably clear and those common but needless repetitions should not occur.

(4) *Avoid labels.* Among our problems with language is the assignment of most thoughts to a good or bad category. We tend to see ideas as absolutes: black or white. As a result, we often assign to our ideas labels which carry with them very strong connotative implications, and we use these labels as if they were valid judgments. For instance, if we talk about "the spendthrift policies of the present administration," or "the disgusting and irresponsible behavior of most of our college students," we assume that these judgments have been established and verified and, by the very nature of the label, they carry undesirable implications. Of course, it is easier to use labels and see the world in terms of all black or all white. It is easier to see problems as having only a

two-sided orientation, but it is not realistic and it will not further the objective of discussion.

The listener in a discussion who hears labels tossed about freely will either tend to discount the reasoning of the person using the labels or will himself begin to use the labeling method so that the discussion process degenerates into a "name calling" situation. Students should be honest in their opinions about the problem, but they should be encouraged to express their feelings in ways that do not arouse the strong feelings of others. *Semantic awareness is the basis of good discussion.*

Leadership in Discussion

Whether we should regard leadership and leader-directed discussion as the major concern or as a secondary function of the process of discussion is a matter of considerable dispute. This matter was first touched upon in the present chapter when we explored the two general orientations to discussion: small group behavior and problem-solving activity. The dispute has been summarized by Cathcart:

> When this type of leadership role, [leadership the focal point in discussion] and all that goes with it, is accepted as an inherent part of the group problem-solving process, then it must follow that students and teachers of group discussion are going to be concerned first with leadership and only secondarily with group deliberation . . .
>
> . . . It is the thesis here that the leadership function in group discussion is basically a secondary function, and training in discussion should place primary emphasis on the *nature* and the *process* of discussion.[15]

Before exploring the merits of each approach, we should consider the classroom situation in which this leadership or absence of it will occur. The typical high school student engaging in discussion for the first time is unaware of his responsibilities and is, almost by the nature of our society, desirous of strong leadership. He has been schooled to expect one power figure to regulate the contributions, to establish the priorities. The major question he asks is not "Should there be a leader?" but "Who should our leader be?" Our experience with group interaction tells us that leadership varies with situations and questions; the individual pro-

---

[15]Robert S. Cathcart, "Leadership as a Secondary Function in Group Discussion," *The Speech Teacher*, 11:222, 225 (September, 1962).

viding it may change but the directing force remains. The function of leadership has been effectively summarized by Gulley:

> In general, then, leadership in discussion consists of performing functions that influence the group to achieve its objectives, and these duties are delegated directly or indirectly to certain individuals because it is in the best interests of the whole group to have guidance, direction, and some degree of control.[16]

The decision of whether or not to appoint the leader for the discussion largely depends upon the length of time allotted for the discussion group activity. Mortenson found that if a group met for less than an hour they were more likely to accept an assigned leader than to take the time to select one of their own.[17] Most of the discussion groups are alloted perhaps one hour to conduct their discussion in front of the class. It would seem appropriate, therefore, to assign the leader for each of the class discussions, and the leader should be the same kind of person the group would select. Even in the case of "leaderless" discussion an organizing and directing force is exerted by some person in the group; this is the type of person who should be designated as the formal leader in classroom discussion.

Function of Leadership. We can identify with some precision the kind of behaviors that should be exhibited by the effective discussion leader. The function of the leader is to initiate discussion, make agenda suggestions, clarify, summarize, and verbalize a consensus or agreement.[18] Another similar, although not identical, list of leadership functions specifies that the leader should regulate, guide, focus, clarify, and point up the discussion.[19] By *regulation*, we mean that the leader should permit and encourage participation by each discussant and draw out the recalcitrant members of the group. *Guiding* refers to the process of adhering to the agenda and proceeding through the problem-solving steps in an orderly fashion. *Focusing* means the sharpening and clarifying of contributions to the very specific phase of the topic which is under examination. *Clarifying* is the function of restating or rewording ambiguous and hazy ideas so that they are briefly and clearly stated. *Pointing up* means emphasizing the significant contributions of members and indicating the relevance of these ideas to the total pattern of discussion.

---

[16]Gulley, *op, cit.,* p. 174.
[17]Calvin D. Mortenson, "Should the Discussion Group Have an Assigned Leader?" *The Speech Teacher,* 15:40 (January, 1966).
[18]Barnlund and Haiman, *op. cit.,* pp. 285-287.
[19]Utterback, *op. cit.,* pp. 60-69.

It would be naive, at best, to expect most high school students of speech to perform each of these responsibilities satisfactorily. It would be foolish to think that a randomly assigned leader could function optimally. What would be most appropriate would be to assign a student who in all likelihood can generally handle these responsibilities. In the course of the discussion he will learn how to exert his influence, if he is not already a highly influential member of the discussion group.

The position put forth here assumes that discussion is being taught as a unit in a course in public speaking; it assumes that there is not a whole semester for training in and exercise of leadership. If an entire semester can be given to discussion training then it would be absurd to assign leaders; the process of learning how to lead and exercising a guiding influence over ones colleagues should be a product of this kind of curricular experience. This is true even when discussion is taught as a unit, but the typical course has such large enrollment that the opportunities for each student to be designated as a leader are very few in number.

There are hazards to the leadership function. When the teacher has assigned the group leader, he may later discover that in the process of the discussion another student actually exerts the leadership. It would be unwise to halt the discussion when leadership changes hands. Leadership in some form must be present in all group activity. The simplest route is to assign a student as leader since there is usually not enough time for the group selection process to function. However, when your judgment is in error and some member of the discussion group begins to function in another capacity, do not interfere. Forcing the "apparent" leader to relinquish his position in favor of the "assigned" leader will discourage participation and damage group morale. As far as possible, the teacher should remain out of the discussion and permit the students to resolve their own problems. This approach assumes that students have had their responsibilities outlined in advance of the actual discussion and that they understand the steps in the discussion and investigation process.

Suggestions for the Effective Teaching of Discussion

(1) Permit and encourage maximum student participation. The idea of discussion is to facilitate interaction. If students feel that the selection of the topic, construction of the agenda, or outcome of the discussion is determined by the teacher or someone outside the group, their commitment to the discussion process will be weak. We should be as concerned with the process of interaction as we are with the outcome of the discussion. When we provide the student with all the answers and directions

we do not involve him in the process. Constructing the agenda to determine the direction the discussion will take is one of the most vital learning phases of discussion. Let the effort be a product of the group based on the direction and guidelines provided by the teacher. As a result of their active participation in the decision-making process, students will be more interested in and believe more in the decisions which they reach.[20]

(2) Diagram the discussion to help students understand the communication flow. There have been several useful techniques developed for determining the type and frequency of individual participation. One such process is the Bales Interaction Profile.[21] By using the categories developed by Bales, it is a relatively simple process to record and thus have a thorough understanding of the quantity and nature of the contribution of each person in the discussion. The following table may help to explain how this method can be used in the classroom.

Discussion Participation					
Number of times for each student	Student 1	2	3	4	5
Showed solidarity			1		1
Showed tension release	2	2		1	1
Showed agreement	1	1	4		3
Gave suggestions	2			1	4
Gave opinion	1	1		4	
Gave information					5
Asked for information	1	2			
Asked for opinion		1			3
Asked for suggestion					2
Showed disagreement	5			6	
Showed tension	1			1	
Showed antagonism	1			3	

Both the individual pattern and the pattern of all members of the group can easily be seen by glancing at this form. In the specimen above, student 1 and student 4 appeared to be in frequent disagreement, frequently voiced their opinion, but provided relatively little information. Student 5, however, relied on information he had collected, asked for

[20]Bernard Berelson and Gary Steiner, *Human Behavior* (New York: Harcourt, Brace & World, 1964), p. 548.

[21]Robert F. Bales, *Interaction Process Analysis* (Reading, Mass.: Addison-Wesley Publishing Co., Inc., 1950).

suggestion and agreement and generally made a constructive contribution to the group activity. Other interpretations could be provided for the other participants, but the procedure should be clear now.

Some teachers elect to diagram the flow of the discussion and the direction of contributions rather than use "hash marks" to categorize the type of contribution made. Each of the circles in Fig. 23 represents a discussion participant. The arrow indicates the flow of the discussion. In this case the chairman had very tight control of the group and all contributions were channeled first through the leader who then made evaluative statements about the contribution. This flow chart provides a very clear picure of a leader-dominated group. A flow chart of an effectively functioning group would have many lines connecting each of the participants with some of the lines going to the leader, but not the inordinate number shown in Fig. 23.

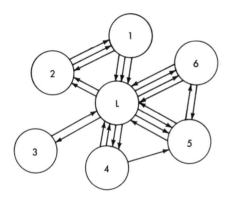

Figure 23. Flow Chart of Leader-Dominated Group.

Both of these methods of analysis enable the teacher to provide more constructive suggestions for improvement than if he were to say, "It seems to me that you need information to clarify some of your thinking." How much more effective such an evaluation would be if the teacher said, "Eight of your contributions consisted merely of you stating your opinion. Wouldn't it make better sense to use, occasionally, some of the information that is in print on this question? That doesn't mean that you need to read it verbatim — just indicate you know it exists."

(3) Present critiques immediately after the discussion. Immediate knowledge of the results has long been acknowledged as one of the principles of sound instruction. Allow enough time between the end of the

class period and the time when the discussion is slated to end (at least ten minutes) for some comments and suggestions for each of the participants and the leader. Make your suggestions positive in nature; offer alternative courses of action. If a student interrupts or attacks the ideas of others, then suggest that he consider the possibility of some approach other than his own. If you do feel negative reinforcement is warranted, then balance it with something positive that the student should do.

(4) Emphasize, at all times, the positive results of discussion. When the course is beginning, you should emphasize the purposes and functions of discussion. It is not wise to toss students into a discussion merely to prove to them that they do not understand how to participate in discussion. A period of instruction, reading, and class interaction on the procedures, purposes, and organization of group discussion should precede active participation in class discussions. Time must be given to agenda development, the process of thinking in a discussion, human relations, etc.

(5) Discussion can be used as a lead-in for other units in a speech course. The process of interaction on topics of common interest will encourage students to reduce their inhibitions and explore a variety of viewpoints. Some teachers use discussion as the initial speaking activity in a public speaking course; students find it much easier to express themselves when they are seated. After losing some of their self-consciousness through discussion, they can present this same viewpoint in a more formal speech. Alternatively, discussion can be used as a subject development activity in which students study a variety of questions and viewpoints and explore their interests in a search for possible topics for speeches.

(6) Make use of the various forms of discussion. For variety you might consider using some of these forms of discussion. *Panel discussion* consists of a moderator or chairman and a group of students, who exchange ideas in front of the class. The panel usually meets previous to the class discussion to plan their analysis and consideration of the problem. It often is necessary for the panel to meet, with the chairman presiding, several times prior to the actual discussion to plot their problem-solving strategy. When the actual discussion occurs, the chairman will introduce each of the panelists and provide the necessary background for the discussion. The discussion then proceeds in the usual manner with the chairman acting as leader.

The *symposium* is a series of set speeches presented by the participants. Usually, a general topic area is provided, such as voter apathy. Members of the symposium then present speeches on phases of the general topic, such as voter apathy in congressional elections, lack of voter interest in local bond issue elections, etc. The chairman acts only to introduce and summarize the presentations.

In the *forum* a panel discussion format is used with audience participation. Some teachers prefer to hold the audience discussion phase until the end of the forum. The forum is most effective when the audience is permitted to participate in all phases of the discussion, but at no time should the audience interrupt or cut off one of the discussants. Their participation should follow the contribution of each of the forum members. This form of discussion encourages participation by all members of the class and forces the members of the panel to think quickly.

An alternative to the more formal, one-hour discussion sessions is the *Phillips 66 format* or an adaptation of it. Groups are assigned to discuss one phase of a problem for six minutes and then report back to the rest of the class. It is rightly called a "buzz session" because there is no time for any kind of lengthy deliberation. In a class of twenty-four students during a forty-five minutes class period, three "buzz" sessions involving each member of the class could be held with approximately two to four minutes permitted for reports following the sessions. This discussion format permits, then, a number of students to become involved in the leadership role and it encourages, although briefly, a highly informal and intimate atmosphere for group interaction.

Discussion Conference. The discussion conference has been rather widely used in high school extracurricular activities. These conferences can be one or two days long and typically use an agenda prepared and distributed to the participants in advance. The high school speech league discussion conference is sponsored by regional and state associations. Its purpose and agenda is a useful illustration of the discussion conference approach.

A Discussion Conference:

What should be the role of public higher education in national security?

Saturday Morning, November 11

9:00-9:30   *Registration.* All schools should check in as soon as they arrive to receive their assignments.

9:30   *Assembly* in the ballroom.

10:00-10:45 *Session I:* Student discussion. Students will meet in the designated groups according to the schedule. (At each session the group will select a student to record the activities of the group and present them to the chairman.)

Step I: What is meant by "national security"?
   A. What are the military aspects of national security?
       1. How important is arms production and development?
       2. How important is scientific development in the space program? Training of scientists?
       3. How important is the training of officers and men for the armed forces?
   B. What are the political aspects of national security?
       1. How important is policy-making, diplomacy, and training of men for these functions?
       2. How important are military and civilian intelligence activities?
       3. How important are the functions of the US Information Agency and other propaganda groups?
   C. What are the economic aspects of national security?
       1. How important is foreign aid?
       2. How important is industrial production?
       3. How important is the nature of the economy as a whole?
   D. What are the ideological aspects of national security?
       1. What are the security problems posed by communism as an ideology?
       2. What are the security problems posed by American attitudes toward communism? (fear, ignorance, complacency)

10:45   *General Assembly.* Synthesis of reports of the student discussions.

11:00-11:45   *Session II:* Student discussion.

Step II: What is meant by public higher education?
   A. What is meant by public support?
   B. What is meant by higher education?

Step III: What is the present relationship between public higher education and national security?
   A. The relation between education and the military aspects.
   B. The relation between education and the political aspects.
   C. The relation between education and the economic aspects.
   D. The relation between education and ideological aspects.
   E. What further relationships exist today?

11:45   *General Assembly.* Synthesis period.

12:00-1:00   *Lunch.*

1:00-1:45   *Session III:* Student discussion.

        Step IV: What problems, if any, does the United States face in the area of national security? What problems may exist in the future?

        A. What problems might we face in the area of actual war?

        B. What problems might we face in the "cold" war?

        C. What nations or geographical area, if any, hold a present or potential threat to our security? (Is the Soviet Union the only one you can think of?)

        D. What attitudes or ideologies, if any, present a threat to our security? (What of communism, fascism, nationalism, race prejudice, etc.?)

        E. What other threats to our security do you recognize?

1:45   *General Assembly.* Synthesis period.

2:00-2:45   *Session IV:* Student discussion.

        Step V: By what criteria might we evaluate attempts to strengthen our security through public higher education?

        A. Should any program involve federal aid to higher education? If so, to what extent and in what way?

        B. Should any program involve a change in present academic structures?

        C. Should any program involve such plans as Reserve Officers Training? Should they be compulsory or voluntary?

        D. Should any program involve a special emphasis on certain areas such as science, international relations, etc.?

        E. Should the establishment of goals be the responsibility of the federal or state government, the individual student, or a combination?

        F. What other criteria might be used to evaluate programs for higher education relative to national security?

2:45   *General Assembly.* Synthesis of reports.

3:00-3:45   *Session V:* Student discussion.

        Step VI: What proposals can we, make, if any, that will strengthen our national security by using public higher education?

               A. How well do these proposals meet the above criteria?
               B. What problems of implementation would any proposals face?
               C. What final selections or decisions can we make?

3:45   *General Assembly.* Synthesis period.
                Reports and announcements.

4:15   Adjournment.

TEACHING DEBATE

Because of the competitive nature of interscholastic debate and the occasional popular misconception that debate is idle academic gamesmanship, debate should be taught in all schools as both vocational training and citizenship preparation.[22] This does not negate the use of forensic training as personality development. The knowledge and skills required for successful competitive debate are a prerequisite for one's own success and the improvement of society. Training and activity in debate is developed toward meaningful and successful interscholastic competition, but the values endure long after the student has left high school.[23]

Debate Programs

Out-of-Class Programs. The most common debate program at the high school level is the extracurricular program. Debate has had a long and distinguished record in our public educational system.[24] The academic debating clubs were the first in a continuing line of organizations which engaged in argumentative speaking outside the classroom. Today, many schools which have not heard of a speech department offer debate training through an active out-of-class program; other schools with established speech departments and communications curricula also provide forensic training outside the classroom.

In schools with large and well established speech programs, the interscholastic and intramural competition is sponsored by the speech or English department. Another method of support in schools where there is sufficient interest in speech activities is sponsorship by a speech club or debate club.

[22]Austin J. Freeley, "An Anthology of Commentary on Debate," *The Speech Teacher,* 9:121-126 (March, 1960).

[23]*Ibid.*

[24]L. Leroy Cowperthwaite and A. Craig Baird, "Intercollegiate Debating," *A History of Speech Education in America,* ed. Karl R. Wallace (New York: Appleton-Century-Crofts, Inc., 1954), pp. 259-276.

Curricular Programs.   Schools with departments of speech frequently offer a semester or a year of in-class training in debate. Occasionally the debate training will be substituted for a course in English or government.

Classes in debate should be two semesters in duration. An attempt to consider adequately all of the units basic to successful analysis and case support requires at least one academic year. This training will be more useful if opportunities for practice debates are provided.

Occasionally, curricular debate training is offered as a unit in other courses. Teachers of social studies or English are fond of using debate as a tool of inquiry and advocacy. More commonly, of course, a unit in debate is taught as part of a first course in speech. There is no doubt about the value of including some curricular training in debate, but for meaningful educational results the program should continue over several years in several courses.

Times of Debate Training.   When debate is taught as a unit in a non-speech area, the timing of its introduction should be governed by the structure of the course. If a systematic attack on the national debate proposition is anticipated in either a course in debate or as another curricular offering, the teacher should start the program at the beginning of the first semester. More time is available for the analysis and development of arguments and cases, and students can thus explore the multitude of arguments and evidence.

In those cases where debate training is extracurricular, training and practice sessions should begin at the start of the school year. The national debate proposition is an excellent vehicle for instruction, and unlike some of the more unusual propositions chosen for practice debates, there is a wealth of published information available for the researcher.

Administrative and Budgetary Problems.   The bane of most debate coaches is money. Preparation of a debate case requires that debaters be exposed to great quantities of printed matter, ranging from *The Congressional Record* to *The Farmer's Almanac*. Most school libraries do not subscribe to all of the useful journals, periodicals, and newspapers which contain materials for case construction. In medium-sized and small communities the city library rarely receives these materials. The coach must then assure himself that there are ample funds available for the purchase of materials. When schools prepare cases on the national debate proposition, materials usually can be ordered either through the state speech league office or from the National Forensic League national office. The printed materials distributed by these organizations are usually sold at or near cost to members.

It is impossible to suggest a minimal budget figure which will permit the purchase of the basic materials for a course or program in debate.

The type of program, the number of students participating, the availability of materials, and the wealth of the community play major roles
in arriving at a dollar figure. Many excellent programs have been
developed on a budget of $25-50 for purchasing materials. Some debate
coaches whose budgets are virtually nonexistent encourage their debaters
to purchase the materials themselves, or the coach or teacher pays for
the materials. Neither of these solutions is desirable, but if materials
cannot be secured from libraries or other free sources, some source
of funds must be found.

Availability of Materials.   If topics other than the national debate
proposition are chosen for debate, is there reason to believe that
adequate resource materials are available? There are a variety of debate
propositions for high school students which are totally unrelated to
the national question but which are rich in available resource materials.
Choose the proposition with the educational goals of debate uppermost
in mind, but remember that for debate to serve as an instrument of
student research, printed materials must be nearby. Again, the question
is one of the type of program. If a competitive interscholastic program
is the objective, then the national proposition must be used; an intramural
or curricular debate program can use any appropriate topic.

Pre-Season Debates.   The "active" debate season for interscholastic
competition usually does not begin before the middle of October. Many
coaches prefer to have their teams "try out" a case on an audience in
their own school or debate before a team or audience at a nearby school.
This approach has the advantage of offering an opportunity for fresh
analysis of the case by opponents or listeners unfamiliar with the
approach. Try to debate other teams as early as possible so that
undetected flaws can be corrected before the tournament trail begins.

Many coaches believe that practice with teams at nearby schools
aids analysis, but the teacher should not ignore the potential within the
student body in his own school. There are many nondebaters who are
effective critical thinkers. They can serve as a sounding board for the
case. If the question used for debate has some economic or political
implications — and virtually all propositions fall into those camps —
the history, political science, or economics teacher may be interested in
a debate before his class. Opportunities such as these arouse critical
questions from listeners not previously exposed to the approach used
by the debate team. A revised and greatly improved case may be the
result of several such debates before classroom groups.

Travel to Other Schools.   When practice debates are arranged with
nearby schools, school transportation frequently is not used. Instead,
because most of the practice sessions involve only one or two teams

from each school, the coach and another teacher or a responsible student drive their own cars. This solution appears to be far simpler than using the school bus or some other school-owned means of transportation, but it is loaded with potential problems. The coach is responsible for the welfare of his students when they are participating in a school-sponsored activity under his direction. The school and its teacher stand *in loco parentis*. The major concern is for the physical safety of all students making the trip; the drivers of the cars must be chosen very carefully, particularly if one of the drivers is to be a student. Frequently, parents of debaters are anxious to be of assistance and will volunteer to drive.

Debaters are highly responsible young adults. But they will behave in a responsible manner only so long as the coach expects them to do so. The "ground rules" for behavior should be outlined before the first practice trip or tournament, and debaters must be advised that they are expected to behave in accordance with the rules. The rules usually are just an extension of the rules of the school, but there is merit in reminding students that they are the guests of the host school and should behave accordingly.

There is one matter that is not part of the rules of conduct in most school systems but it is critical to good school and personal relations. *Under no circumstances should a debater ever argue with a judge about a decision.* There is nothing to be gained from cornering a judge after the team has received an unfavorable decision and making unsolicited observations about his sanity or lineage; this advice applies to debaters and coaches alike. In perhaps one case in one hundred the judge will be receptive to disagreement of this type; in the other ninety-nine irreparable damage is done to the image and future success of representatives of the school. Teams which dispute decisions acquire a reputation which is then transferred to their schools. Often, debaters overhear their coaches questioning a judge's decision. The coach should serve as a model of proper behavior for his team, accept decisions even though he may feel they are incorrect ones, help his team rebuild the weaknesses in their case, and look forward to meeting the same team again.

Participation for Many. A debate program should serve as an educational tool for all students who wish to participate rather than as a public relations or prestige activity for only a few.[25] We encourage communities to start and support debate programs as part of the total education of the child. If we encourage only the proficient to become active in the program, we violate our own case for debate. One of the

---

[25]Michael M. Osborn, "A Blueprint for Diversity in Forensic Programs," *The Speech Teacher,* 14, No. 2:110-115 (March, 1965).

most successful football coaches of our time has said that as long as a player is willing to go through the drills and exert every effort to become a member of the team, he will be issued a uniform and will dress for every game. Not every student who is interested in debate can become a member of the varsity team, but he must be given the opportunity to participate. All of the school's resources for debate should be directed toward participation for all interested students. It is much more educationally defensible to have twenty debaters attending two tournaments than to have an extracurricular activity which sends four debaters to fifteen tourneys. It is possible to have excellence quantitatively and qualitatively.

Administration of the Program. The paper work connected with the direction of a debate program, and particularly an extracurricular one, is bothersome but never overwhelming. Records of expenditures for materials, transportation costs, meals (if the school pays for meals when students attend tournaments at other schools), and entry fees must be maintained. A specific discussion of the expenses associated with directing an out-of-class program appears in Chapter 12. It is unusual for a teacher to be given *carte blanche* disbursement of funds allocated to debate programs, so coaches should keep records of all expenditures connected with the activity. This accounting will enable the students to use all the funds assigned to the activity; unused funds usually revert to the general school fund and frequently the unused portion of the budget is deducted from the funds assigned to the activity for the succeeding year.

Debate and the Student. The very nature of competitive problem-solving activity requires above-average mental ability if the student is to be successful. We attempt to train all students, not just those engaged in debate, in the techniques of creative problem-solving, but the complex nature of the national high school debate proposition demands that students have above-average abilities.

The students for whom debate has the greatest value are the upper twenty per cent, or the gifted and near-gifted. They will find argumentation a challenging process and one providing demands on their intellectual abilities that are perhaps greater than any academic subject they take. Debaters usually are among the leaders in school life.

There are significant values to be derived from the participation of the upper fifty per cent of the student population. It is for these above-average but not brilliant students that debate programs are most needed. We must realize that the program should be extended to all those who will benefit from debate training, but we should concentrate out efforts on the upper fifty per cent.

We should include as many students as are interested in the program. Besides the obvious value of exposing more students to an intellectually demanding process, the large program encourages teamwork in analyzing the proposition and collecting the evidence. Coaches can develop a team spirit concept in which there are no "stars" but only a closely knit group of students whose concern is for the squad and not for their own personal record. The legendary Vince Lombardi, who coached the Green Bay Packers to three consecutive National Football League championships and two world championships described this quality as "love" — love of team members for each other. Students may call this feeling "concern" or "identification." Whatever name you choose to give to it, it represents the close feeling of each member of the team for all other members, a knowledge of others' expectations, and a realization that success is determined by the energies of all members. A debate is not won by a single person; it is a team effort. The first aim of any coach must be to develop an *esprit de corps;* after that other problems are solved easily.

Objectives of Teaching Debate

The primary concern of the debate coach must be with the long term effects of debate training upon his students. These effects can be expressed as the objectives of debate training: (1) to develop the student's ability to find answers to his problems through research, reasoning, and conference, (2) to develop a respect for competent authority, (3) to develop an awareness of speaking techniques and the use of evidence which will improve discrimination and evaluation of public propositions, (4) to improve the skills of definition, analysis, and the structuring of problems into workable forms, (5) to develop the awareness that complex problems have more than one solution and that workability as well as causes are factors in solving problems, (6) to develop skills in the selection, organization, and presentation of ideas in defense of his own point of view, and (7) to develop the ability to participate in controversial problem-solving at the conversational, discussional, or formal debate level.

Debate is a productive intellectual activity resulting from what McBath calls critical deliberation and persuasive argumentation.[26] This critical deliberation and persuasive argumentation has enduring value for the student because

---

[26]James H. McBath, "Introduction to Argument," *Argumentation and Debate: Principles and Practices,* ed. James McBath (New York: Holt, Rinehart & Winston, Inc., 1963), pp. 6-7.

1) arguers may contribute facts, interpretations, or judgments unknown to others,
2) new ideas may emerge from the pooling of information and the contest of ideas,
3) errors may be exposed, since arguments are subjected to rigorous tests of their proof and consistency, and
4) arguers may be jarred loose from rutted, unproductive patterns of analysis.[27]

If training in debate is to be of value, the skills learned must be transferred to everyday experiences to enable students to incorporate new patterns of behavior which will assist in the discovery of new facts, new ideas, valid reasoning, and effective analysis.

Types of Debate Propositions. There are three general categories into which debate propositions can be placed: (1) propositions of fact, (2) propositions of value, and (3) propositions of policy. Most interscholastic and intercollegiate questions are policy propositions, but class and intra-school debates frequently use one of the other two types of questions.

A proposition of fact alleges the existence of a set of relationships or events, or an interrelationship of events and objects. More simply stated, a proposition of fact might be, "Chicago is the midwestern center of the Mafia." This proposition is one of fact, but it is not likely that this question is subject to final proof; there is conflicting evidence. Most propositions, regardless of their type, have this limitation. There are a few instances where the question can be evaluated more objectively. "Lee Harvey Oswald shot President Kennedy," although a controversial proposition, is more capable of objective analysis and proof than the preceding proposition (although critics still assert that the evidence is not conclusive). Court cases are cases of fact.

Propositions of value are concerned with a judgment about facts: whether an idea, person, event, or movement is good or bad, worthwhile or worthless. Topics for intra-school debates could deal with the value of a course in the curriculum, for instance English or mathematics. The debate would center on evidence and reasoning which would enable us to determine if there is value in a particular academic field.

Debate propositions which assert that a specific course of action should be undertaken are propositions of policy. Most of the problems which we face are concerned with what we should do: raise taxes, execute criminals, permit 18-year-olds to vote, resume nuclear testing,

---

[27]*Ibid.,* p. 12.

or nationalize basic industries. Basic to analysis are matters of fact and value. We explore the question to determine what factual information exists, and then incorporate the facts and our interpretations of them into a value judgment. The value judgments, after they have been summed up, suggest the course of action we should take.

Your career as a debate coach will be concerned with a host of propositions of policy. These have been as diverse as the formation of a federation of nations and the support of farm prices at ninety per cent parity. When we discuss cases and the structure of arguments for debate speeches, we will concentrate on the proposition of policy.

Debate Formats

Traditional Debate. The most widely used approach consists of four ten-minute constructive speeches, with the affirmative delivering the beginning speech followed by a negative speech, another affirmative presentation, and a second negative. There is often a five-minute break between the end of the constructive and the beginning of the rebuttal speeches. Rebuttal speeches are five minutes long and are begun by the negative. All speakers are heard; the debate is concluded by a five-minute rebuttal speech by the second affirmative speaker.

Cross-Question Debate. The cross-examination format has had widespread acceptance and use at the high school level. The distinctive feature of cross-examination is the opportunity for each team to question the constructive speaker of the opposition. Since the questioning period follows each of the constructive speeches, there is more of an opportunity for a direct clash on issues. One of the more common arrangements of speeches for a cross-exam debate is the following:

> First affirmative constructive speech
> Cross-examination of first affirmative speaker by the second negative
> First negative constructive speech
> Cross-examination of the first negative speaker by the first affirmative speaker
> Second affirmative constructive speech
> Cross-examination of the second affirmative by the first negative speaker
> Second negative constructive speech
> Cross-examination of the second negative speaker by the first affirmative
> Negative rebuttal
> Affirmative rebuttal

There is only one rebuttal speech for each side.

Although many high school teams participate in cross-examination debate, few understand or use the question period properly. Their problems usually arise from a failure to prepare questions in advance or to make use of earlier statements as a wedge for new questions. The following guidelines should assist debaters in developing and using questions.

1) Have a purpose for each question.
2) Always prepare questions in advance and then use those questions which are appropriate.
3) Be reasonably certain of the answers that will be given.
4) Begin with common ground areas and then proceed to areas of disagreement.
5) Never ask an important question until you have laid the ground for it.
6) Inquire rather than tell.
7) Don't make inferences and draw conclusions during the question period.
8) Make questions brief and understandable.
9) Avoid a belligerent attitude.

Besides raising the appropriate questions and using the results of the question period in constructive and rebutting presentations, the debater must respond to the opposition's questions as astutely as possible. Coaches should encourage their debaters to follow these principles when they are being questioned:

1) Answer any reasonable questions.
2) Request clarification of vague questions before attempting to reply.
3) Don't answer a question with another question.
4) Loaded questions should not be answered.
5) Be brief in your replies.
6) Yield quickly on indefensible points.
7) Don't hesitate to admit you don't know all the answers.

Legislative Debate. This form of debate is also called parliamentary, largely because of the similarities between it and the procedures in public legislation. *Robert's Rules of Order* governs procedures. Before the beginning of actual debate, the class members sit on the side of the aisle corresponding to their feeling. For instance, on a proposition like "Resolved: That this house believes that eighteen-year-olds should be given the right to vote," two-thirds of the class might sit on the affirmative side of the aisle while one-third might sit on the negative side. As the debate progresses, members may move to the other side of the aisle to indicate a change in their feeling about the topic.

Speakers usually are restricted to three or four minutes for their presentations and the debate is begun by the author of the resolution speaking on its behalf. In most legislative debates an affirmative speech should alternate with a negative speech. With the permission of the chair, speakers may be interrupted and asked either to yield to a question or to yield the remainder of their time to another speaker.

Since the proceedings are governed by *Robert's Rules,* a motion to close debate may be crucial in determining the passage or failure of the resolution. Sometimes the author is given the final opportunity to speak on behalf of his resolution.

Legislative debate is an excellent forum for training in extemporaneous speaking and practical use of parliamentary procedure. It is not necessary for resolutions used in legislative debate to be only matters that are likely to be considered in national or state legislatures; the topics should be timely and consider the interests and abilities of the students.

Problem-Solving Debate. The objective of most debating is the solution of difficulties, but we often lose sight of this goal by developing a competitive atmosphere. The ballots for problem-solving debate vary from those used in the traditional and cross-question styles. The criteria used for evaluating problem-solving debate emphasize analysis, solution, and evaluation rather than "slick," devious cases.

Teams in problem-solving debate consist of two or three members. The first speaker, who is allotted ten minutes, should analyze the question, introduce all relevant facts, and attempt to identify the basic issues in the problem. The first speaker on the opposing side then gives his team's analysis. The solution speeches, each twelve minutes in length, are presented by the second speaker for each side; these solutions must apply to the analysis introduced by that team and demonstrate a superiority over other solutions. The third, the evaluation speech, is eight minutes long and has as its goal the objective analysis and consideration of the cases of both teams. If clarification of ideas is needed, the third speaker may request information from either team, but his concern is not to extract damaging admissions from his opponents nor to strengthen his own case. He is attempting to evaluate objectively the contributions of both sides.

There is neither an affirmative or negative team in problem-solving debate, so the first team to speak is chosen by lot just before the debate begins. Since the goal is problem-solution and not just presentation of an analysis and solution to win a contest, decisions are not given. Speakers may be ranked in skill in this style of debate.

Direct Clash. Traditional debates often bog down over irrelevant or insignificant issues. The direct clash approach forces debaters to concentrate their arguments in areas where there is a difference of opinion between the two teams. The direct clash is particularly useful for practice sessions to force debaters to introduce and exhaustively consider a single issue at a time. There are few high school tournaments which use the direct clash format.

The direct clash debate is begun by the first affirmative who spends five minutes presenting a definition of the proposition, discussing basic arguments and presenting the plan. Equal time is then given to the first negative to accept or reject the analysis, introduce any new issues, and if desired, present a counterproposal. After the negative speech each team is usually given two or three minutes to clarify the basic issues. At this point the judge will rule on the issues for debate; these issues are the ones on which the two teams differ. Definition of terms may be an issue, but clashes are normally confined to differences in need and plan. It is possible, but unusual, for a judge to award a decision at this point. Normally, he will identify the issues on which the debate is to concentrate and state which issue will be considered first.

When debate is begun on the issues, the affirmative speaks first and one member of the team has four minutes to present his argument. The negative is then given two minutes to reply, and succeeding speakers alternate for two minutes each until both sides have spoken three times. The affirmative is then given two minutes to summarize and, if a decision has not been given during the clash, the judge then awards the decision. If there are additional issues on which to clash, the debate proceeds in the same manner for each issue. When all issues have been debated or when one team has won three clashes, the decision for the debate is given.

Heckling Debate. One of the major difficulties in the use of the heckling style is that it tends to disorganize and disturb a large proportion of the participants. Unless your debaters are experienced and well poised, this format could seriously damage their attitude and confidence in the debate situation. The heckling debate, because it consists of constructive speeches studded with interruptions and questions from the opposition, does little good for anyone but the experienced debater. Teams consist of two debaters and each speaker speaks for approximately fifteen minutes. The heckler then may ask questions of the speaker until he receives what he considers a satisfactory answer.

Mock Trial. Although it is rarely used in the high school situation, the mock trial, through creating a courtroom atmosphere, is very appealing to student groups and is highly effective for audiences of from 50-75 persons. Students may take the roles of judicial officials, witnesses, or jury; in all: bailiff, Attorney-General of the US, presiding judge, attorney, six witnesses, and twelve jurors.

Split Team. Split team debaters pair colleagues from different schools in a traditional debate format; the teams usually are not formed until shortly before the first round. Such last minute formation of teams can lead to a superficial analysis. But if the participants are unable to engage in several lines of analysis before coming to the tournament and are incapable of adapting their arguments to a new or revised thesis, then the claims made that debate is a training ground for effective thinking and adjustment may indeed be only claims.

DEBATE TECHNIQUES

In this section we shall explore the criteria for selecting a debate proposition, analyzing and defining the problem, researching the case, organizing materials, and deciding strategy. This section is not designed to be a brief on how to win debates; it is not aimed solely at the development of a sucessful interscholastic forensics program when the name of success is victory. The aim is to enable students to use debate as an educational instrument with all the often-claimed advantages which accrue. There is nothing shameful about developing a successful competitive debate program, but there is something less than desirable about a program which makes victory rather than educational experiences for the participants the major objective. Good debate training may result in victory, but training for victory alone does not frequently cultivate success.

Selection of the Question. Debate propositions result from systematic human problem-solving behaviors. In the exploratory stages of conversation and discussion, we are searching for all the available approaches, submitting our theses to tests and examining, evaluating, and reexamining. Then we determine that we have approached our goal; a tentative answer to the discussion question has been reached. Now we are prepared to research even further the answer we have selected through sifting all the available evidence, evaluating it, and examining and exploring its relationship to the thesis we will defend. It is possible that highly stimulating and useful debate propositions will arise from discussion and questions in the classrooms; debate is the product of the inquiring mind as it moves from questioning and searching to advocacy and belief. Intramural debate, in particular, can formulate propositions for debate in this manner. Classroom discussion of contemporary issues will indicate the kind of question which interests the class. As part of the problem-solving process, the class may wish to explore very quickly all the questions which may be of interest, select two or three which are of primary interest, and then after discussing each of the questions, phrase one or more debate propositions from the questions. You, as the teacher, may find it useful to follow the pattern outlined above in your attack upon a useful question for class investigation, but instead of relying upon a committee to prepare a national question, you may wish to word a proposition indicating the specific interests of your students.

Selection of the Proposition by National Committees. The propositions used for most invitational and qualifying tournaments are the ones prepared by the National University Extension Association. The procedures to be followed in preparing and developing these topics are discussed in Chapter 12, which deals with extracurricular speech activities. These questions are always issues of national or international importance, but you may wish that your debaters not restrict their attention to several topics selected from the same problem area for an entire season. If you wish variety in problem selection, then selecting an alternative proposition via problem-solution methods would be appropriate.

Preparing for Debate

Selection of the Proposition. Before the wording of the proposition is considered, the general topic area must be evaluated. There are a number of questions to be asked about the general area and the very specific propositions which result from analysis of the area. The most significant criteria to be considered are:

1) Is the subject of nationwide interest?
2) Is a discussion of the subject in the public interest?
3) Is the proposition to be worded from the subject likely to be removed from the realm of debate by being solved or exhausted during the debate season?
4) Are adequate research materials available, or can they be made available?
5) Is the subject interesting to young people?
6) Will audiences be interested in it?
7) Can a suitable proposition be phrased on this subject?[28]

---

[28]James H. McBurney and Glen E. Mills, *Argumentation and Debate: Techniques of a Free Society* (New York: The Macmillan Company, 1964), pp. 33.

When the proposition is to be used only in intramural debates, the first criterion does not apply. But even with local issues there will probably be an abundance of materials available, the debate will probably be in the public interest, and the question may be solved during the time the proposition is being used. Perhaps most importantly the subject should be of interest to students and those who participate in the debates. Such questions as

"There should be fair housing for all the citizens of Milwaukee."

"Fluoridation of the water supply in Indianapolis will benefit the children."

"The proposed 9:00 p.m. curfew for persons below the age of 16 should be enacted."

will certainly be of interest to students in the affected communities. Of the criteria cited, the only ones which may not be satisfied by the use of local issues are the adequacy of materials and the exhausting of major issues after a few practice sessions. But resourceful student debaters will continue to find either new issues or new ways of examining old issues each time the proposition is debated. Both local and national questions can satisfy all of the criteria cited for effective debate topics.

Wording the Proposition. There are several points to consider in phrasing a debate proposition. First, the question should be affirmatively worded. Within the proposition, the wording must specify an action or procedure to be undertaken — what the affirmative wants done. A proposition, such as "Resolved: That the President of the United States should be elected by a direct vote of the people," tells exactly what the affirmative will support. With negative wording of the debate proposition the affirmative must take a negative stand and contend that no problem exists or that a change other than that proposed by the proposition should be made. For example, a proposition like "Resolved: That the present system of electing the President should not be changed" would mean that the affirmative agrees "Yes, the present system should not be changed." Imagine the confusion in such a debate!

Second, all debate propositions should be precisely worded and free from question-begging statements. Not all propositions meet these requirements. In fact, one of the interscholastic propositions was that the United States should substantially reduce its foreign aid. Debaters and judges alike were confused by the term "substantially" which permitted unusual and often unreasonable interpretation. In some debates, substantially was considered anything over two million dollars, while in others no figure less than fifty million was acceptable.

Question-begging statements are not often found in debate propositions, particularly in questions which are used in interscholastic competition. Phrases such as "improper emphasis" or "wasteful spending"
assume that the statement has been proven and suggest that these
attributes are undesirable. Most coaches would agree that, if these
allegations can be proven, the course of action suggested should be
taken. But the proposition must never use this kind of loaded language.

Third, the proposition should refer to only a *single* course of action.
For example, the proposition "That our currency should be supported
by gold and the dollar should be devalued" is two questions. Although
both are highly legitimate matters and have many significant problems,
they should be debated as separate propositions. Debaters have enough
difficulty in sticking to a single proposition; we should not multiply
their problems by allowing them to clash on two propositions at once.

Fourth, propositions should be phrased so that the affirmative must
support the adoption of a new policy and must assume the burden of
proof for undertaking this new approach. The proposition "That the
state of Nebraska should establish a unicameral legislature" does not
meet this requirement since there is already a unicameral legislature in
Nebraska. If we altered the proposition to read "The state of Nebraska
should establish a two-house legislature," the proposition would meet
the requirement since the affirmative team is supporting a resolution
which is a new policy.

Defining the Proposition. Once a satisfactory proposition has been
chosen, the first task before a season begins is to define the proposition.
Research on the definitions of all crucial terms must be the first order
of business. If the debaters cannot first arrive at some reasonable
description or definition of the problem, then no useful analysis and
research can occur.

There is an impression that all the terms in a debate proposition must
be defined. *Those terms which need definitions are the ones with which
disagreement or confusion may result.* Except for those just beginning
to debate, the term "should" is understood by all debaters to mean
"ought to but not necessarily will." The nature of the proposition and
its wording will determine which words are crucial to the understanding
of it. It is always wise to define too many terms instead of too few, but
experience is the most reliable guide in determining which terms justify
formal definition.

The importance of definition in debate cannot be stressed too much.
Every coach can probably recall a member of his squad coming to him
after a debate and reporting that the opposition had defined the question

in such a way that they had limited the proposition to areas that were not acceptable, or that the definition was presented so skillfully that its implications did not become apparent until after the definition was accepted and the actual debate had begun. Debaters should be encouraged to interpret the proposition legitimately. The importance of attention to the definitions introduced by opponents is evident when the negative complains, "But we never heard you define that term," or "I didn't understand your definition of that term." These charges usually arise from a failure to listen to the definition or to consider its meaning relative to possible negative cases. The definition period is an agreement to disagree; if there is no agreement on what constitutes the disagreement, then there can be no orderly procedure of analysis and consideration.

There are five basic methods of defining propositions. *Definition by etymology* involves tracing the term being defined back to the origin of the word. The term "parity" defined in this way could be traced back to late Latin *paritas,* from which the words *par* and *paris,* meaning "equal," are derived.

The method of *contextual definition* involves considering the term with regard to the words which precede or follow it, as in "The powers of the Department of State should be increased." Here "powers" has a specific reference and meaning.

Definition by illustration cites a specific case. In defining the term "non-communist nations of western Europe," a debater would mention France, Switzerland, West Germany, Italy, and others he wished to include as non-communist nations (illustrations of the countries which are in the category being defined).

Definition by negation considers what is *not* meant by the term. Although it may represent an extreme case, some debaters define "law enforcement agencies" as not being the Federal Narcotics Bureau, the Treasury Agents, or the Secret Service. Frequently an alternative definition is provided by stating that the term has been described and discussed as to what it is *not,* and now we shall move on to what it *is.*

The use of *synonyms* is perhaps one of the easiest methods of definition to understand. Debaters cite or quote synonyms for the term being defined, such as equating "election by direct vote of the people" with its synonym, "election by popular vote for the candidate."

Analysis of the Proposition. For reasons which by now are apparent, analysis must follow definition since definition determines the nature of the analysis. The most easily understood approach to analysis involves what are called *stock issues.* By *stock* we mean a method for determining the general issues present in any proposition of policy. Other approaches exist which are used to determine the issues in a proposition of fact or value, but since most debates are concerned with policy questions, this discussion will focus on analysis of that type of question. Stock issues, which apply to all propositions of policy regardless of the wording of the proposition, include: (1) *Is there a need for a change?* (2) *Will the proposed change correct the problems inherent in the present system?* (3) *Are there serious disadvantages in the adoption of the proposal?* A more detailed discussion of these issues will enable us to see how debaters incorporate them into the analysis of a proposition and the preparation of a case.

Ehninger and Brockreide offer four subissues which are essential in determining if there is a need for a change:

> (*a*) Do serious problems actually exist? (*b*) Do such problems result in enough harm to require a change of policy? (*c*) Is the present policy to blame for the alleged problems? (*d*) Is any policy short of the one proposed inherently incapable of mitigating the alleged problems?[29]

Let us examine a debate proposition to see how these stock subissues apply to all propositions of policy. The proposition is *Resolved: That the United States should adopt a program of compulsory health insurance for all its citizens.* First, to determine if there is a need for a change we must establish whether there are serious problems in the present system of health care. Are all people receiving adequate medical assistance? Are all people able to afford minimal health care? (Is there the danger of epidemics or significant health hazards because of inadequate health care?) Are the rich healthier than the average and the poor? Are the poor the ones with the greatest need but the least likelihood of assistance? These are the types of questions which must be raised and answered in analyzing the proposition.

If, after considering the proposition in light of these questions, your debaters can accept and support with the various forms of evidence this aspect of the proposition, then they are prepared to move on to the second subissue. Are these harms of sufficient magnitude to change our policy in respect to health care for all citizens? Do epidemics, major health hazards, and disproportionate illness in the lower classes constitute such a problem that we ought to change our total policy toward medical care for the affected individuals? Naturally, much of the proof related

---

[29]Douglas Ehninger and Wayne Brockreide, *Decision by Debate* (New York: Dodd, Mead and Company, 1963), p. 224.

to this question will be introduced as the debater shows the seriousness of the problem. The entire matter of demonstrating the seriousness and significance of the problem is handled at one time.

For high school debaters the matter of *inherency* is a common stumbling block to establishing a need. Inherency is not a difficult concept to grasp; the misuse of the term by debaters leads to much misunderstanding. *Inherency refers to critical attributes without which the system could not function — the essential or fundamental characteristics within a policy which, if they were eliminated, would lead to an entirely new system or policy.* For instance, the opportunity for discrimination in housing is inherent in present state statutes. There is no legislation in many states specifically designed to prevent this action, so the opportunity is inherent — it is a characteristic of the present system. Now, applying this approach to the subissues mentioned earlier, we have "Will any policy short of putting new legislation on the books result in the type of change which is desirable and necessary?" An affirmative team should demonstrate that any other approach cannot, because of its fundamental features, induce a change and thereby solve the problem.

This question of inherency in a debate case is also critical to the second stock issue: Will the proposed system correct the deficiencies inherent in the present system? First, the inherent deficiencies must be identified in the first affirmative presentation. Then any discussion of a proposed solution must be based upon the elimination of these problems. This phase of the affirmative case will usually be presented by the second affirmative who is responsible for the introduction and justification of the proposal. We also need to ask: Should the solution be put into operation? It is *not* a matter of *will* but of *should*. High school debaters frequently become confused about the obligations of the affirmative. The affirmative is obligated to demonstrate that their proposal ought to be adopted and not that it will; they must only attempt to prove that a program of compulsory health insurance for all citizens should be adopted, not that this country will adopt it. Of course, there are some practical concerns here; legal problems, philosophical difficulties, and so forth, connected with a given proposal may be crucial in deciding if that proposal *should* be adopted.

Is this approach practical and workable? The downfall of many otherwise sound cases has occurred here. If the solution will cost fifty billion dollars per year, require us to relocate entire populations, or force us to abandon our commitments to other countries, then the proposal may not be as workable or practical as the system replaced.

Finally, we must ask, are there other serious disadvantages to the proposal? Although the price of the change may not be impractical, five billion dollars may be a significant disadvantage if the benefits are not great. The creation of a neighborhood vigilante corps, while perhaps being practical and workable, may have the disadvantage of taking law enforcement responsibility out of the hands of trained professionals who have a responsibility to the community and giving it to self-appointed guardians of public rights. Most skilled affirmative debaters will admit that there may be a few disadvantages to their proposal, but they should and usually will attempt to show that the advantages grossly outweigh the problems and that their proposal ought to be adopted.

Developing the Tools of Research and Analysis

Successful debating is largely determined by the amount of preparation; the effective researcher has a much greater likelihood of success. Students should be required to research the topic thoroughly and to base their case preparation upon materials encountered in their reading. Debate must remain a disputation of substance, and the only means for acquiring substance is through the use of research tools.

Free Materials. There is no need for large sums of money to be invested in debate materials or resource information. Although there are several publications which annually publish editions aimed at high school debaters and their proposition, there is a host of printed matter pertinent to the question in nearly every high school or public library.

The student researcher should first investigate the *Reader's Guide to Periodical Literature* for references on the proposition. Among the periodicals which are most likely to contain information on current national or international questions are *Time, Newsweek, U.S. News and World Report, Fortune, Business Week,* and *Current History.* Some publications publish a special issue devoted to an analysis of the high school question; these may be available in your library. *The Congressional Digest* and *The Annals of the American Academy of Political and Social Sciences* are two of the most popular of these publications. If they are not available in your library, they can be purchased at a minimal cost from the publishers. These are two of the most valuable sources of information for beginning and advanced debaters.

Current newspapers as well as back editions of papers such as the *New York Times,* the *Wall Street Journal,* the *Christian Science Monitor,* the *National Observer,* the *St. Louis Post-Dispatch,* the *Cleveland Plain-Dealer,* the *Louisville Courier-Journal,* the *Denver Post,* and the

Detroit Free Press are well known for their thorough treatment of contemporary affairs.

Low-Cost Materials. Because of the interest and participation in interscholastic debate, there is a wealth of materials written on the proposition of the year. If the school in which you teach is a member of either the state high school league or is affiliated with the district National Forensic League, order blanks for many of these materials will be provided through the state organization or the NFL. These associations usually provide the materials at cost to their members. The price charged for the materials ranges from 25 cents for a pamphlet to approximately five dollars for a book-length publication on the proposition. Most of the materials necessary for an intelligent analysis of the question cost between 70 cents and $1.75. Because these materials are prepared primarily for the issue chosen as the debate proposition, they frequently are not purchased by school or public libraries; for that reason you may need to purchase the publications.

Several companies prepare a handbook with sample cases and ample evidence to get the debater started on analysis and case preparation. These handbooks are useful devices for indicating the directions and types of analysis which may be utilized, but coaches should not encourage their debaters to rely upon the hardbook for year-long analysis and evidence. The "canned cases" (those lifted from published guides to the proposition) are rarely useful after substantial analysis of the proposition has been performed. If debate is to teach the principles of organization, analysis, refutation, and research, the debaters handbook should be used only as an instrument for providing direction for student investigation. Two of the more popular handbook publishers are J. Weston Walch, Box 1075, Portland, Maine, and The Mid-West Debate Bureau, Normal, Illinois.

Evaluating Sources of Evidence. Beginning debaters are, understandably, naive about printed matter. There is a common belief among the uninitiated that "if it's in print, it's true." The value of research will be increased if you will devote some time to criteria for evaluating sources. Even after the criteria are provided, the matter of critical judgment in application (degree and type) removes evaluation from the exact sciences.

Some of the tests offered by McBurney and Mills[30] describe how to evaluate the sources and the reporting of the information. First, and perhaps of greatest importance, do the authors qualify as experts? Second, does the medium have high credibility? Credibility, in this case, is inti-

---

[30]McBurney and Mills, *op. cit.,* pp. 105-111.

mately related to the comparative objectivity of the source. While it is impossible to find a totally objective source, evidence is most acceptable and useful in debating situations when it comes from reasonably objective sources. Third, is the reporting of the information clear and fair? Exaggeration in print is unfair treatment, and inaccurate or untrue statements should not be used by debaters. One recent case involved a group of psychiatrists who, without personally contacting the persons they were analyzing, made judgments about personality disturbances. These alleged personality disorders were then made public in the pages of a controversial popular magazine. Information of this type is not the result of clear and fair reporting and should not be used as debate evidence.

A word of caution regarding student behavior in the collection of evidence is in order. In their effort to find information which supports their case, debaters sometimes take portions of printed material out of context and then introduce the information in the debate as if it were not qualified by its surroundings. For instance, one political candidate was rumored to have said, "My opponents say that I am a liar and a cheat. Nothing could be further from the truth." His opponents did quote him on this matter, but they took his words out of context and cited him as saying, "I am a liar and a cheat." The surroundings make a significant difference in the meaning of statements, and debaters should be urged to use only that evidence which is an accurate representation of the intention and feeling of the author.

Recording Information.   There are numerous methods for recording information. The one you should have your students use is the one which is most acceptable to you.

The importance of a systematic approach to data recording is obvious to anyone who has researched for a term paper or speech. It is common for the researcher to discover after he sits down to prepare the paper or speech that he has failed to note, for instance, the source or the date of publication, the volume number, or perhaps the page number. The serious scholar then returns to the original work and takes down the information he had originally ignored; time and energy are wasted because of this failure to use a systematic approach to data recording.

Cards rather than sheets of paper should be used for recording the information. Cards are not as easily torn, can be filed easily, and are more compact and usable. Five by eight cards are widely used by debaters because of the large amount of available space.

When recording information, the debater should note at the top of the card the author, the article title, the publication in which it appeared, the date of the publication and the volume number, and the page or pages on which the article appeared. An illustration follows.

TELEVISION REGULATION
(AFFIRMATIVE)

Harold E. Fellows,
"The Television Industry Can
Regulate Itself." Statement
before the Federal Communications
Commission, 1960. Appearing in
Issues of the Sixties, ed. Leonard
Freedman and Cornelius Cotter,
Belmont, Calif.: Wadsworth Publishing
Co., 1961, p. 123

"Good advertising will always be to the benefit of broadcasting for
it will enable broadcasting to constantly build and improve its
facilities and its product for the American viewing and listening
audiences. Advertisers, through their use of broadcast facilities,
themselves are performing a public service by describing their merchandise, by increasing the sale of such merchandise and thus by
creating and stabilizing employment."

For economy in filing cards and for rapid retrieval, it is useful to place
a notation of the general category into which the information fits in the
upper right-hand corner. It also may be helpful to note whether the evidence is affirmative or negative.

Early in the season, debaters should be encouraged to develop "categories" for major pieces of evidence and argument. Once these rather
broadly labelled "pigeonholes" are established, research can proceed
more efficiently, e.g., by finding more information in a special category
or by organizing material already collected in a systematic fashion.

We must also have an understanding and agreement about the basic
kinds of issues present in the proposition. Otherwise, the debater will
wander through his research, wondering if the evidence collected will fit
into any kind of case, and lacking a well organized and systematic approach to the matter of research. Analysis should precede research; research then grows out of the issues discovered in the analysis phase. Not
all relevant issues can be discovered through the stock issues approach
discussed earlier in this chapter. Stock issues do provide the major issues
inherent in all propositions of policy and are useful as a point of departure. Debaters, after extensive work with a proposition, may evolve issues
that are peculiar to the specific question under consideration. But you
and your students will find research more fruitful if you begin with the
stock issues and then "grow into" the additional analysis required.

Specimen Brief[31]

I. The United States must seek improved relations with Red China.
   A. China is the major nation in Asia.
      1. According to the *New York Times*, April 18, 1965, "China is, even in her present underdeveloped state, the dominant power in Asia. She is this by virtue of the quality and quantity of her population, her geographic position, her civilization, her past power remembered, and her future power anticipated."
   B. Failure to improve relations with China encourages Chinese hostility.
      1. Dr. Alexander Eckstein, Professor of Economics at the University of Michigan said, "Continuing efforts to isolate China are bound to reinforce the regime's implacable hostility to the United States and its determination to wage an unrelenting campaign to isolate the United States in Asia."
II. The United States can safely seek improved relations with Red China at this time.
   A. China is weak economically, politically, and militarily.
      1. China lacks the industrial capacity to support a modern war.
         a) Ralph Powell, Professor of Far Eastern Studies at the School of International Service, American University, said: "Chinese factories cannot yet build all the heavy and sophisticated weapons necessary for a major conventional war."
   B. Politically, the split with Russia hampers China's ability to support a modern war.
      1. The United Press International reports Western military experts believe the Chinese army is now in no shape to fight because of shortages of planes and transportation equipment resulting from Russia's cutting off of armaments in 1960 following the growth of the Sino-Soviet quarrel.

The preparation of the debate case, the structuring of evidence, and the development of arguments is called "briefing the case." This is the matter of outlining the affirmative or negative constructive speech. Prin-

---

[31]Adapted from "1967 N.D.T. Final Debate," *Journal of the American Forensic Association*, 4, No. 3:118-119 (Fall, 1967). Reprinted by permission.

ciples of outlining such as subordination and indentation should be observed and, if the brief is to be used in actual debating situations, it must use complete sentences. (See the specimen brief.) The specimen brief illustrates the principles of briefing in including the major contentions, the evidence, and the subcontentions. Although most debaters prefer to work with evidence cards which contain the outline and major contentions of the case, they should be encouraged to commit the entire case to a brief format so that they may observe the case and arguments in relation to all ideas and evidence introduced.

The affirmative brief can be more "fixed" than the negative since any valid negative presentation must be adapted to the affirmative case. A flexible negative position does not prevent briefing the case to include the negative stand on all of the major stock issues discussed earlier. Since the stock issues are present in all affirmative cases, a brief which refutes these issues will have portions which are relevant to all affirmative need and plan contentions. The rationale for the brief for both sides is the same as that requiring students to prepare an outline for each speech they present in a public speaking course; structure, subordination, and unity are essential to the understanding of any communication.

The Form of a Debate

The placement of materials and arguments in their proper sequence assumes a knowledge of the responsibilities of each speaker in the debate. There is a standard set of responsibilities for each debater on most questions of policy. The format of a ten-minute constructive debate follows.

FIRST AFFIRMATIVE (10-minute constructive speech)
Introduction
1. Explain why the subject is of vital interest to the listeners.
2. Explain why this proposition should be debated in the light of current events.
3. Statement of the proposition and definition of terms.
4. Present the main issues in the question.
    a) Indicate the portions which you will cover.
    b) Indicate what your colleague will do.
Discussion
1. Identify the problems in the present system which warrant a change.
2. Develop your first contention and prove it through
    a) examples
    b) statistics, and
    c) authorities.

3. Summarize your first contention.
4. Present and prove other contentions which you support, if there is more than one.
5. Clarify the relationship of each of the contentions to the proposition.

Conclusion
1. Summarize your case.
2. Repeat the affirmative position.
3. Restate the contribution of your colleague.
4. Conclude your presentation.

FIRST NEGATIVE (10-minute constructive speech)

Introduction
1. Briefly review the speech of the first affirmative speaker.
2. Accept or change the affirmative speaker's definition of terms and their analysis.
3. State points of agreement and disagreement on the major issues.

Discussion
1. Make the position of the negative team clear:
   a) deny the existence of a need, or
   b) if you admit a need for a change, introduce a counter-proposal, or
   c) deny the existence of a need sufficient for adoption of the affirmative proposal.
2. Attack the first major point of the affirmative.
3. Prove your contention (while disproving the affirmative). Adapt your case to any portion of the affirmative which is inconsistent with the negative stand. Use proof such as
   a) examples,
   b) statistics, and
   c) authorities.
4. Proceed through the remainder of the case in the same way.

Conclusion
Summarize your case and show its strength relative to the affirmative case.

SECOND AFFIRMATIVE (10-minute constructive)

Introduction
1. Review the case of the first negative speaker.

Discussion
1. Refute those points of the negative which are most in conflict with your case.
2. Restate and emphasize your colleague's contribution.
3. Present the affirmative plan.
4. Show how your proposal will eliminate the evils of the present system while contrasting this solution with the negative approach.

5. Show that your plan is workable and that advantages will accrue from its adoption.

Conclusion

1. Summarize the affirmative case.
2. Present your conclusion.

SECOND NEGATIVE (10-minute constructive)

Introduction

1. Briefly review the affirmative case.
2. Show how your colleague disproved the affirmative case.

Discussion

1. Refute the affirmative need case.
2. Examine and refute the affirmative plan.
3. Emphasize the weak points in the opposition's case by showing the inconsistencies between the need and the plan.

Conclusion

1. Show how the affirmative proposal is undesirable.
2. Show how the need case does not stand.
3. Summarize the negative stand.[32]

These are the duties of each of the speakers during the constructive phase of the debate. Note that in a discussion of the choices available to the negative the status quo (or existing system) with repairs alternative was chosen. The directions for case construction for each side are of sufficient importance that they will be presented in detail here.

Types of Affirmative Cases. (1) *Need-plan.* Many coaches feel that the only approach to affirmative debating is the standard "need-plan" attack. It considers the present system as inadequate because of several fundamental shortcomings. Those problems are then developed as inherent needs, problems which reside in the present system because of its very nature. The affirmative will contend that a more satisfactory solution must be elected because of these deficiencies. The affirmative "plan" then outlines the most desirable solution to the difficulties, identifying the problems, and illustrating how this proposal will overcome the shortcomings of the present system. From the adoption of this solution will come a set of advantages which are additional reasons for adopting the proposal.

(2) *Comparative advantages.* This case is often misunderstood because only certain kinds of propositions lend themselves more readily to a comparative advantages case. Kruger describes the comparative advantages case in the following way:

---

[32]Adapted from Paul A. Carmack, "The Debaters Blueprint," *The Ohio High School Speech League Newsletter,* 1960-61.

As I understand it, the affirmative need not show any compelling
and inherent need, that is, the existence of a significant problem
stemming in whole or in part from the present policy whose removal
is being advocated. It may contend simply that, although there is
no real problem at present, the affirmative proposal would be
slightly more advantageous in achieving certain goals than the
existing policy and that its adoption, therefore, would be warranted . . . The chief contentions of the comparative advantage
advocates seem to be these:

1. Some propositions lend themselves to this type of analysis,
   which is to say they can be more effectively developed by it.
2. The element of surprise is good strategy.
3. It is a refreshing change from the traditional need-plan
   analysis.[33]

If this case is difficult to understand, perhaps an analogy could be
used. Imagine that you have a car which is four years old and has racked
up 65,000 miles. At this moment there are no inherent difficulties in this
car, but you are considering the purchase of another car. When you
compare the value of purchase to the present vehicle, you can see that
there is the possibility of failure in the present car due to the very age
which it has reached: it may need new tires, piston rings, wheel bearings,
or automatic transmission seals. At this moment, none of these items has
failed and they are not inherently faulty. But if you were to purchase a
new car you would be in a comparatively more advantageous situation
than you are with your present four-year-old car. This type of reasoning
and rationale applies to the comparative advantages affirmative case.

   Types of Negative Cases. (1) *Status quo.* Defense of the present
system as the best solution to any of the affirmative needs is still a
common negative approach. This case says that the present system can,
without change, best operate to overcome any problems.

   (2) *Status quo with repairs.* Most competitive debate teams elect this
negative case in which they endorse the basic nature of the present
system to overcome problems but agree that perhaps some minor mod-
ifications are necessary to deal with a few unforseen problems. The key
to this case is that the changes to be made are not basic ones but represent only slight changes. It permits the negative to use the strengths
of the present system in their defense while still allowing for minor
change to meet all situations.

   (3) *Counterplan.* When the negative feels that the present system has
certain fundamental weaknesses, they may choose the counterplan ap-

---

[33]Arthur N. Kruger, "The Comparative Advantage Case: A Disadvantage," *Journal of the American Forensic Association,* 3, No. 3:104-105 (September, 1966).

proach. The negative may agree with the affirmative need case, or they may elect to develop and prove a different type of need case. After establishing their needs, the negative then introduces, proves, shows the operation and advantages of accepting their proposal.

(4) *Straight negative.* Refutation of the affirmative need and plan contentions and denying all portions of the affirmative case is the heart of this approach. The negative will contend that the need is not adequate nor well proven and that, even if it were, the affirmative need could not and would not be workable or acceptable.

The Process of Refutation and Rebuttal. All debaters know the significance of refutation and rebuttal although debaters and coaches alike sometimes fail to differentiate between them. Refutation is the process of tearing down the opposition's case; *rebuttal* is the process of rebuilding your own case. As we practice it, however, in the act of refutation a debater also engages in rebuttal, and during the rebuttal period there is both refutation and rebuttal.

"Running refutation" is basic to effective debating. This involves refuting the opposition case during your constructive case. It requires flexibility and maximum adaptation. Ideally, all debaters would incorporate running refutation into their case, but only those who are well researched and effective are capable of it.

Refutation technique includes (1) stating the point to be refuted, (2) showing its significance to the opposition case, (3) proving your position, and (4) summarizing the issue. Or more aptly phrased by some coaches, "Name it, explain it, prove it, conclude it." The effectiveness of some outstanding debaters has been a result of their skill in emphasizing the significance of ideas to be refuted, the ability to make the opposition's arguments appear to be based upon the idea to be considered, and then refuting and destroying the case of the opposition.

The Importance of Summaries. Since the final summary of each speaker is the best opportunity for him to emphasize the result of the evidence and argument presented and shift the balance of the debate to the strengths of his presentation, the summary often weighs heavily in judges' decision-making. The final duty of each speaker in the debate, both in rebuttal and in the constructive period, is to summarize his efforts and those of his colleague. But the type of summary is significant. The debater must take the offense. He must demonstrate the weaknesses of his opponent's position while contrasting them with the strengths of his side. In the summary the speakers should boil down the information provided by their teams, emphasize its significance, and capsule the position of their side at the time of the summary. The final affirmative rebuttal speech is merely an extended summary; the affirmative speaker discusses the debate, highlighting the contributions of each team and spotlighting deficiencies and strengths. Naturally, the affirmative summary should present the debate from the affirmative point of view.

Classroom Approaches to Teaching Debate

The discussion of debate preparation and competition has largely emphasized the extracurricular feature of the activity. It has been assumed that many effective co-curricular forensic and debate programs have their genesis in a dynamic curricular speech program. Because many of the debaters originally become involved through classroom participation and interest in debate when it is offered as part of the instruction in a course in public speaking, let us examine a few of the methods used to teach debate in the classroom.

Subjects Developed from Units. Topics which are the most useful and productive to novice debaters are those which are closely related to their interests. These propositions can be taken from questions discussed by students during a speech. Some of the significant social questions discussed by students such as "Teenagers are responsible" or "Why the races don't live together" could be rephrased as "Resolved: That adults should treat teenagers as responsible persons" and "Resolved: That all Americans should live in integrated neighborhoods." These propositions could then be used for classroom debates.

It would be foolish to expect all questions which are used for debate propositions to be national or international problems. The use of a community or school issue as the basis for debate will arouse more interest and demonstrate the values of debating to students more rapidly than would debates on "the economic status of the satellite nations."

Generating Materials. Some descriptions of the effective debater include the phrase "well read." Skill in the use of printed materials naturally requires familiarity with the materials and publications. This does not mean that each debater must do all his research independently of his colleagues. The debate teacher or coach should urge students to pool their resources early in the year to avoid unnecessary duplication of effort. There is no stigma attached to research done by another member of the team or school provided that the research cites material accurately and in context. An outmoded belief exists which says that unless the debater has gone to the original source himself and has read and extracted the printed materials from the source, then the evidence is ill-gotten. If we perceive debate as a learning process and if each of our students can examine five times as much material through cooperative research and learn perhaps twice or three times as much about the question, then the case for group research is made.

Team Research. After preliminary analysis of the proposition, the teacher should assign teams of researchers to investigate each phase of the proposition. For instance, one team might explore the matter of US gold reserves if a question on the "balance of payments deficit" were the debate proposition. Another team might do research on the World Bank as an agency involved in international finance. The proposition could systematically be analyzed to discover other major topics which warrant research. As the teams collect information and record it in a standard form, it becomes available to all other members of the squad. The only effort required by the rest of the team is that they must copy the evidence cards for their own use. If each member of the class collects three items of evidence and there are fifteen students in the class, then all members who are willing to copy the information for their own use then have forty-five pieces of evidence.

Even when this approach is followed, the superior debaters will secure more evidence than that provided by the squad in general. Remember that class research has the limitation of providing easily available information, data which may be chosen from other than highly reputable sources and which may not be usable in most debate speeches. A great variety of materials can be secured in this way, but debaters must be careful in their use of these kinds of source materials.

Debating Both Sides. The ethical matter of "Is it proper to debate both sides of a proposition?" was for some time a hotly contested issue. In an attempt to investigate the opinions of both high school and college coaches of debate, Klopf and McCroskey surveyed 393 National Forensic League and American Forensic Association teachers and coaches. They found that only 3.5 per cent of the number surveyed thought debating both sides is unethical.[34] Much of the cited controversy revolves around the matter of what the authors call "the relative versus the absolute ethic." The position of some teachers and coaches is that a debater should be committed to that case which he presents, much as the public speaker should speak only on behalf of a proposition to which he is personally committed. Those favoring debating both sides of the proposition believe that debate is essentially an educational endeavor, "a relative ethic," and that interscholastic and intercollegiate debate exist as a training ground for investigation and evaluation of issues and evidence. Obviously, the latter school has prevailed.

Many of the high school tournaments are "switch-sides"; a team will uphold the affirmative side in one round and the negative side in the next round. Such an arrangement requires the debater to be well informed on

---

[34]Donald W. Klopf and James C. McCroskey, "Debating Both Sides Ethical? Controversy Pau!", *Central States Speech Journal*, 15, No. 1:36-39 (February, 1964).

both sides of the question, the major objective of debate training. There are a number of tournaments in which schools bring four members for each team; two members take the affirmative in each round while the other two debaters comprise the negative team. The beginning debater generally is more successful with the standard approach of debating only one side of the proposition since he is awkward in his technique and has difficulty with research and analysis. By debating only one side, he has time to learn debate style and perform a thorough amount of research. After a year or so of debating one side, the debater may move to the "switch-sides" format and from then on move with relative ease from one side to the other.

The switch-sides approach has the disadvantage of reducing the number of students who can compete. When the number of invitations to a tourney is limited, each school will usually be permitted to bring only one team in each division. If the tournament is a four-man team affair, there is a greater opportunity for more students to get tournament experience than when it is only a two-man tourney. However, from the analysis position the student gains more useful experience participating in switch-sides debate, since the best understanding of the question is gained by an exposure to arguments and analysis of all phases of the proposition.

Developing the "Horses."   Nothing succeeds like success and nothing arouses a greater interest (and likely future success) in debate than a successful team. The requirements for a debater are certainly far different from those for a good football player; we do not need giant specimens with speed, moderate intelligence, desire, and innate ability. But our requirements in many respects parallel those of the football coach. A good debate prospect is mentally fast, has moderate or high intelligence, and possesses a desire to succeed. It is possible for us to describe the characteristics of a person whom we believe will have success in this activity. But how can we encourage persons like these to participate?

Early identification of talented students is a *sine qua non*. A sound and educationally defensible speech program begins at the junior high school level and helps to foster the identification and education of all students who could be helped by or make a significant contribution to the program. If a program is designed to be competitively successful, then the best available talent must be secured each year, probably from students voluntarily joining a speech club or course, or through invitation to participate.

A "feeder" type program will help to cultivate talent. Beginning with the seventh grade, students showing average or above-average abilities in speech activities should be referred to the speech teacher and encouraged to attend debate or speech meetings. They also may be permitted to observe and participate in after-school debates. Do not be reluctant to place them in competition with students who are a year or two ahead of them; this kind of competition often will spur them to achievement they otherwise would never think possible.

Since frequent competition enhances existing abilities, the teacher must provide either intramural or interscholastic opportunities for debate with other students. There is nothing which will stimulate a successful program as much as an interested teacher who personally encourages each participant to continue and praises him for his efforts as well as suggests directions for improvement. If students experience this kind of positive reinforcement and if they are stimulated through a constructive program of curricular and co-curricular activities, there is no need to worry about developing a pool of talented participants.

A Deep Yet "Broad" Squad. Do not be misled by the discussion of the development of a high quality squad. It is possible to be successful in competition and also provide a broad array of experiences for interested students. If a program has weekly or biweekly meetings and opportunities for practice debates between members of the squad, if all members of the team are given an opportunity to attend one or more tournaments, and if the speech classroom becomes a forum for the interchange of ideas and in-class debates, then debate activities will be a broad, in-depth program. To a great extent, we regard debate as an educationally broadening experience designed to assist the greatest possible number of students to increase their abilities to communicate and participate meaningfully in our society. If this is our concern, then the program will have to be broadly based, will use successful competition as a stimulus to greater achievement and effort, and will result in the greatest value for the greatest number of students. Trophies and awards should not become the goal of the program; they are useful only as incentives for achievement. There are, however, too many coaches who live for the collection of "hardware." They may point with pride to their array of trophies, all of which may have been won by only two or three "experts." Instead, a program which has won no trophies but has provided an opportunity for twenty students to participate in effective communication experiences is much more educationally sound.

One of the recent innovations in forensics is the use of a variety of contemporary topics to involve students more deeply and increase the extent of participation in the program.[35] It involves students from three or four schools in a debate on a topic of current interest, such as "That

---

[35]One application of the general approach is described in Owen Peterson, "Forum Debating," *The Speech Teacher*, 14, No. 4:286-290 (November, 1965).

more stringent law enforcement should be practiced by the police" or "That students involved in protest movements should be suspended from school." Topics of this type have the advantage of exciting more students and being in tune with the dynamic nature of our society. Instead of having the participation of only a few skilled craftsmen on a single proposition for an entire year, we have an opportunity to involve a large group of students on a topic of contemporary interest. With this approach the proposition may be used for only one or two meetings or contests; topics are changed frequently to encourage excellence in research and variety in materials. Debate thus becomes a forum for current affairs—the kind of training ground for citizenship and participation that we have so long claimed it is. An approach of this character also encourages opportunities for the use of classroom debates in other curricular courses. Government and history courses are an excellent forum for this activity. If we bring our activity more in tune with the needs of society today, we shall find an increasing demand for our activity and profession. The "hippy" accuses the "traditional" members of society of being irrelevant. In the eyes of many, the same kind of charge pertains to debate. We can make it more relevant; the method suggested here may be the most immediate and appropriate approach.

Model Debates. Schools which are beginning a debate program or institutions which want to stimulate participation and interest may schedule a demonstration or "model" debate for a school assembly or debate club meeting. If you contact a nearby school, you will probably find that they have a team or teams which are able to present a demonstration debate. Some coaches and teachers assume that the best demonstration can be presented by a college team from a nearby university. College debaters use a somewhat different style in presenting the analysis of their case, but that is not the main reason for discouraging demonstration debates by collegiate teams. Students usually perceive the college student as representing a goal which is virtually unattainable for them. Instead of seeing the demonstration as a model of debate technique, they consider it to be an academic exercise only for the brilliant and sophisticated adult. These students become impressed with the delivery, the urbane manner, and the skillful use of evidence and conclude that all debaters, even the beginner, should behave in this manner; with their limited experience they decide that they could never compete successfully. The result of a demonstration by a college team may discourage students from participating rather than encouraging them.

Students from another high school have nearly the opposite effect. Although the listeners may be impressed, if they are told that the debater once had no experience or skill in debating and that this performance is a result of two years participation, they may be much more likely to become interested in debate. Finally, interschool rivalry (regarding anything done by a rival school as basically inferior to that of the home school) will serve as a stimulus. If you have a choice, invite a high school team to present a demonstration debate.

Motivational Factors. For some students, participation is an opportunity to "belong." They become part of a select group whose membership is determined both by desire and ability. Group spirit and the hope to remain a contributing member of the squad causes some to work far into the night or rework their materials an endless number of times.

Trophies, medals, certificates, and plaques are our most frequently used motivational tools. The teenager will labor for hours just to win a ten-cent medal, but he might not try if no reward were provided. Any coach who has seen his students gaze at the trophies on display at the registration desk of a tournament or has watched debaters examine the medals to be presented to members of the winning squad is aware of the strong motivation provided by these awards. In his development of a theory of motivation, Maslow identifies the esteem needs as

> ... [partially] what we may call the desire for reputation or prestige (defining as respect or esteem from other people) ... Satisfaction of the self-esteem need leads to feelings of self-confidence, worth, strength, capability, and adequacy of being useful and necessary in the world.[36]

The trophies should never become the end themselves, but they can offer the incentive for successful participation. Trophies often serve more strongly as instruments of motivations for the coaches than for the debaters; witness the fraternity of coaches who journey forth on weekends in search of "hardware."

Surprising as it may seem, travel to different cities and towns acts to encourage student participation. In many debate programs each year there is a trip to a somewhat distant city in the state (perhaps a three- or four-hour drive), a city which many of the students have not visited. The adventure of travel (and perhaps travel via a crowded schoolbus where horseplay and spirit are sometimes boundless) helps to attract debaters.

---

[36]A. H. Maslow, *Motivation and Personality* (New York: Harper & Row, Publishers, 1954), pp. 90-91.

Basic Rules of Debate

Staging the Debate.   Debates should be scheduled in a room with a table and lecturn. There should be enough chairs for each of the four debaters and additional chairs for the timekeeper and the judge. Rooms designed specifically for debates are not necessary; any experienced judge can recall listening to debates in zoology laboratories and physics class-rooms. The room should be located so that the debaters will not be interrupted during their speeches.

Definitions of Terms.   One of the obligations of the first affirmative speaker is to offer an affirmative interpretation of the proposition for consideration. The affirmative definition should be either accepted or rejected by the first negative speaker; in the event that the negative chooses to reject or modify the affirmative definition, they should be prepared to support and defend their interpretation of the proposition. If the affirmative does not assume this obligation, then the negative is entitled to offer a definition of terms which will stand unless challenged by the affirmative.

Debaters should be urged to listen carefully to the definition of terms. The remainder of the debate will include these terms and if the challenge of a faulty definition is not offered early in the debate, the side present-ing the original definition is totally justified in refusing to accept a late change in the definition.

Proposed Plans.   On the affirmative side, two approaches are possible. The first approach concerns teams which follow what we could call the "standard" analysis pattern: need-plan. A case of this type would intro-duce and defend the plan, in most instances, in the second affirmative presentation.

The comparative advantages case, however, requires a different approach:

> ... because it compares the present plan with the affirmative pro-posal on the basis of results. The cause-for-action or "need" argu-ment is given much less importance and is handled indirectly.[37]

Since most of our high school competition involves propositions of pol-icy, the bulk of the first affirmative speech will be spent in establishing criteria for a judgment and in demonstrating how the action proposed meets the criteria.[38]

---

[37]McBurney and Mills, *op. cit.,* pp. 195-196.
[38]*Ibid.,* p. 196.

Counterplans make the obligations of the negative more substantial than normal. The location of the plan depends upon the affirmative need case. In the event that affirmative analysis reveals a need identical to that which the negative intends to propose, there is little value in duplicating the affirmative. The negative counterplan could then be presented in the first negative constructive speech.

Usually, the negative will not find the affirmative analysis of the present situation adequate and the first negative speaker will spend his constructive presentation establishing an indictment of a different type than the affirmative. Then, in the constructive period, the second negative will present the counterproposal. Under no circumstances should the plan be introduced during the rebuttal period.

Burden of Proof. This is one of the most widely misunderstood concepts in debate. Burden of proof "rests with the party who has the presumption against him."[39] The affirmative bears a greater burden of proof than does the negative; the affirmative is first obligated to present a *prima facie* case, a case sufficient to establish a fact or establish the fact in question unless refuted. If on the surface the proposition is not acceptable or proven after the first affirmative speech, the affirmative has not met its burden of proof. For each successive speech the debaters bear burdens of proof; the negative must counterbalance the affirmative presentation.

The affirmative has a greater burden since the presumption is against the affirmative team; they must demonstrate the acceptability of the debate proposition. This burden is further borne out when we examine the judging process. In case of a tie (where the affirmative has not adequately assumed its burden of proof and neither side appears to carry the issue or the debate), the decision is granted to the negative.

Rebuttal. The formal rebuttal period, consisting of a five-minute block of time for each debater, is the rebuilding phase of the debate. Its purpose is to reestablish the position of each party to the debate, so no new issues may be introduced in the rebuttal period. High school debaters often confuse the use of new evidence with the introduction of new issues. New and additional evidence should be presented each time an issue is reused; otherwise the debate degenerates into an almost endless repetition of the same quotations and statistics. However, judges will and should penalize a team which introduces in their rebuttal speech an issue which had not previously been presented in the debate.

---

[39]Wayne C. Eubank, "Developing the Case," *Argumentation and Debate: Principles and Practices,* ed. James H. McBath (New York: Holt, Rinehart & Winston, Inc., 1963), p. 106.

Right to Question or Challenge.   Only in a parliamentary type debate can a point of order or direct question be asked of one of the opposing team members. Since most of the high school interscholastic tournaments are not conducted using the parliamentary approach, there is no proper or appropriate method for directly questioning members of the other side or objecting directly to the evidence they introduce.

The proper method for objection is to raise the issue during your constructive speech, identify the problem, cite the evidence, introduce the appropriate reasoning, and leave the issue in the hands of the judge. The judge will not render a decision on the issue at that time, but his decision will be made when he weighs the evidence to arrive at a decision on the total debate.

From an ethical position, debaters should not approach the judge after the conclusion of the debate and attempt to introduce the "right" interpretation of the opposition's case; they should rely upon the merits of their case as presented to make the problem clear to the judge. The debate is concluded, finally and officially, at the conclusion of the second affirmative rebuttal speech.

Arousing Interest in Debate

The following principles offered by O. J. Wilson[40] are useful in stimulating student and community interest in debate.

1. *Correct erroneous misconceptions about debate.* In some schools and communities there is a belief that debate is "elocution" and that like elocution it is out of date. Your best tool in refuting this misconception is through assembly programs, community activities, and newspaper items which demonstrate the usefulness of debating skill.

2. *Sell the program to your school administration.* Many principals and superintendents are not hostile to speech and debate but maintain a generally passive attitude toward it. Effective public relations by the coach and in-service training programs for the school administrators in the form of continuing information about the accomplishments of debate students and the value of their training will help to overcome the administration's apathy. A debate coach or teacher must be the best salesman for his activity in the school and community.

3. *Get the cooperation of other teachers.* The social science teachers usually are very interested in and willing to help support a debate program. In the sciences there is less knowledge about the debate and its values. The debate coach might help explain the program to these teach-

---

[40]O. J. Wilson, "Techniques for Stimulating Interest in Debate," *American Forensic Association Register* [n.d.].

ers and at the same time ask if the teacher knows of any potentially promising students who might work into the program.

4. *Organize a debating club.* A group with a common interest in speech offers an incentive for students to continue their participation beyond the classroom. With the incentive of its activities, offices, and recognition the debate club will be an effective supplement to the program.

5. *Attend debate tournaments.* The stimulation from just observing a debate tournament often brings students to debate activities. After the program is established, participation in tournaments brings with it the excitement of competition and the winning of awards. Try to involve each student who wishes to be in tournament activity; don't restrict tournament activity to just your best debaters.

6. *Encourage local leaders to establish awards and prizes.* If you can induce members of the community to provide the trophies or the money for a competitive event, the publicity and interest in debate will soon arouse more interest and result in more community awareness of the activity. Use the school and local newspaper to publicize the awards and the results of the competition.

7. *Arrange for debaters to appear before community organizations.* Organizations such as Kiwanis, Lions, Rotary, Sertoma, League of Women Voters, and Junior Chamber of Commerce are in search of material for programs at their weekly or monthly meetings. This demonstration will help create more awareness of the values of the program, and the interest and support which these community leaders give to the debaters as a result of their appearance is a great morale booster.

8. *Publicize debate activities.* The debate coach must sell his program to his community. Publicity will sell the program. Send all information about participation in contests, announcements of demonstration debates before service clubs, tournaments to be attended, awards won by students, or any item with any news potential to the newspaper. Students and parents will scan the paper for news of the program. Recognition in the local newspaper stimulates student interest and creates community awareness and appreciation of the program.

Suggested Projects

1. How would you explain to an administrator the value of teaching conversation in the classroom? Is it anything more than a useful social technique? Why?

2. Design a conversation unit for classroom use. What kind of practical situations are essential? How does the design of a unit in conversation differ from any of the units in a public speaking course? Be prepared to defend your reasons.

3. Are any of our real-life situations ones in which discussion plays a significant role? Identify and analyze three situations showing how discussion plays a critical part in exploring and resolving problems.

4. What format would you follow if you were asked to design a discussion conference? Would you present awards to outstanding discussants? How would you determine which participants made the most significant contributions? What kinds of rating instruments and what criteria would you use in arriving at judgments about the excellence of participation?

5. Which approach to discussion do you feel will be of the greatest value to students being prepared for citizenship twenty years from now? Is this a significant change from the present approach? Will society differ substantially at that time? Should discussion reflect the changing character of society?

6. Design a unit in the teaching of debate. Can you justify the teaching of debate to students who will probably not further their formal education after high school?

7. Is debate only idle academic gamesmanship? How might we alter our debate format to make it more applicable to the needs of students? Are we teaching students to use jargon and technique that are useful only when presented to an "expert" judge?

8. If you were asked to establish a forensics program in a high school that had never offered any formal speech training, what course of action would you follow? Who would be your most promising academic allies? How would you enlist their assistance?

9. Select questions from Chapter 6 and assign individual students to classify them and reword them into the types of good discussion questions presented on pages 258-260.

10. Select questions from Chapter 6 or from current events which are worded as policy problems. Reword them into debate resolutions of value.

References

Becker, Samuel L., Bowers, John Waite, and Gronbeck, Bruce E. "Instructional Uses of Videotape, II. Videotape in Teaching Discussion," *The Speech Teacher*, 17:104-106 (March, 1968).

Behl, William A. "A New Look At the Debate Brief," *The Speech Teacher*, 10:189-193 (September, 1961).

Boaz, John K. and Ziegelmueller, George. "An Audience Debate Tournament," *The Speech Teacher*, 12:270-276 (November, 1964).

Cartwright, Dorwin and Zander, Alvin. *Group Dynamics, Research and Theory*. New York: Harper & Row, Publishers, 1953.

East, James R. and Streifford, Howard. "Competitive Discussion: A Literary Approach," *The Speech Teacher*, 11:136-140 (March, 1962).

Ehninger, Douglas. "Debate as Method: Limitations and Values," *The Speech Teacher*, 15:180-185 (September, 1966).

Fausti, Remo P. and Luker, Arno H. "A Phenomenological Approach to Discussion," *The Speech Teacher*, 14:19-23 (January, 1965).

Geiger, Don. "The Humanistic Direction of Debate," *The Speech Teacher*, 14:101-106 (March, 1965).

Giffin, Kim. "Interpersonal Trust in Small-Group Communication," *The Quarterly Journal of Speech*, 53:224-234 (October, 1967).

Gulley, Halbert E. *Discussion, Conference and Group Process*. 2nd ed.; New York: Holt, Rinehart & Winston, Inc., 1963.

Hare, A. Paul. *Handbook of Small Group Research*. New York: The Free Press, 1962.

Hare, A. Paul, Borgatta, Edgar F., and Bales, Robert F. *Small Groups: Studies in Social Interaction*. New York: Alfred A. Knopf, Inc., 1962.

McBath, James H. (ed.). *Argumentation and Debate: Principles and Practices*. Rev. ed.; New York: Holt, Rinehart & Winston, Inc., 1968.

McBurney, James H. and Mills, Glenn E. *Argumentation and Debate*. 2nd ed.; New York: The Macmillan Company, 1964.

Roberts, Mary M. "Improving Speech Programs: Needs, Trends, Methods, Part II, Planning a Forensic Workshop," *The Speech Teacher*, 12:115 (March, 1963).

Scheidel, Thomas M. and Crowell, Laura. "Feedback in Small Group Communication," *The Quarterly Journal of Speech*. 52:273-278 (October, 1966).

Utterback, William. *Group Thinking and Conference Leadership*. New York: Holt, Rinehart & Winston, Inc., 1960.

Watkins, Lloyd. "Some Problems and Solutions in Teaching Group Discussion," *The Speech Teacher*, 10:211-214 (September, 1961).

10

Theatre

Theatre is the most comprehensive form of art developed by man. It utilizes every other art form in selective ways—the arts of the actor, designer, and playwright—and presents this total production with accompanying music and dance before an audience. More than this, it puts to work all of our most recent ideas in communication theory to bring about *empathy,* the artistic involvement of the audience. Artistic communication (idea, encoding, transmission, reception, decoding, and finally feedback) has found its basic media in the theatre. The statistical proof of the millions of viewers throughout the world has helped our modern advertisers to verify the empathy that theatre people have known since the time of the Greeks.

THEATRE: SOME PROCESS DEFINITIONS

The teacher of theatre needs to be well informed about the basic elements of theatre and the terms used to describe them. Because theatre is basic to man and because it has proven useful as entertainment, commentary, and therapy, we find drama discussed in books and journals ranging from commercial theatre through sociology, psychology, education, and commerce. Terms such as role-play, sociodrama, psychodrama and creative drama fill modern journals of therapy. Discussions of simulation, role-play, and improvization share educational and management bulletins with those on T-group and sensitivity sessions. Indiscriminate use of such terms forces professional theatre workers (educational and commercial) to reanalyze their own definitions and processes. What is theatre? drama? creative dramatics? How are these related to therapeutic types? Under what conditions does drama become theatre? What is creativity? talent? artistry? What is the relation of talent to creativity? to artistic performance?

Let us subscribe to the established definition that *a play is a story told to an audience through action* (by actors or dancers) from some type of a stage. Drama, we will assume, differs from a novel or poem (as a literary form) by a combination of elements including *action, conflict, suspense, characterization,* and *dialogue.* We must then be ready for the arguments of teacher-artists who advocate that the audience is unnecessary, that they get in the way of creative art in the theatre. These arguments are often heard from studio artists and musicians; the artist wishes to express himself, does so, and that is the end of it. If the audience likes the work of art, fine; if not, some other audience might, or else the work is ahead of its time.

Directors are very recent in the history of theatre. Modern theatre knows them as "an audience of one,"[1] hired to represent the audience until it shows up. To a student of theatre this notion implies that, when a play is poorly received, it is (*a*) poorly chosen for this specific audience, (*b*) poorly directed, or (*c*) beyond the ability of the cast. In any case, it is not the fault of the audience. A second thought to ponder relates communication to the theatrical effort. The late Wendell Johnson[2] stated that most of us speak those things we like to hear ourselves say, but we hope to hear applause for our wisdom from listeners. Herein lies the heart of the argument: Does theatre occur before any audience is present? With regard to communication, we sometimes talk to ourselves to clarify our thinking, to select language for some anticipated discussion or to rethink past discussions. But even in terms of communication, only a fool would talk nonsense to himself. Many modern contributors of

---

[1]Joshua Logan, "The Art in Yourself," *Directing the Play,* ed. Toby Cole and Helen K. Chinoy (Indianapolis, Ind.: The Bobbs-Merrill Company, Inc.), pp. 210-17.

[2]Wendell Johnson, *Your Most Enchanted Listener* (New York: Harper & Row, Publishers, 1956).

painting, music, and theatre seem to be babbling. Art is based upon order and form; creative artists may find a new order and arrangement, but the order still exists. It is the job of the director to find the order and form of a play and prepare it for the audience expected.

Theatre as Language Development

Theatre provides many opportunities for the embellishment of ideas through language that is beautiful, profound, and powerful. Research in language development indicates that personal language is the result of the environment of the user. Both amateur and professional actors find dialogue from past plays creeping into their daily conversations. Often we become aware of a phrase or idea spoken in a style beyond the colloquial level of language. After some thought we can trace the idea to a play or piece of literature which we have committed to memory. If we wish to improve the language of students, we might well involve them in many theatrical opportunities to enrich their ideas and vocabulary. We should recognize, however, that the selections we make will have considerable influence on their style of language. It is with some hesitation that we consider such plays as *Who Is Afraid of Virginia Woolf?* or *Endgame.*

Churchill marshalled the language of Shakespeare into an instrument of war and used it to defend the world. Modern theatre seems to be attacking the ideas of form, continuity, and theme with the language of the gutter. The history of theatre has recorded the development of ideas, the power of language, and the beauty of spectacle. It has also recorded cycles of decay, ideas unworthy of development, substitution of language for ideas, and indecent display of words and action as a substitute for ideas or linguistic power. In any event, future historians will make the final evaluation of the cycles through which theatre has passed. The theatre has acted as a mirror of nature, recording the part of the culture that the mirror is focused upon. Perhaps *Theatre of the Absurd,* the theatre of sensation, and the theatre of the obscene are true images of our culture. They might merely reflect the distortions furnished by the master comics of our time—like mirrors at a funhouse, deliberately distorting ideas and language as a means of ridicule. If it is in fact the distorted views of a small group of people, they might better spend their time studying Johnson's *People in Quandaries,*[3] which so well develops the concept that we talk ourselves into our own mental illness. Students

---

[3]Wendell Johnson, *People in Quandaries* (New York: Harper & Row, Publishers, 1946).

of drama should compare the world they see with that described in the new plays and judge for themselves if the ideas, the language levels, or the characters represent the culture. Fantasy generally portrays a world we would like to escape to. Is the modern theatre fantasy, or is it a world one would wish to escape from? At any rate, the teacher should be concerned in selecting a play for study and production about whether the play will help students improve themselves, or furnish a blueprint for deterioration. Those ideas and words used most frequently eventually become a part of the working vocabulary. Theatre can provide improvement in language usage.

We established the theory in Chapter 1 that an institution has a basic *raison d'etre* (reason for existence) and that all curricular offerings must find their context and reason to exist within the institutional objectives. We submit that a knowledge of theatre, its historic contribution to art and language form, and its processes of using language in poetic and prose dialogue are valuable contributions to the total education. Furthermore, within the best objectives of the public school, theatre should be included at every grade level from kindergarten through college. We further believe that the study of theatre should include play making, play reading, play analysis, play production, and play attendance. Study of the theatre should be active rather than passive. A course based upon play reading is comparable to a course on cooking with the food catered, or a course in physical education in which the exercises are merely demonstrated. Students should experience the total theatre process: acting, design, building of models, rehearsal and production, stagecrafts, play writing, audience analysis, and play attendance.

Theatre as Community Preparation

Many students are active in community theatrical ventures sponsored by their church and other civic organizations. If the school program is complete in its development of processes, skills, and conceptual understandings, a production team could work efficiently with such an organization to produce plays of quality. One-act plays presented as an alternate to noon hour movies may provide directing experience for mature students in the drama class while others may gain considerable experience as cast members. Working with basic scenery in this "workshop" setting would increase the student's flexibility in the use of many staging techniques. Experience with one-act plays and scenes from longer plays would provide considerable variety in the types of characterizations for each actor, which is often not possible in the limited number of school- and class-sponsored plays. Such an instructional laboratory may push near the edges of the cast's and director's ability and help with the concept that any producing group can select productions beyond the ability of cast, director, or plant. Another valuable learning process develops in realizing the amount of time needed to polish any play sequence, or in building a stage prop from design to tested use. The final test for the school theatre, however, is not the productions in the school laboratory, or even the major school productions, but the ability of the students to bridge the gap between the school and the community. The final evaluation includes itemizing the number who help to sponsor, direct, participate in, and shoulder the technical duties of community productions.

Occasionally the teacher is rewarded with a good play, written by a cast member, a play worthy of publication. Many original skits, variety shows, and reviews are sponsored in any community and may be improved through professional school leadership and practical training. American theatre has been helped little by those who have run from the problems in hopes of finding facilities and financing in New York. The hope of theatre in America lies in the leadership of college-trained students who are willing to establish programs and facilities over several years, producing quality performances in theatre for children as well as adults.

Drama as Human Behavior

If we probe the primitive culture from which man has come, we find the continuous rebirth of drama in the making. The leading characters are all there and the basic situations cause dramatization to develop from the desire to express oneself with sound and the play on sound to develop four-dimensional theatre (story, actor, stage, and audience). The curtain opens revealing a primitive cave or tent group. Long famine and drought has made foraging for food less productive than in the past. Rain is needed to feed the wild roots and animals. Each small family cries out to their gods for help in easing famine. One or two members of the community, it seems, have better "communication" with the listening gods than others. The community pleads with them to share their methods of prayer so that all may find life more bountiful. Whether the process of prayer is the cause, effect, or accidental coincident of the desired event is not the point at issue. The point is that some seem to time the dramatized message more directly with the desired response.

At first this lucky communicator is hesitant to share his secret because he is not sure what it is he does. In an attempt to refine his method he sneaks away to sing his prayers (incantations) and dance his dances in private. In this process he is like the playwright, reworking his plots, revising his lines, and rearranging his episodes. Curious neighbors, wishing to share in his success secretly follow to learn the words, steps, and timing of his "medicinal message." As they watch they become so involved in his movements and pleas that they join or applaud. Finding the support and applause to his liking, empathy is born, an actor is created, and the need to move to higher ground or place his audience on the hillside grows as the audience grows. While time for meditation is needed, the desire to share in language, music, and movement is basic to man. Even the most meditative and quiet form of religious ritual becomes staged ceremony. Such ceremony enhances, enriches, and embellishes man's most sacred events. For many people there would be little religion left if the dramatic embellishments were omitted from religious ceremony. Dramatization is basic human behavior.

Drama as Self-Therapy

Dramatization serves man in a second dimension as a means of playing out his problems with other men and women. The man on the way to the office rehearses the breakfast argument relating to his son's long hair and his daughter's short skirt. The verbalization is often the second draft of the earlier disoriented plot. Taken by surprise at breakfast, he now finds more time and less interruption as the new outline allows him to arrange his arguments, pose rhetorical questions, and culminate with oratorical flourish. A second version of the same discussion is likely taking place as his wife is pushing the vacuum into dark corners, chasing every particle of dust as a symbol of the antagonists she met at breakfast. These characters differ in precise degrees from those striding the stage in the husband's version. In some ways they may seem like the miniature forms of the same scheming, unappreciative soul who left her table to mumble his way to the office. The family cat, dog, and canary may even be utilized as momentary members of the cast as she focuses logical, emotional, and ethical arguments upon them. Like the characters in a play, they may have been planted to provide a listener or an occasional questioner. The dialogue seems real since it provides an opportunity for the exposition of previous happenings, inner thoughts, and other involvements needed to round out the play, provide the necessary conflict, suspense, and particularly the identity of the protagonist. Meanwhile on the other side of the forest, the two offspring are walking to school kicking rocks and likewise talking up their post-breakfast version, each cast as the leading but misunderstood protagonist. This vicarious living through verbalization proves as valuable as the normal individual's psychiatric service. It is much cheaper, and no records are kept. Inadequate solutions are identified and omitted.

Drama as Functional Simulation

Not only is the use of dramatization an excellent form of *post-action evaluation,* industry and professional groups have recently developed this process as a means of *pre-action evaluation* of organizational forms and problem-solving. Complete departments and personnel are reshuffled to "improvise" new possible alignments and to create for visible and oral measurement the new problems which will occur if the new personnel packaging materializes. The teacher of theatre now needs to be an expert in the use of drama as a discipline for industrial planning in anticipatory problem-solving. His students should be prepared for industrial "simulation." No longer are we confined to running account commentary or post-operative reporting. With industry and professions leading the way the drama specialist must run to keep up. The process of drama makes "simulation" a valid measurement of new administrative arrangements. Basically, *the simulation must provide the necessary conflict* which the new forms will create. The characters and the dialogue must reflect the backroom beefing and corridor action which reflect new frictions. The trained dramatist should help get the simulation group past the stage of the polite etiquette-mongers to the subtle satire and ironies which precede political bloodletting. *The process of dramatization* is the craft and artistry expected of the teacher of drama. He should understand the various purposes of drama, which may be summarized as *entertainment, vicarious experience, release of creativity, experiments in personality, development, catharsis, stimulation of thought, escape, commentary on society and life, reporting, and criticism.*

Drama and Creativity

One of healthiest developments in dramatization has been the renewed emphasis on *creative dramatics* in all levels of educational theatre. For too long there has been blind worship of the established plays, often "reproduced" in blind imitation of the first successful commercial production. Frequently this resulted in no creative development for the cast, crew, or even the director. Even the stage setting became a slavish photograph of the original. Creative drama encourages producing groups to utilize new ideas in artistic arrangement, movement, motivation, and even originality in play writing. To understand *creative dramatics* one must understand the concepts involved in the two terms. We have long maintained that *one of the purposes in teaching drama is to find and develop creative talent.* What then are we looking for? What criteria will be used for identification? Are we capable of recognizing creativity when we see it?

Creativity. During the past two decades the need for leadership has caused considerable research into the identification and behavioral patterns of "gifted" and "creative" individuals.[4] A few generalizations may be listed as criteria for identification of these patterns.

A creative person
1) has multi-response to a given stimulus,
2) is independent enough to isolate himself from crowd opinion or action to pursue his own interests and activities,
3) is motivated by a sense of destiny and will solve problems using new approaches, or new materials if the original approaches or materials are not available,
4) is perceptive and curious about many things,
5) will risk failure in a desire to make new alignments of materials or ideas,
6) is skeptical and prone to ask questions which probe the unknown,
7) has a high sense of humor and may use satire and irony in forcing the improbable into probable situations,
8) is more interested in meanings and implications than with small detail, and
9) shows little direct correlation with intelligence above the level of IQ 120.

Let us apply some of these criteria to the identification and development of creative talent in drama. A play is a story told in action, utilizing conflict, suspense, characters, and dialogue. A playwright selects an event or established story as his point of departure. The *gifted* person, representing the upper two per cent (or five per cent of the population according to intelligence tests), behaving in typical fashion, will re-create the story or incident with photographic accuracy. In contrast, the creative

---

[4]Donald W. Mackinnon, "Characteristics of the Creative Person: Implications for the Teaching-Learning Process," paper presented at the Sixteenth National Conference on Higher Education (March 6, 1961). Also reported in the *New York Times,* Oct. 21, 1961, and in the network television program "The Explorer, The Creative Individual," University of California, Broadcast No. 5025, January 28, 1962.

person will reject the reproduction and immediately start a series of alternate responses. He may decide to satirize or ridicule by overexposure of the realities left out of the original story.

Let us turn to *"Cinderella"* as an example. Historical or literary customs cause us to identify with the little pot girl, suffer with her in her labors at the hearth, weep with her as the mother and older sisters leave for the ball, and rejoice as the prince fits the slipper on her dainty foot. What are the alternatives? Have you ever had the responsibility of supervising a younger brother or sister in the menial tasks of cleaning a room or helping with the household chores? What duties are within the reach of a ten-year-old who can't be trusted with scalding water or hot ovens? Well, Cinderella was dusting. Was she satisfied with the freckle-faced boy next door? No, she wanted to attend the junior prom with the star halfback (prince) while an older sister danced with the freckle-faced, pimpled jerk who played second-string end. Why didn't Cinderella take out her feelings on her own mother and sisters? Oh, our culture doesn't encourage such feelings against the next of kin, but it *is* kosher to dislike the *step*mother and *step*sisters. Let us reenact this story from the point of the older sister, saddled with the responsibilities of getting the housework done, trying to explain the appropriateness of a ten-year-old going to the biggest dance of the year and the possibilities of dating the only boy acceptable to her childish mind. Or should we replay the story from the point of view of the mother, trying to make a home for the child, conditioned by cultural biases and reinforced by in-law cousins and their aunts to dislike all "step" relations. Let us see this through the eyes of the other members of the family.

The creative dramatist would rather tell the story of "Jack and the Beanstalk" from the point of view of the tenement house dwellers living on the beanstalk. Did you ever contemplate trying to keep house and home together while a scrawny kid and a giant run back and forth over your house carrying chickens which are in the process of laying eggs of gold? *If creativity and the development of creative talent is the goal, then a climate must be established for the alternate response,* in which students are encouraged—almost required—to look for other solutions, where one may risk the error in an effort to find new arrangements, movements, and sounds.

Drama as a Process

At this point we might chart some of the basic features of two dramatic processes. The first involves those processes which are still in the formative stages — flexible, open to change in story line, characters, selection of protagonist, language, and outcome. The second is the theatre as most students have been introduced to it. Here the play is already written, lines are fixed, and situations are ordered. The final process is to select the necessary cast, director, and crews and to reproduce the play within legal limits, psychologically set to "conform to the intent of the playwright." Surely we cannot claim to have presented Lawrence and Lee's *Inherit the Wind* if we have taken liberties with the interpretations of basic lines or major characters. Changes of degree may result from interpretation, but in the formal theatre the intent of the author must be respected if the play is to be produced. In the process of creation all options are open and may be reversed, recalled, reordered, and respoken.

A chart of these processes is shown in Fig. 24. One must not oversimplify the process chart. During opening seasons, plays are often rewritten; the playwright may be recalled to edit or change a segment of a play which is faulty. Motivation may be needed to provide believability for a movement or cycle. One should also note that the three therapeutic forms demand special training in psychology, sociology, or psychiatry, or they be carried on under the direct supervision of such

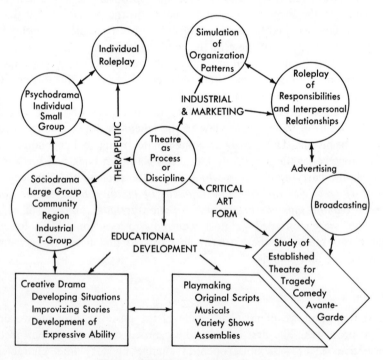

Figure 24. Theatrical Applications

qualified personnel. Extensive case work is a prerequisite to any administration of these therapeutic techniques. A thorough knowledge of the relation of family or community members to the person undergoing therapy can only be interpreted by a competently trained person.

At this point we might recognize the term "role-playing" as a synonym for creative dramatics in many elementary education books. The varying uses of the term in sociology and economics relate to one's role as a vice-president, teacher, board member, or mother. This term is ambiguous and is often used in the sense of improvisation, or simulation—"believing and playing your part" in the *role* assigned.

You are now the superintendent of schools. The town is suburban; there are no industries, only limited recreation facilities, but an expanding school enrollment; bond issues and operating levies have been defeated in the past two elections. You have just been hired and must present your school program to the board of education. Play the role of the superintendent and solve the following problems: (1) . . . , (2) . . . , (3) . . . These problems will be brought to you by selected groups of students, parents, teachers, and members of the board of education. You will need to recognize personalities precisely for each *individual* on each committee. This process of educating school administrators has been in practice during the past decade.

OBJECTIVES OF TEACHING THEATRE

If drama is to concern itself with identifying and developing creativity, and is to aid in the development of man's ability to cope with problems related to himself, his family, and his community, it is certainly more than a "frill" as it is so often labeled by those knowing little of its process. If man is able to utilize the dramatic process to analyze his problems, ridicule his mistakes, and maintain perspective regarding his desires, goals, ethics, and ideas—if he is able to do all this while presenting his ideas now, in three dimensions, in highly artistic as well as functional form—then this part of the curriculum is demonstrably fundamental to total education. In this way we can study problems so flexible that they cannot be treated using scientific procedures needing more rigid controls. In fact, most socioeconomic problems which excite and bedevil man must be measured under the flexibility of instruments which can tolerate different solutions with each administration. A study of drama should therefore

1) explore the contribution of drama to civilization in the historical dimension, relating the type, style and physical theatre to the society in which it finds itself,

2) make an analysis of ideas, indicating the major themes of mankind and the relevance to ethics, morals, living habits, and their relation to institutions such as governments, churches, marriage, courts of justice, etc.,

3) provide opportunity to develop skill in use of language and the embellishment of ideas through the study of great playwrights as they differ in diction (in the classic sense), demands for fluency, and precision in ideas and symbolic forms,

4) provide ample opportunity to develop original dramatizations, with the built-in discipline of rewriting, redesigning, and editing and with the goal of recognizing the wide-spread talent of potential playwrights and other necessary theatre personnel,

5) provide extensive audience situations so that the student experiences total theatre (Such audiences should include various age groups so that basic differences may be understood.),

6) provide criteria for the analysis and evaluation of all types of theatre experienced by society, including the broadcasting media,

7) provide challenging opportunities to create in the related arts necessary to quality production, including lighting, painting, costuming, dancing, architectural forms, and three-dimensional sculpture in motion, and

8) above all, provide the laboratory for developing the voice and body as an instrument for functional and artistic expression.

If we are to accomplish these objectives we must reassess the theatre concepts so frequently expressed by laymen and theatre people alike. What is the theatre of the American people? Where do we find it? What is its quality?

Theatre: Where Do You Find It?

We have already mentioned the innate desire to dramatize. The desire to be recognized and applauded is equally as strong. The Walter Mitty's among us quietly bow to the applause of their unseen audiences. Modern television plays upon the empathic urges of us all. One of the great myths of America is that the American theatre is on Broadway. Only a few (less than sixty) new plays open each year. Seldom does a New York producer risk his commercial investment by presenting a "museum piece" from the great historic library of theatre. The play must first of all be a "commercial success"—a small idea, greatly embellished with musical reviews. One must be careful to note that this does not always mean music as defined by a musician.

Campus-Oriented Theatre. If one wishes to see some great Shake-speare, Ibsen, Sophocles, or even O'Neill, he must venture off-Broadway to the universities and colleges of our nation where the actors may be less experienced but often much more willing to study their roles in rela-tionship to the play. Hidden away on the campuses, the professionally prepared staff often exceeds in training and experience the "commer-cially successful" staff in the larger cities. Often the staff of a university includes from five to fifteen scholar-directors who direct three to five productions each season, representing historical variety far beyond the limited opportunities of the commercial director. With approximately 2000 universities and colleges producing from five to fifteen plays per year (each with multiple performances), it would seem that we might look for the American theatre on these campuses. These play to audi-ences who seldom go to a major metropolitan area to see a commercial production. In terms of the quantity and the quality of the preparation of capable staff, the American professional theatre is campus-oriented.

Quality in Educational Theatre. For many years another myth con-tinued concerning theatre in the secondary schools. It was often said that *Simon Slick of Punkin Creek* was the most frequent production presented by high school producing groups. During the past three decades the National Thespian Society has furnished fine leadership through its National Honorary Society for students in theatre. Each year its approximately 1800 member schools report the productions of the past year. The two lists and the tabulation which follow indicate the quality of these fine producing groups. One will note that *Our Town* has ranked in the top three plays for almost thirty years. Many schools not affiliated with National Thespian produce these same quality plays. While prone to emulate the recent Broadway successes and musical variety types (one each year), they represent a far richer literary quality than may be found in the commercial theatre in any given season. While many producing groups must adapt the play to limited facilities, others have plants which would be envied by commercial producers. In short, the facilities and salary for the resident theatre director (on the staff as a teacher) in-cludes a plant, a casting pool, and a school for training the cast over a longer period than the commercial producer can afford. The educational theatre is heavily subsidized and need not use the questionable practice of type casting. Again, the public school theatre plays to an audience which may never attend either the commercial theatre or even the distant university theatre. We might then ask if 200,000 performances per year presented by high schools to such an audience should not be considered a vital part of the American theatre. Good, bad, or indifferent, it is an

active part of the theatre and should undergo a constant improvement
to be worthy of its calling. We need to involve more students in production experience, original skits, assemblies, and variety shows. We might
yet develop the best new scripts by encouraging the use of creative dramatics throughout public schools at all levels and by utilizing this process
in developing new playwrights. Twelve plays in the 1967-68 listing from
National Thespian represent 219 schools producing multiple performances of Children's Theatre. This field is a rich market for amateur
playwrights.

Frequently Produced Plays (1959-1960)[5]

The following are the most frequently produced three-act plays
by Thespian affiliated schools during 1959-1960. This list was tabulated from the Annual Reports of 1581 Thespian affiliated schools.
Publication of this list is not to be interpreted as a Thespian recommended playlist, nor does it represent overall statistics of the
national secondary school theatre.

Title	Number of Productions
Our Town	81
Curious Savage	71
Diary of Anne Frank	67
Night of January 16	61
You Can't Take it With You	50
Our Hearts Were Young and Gay	42
The Man Who Came to Dinner	41
Arsenic and Old Lace	32
Harvey	31
Time Out for Ginger	30
Teahouse of the August Moon	30
Gidget	29
Meet Me in St. Louis	29
Cheaper by the Dozen	26
My Three Angels	25
The Matchmaker	24
Charley's Aunt	23
Dino	23
The Importance of Being Earnest	22
I Remember Mama	21
The Little Dog Laughed	21

---

[5]*Dramatics*, 31:32 (Cincinnati, Ohio: The National Thespian Society, October, 1960).

Title	Number of Productions
Onions in the Stew	20
Rebel Without a Cause	18
Remarkable Incident at Carson's Corners	18
Ten Little Indians	17
The Thread That Runs So True	17
Blithe Spirit	16
The Family Nobody Wanted	16
Gentlemen Prefer Blondes	16
The Glass Menagerie	16
A Roomful of Roses	16
Little Women	16
Dear Ruth	15
The People vs Maxine Lowe	15
January Thaw	15
Mother is a Freshman	15
Nuts in May	15
Stage Door	15
Take Care of My Little Girl	14
The Unguided Miss	14
The Great Big Doorstep	14
Curtain Going Up	14
Antigone	13
Green Valley	13
No More Homework	13
Flight into Danger	12
A Man Called Peter	12
Nine Girls	12
Pygmalion	12
Annie Get Your Gun	11
The Egg and I	11
George Washington Slept Here	11
I Was a Teenage Dracula	11
Sabrina Fair	11
Death Takes a Holiday	10
Double Door	10
Father Knows Best	10
Goodbye My Fancy	10
Life With Father	10
Lute Song	10
Mrs. McThing	10
Seventeenth Summer	10
Stardust	10

Summary of the 1963-64 Thespian Season[6]

Number of Thespian affiliated schools	2561
Number of schools reporting	1958
Number of full-length plays reported	3210
Average number of full-length plays by schools reporting	1.69
Estimated number of major productions by *all* member schools 1963-64	4328

Distribution of productions among schools reporting:

Schools	Number of Productions
228	0
597	1
872	2
204	3
40	4
10	5
3	6
3	7
1	8

Number of one-act plays produced during the season (includes class work)	3776
Number of reported productions of musicals, operettas, pageants, etc.	1290
Number of reported Children's Theatre productions	255
Number of schools reporting participation in play contests and festivals	799
Number of schools reporting participation in radio broadcasts	137
Number of schools reporting participation in television broadcasts	73
Number of schools reporting participation in films	2

Frequently Produced Full-Length Plays (1967-68)[7]

The following are the most frequently produced full-length plays (all categories) by Thespian affiliated schools during the 1967-68 school year. This list was tabulated from the Annual Reports of 1775 Thespian affiliated schools. Publication of this list is not to be

---

[6]*Dramatics*, 36:31 (October, 1964).
[7]*Dramatics*, 40:39 (November, 1968).

interpreted as a Thespian recommended playlist, nor does it represent overall statistics of the national secondary school theatre.

Title	Number of Productions
You Can't Take It with You	77
Our Town	76
Harvey	60
The Diary of Anne Frank	58
The Miracle Worker	53
The Crucible	48
The Man Who Came to Dinner	43
South Pacific	43
The Curious Savage	47
The Mouse That Roared	46
The Music Man	44
Arsenic and Old Lace	43
Oklahoma!	43
Brigadoon	41
The Wizard of Oz	39
Bye Bye Birdie	38
Cheaper by the Dozen	36
The Night of January 16th	30
Our Hearts Were Young and Gay	30
The Sound of Music	30
Teahouse of the August Moon	30
My Fair Lady	29
Antigone	28
Charley's Aunt	28
The Glass Menagerie	28
Li'l Abner	27
The Importance of Being Earnest	26
Hip Hippie Hooray	25
The Madwoman of Chaillot	25
Oliver	25
Blithe Spirit	24
1984	24
Time Out for Ginger	24
Camelot	23
Guys and Dolls	22
Skin of Our Teeth	22
Alice in Wonderland	21
Annie Get Your Gun	21
Inherit the Wind	21
Snow White and the Seven Dwarfs	21

Title	Number of Productions
The Boy Friend	20
Cinderella	20
A Midsummer Night's Dream	19
Tom Jones	19
Barefoot in the Park	18
Hansel and Gretel	18
The Imaginary Invalid	17
Pillow Talk	17
Rally Round the Flag, Boys	17
See How They Run	17
Ten Little Indians	17
A Thurber Carnival	17
Carousel	16
Life With Father	16
Spoon River Anthology	16
David and Lisa	15
Pygmalion	15
Winnie-the-Pooh	15
George Washington Slept Here	14
The King and I	14
West Side Story	14
The Fantasticks	13
Finian's Rainbow	13
I Remember Mama	13
Little Mary Sunshine	13
Bell, Book and Candle	12
Carnival	12
Get Witch Quick	12
My Three Angels	12
Rumpelstiltskin	12
Take Her, She's Mine	12
Twelve Angry Jurors	12
The Unsinkable Molly Brown	12
Amahl and the Night Visitors	11
Dark of the Moon	11
How to Succeed in Business, etc.	11
Night Must Fall	11
Pajama Game	11
Aladdin and His Wonderful Lamp	10
Ask Any Girl	10
The Clown Who Ran Away	10
Everybody Loves Opal	10
Out of the Frying Pan	10
Trial by Jury	10

Theatre and the Amateur

Theatre is not necessarily bad because it is amateur, nor is it necessarily good because it is professional. Quality is an outgrowth of talent, knowledge, and hard work. Talent is available in various degrees in most people and a successful theatre program could be developed using at least eighty out of one hundred people. Given time and training many with limited capability could develop greater potential as actors, directors, or technicians. One might develop the theme that while many could learn to appreciate theatre, not more than a few in a group should ever try to work as actors. Such a position it seems is self-defeating. The capable few may choose to become doctors of medicine, or engineers, or lawyers. Too often the theatre is left with the academic and emotional derelicts who turn to the theatre as an outlet for their maladjustments. Talent, we know, seems to "cluster," and most individuals with high ability in one area are also talented in others. If the theatre is to portray society, it may be very healthy to utilize the talented whose personal choice may lead them into a wide variety of trades and professions. The theatre mirrors society and therefore must maintain a scholarly observation and participation in society. The competent theatre worker cannot remove himself to the garret to contemplate but must make a continuous study of people. In this sense he cannot join *the cult of the amateur*. Stanislavski was concerned with intellectual observation, not emotional binges. Great plays are concerned with the total society. Few plays of quality are about theatre people. The theatre is interdisciplinary and needs the knowledge and processes of other arts and disciplines.

Theme and Subject

Selected plays should be used in play reading for high school seniors as examples of subject or theme treatment in play writing. The following are representative of problems treated by playwrights for centuries.

Lysistrata	Aristophanes
Peace	Aristophanes
The Trojan Women	Euripides
Journey's End	Robert Sheriff
What Price Glory?	Maxwell Anderson and Laurence Stallings
Bury the Dead (one act)	Irwin Shaw
Johnny Johnson	Paul Green
Key Largo	Maxwell Anderson
Idiot's Delight	Robert Sherwood
There Shall Be No Night	Robert Sherwood
Mr. Roberts	Thomas Heggen and Joshua Logan

The Cid	Pierre Corneille
The Silver Cord	Sidney Howard
Saturday's Children	Maxwell Anderson
The Little Foxes	Lillian Hellman
I Remember Mama	John van Druten
The Glass Menagerie	Tennessee Williams
All My Sons	Arthur Miller
Death of A Salesman	Arthur Miller
Medea	Euripides
Hamlet	William Shakespeare
Othello	William Shakespeare
Andromaque	Jean Racine
Emperor Jones	Eugene O'Neill
Oedipus Rex	Sophocles
Antigone	Sophocles
The Silver Box	John Galsworthy
An Enemy of the People	Henrik Ibsen
Winterset	Maxwell Anderson
Inherit the Wind	Jerome Lawrence and Robert E. Lee
The Visit	Frederick Durrenmatt
The Weavers	Gerhart Hauptmann
Strife	John Galsworthy
Pygmalion	George Bernard Shaw
Waiting for Lefty	
(one act)	Clifford Odets
The Hairy Ape	Eugene O'Neill
The Merchant of Venice	William Shakespeare
Major Barbara	George Bernard Shaw
Native Son	Paul Green and Richard Wright
Wingless Victory	Maxwell Anderson
Home of the Brave	Arthur Laurents
West Side Story	Arthur Laurents
The Male Animal	James Thurber and Elliott Nugent
The Clouds	Aristophanes
A Doll's House	Henrik Ibsen
Ghosts	Henrik Ibsen
Rosmersholm	Henrik Ibsen
Hedda Gabler	Henrik Ibsen
Candida	George Bernard Shaw
Our Town	Thorton Wilder
Tea and Sympathy	Robert Anderson

Teachers should be able to lead a discussion about these plays dealing with the subject discussed, the theme, and the style and manner in which the playwright chose to develop his play. Some plays about war are pacifistic, others promotional, others discuss the social and economic problems caused by war. Many plays develop problems of parent-child relationships in a comic manner while others help us see the tragedy in these same relationships. Justice, suspicion, responsibility, and freedom of the individual are all worthy subjects for themes. The teacher should be able to differentiate between theme and the vehicle used to develop it. While sex is used as a vehicle, there is little question that *Lysistrata* is a play denouncing war. A director who emphasizes the bawdy and lusty action in *Romeo and Juliet* may find the pantomime interfering with the love story or the tragedy of war-torn families. He may completely miss the relevancy of this story to the family alignments of those supporting Elizabeth I in contrast to those supporting Mary, Queen of Scots, so comfortably detained in the Tower.

PRODUCTION AND INSTRUCTION

The theatre director in a school is first employed as a teacher. This position involves the selection of objectives related to conceptual, content, skill, and behavioral goals. In order to accomplish these goals the teacher must be knowledgeable about the materials as well as the activities by which the objectives may be achieved. It is recognized that many theatrical activities take place during time other than that of the classroom. We wish to reiterate that in terms of institutional goals all courses and activities must meet the criteria of the institutional objectives.

Theatre activities and productions must, under these standards, help the school meet the high objectives discussed in Chapters 1, 2, and 3. Primarily, the objectives of teaching students to think and utilize language at functional and artistic levels must take priority. Closely aligned to this problem is the relating of social and economic behavior to social and economic responsibility. Such objectives place qualitative decisions on the selection of plays produced by the drama class, club, or workshop. Plays sponsored by the junior or senior classes should meet the same high quality of excellence in script and production as those sponsored by the institution. It is likewise important that the classes in drama extend the laboratory so that it may provide multiple opportunities for experience for all the students in "workshop" productions—designed, lighted, directed, and even written by students. Here is the valuable use of creative dramatics as a means of trying on ideas and developing thinking artistic talent. Creativity is often expressed in new arrangements of old forms, which suggests the expansion of the "workshop" into blends of music, interpretation, and dance into original productions of chamber theatre or Readers' Theatre.

Sources of Materials

The theatre teacher must be well informed regarding the many types of material utilized in classroom instruction and in production schedules. With continual mergers in the business world, one must keep abreast of new companies specializing in staging materials (costuming, scripts, lighting, draperies, and publicity). Current suppliers and service companies are listed in the bibliography. Students are easily motivated to more intensive study of historical aspects of theatrical scripts, criticism, and styles if involved in the physical apparatus of the theatre. For this reason and in order to keep their dreams in the area of reality, they should be encouraged to study the trade journals and catalogues regarding the prices of lighting instruments, scrims and draperies, royalties, and the many implications these concepts create. Many students are totally unaware of the amounts or reasons for royalties and expect to pirate songs and stories and parody them for use in fund-raising drives. The same creative response might be justifiable in the classroom but the marketing of such activities raises important questions of ethics. We might also point out that students interested in sciences are often attracted to the theatre through study of commercial bulletins showing the creative application of new scientific concepts such as the SRC, the Davis multi-brush dimmer, and vacuum tube dimmers. The remote control of massive instrument groups also initiates additional study.

Script catalogues from the various publishers of plays can be used as instructional devices. These range from brief descriptions of plot and royalty rates to longer sketches of plot and the relationships of character to character. Students may gain considerable mental and emotional maturity in studying the variety of characters needed. They may also find that some plays were written as vehicles for a particular performer (for instance, Le Gallienné's *Alice in Wonderland*) in contrast to some devoted to the development of the story or the theme.

Professional leaders in speech education have concerned themselves with resources and content of theatre courses for the past three decades. Complete course outlines and model units can be found in quantity in *The Quarterly Journal of Speech, The Speech Teacher, The Educational*

Theatre Journal, and various regional and state journals of speech. The National Thespian Society's *Dramatics Magazine* publishes many articles of high motivational value to students and furnishes guides to objectives, content, and activities in drama instruction which the teacher can use. Reprints on many subjects are available, some of which are listed at the end of this chapter. *The Bulletin of the National Association of Secondary School Principals* devoted a complete issue to "Dramatics in the Secondary School." This is a good source to help educate the administration regarding the objectives of theatre and its processes. A recent monograph, *Teacher's Guide to High School Speech,* published by the Indiana State Department of Public Instruction in cooperation with the Indiana English Curriculum Study Center may prove equally valuable in providing qualitative support of educational theatre to our colleagues in English. Sixty pages of theatre material are provided.

One is impressed with the depth of study expected and the scope of theatrical knowledge included in all lists created by responsible committees and individuals who have contributed to the professional journals available to the teacher. Whether we turn to the early or late course outlines created by AETA committees (1950, 1963, 1968), or to the excellent outline by Evelyn Konigsberg,[8] we find considerable agreement as to objectives and content. Both stress that at least one-third of the course should be devoted to the development of understanding of theory through practice. It might be noted that the theory might be drawn from practice but in any case must be developed. Courses in drama cannot be justified on the basis of quantitative activity. Units or areas of study in theatre listed above include the following:

I. *The World of the Theatre as Seen by the Student*
II. *Evaluating Plays and Performers* — in the theatre, on television, in movies, on radio. This should include analysis of audience contribution and use of imagination.
III. *Interpreting Through Action and Language*
    Reading for meaning
    Improvising
    Revising characters, order of incidents, meaning
    Memorization of incidents, lines, and action
IV. *Analysis of Structure in Theatre*
    Identification or establishment of plot
    Rising action, climax as compared to crisis, purpose of exposition, complication, suspense

---

[8]Evelyn Konigsberg, "An Outline Course of Study in Dramatics," *The Speech Teacher,* 4:27-31 (January, 1955).

Implication for reordering incidents or selection of pro-
  tagonist and antagonist, supporting characters
Complexity of characterization, dialogue, language levels
Contribution of setting to the structure
  V. *Types and Styles of Drama*
Tragedy: historical definitions
Comedy: historical definitions and types
  Satyr plays
  Comedy of manners
  Plautus's contributions to Spanish and Elizabethan
  Farce
  Romantic drama
  Fantasy
  Sentimental comedy
  Social comedy or drama
  Melodrama
Styles: Classical, romantic, symbolic, realistic, naturalistic,
  expressionistic, and avant-garde
  VI. *History of Drama:* all major periods and representative plays
    and playwrights, with particular emphasis on the Greeks
    and Shakespeare
  VII. *Acting:* pantomime and voice and language development in-
    cluding pacing and durability in the use of the vocal
    instrument
  VIII. *Production Techniques*
Play selection based upon limitations of director, cast, and
  plant
Scene design using models, sketches, and working drawings
  and their relation to order forms and total cost
Light design in relation to costuming and set, including
  mounting, focus, color, and cues
Costuming and its relation to lighting and set colors, de-
  cisions to rent or construct
Casting and rehearsal techniques including various tech-
  nical rehearsals for costume, lighting, scenery movement,
  and make-up
Publicity, tickets, house control, and financial reports
Performances and evaluation
  IX. *Motion Pictures* as theatre, relevancy to units above
  X. *Radio and Television* as theatre, history, technical skills, and
    equipment; new developments and relevance to live theatre
    in above units

A selected list of terms will indicate a few of the minimal concepts to
be developed. Working process definitions should be developed so that
the student understands the contribution made to theatre by the particular personnel or theatrical technique.

Basic Terms for Production Analysis[9]

Descriptive Terms
drama
play
commedia dell'arte
situation
crisis
climax
plot
unities: time
        place
        action
main characters
dramatic unity
motivation
involvement
desire (will)
excitement
audience climate of opinion
foreshadowing
falling action
rising action
exposition
expectation
gratification
cause and effect
   situation motivation
   obligatory scenes
denouement
rapprochement
primacy of the play

Types of Drama (defined historically)
  Tragedy
    Serious drama
    Tragicomedy

  Comedy
    Farce
    Melodrama
    Sentimental comedy
      Meler-dramer
    Comedy of character
    Domestic comedy
    Romantic comedy
    Comedy of manners
    Comedy of intrigue
    Comedy of humours
    Aristophanic comedy
    Non-Aristophanic comedy
  Chronicle plays (historical)

Elements of Drama
Action
Contention
Suspense
Characterization
Dialogue

Styles of Drama
Non-illusionistic: non-realistic
                  presentational
Illusionistic: representational of
    life in natural background

Particular Styles
Classical
Neo-classical
Aristophanic comedy (old)
Non-Aristophanic (new)
Morality
Mystery
Miracles
Romantic
Realistic (naturalistic)
Symbolistic
  Expressionistic
  Epic
  Constructivistic

Theatre Styles
Non-illusionistic
Illusionistic

Basic Styles
Oriental
Classic
Medieval
Renaissance
Elizabethan
Neo-classic
Realistic (naturalistic)
Restoration
Selective realism
Symbolism
  Expressionism
  Formalism
  Constructivism
  Demonstrational

---

[9]See John Gassner, *Producing the Play* (rev. ed.; New York: Holt, Rinehart & Winston, 1953), pp. 1-100, and *Masters of the Drama* (New York: Dover Publications, Inc., 1954).

The Teacher as Producer

In the theatre the producer is responsible for all materials, space, and personnel to make possible the opening of a show. This task begins with the decision to (*a*) select a play, a director, technical staff, and cast, (*b*) provide facilities for rehearsal and production, (*c*) provide a business office to handle all purchases of scripts, materials for scenery, and lights, (*d*) make all financial arrangements for budgets, royalties, payrolls, deductions, and insurance, and finally (*e*) provide the necessary advertising to attract an audience to the play. At the end of production he is also responsible for clearance, disposal, or storage of all supplies and equipment and for having the production returns audited.

Production Responsibilities. As one will quickly note, many of the above responsibilities have been assumed by the board of education and delegated through the regular administrative offices of the school. Some of the duties are delegated to the teacher of theatre as a direct and understood obligation which is attendant upon the contract to teach. Auditorium facilities and rooms for rehearsal have been provided by the board but must be scheduled through the office of the school principal. Such schedules should be double checked to avoid accidental conflicts with other major events utilizing the same building facilities, or more importantly the same potential audience. The teacher begins then as an administrator, dealing with very practical problems of space utilization. Seldom does the teacher-producer have to search a community for an auditorium to rent or lease. But space for building, painting, and storage of scenery may create problems. One of the first duties of a new teacher is to inventory facilities and equipment to determine the complexity limitations on the first plays to be produced.

Production Scheduling. A major challenge to the teacher-producer is the scheduling of many parallel interrelated activities. A commercial producing group may make the decision to produce and then begin schedules for construction facilities, personnel, and rehearsal simultaneously. The teacher-producer frequently must schedule production, rehearsal, and construction facilities early in September for productions scheduled in March. An organizational chart for scheduling is given in Fig. 26. Storage space may dictate the delay of sets until the production is nearing the completion of rehearsals. Such simultaneous operating of A, B, and C should be attempted only with several adults supervising the production. Business management might be absorbed by the school office or business education classes, and the construction may be as-

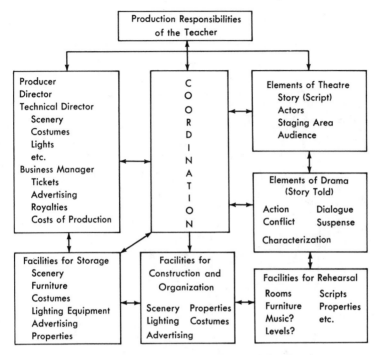

Figure 25. Production Responsibilities of the Teacher

signed to technical staff working closely with the director. The design of sets, costumes, lights, and direction must work in harmony.

Each stage of the production schedule presented in Fig. 26 can be subdivided into time-oriented job assignments. Any production may schedule differently based upon available facilities and the desires of the director. Some directors like to conduct blocking rehearsals prior to line rehearsals; others prefer to have blocking evolve from the lines. Fig. 27 indicates the breakdown of design and rehearsal schedules in terms of performance time minus the number of days for any stage of production.

Inventories. Modern school architects often provide equipment for *general lighting* but fail to furnish either instruments or control for *specific lighting.* With three (or sometimes four) color borders the stage may be bathed in any color of light but not faded or blended into any combinations. The scenery may be lighted but not the acting areas. Such facilities place serious limitations upon the most frequently produced

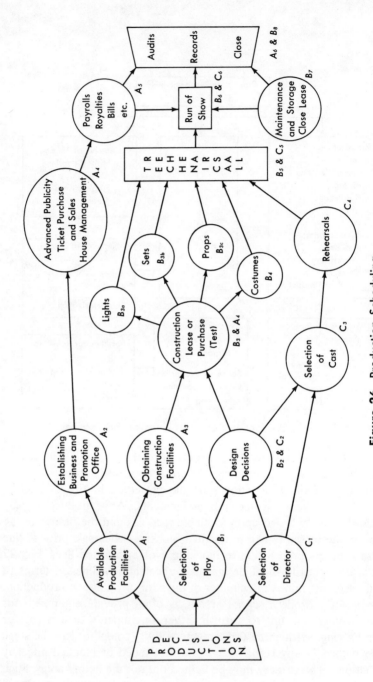

Figure 26. Production Scheduling

A = Business management   B = Design and construction   C = Direction and performance

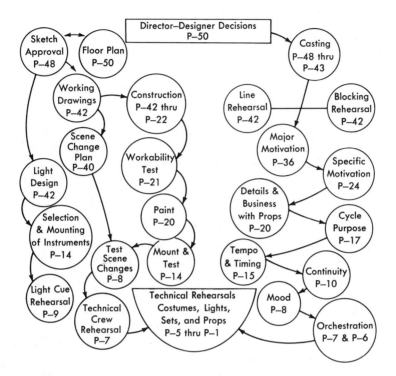

Figure 27. Breakdown of Design and Rehearsal Schedules

The notation P—50 means "performance time minus fifty days," or fifty days before the performance. The numbers given here are flexible, dependent upon the order desired by the director and the experience of the cast and crew.

play, *Our Town.* Further inventory may indicate no rigid scenery, and a set of draperies, once regarded as an interior box set, has shrunk and inadvertently provides a view of feet and legs from behind the supposed scenery. An inventory of the available production materials helps to base the plans of the producing group on realistic considerations. Inventory should also take in the potential casting pool and policies regarding the expansion of the casting pool or rehearsal arrangements. The teacher-producer must know if this policy may be changed without the advice or decision of certain committees, members of classes, or possibly established precedent. Staging and designing may already be the responsibility of personnel outside the theatre or else should be assigned to the theatre producing group. Such personnel may include teachers of art, home economics, physics, and industrial art. This inventory might well become a part of the prospective teacher's interview with the hiring superintendent. If you wish to have some freedom to select quality plays which are a challenge to the learning of the students in terms of literature, design, costume, lighting, and acting, you might well begin with a complete inventory of equipment, space, personnel, and policy. Help is appreciated, but flexibility is important. It is important to know what has been delegated and to whom.

Many schools would like to employ teachers familiar with the necessary equipment. Most of you will find that plays may be selected to expand the lighting inventory on one production (*Our Town*), draperies and scrims on another (*Sing Ho for the Prince*), and possibly levels on still another. Eventually a well equipped stage should include:

1. *Stage area:* Proscenium opening of thirty to thirty-six feet, with adequate room offstage to strike and store flats, parallels, and tracked draperies. In addition there should be space for set properties and still enough space to allow movement of acting personnel. The depth from the grand drapery should not be less than twenty-two feet and should allow for sky drops and movement from one side to the other without interfering with a scene in progress. The back wall should be free of electrical outlets, heat vents, and other obstructions. It can be painted light blue and used as a sky drop for deep scenes if movement backstage can be handled. The flying area should have an adequate counterweight system or pin rail, but adequate trackage and new developments in flexible switching techniques will work if sufficient storage and offstage space is available for draperies. (See switch-it and adapta-units in which leg drops may be turned parallel to proscenium or upstage.) Special note: While one or two plays may be presented in a set of draperies, these must not become a substitute for rigid scenery. An instructional program includes plays with exterior and interior sets. It is also desirable to have a trap system, which can be easily adapted into most stage floors by mounting a lid flush with the floor, resting on supports attached to floor supports.

2. *Space for scene construction and storage:* This space should be as close as possible to the stage, preferably to one side. The same space might be used as an instructional facility in the speech program. Cabinets for tools, paint, and hardware, sinks with hot and cold water, and a wall area high enough for painting scenery in standing position is needed. If the stage area is used for such painting, drop cloths and increased supervision are necessary. If the construction area is away from the stage, damage to paint and walls may result as scenery is

moved. Once the scenery is built, storing it on stage is highly desirable. Draperies may be "tracked" into the storage area with dust covers, and flats may be compactly stood in the scene dock. Provisions should be made for repainting and adding to the scenery to avoid the monotony of producing many plays with the same settings, as is done with permanent drapes.

3. *Lighting control and instruments:* Modern light control is based upon flexibility. This means that the control board may be used to dim the house, and then control may be transferred to the stage lights by use of a transfer switch. At least one hundred twenty circuits are needed and should lead to a flexible plugging panel where they may be ganged in any combination. The plugging panel should be flexible enough so that, when it is attached to the control board, any circuit or group of ganged circuits can be attached to any dimming unit. Dimming units should provide variety in quantity control (0–6000 watts) and be capable of handling master dimming of several dimming units. The instruments should be flexible so that any instrument can be plugged into any circuit at the position of mounting. At least twelve circuits should be available at the position of the first beam (in front of the proscenium); six circuits at this position is the absolute minimum. These circuits should be rated at 750 watts or more, depending upon the distance of mounting from the front acting areas. Catalogues from the respective lighting companies indicate the amount of illumination at given distances. At least twelve circuits, with flexible mounting for 500- or 750-watt fresnel instruments, should be located at the first pipe position (immediately behind the grand drape). A second pipe position providing for six or more individually circuited instruments should be provided at approximately six to eight feet back of the first pipe. Three heavy circuits, attached to the three-color border (red, blue, and green) should be mounted adjacent to the first pipe and should parallel the second pipe mounting. Additional circuits for portable three-color striplights, scoops, and special spotlights are needed at pipe and floor positions where one might expect to hang scrims, sky drops, tormentor, or backlighting. It is highly desirable that the control board for all of this be placed at the projection booth position in the rear of the auditorium.

4. *Stage ladders and rolling equipment:* Often a permanently stored ladder can be placed on the stage by the custodial staff. This should be mounted on a small wagon (dolly) and used for all adjustments of lighting and draperies. Expensive equipment is often damaged through

the use of makeshift working equipment. Uncastered ladders result in the loss of time for students and teacher, time which could be better used in teaching, studying, or creative work. This dolly may be constructed to provide locked space for tools specifically needed for lighting and drapes.

5. *Platforms, parallels, and towers:* By previous scheduling the flexible risers used by the chorus and the tubular towers used by painters and custodial staffs may be made available for staging purposes. This might be investigated as part of the inventory. Paired, movable stairs (three and five steps high) should be a permanent part of stage equipment. These can be used with lids or on wagons to supplement the need for parallels and other units where levels will be needed. They also simplify the construction of staircases and light towers in tormentor positions.

6. *Property construction and storage:* Most school facilities are much too crowded to allot space for storage of stage properties. When every space large enough for a classroom is needed by two groups of students, one finds the justification for storage difficult. Many properties might best be built or borrowed for each production. This may also prove a valuable part of the instructional process. Certain types of furniture, period and modern, is needed for an on-going production group. The teacher of theatre may well establish policy and keep inventory on a variety of period furniture suites. One ladies' faculty lounge may be furnished with Danish modern, while an instructional set in home economics might be furnished with colonial or Chippendale. The men's lounge may be furnished with modern tubular plastic chairs and couch, and the guidance office may furnish still another period setting. Freedom to recover with selected fabrics may furnish the necessary variety throughout a number of productions. The inventory should identify the availability and policy regarding the use of such equipment. As a final resource, local furniture companies may rent or loan the desired furniture for program credits. A producing group, however, must be ready to stand behind the cleaning and purchase of equipment which is broken or soiled by carelessness or misjudgment in direction. Temporary storage may be provided in garages or storage buildings.

7. *Dressing rooms and costume storage:* Producing groups moving into children's theatre are immediately faced with the storage of costumes representing Oriental, Gothic, and other periods which are not easy to rent and which may be reused with frequency. The instructional

room for speech or a room close to the stage area of the auditorium may provide space for permanent costume storage. Costumes for children's theatre can frequently be constructed for the price of rental. A variety of plays produced over a two-year period can provide a permanent costume supply. Modern plays, frequently produced by high schools, are best costumed through local supply from parents and community, backed with an adequate cleaning budget. Space for costume changes within easy walking distance of the stage is needed. The availability of these areas should be cleared for times of production as part of the inventory. If dressing rooms are constructed as a part of the auditorium one must be sure they have not become permanent storage facilities for musical instruments, dance decorations, or parade materials. It is often best to incorporate such space into the instructional facilities for line rehearsal, debates, or practice areas for speeches and broadcast programs.

Planning Systems. Check sheets are valuable in the production of plays and also in teaching young crew chiefs. Beginning with an inventory of available space and equipment (lighting and scenery), one is able to see the feasibility of several possible scripts. The final choice may be made by a student or faculty committee from those within the capabilities of the director, cast, and potential crews. It is extremely important that decisions on crews and scenery be made before the cast is selected and rehearsals started. Reversing this order may result in a production which is ready to open in terms of cast but unable to open because materials for construction have not arrived, are on back order, or may take longer to construct than anticipated. Space may have been taken by other school or community groups and construction may need to be planned around them.

Since the teacher-director-producer is responsible for many tangental units, he must have some type of organization form. The play preparation check sheet below is designed to recognize the assignment of personnel to all key jobs (Part I). Some of these assignments may be delayed or two posts might be held by a single individual (for example, business manager and publicity), but once assigned, the job is clarified and assistants are to report to the appropriate crew chief. An assistant to the director may be assigned to post all notices and assignments in addition to checking the levels of development (assigned, started, completed, tested). In this way delay in construction can result in reassessment and double crews if something started goes beyond the date for completion.

Play Preparation Check Sheet

Name of play_____Date first performed_____

Director_____Place first performed_____

I.   *Personnel*
   1. Stage manager_____
   2. Stage carpenter_____
   3. Property master_____
   4. Electrician_____
   5. Assistant_____
   6. Assistant_____
   7. Assistant_____
   8. Business manager_____
   9. Ticket clerk_____
   10. Doorman_____
   11. Head usher_____
   12. Usher_____
   13. Usher_____
   14. Usher_____
   15. Scene designer_____
   16. Musical director_____

II.   *Cast* (See attached sheet)   A S C T

III. Rehearsal Schedule_____
   1. Performance
      Office schedule

IV.. *Scenery*
   1. Scene sketches
   2. Scene models
   3. Scene plots
   4. Equipment
      1st set
      2nd set
      3rd set
      4th set
      5th set
      6th set
   5. New construction
   _____
   _____
   _____
   6. Painting
   _____
   _____

V.   *Properties*   A S C T
   1. Stage props   (see
   2. Hand props   list)
   3. Stage effects

VI. Lighting
   1. Light plots
   2. Equipment
   3. Color media
   4. Special effects

VII. *Make-up* (See attached)
   1. Make-up plots
   2. Grease paints
   3. Cold cream
   4. Spirit gum
   5. Tools
   6. Kleenex
   7. Hair goods
   8. Wigs

VIII.   *Costume* (See attached)
   1. Costume plot
   2. Made costumes
   3. Rented costumes
   4. Costume returned

IX.   *Business Management*
   1. Publicity set-up
   2. Ticket sale
   3. House
      accommodation
   4. Receipts checked
   5. Bills paid

X.   *Music* (See attached)
   1. Between acts
   2. Incidental
   3. Special numbers

XI.   *Specialties*
   1. _____
   2. _____
   3. _____

XII.   *Royalty*
   Notes_____

LEGEND: A = assigned, S = started, C = completed, T = tested.

A sample of a second working check sheet is the play analysis from below. Again a student or student committee may perform the analysis and filling out of the form. This form is useful during the process of play selection with regard to plant and equipment facilities. The upper part of the form is used to identify the play, the number of settings, the number of scene changes and their order, and the number and types of characters. The form has been useful in children's theatre where *The*

Play Analysis Form

Name of play   Author   Type

No. of settings_____   Type and order_____
No. of scene changes_____
No. of characters_____
     men_____
     women_____
     children_____   Others (list) _____
                                                 _____
                                                 _____

Properties: (by acts) number of each

Standard   Description if important   Special description

Special light and costume problems: List and attach

Christmas Carol calls for five settings and fourteen scene changes in a complicated order, while *Reynard the Fox* lists only animals for characters. *The Land of the Dragon* lists multiple settings; several male, several female characters, and a dragon. Children's theatre also pays special attention to properties, light, and sound problems, where objects must appear and disappear magically. Several plays may be so analyzed, and the final choices might be determined from equally challenging productions by the availability of equipment and the training and efficiency of the potential director, cast, and crew. Few plants have the facilities to produce *Peter Pan* if one feels that the flying scenes are obligatory. Even as an instructional device this form is extremely valuable in helping students realize the meaning of total production. Sketches, models, and working drawings may be required as a part of the production analysis before final selection is made. Such analysis may also lead to discussions of various means of flying, rolling, or running scenery. Students may discuss the impact upon the play of adapting it to leg-and-drop, wing-and-drop, unit set, or space staging. The check sheet assists in bringing all problems of production into the discussion.

The production cost sheet shown below provides a means to lay out the total expected budget before the producing group is committed. Established inventories may prove that the necessary scenery and lighting equipment is available. Working drawings and construction processes must be completed to make accurate requests to the administration for materials to be purchased. All requests should include number of pieces, composition (white pine), size, and model numbers (lighting equipment).

Royalties. Legal and financial responsibilities demand precise action and record-keeping. Although the payment of royalties is the responsibility of the office of the superintendent, the teacher-director is responsible for the choice of the play, the negotiations to gain permission to produce, and the agreement as to royalty rates. Royalties are paid to the publisher owning the producing rights, which are extended to producing groups under definite agreements. Rates vary from commercial to educational groups and may vary on a particular play. Play catalogues generally list the rate for amateur groups and may list a reduced rate for second and third performances. One-act plays of quality may be listed for five to fifteen dollars for each performance, while major plays may be listed for fifty dollars for the first performance with twenty-five dollars for each succeeding performance. Most play publisher contracts call for the payment of the royalty one week in advance of the opening. The director should initiate this order.

Educational objectives are best reached with multiple performances to small audiences rather than a single performance to one large audi-

Production Cost Sheet (estimate and final)

Production_____ Dates_____

Director_____ Technician_____

Scenery:
    Lumber
    Muslin
    Hardware
    Miscellaneous
    Paint

Costumes:
    Materials
    Rentals

Make-up:

Properties:
    Materials
    Rentals

Lights:
    New equipment
    Replacements
    Rental

Printing:
    Tickets
    Programs
    Placards

Advertising:
    Periodicals
    Posters
    Post cards
    Direct mail
    Photographs
    Miscellaneous

Scripts:

Royalty:

Tax:

Total

ence. For this reason the teacher-producer might investigate *playbox quotations*. Under *playbox* the teacher arranges to present several performances (generally five or more) within one week, or on two weekends. Rates are based upon the size of the expected house. In this way five performances to a house of 300 for each performance might not exceed the royalty of two performances each to a house of 700. Royalties for musicals are exceedingly high, are based upon the size of the house and the price of tickets, and include a rental and use fee for musical scores plus a deposit for lost or damaged scores. Typical royalty quotations for modern musicals begin at 150 dollars plus an 80-dollar use fee, and a 100-dollar deposit. They may range as high as 500 dollars for each performance with additional rental and deposit. Budget royalties should be explored and are explained in most of the catalogues of play publishers.

The Teacher as Director

Among the direct responsibilities of the teacher-producer we find (*a*) the direction of the play, (*b*) often the selection of the play, and (*c*) the schedule of rehearsals. In a school setting, plays are produced to develop the talent and analyzing ability of the students. Teacher-directors who involve students in play selection, in planning and making rehearsals effective, and in responsibilities for scheduling, advertising, and public relations with other teachers, students, and the administration thus find the job much more pleasant and effective. Although considerable professional growth for the director occurs with every successful production, the school does not hire a director to develop his talents or to exploit the school's facilities and students to embellish his own reputation. Professional reputations are a direct outgrowth of the number of students successfully taught, and in many ways the high degree of excellence of seasonal productions. The selection of plays with small casts can be occasionally justified, but the teacher who produces *Glass Menagerie* and then turns to two more small cast plays has neglected the basic purpose of theatre in the secondary school. If he selects a number of plays within the reach of the plant and his ability to direct, and within the ability of available cast, he can then leave the final selection from that list to the students. Such maturity in the teacher will lead to more freedom and flexibility in the programming. Delegation is often the direct result of keeping all concerned people informed and responsibly involved.

The director's greatest task is that of leading students through play analysis, for classroom learning as well as for production. In a learning context the process of super-marionette manipulation can hardly be supported. Students must learn to find within the play its meanings, crises, climaxes and the interrelationships of the characters to each other and to

Character Analysis

I. *Character relationships:*
   A. What is the turning point of the play?_____
   B. What is the theme of the play?_____
   C. What is the most dramatic scene?_____
   D. What does my character contribute to it?_____
   E. List all characters with whom this character is in contact in the story of the play (include offstage incidents shown in the lines) and mention the attitude toward these characters and the counterattitude. Note changes of attitudes.

Character	Attitude toward	Attitude of other character (counter)

II. *Attitudes, traits, and abilities:*
   Racial characteristics_____
   Family background_____
   Educational background_____
   Social position_____
   Economic position_____
   Philosophy of life_____
   Moral standards_____
   Temperament_____
   Dominant emotions_____
   Outstanding personality peculiarities_____

   Attitude audience should have toward character_____

III. *Research:* Character played professionally by_____

IV. *Remarks of critics* on past performances of this play or character:

V. *Bibliography* of character

VI. Describe yourself by physical characteristics of the character as you see him: age, height, weight, build, posture, walk, health, mannerisms, dress; facial characteristics and vocal characteristics (this only after you have worked the part up to an understanding).

the structure of the play. You will note by the character analysis sheet which follows that physical characteristics and mannerisms are one of the last things to be considered and take precedence only on rare occasions to the contribution which this character makes to the plot. Bibliographies about those who have played the part may result in a cheap imitation with young actors and may thus be omitted. Viewing a recent movie may be reason enough to select a different play. Some directors prefer to tell actors what they are like and how to perform, but they seldom achieve the excellence gained by interrogation and inquiry where the actor must do the thinking and establish the role. We can gain insight into this problem from the recent experiments done on group direction, as reported in Supplement 8.

Supplement 8.

Some Recent Experiments in Group Direction at E.M.U.*

Mitchel Roberts McElya

As recent as thirty years ago, the average educator's task was considerably more simple than is his counterpart's today. There was a tradition of method, an acceptable catalogue of information, and a manageable number of relatively docile students. With the enormous increase in knowledge, the average educator now finds himself with a much more bewildering task. He must select rather than merely transmit information, and he has been forced, because of more numerous and less naive students, to question traditional methods. The job has been difficult for us all, but probably more difficult for those of us in the more abstract disciplines than for our colleagues in comfortably concrete studies. At least we would like to think that approaches are more various, content is more flexible, and motivation more elusive in Aesthetics, say, than in Botany. No doubt there are aesthetics in Botany and structural principles in Aesthetics — indeed, cross-fertilization of the disciplines is one of our most interesting and most neglected educational challenges — but understanding the flower in someone's hand is a more obvious process than understanding what he thinks about holding it.

Those of us in educational theater have been trying new ways of justifying it on its own level. If it is not merely the recreation that some administrators would have it, and if it is not the preprofessional training better handled by the conservatory, what functions does it have which will place it squarely on the side of legitimate subjects of the Institute? Are there darker sides to fun

*Appeared in *Newsletter* of the Theatre and Drama Interest Group of SAA (August, 1968). Reprinted by permission of the author. For a complete presentation see Joseph Del Giudice's Master's thesis, Eastern Michigan University, 1968.

on the one hand and money on the other? What can educational theater do that no other kind of theater can do so well? We are convinced that the values of theater go beyond recreation, though some of us are too apt to dismiss the oneiric values of games; and we are equally convinced that the theater will be healthier if its people know something about history and botany and art and physics: otherwise we would cast our lot with the conservatory. In an attempt to explain this rather vague set of beliefs, many of us pepper our arguments with "service" — to the annoyance of empirically minded curricular committees. The point is a good one. It's time we developed more support for it.

The idea of service to the community is unassailable, but it is frequently a two-edged sword. Freed from the outrageous economic demands of professional theater in this country, we can afford to present meritorious dramatic literature, either classic or original, which the audience would not be likely to come across otherwise. Though the intent is specious, the practice must frequently be answered for. If you are to serve an audience, the audience must come, and very few of us are fortunate enough to have an audience which prefers Marlowe to Neil Simon. One of our strengths *should* be that we can present material the audience is not likely to see on the road, in stock, on television, or in the movies. That the comfortable, familiar play is precisely what many of our audiences most *want* to see presents a dilemma that can considerably reduce our argument that we serve the community. Whatever form this discussion takes in local variations, its lines of debate are at least clearly drawn. In its most futile form we're forced to defend Shakespeare exactly as though we had been caught introducing a mild purgative into the local water supply: a dose of him will do you good, whether you like it or not.

Less powerful, because more vague, is the notion of service to the individual who participates in educational theater. We do not tell him simply to enjoy himself, nor do we tell him to have his teeth capped and get an agent. Yet we all know that during the production of a play something *besides the play* happens to its participants. Occasionally what happens is detrimental; usually it leaves them better people. Each of us has a favorite name for this effect: "we worked well together," "co-operation," "dependability," "discipline," "a broadening experience," "leadership," are some of the favorites; and we can cite statistics, if pressed, to show that those who participate in co-curricular activities are demonstrably better students than those who do not. Might not this beneficial result be explored further and controlled more? Some of us have begun to deal with this possibility. The inspiration has largely come from investigations in Psychology and Sociology of how groups serve their individual members.

Borrowing Carl Rogers' idea that the client has insights into his own needs, some of us at Eastern Michigan University embarked on an attempt to discover how student participants in drama would *like* to be served. Through a set of fairly haphazard experiments in productions both on the main playbill and in the experimental theater, we find that students have most artistic and personal development in proportion to their participation in decisions affecting the production. This has led to: 1) a more limited definition of the role of the director, and 2) a corresponding increase in the responsibility of the participants.

In the most loosely organized of these experiments, the main approach was through blocking. The production was Marlowe's *The Tragical History of Dr. Faustus*, a play replete with episodic and textually unmotivated entrances and exits. The director's decision was to refuse the traditional role of traffic-manager, and try to use blocking as a method of increasing the actors' commitments to their roles. To that end, the director gave no blocking, though through the first two-thirds of the rehearsal time of ninety hours he constantly demanded logic in the actors' blocking, as any critical audience member would. A sampling of his questions during an evening's rehearsal might be:

Why did you come onto the stage?

Why did you move at this line last night and not move tonight?

Why did you go there?

Why do you finish scene twelve down left and begin scene thirteen in the same place?

Why do your words say "triumph" while your body says "bored"?

Because the actors created their own relationships on the stage, their movements never had the artificial quality so often associated with rote learning. Because they had to justify themselves in terms of plot, character, and audience, they developed a respect for stage movement impossible to communicate in so relatively short a time by more traditional methods.

The most far reaching and provocative of these experiments was the double production of John Mortimer's *I Spy*,[10] in which the roles of the directors were polarized. One group took as its guideline the traditional approach that all decisions belonged ultimately to the director — a theory familiar to all of us. The other group took the position that all decisions belonged to the group as a whole. The first group's production was unified and enjoyable. The second group's, though quite different, was no less so. The effect on the actors, however, was strikingly divergent. Group A (the traditional group) felt constrained and frustrated; they were glad when the play ended. Group B developed too strong a feeling of commitment *not* to enjoy their play, for they had been responsible for all directorial, technical, and administrative decisions.

So far as direction was concerned, they decided on characterization, blocking, reblocking, line deadlines, rehearsal times, and kinds of rehearsals. They decided on the director's role, which became essentially "when we decide what we want to do, give us suggestions on ways in which we can augment it technically," and they decided whether and when they wanted the director to attend rehearsals. In an absolute fever of creative inventiveness, rehearsals

---

[10]For a detailed account, see the M. A. thesis of Joseph Del Giudice, Eastern Michigan University, June, 1968.

could take any form, and relied heavily on sensitivity training at times: rehearsals in the dark, rehearsals to music. One rehearsal period was given over to drawing their characters in chalk. They often switched roles in rehearsal, the better to appreciate another character's feelings and functions. Nearly every rehearsal began with a game of tag, to loosen them up physically and emotionally, and make them interrelate. They were allotted sixty hours of rehearsal time, and elected to triple that. Though many of their approaches might seem superfluous to us, they did not to them, and they debated each method seriously before electing it. Many other techniques (most notably a twenty-four-hour marathon rehearsal which they mercifully abandoned) were voted down because they could see in them no direct contribution to the play.

Technically, they decided on their costumes, make-up, scenery, lighting, sound, and properties. Though their approaches were at times unusual, the results were more or less traditional. They did successfully integrate their unified approach to the play.

Administratively, their responsibilities included deciding on programs, performance dates, whether or not there was to be an audience, whether or not they would allow observers to their rehearsals, and so on. One of the major values of the experiment was simply that they discovered how many decisions were involved in the production of a play, and how easily an arbitrary decision could fracture the unified approach that they felt was essential to the communication of the author's meaning.

In such experiments, the director's role becomes more one of counselor than dictator. He uses traditional answers only if they honestly serve the needs of the particular case. He makes the company decide what it wants to do, and then suggests different ways in which they might proceed. He points out what set of responsibilities go with specific decisions; for instance, if they decide to perform before an audience, they owe the audience such things as clarity of voice, clarity of sight, unambiguous focus, interesting compositions, and logical developments. As a member of the producing group, the director, too, has a voice in decisions which affect the whole. If he selects the play and the cast, as he usually must, he is the authority on the play and the arbiter between the company and the administration.

For the company, such experiments go much deeper than the usual productions, and result in true service: advantages more long-lasting and more pervasive. The production itself gives them more mutuality of acting, more security in their roles, and more reward from the audiences' reactions than do traditional methods. By having to unify, but committing themselves to all facets of a problem, by deciding to communicate, and by investigating as many ways as possible to achieve communication, "what happens'" to them in the production of a play does not die with the production.

Rehearsal Block Sheet. One of the students should work out a rehearsal block sheet prior to casting. A rehearsal block sheet is shown below. This device aids in the planning of rehearsals. Characters

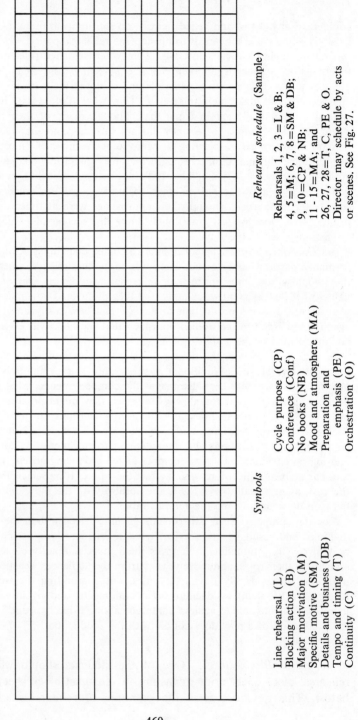

Rehearsal Block Sheet

Characters   *Page* 1 2 3 4 5 6 7 8 9 10 11 12 13 14 15 16 17 18 19 20 21 22 23 24 25 26 27 28 29 30

Symbols

Line rehearsal (L)
Blocking action (B)
Major motivation (M)
Specific motive (SM)
Details and business (DB)
Tempo and timing (T)
Continuity (C)

Cycle purpose (CP)
Conference (Conf)
No books (NB)
Mood and atmosphere (MA)
Preparation and
    emphasis (PE)
Orchestration (O)

Rehearsal schedule (Sample)

Rehearsals 1, 2, 3 = L & B;
4, 5 = M; 6, 7, 8 = SM & DB;
9, 10 = CP & NB;
11 - 15 = MA; and
26, 27, 28 = T, C, PE & O.
Director may schedule by acts
or scenes. See Fig. 27.

represented in the play may be recorded on the rehearsal block whenever present, page by page, or two symbols might be used (a solid block ■ on stage and speaking, and an *X* if on stage but not speaking). A rehearsal block for *The Elves and the Shoemaker* would indicate that the elves dominate the stage alone for many pages, while the court citizens dominate many other pages. Occasionally the elves are on stage in pantomime during a scene of the citizens. Such a picture dictates the use of two student directors, and separate rehearsals for the elves and the citizens, except for the combined scenes. Thus the teacher-director can better utilize rehearsal time and space. One student director might run *line rehearsals* while *blocking rehearsals* are under way with the director. Later rehearsals might concentrate upon major or specific motivation, tempo, mood, pointing up of ideas or lines, orchestration, or technical matters.

Prompt Book. A prompt book of each production must be turned in not later than two weeks after the final performance. It is the joint responsibility of the stage manager and the assistant to the director. The assistant to the director is responsible for everything concerning the script proper — charting movement, recording business, and technical cues. The stage manager is responsible for assembling and preparing all other material and operating with the assistant in the final compiling of the book. The function of the prompt book is that of keeping an accurate record of each production. Since it will be used as the guide to subsequent performances, all terminology must be consistent and all statements must be brief and concise.

Prompt Book

1. Title page
2. Table of contents
3. Copy of the printed program
4. Actors
    a) Description of each character; nature, personality, etc.
    b) Costumes worn by each actor.
    c) Make-up used by each actor.
    d) Charts of characters appearing on stage by scenes.
5. Settings
    a) Description of each setting from the audience viewpoint.
    b) Ground plans for each setting as used in rehearsals.
    c) Picture of each setting.

> *d)* List of set props, by scenes.
>
> *e)* List of hand props, by scenes.
>
> 6. Description of the lighting of each scene from the audience viewpoint, together with all cues.
>
> 7. Description of music and offstage sound effects used together with all cues.
>
> 8. Script
>   *a)* The printed or typewritten script as used in the production is mounted on the left-hand pages of the book.
>   *b)* The right-hand pages of the book are divided into three columns. The first column contains a detailed *written* description of all movement and business. The second column contains at least one stenciled drawing of the set in which the movement is *charted*. The third column contains the warnings and cues for curtains, sound effects, and lights.
>   *c)* The script is preceded by a page which explains all symbols, colors, and terminology.
>
> 9. Rehearsal data
>   *a)* Address and phone number of all members of the cast.
>   *b)* Record of each rehearsal, showing date, place, and time.
>
> 10. Performance data, including the time sheets for all dress rehearsals and performances.

Problems and Safety.   The most troublesome scenes for the beginning director involve fight and love scenes. Some practice in judo may make a fight scene believable. People of all ages have seen enough to know the phony and dangerous positions of a would-be assassin. Holding a knife blade down in the heal of the hand appears artificial; a well placed foot would reduce such an attack to the ridiculous. With the knife held with the blade forward from the thumb the scene appears dangerous and is, but the attack can be covered to expedite the fall of the victim. The use of guns on the stage can be extremely dangerous, resulting in injury even with blank cartridges. Starting pistols are best, but guns should never be pointed directly at an actor. Double safety supervision should be made of all guns used. They should never be placed on the general property table and left to the devices of practical jokers. A demonstration should be conducted in a darkened room to show the length of the firestream from a blank cartridge 22-calibre pistol. Such a demonstration may increase the desire for safety. Sword fights must be rehearsed until every movement is perfected and must be conducted on set cues for each movement. Face masks and body protection must be worn until perfection is reached. Love scenes can often be improved by using dance positions in which two persons move from open to closed positions rather naturally. A tender, affectionate kiss might then be accomplished before friends in the audience have time to add unwelcome sound effects.

The Teacher as Censor

Newspapers occasionally tell of drama directors who have chosen to resign or have been informed by educational boards that their contracts would not be renewed. Charges range from swearing and obscenities in plays to improper attire and hair styles. Several years ago a study was made asking whether the play director would edit or omit a play dealing with the criteria in the form which follows.[7] Several generalizations can be drawn from the five hundred returns: (1) Swearing, profanity, and cursing are synonomous to many play directors, (2) drinking scenes are often directed to be ridiculous and detract from the play, (3) racial and religious references are not problems if handled with good taste, and (4) directors who know their communities well have few problems. The comments added to the return that the following ideas need consideration:

1. If an actor cannot swear or curse without making it sound precocious, it should be edited. Few plays within the reach of secondary school actors are helped by swearing. Profanity is objectionable to most audiences when heard from the stage uttered by teenagers. This is true even when parents swear and use profanity at home.

2. Good taste in play situations and in direction can handle most problems of racial, religious, or sexual references.

3. Love scenes detract from the play and the feeling of sincerity if directed at physical levels.

4. If the director understands the audience (teenage or parent), he can utilize dance movement, variety of stage positions, and other techniques to keep the audience from interfering, or overreacting to love scenes.

5. A study of the play lists used by National Thespian directors indicates little censorship on the part of administration or community.

6. Most censorship is in the mind of the directors themselves. If the director is unsure, the administration will recommend a different choice. If, however, the director suffers from a messiah complex, determined to introduce a community to the modern world of sex, sin, and swearing, he can expect controls.

---

[7] Albert Lynn Briggs, "A Survey of Content Problems in High School Play Selection," Master's thesis, Department of Education, The Ohio State University, 1961.

Censorship in High School Theatre

Check the appropriate box if you would edit or omit. Then circle the number to indicate the degree of your concern. The number 1 indicates a strong, positive reaction and the number 5, a weak or negative reaction.

	Edit	Omit	Farce and comedy	Drama and tragedy
I. Smoking, drinking, swearing				
1. Using the Lord's name in vain			1 2 3 4 5	1 2 3 4 5
2. Use of swearing: damn, hell, etc.			1 2 3 4 5	1 2 3 4 5
3. Reference to alcoholism: "drunk as an owl," "three sheets in the wind," etc.			1 2 3 4 5	1 2 3 4 5
4. Use of social drinking: cocktails, highballs, etc.			1 2 3 4 5	1 2 3 4 5
5. Use of heavy drinking: a drunken character, or a character getting drunk on stage			1 2 3 4 5	1 2 3 4 5
6. Use of smoking			1 2 3 4 5	1 2 3 4 5
II. Racial-religious reference				
1. Derogatory racial reference: "wop," "nigger," etc.			1 2 3 4 5	1 2 3 4 5
2. Derogatory religious reference: "fish-eater," "soul-saver," "psalm-singer," etc.			1 2 3 4 5	1 2 3 4 5
III. Sex reference				
1. Reference to premarital relations			1 2 3 4 5	1 2 3 4 5
2. Reference to extramarital relations			1 2 3 4 5	1 2 3 4 5
3. Prolonged or heavy love-making			1 2 3 4 5	1 2 3 4 5
4. Reference to approved marital relations			1 2 3 4 5	1 2 3 4 5
5. Assault action			1 2 3 4 5	1 2 3 4 5
6. Actual nudity or seminudity			1 2 3 4 5	1 2 3 4 5
7. Offstage or out-of-sight sound effects or dialogue referring to sex action			1 2 3 4 5	1 2 3 4 5
8. Reference to pregnancy			1 2 3 4 5	1 2 3 4 5
IV. Sociopolitical reference				
1. Reference defaming American political system			1 2 3 4 5	1 2 3 4 5
2. Reference supporting political systems other than American system			1 2 3 4 5	1 2 3 4 5
3. Reference defaming political systems other than American system			1 2 3 4 5	1 2 3 4 5

	Edit	Omit	*Farce and comedy*	*Drama and tragedy*
4. Satirization of professional people or groups			1 2 3 4 5	1 2 3 4 5
V. Mental health				
1. Reference to insanity			1 2 3 4 5	1 2 3 4 5
2. Characterization of insanity			1 2 3 4 5	1 2 3 4 5
3. Murder acts on stage			1 2 3 4 5	1 2 3 4 5
4. Reference to juvenile delinquency: e.g., *Dino*			1 2 3 4 5	1 2 3 4 5
5. Emotional instability within a family situation: e.g., *Ladies in Retirement*			1 2 3 4 5	1 2 3 4 5

If you concede that the above references do influence your selection of a play, do you feel that this in any way thwarts your work in high school theatre?

The Teacher as Technical Director

Until recently we have been limited in quality materials for teaching technical theatre. The Olesen Company (1535 Ivar Avenue, Hollywood, California) is representative of suppliers of new and excellent filmstrips, catalogues, and services available to teachers. The following materials are quoted directly from Olesen's basic catalogue and prices may be obtained directly from the company. Other suppliers, listed in the chart which follows, will furnish catalogues and brochures to interested schools and institutions. Selection should be made according to the objectives and sophistication of class experience.

Theatre is not adequately taught without involving students in production problems. While rental of scenery may be justified for some productions, the total concept of theatre is learned through scene construction and the development of experience in lighting projects. This can be accomplished in a small workshop theatre or with major productions. The teacher becomes a supervisor in this process. Students are capable of doing all the building, plotting, focusing, and operational tasks of play production. Even junior high students can do these processes well, if properly taught. The teacher who does this work robs students of valuable experience and fails to accomplish the objectives for which he was hired — *to teach*. The teaching aids listed below may accelerate the learning. The building of models should precede actual construction, which should be the final experience, tested on stage under the critical eye of the audience. Prices on lumber, muslin, and basic electrical materials should be obtained locally. Only those unique to the theatre should be purchased from theatrical sources, since shipping costs may equal the cost of the product.

Theatre Crafts Filmstrips

Educational aids to assist the beginning theatre
student to learn stage production techniques

SCENERY CONSTRUCTION

Seven 35-mm color filmstrips with captions by Robert H. Johnson of the University of Southern California. Color photographs and captions combine to describe the step-by-step procedures in building and handling stage flats. Covers various construction methods, flat sizes, and almost every situation where elevations are used in stage application. Stage terminology is explained and used in context. A complete unit, simple enough for the beginner to follow.

Part I   – The Simple Flat (67 frames)
Part II   – Complex Flats (49 frames)
Part III – Handling Flats (32 frames)
Part IV   – Platforms (26 frames)
Part V   – Parallels (33 frames)
Part VI   – Stairs (34 frames)
Part VII – Ramps (29 frames)

BASIC TECHNIQUES OF SCENERY PAINTING

Six 35-mm color filmstrips by Robert Corrigan of the University of California at Los Angeles. Covers in a complete, step-by-step manner the painter's tools, methods of applying paint, such as scumbling, stippling, appliquéing, etc., and the uses of these techniques to produce realistic effects in paint. It also covers the special problems involved in transferring large scenic subjects from drawing to drop or scrim.

Part I   – Material and Equipment
Part II   – Prime and Base Coat Techniques
Part III – Overbase Coat Techniques, I
Part IV   – Overbase Coat Techniques, II
Part V   – Special Techniques
Part VI   – Painting the Drop and the Scrim

ELEMENTARY SET DESIGN

Five 35-mm color filmstrips with captions by Dr. Wendell Cole of Stanford University. Elementary discussion of the physical problems of designing the set, combined with the basics of need to incorporate the mechanical limitations with the requirements of the play. Fundamental principles of the use of line, color, and mass are discussed in respect to their use in developing mood and characterization. The uses and need for working drawings, plus the simple solutions of certain types of special problems, such as outdoor settings, are covered.

Part I   – The Physical Stage and Basic Set Units (32 frames)
Part II – Basic Elements of Design (55 frames)
Part III – Drafting for the Proscenium Stage (37 frames)
Part IV – Styles of Scenery (32 frames)
Part V – Special Types of Settings (33 frames)

BASIC PRINCIPLES OF STAGE COSTUMING

Six 35-mm color filmstrips with captions by Patricia Hungerland of the University of California at Los Angeles. This series is designed to help the beginning stagecraft student achieve a better understanding of the problems involved with the design and organization of the costumes for a production. Covers such things as script breakdown, measuring fitting, source materials, basic sewing and workroom facilities.

Part I   – General Organization of Script (33 frames)
Part II – Application of General Design Principles (41 frames)
Part III – Sketches and Use of Textiles (31 frames)
Part IV – Workroom Facilities and Basic Sewing Techniques (31 frames)
Part V – Patterns and Fitting (42 frames)
Part VI – Special Problems (36 frames)

ELEMENTARY STAGE MAKE-UP

Four 35-mm color filmstrips with captions by Jane Rasche of Max Factor & Company and University of Southern California. Demonstrates elementary techniques of applying stage make-up for the beginning actor. Explains the fundamental principles of color, use and handling of various make-up materials; covering application of grease paint, lining colors for highlight and shadow, false eyelashes, false noses, wigs, and beards. An independent unit which assists the student in creating a competent stage make-up.

Part I   – Straight Make-up for Men (33 frames)
Part II – Straight Make-Up for Women (30 frames)
Part III – Making-Up Youth for Old Age (30 frames)
Part IV – Use of False Hair and Nose Putty (30 frames)

LIGHTING FOR THE THEATRE

Three 35-mm color filmstrips with captions by Robert C. Todt and William C. White. Primer on stage lighting presents captioned exterior and interior photographs, diagrams of the optical systems, and examples of the area of throw for the most commonly used lights. Explains the principles of area lighting and back, side, and fill lighting. Included also are types of lamps, lenses, connecting devices, mounting devices, beam control devices, diaphragms, plugging gutter, dimmers, patching panels, and dimmer boards. Used together these filmstrips contain the information for a basic approach of how to light the typical stage production.

Part I   – Basic Stage Lighting Equipment (40 frames)
Part II – Area Lighting (36 frames)
Part III – Back, Side, and Fill Lighting (36 frames)

WORKING AIDS FOR THE THEATRE TECHNICIAN

Three 35-mm color filmstrips with captions by Robert H. Johnson of University of Southern California. Thoroughly covers machinery, equipment and tools for the stage and shop, and hardware used on scenery, and identifies and explains uses and shows applications of a complete inventory of working aids found in the educational, community, and professional theatre.

Part I   – Stage Machinery and Equipment (71 frames)
Part II – Stage Hardware (53 frames)
Part III – Shop Machinery and Tools (40 frames)

Theatre History Filmstrips

For theatre and art history classes, as an aid to textbooks to show visually the development of the theatre from the past to the present day

THE DEVELOPMENT OF THE PHYSICAL THEATRE
(5th Century B.C. to 20th Century A.D.)

One 55-frame 35-mm black and white filmstrip by Dr. James H. Butler and Desmond P. Wedberg of the University of Southern California. Pictures the development of the threatre through close-up illustrations of authentic scale models. Types of theatres include classical Greek and Roman; stages for medieval mystery and miracle plays; Coventry pageant wagon cycle; Commedia Dell'Arte; Teatro Olimpico; Elizabethan theatres including the Globe and Fortune, and a Masque theatre; 18th and 19th century French and English theatres; Japanese Kabuki; 19th century American; and 20th century German. Teaching manual — narrative script discusses each theatre in detail.

GREEK AND ROMAN THEATRES OF THE ANCIENT WORLD

Five 35-mm color filmstrips with captions by Dr. James H. Butler of the University of Southern California. A definitive study of important classical theatres and the development in staging the ancient world's drama. Color drawings and photographs from Greece, Turkey, and France combine to reconstruct the development of the theatre from the sixth century B.C., including views of classical tragedies as performed then and now.

Part I   – Ancient Greek Theatre of Epidauros (56 frames)
Part II – Theatre of Dionysus, I (39 frames)
Part III – Theatre of Dionysus, II (39 frames)
Part IV – Hellenistic Theatre of Priene (43 frames)
Part V   – Roman Theatre of Orange

THE HISTORY OF THE PHYSICAL THEATRE; FROM THE ANCIENT GREEKS TO THE CONTEMPORARY THEATRE

Four 35-mm color filmstrips with captions by Dr. James Butler of the University of Southern California. A broad survey of the evolution of theatre buildings and arenas from the first theatre at Knossos in ancient Crete to modern Melodyland in Southern California. Through the use of colored photographs, art work and reconstructions, Dr. Butler shows the changes that have taken place in the playhouse itself, as influenced by the times and interests of civilization. A basic view of the history of the theatre, this series is excellent for high school classes and college courses of an elementary nature.

Part I – The Ancient Greek, Roman, Medieval, Spanish, and Italian Renaissance Theatres (50 frames)

Part II – The Elizabethan and 17th-Century French Theatres (52 frames)

Part III – The English Restoration; English, European, and American Theatres of the 18th and 19th Centuries (53 frames)

Part IV – 20th-Century Theatres (50 frames)

SOPHOCLES' *ELECTRA*

One 35-mm color filmstrip of 30 frames with captions by Dr. James H. Butler of the University of Southern California. Scenes from the production illustrate the action of the famous Greek tragedy by Sophocles. Models of the stage setting and costume plates are included to help you produce classical plays. A teaching manual includes a discussion of Greek tragedy and the House of Atreus; the story of the play; a critical analysis of the play; and an annotated bibliography on Greek theatres, Greek Tragedy, Sophocles, and mythology.

ROMAN CIRCUSES, NAUMACHIAE AND AMPHITHEATRES

Part I and II (52 frames each part), directed and written by Dr. James H. Butler. A fascinating visual and written description of Roman hippodromes, amphitheatres, circuses, and naumachiae. Each ancient form of Roman theatre is explained in an interesting and informative manner. Dr. Butler vicariously places you among the tremendous throngs that watched swift and exciting chariot races, gladiator contests, animal baiting, and other ancient forms of entertainment.

SHAKESPEAREAN PLAYS

A group of five of the most important plays, produced by Lexington Records of New York from various productions. 35-mm color filmstrips, with teaching guides for classroom visualization in secondary schools or theatre survey classes.

23000 *Hamlet*
23005 *Julius Caesar*
23010 *Macbeth*

ENGLISH PLAYHOUSES OF THE RESTORATION, 18th and 19th Centuries

Six 35-mm color filmstrips with captions by Dr. James Butler of the University of Southern California. Covers the history of the great English playhouse in chronological order. Through the use of historical etchings, shows the development of such great theatres as Drury Lane, Covent Garden, The Royal Opera House, the Haymarket, and Sadlers Wells. It discusses the contributions made in design by Sir Christopher Wren, William Davenant, Inigo Jones as well as the great advancements in stage scenery and lighting.

Part I   – Restoration Theatres (45 frames)
Part II   – Early 18th-Century Theatres (47 frames)
Part III – Late 18th-Century Theatres (64 frames)
Part IV   – Early 19th-Century Theatres (50 frames)
Part V   – Middle 19th-Century Theatres (50 frames)
Part VI   – Late 19th-Century Theatres (47 frames)

HISTORY OF COSTUME

(From the Atomic Age to the Time of the Magna Carta)

Two 35-mm color filmstrips with captions by the late Fred Kuwalski, director, Stage and School Departments, Western Costume Company, Hollywood. Photographs of models in authentic costumes and wigs trace the development of men's and women's costumes, generation by generation, from modern streetwear to the knights and ladies of the thirteenth century. A teaching manual discusses each costume in detail and lists plays in which specific costumes are worn.

Part I   – Men's Clothing of the Western World (35 frames)
Part II – Women's Clothing of the Western World (28 frames)

THE ITALIAN RENAISSANCE THEATRE

A history of the stage architects and engineers who built such legendary theatres as the Teatro Olimpico 16 years after the death of Michelangelo. Carefully prepared by Dr. James Butler, you'll see the first light dimmers, the first attempts to float ships across the stage, and the first cloud effects. This period exerted an indelible impression upon Shakespeare and his fellow Elizabethan dramatists.

Part I   – Theatres and Stage Scenery
Part II – Stage Scenery, Stage Machinery, and Stage Lighting
Part III – The Commedia Dell'Arte

THE AMERICAN THEATRE

Two 35-mm color filmstrips with captions by Dr. James Butler of the University of Southern California. A history of the first 150 years of American theatre, starting with the first building in Williamsburg in 1718. By means of art work and photograph, this series shows how the American theatre began to develop from productions and actors imported from England to the position of New York City as a theatrical metropolis by the building of large numbers of theatres. It covers the earliest American theatrical stars and some of their most noted roles.

Part I – The Late 18th-Century and Early 19th-Century American Theatre (49 frames)

Part II – The 19th-Century American Theatre: 1826 to 1950 (60 frames)

Motion Pictures

YESTERDAY'S ACTORS

By Dr. Edwin Burr Pettet, Brandeis University. A 16-mm sound motion picture, on styles of acting from Shakespeare's day to the present, in black and white; running time – 30 minutes. In parody, Dr. Pettet delivers the "To be or not to be" soliloquy from Hamlet as it might have been performed through theatrical history by these leading actors: Edward Alleyn, David Garrick, John Philip Kemble, Edmund Kean, Sir Henry Irving, Leslie Howard, and Marlon Brando. After providing that the serious business of acting can best be illustrated by humorous exaggeration, actor Pettet concludes with an interpretation of the soliloquy "as, perhaps, the Bard intended it to be performed."

Selected Equipment Suppliers

Lighting Equipment (instruments, control, accessories, consultation services)

American Stage Lighting	1331c North Ave.	New Rochelle, N.Y.
Century Lighting, Inc.	3 Entin Road	Clifton, N.Y.
Electro Controls	2975 S. Second West	Salt Lake City, Utah
Electronics Diversified	0626 S.W. Florida St.	Portland, Oregon
Gothic Color Company	90 Ninth Avenue	New York, N.Y.
Hub Electric Company	2255 W. Grand Ave.	Chicago, Illinois
Kliegl Brothers	32-32 48th Avenue	Long Island City, N.Y.
Little Stage Lighting	10507 Harry Hines Blvd.	Dallas, Texas
Major Corporation	P.O. Box 359	Crystal Lake, Illinois
Olesen Company	1535 Ivar Ave.	Hollywood, California
Paramount Theatrical Supplies	32 West 20th St.	New York, N.Y.
Rosco Laboratories	Harrison	Harrison, N.Y.
Skirpan Electronics, Inc.	41-43 24th Street	Long Island City, N.Y.
Strong Electric Corp.	87 City Park Avenue	Toledo, Ohio
Superior Electric Company	2807 Cann Street	Bristol, Connecticut
Theatre Production Services	52 West 46th	New York, N.Y.
Times Square Lighting	318 W. 47th Street	New York, N.Y.

Costumes and Properties (materials, design, rental, novelties)

American Costume Co.	810 Broadway	New York 3, N.Y.
Central Shippee Inc.	24 West 25th St.	New York, N.Y.
Costume Associates, Inc.	68 East 153rd St.	Bronx, N.Y.
Eaves Costume Company, Inc.	151 West 46th St.	New York, N.Y.
Giesen	389 St. Peter	St. Paul, Minn.
New York Costume Co.	10 West Hubbard St.	Chicago, Illinois
The Armoury	2122 Fillmore St.	San Francisco, Cal.

Stage Equipment (hardware, rigging, draperies, track systems)

Art Draperies Studios	2766 N. Lincoln Ave.	Chicago, Illinois
Automatic Devices Co.	2121 S. 12th St.	Allentown, Pa.
Olesen Company	1535 Ivar Ave.	Hollywood, California
Theatre Production Service	52 West 46th St.	New York, N.Y.
True Roll Corporation	622 Sonora Ave.	Glendale, California

Music and Sound Equipment

Dept. A, Music For Theatre	425 Central Park W.	New York, N.Y.
Sony	8150 Vineland Ave.	Sun Valley, California
Sound Associates	432 West 45th St.	New York, N.Y.

Tickets and Publicity

National Ticket Co.	1564 Broadway	New York, N. Y.
Package Publicity Service	1564 Broadway	New York, N.Y.
Ticketron Corporation	Fort Lee	Fort Lee, N.Y.

Suggested Projects

1. Assume you have been employed to teach speech and theatre in a senior high school and your initial inventory provides you with a "bare stage" with the exception of a front curtain (grand drape). You are expected to produce two plays during the year. The first may be a single set with levels, or a unit set with levels (*Death of a Salesman, On Borrowed Time, Look Homeward Angel,* or *The Diary of Anne Frank*). The second requires space staging with multiple areas of interiors and exteriors (*Our Town, The Christmas Carol,* or *Carousel*).

   a) Work out complete designs, working drawings, and production plans for technical rehearsals: floor plans, sketches, detail drawings on stairs, parallels, color renderings, costuming, and light plots.

b) Itemize all items to be purchased in terms of quantity and quality (lumber by number, length, and size; fabric by yards, width, and color; lighting instruments by number, type, and model; paint by color, type, and gallons, etc.). Indicate source of supply (local and out of town) and price per unit.

c) Turn in the total project (*a* and *b* above) to your instructor and present to the class a rationale for all purchases. The class and the instructor represent the budget committee for the school. Estimate the time of order to the date of production.

d) Be sure to include quotations for play books, royalties, and all publicity plans.

e) Work out a plan for casting, rehearsal, and schedule of facilities. Anticipate football, basketball, and music schedules along with major class proms.

f) Assuming you plan to make the theatre plant adequate for any production within five years, work out a program of budget and construction for an adequate control board, spotlights at beam and pipe positions, three-color strip or borders, a supply of basic scenery, and an adequate system of velour draperies mounted upon a flexible track system.

g) Work out a complete design and working drawings for a similar play needing multiple sets, but set upon a rotary stage with levels (*Niccolo and Nicollette*, *Twelfth Night*, etc.)

2. Describe the use of the following as a means of solving your staging problems and provide sketches of their use in changing scenery. You may wish to use models rather than sketches.

roll drop	leg drop	cut-out drop
sky drop	scrim	flying
trip flying	running a set	wagon stage
jack knife stage	rotary (disc) stage	traveller track
box set	unit set	wing and drop set
screens (3-fold)	unit set with plugs	

3. Furnish a diagram for a simple bell system to be constructed by a student. Add to this variations of manually operated sound for thunder, rain, and wind.

4. The administration is willing to purchase a control system for stage lighting. Explain the differences between a resistance, a transformer, and an SRC type installation. Also explain what is meant by flexibility in a lighting system.

5. Using large posterboard, make a diagram of various types of lamp bases by size and type and explain the importance of this to production planning.

6. Develop a lesson plan to clarify the use of "cross-spot" technique in stage lighting and its rationale for artistic production.

7. Develop a unit on the history of theatre in terms of play structure. Develop particularly the meanings of tragedy and comedy and the changes

in these historically. Relate social comedy, comedy of manners, farce, tragi-comedy, melodrama, and sentimental comedy to the historical aspects of tragedy and comedy.

7. Develop poster-sized drawings to guide students in constructing a basic flat, a doorway flat, and a flight of stairs (five steps high). Include detail blow-up drawings of butt joint, rabbit joint, mitre joint, mortise and tenon joint, half joint, and scarf joint and indicate where each might be used in constructing scenery.

8. Develop a diagrammed instruction on the assembly and folding system for a parallel. Particularly stress the safety features.

9. You have your scenery constructed. Work out complete instructions for the students to paint the set. Clarify the following terms:

stippling	sponging	spattering
spraying	whipping	triangulation (snap-line)
flameproofing	drybrushing	laying in
lining	stencilling	opaquing
transparency	whiting	dry pulp pigments

10. Develop job descriptions for the following theatre personnel:

stage manager	assistant director	property manager
costume manager	publicity manager	sound man

11. You have selected a Children's Theatre play and plan three perfor-mances per day for each of three Saturdays. Costumes include two rabbits, a fox, a bear, a wolf, a possum, an owl, and several terrapins. The action will be vigorous and the lines must be heard and understood. Design the costumes including heads so that these features are provided.

12. Assuming you are limited to a gymatorium and wish to produce *Inherit the Wind,* design a production utilizing the gym floor with the audi-ence seated in bleachers on two sides. React to the charge that teaching science is no longer on trial but teaching religion is. Would making Brady the protagonist destroy the play?

13. Assume a season of plays including *Teahouse of the August Moon, Ali Baba and the Forty Thieves,* and *Music Man.* Through study of the publishers catalogues or letters to the publishers determine the royalties for three performances of each in contrast to a five-performance schedule under playbox billing. You may get your prices on an estimated house of 1000 for regular billing and 400 for each performance on the *playbox.* Using a ticket price of $1.00 per seat on the adult plays and $.50 per seat for the children's theatre production, make a pre-season estimate of income and expected costs. (Include estimates of building, rental, maintenance, sets, lights, costumes, and properties.)

14. "The story of the theatre is the story of both the playhouse and the play. Drama cannot be studied without considering the physical theatre; a theatre is meaningless apart from the drama it presents."*

With the above quotation the authors set their focus upon the physical theatre. The present material is presented in the firm belief that the desire to

---

*Kenneth Macgowan and William Meinitz, *The Living Stage,* Englewood, N.J.: Prentice-Hall, Inc., 1955.

dramatize stems first from the desire to create in dramatic form for an "audience." The playwright then hopes that others will approve of his creative effort and seeks a staging area consciously or unconsciously. The type of staging area depends upon the materials available, the form the idea takes, and the engineering ingenuity of the dramatist. Some plays have been written for a specific type of stage. The struggle begins, however, with an idea or action to be expressed.

Although the ideas have hundreds of variations most are recurring themes. Various dramatists have looked upon these problems, or ideas, from a variety of windows, shaped by the cultural architecture of the world in which they lived. Some of the windows are high and narrow, pointed like those in Gothic cathedrals. Others are broad and gregarious like openings of the Left Bank cafes. Some reek like the soil and mildewing out-buildings along Tobacco Road, while others furnish the limited view of tenements where present and past is seen between the elbows of crowded tenants fighting for employment and satisfaction. Some of the windows are a confused distortion of the maladjusted seeking a mate or security in a world of sophisticated dogs, each guarding against fearful but desperate challengers. Theatre has treated such problems from the time of *Prometheus* and *Antigone* to *Death of a Salesman, The Visit,* and *Endgame.* Dramatists have cried out *for justice* and *against war.* Plays have *decried slavery* of women, the rich, the poor, and children. Prejudice of race has not been as frequent as prejudice of the rich against the poor, the poor against the rich, the citizen against the immigrant, established religion against the searcher. These are but a few of the problems about which dramatists have written. The style and the available materials determine the staging, within the imagination and creativity of the writer and producing team. Only by knowing more about the message of the dramatist can we intelligently stage his work.

Following is a list of "classic" and modern plays frequently mentioned in production lists and discussions where theatre is considered a contribution to the culture of mankind. Many modern plays have focused upon a "social problem." It is interesting to note that these problems were the central theme or the vehicle for discussing another theme in the classic plays. The mature student should develop reading habits which would help him visualize production in terms of subject, theme, or style of a number of plays from various periods which deal with the same or similar problems. In order to understand the play, the student must know something of the social, economic, and philosophic trends of the time in which the play was written. Undergraduate students should be familiar with those plays marked (*), while graduate students should be familiar with and conversant about all in the list. The ability to associate the title with author and subject is a valuable reference technique. The present list does not represent all of the "good" plays. It does not even attempt to classify by quality. It is a list of these most frequently mentioned when theatre is discussed in terms of ideas. The titles have been briefed to save space.

Assignments:

    a) Identify authors with plays they have written.

    b) Identify the period with the types of plays written.

c) Now that you have associated the author with titles, time, place, and style, you are ready to consider the author's significant contribution to mankind. Some authors discussed a single subject, with its peripheral relations to other subjects throughout the productive period of writing; other dramatists dealt with a number of subjects. The purpose of this assignment is to focus upon a number of the major concerns of mankind as treated by dramatists. Several have written plays discussing the value or lack of value of war. Others have concerned themselves with the dignity of man, or the relationship of parent to child. Still others have concerned themselves with justice, responsibility of public leaders. Using this list of plays, you should classify them according to the subject matter with which they deal. Choosing several plays dealing with a single subject you should contrast or compare the treatment given a subject by the various authors.

The Time of Your Life	*The Dark at the Top of the Stairs*
The Voice of the Turtle	*Cat on a Hot Tin Roof*
The Hasty Heart	*Tall Story*
Death of a Salesman*	*The Rope Dancers*
The Fall of the City*	*The Rose Tatoo*
Life with Father	*The Gazebo*
A Majority of One	*Kiss Me Kate*
Look Homeward Angel	*The Man Who Came to Dinner**
Inherit the Wind	*All My Sons*
Green Pastures	*The Three Sisters*
World of Suzie Wong	*The Cherry Orchard**
The Crucible	*King Hunger*
A Raisin in the Sun	*The God of Vengeance*
J.B.	*The Second Mrs. Tanqueray*
West Side Story	*The Liars*
South Pacific	*Candida*
Look Back in Anger	*Major Barbara*
Suddenly Last Summer	*Heartbreak House*
I Remember Mama*	*The Admirable Crichton**
A Streetcar Named Desire*	*The Tragedy of Nan*
Arsenic and Old Lace*	*The Pigeon*
Member of the Wedding*	*The Circle*
The Male Animal*	*The Vortex*
Sabrina Fair	*Blythe Spirit**
Requiem for a Nun	*The Green Bay Tree*
My Fair Lady	*The Plough and the Stars**
Auntie Mame	*Beyond the Horizon**
Night of January 16th	*Strange Interlude*
Pleasure of His Company	*Desire Under the Elms**

Rain
What Price Glory*
Elizabeth the Queen
Wingless Victory*
The Silver Cord*
You Can't Take It With You*
Johnny Johnson*
Biography
Dead End*
Golden Boy*
Three Men on a Horse*
Of Mice and Men*
Idiot's Delight
Stage Door*
Picnic
Two for the Seasaw
Girl Crazy
The Captive
Bonds of Interest
The Visit*
Sweet Bird of Youth
A Touch of the Poet
Rashoman
Witness for the Prosecution
Summer and Smoke
The Disenchanted
Oklahoma
Flower Drum Song
Sunrise at Campobello
The Sound of Music
Saint Joan*
What Every Woman Knows*
Justice
Our Betters
Outward Bound
Fumed Oak
Juno and the Paycock
The Great Divide
Anna Christie
Ah, Wilderness
The Adding Machine*
The Show Off
Saturday's Children*
Winterset*
Key Largo

Beggar on Horseback
In Abraham's Bosom
The Little Foxes*
Green Grow the Lilacs
Awake and Sing
The Detective Story
The Petrified Forest
Abe Lincoln in Illinois*
Tobacco Road*
Born Yesterday
The Glass Menagerie*
Watch on the Rhine*
A Month in the Country
The Kingdom of God
The Power of Darkness
The Sea Gull
The Lower Depths*
He Who Gets Slapped*
Lady Windemere's Fan*
Michael and his Lost Angel
Widower's Houses
Caesar and Cleopatra*
Androcles and the Lion*
Back to Methuselah
Peter Pan*
Strife
Loyalties
Abraham Lincoln
Ways and Means
Journey's End
The Playboy of the Western World*
Shadow and Substance*
Emperor Jones*
Mourning Becomes Electra
The Hairy Ape
Street Scene*
Craig's Wife
Both Your Houses
High Tor*
Yellowjack*
Of Thee I Sing
The Children's Hour*
End of Summer
Philadelphia Story
Bury the Dead*

The Jew of Malta*
Twelfth Night
Hamlet*
King Lear*
Anthony and Cleopatra*
Cymbeline
The Tempest
The Woman Killed with Kindness
The Indian Queen
The Way of the World*
The London Merchant
The Contrast
Phaedra
The Imaginary Invalid*
William Tell
Richelieu*
The Outer Edge of Society
The Pirates of Penzance
A Doll's House
Rosmersholm
Brand
The Father*
The Lady from the Sea
The Weavers*
The Awakening of Love
The Green Cockatoo
The Guardsmen
The Goat Song
Damaged Goods*
Pelléas and Mélisande
L'Aiglon
Prometheus Bound
Medea*
The Clouds*
The Captives

The Four P's
The Spanish Tragedy
The History of Friar Bacon and
  Friar Bungay
Othello*
Macbeth*
Coriolanus
The Winter's Tale
Volpone*
The Duchess of Malfi*
The White Devil
The Country Wife
The Conscious Lovers
The School for Scandal*
Life is a Dream*
The Would-Be Gentlemen
The Mistress of the Inn
Faust, Part I
Fashion*
Caste*
Chantecler
Gioconda
Cradle Song
The Inspector General*
Ivanov
Uncle Vanya*
The Life of Man
The Dybbuk
The Importance of Being Ernest*
Mid Channel
Man and Superman
Pygmalion*
Six Characters in Search of
  an Author

References

Creativity

Fitzgerald, Burdette S. *World Tales for Creative Dramatics and Story-telling.* Englewood Cliffs, N. J.: Prentice-Hall, Inc., 1962.

Getzels, Jacob W. and Jackson, Philip W. *Creativity and Intelligence.* New York: John Wiley & Sons, Inc., 1962, pp. 13-76.

Gruber, H. E., Terrell, Glen, and Wertheimer, Michael (eds.), *Contemporary Approaches to Creative Thinking.* New York: Atherton Press, 1962.

Guilford, J. P. "Creativity," *American Psychologist,* 5: 444-454. (1950).

Kerman, Gertrude. *Plays and Creative Ways With Children.* Irvington-on-Hudson, N. Y.: Harvey House, Inc., Publishers, 1961.

Koestler, Arthur. *The Act of Creation* New York: The Macmillan Company, 1964.

Lewis, George L. "Special Problems in Teaching Artistic and Creative Activities in Speech," *The Communicative Arts and Sciences of Speech,* ed. Keith Brooks. Columbus, Ohio: Charles E. Merrill Publishing Company, 1967, pp. 542-563.

Lowry, W. McNeil. "The University and Creative Arts," *Educational Theatre Journal,* 14:99-112 (May, 1962). Reprinted in *The Superior Student,* The Newsletter of the Inter-University Committee on the Superior Student, 5:4-9 (May, 1963).

Mackinnon, Donald W. "Characteristics of the Creative Person: Implications for the Teaching Learning Process," paper presented at the Sixteenth National Conference on Higher Education, March 6, 1961.

————. "What Makes a Person Creative," *Saturday Review* (February, 1962).

McQuigg, Ruth. "An Experimental Study of the Effects of Certain Directed Activities on Oral Communication Behavior of First Graders." Master's thesis, The Ohio State University, 1962.

Mearns, Hugh. *Creative Power: The Education of Youth in Creative Arts.* New York: Dover Publications, Inc., 1958.

Rusch, Reuben, Denny, David and Ives, Sammie. "Development of a Test of Creativity in the Dramatic Arts, A Pilot Study," *Journal of Educational Research,* 57, No. 5: 250-254 (1964).

Siks, Geraldine B. *Creative Dramatics: An Art for Children.* New York: Harper & Row, Publishers, 1958.

Ward, Winifred. *Drama With and For Children.* Washington, D.C.: U.S. Department of Health, Education, and Welfare, Bulletin No. 30, 1960. United States Government Printing Office, 1962.

————. *Playmaking with Children.* New York: Appleton-Century-Crofts, 1957.

Theatre Programs and Courses of Study

A Suggested Outline for a Course of Study in Dramatic Arts in the Secondary School. Stanford, California: American Educational Theatre Association, 1950.

A Suggested Outline for a Course of Study in Theatre Arts: Secondary School Level. Washington, D.C.: American Educational Theatre Association, 1963. Rev. 1968.

Ball, M. E. "Drama and the Community," *Dramatics,* 24:12-13 (May, 1953).

Bavely, Ernest. "Dramatic Arts in Secondary Education," *The Quarterly Journal of Speech,* 32:40-47 (February, 1946).

————. "Play Standards at the High School Level," *The Quarterly Journal of Speech,* 26:89-97 (February, 1940).

————. "Suggestions for Improving Drama Festivals and Contests," *The Quarterly Journal of Speech,* 28:327-332 (October, 1942).

Bouee, M.E. "Allied Activities and Dramatics," *Dramatics,* 24:6-17 (October, 1952).

Braden, Waldo W. *Speech Methods and Resources: A Texbook for the Teacher of Speech* New York: Harper & Row, Publishers, 1961, pp. 346-366.

Cartright, E.S. "Selecting, Casting, and Rehearsing the High School Play," *The Quarterly Journal of Speech,* 29:443-51 (December, 1943).

Committee on Curriculum Planning and Development. "The Arts in the Comprehensive Secondary School," *The Bulletin of the National Association of Secondary School Principals,* 46:1-19 (September, 1962).

"Dramatics in the Secondary School," *"The Bulletin of the National Association of Secondary School Principals,* 33 (December, 1949).

Elkind, S. "Principles of Learning: Their Application to Rehearsal," *The Speech Teacher,* 5:51-59 (January, 1956).

Heffner, Hubert C. "Theatre and Drama in Liberal Education," *Educational Theatre Journal,* 16:16-23 (March, 1964).

Konigsberg, E. "An Outline Course of Study in Dramatics," *The Speech Teacher,* 4:27-31 (January, 1955).

Lewis, George L. "Children's Theatre and Creative Dramatics: A Bibliography," *Educational Theatre Journal,* 7:138-146 (May, 1955).

————. "Do You Know Your Plays and Playwrights?" *Ohio Speech Journal,* 1:42-50 (1962); 2:149-154 (1963).

————, and Schoen, Kathryn T. "The High School Drama Course: A Project in Test Item Analysis," *Ohio Speech Journal,* 2:161-180 (1963).

Michielutte, Robert. "Secondary School Students' Perceptions of Actors," *The Speech Teacher,* 18:30-38 (January, 1969).

Mitchell, W.B. "Issues and Developments — Theatre Arts." *The Bulletin of the National Association of Secondary School Principals,* 47:51-56 (November 1963).

Ogilvie, Mardel. *Teaching Speech in the High School.* New York: Appleton-Century-Crofts, 1961, pp. 285-325.

Robinson, Karl F. and Kerikas, E.J. *Teaching Speech: Methods and Materials.* New York: David McKay Company, Inc., 1963, pp. 454-478.

Theatre History and Theory

Albright, H.D., Halstead, W.P., and Mitchell, Lee. *Principles of Theatre Art.*
Boston: Houghton Mifflin Co., 1955.

Bentley, Eric R. *The Playwright as a Thinker.* New York: William Morrow
& Co., Inc., 1946.

Bieber, Margarete. *The History of the Greek and Roman Theatre.* Princeton,
N.J.: Princeton University Press, 1939.

Brown, John Mason. *The Modern Theatre in Revolt.* New York: W.W.
Norton and Company, Inc., 1929.

Cheney, Sheldon. *The Theatre: Three Thousand Years of Drama, Acting and
Stagecraft.* New York: Longmans, Green and Company, 1929.

Cole, Toby and Chinoy, Helen Krich (eds.). *Actors on Acting.* New York:
Crown Publishers, Inc., 1949.

————. *Directing the Play.* Indianapolis, Ind.: The Bobbs-Merrill Company, Inc., 1953.

Cooper, Lane. *The Poetics of Aristotle.* Ithaca, N.Y.: Cornell University
Press, 1956.

Downer, Alan. *The Art of the Play.* New York: Holt, Rinehart & Winston,
Inc., 1955.

Else, Gerald Frank. *Aristotle's Poetics: The Argument.* Cambridge, Mass.:
Harvard University Press, 1957.

Fergusson, Francis. *The Idea of a Theatre.* Princeton, N.J.: Princeton University Press, 1949.

Freedley, George and Reeves, John A. *A History of the Theatre.* New York:
Crown Publishers, Inc., 1941.

Gassner, John. *Form and Idea in the Modern Theatre.* New York: Holt, Rinehart & Winston, Inc., 1956.

Hewitt, Barnard. *Theatre, U.S.A., 1668-1957.* New York: McGraw-Hill Book
Company, 1959.

Kernoldle, George. *From Art to Theatre.* Chicago: University of Chicago
Press, 1944.

Krutch, Joseph Wood. *"Modernism in Modern Drama.* Ithaca, New York:
Cornell University Press, 1953.

Levin, Richard. *Tragedy: Plays, Theory and Criticism.* New York: Harcourt,
Brace & World, 1960.

MacGowan, Kenneth, and Melnitz, William. *The Living Stage.* Englewood
Cliffs, N.J., Prentice-Hall, Inc., 1953.

Meyers, Henry Alonzo. *Tragedy: A View of Life.* Ithaca, N.Y.: Cornell University Press, 1956.

Nicoll, Allardyce. *Theory of Drama.* New York: Thomas Y. Crowell Co.,
1931.

————. *The Development of the Theatre.* Rev. ed.; New York: Harcourt,
Brace & World, 1947.

Seyler, Athene and Haggard, Stephen. *The Craft of Comedy*. New York: Theatre Arts, Inc., 1946.

Simonson, Lee. *The Stage is Set*. New York: Harcourt, Brace & World, 1932.

Stebbins, Genevieve. *Delsarte System of Expression*. New York: Edgar S. Werner Publishing and Supply Company, Inc., 1902.

Stanislavsky, Konstantin. *An Actor's Handbook*, ed. and trans. Elizabeth Reynolds Hapgood. New York: Theatre Arts Books, 1963.

Theatre: Style-Aesthetics and Criticism

Beerbohm, Max. *Around Theatres*. New York: Alfred A. Knopf, Inc., 1930.

Bentley, Eric. *The Dramatic Event: An American Chronicle*. New York: Horizon Press, 1954.

_____. *What is Theatre?* New York: Horizon Press, 1957.

Boyle, Walden. "On the Nature of Artistic Representation in the Theatre," *The Quarterly Journal of Speech*, 30:316-328 (1944).

Brockett, Oscar. *The Theatre: An Introduction*. New York: Holt, Rinehart & Winston, Inc., 1964.

Brown, John Mason. *The Art of Playgoing*. New York: W. W. Norton & Company, Inc., 1936.

Bullogh, Edward. "Physical Distance as a Factor in Art and as an Esthetic Principle," *British Journal of Psychology*, 5 (1913).

Coleridge, Samuel Taylor. "Progress of the Drama," *European Theories of the Drama*, ed. Barrett H. Clark. New York: Crown Publishers, Inc., 1947, pp. 425-427.

Esslin, Martin. *The Theatre of the Absurd*. New York: Doubleday & Company, Inc., 1961.

Gassner, John. *Form and Idea in Modern Theatre*. New York: Holt, Rinehart & Winston, Inc., 1956.

_____. *The Theatre in Our Times: A Survey of the Men and Materials and Movements in the Modern Theatre*. New York: Crown Publishers, Inc., 1954.

Gorelik, Mordecai. *New Theatres for Old*. New York: Samuel French, Inc., 1940.

Ommanney, Katharine. *The Stage and the School*. New York: McGraw-Hill Book Company, 1960.

Shaw, George Bernard. *Plays and Players: Essays on the Theatre*, ed. A. C. Ward. London: Oxford University Press, 1954.

Wright, Edward A. *A Primer for Playgoers*. Englewood Cliffs, N.J.: Prentice-Hall, Inc., 1958, pp. 31-51.

Young, Stark. *Immortal Shadows: A Book of Dramatic Criticism*. New York: Charles Scribner's Sons, 1948.

Dramatic Production

Adix, Vern. *Theatre Scenecraft.* Anchorage, Kentucky: Children's Theatre Press, 1956.

Barton, Lucy. *Historic Costume for the Stage.* Boston: Walter H. Baker Co., 1938.

Blank, Earl (ed.). *How They Were Staged.* Cincinnati: *Dramatics,* National Thespian Society, 1945 and serially.

Boyle, Walden P. *Central and Flexible Staging.* Berkeley, California: University of California Press, 1956.

Bretz, Rudy. *Television Production.* Rev. ed.; New York: McGraw-Hill Book Company, 1962.

Bretz, Rudy, and Edward Stasheff. *The Television Program: Its Direction and Production.* New York: Hill & Wang, Inc., 1962.

Cole, Toby (ed.). *Actors on Acting.* New York: Crown Publishers, Inc., 1949.

————. *Directing the Play.* Indianapolis, Ind.: The Bobbs-Merrill Co., Inc., 1953.

Corson, Richard. *Stage Make-up.* New York: Appleton-Century-Crofts, 1949.

Davis, Jed H. and March, Jane Watkins. *Children's Theatre, Play Production for the Child Audience.* New York: Harper & Row, Publishers, 1960.

Dean, Alexander and Carra, Lawrence. *Fundamentals of Play Directing.* New York: Holt, Rinehart & Winston, Inc., 1965.

Dolman, John J. *The Art of Play Production.* Rev. ed.; New York: Harper & Row, Publishers, 1946.

Factor, Max. *Make-up Leaflets.* Hollywood, California: Factor Studios. 9 booklets, 50¢ a set.

Gassner, John. *Producing the Play.* Rev. ed.; New York: Holt, Rinehart & Winston, 1953.

————. *Masters of the Drama.* New York: Random House, Inc., 1954.

————. *Best Plays of the Modern American Theatre.* 5 vol. New York: Crown Publishers, Inc., 1939, 1947, 1949, 1952, 1960.

————. *A Treasury of the Theatre.* New York: Simon & Schuster, Inc., 1951.

———— and Allen, Ralph G. *Theatre and Drama in the Making.* Boston: Houghton Mifflin Company, 1964.

———— and Sweetkind, Morris. *Introducing the Drama.* New York: Holt, Rinehart & Winston, Inc., 1963.

Gillette, Arnold S. *Stage Scenery: Its Construction and Rigging.* New York: Harper & Row, Publishers, 1960).

Hartnell, Phyllis. *The Oxford Companion to the Theatre.* 2nd ed; London: The Oxford University Press, 1957.

Heffner, Hubert, Seldon, Samuel, and Sellman, Hunton D. *Modern Theatre Practice.* 4th ed.; New York: Appleton-Century-Crofts, 1959.

Hewitt, Barnard. *Art and Craft of Play Production.* Philadelphia: J.B. Lippincott Co., 1959.

Howard, John. *Practical Stage Lighting.* Los Angeles: Los Angeles State College, 1960.

Larson, Orville K. *Scene Design for Stage and Screen.* East Lansing, Mich.: Michigan State University Press, 1961.

Nelms, Henning. *Play Production.* Rev. ed.; New York: Barnes & Noble, Inc., 1961.

—————. *A Primer of Stagecraft.* New York: Dramatists Play Service, 1941.

Ommanney, Katharine. *The Stage and the School.* 3rd ed.; New York: McGraw-Hill Book Company, 1960.

Peterek, Josephine D. *Costuming for the Theatre.* New York: Crown Publishers, Inc., 1959.

Phillipi, Herbert. *Stagecraft and Scene Design.* New York: Houghton Mifflin Company, 1953.

Plummer, Gail. *The Business of Show Business.* New York: Harper & Row, Publishers, 1961.

Simonson, Lee. *The Stage Is Set.* New York: Theatre Arts, Inc., 1962.

Selden, Samuel, and Sellman, Hunton D. *Stage Scenery and Lighting.* 3rd ed.; New York: Appleton-Century-Crofts, 1959.

Walkup, Fairfax P. *Dressing the Part: A History of Costume for the Theatre.* New York: Appleton-Century-Crofts, 1950.

AETA Publications

American Educational Theatre Association
726 Jackson Place, N.W.
Washington, D.C. 20566

Abrams, Dolores M. (ed.). *Theatre in the Junior College.* 1965 (paper), 58 pp.

Ayers, Richard G. *Directory of American College Theatre.* 1967 (paper), 195 pp.

Batcheller, David R. (ed.). *Films for Use in Teaching Theatre.* 1967 (paper), 78 pp.

Biddulph, Helen R. and Hailer, Julia H. (eds.). *Bibliography of Books, Pamphlets and Magazines Relating to Community Theatre.* 1966 (mimeo.), 21 pp.

Bowman, Ned A. and Engel, Glorianne (eds.). *Recent Publications on Theatre Architecture.* Oct. 1960-Feb. 1966 (mimeo.), 55 pp.

Busfield, Roger M., Jr., *Theatre Arts Publications in the United States, 1953-57.* 1964 (cloth), 188 pp.

Course of Study in Theatre Arts for High Schools. SSTC, 1968.

Dodrill, Charles W. (ed.). *Theatre Management Selected Bibliography.* 1966 (mimeo.), 10 pp.

Downer, Alan S. *Conference on Theatre Research.* 1967 (paper), 76 pp.

Dukore, Bernard F. *Bibliography of Theatre Arts Publications in English.* 1965 (paper), 82 pp.

Edyvean, Alfred R. (ed.). *Religious Drama Play List.* 1965 (mimeo.), 24 pp.

Eek, Nat (ed.). *Touring Manual.* 1965 (mimeo.), 28 pp.

Graham, Kenneth L. (ed.). *Relationships Between Professional and Educational Theatre: Actor Training in the U.S.* 1966 (paper), 76 pp.

Litto, Frederic M. (ed.). *Directory of Useful Addresses.* 1966 (mimeo.), 19 pp.

Melnitz, William W. *Theatre Arts Publications in the United States.* 1959 (cloth), 188 pp.

Miller, Dale E. (ed.). *Summer Theatre Directory.* 1967 (paper), 44 pp.

Plays Recommended for High Schools (3-act). SSTC, 1967 (mimeo.), 8 pp.

Preliminary List of Children's Theatres in the U.S. CTC, 1966 (mimeo.), 22 pp.

Pritner, Calvin L. (ed.). *Secondary School Theatre Bibliography.* 1968 (mimeo.), 72 pp.

Welker, David (ed.). *Educational Theatre Journal, Ten Year Index, 1949-1958.* 1959 (paper), 84 pp.

11

Broadcasting

Rapid changes in local and international broadcasting have resulted in viewing habits for students which make this media more effective as a source of entertainment and information than the combined offerings of all other communication media. Few cars or homes are without radios, and multiple television sets in the home have reduced parental control over the listening habits of children. Recent studies indicate that active listening decreases during good weather and scheduled sporting events and that much of the listening is passive (divided among other interests going on in the home). One study checked active televiewing each of several days across three months against the actual programs listed and found the televiewing time significantly below the hours listed in the many popular studies by Witty and others. Still the listening and viewing is frequent and often consumes long hours when competition is lacking. Such facts make imperative a knowledge of the function of these media with the hope of creating a more critical audience. Many believe that quality is directly related to what the audience will accept; they assume that educating the consumer is a better approach to quality than relying on the integrity or responsibility of the advertising sponsors.

OBJECTIVES

A course in broadcasting encompasses values based upon the following assumptions: (1) A broadcasting course must provide concepts and
practice designed to improve processes of oral communication. (2) An
adequate course in speech, oral communication, or broadcasting is concerned with preparation, presentation, and evaluation of ideas. (3) Such
a course will include instruction about and refinement of communication
models and processes, including problems of encoding (language symbols), transmission (media), reception (media), decoding (analysis and
semantics), and valid methods of measuring feedback. (4) A course in
broadcasting is as much concerned with a study of listening as with
preparation and presentation of ideas. Knowing the barriers to listening
and the semantic implications of interpreting messages is necessary in
audience analysis if successful communication is to take place. (5) Broadcasting in the United States is predominantly commercial and is therefore controlled as a means of selling products and ideas. Such a course
must, therefore, include instruction in direct and indirect techniques of
propaganda, interdisciplinary tools (such as semantics), tests of reasoning, knowledge of listening related to attention span, association, and
motivational research. (6) Learning is achieved through personal involvement in analysis and practice; therefore, this course should be implemented through a combination of studies of actual broadcasts in a climate
of free inquiry and actual practice in preparing and presenting programs
which emulate the originals in purpose or in parody. Critical analysis is
creative and thus permits the freedom of a multiple response to any
given stimulus — the right to ridicule as well as praise. (7) Finally, careful analysis dictates the ability to classify and describe. Students should
be expected to analyze weekly, monthly, or seasonal offerings by contrasting and comparing them with other media of communication and
entertainment. Such a course should aid in processes of selection and
evaluation. It is believed that practice in student-created programs may
equal critical analysis of available professional efforts as a good utilization of time. The motivation of students can remain high if such analysis
is furnished through active participation rather than through lectures by
teachers.

Creativity and Broadcasting

Once models are instituted as a means of learning we risk the danger
of only imitating. After models are used to acquaint the student with the
facilities and the methods of response, the major effort should be to en-

courage new formats, new approaches to advertising, and alternate uses of established material. Unfortunately each new idea established is copied with such frequency that the new is often the most conforming style within weeks. Some examples of mass conformity in radio and on camera are the comedy style of advertising copy, long hair and beads on men, and the desire to get the camera inside the violence in every riot or assassination. Many of our best innovators try their ideas off camera in the privacy of a study or small studio. Here the idea can be developed, refined, improved, or rejected. The broadcast classroom is excellent for such experimentation. Students need wide variety and should not be allowed to waste hours of valuable class time or personal time playing disc jockey recordings of current hits. A few programs from this type can be used to note a passing fad, but the total spectrum of the media must be studied if the course is to contain the scope needed. One part of the spectrum is to study or search for forms not now included. Even some new combination of old forms may prove valuable.

Broadcasting as a Phenomenon

Students should study broadcasting as a changing phenomenon. The immediacy of information from all parts of the world has increased chances for war and peace within moments. No longer do we anticipate continuing battle weeks after the signing of an armistice due to lack of communication. Rumor, however, may cause further problems due to irresponsible reporting. Children of lower elementary grades have a knowledge of the world (geographically, economically, and socially) which exceeds that of their parents when they graduated from college in the late forties. Children have watched funerals of great leaders, with international leaders honoring the dead. The face of de Gaulle is as well known as that of the local mayor. The media is capable of bringing us information about our leaders which builds them up or diminishes them in our judgment, often information which we question our right to know. Students should give serious consideration to the current changes in the right to privacy for those in public office. "Reliable sources" of information should be discussed and verified. News managing has been attacked by journalists who in turn might also be involved in news managing to fit their own needs. Students should also investigate the efficiency of packaged educational broadcasting (such as MPATI, Midwest Programs on Airborne Television Instruction, Purdue University). Much has been made of the "team teaching" innovation, with a master teacher on TV, followed by master teachers and their teams at local levels. How effective are such programs, compared to the assignment of the same personnel to smaller sections and classes? How effective is the use of mass media libraries where valuable taped shows are stored and distributed? Students should understand network and local concepts of programming and administration, and the efforts of teams to get competent reporters and administrators to the "current newsbreak." In short, students need massive information about broadcasting in order to behave rationally in a world so influenced by it.

Rhetoric and Broadcasting Purposes

In a world so dominated by broadcast media the student has a considerable need to understand the goals, processes, and skills which take so much of his time and involve him so directly as a decision-maker and action-taker in the education and commerce of his country. He is further challenged by the modern theorists of communication who are finding new approaches of analysis which indicate a much more complex relationship between the speaker and the listener. Recognition of *semantic response* at various stages of the message is much different than the delayed response expected from the call to action through well ordered oration. Further complications arise as the modern theorists pay homage to the classical *purposes* of a speech or message (to *interest* or *entertain, inform, stimulate, convince,* and *actuate*) and yet confuse the issue by assuming that the purposes of broadcasting are to *inform, educate,* and *entertain.* Even the rhetoricians who have reduced the purposes of speaking to three (to *interest, inform,* and *actuate*) find some problems in following this new format. A third approach, discussed in one of the most recent texts for high school students, states the purpose of speech is *to impart knowledge, to persuade,* or *to build social cohesion.*[1]

Such a change in direction causes the teacher to review basic texts representing various schools of thought on *purpose* in speaking. You will note that many argue that *stimulating* and *convincing* are degrees of *activating,* thus reducing the five-step list to three. To what extent is *educating* different from *informing?* How does *building social cohesion* differ from gaining a desired audience response from a group or an individual (actuating)? Is there a place for a speaker to "cool it" by destroying social cohesion and getting an audience to act as individuals, responsible to themselves only, which actions are apart from social cohesion? Or is this merely a different kind of social cohesion? If the purposes are

---

[1]R.R. Allen, Sharol Anderson, and Jere Hough, *Speech in American Society,* Columbus, Ohio: Charles E. Merrill Publishing Company, 1968, pp. 100-103, 161-163, 216-246.

to impart knowledge, to persuade and *to build social cohesion,* how do we classify the speech to entertain which has so long been a part of rhetorical purpose? Are the purposes of broadcasting basically different from those of rhetoric and drama? It would seem that all three have one common purpose, and that is to get a predetermined response from a listener. Broadcasting has helped speakers, directors, playwrights, and actors focus upon that process and determine if such a response took place.

We have learned much about the *validity of samples* from various types of polls and information retrieval techniques. We have also learned about *active* and *passive* persuasion as measured by listeners and those who purchase at the marketplace. What types of products, or ideas, can be profitably "pitched" at teenagers? at childen? Does public service programming result in the purchases expected? It may be that the public service function and the marketing function are not adequately coordinated. Is it possible that hard-sell techniques and frequent interruptions for advertising destroy the consumer's willingness to buy? Teachers and students may well analyze the various purposes of many types of broadcast speaking. As consumers of *educational* and *commercial programming,* it is important that we understand the motives of the identified and the hidden persuaders who would have us *buy things we don't need to influence people we don't like and pay for it with money we don't have* (which they are willing to loan at high interest).

Raw Materials Needing Analysis

If critical analysis is to permeate a course of study, we must establish a climate of free inquiry and even invite open attack of practices, encourage dissent from critics, and expose or support invested interests. In this setting the students must learn the tools of research (the gathering of facts, processes of verification, identification of working policies, etc.) to verify or repudiate charges made against the system. There is no need to hunt for artificial charges. The student should learn to refine, define, and verify the raw charges so often heard in the home, in school, and at public meetings. The following critical statements and questions are taken from public utterances. Research may prove some false and support others.

American radio and television is inferior to European programming. What are the differences? Is the best talent in America now involved in writing and performing the commercials? Are the commercials more entertaining than the scheduled entertainment?

Why is the news confined to multiple repetition of the headlines? Is there no longer a news analyst providing "in-depth" commentaries? Who are the modern equivalents, if any, of Edward R. Murrow? In what ways are news broadcasts a public service? How are they used primarily as advertising bait?

Why are the best programs scheduled against each other? How do some of the worst ones get on the air and how do they stay on? What is the effect of program duplication on competing networks ("Hogan's Heroes," "F Troop," and "McHale's Navy")?

Is it possible to avoid solid schedules of athletic games (baseball, football, golf, and soccer), soap opera, and Sunday sermons? Could these be varied to provide a choice? Such programming has a detrimental effect on American culture.

Broadcasting, as handled in America, has provided increased knowledge of the world to the masses at little expense to them. The price is eventually paid by the consumer in advertising costs buried in the price of the product.

Broadcasting has increased (or decreased) the levels of language proficiency in vocabulary and appropriate grammatical usage. It has also helped establish a common pronunciation within acceptable standards. The level of language used in "inferior" western and gangster shows is above (or below) the level of street language used by students.

All summer programs are reruns. To what extent does the audience actually watch a program willingly for a second or third time? Is the summer audience a different audience? Does the rerun audience represent people who would go to the same movies more than once?

Which programs are packaged (writing, production, and talent provided by outside advertising agencies) and presented over the station by buying broadcast time? How would the broadcasting agency control policy for such productions? Under what conditions and with what frequency does the local station or network act as an advertising agency, furnishing all design, copy, format, and talent for major companies? What is the relationship of direct mail, billboard, newspaper, and magazine advertising to that presented in the broadcast media? What is the meaning of pioneering, sustaining, and institutional advertising?

The microphone and camera are like microscopes and increase stage fright. I sounded (or looked) so horrible that I'll never get up again.

How is music used in a position of prime importance? In what ways is it used as a support for other ideas? Is great music being destroyed by using it as a prop for advertising? What is meant by bridges, moods, interludes, fades, etc.?

What is the effect of broadcasting upon the democratic process? The desire to be on the bandwagon should restrict all announcements of elections until the last voting booth is closed in Hawaii. Broadcasting destroys the democratic process by actively participating in the selection of candidates, making it impossible to find competent, unbiased juries, by participating in *trial by media*, and by encouraging violence.

If broadcasting can be studied as a source of news, music, information, religion, politics, advertising, or entertainment, what contribution has it made which is unique to broadcasting?

The High School Course of Study

The above questions make it necessary to establish a series of structured units or projects to carry out the inquiry. One might utilize a problem-solution approach with a simulated station for dissemination of information as a means of providing speaking experience, or one might establish a working station with typical daily and weekly programming. To keep the projects or programs relevant, it would be necessary to maintain a constant comparison of the school laboratory to programs available through networks and local stations. A topic outline for such a course follows:

I. Objectives

1. To develop an awareness of broadcasting media through analysis of the history of the industry as a means of communication.
2. To acquire an understanding of radio and television processes as a means for improving standards for appreciative, informational, and critical listening.
3. To provide instruction and practice in fundamental techniques of (*a*) audience analysis, (*b*) listening, (*c*) announcing, (*d*) writing, and (*e*) production.

4. To develop speaking skills appropriate for a variety of broadcasting situations.
5. To become familiar with and recognize the value of equipment
used in broadcasting, and to develop skill in using such equipment.
6. To recognize purposes, characteristics, and structure of various
types of programs and provide laboratory experiences in creating
each.
7. To become familiar with the relationship and importance of *time*
to broadcasting.
8. To develop an understanding of the reciprocal impact of broadcasting upon other communication media.
9. To develop an understanding of the relationship of marketing
principles to broadcasting and the validity of various program
evaluation services.
10. To recognize broadcasting as a major industry and understand
the sound business principles involved in diversified markets and
stock-owner control. Include in this the importance of development and maintenance of a market for the industry through
self-promotion.

II. Content

(The order of these areas may be varied to fit the desires of the instructor. The order given suggests capitalizing upon the desire to
become active in the use of equipment. Some units may be anticipated and thus provide time for students to gather and analyze
information and opinion.)

A. Broadcasting equipment, studio, personnel
  1. Microphone types, purposes, limitations
  2. Radio and television studios, control rooms: similarities and
differences
  3. Camera types, uses, basic shots, and editing
  4. Producer, director, floor men, others
  5. Special facilities: mobile units, projection and taping techniques
  6. Broadcasting vocabulary for radio and television

B. Announcers and "talent"
  1. Talent: personnel on camera or microphone, regular and
special
  2. Announcer: duties, characteristics, image, role, preparation
  3. Speech and delivery for radio and television
    a) Voice and diction
    b) Breathing, placement, resonance, projection

    c) Pronunciation, articulation, enunciation, rate

    d) Emphasis, phrasing, rhythm, inflection

    e) Bodily action, facial action, and camera appearance

    f) Memorization, correlation with picture

    g) Use and marking of script or "idiot" cards for cues and interpretation

C. Program analysis and classification
1. Program idea and specific purpose
2. Title: purpose, structure, attention devices
3. Program proper (analysis according to type: variety, drama, music, etc.)
4. Closing: purpose, hook or teaser, credits
5. Commercials: placement, integration with program or talent, etc.
6. Program routining
7. Audience appeals
8. Production design, styles, and techniques including scene transitions

D. Sound and music effects in broadcasting
1. Manual, recorded, and vocal types
2. Function in establishing locale, mood, transition, or bridge
3. Selection, timing, cuing, and synchronization
4. Music as theme, montage, mood, atmosphere, or transition
5. Music terminology
6. Sources of music and classification indexes. See Henry M. Katzman, *Recorded Bridges, Moods and Interlude* (New York: Broadcast Music, Inc., 1953).

E. Analysis and writing of various program types. (This section should be based upon an analysis of program listing, viewing, and auditing over a period of several weeks. Writing and presentation should then be practiced in each of the various types. Typical programs of several types might be listed.)
1. Interview types: opinion, information, personality
    a) Mechanics of script form
    b) Questioning and discussion leadership techniques
    c) Adapting to use of microphone or camera
    d) Pre-broadcast preparation of materials and talent
    e) Women's page or society discussion (relates to newspaper)
2. Newscast types and structure
    a) Number and length of items
    b) Arrangement and transitional materials
    c) Brevity or depth reporting (headlines only?)
    d) Color interest and editorializing
    e) Use of wire services

f) Presentation

g) Use of visuals, and size of staff and talent for television

3. Sports program types and structure
   a) On-the-spot broadcasts, including playbacks with commentary
   b) Pre-game and post-game resumé
   c) Dramatized sport programs
   d) Daily sport show
   e) Filmed and pre-taped events for later release
   f) Preparation and presentation: rules, vocabulary, plays and players, press releases, slogan phrases, and ad-libbing

4. Music program types and structure
   a) Live talent
   b) Recorded or transcribed
   c) Filmed, music dubbed in for later release
   d) Planning music programs: copyright regulations, program format, audience analysis
   e) Types: classical, pop, jazz, rock, R & B, country and western, folk
   f) Writing continuity for various types of music programs
   g) Production techniques and problems: cuing, cross-fading timing, studio production

5. Dramatic Types and Structure
   a) Originals written for the media
   b) Adaptations from novels, plays, movies
   c) Editing to fit time, commercials, series segments
   d) Dialogue and exposition needs
   e) Plotting script: situation, order of events (use of music and sound to enhance mood, conflict, suspense), crisis, conflict
   f) Determination of type and purpose: variety, farce, melodrama, serious drama, tragedy, sentimental comedy, etc.
   g) Selection of talent: acting, characterization
   h) Special problems: synchronizing people and cartoons

F. Development of Broadcasting in America
   1. Radio development pre-1920 no advertising; compare with European systems and governmental monopoly. Network development.
   2. Technical advances of the 1930's. Important programs of the period.
   3. Wartime network and program policies.
   4. Development of television: early programs.
   5. Changing status of radio at local and network levels. Change of types of programs in news, drama, sports.

6. Development of new techniques: color, video-tape, vidicon tubes, hand cameras, and competition techniques in program types. Use of movies, audience saturation, rising costs, quiz programs, and scandals.
7. Standards of evaluation and criticism: control of advertising content, various rating and polling services, federal regulation and critics from other media (Seldes, Schram, Gould, Siepmann, Minow, and FCC).
8. Regulations and controls: self-regulation, FCC and FTC "truth in advertising," industry and network codes concerning sex, indecency, religion, minority groups, family life, etc., balanced programming, public interest, and public issues.
9. Development of educational television: scope and limitations.

G. Appreciative, Informational and Critical Listening
   1. Active and passive listening
   2. Problem-solution listening
   3. Listening based upon established skills in arts, music, and ideas
   4. Recognizing the properties of propaganda
      a) *Name-calling* (labels to gain negative response)
      b) *Glittering generalities* showing positive relation to speaker's point of view: "freedom-loving," "equal," "democratic," "efficient" (hides reasoning)
      c) *Transfer:* use of an authority respected by the listener implying that this authority agrees with the speaker
      d) *Testimonial:* Is the person an authority on the thing quoted?
      e) *"Plain folks"* approach, very persuasive
      f) *Card-stacking:* all evidence included, but to the advantage of the speaker
      g) *Bandwagon:* based upon the desire not to be left out; appeals to status-seekers
   5. Tests for validity
      a) Timeliness
      b) Competency
      c) Prejudice
      d) Completeness

H. List of audience size measurement services (excerpted from ARF's Directory of Audience Size Measurement Services)
   1. Study methods used in sampling
   2. Analyze for validity on slanting, socioeconomic distortion limited to telephones, etc.
   3. List of companies:

American Research Bureau, Inc.
National Press Building
Washington, D.C.

Robert S. Conlan and Associates, Inc.
1715 Wyandotte Street
Kansas City 8, Missouri

C.E. Hooper, Inc.
10 East 40th Street
New York 16, New York

A.C. Nielsen Company
2101 Howard Street
Chicago 45, Illinois

The Pulse, Inc.
15 West 46th Street
New York 19, New York

Trendex, Inc.
347 Madison Avenue
New York 17, New York

Videodex, Inc.
342 Madison Avenue
New York 17, New York

I. Current poll services for public figures and agencies:
    Gallup, Lou Harris, Muchmore, Quayle, Kraft, Bucci, Field.

Suggested Projects

III. Inductive Learning Activities

1. Students start a broadcasting notebook. Include the following:
   a) Notes taken in class
   b) Evaluation and critique sheets of viewed or audited programs
   c) Program critiques from *Time, Newsweek, US News*, etc.
2. Class discussion regarding the various aspects and effects of broadcasting upon our lives. Questions dealing with the beginnings of radio or television might be brought forth.
3. Assign short talks on radio and television history to be given on the microphone.
4. Instruct the students in the basic organization of the radio and television station.

5. Prepare a sheet on radio and television observation to be used by students touring a radio or television station.
6. Bring several kinds of microphones into the classroom. Explain their construction. Have students speak into each microphone. Decide which type of microphone is better for a specific purpose.
7. Discuss microphone usage for radio and television.
8. Inform students on the school's broadcasting equipment.
9. Prepare and demonstrate a list of radio signals.
10. Instruct students in the mechanics of oral reading. Provide drill work.
11. Discuss symbols which could be used in marking copy.
12. Secure tapes or records of well-known radio voices. Play for student analysis.
13. Give listening assignments involving the evaluation of local radio and television voices with rating scales.
14. Prepare and demonstrate a list of radio signals.
15. Evaluate tapes of student's voices.
16. Prepare two pages of announcer's copy using various reading styles for preparation and presentation.
17. Demonstrate how sounds can establish locale, advance action, and create mood using sound records and dialogue.
18. Have the students write an analysis of the use of sound effects and music from radio or television.
19. Assign certain manual sound effects to be produced or constructed and then presented in an original scene to be taped.
20. Prepare an information sheet on the mechanics of writing and standard script form for radio and television.
21. Instruct the students on the mechanics of program timing
    a) Marking the script for timing
    b) Including stretch material
    c) Use of run-down or timing sheets
22. Divide the class into groups. Have each group prepare a script for two people with the third person of the group used as the director.
23. Secure news copy from a local radio station. Have every student read aloud the copy.
24. Divide the class into small groups. Have them work together in preparing a 12:30 television news summary program.
25. Obtain film footage which shows a sports event in progress. Have students take turns in describing the game for radio and for television.
26. Instruct the students in the various program formats for music shows. Discuss routining on a music show.

27. Provide drill work in reading continuity for different types of music shows.
28. Make a radio or television drama listening assignment. List specific elements of the show for evaluation.
29. Secure copies of several radio drama scripts for class production. Divide the class into groups. In each group assign a program director, an engineer, and a sound effects technician. Give time to each script. Music and sound effects should be used. Commercials and closing credits should be incorporated. Give a production date to each group. Have the students rehearse and present the scripts for class. Written or oral comments could be made.
30. Make a study of job opportunities in commercial and educational broadcasting. Include salaries, job descriptions, turnover, promotion, etc.
31. Give a two to three-minute talk on some phases of radio or television history. Take notes in broadcasting notebook on radio history. Question fellow students after presentations regarding their topic.
32. Plan and carry out a trip to a local radio or television station. Use your "observation" form.
33. Become familiar with your school's broadcasting facilities. Learn the operation of the school's central sound system. Classify your studio setup as to acoustical construction. Locate the live and dead areas.
34. Add your list of radio and television terms and hand signals to your notebook. Use both in class discussion and class work.
35. Select a paragraph of appropriate reading and test your ability to use the microphone correctly. Pay attention to the following:
    a) The way you hold and handle your script
    b) Your distance from the microphone
    c) Your maintenance of position
    d) Breath control in reading
    Evaluate the results in class discussion.
36. Make a one-minute tape with the microphone, reading appropriate material. Listen critically to your voice, and with your teacher's help, decide how you can improve your reading.
37. Take a script that gives practice in changing volume, rate, and inflection and that makes use of the pause. Listen to and analyze the script.
38. Read and practice lists of commonly mispronounced words. Have a "pronouncing bee" with them.
39. Listen to the voices of local radio and television personalities. Listen to tapes or records of well-known voices. Evaluate.

40. After class discussion of reading style, prepare and rehearse the announcer's copy given to you. Mark your copy. In reading, go from item to item using the appropriate reading style. Read on mike and tape. An evaluation of the reading will be made.

41. Listen to and write an analysis of a specific program. Consider the following:
    a) Use of program title
    b) Opening
    c) Closing
    d) Other conventions of program structure

42. Listen to a radio or television drama. Write an analysis of the use of sound effects and music.

43. Demonstrate the production of some sound effect which is used on radio or television. Write a short script using that sound effect. Present the script using the recording facilities for class comments and criticisms.

44. If you have music albums or records available in your studio, classify them for possible future use.

45. Write a radio interview for two people. You may want to include music sound effects. The interview should be exactly 4:30. Use the correct form for typing the script. Work in groups of three; two people will produce the show and the third person will direct it.

46. Read on microphone the wire service news copy given to you. Before reading go through the following process:
    a) Edit the copy and mark all changes
    b) Determine your most effective news reading rate
    c) Check pronunciation

47. Work together in small groups and present a 14:30 television news summary program. You may want to consider the following as separate assignments for each member of your group: presentation of national and international news, local news, sports news, weather report, commercial. An announcer and a director would also be needed. You may use the newspaper and magazines for information and for visual material.

48. Prepare a 1:30 script of "color description" for any sports event. The event may take place at your school, on a college campus, or in the community.

49. You are a disc jockey. Plan a 14:30 disc jockey program to be presented on radio for a 4:00 p.m. audience. Decide on a program format. Select your records and write your continuity. Present the program. (You need not play the records all the way through.)

50. Evaluate a radio or television drama in terms of the following:
    a) The story presented

      b) The characterizations
      c) The production techniques
      Discuss the show in class.
51. Plan, rehearse, and present a radio drama for class presentation. The script will be provided.
52. Take the plot of *Hamlet* or *Macbeth* and build a television show staged on the Ponderosa with the characters from *Bonanza*. Is the plot adaptable? How can the ambition theme be developed? Is the revenge theme possible in the new setting? Are there ample opportunities for character development? Identify the *kingdoms, crowns, positions*.
53. Using talent from the student body, select a theme and build a variety show using the program format of:
      a) Mike Douglas
      b) Ed Sullivan
      c) Red Skelton
      d) Danny Kaye
54. Make a comparative analysis of time utilization and content of a movie from an educational television station and commercial station.

IV. Equipment for Classroom Studio and Broadcasting Station

A. Ideal equipment
   1. Tape recorder
   2. Radio receiver adapted to the P.A. system and console if broadcasting is to be done (necessary)
   3. Two mikes and mike lines
   4. Turntable for sound effects, and two if using commercial stations as outlets (necessary)
   5. Portable recording machine for cutting and playing back records (very desirable but not actually necessary)
   6. A P.A. system in the school (absolutely necessary)
   7. One studio, with control room adjoining and classroom in conjunction
   8. Television set for viewing and analysis; kinescope desirable
B. Operators
   1. Students participating in the radio unit, trained in the department to set up and operate equipment
   2. The teacher of the unit (the teacher should be able to operate the equipment and supervise its use.)
C. Textbooks
D. Radio scripts; samples of used and usable models from networks.

E. Library of tapes from each type of programs to be used for analysis.

F. File of critiques on past seasons including all types of programs, reruns, etc.

References

V. Selected Resources for the Teacher and Student

In the following bibliography general studies are listed in preference to specialized works of more limited scope. Most works listed are available in metropolitan or larger school libraries. Many are not new. The value of many pioneer volumes on radio and television should not be overlooked.

There is not as yet a comprehensive history of radio, a complete history of television, an adequate analysis of radio or television programming, or a complete economic description and definition of broadcasting's relationship to the other media and to society.

Adams, Harlen M. and Pollock, Thomas. *Speak Up.* New York: The Macmillan Company, 1964.

Allen, R. R., Anderson, Sharol, and Hough, Jere. *Speech in American Society.* Columbus, Ohio: Charles E. Merrill Publishing Company, 1968.

Barnhart, Lyle D. *Radio and Television Announcing.* Englewood Cliffs, N.J.: Prentice-Hall, Inc., 1953.

Becker, Samuel L. and Harshbarger, H. Clay. *Television Techniques for Planning and Performance.* New York: Holt, Rinehart & Winston, Inc., 1958.

Berry, Minnie H. "Developing a High School Radio Program, *The Southern Speech Journal,* 21:52-55 (Fall, 1955).

Chester, Giraud, Garrison, Garnet R., and Willis, Edgar E. *Television and Radio.* 3rd ed.; New York: Appleton-Century-Crofts, 1963.

Costello, Lawrence and Gordon, George N. *Teach with Television: A Guide to Instructional TV.* New York: Hastings House, Publishers, Inc., 1961.

Crews, A. R. *Professional Radio Writing.* Boston: Houghton Mifflin Co., 1946.

Curran, Charles W. *Screen Writing and Production Techniques: The Non-Technical Handbook for TV, Film and Tape.* New York: Hastings House, Publishers, Inc., 1958.

Duerr, Edwin. *Radio and Television Acting; Criticism, Theory and Practice.* New York: Holt, Rinehart & Winston, Inc., 1950.

Elson, E. F. and Peck, Alberta. *The Art of Speaking.* Boston: Ginn and Company, 1957.

Hastings House, Publishers, Inc., "Communications Arts Books," a descriptive catalogue by the publishers of the most comprehensive list of standard titles on television and related fields.

Head, S. W. *Broadcasting in America: A Survey of Television and Radio.* Boston: Houghton Mifflin Company, 1956.

Hibbs, Paul, *et al. Speech for Today.* New York: McGraw-Hill Book Company, 1965.

Hilliard, Robert T. *Writing for Television and Radio.* New York: Hastings House, Publishers, Inc., 1962.

Holt, Robert T. *Radio Free Europe.* Minneapolis, Minn.: University of Minnesota Press, 1958.

Hyde, Stuart W. *Television and Radio Announcing.* Boston: Houghton Mifflin Company, 1958. Record to accompany text.

Journal of Broadcasting, quarterly publication of the Association for Professional Broadcasting Education, University of Southern California, University Park, California.

Katzman, Henry M. *Recorded Bridges, Moods and Interludes.* New York: Broadcast Music, Inc., 1953. (87 pp.; last two thirds of book is an alphabetical index covering 570 moods from major musical compositions frequently used in broadcasting.)

Kaufman, William I. (ed.). *How to Announce for Radio and Television.* New York: Hastings House, Publishers, Inc., 1956.

Lawton, Sherman P. *The Modern Broadcaster: The Station Book.* New York: Harper & Row, Publishers, 1961.

Lewis, Philip. *Educational Television Guidebook.* New York: McGraw-Hill Book Company, 1961.

Lynch, James E. (ed.). "Radio and Television in the Secondary School," *The Bulletin of the National Association of Secondary School Principals,* 50, No. 312 (October, 1966). Papers assembled for *The Bulletin* by a special editorial committee of The Speech Association of America. Committee members include: James E. Lynch, chairman and editor, Gale R. Adkins, Samuel Becker, George Johnson, George L. Lewis, Wanda B. Mitchell, Joseph M. Ripley, Juanita Jane Rucker, John R. Shepherd, J. Clark Weaver, and Edgar E. Willis.

McMahan, Harry Wayne. *Television Production: The Creative Techniques and Language of TV Today.* New York: Hastings House, Publishers, Inc., 1957.

NAEB Journal, bimonthly publication of the National Association of Educational Broadcasters, 14 Gregory Hall, Urbana, Illinois.

Norris, R.C. "Audience Oriented Television for Education," *The Speech Teacher,* 3:188-192 (September, 1954).

Ommanney, Kathryn. *The Stage and School.* New York: McGraw-Hill Book Company, 1965.

Oringel, Robert S. *Audio Control Handbook for Radio and TV Broadcasting.* New York: Hastings House, Publishers, Inc., 1956.

Packard, Vance. *The Hidden Persuaders.* New York: David McKay Company, Inc., 1957, and Simon & Schuster, Inc., Pocket Books, 1958.

_____. *The Waste Makers.* New York: David McKay Company, Inc., 1960, and Simon & Schuster, Inc., Pocket Books, 1963.

Paulu, Burton. *British Broadcasting in Transition.* Minneapolis, Minn.: University of Minnesota Press, 1961.

_____. *British Broadcasting: Radio and Television in the United Kingdom.* Minneapolis, Minn.: University of Minnesota Press, 1956.

Postman, Neil. *Television and Teaching of English.* New York: Appleton-Century-Crofts, 1961, pp. 138.

Reinsch, J. Leonard and Ellis, Elmo. *Radio Station Management.* 2nd rev. ed.; New York: Harper and Row, Publishers, 1960.

Roth, Lucile M. "Integrating English Literature with Radio, *The Speech Teacher,* 5:47-50 (January, 1956).

Siepmann, Charles A. *Radio, Television and Society.* Oxford: Oxford University Press, 1950.

Stasheff, Edward, Tincher, Ethel, and Willis, Edgar E. "Radio and TV Speech, A Course of Study for High Schools," *NAEB Journal,* 17:6ff (January, 1958).

"Teacher's Guide to High School Speech." Indianapolis, Ind.: Indiana State Department of Public Instruction in Cooperation with The Indiana University English Curriculum Study Center, Bulletin 503, 1966, pp. 201-214, 237-242.

General Introductions and Surveys

Becker, Samuel L. "Radio and Television," *Introduction to the Field of Speech,* ed. Ronald F. Reid. Glenview, Ill.: Scott, Foresman and Company, 1965.

Broadcasting Primer: Evolution of Broadcasting. Washington, D.C.: Federal Communications Commission, Office of Reports and Information [n.d.].

Brooks, Keith (ed.). *The Communication Arts and Sciences of Speech.* Columbus, Ohio: Charles E. Merrill Books, Inc., 1966. (Television and radio section, Chapters 22-26.)

Chester, Giraud, Garrison, Garnet, and Willis, Edgar. *Television and Radio.* New York: Appleton-Century-Crofts, 1963.

Gould, Jack. *All About Radio and Television.* New York: Random House, Inc., 1958.

Head, Sydney W. *Broadcasting in America.* Boston: Houghton Mifflin Company, 1956.

Hilliard, Robert L., *et al. Understanding Television: An Introduction to Broadcasting.* New York: Hastings House, Publishers, Inc., 1964.

Lawton, Sherman P. *The Modern Broadcaster: The Station Book.* New York: Harper & Row, Publishers, 1961.

The Business of Broadcasting

Agnew, C. M., and O'Brien, N. *Television Advertising*. New York: McGraw-Hill Book Company, 1958.

Careers in Radio. Washington, D.C.: National Association of Broadcasters, 1965.

Careers in Television. Washington, D.C.: National Association of Broadcasters, 1965.

Lerch, John (ed.). *Careers in Broadcasting*. New York: Appleton-Century-Crofts, 1962.

Reinsch, Leonard, and Ellis, Elmo I. *Radio Station Management*. New York: Harper & Row, Publishers, 1960.

Roe, Yale (ed.). *Television Station Management*. New York: Hastings House, Publishers, Inc., 1964.

Seehaefer, Eugene, and Laemmar, Jack. *Successful Television and Radio Advertising*. New York: McGraw-Hill Book Company, 1959.

Content: Programs and Programing

Bluem, A. William. *Documentary in American Television*. New York: Hastings House, Publishers, Inc., 1964.

————, Cox, John F., and McPherson, Gene. *Television in the Public Interest*. New York: Hastings House, Publishers, Inc., 1961.

CBS News Department. *Television News Reporting*. New York: McGraw-Hill Inc., 1958.

Gaskill, Arthur L., and Englander, David A. *How to Shoot a Movie Story: The Technique of Pictorial Continuity*. Hastings-on-Hudson, N.Y.: Morgan & Morgan, Inc., 1960.

Hyde, Stuart W. *Television and Radio Announcing*. Boston: Houghton Mifflin Company, 1959.

Newsfilm Standards Conference, Radio Television News Directors Association. *Television Newsfilm Standards Manual: A Guidebook and Working Manual for Students and Professionals*. New York: Time-Life Books, a Division of Time, Inc., 1964.

Reisz, Karel. *Technique of Film Editing: Basic Principles for TV*. New York: Farrar, Straus & Giroux, Inc., 1953.

Spear, James. *Creating Visuals for TV: A Guide for Educators*. Washington, D.C.: National Education Association, 1962.

Stasheff, Edward, and Bretz, Rudy. *The Television Program*. New York: Hill and Wang, Inc., 1962.

Summers, Harrison B. *Radio Programs Carried on National Networks, 1926-1956*. Columbus, Ohio: Department of Speech, Ohio State University, 1958.

Zettl, Herbert. *Television Production Handbook*. Belmont, Calif.: Wadsworth Publishing Co., Inc., 1961.

Audiences and Audience Effects

Glick, Ira O., and Levy, Sidney J. *Living with Television*. Chicago: Aldine Publishing Co., 1962.

Klapper, Joseph T. *Effects of Mass Communication*. New York: The Free Press, 1960.

Schramm, Wilbur. *The Effects of Television on Children and Adolescents*. New York: UNESCO Publications Office, 1964.

Steiner, Gary. *People Look at Television: A Study of Audience Attitudes*. New York: Alfred A. Knopf, Inc., 1963.

Regulation and Responsibility

Emery, Walter B. *Broadcasting and Government: Responsibilities and Regulations*. East Lansing, Michigan: Michigan State University Press, 1961.

Radio Code of Good Practices. Washington, D.C.: National Association of Broadcasters, revised 1966.

Schramm, Wilbur. *Responsibility in Mass Communication*. New York: Harper & Row, Publishers, 1957.

The Television Code. Washington, D.C.: National Association of Broadcasters, revised 1966.

Broadcasting History

Archer, Gleason L. *Big Business and Radio*. Chicago: American Historical Company, Inc., 1939.

Archer, Gleason L. *History of Radio to 1926*. Chicago: American Historical Society, 1938.

Banning, William P. *Commercial Broadcasting Pioneer: WEAF*. Cambridge, Mass.: Harvard University Press, 1946.

Blum, Daniel. *Pictorial History of Television*. Philadelphia: Chilton Book Company, 1950.

Settel, Irving. *A Pictorial History of Radio*. New York: Citadel Press, Inc., 1960.

Weinberg, Meyer. *TV in America: The Morality of Hard Cash*. New York: Ballantine Books, Inc., 1962.

White, Llewellyn. *The American Radio*. Chicago: University of Chicago Press, 1947.

World and International Broadcasting

Codding, George A., Jr. *Broadcasting Without Barriers*. New York: Columbia University Press, 1959.

Costello, Lawrence F. and Gordon, George N. *Teach with Television: A Guide to Instructional TV.* New York: Hastings House, Publishers, Inc., 1961.

Educational Television: The Next Ten Years. Stanford, California: Institute for Communication Research, Stanford University, 1962.

Griffith, Barton L. and MacLennan, Donald W. *Improvement of Teaching by Television.* Columbia, Mo.: University of Missouri Press, 1964.

Lewis, Philip. *Educational Television Guidebook.* New York: McGraw-Hill Book Company, 1961.

Postman, Neil. *Television and the Teaching of English.* New York: Appleton-Century-Crofts, 1961.

Powell, John W. *Channels of Learning: The Story of Educational Television.* Washington, D.C.: Public Affairs Press, 1962.

Schramm, Wilbur, editor. *Impact of Educational Television.* Urbana, Ill.: University of Illinois Press, 1960.

Schramm, Wilbur, Lyle, Jack, and Pool, Ithiel de Sola. *The People Look at Educational Television.* Stanford, Calif.: Stanford University Press, 1963.

Broadcasting and Society

Bachman, John W. *The Church in the World of Radio and Television.* New York: Association Press, 1960.

Bogart, Leo. *The Age of Television.* 2nd ed.; New York: Frederick Ungar Publishing Co., Inc., 1958.

Dexter, L.A., and White, D.M. (eds.). *People, Society, and Mass Communications.* New York: The Free Press, 1964.

Elliot, William (ed.). *Television's Impact on American Culture.* East Lansing, Michigan: Michigan State University Press, 1956.

Himmelweit, Hilde T., *et al. Television and the Child: An Empirical Study of the Effect of Television on the Young.* New York: Oxford University Press, 1958.

Jacobs, Norman (ed.). *Culture for Millions.* Princeton, N.J.: D. Van Nostrand Co., Inc., 1961.

Kraus, Sidney (ed.). *The Great Debates.* Bloomington, Indiana: Indiana University Press, 1962.

McLuhan, Marshall. *The Gutenberg Galaxy: The Making of Typographic Man.* Toronto, Ont.: University of Toronto Press, 1962.

Rosenberg, Bernard, and White, David M. (eds.). *Mass Culture: The Popular Arts in America.* New York: The Free Press, 1957.

Schramm, Wilbur (ed.). *Mass Communications.* Urbana, Ill.: University of Illinois Press, 1960.

Skornia, H. J. *Television and Society: An Inquest and Agenda for Improvement.* New York: McGraw-Hill Book Company, 1965.

Wright, Charles R. *Mass Communications: A Sociological Perspective.* New York: Random House, Inc., 1959.

Bibliographies

Adkins, Gale R. *Books on Radio-Television Film.* Lawrence, Kan.: University Press of Kansas, 1962.

Blum, Eleanor. *Reference Books in the Mass Media.* 2nd ed.; Urbana, Illinois: University of Illinois Press, 1966.

Cole, B. and Klose, A. "Selected Bibliography on the History of Broadcasting," *Journal of Broadcasting* (Summer, 1963).

Golter, Bob J. *Bibliography of Theses and Dissertations Relating to Audio-Visuals and Broadcasting.* Nashville, Tenn.: Methodist Publishing House, 1958.

Hamill, Patricia Beall. *Radio and Television: A Bibliography.* US Department of Health, Education, and Welfare, Office of Education. Washington, D.C.: Government Printing Office, 1960.

Harwood, K. "Entries on Broadcasting in Sociological Abstracts, 1953-1963," *Journal of Broadcasting* (Summer, 1961).

————. "World Bibliography of Selected Periodicals on Broadcasting," *Journal of Broadcasting* (Summer, 1961).

Knower, F. "Graduate Theses and Dissertations on Broadcasting..." *Journal of Broadcasting* (Winter, 1959-60; Fall, 1961; Summer, 1963).

Smith, D. "Books on Broadcasting in the Library of Congress: Scripts, Performance, Production, Writing." *Journal of Broadcasting* (Fall, 1965).

Summers, R. "Graduate Theses and Dissertations on Broadcasting: A Topical Index," *Journal of Broadcasting* (Winter, 1957-58).

Television and Education: A Bibliography. New York: Television Information Office, 1962.

Television: Freedom, Responsibility, Regulation: A Bibliography. New York: Television Information Office, 1962.

Television in Government and Politics: A Bibliography. New York: Television Information Office, 1964.

12

Out-of-Class Activities

In many schools, much speech training consists of activities conducted outside the classroom. It is not uncommon for these programs to be directed by the speech teacher without the benefit of school funds, payment for direction of the activities, or school time provided for meetings and practices. Parents and community leaders take pride in the performance of students in plays and debates, and these activities help citizens and school administration develop an appreciation of the significance of speech education. Community awareness of the value of speech participation usually leads to increased support for the program.

Some communities already provide the substantial financial and administrative support for the out-of-class program because of the close school–community relationships which are developed. In most cases these effective and well funded out-of-class programs are a product of an energetic curricular program. However, in schools where speech is not a part of the formal curriculum, the co-curricular program may create an awareness of the needs for and values of speech and communication training and may shortly lead to course offerings in speech and drama.

The attempt here is not to suggest that an out-of-class program is the opening wedge in a battle to develop speech as a curricular offering, nor should prospective teachers feel an effective co-curricular program must be very expensive. Co-curricular programs should be of sufficient quality to arouse popular support for formal speech training with, of course, a gentle nudge from the speech teacher, and the program need not be lined with money. Some effective out-of-class activities operate on a minimal budget because of the ingenuity and contagious enthusiasm of the speech teacher and a few student leaders.

THE SIGNIFICANCE OF OUT-OF-CLASS SPEECH PROGRAMS

One way of answering the perennial question "Why should our school participate in out-of-class speech activities?" is to explore the values of student involvement. Development of the communication skills of the student is our primary concern. These talents can be manifested through a debate, an extemporaneous speech, one-act play performances, or the reading of a radio script; they can be devoted to the transmission of information, the changing of attitudes, or the interpretation of a role. Participation refines the skills of communication and develops, through the communicative act, improved understanding of man and society.

A sound out-of-class program must complement curricular speech training, and the goals of the extracurricular program must parallel the objectives of the course offerings in speech. Briefly, the objectives of the out-of-class program are (1) to increase student facility in the act of oral communication, (2) to develop aesthetic appreciation of literature and drama through participation in dramatic production and interpretation, and (3) to stimulate critical thinking and organizational skills through forensic and public speaking competition.

An educationally sound out-of-class program offers interested students an opportunity to develop talents which may have been identified through class participation in speech-oriented activity. And in schools where speech is not part of the curriculum, the out-of-class program must serve as the vehicle for all speech instruction.

If we were to evaluate the soundness of speech education provided by high schools in any state or region, the most effective programs would be those which include and encourage extensive out-of-class participation by students. There is no substitute for a soundly conceived and thoroughly developed curricular program, but the out-of-class activities provide a continuing and stimulating opportunity for application of speaking behavior in practical, "real life" situations. The student is made more aware of the need for and values of communication training, and he is given an opportunity to enhance his facility and increase his success in speech-related activities.

PLAY PRODUCTION

Dramatic presentations are the most common form of extracurricular speech activity. Schools in communities which have never heard the term "speech" may produce several plays each year, perhaps under the direction of the English teacher. Productions range from a highly polished version of "Kismet" with complex lighting, several sets, a large cast, and the school orchestra to the bare stage, few props, and modest cast of "Our Town." All dramatic productions, regardless of the type or complexity of the presentation, should be consonant with the objectives of educational dramatics which follow:

> 1. To secure for all students understanding, critical standards, and skills with which they may judge drama as literature and dramatic production — in theatre, television and motion pictures — as a fine art.
> 2. To improve student understandings of the dramatic and theatrical tradition as a cultural force in the history of man.
> 3. To continue, in common with other programs in the school, to improve the student's ability to effectively use his expressive mechanisms and to grow in leadership ability as well as in understanding of the responsibilities and disciplines of cooperative endeavor.[1]

Play production also serves as a useful channel for fostering healthy relationships between school and community. The class or all-school play is tradition-bound and its production often is a significant cultural event. It may be the only time during the school year that members of the community can observe student participation in a non-athletic activity. Parental pride and community interest in dramatic productions is nearly universal, and the play often is the most effective instrument for demonstrating the values of education and training in speech and dramatic art. Dramatic productions also should increase popular understanding and appreciation for theatre as a medium of communication.

The discussion which follows is concerned *only* with *general problems* encountered in all-school productions, class, and organizational plays.

---

[1] *Teacher's Guide To High School Speech* (Indianapolis: Indiana State Department of Public Instruction, Bulletin No. 503, 1966), p. 144.

Specific information on play selection, blocking, set construction, etc., can be found in Chapter 10, "Theatre."

All-School Plays

Many schools have adopted the practice of presenting several three-act, all-school dramatic productions each year. Usually, the type of play to be presented is a product of long-standing policies. For example, tradition may establish that the first all-school production of the year is a comedy, the second a mystery, and the third a musical.

The large high school is more likely to embark on an ambitious and successful play production schedule. Interested and talented students are available for acting and production roles and in most metropolitan and suburban systems one teacher is assigned responsibilities for the direction of the major dramatic productions of the year. When the director can devote his non-classroom school time almost exclusively to play production, it is possible to present several all-school productions during a single school year.

In some city systems and particularly in smaller single high school communities, one teacher may direct all the dramatic productions, coach the debate team, organize school assemblies, and act as sponsor for one of the classes. These and other demands on the teacher's time must be considered when deciding how many all-school plays can be presented. Most rehearsals will be held after school or in the evening; classes must still be taught, papers graded, meetings attended, and other responsibilities discharged. Students may express interest in several all-school productions in addition to class plays, but the wise teacher in this situation should undertake the direction of only one or, at the most, two all-school productions a year.

Since talent can be drawn from all segments of the student population, the director can choose plays which need not be tailored to the limited abilities of, for example, the senior.

The cast for dramatic productions should be selected by tryouts. Some directors choose the play only after they have decided on the casting of the key roles. This practice raises serious questions about the intent and educational value of the production. The play should be an educational experience for the participants, and an effective out-of-class speech program should encourage participation by those with demonstrated skills and identify persons with talent who have not, as yet, become active in speech activities. These objectives cannot be achieved if the dramatics program concentrates on developing the skills of a few already experienced actors rather than serving as an educational instrument for all interested students. Tryouts encourage participation by all students in dramatic activities and result in the selection of the best available cast for the play.

Because many all-school productions are ambitious undertakings, involving not only students with acting skills but dancers and singers as well, the director must cultivate good relationships with the music and physical education departments. Their judgments about the availability of talent will be crucial in the choice of the production.

Major roles often represent a compromise between, for instance, substantial musical talent and moderate acting ability, while in other productions the lead may be played by a student who has significant acting skill but only minimal musical talent. The characteristics of the play will suggest criteria for cast selection.

A word about production expenses is in order. The play sometimes is the major fund-raising activity of the school year. School systems occasionally *expect* sizeable proceeds from the production so that new books may be provided for the library, new curtains can be purchased for the stage, or other equipment not normally in the school budget can be provided. The educational objective is of primary importance, but to achieve this financial goal as well, the director should determine probable production costs before selecting the play. Keep in mind that the following expenses must be deducted from the receipts before funds are available to the school: printing of tickets, printing of programs, advertisements in the local newspaper and posters, all set construction expenses, and royalty payments. Royalties will probably be the greatest single expense, and recent and highly popular plays command the largest royalty payments.

Class Plays

If there is a type of dramatic production which is nearly universal in American public education, it is the class play. School calendars in scores of communities are constructed around the class plays and these productions become major cultural events of the academic year.

Class plays, in general, are concerned with two objectives: cultural enrichment experiences and, occasionally, raising funds for the sponsoring class. In some areas, the theatre director must take care to avoid having the educational value subordinated to the fund-raising goal. But, in most communities, the financial success of the play is of minor importance because school administrators are abandoning the position that the play should operate basically as a fund-raising exercise. Related to this posture is the belief that play quality has minimal impact upon attendance at performances. The student body will attend, en masse, one of the matinee productions, and parents and friends of the actors and those in the community interested in dramatic activities will appear at the evening performances. This "gate" can be accurately predicted, so the feeling that a frothy, uncomplicated comedy is the ideal vehicle because it will attract more patrons is largely fallacious. But most important, educators and the public alike now regard educational theatre as an instrument of cultural development for students and the community at large. This crucial objective is most readily served through judicious play selection; the educational and cultural goals must therefore be uppermost in the mind of the director when he selects the play.

When the class play is a musical production, the considerations mentioned earlier — availability of talent and coordination with other departments — should be observed. Because of talent limitations, it is usually not desirable to choose a musical as the class production.

Since the play is the major class undertaking of the school year, a large number of students will attend tryouts and play rehearsals even if they are not or do not hope to be involved in the production. Finding a role for everyone evincing a desire to become involved, whether in the cast or as a member of one of the committees, will lighten the load carried by the director and provide a sense of belonging and achievement for the students. After the tryouts are held and casting announced, it often is useful for the director to contact students who read for parts but were not chosen for the cast and ask them to serve as members of some of the production committees.

Although the class plays typically are three-act productions, the one-act play, a series of one-act plays, or cuttings from several full-length plays are other possibilities. They offer an opportunity for several types of dramatic presentation and a chance for many members of the class to appear as actors. In selecting a program of one-act plays or cuttings for the annual class production, the director should strive for variety in the types of plays chosen, or he may build the plays around a single theme.

Organizational Plays

School organizations, such as the Drama Club or the Shakespeare Club may undertake a three-act play. Usually they will approach their advisor, who is often the speech teacher, for help in the choice and direction of the play. Members of these groups are often highly motivated and familiar with plays and their production, so it is appropriate to encourage maximum student involvement through a show directed and produced by students. Matters of direction can be placed in the hands of the student director, but the speech teacher should be immediately available to lend counsel. Direction itself will be a sufficient challenge for the student director, so a technical director should also be selected. These two students can then schedule tryouts, cast the play, organize committees, and handle other production details. A student directed and produced play affords interesting challenges, even for students with substantial dramatic experience.

Other student groups, such as the FFA, the Spanish Club, or the Home Economics Club may decide they wish to produce a play. Their motives vary from fund-raising to a seasonally oriented community service production, such as a Christmas play. Their membership may lack the talent or interest needed for a three-act play; one-act plays are usually the best vehicle for these organizations. The play selected should have a simple set and a small number of clearly defined characters; a study of the talents and energies of members of the organization will suggest how simple and how small. The play should be a low or no royalty production and its selection should be a joint effort of interested members of the group acting with the advice and guidance of the speech teacher. In some cases, the advisor of the organization will direct the play, occasionally requesting the assistance of the speech teacher; but in many schools the speech teacher is expected to direct or supervise all student productions.

DRAMATIC ART AND SPEECH CLUBS

There are several national and state organizations which have as their primary purpose the promotion of student participation and education in speech and dramatic art. They operate in conjunction with local groups or chapters to improve the skills, strengthen the interest, provide appropriate information, and offer the guidance needed to establish and maintain a dynamic curricular and co-curricular speech program.

The National Thespian Society

Established in 1929, this organization has as its aims "(1) to establish and advance standards of excellence in all phases of dramatic arts, and (2) to create an active and intelligent interest in dramatic arts among boys and girls in the high schools."[2] A local affiliate, called a troupe, can be established when at least eight students meet the qualifications for mem-

---

[2]*Information: The National Thespian Society* (Cincinnati, Ohio: The National Thespian Society, 1967), p. 3.

bership in the national organization and when there is evidence of a continuing interest in dramatic activities, as specified in the membership requirements of the organization. The society provides advisory service on play production to its membership without charge and, through its contacts with leading play publishers, offers member schools the opportunity to apply for royalty adjustment when door receipts are limited. Student membership qualifications are based on a scale of points assigned for work done. After membership is obtained, the student can receive additional recognition from the society by continuing to participate in dramatic arts. The official publication *Dramatics Magazine*, contains articles on all phases of theatre education and is published eight times each year. Information on the services and activities of the organization may be secured by contacting the Secretary-Treasurer, Ronald L. Longstreth, College Hill Station, Cincinnati, Ohio 45224.

National Forensic League

Since its formation in 1925, the National Forensic League has been a significant force in the establishment and improvement of interscholastic speech competition. Membership in the organization is restricted to students and coaches who accumulate a minimum number of participation points, according to a credit point schedule developed by the NFL. Local chapters can be established when an application is submitted to the national office, certifying that an effective and continuing extracurricular forensic program exists at the applying school.

Member schools are placed in geographical districts; currently there are 1,065 chapters in 42 districts. Each district conducts tournaments in debate, extemporaneous speaking, original oratory, and dramatic interpretation. Winners of these district contests become eligible for participation in the national tournament sponsored by the organization each summer. To stimulate excellence in forensic participation, several "degrees" can be earned by members, based upon points awarded by the organization for success in contest competition.

In addition to sponsoring district and national tourneys and awarding membership to those proficient in forensic activities, the league communicates with its membership through the *Rostrum*, which is published each month during the school year.

The National Forensic League has done much to stimulate interschool competition in speaking activities; it is, however, designed to assist schools with established forensic programs. Teachers interested in further information about the league should contact the secretary, Ripon College, Ripon, Wisconsin 54971.

State Speech Leagues

Most states with extracurricular programs have established speech leagues which supervise and conduct district and state championship tournaments and provide information and assistance to all the members. Typically, membership in the state organizations is open to all high schools in the state, is voluntary, and must be renewed annually. The state leagues are uniquely situated to provide the most useful channel for guidance and help in establishing a speech program; their goal is the establishment and furtherance of speech education in the schools of the state. Schools with mature co-curricular programs are also associated with the honorary speech organizations, such as the National Forensic League, but the primary goal of most state leagues is to establish new programs in the high schools and cultivate excellence in existing programs.

Some of the services provided by the state league are (1) conducting state championship tournaments in all speech events, (2) distributing debate and discussion materials, (3) holding student debate and drama clinics, (4) acting as the coordinating agency for all extracurricular speech activities in the state, (5) assisting schools which are initiating curricular or co-curricular speech programs, and (6) representing the speech profession to the secondary schools of the state through relationships with school administrators and teachers.

The more populous states have the most active and strongest leagues; Texas, Michigan, California, Ohio, Missouri, Indiana, Oklahoma, Florida, Pennsylvania, and Wisconsin are outstanding.

The office of the state organization characteristically is located on the campus of the major state-supported university. Membership fees are minimal and a teacher who is initiating co-curricular activities or is continuing an already established program should seek affiliation with his state organization.

Local Clubs

Most schools have one or more organizations concerned with speech or dramatic art but not associated with any national society. Such groups as Drama Clubs, Debate Clubs, Thespians, and Masque and Gavel offer an opportunity for interested students to meet and share their concerns and energies for speech activities outside the classroom. Because national organizations establish rules and procedures for the establishment and maintenance of a chapter, schools may find it desirable to organize a local club with activities and interests peculiar to that school. A strong local club may lead to national affiliation, but local club development is one of the best avenues for student involvement and enthusiasm for the goals and activities of speech and dramatic art.

CONTESTS

A well rounded speech program will provide opportunities for student participation in speech contest work. Competition and the desire for achievement are the ingredients of contests in speech activities, but the desire to win must be subordinated to the educational objective: the development of facility in oral communication behaviors through inter- and intraschool competition. In developing a sound speech program for the secondary school, the director should urge all interested students to participate in contest activities. He should not attempt to establish a program which stresses participation and excellence only for those already highly trained in competitive speech work. The success of the program should be measured by the number of students participating, their enthusiasm for speech activities and their competitive achievements.

Debate

Perhaps the single most popular competitive speech event is debate. Schools with co-curricular speaking activities typically field one or more debate teams and at schools with a well established forensic program it is common to have fifteen or twenty students participating in debate. From the second or third week in October until mid-March, interschool debate tournaments are held, on Saturdays, at various locations throughout the state. Each week, a different school acts as host for the practice tournaments which generally use the national debate topic for the tournament proposition. At this point it will be useful to discuss how the national debate topic is selected.

The National Debate Topic. At its annual meeting in December the National University Extension Association and its state league affiliates discuss possible debate topics for the succeeding school year and the field is narrowed to three topic areas. Three separate debate propositions are prepared for each of the topic areas, with the propositions representing different facets of the general areas.

During February most of the state league offices poll their membership to determine which of the three topic areas is preferred, and the results are reported to the NUEA. The votes of all the states are tallied by the association, and the topic area selected by a plurality of states becomes the *area* for debate during the next school year. Schools participating in debate are encouraged to prepare cases on each of the three propositions within the topic area. This procedure is designed to provide an extensive background through examination of all facets of the problem area.

In November, the state leagues again poll their membership to discover which of the three propositions in the selected area is the best single topic for debate during the remainder of the academic year. At the December meeting of the NUEA the state leagues cast their ballots for the propositions according to the outcome of the selection process in their respective states. The results of balloting by the states are submitted to the advisory council of the NUEA which then chooses the national debate proposition. Officers of the state organizations communicate the results of the meeting to their members; with few exceptions, states use the national proposition in the practice contests during the rest of the school year and, particularly, in the state championship competition.

Interschool Tournaments. The typical debate tournament is a one-day, three-round contest sometimes held in conjunction with other individual speaking events. Large tournaments offer competition in several classes of debating proficiency: novice for the beginning debater, intermediate for the debater with approximately one year of experience, and varsity for the first-line teams from each school. It is not necessary, however, to have more than one classification of debate in a tournament.

Most tournaments are held for schools in the immediate geographical area: travel of over 150 miles for a Saturday tournament is unusual. The host school should clear the date for the tournament with the state speech league office so that a conflict with another contest in the same region can be avoided. Approximately three to four weeks in advance of the tournament, invitations are mailed to all schools in the area with active extracurricular speech programs. Teachers at schools which are interested in tournament competition but who have not received invitations to tourneys should contact their state speech league office for a schedule of tournaments throughout the state and should then write to the host schools indicating their interest. Tournament directors are willing, almost without exception, to invite any school interested in participatng.

Debate tournament competition is usually between four-man teams: two negative and two affirmative speakers. Four-man debate has the advantages of providing an opportunity for participation by more students and of enabling the participant to specialize on the side of the question where his convictions lie. However, more and more high school tournaments are being held for the two-man team in which, in alternate rounds of competition, debaters uphold the affirmative and then the negative side. The "switch-sides" format makes a broad knowledge of the proposition imperative and its proponents assert that the debaters derive more value from this approach because they are forced to investigate both sides of the question intensively. The morality of debating both sides remains unsolved in spite of extensive publication and discussion on the question.[3] But veteran coaches, when evaluating the success of their students with the two approaches, feel that inexperienced debaters are more successful in four-man debate while veteran debaters find two-man debate more challenging and valuable.

Hosting a Tournament. Some schools with established programs host a tournament to increase student interest and participation in the speech program and to demonstrate to the community and the school administration the values of speech training. The debate tournament is a major school event, requiring most of the rooms in the high school and assistance from all available students. The sight of scores of pupils from surrounding communities participating enthusiastically in a competitive intellectual activity is powerful ammunition in the battle for student and community support of a co-curricular speech program. However, no teacher should plan to hold a debate tournament as a method for avoiding travel or for securing funds for the support of the debate program; running a tournament is an exhausting experience and the financial rewards are usually trifling.

A successful tournament is based on planning. The discussion which follows describes the planning activity of the host school; the teacher who hopes to conduct a successful tournament should follow the steps in the order presented.

1. *Determine if your school has sufficient space for a tournament.* If four-man teams will be competing, one room for each competing team will be necessary. Two-man debate competition will require only half the number of rooms, one room for each two teams. Both of the preceding methods for determining the number of rooms required assume that only one entry from each school will be accepted in the tourney. Coaches not experienced in directing a tournament should keep the first tourney small, permitting only one team from each school to enter.

---

[3]For example, see Nicholas M. Cripe, "Debating Both Sides in Tournaments is Ethical," *The Speech Teacher*, 6, No. 3:209-212 (September, 1957); Richard Murphy, "The Ethics of Debating Both Sides II," *The Speech Teacher*, 12, No. 3:242-247 (September, 1963); and Donald Sikkink, "Evidence on the Both Sides Debate Controversy," *The Speech Teacher*, 11, No. 1:51-54 (January, 1962).

2. *Secure permission to hold the tournament from the principal of the high school.* It is unwise to approach the principal until there is assurance of sufficient space, but his permission should precede any other planning for the contest.

3. *Choose a date for the tournament.* When the principal is contacted, several possible dates for the tournament should be proposed. Most schools have a crowded calendar of activities and it may be necessary to select a date or dates three, four, or even five months in advance of the tournament. Conflicts with tournaments at other regional schools can be avoided if the director will first check with the state speech league office to determine the date and locations of tournaments scheduled during the school year. When contests are held at neighboring schools on the same date, the probabilities for good attendance at either meet are severely limited. If possible, do not host a tourney on a date when another tournament is being held within one hundred miles of your school.

4. *Be certain there are eating facilities* available either in the school or nearby. A Saturday tourney makes it imperative that any plans for use of the school cafeteria be made well in advance and with the appropriate school authorities. If school facilities cannot be used, local restaurants are a possibility, but they usually are a time-consuming alternative. Some tournament directors arrange with a youth group at a nearby church to provide lunch. Regardless of the type or location of the eating facilities, not over an hour and a half should be provided in the time schedule for lunch.

5. *Estimate probable expenses.* It may seem unusual to expect a tournament director to determine the cost of the tournament prior to mailing invitations, but a reasonable estimate of expenses must be made so that entry fees sufficient to defray expenses can be specified. The expenses usually incurred in hosting a tournament are the cost of awards, postage, and secretarial supplies. Typically no charges are made for use of the school facilities, the services of a custodian, or equipment owned by the school used during the meet. Some tournaments are designed as money-making endeavors for the host school, but an unreasonable entry fee will discourage schools with low budgets from attending. A fee of from 50¢ to $1.00 per participant is reasonable and common.

6. *Prepare letters of invitation and entry blanks.* The letter of invitation should provide all relevant information including a statement of entry fees, the date of the contest, the location of the contest, entry blanks, directions for finding the school (if necessary), a tentative time schedule, and the deadline for return of the entries. A specimen letter follows.

New Dover High School
New Dover, Ohio
November 10, 19—

Dear Debate Coach:

You are cordially invited to attend the third annual New Dover Invitational Debate Tournament to be held at the high school on N. Dewey Lane on Saturday, December 18. There will be three rounds of debate on the proposition: Resolved: That all agricultural prices should be supported at not less than 90 per cent of parity.

ELIGIBILITY: Entries will be restricted to one four-man team per school. Only debaters with fewer than two years debating experience are eligible for competition.

ENTRY FEE: The entry fee, which includes luncheon tickets for the squad and coach for the Saturday meal in the school cafeteria, is $6.50 per school.

JUDGES: Each school must provide one experienced judge. If your school cannot send a judge with the team, a limited number of qualified judges is available at a charge of $15 per judge. All requests for the hiring of judges must accompany the entry blank and payment of the fee must be made in advance.

DEADLINE: The completed entry blank must be received not later than December 11.

AWARDS: Trophies will be awarded to the first, second, and third place teams. Medals will be given to members of the first place squad.

SCHEDULE:
    8:30- 8:55   Registration in auditorium
    9:00- 9:15   Assembly and announcements (auditorium)
    9:30-10:45   Round I
  11:00-12:15   Round II
  12:15- 1:15   Lunch (school cafeteria)
    1:15- 2:30   Round III
    3:00   Announcements and awards

I hope that you can be with us and help make this our most successful tournament ever.

R____ L____
Director of Debate

The date for return of the form should be clearly specified and strictly enforced. Debate coaches are notoriously forgetful where entry blanks are concerned, and their failure to submit entries until after the deadline is well known.

7. *Mail the letters of invitation and entry blanks to schools.* Invitations should be placed in the mail approximately four or five weeks prior to the tournament. If the names of schools in the region interested in competitive debate are not known to the director of the tournament, a list can usually be secured either by writing to the state speech league office or by contacting the regional National Forensic League chairman. Schools wishing to compete in the tourney should be instructed to mail their entries to the tournament host at least one week before the contest.

8. *Order the awards.* One of the attractions of competition in debate is the collection of "hardware," and virtually all interschool tournaments offer some tangible evidence of accomplishment to the winning school(s). Awards, for economic and incentive reasons, should not be presented to more than the first, second, and third place teams.

9. *Contact school service organizations for assistance.* The Key Club, Honor Society, Speech Club, Drama Club, and fraternities and sororities are able and usually willing to provide students who will act as timekeepers, assist at registration, and carry messages and debate ballots. Students active in speech activities will serve as the nucleus of the tournament organization, but only a very large co-curricular speech organization could hope to provide enough persons to perform all the tasks involved in the conduct of a tournament.

10. *Prepare materials.* Ballots for decisions, a set of time cards for each debate, a map of the building or grounds (if debaters might have difficulty in finding rooms or buildings), and a final time schedule are materials the tournament director can prepare before the entries arrive. The ballots can be stuffed in envelopes several days before the tournament, and then three of the envelopes, carbon paper, scratch paper, and a pencil should be placed in a manilla envelope to be distributed to each judge prior to the beginning of the first round. Tournament directors often find it helpful to include time schedules, general instructions, and a map in the packet as well. Time cards are expendable and can be prepared using blank, unruled 3 x 5 file cards. Printed ballots can be purchased from the American Forensic Association, or the ballot commonly used in state contests can be secured from the state league office or from nearby member schools.

11. *Prepare the debate schedule.* After the deadline for entries has passed, the tournament director should prepare a *tentative* schedule of

debates. It must be a tentative schedule since one or more schools registering for the tournament may be prevented, for health or other reasons, from participating.

There are several systems for determining the pairings in a multischool debate tournament. The system shown below can be used at tournaments in which each school brings one four-man team and one judge. In this system, the negative teams move one place each round and the judge moves three places. No school meets another school more than once. Judges use the same number as their school team.

| Round I | | | Round II | | | Round III | | | Round IV | | |
Aff	Neg	Judge	Aff	Neg	Judge	Aff	Neg	Judge	Aff	Neg	Judge
1	2	6	1	3	9	1	4	12	1	5	3
2	3	7	2	4	10	2	5	1	2	6	4
3	4	8	3	5	11	3	6	2	3	7	5
4	5	9	4	6	12	4	7	3	4	8	6
5	6	10	5	7	1	5	8	4	5	9	7
6	7	11	6	8	2	6	9	5	6	10	8
7	8	12	7	9	3	7	10	6	7	11	9
8	9	1	8	10	4	8	11	7	8	12	10
9	10	2	9	11	5	9	12	8	9	1	11
10	11	3	10	12	6	10	1	9	10	2	12
11	12	4	11	1	7	11	2	10	11	3	1
12	1	5	12	2	8	12	3	11	12	4	2

The prudent host will prepare three schedules — one for the number of schools registering for the tournament, one for the number of teams registered less one, and one for the number of teams registered less two. The labor involved in the preparation of the extra schedules is small compared to the confusion that can develop when pairings are prepared in the final five minutes prior to the first round. When the schedules have been checked for errors, they should be transferred to ditto masters.

Difficulties in pairings will be minimized if numbers are used instead of school names. This approach facilitates preparation of the schedule and enables conflicts and duplications to be identified easily. When the schools register the morning of the tournament, they can draw a number which will serve as their school identification for the remainder of the day. The competition for each team, then, is not determined until the day of the tourney, by lot of the coaches.

12. *Prepare results sheets.* A day or so before the tournament, a results sheet for the decision from each round and total wins and losses should be prepared on ditto masters. Again, use the number system with

space provided beside each number for a school name. When numbers have been drawn, names can be written in the blanks. Results can be copied on the ditto master, thus expediting tabulation of wins and losses and announcement of the winner.

Specimen Results Sheet

Team No. and School		Rd I		Rd II		Rd III		Rd IV		Total
		A	N	A	N	A	N	A	N	
1	Uinta	W	W	W	W	L	L	W	W	6-2
2	Wyoming	L	L	W	L	W	W	W	L	4-4
3	North	L	L	L	L	W	L	W	L	2-6
4	Princeton	W	L	W	L	W	L	L	L	3-5
5	West	W	L	L	W	L	L	W	L	3-5
6	Louisville	L	W	L	L	W	W	W	L	4-4
7	Marysville	W	W	W	W	W	W	W	L	7-1
8	East	L	L	L	L	W	L	W	L	2-6
9	Fairmont	W	L	L	L	L	W	W	W	4-4
10	Willis	W	W	W	W	L	W	W	L	6-2
11	Oakwood	W	W	W	W	L	L	W	L	5-3
12	South	L	L	L	W	L	W	L	L	2-6

13. *Secure student assistants for tabulation of results.* Three or four energetic and highly competent students should be selected, several days prior to the tournament, to assist the director in tallying results. Some tournament directors also enlist the help of a highly experienced coach from another school for guidance if problems arise.

14. *Hold a brief general meeting* before the debates begin for announcements and general instructions. The drawing of team numbers can precede the assembly or be done during the meeting. (Judges should be advised of the method to be used for returning ballots and be requested to return their ballots at the end of each round.) The floor plan of the building(s) in which the debates are to be held should be explained if necessary, and the location of the cafeteria (if it is to be used for lunch) should be made clear. Any rules or procedures peculiar to the tournament must be mentioned and explained at this assembly because it is the final opportunity, before debates begin, to clarify the tournament procedures.

15. *Tally the results.* The timekeepers or chairmen for each debate (if you can secure enough student help to have chairmen) should return the completed ballots to the tournament headquarters after each round. All ballots should be checked by the student assistants and again by the

tourney director for consistency between speaker points and the awarding of the decision before the result is recorded on ditto. While the director and one or two students are tallying results, several other student
helpers can place copies of each decision on a table beneath the school
number. One copy of the ballot should be given to the participating
negative team and one copy to the affirmative team. When ballots for all
the debates have been distributed, a packet should be prepared for each
competing school. These packets will bear the names and numbers of the
schools and should contain ballots for each debate in which the school
participated and a copy of the results sheet. The packets will be distributed to the schools following the awards meeting.

If at the end of the three rounds of debate two or more teams are tied
for first place, the tie can be broken by totalling the speaker points of
each team, or additional debates can be held between the tied teams. This
solution is rarely used to break ties because (1) a fourth round of debate
would delay the awards meeting and schools not involved in the tie-
breaking debate would leave for home, (2) tournament directors experience substantial difficulty in finding a judge or judges willing and able to
stay at the host school for another round of competition in which their
students are not involved, and (3) there is minimal educational value for
the competing schools in debating a fourth round.

The method for breaking ties for award purposes must be announced
prior to the beginning of the first round; it should be a reasonable and
practical approach. One method used is to record, for each round, the
speaker points for each team as well as the decision. Then, when total
wins and losses are known and a tie for one of the awards develops, the
points accumulated by the teams involved can be summed easily.

Intraschool Debates.   In some schools the forensic program consists
primarily of debates between school organizations or classes. These debates, although they can utilize the national high school proposition,
usually are on topics related to the school, organization, or persons involved in the debate.

Often, the debate coach is approached by members of one or more of
the school organizations for advice on a topic suitable for a debate and
for general instructions about debate procedure. Several female members
of the junior class may challenge a group of junior boys to debate them
on a topic such as "Resolved: That all boys in this high school should be
required to take home economics." The team members probably would
not phrase the proposition in the form presented above, but the wording
of the topic and general development of the affirmative and negative
speeches should be the product of several meetings between the debate
coach and members of each team. Procedures used in intraschool debates

should not be those used in contest competition, for the experience should be a somewhat informal introduction to argumentative speaking. Although basic rules should be observed, the participants should not feel that stilted terminology and rigid procedure are fundamental to the debate.

A program of this type may serve as the foundation for subsequent interschool debate participation but that should not be the objective of an intramural debate program. It must provide an opportunity for students to engage in argumentative speaking on a topic of interest to them. If their experiences in intraschool debates are rewarding ones, the groundwork for participation in interschool debating has been laid.

Public Speaking

Intraschool. Contests of this type held within the school often are sponsored by a community organization, such as the American Legion, the Daughters of the American Revolution, or the Women's Christian Temperance Union. Information about the contest is usually sent to the principal or to the teacher in charge of speech activities several months before the date of the competition. When the contest is for qualification in a national competition, such as the Veterans of Foreign Wars "Voice of Democracy" contest, the sponsoring organization will specify the type of speech, its length, and occasionally the specific topic area. Persuasive speeches are the most common forms of speaking used, and they range from ten to twenty minutes in length.

Extemporaneous Speech. Interschool tournaments which provide individual events competition nearly always include *extemporaneous speaking*, an event which enables the student to develop and sharpen his organizational skills while placing substantial emphasis upon the ability to "think on one's feet." Debate coaches feel that there are numerous similarities between effective extemporaneous speaking and good debating, and that the skilled debater should be a good extemporaneous speaker and vice versa. The most successful participants are students who are well informed on current affairs, are articulate, and possess above-average organizational ability. The procedures followed in extemporaneous speaking contests are more complex than for most other individual speaking events and for that reason they will be discussed in detail here.

Extemporaneous speaking comes from the Latin *ex tempore*, meaning "from a time." Contestants have a specified period of time in which to prepare a 5-7 minute speech on a selected topic. The participant, however, cannot choose any topic that suits his fancy; the topics for the speeches deal with current events and are prepared by the tournament director before the contest. The common practice of tourney directors is to select topics which have been discussed during the most recent three months period in *Time Magazine, Newsweek,* and *US News and World Report.*

Approximately 45 minutes prior to the time when he is scheduled to speak, the contestant selects three topics from the pool of questions provided by the tournament director. The cards or strips of paper bearing the topics are turned face down on a large table so that the selection is made completely in the blind. From the three topics drawn, the contestant chooses the one on which he will speak. He may then go to the area set aside for preparation and consult recent issues of the magazines mentioned above for information pertaining to his subject. Most contestants maintain a card index of subjects discussed in those publications for convenience and speed in speech preparation. Contest rules vary. Occasionally, speakers are permitted to use a brief outline when speaking, but extensive notes are not allowed.

Extemporaneous speaking competition, in addition to being an event in numerous invitational speech tournaments, is one of the activities in all NFL district contests and most state league championships.

Original Oratory. Interschool and intraschool competition is frequently offered in this event. The oration usually is persuasive in form and consists of the original thoughts of the participant on a topic of social, political, or religious significance. To insure that the speech presented is the original work of the contestant, most contest directors specify the maximum amount of quoted material which may be used; typically it is one hundred fifty words. Orations vary in length from seven to ten minutes for contest purposes, with evaluation based upon the originality and uniqueness of the thought and its development and presentation.

Oratorical Declamation. This speaking activity, which involves the memorization and presentation of a published speech previously delivered, is another competitive event. It provides the student with a model of effective speaking and stresses the ability to communicate the meaning of another author to the audience. Coaches interested in purchasing copies of orations and declamations which have proved successful in contest competition should write for the catalogue of Edna Means Dramatic Service, 610 Harmon Street, Tama, Iowa 52339, or Wetmore Declamation Bureau, Box 2595, Sioux City, Iowa 51106. It would also be helpful for students and coaches to secure a copy of *Winning Orations,* an annual publication of successful collegiate orations published by the Interstate Oratorical Association.

INTERPRETIVE SPEECH ARTS

Oral Interpretation

Contest competition includes the reading of several works, whether on a single theme or of one author. The sole requirement in choosing material for this type of presentation is that the selection must have literary merit. Most contest activity in interpretation is restricted to poetry reading, but the director of a tournament may choose to call the event "oral interpretation" and thus permit the reading of prose selections. But because competition of this type is rare, this discussion will be restricted to poetry reading as the contest form of interpretation. Although most students choose works of well-known authors, it is not mandatory to do so. It is unusual and generally unwise for students to use their own compositions in contest activities.

Examples of the kinds of programs or readings which can be presented may be helpful. First, consider a group of readings representing the work of a single author. The following poetical selections from the work of Carl Sandburg exemplify this approach: "Chicago," "I Am the People, the Mob," "Grass," and "Cool Tombs." It is possible to build the works of Sandburg around a theme; the selections above could be introduced and developed on the theme of the brawling and lusty nature of man and his products contrasted with the peace that reigns upon his passing. Another approach is to choose works from various authors, all concerned with a single theme such as "seasons," "love," "death," or "moods."

Each reading should be preceded by introductory remarks which may provide some information about the author, the reason for choosing the selection, and perhaps expression of the feeling of the reader about the work. The interpreter must be familiar with his materials and may, if the rules of the contest permit, present his reading strictly from memory. Students should be encouraged to take the book from which the works are selected with them when they read; it not only eliminates any fears of forgetting, but stress and phrasing marks are available for ready reference during the presentation.

Humorous Declamation. Participation in this event involves the presentation, from memory, of published material of a humorous or entertaining nature. Materials often consist of "cuttings" from a well-known, popular work, such as "The Secret Life of Walter Mitty" or "The Proposal." Contest declamations are usually limited to ten minutes. There has been some disagreement about the distinction between the interpretation of a role and acting. Most contest directors permit participants to "suggest" a character, through mannerism, dialect, and other behaviors, but apparel designed to assist in evoking the desired response is not allowed.

Dramatic Declamation.   Materials used for contest work include cuttings from full-length plays, novels, and occasionally short stories. As with other declamation events, dramatic declamation is designed to expose the student to significant literary works and to heighten his appreciation and understanding of them through extensive study and presentation. The guidelines specified for humorous declamation are applicable to dramatic declamation also. Materials are memorized and should be approximately ten minutes long.

Radio Announcing.   Competition usually is based on the reading of news copy selected from recent wire service releases. The following format for contest participation is used by one state league. Twenty minutes prior to actual reading, the contestant is given the script he will read "on the air." The copy is six minutes long, and the students may refer to a pronouncing dictionary during their preparation period. The material used is similar to that read by newscasters and includes straight news items, a few passages containing musical terms and artists' names, and several commercial messages. Contestants are evaluated on pronunciation, voice quality, rate, pitch, enunciation, intensity, breath control, vocal enthusiasm, and rate of delivery. When material requires contestants to switch from narration to interpretation, their skill in the communication of feeling and their ability to change vocally from character to character become evaluative criteria.

Television Announcing.   While television and radio announcing use many of the same criteria for evaluation of performances, physical behavior is considered in television because it is a visual medium. Most invitational speech tournaments do not provide competition in this event because of the dearth of facilities and the complex nature of the contest. More and more state leagues are, however, including television announcing as one of the interpretive speech activities in championship competition. Because of its recent appearance as a competitive event, the format for contest work remains fluid. Contestants are usually required to submit the script for their performance to the tournament director several days in advance of the competition so that copies may be distributed to the technical personnel and arrangements made for camera movements and props. If at all possible, the director should schedule one "dry run" prior to the performance. The length of the performance will vary according to the contest rules but they are frequently from five to seven minutes long. Since deviations of more than ten to fifteen seconds from the specified limits are penalized, the contestant must have his material timed exactly.

The following criteria and guidelines for preparation were used by a representative speech league in its television announcing contest:

Criteria
1) Planning and organization of material (Was it developed in an easy to follow, logical pattern?)
2) Selection and integration of visual material
3) Presentation on camera (Was there an informal, conversational approach? Was there good eye contact? Was there ease of movement?)
4) Appearance
5) Neatness and clarity of script preparation

Script Preparation Tips
1) Put what is to be seen on the left half of the page and what is spoken on the right side.
2) Capitalize everything that is not spoken, such as the description of what is seen, any action by the speaker, any designation of speakers *(ANNCR:* or *NARR:* or *HOST:* or *SPEAKER:),* any *MUSIC* or *SOUND EFFECTS.* Everything that is spoken should be in lower case.
3) Double space all your written material.
4) Put any video (visual) description opposite the spoken work it refers to.
5) Type your scripts and make them clean and neat.

Tips for Preparation of Visuals
1) Bring live objects for demonstrations whenever possible.
2) If you use still pictures, try to get them in a 3 by 4 ratio (3 vertical and 4 horizontal) and mount and center them on hard poster board (11 by 14 inches).
3) If you do any lettering on cards, don't have them any smaller than ½ inch high and don't have them any larger than 1 inch high (on an 11 by 14-inch card).
4) Look for good contrast in pictures, a proper balance of black and white.
5) Use visuals only when they will add to the understanding of your material.

Readers' Theatre. One of the newest competitive activities at district, regional, and state levels is Readers' Theatre. This contest is a presentation of a cutting from some popular story or play, staged with lecterns or stools on a formalistic stage, sometimes with the aid of spacelighting. The time may vary from contest to contest but is generally about thirty minutes. One must be particularly flexible because of the wide variety of rules for this competition. Since some host institutions may attempt to implement the dogma of oral interpretation enthusiasts, the performance may be rated low due to memorization of lines, characterization, blocking, or costuming of any kind. Other institutions may decide to limit the movements of the performers yet favor a common costume for all and overlook memorization. This form is a welcome relief from the oral interpretation presentation, which has reduced itself to *reading aloud*. Further, *restrained acting* is considered good acting because it simply suggests, leaving the completion of the artistic idea to the imagination of the audience.

The judging of this competition varies from awarding those who "read" best to awarding those who "appeared to read." The cast of a Readers' Theatre group who were successful in a recent contest dressed in dark pants or skirts and turtle-neck sweaters. They demonstrated little need for the script as they appeared to read from Edgar Lee Masters' *Spoon River*. Their polished performance was restrained but without visible crutches.

PRODUCTION

One-Act Plays

Participation in one-act play contests or festivals should include students who have demonstrated their abilities as actors; usually the cast will be composed of members of a drama class, the Thespian Society, or the Drama Club. Rules in some contests specify that the work selected must be a one-act play, but selected cuttings from a full-length play usually are permitted. Contest play selection presents unusual problems. The contest play must be technically simple, provide opportunities for varied characterization, demonstrate dramatic significance, have a logical plot and theme, and be within the capacity of the director and the students. It is not desirable to choose a play primarily because it requires no royalty payment. Many publishing companies permit one-act plays to be presented royalty-free when there is no admission charge.

Technical considerations are critical since performances will be given on stages at other institutions with only minimum facilities made available. The following criteria should be considered in a play chosen for contest presentation:

> 1. Because of the difficulties involved in taking a production on tour and because of the various types of theatres encountered, a

presentational style production using a minimum of realistic necessities such as walls, doors, windows, and hand props would be advisable.

2. A show which makes imaginative use of costumes is always impressive. This does not mean that great expense is necessary, nor does it mean that the show must be a period piece or historical and antiquarian study. However, some sort of formalistic costuming or theatrical costuming is something you can easily transport and is always interesting to the eye of the spectator.

3. In many theatres there are aprons, forestages, proscenium doors, and other aspects which are theatrical and help to break down the overworked realistic conventions of the picture frame stage. An interesting and imaginative use of these areas and of various collapsible levels and steps without overdoing it can make a show more interesting visually than the old-fashioned box set.

4. Imaginative and theatrical stage lighting can be done easily and with a minimum of spotlights or even with simple floods or strip lights. However, beware of substituting a dim stage for mood lighting. The audience must see the actor; and mood may be created with color and bright light more easily than with a dim, dull glow.

5. Try to choose a play or a cutting that has crisp theatrical qualities. This means it could be either Tragedy, Comedy, or Drama, but it should not be a piece that requires dreary moody situations or complete histrionics to create any conflict.

6. Finally, don't overtechnicalize your production. It is better to have a finely directed show with an interesting script and good acting than a weak show that depends on lighting or scenic efforts to create any interest.

There are numerous plays available and appropriate for contest presentation, but titles in the following list are among the most popular and effective contest plays:

Suggested One-Act Plays

Antic Spring by Robert Nail
The Bad Penny by Rachel Field
Barbara's Wedding by J. M. Barrie
The Birthday of the Infanta by Vail Motter
The Chairs by Eugene Ionesco
The Darkest Hour by Charles George
The Devil and Daniel Webster by Stephen Vincent Benet
Gammer Burton's Needle by William Stevenson
Fumed Oak by Noel Coward

If Men Played Cards as Women Do by George F. Kaufman
In the Zone by Eugene O'Neill
The Lord's Will by Paul Green
The Marriage Proposal by Anton Tchekoff
The Monkey's Paw by W. W. Jacob and Louis N. Parker
The Old Lady Shows Her Medals by J. M. Barrie
The Patchwork Quilt by Rachel Field
Pink and Patches by Margaret Bland
The Pot Boiler by Alice Gerstenberg
Riders to the Sea by J. M. Synge
Submerged by H. Stuart Cottman and LeVergne Shaw
The Trysting Place by Booth Tarkington
The Ugly Duckling by A. A. Milne
Where the Cross Is Made by Eugene O'Neill
The Wonder Hat by K. S. Goodman and Ben Hecht
A Young Lady of Property by Horton Foote

Directors wishing to refer to a more complete list of one-act plays which are endorsed by the American Educational Theatre Association should consult *Dramatists' Guide to Selection of Plays and Musicals*, by Gail Plummer, published by William C. Brown Company, Publishers, Dubuque, Iowa, 1963.

Radio Program Production

Most practice tournaments and school-sponsored festivals do not include radio program production, but many state leagues do offer competition in this event. The competing schools prepare tape-recorded programs, ranging in length from fifteen to thirty minutes, and submit them to the contest director. Programs can be recorded at the time of presentation on the air, but they do not need to be broadcast programs. In many cases, they are recordings prepared in speech or radio classes. Competition may be provided in the categories of dramatic program, documentary program, discussion program, or variety program. Judging of the programs is typically done by a panel of expert judges who listen to the tape and evaluate the quality of the presentation, using the following criteria:

Program Evaluation Form

1. *Unity*
   Aside from selling the sponsor's product (if any), did the program contain a clearly obvious purpose? To what extent did the program achieve this purpose? Was there a consistent mood

throughout the program? Did a single feature personality emerge? How effective were lead-ins and transitions from one program segment to another? Were commercials (if any) appropriately handled?

2. *Opening and Closing*
Did the title of the program provoke interest? Did the title suggest the general nature of the program? Was the standard opening of the program strong in motivating audience interest? Did the closing adhere to standard content (cast of characters, musical signature if appropriate, list of production staff, etc.)?

3. *Beginning of the Program Proper*
Aside from the standard opening, did the program proper get under way immediately? Would the first segment of the program catch and intensify audience interest?

4. *Program Structure*
Did the program "drag," or did it create the impression of moving fast? Were specific segments within the program relatively short? Was there variety from one program segment to another? Was there constant building of interest to a climax or high point within the program?

5. *Presence of Psychological Appeals*
To what extent did the program take advantage of psychological appeals (conflict, comedy, information, sex, emotional stimulation, human interest, importance) to sustain audience interest?

PROGRAMS AND ACTIVITIES

Assembly Programs

The principal often asks the speech teacher to assume the responsibility for the planning and programming of school assemblies. When possible, plans for all the assemblies should be made at the beginning of the school year. The planning of the programs may be the assigned responsibility of the speech teacher, but it will be helpful to have a board of students act in an advisory capacity to the teacher in assembly planning and preparation. The student members of the board can either be elected by their class or appointed by the school administration.

Because these school meetings may involve participants with musical and dance talents, as well as dramatic, oratorical, or interpretive skills, close relationships with the music and dance (physical education) areas should be cultivated. The nature of the assembly will be, to a large degree, dictated by the occasion and purpose, but a school assembly on Veterans Day might involve the reading of several poems, a short speech paying tribute to the veterans of all wars, and a group of choral selections. The more effective assemblies utilize more than one communicative art form, and many will incorporate choral or instrumental music, modern dance, poetry readings, and perhaps an excerpt from an appropriate dramatic work. Other possible assembly programs include choral speaking, dramatization of a literary work, demonstration or practice debates, and skits.

Even in schools where the speech teacher is not assigned the duty of planning assembly programs he will play a key role in the preparation since he is able to identify those students with speaking and acting talents.

Speaker's Bureau

In response to the desire of students to speak before public gatherings and because of the need of numerous community groups for interesting programs for their meetings, some schools establish a speaker's bureau. The bureau is a community service endeavor of the speech department, providing speakers for group meetings usually at no charge to the organization.

The first step in organizing such a service is to identify those students who have speaking capabilities and interests; these may be students who already are engaged in co-curricular speech activities. With the teacher screening topics for appropriateness, students may be asked to prepare a ten- to fifteen-minute speech on a question of interest to them. The following topics, selected from titles used by students in the Wabash College Speaker's Bureau, represent questions which are appropriate for students and the organizations to which they speak: "The Public Opinion Pollsters," "Why Study History?" "Are You Being Cheated on Your Taxes?" "How We Got Indiana From the Indians," "Advertising, a Multi-Billion Dollar Business," "God Is Dead?" "That Modern Math," "What's Going On In Our Skies?" "How We Named Our Towns," "Is Peace Possible?" and "Does Indiana Need Capital Punishment?" For other topics see the section in Chapter 6 entitled "Current Events as Resources."

When the speeches have been prepared, local service organizations should be advised that speakers from the bureau are available. Requests for speakers then can be made, at least three weeks in advance of the meeting, to the speech teacher, who serves as the coordinator of the activity.

Joint Productions with Other Departments

The services of the speech department are sought for numerous programs and activities sponsored by other areas: operettas, dance productions, fashion revues, and pageants all require the assistance and cooperation of the speech teacher.

Operettas are commonly a production of the music department, but the speech teacher often is asked to help select the cast and to advise on technical production matters. Costume selection may be a mutual concern of the speech and home economics departments. Sets may be designed by the art department and erected and painted by students in speech or stagecraft courses. Stage crews will usually be furnished by the speech department. The speech teacher's advice will probably be sought in blocking the production, achieving balance in stage composition and the techniques of acting.

Dance productions are in the domain of the physical education department, but again the speech teacher's assistance may be requested on lighting, set construction, and general matters related to staging.

Fashion revues presented by the Home Economics department may call for technical services provided by the speech department. The speech department may also be asked to provide a commentator for the show, in addition to the stage personnel.

Pageants are, generally, rather ambitious undertakings and substantial assistance from the speech teacher often is requested. Easter and Christmas pageants usually are joint undertakings of the music and physical education departments, as is the Thanksgiving program. Here too, the speech area provides direction in the selection of dramatic materials to be presented, choice of the cast, direction, and staging. The speech teacher can expect to be approached by teachers in other departments for technical assistance and advice, directional help, and information on characterization even when the production is one in which the speech department is not involved. As a service agency of the school, the speech department is actively involved in virtually all school programs.

FINANCING THE OUT-OF-CLASS PROGRAM

The cost of participation in out-of-class speech activities is high. Some activities, such as full-length and one-act plays may, through box office receipts, pay their royalties. Even in the case of dramatic productions, however, the total production cost is seldom met through admission charges, and supplementary revenue sources must be found. A co-curricular program in radio is extremely expensive because of the high cost of electronic equipment, but this phase of out-of-class activities generates no revenue to offset the equipment expenditures.

Attendance at tournaments and festivals also is an expensive matter. Transportation must be secured and paid for; it often involves the use of school buses and the hiring of bus drivers. Entry fees at tournaments can be substantial, particularly when the minimum fee is fifty cents per participant. When one adds to this the cost of hotel rooms (when it is a 2-day tournament) and meals for all contestants, entry in a tournament becomes a costly matter.

In many communities, the out-of-class program is supported by funds appropriated by the board of education expressly for the purpose of maintaining an active co-curricular program. Occasionally as much as $800-1000 is allocated through the principal's office, but more often the funds are in the range of $200-500. Without being miserly, a budget-minded speech director can stretch poorly funded programs by selecting nearby all-events tournaments and entering students in contests only once or twice a month during the competitive forensic and dramatic season.

It is not unusual for an out-of-class program to be funded through the operation of a concession at the school athletic contests. In these cases, the speech club is permitted to retain all earnings from concessions sales at football and basketball games.

Perhaps the least frequently used method for supporting the speech program is through box office receipts at school plays. Most productions call for substantial expenses in addition to the royalty payments; paints, costumes, wood, muslin, properties, and play books are only a few of these costs. Several well attended performances are required merely for the play to meet its costs. Few schools are successful in using the play as an instrument for raising funds for the speech program.

The most desirable approach to financing the program is through school board allocation of funds. Speech teachers and other members of the faculty hope that members of the board are aware of the values and sensitive to the needs of the co-curricular program. Where they are not and where funds have not been made available, it is incumbent upon the speech director to demonstrate the lasting values of student participation.

Many dedicated teachers have secured community financial support only after they have invested heavily of their own resources to maintain the program while student interest and community support is being cultivated. Our opulent society is able to provide worthwhile educational endeavors with the finances needed; out-of-class speech activities are in the forefront of such programs. Time and time again the effective teacher, working with enthusiastic students, can create the favorable community climate needed for financial aid. It can and should happen in all school systems.

Suggested Projects

1. Prepare a schedule for a one-day debate tournament involving fifteen schools meeting under the following conditions:
   a) each school may bring only one four-man team,
   b) no school should meet any other school more than once,
   c) there will be three rounds of debate, and
   d) the rules will provide for methods of breaking ties on the basis of win-loss records.

2. Read several articles in *The Speech Teacher* and *The Quarterly Journal of Speech* and then write a concise paper on
   a) the merits of debating both sides of the question,
   b) the significance of debate training in secondary education,
   c) the place of debate as a co-curricular activity,
   d) the importance of speech clubs and honorary organizations in stimulating excellence in speech activities, and
   e) the values of tournament competition.

3. Outline the significant values of extemporaneous speaking activity.

4. You have been assigned the responsibility of directing the junior class play. What major considerations determine the selection of the play and the date of presentation? How much time should be allotted for rehearsals? What information or advice do you need from your principal? Is it advisable to assign a student director?

5. What are the values in competitive discussion? How would you organize discussion competition?

6. What arguments would you use to request a 100 per cent increase in the budget for co-curricular speech activities if you were asked to appear at a board of education meeting to justify such a request?

7. How would you stimulate student interest in community-sponsored speaking contests such as "I Speak for Democracy," or "The Prince of Peace" competition? What are the public relations value of participation?

References

Blanding, Donald C. "The Speech Contest: Medium of Public Relations," *The Speech Teacher,* 6, No. 3:193-195 (September, 1957).

Boaz, John and Ziegelmueller, George. "An Audience Debate Tournament," *The Speech Teacher,* 13, No. 4:270-276 (November, 1964).

Carmack, Paul. "State Forensic Leagues," *Argumentation and Debate,*

Principles and Practices, ed. David Potter. New York: The Dryden Press, Inc., 1954, pp. 423-453.

Gehring, Mary Louise. "The High School Oration: Fundamentals," *The Speech Teacher,* 2, No. 2:101-104 (March, 1953).

Gilbert, Edna. "Oral Interpretation at Speech Festivals," *The Speech Teacher,* 5, No. 2:117-120 (March, 1956).

Hance, Kenneth. "Newer Types of Extracurricular Activities in Public Speaking," *Bulletin of the National Association of Secondary School Principals,* 36:132-187 (May, 1952).

Klopf, Donald W. and Rives, Stanley G. *Individual Speaking Contests.* Minneapolis, Minn.: Burgess Publishing Co., 1967.

Knower, Franklin (ed.). "A Speech Program for the Secondary School," *Bulletin of the National Association of Secondary School Principals,* 38, No. 199: whole issue (January, 1954).

Kruger, Arthur N. "The Extempore Speaking Contest," *The Speech Teacher,* 5, No. 3:214-222 (September, 1956).

Lynch, James (ed.). "Radio and Television In the Secondary School," *National Association of Secondary School Principal's Bulletin,* 50, No. 312: whole issue (October, 1966).

Niles, Doris. "The Beginning Speech Teacher as Director of the High School Assembly," *The Speech Teacher,* 10, No. 4:291-297 (November, 1961).

Smith, William S. "Co-ordinating Classroom Instruction in Debate with Extra-Curricular Program," *The Speech Teacher,* 6, No. 3:213-216 (September, 1957).

Sorber, Edna. "Tournaments: For Better and Better," *The Speech Teacher,* 8, No. 1:49-52 (January, 1959).

Wilmington, S. Clay and Swanson, Linda. "A Televised High School Debate Tournament," *The Speech Teacher,* 15, No. 4:299-302 (November, 1966).

13

Professional Organizations

The effective teacher soon realizes the need for exposure to current developments in education in general and in his academic field in particular. Any experienced teacher will readily testify to the numerous times he has felt inadequate in handling a discussion of a difficult subject in the classroom or of rating or grading performances. Regardless of the excellence of your educational preparation, you will find that you need additional information about the philosophies of instruction in speech, recent research findings, and resource materials. Your professional speech organizations, through their publications and services, exist to solve these needs. Our discussion will deal generally with the purposes of professional organizations and specifically with the services and operations of speech organizations.

GENERAL OBJECTIVES OF PROFESSIONAL ORGANIZATIONS

Professional organizations serve their membership in the following ways: (1) They represent the professional interests of their members to the community in which instruction is offered and to the educational community at large. (2) They offer services to their membership. These services consist of job placement bureaus and professional consultation to assist in securing adequate employment as effective classroom instructors. They also act as a clearinghouse for resource material used in subject matter teaching. (3) They publish journals which report new theories, philosophies, and methodologies in subject matter teaching, and they offer through these journals reports of research investigations in the field.

FUNCTION OF PROFESSIONAL SPEECH ASSOCIATIONS

The general welfare of secondary teachers is the concern of several educational associations. The National Education Association and the state teachers organizations have done an effective job of representing the needs and objectives of American public education to the people of this country. However, each academic discipline is concerned with materials, objectives, and methodologies peculiar to its field. Although the education associations are admirably equipped to promote and represent teachers in general, the professional organizations of each academic area are best equipped to meet the needs of teachers in their area of specialization.

The field of speech, as far as American education is concerned, is a comparatively new and recently accepted area of academic investigation. Because speech is an interdisciplinary field drawing on the disciplines of psychology, sociology, physiology, history, English, and so forth, the difficulties which the teacher of speech faces in his search for materials and resources are compounded. The literature of interest to us is scattered throughout the publications of each of the disciplines which we study. Thus, one of the purposes of the journals in our field is to unify a highly diverse profession by reporting results of research in relevant areas and by providing a single source to which scholars and teachers in speech can look for information critical to their area of concern.

The diversity of sources of material which apply to our field is even more evident when the list of publications of major book firms is examined. Our "publication explosion" makes it impossible for even the most serious scholar to keep up with the literature in his own field. The book reviews which appear in the more prominent speech journals assist the speech teacher by providing capsulized evaluations of the approach, discussion, and value of most major publications relevant to our discipline.

As previously noted, our discipline has only recently been accepted by many of our fellow educators. It would be inaccurate to attribute this acceptance primarily to our professional organizations, but they have been instrumental in enabling us to secure the understanding and respect of our teaching colleagues. Our organizations will continue to speak for our profession.

The field of speech has generated the formation of a host of professional organizations dedicated to the enhancement of various areas of the discipline. Our discussion will be limited to the major national and regional organizations, but we should not ignore the size and importance of the state and local arms of our profession. Nearly all states with active college or high school programs in speech have at least one organization devoted to the promotion of speech and speech education in the public and private schools of the state. These organizations and their officers work closely with state and local school administrators to articulate the needs and values of communication training. They coordinate local and state conferences and colloquia which consider the problems and the future of education in our field. Many of the state organizations publish newsletters which inform the membership of recent developments in speech affairs in the state. In states which have a substantial speech education program and where the membership is large enough to provide financial backing, a state speech journal may be published. The journal is usually distributed to the total membership and typically contains both theoretical and methodological articles.

National Organizations

Speech Association of America. Founded in 1914 by a group of college teachers of speech who felt that departments and courses of study in speech should be independent of English departments, SAA has attempted to develop a membership drawn from all areas of the field. Although the executive secretary and the executive council of the association are responsible for the business and professional matters, the general membership of the association exercises its voice through an elected Legislative Assembly. The following selected listing of groups operating within the association indicates the diversity of interests represented by the organization: American Forensic Association; phonetics, linguistics, and voice science; radio, TV, and films; speech in the secondary schools; speech in the elementary schools; rhetoric and public address; behavioral sciences; theatre and drama; and undergraduate speech instruction.

Each year the association sponsors a national convention. This meeting serves two major functions: (1) meeting of the Legislative Assembly to transact business, and (2) presentation of research and philosophical papers at sectional meetings sponsored by each of the interest groups. The convention also affords teachers, researchers, and others seeking new positions an opportunity to meet prospective employers and discuss job opportunities. The SAA Placement Service coordinates this phase of the organization activity and publishes and distributes to members of the service a listing of job vacancies. It also maintains a file of the credentials of its subscribers and it will make these credentials available to prospective employers.

The association publishes three journals. *The Quarterly Journal of Speech* contains articles dealing with all aspects of the field of speech and reviews of recently issued books in the field. *Speech Monographs* is a quarterly publication which prints articles emphasizing research investigations in speech. Articles devoted to methodology and research in speech instruction are printed in *The Speech Teacher*, also a quarterly publication. A publication of the association that many students find useful is the *Table of Contents* of articles appearing in *The Quarterly Journal of Speech, Speech Monographs,* and *The Speech Teacher* from 1915 to the present. Articles are indexed by title, author, and area discussed.

American Educational Theatre Association. This organization has specified its purpose as the promotion of the highest standards in theatre practice, teaching, scholarship, and research, the stimulation of creativity in theatrical affairs, and the creation of understanding and appreciation of theatre. AETA has three internal divisions — the American Community Theatre Association, the Children's Theatre Conference, and the Secondary School Theatre Conference. Each of these divisions operates nearly autonomously since each elects its own officers and governing board, has its own regional organization, and holds its own national convention.

The Educational Theatre Journal is published quarterly and is sent to all members of the association. Special issues of the journal are published as warranted on topics of considerable importance to theatre. Each division of the association also publishes a periodical which is distributed to the membership of the division. As a further service to its membership and to those interested in the study of theatre, "Theatre Arts Publications" and other bibliographies, teaching aids, and courses of study are published and distributed by AETA.

The annual convention of the association provides an opportunity for those interested in theatre to meet and discuss theatrical trends, interpretations, and productions and to examine recent commercial products and publications in the theatre area.

Because AETA includes on its membership rolls not only theatre educators but professional artists and amateur workers, the projects of the association are diverse. Included in current projects are: Afro-Asian theatre, experimental research, playwrights' program, stage design and technical developments, theatre administration, and theatre architecture. The association headquarters are located in the John F. Kennedy Center for the Performing Arts, 1701 Pennsylvania Ave., Washington, D.C.

American Speech and Hearing Association. The major objectives of this organization are to encourage the study of human speech and hearing and to promote the investigation of speech and hearing disorders. Requirements for membership are more stringent than for most other professional organizations either within or outside the field of speech. Members must hold either a Master's degree or the equivalent with a major in speech pathology, audiology, or speech and hearing sciences and must display interest in research in human communication.

ASHA provides clinical certification for members in either speech pathology or audiology. After submission of evidence that the candidate is qualified to conduct clinical services and train others in the profession, the association officially certifies the member as clinically competent in either of two areas.

Through its three major journals — the *Journal of Speech and Hearing Disorders,* which is issued quarterly, the *Journal of Speech and Hearing Research,* also a quarterly publication, and *ASHA,* a monthly journal — the association serves as a continuing source of professional information and research in speech and hearing. Two other publications, *ASHA Monographs* and *ASHA Reports* are issued by the association but on an irregular basis.

The association also established, in 1959, The American Boards of Examiners in Speech Pathology and Audiology. The boards evaluate the educational programs and organizations which offer clinical hearing and speech services and issue certificates indicating the competency of the training provided.

Information describing the association and its functions can be secured from the Executive Secretary, 9030 Old Georgetown Road, Washington, D. C.

National Society for the Study of Communication. Interdisciplinary in character, this society is concerned with the improvement of human communication through a study of the nature of communication and its functions. It also acts as a distribution and exchange center for those educators, businessmen, journalists, labor leaders, and myriad others who are concerned with the removal of barriers to the successful sharing of thoughts in contemporary society. Because of the plethora of individuals involved in activities based upon communication behavior, the NSSC includes on its membership rolls persons in fields such as public relations, personnel management, psychiatry, engineering, law, medicine, the ministry, and industrial communication.

The Journal of Communication, a quarterly publication devoted to an interdisciplinary approach to the study and research of communication activities, is distributed to all active members of the society.

The society sponsors two major meetings per year. The annual summer conference is devoted to the discussion and evaluation of current research and theory on communication, while the winter meeting of the organization, usually held in conjunction with the Speech Association of American convention, is concerned with the report of recent findings and implications of theory and research in human communication.

American Forensic Association. This association directs its activities and publications toward the needs and interests of teachers and coaches of debate. In recent years, AFA has made a concerted effort to enlist the interest and participation of more high school directors of forensics in the activities of the organization.

All of the efforts of the association are concerned with the promotion of excellence in forensics and, to that end, several publications and services are provided. *The Journal of the American Forensic Association* is published in both regular and special issues and distributed to all members of the association. Articles in the journal are concerned with the practical problems of persons engaged in forensics work, ranging from the direction and scheduling of tournaments to the ethics of debating both sides of a proposition.

Membership in AFA automatically carries with it membership in one of the regional forensic associations. These regional organizations sponsor research on matters pertinent to the direction of forensic activities and in some sections of the country have sponsored a debate tournament organized on an experimental format; *i.e.,* debaters list the topics they feel are critical to the decision of the judge before the decision is known. These judgments about the selection of issues are then related to the win-loss record of the participants, and in turn, this total record is examined in light of the organizational skills of the debaters.

Standardized debate ballots are available at low cost to high schools and colleges through AFA. The association has also sponsored a series of television debates between outstanding college teams over one of the educational networks. During the Speech Association of America convention, AFA sponsors programs dealing with debate theory, case development, direction of forensics programs, and other matters of concern to forensic coaches and participants. The association is also represented in several professional activities such as the Legislative Assembly of SAA and the Committee on Intercollegiate discussion and Debate.

Regional Speech Associations

The regional speech associations were established in an attempt to promote the study of speech through more direct contact between members of the profession. Each of the regional organizations is concerned with the study of all areas of speech. One of the major advantages of the regional association is that the members are in geographical proximity to each other and share interests and problems peculiar to their section of the country. Each of the associations, then, has a slightly different orientation dictated by the nature of the study of speech in the area.

Speech Association of the Eastern States. Members of this organization are in the territory bounded by Maryland and Pennsylvania on the south and west and New York and New England on the north. The journal *Today's Speech* is the official organ of the association and carries articles of professional interest. In addition, the association publishes a newsletter, operates a placement service at the annual convention of the organization, and publishes a directory of its membership.

Southern Speech Association. Historically, the SSA has been identified more with regional interests and activity in speech than any of the other associations. The *Southern Speech Journal,* a quarterly, has mirrored this concern over the years by concentrating on articles dealing with oratory, rhetoric, and theatre in the South. SSA territory is bounded by the Ohio River on the north and Texas and Arkansas on the west. The association holds an annual convention to present reports in scholarly research and establish contacts for professional positions. Membership in the association is open to high school and college teachers as well as graduate students in speech.

Central States Speech Association. Including virtually all the states where speech education has received the greatest academic support, CSSA is the largest in number of members of any of the regional associations. The central states range from Ohio on the east to Missouri and Oklahoma on the south and the Dakotas, Nebraska, and Kansas on the west. *Central States Speech Journal* is the quarterly publication of the association; this journal and the directory are sent to members of the organization. The annual association convention is held, like all the other regional conventions, in early April and features programs reporting the results of research in speech and presenting an opportunity for employers and employees to meet through the placement service of the association.

Western Speech Association and Pacific Speech Association. These two associations share professional leadership in states from the Rocky

Mountain area to the Pacific (Montana, Wyoming, Colorado, New Mexico, Arizona, Utah, Idaho, Washington, Oregon, California, Alaska, and Hawaii). Geographic distance has dictated a need for professional contacts, conferences, and consultation services with shorter travel arrangements. Both associations publish journals under their respective names which represent very active interests in teaching and research. Teachers in these states may contact these associations through the leading universities in each state.

When the teacher accepts his first position, he will be strongly encouraged to join the state education association and, in some systems, the NEA. The values of these associations are apparent, but the secondary teacher must, if he hopes to remain an effective teacher and representative of his profession, remain abreast of his field. The professional speech organizations are the best route to this goal.

Suggested Projects

1. What are the national and regional speech organizations in your area of interest?

2. Compare the values of affiliation with professional speech organizations and professional education associations. Which are of more immediate concern to you? Do the organizations differ basically in their objectives?

3. Which speech journals would be of maximum value to the secondary teacher? Why?

4. If you wished to determine if an article on "The Use of Multiple-Choice Test Items" had been published in one of the major speech journals, what would be the most efficient method for reviewing published articles? Do most of the major associations or publications provide an index of published materials?

5. Other than the legal responsibilities, what responsibilities do you have to keep up with your discipline? What means have you used thus far?

References

Callaghan, J. Calvin. "Why on Earth Do People Go to Conventions?" *Today's Speech*, 8:10-12 (February, 1960).

Crocker, Lionel. "The Professional Spirit," *Central States Speech Journal*, 6:20-22 (Fall, 1954).

Hall, Robert N. "Seeking Employment: Placement Services, Letters, Interviews," *The Speech Teacher,* 17:71-74 (January, 1968).

Hitchcock, Orville A. "How to Get a Job as a Teacher of Speech," *The Speech Teacher,* 4:225-230 (November, 1955).

Smith, Raymond C. "The Dignity of a Profession," *Central States Speech Journal,* 14:83-87 (May, 1963).

Timmons, Jan and Giffin, Kim. "Requirements for Teachers of Speech in the Secondary Schools of the United States," *The Speech Teacher,* 13:96-98 (March, 1964).

Index